NEGOTIATING
INTERNATIONAL
BUSINESS

NEGOTIATING INTERNATIONAL BUSINESS

The Negotiator's Reference Guide
to 50 Countries Around the World

Lothar Katz

www.negintbiz.com

ISBN 1-4196-3190-X
Library of Congress Control Number 2006903917
Second edition, 2007

Booksurge, LLC   Charleston, SC

To order additional copies, please contact
www.booksurge.com
1-866-308-6235
orders@booksurge.com

To contact the author, please e-mail lotharkatz@negintbiz.com

Table of Contents

Part III: Negotiate Right in Any of 50 Countries 111

Preface

Who Should Use This Book

Negotiating International Business is a reference for businesspeople negotiating with counterparts in/from other countries. Whether such a negotiation takes place abroad or in the reader's home country makes little difference. The need to understand how to negotiate across the cultures remains the same.

The information given in this book focuses on professional business negotiations. That includes interactions large and small, from preparing multi-billion-dollar corporate mergers and acquisitions to engaging with small local distribution companies. However, we may not always cover typical tourist interactions, such as bargaining in a street market or haggling over the price of a cab ride. Street merchants and other vendors in foreign cultures, especially in third-world and emerging economies, often resort to extreme negotiation techniques that would be inappropriate within the country's business culture. We chose to focus on practices that people are likely to use in business settings.

This book is a tool for anyone seeking to boost his or her success in international negotiations. However, we would like to point out that it is not written for the novice. If you are unfamiliar with the fundamentals of effective negotiation and have little or no negotiation experience, we encourage you to check out some of the *References* listed on page 453.

How This Book is Structured

Depending on your previous negotiation experience, we invite you to read all of it or only those parts that serve as an essential reference.

Part I describes how culture impacts negotiations, explaining which factors influence how members of a given cultural group prefer to negotiate. We also take a close look at the framework and structure of the international negotiation process, reviewing each of the phases that negotiations go through.

No matter what your experience level, we urge you to read at least Chapters 2, 3, 4, and 6. Without understanding some fundamental cultural concepts that explain the difference between international negotiations and domestic ones, negotiating with people from other cultures will be left to chance and you rarely get the best deal you could.

Part II lists numerous techniques negotiators around the world use. While many of these may also be applied in domestic negotiations, we discuss each in its international context, reviewing

- how the technique works,
- how to counter it,
- who likely uses the technique,
- who will not likely use the technique,
- when using the technique may be effective, and
- when using the technique may not be effective.

We suggest at least to speed-read this part. Even experienced negotiators can increase their effectiveness through identifying and leveraging the most powerful international negotiation techniques. The country-specific information in Part III of the book frequently refers to these techniques.

Part III serves as a reference for negotiators working in, or with people from, any of fifty different countries. Most readers may choose to read only those pages that are specific to the culture or cultures they are interacting with. Each country section covers these seven topics:

Relationships and Respect explains the relevance of relationships in the culture and the process through which local businesspeople may expect to get to know their counterparts. It also discusses individual characteristics that command respect in the country.

Communication introduces must-know aspects when starting to communicate with people from the culture. This includes language abilities, requirements for interpreters, whether people prefer direct or indirect communication, how non-verbal communication works, and so on. Matters of etiquette are mentioned if they may have a significant impact on the success of a negotiation.

Initial Contact & Meetings describes expectations members of a culture have of foreign businesspeople and reviews other aspects that are critical to know to start a negotiation the right way. This includes such topics as punctuality, the exchange of business cards, small talk, presentations, and many more.

Negotiation reviews negotiation styles, bargaining and haggling preferences, and how long it may take before the negotiation might reach closure. Next, we discuss which negotiation techniques to expect and which to use in the country, including techniques that are rare and those that are best avoided. The section further analyzes the decision-making process, explains the roles of the primary stakeholders, and summarizes considerations upon which decisions are based.

Agreements and Contracts discusses how agreement is established and documented in the culture, how dependable commitments are, what role written contracts play, and what expectations the other side will have after one has been signed.

Women in Business addresses topics such as the distribution of roles between genders in a country's business environment and how to best establish credibility as a visiting businesswoman. For some countries, it also discusses how to greet local women properly as a male business visitor.

The final section, *Other Important Things to Know*, provides additional information about the country that negotiators need to be aware of.

Definitions: Regions of the World

As long as cultural stereotyping is avoided, it can be helpful to refer to groups of countries or geographic regions if the majority of their people share certain values and behaviors. Keeping in mind that there remain important cultural differences between members of each group, we occasionally use the following terms throughout this book:

- *Arab countries* refers to the Gulf Arab countries of Bahrain, Kuwait, Oman, Qatar, Saudi Arabia, the United Arab Emirates, and Yemen, as well as the Levantine Arab countries of Lebanon, Syria, and Jordan.

- *Middle East* refers to all Gulf and Levantine Arab countries, plus Egypt, Iran, Iraq, and Israel.

- *Europe* includes the Eurasian border countries, such as Russia, Ukraine, and Turkey.

- The *Nordic countries* or *Nordics* are Denmark, Finland, Iceland, Norway, and Sweden. We sometimes refer to their people as *Northern Europeans*. The three countries of Denmark, Norway, and Sweden may also be referred to as *Scandinavia*.

- *Southern Europe* refers to several of the European countries around the Mediterranean Sea, namely Cyprus, Greece, Italy, Malta, Portugal, Spain, and Turkey.

- *Slavic countries* refers to Belarus, Bulgaria, Croatia, the Czech Republic, Macedonia, Moldova, Poland, Serbia, Slovakia, Slovenia, Russia, and Ukraine. The countries of Albania, Bosnia and Herzegovina, Hungary and Romania are not Slavic but may show cultural similarities.

- *Latin America* in the context of this book refers to all countries on the American continents with the exception of Canada, Mexico, the United States, and the numerous countries of the Caribbean Islands. We always use the term *Latin Americans*, rather than simply saying *Americans*, when referring to the population of these countries. This choice of language reflects our attempt to keep with terms most readers can easily recognize. It means no disrespect to people from Latin America, who may be quick to point out that they are Americans, too.

- We use the term *Americans* to describe those citizens and residents of the United States who, to a large degree, share distinct cultural values and preferences, such as individualism, achievement orientation, a sense of urgency, directness, and a distrust of formal authority.

  A large group of people in the United States are either first-generation immigrants, or they grew up in one of the country's many subcultures, such as the sizeable Hispanic community. While these residents usually blend in well, they nevertheless often hold on to a different set of values. Without meaning disrespect to this or any other group, the term *Americans* as used in this book does not include these individuals.

Acknowledgements

Writing *Negotiating International Business* would not have been possible without the help of many others who provided ideas and suggestions, reviewed chapters and country-specific information, and trusted me with their open and candid feedback. These great people, who have lived and worked in many places around the world, contributed their experiences and profound insights, making this book much more valuable than I could ever have hoped it would become.

Specifically, I would like to thank the following friends and colleagues for their help:

Dr. Hans-Joachim Adler
Niels Anderskouv
Michel Arnoux
Hanna Bachmann
Mark Bachmann
Mike Bartlett
Christian Blackwell
Chris Bussey
Vincent Chan
Vince Chapa
Wayne Chou
Jim Davidson
Anthony Dell
Selan Diraviyam
Chris Elliott
Thomas Finkbeiner
Christoph Fischer
Dr. Sue Freedman
Maly Friedel
Gabriele Gross
Sam (Shaoul) Hai
Klaus Haidacher
Elke Harrison
Dr. Sandra Haudek
Brian Hinchcliffe

Cornelia Hüllstrunk
Hamilton Ignacio
Dr. Zareen Karani Lam
    de Araoz
Pavel Kharitonov
Chris Koski
Ola Luboinska
Igor Mashkevich
Valeriya Mashkevich
Lourdes Menendez
Glenn Merkel
Günther Mielke
Dr. Hans Moormann
David Mulcahy
Vandana Mysore
JJ Nanez
Suman Narayan
Milton Nee
Roman Neumeister
Dr. Ted Pait
Bill Parker
Ektor Polykandriotis
Fredrik Prince
Dr. Rüdiger Reitzig
Sannamari Riekkinen

Donald Ritter
Derrick Robinson
Christina Robinowitz
Steve Ruddell
Hans G. Schlegel
Frank Schulze
Zoltán Simon
Oliver Sintobin
Jean-Claude Soroka
John Stich
Dr. Gabor Szalai
Alex Tessarolo
Maria Tessarolo
Rob Timmermans
David Troncoso
Dr. Gerald Turner
Roemer Visser
Keith Wangle
Ted Wilson
Cathy Witte
Thomas T. Wu
Shawn Yang
Dr. Zhen Yu

In addition, I would like my wife Annette to know that I am eternally grateful for her strong and loving encouragement, as I have been during the last twenty-seven years. I love you.

Part I: International Negotiations

Chapter 1: Take On The Challenge

The Stakes are High, And So is the Risk

Watch a few old *James Bond* movies, and you may come away thinking that cultural differences are no big deal. In the secret agent's world, natives of all countries speak English with only a trace of a local accent (unless, of course, they are Russian), most people seem to prefer British or American manners and etiquette, and except for a few folkloristic customs here and there, everyone readily understands even the most subtle expressions and gestures.

Experienced business travelers know that the real world is not like that. While countless people around the globe speak at least some English, language gaps still can be huge barriers. Manners and etiquette vary greatly across cultures, and their influence on the way people perceive others is often substantial. Entire business deals have dissolved solely because company representatives spoke or behaved in ways deemed inappropriate within their host culture. Many a negotiator has failed to reach agreement or to achieve the desired results because they did not prepare well for these and many other challenges of doing business in foreign countries or with foreign representatives.

This mistake can become incredibly expensive. The potential impact of international negotiations to the strategic and financial success of a company is hard to overestimate. Whether the goal is a product sale, a turnkey project, a licensing agreement, a BPO (business process outsourcing) engagement, a joint venture, a service contract, or any other kind of business deal, two factors can make negotiating across cultures a high-risk undertaking:

- *The financial stakes are high.* Since the outcome of an initial negotiation often determines the strategic position of a company in a particular country or region of the world, failure to reach agreement hugely impacts factors such as market access, resource availability, or required financial investments.

- *Most companies' cultural competence when engaging in a new territory is low.* Few or none of their executives and middle managers may have a sufficient understanding of effective negotiation approaches in the 'new' country's culture, which substantially reduces the odds of winning great deals and reaching favorable terms.

Cross-cultural negotiations combine high stakes with high risks, which creates a powerful incentive to learn how to 'make things happen' the right way. Competitive pressures in many international markets have increased considerably over the past decades. Countries whose economies were historically either closed or were accessible to only a few foreign players have become level playing fields, attracting trade partners from all around the world. Success in this competitive environment often requires differentiating oneself by adjusting to local mentalities and cultures. It is no surprise that businesspeople who are good at crossing cultural boundaries, such as many British, Dutch, and Singaporean negotiators, tend to achieve superior outcomes in global trade negotiation.

Some argue that the effects of globalization have mostly eliminated the need to prepare for cultural differences. To support this position, they may emphasize that more people than ever have extensive international experience, or they might point to the numerous brands and icons of popular culture, from retail chain Starbucks Coffee to singer Britney Spears, who managed to establish a global presence with a huge following in many different countries. We believe that these arguments are misleading. Studies have shown that instead of disappearing, disagreements in cultural values among employees in different country subsidiaries of multinational companies are usually more pronounced than those between employees working for domestic companies in these countries. This indicates that people who had greater opportunity to learn about other cultures may cling on to their own one more strongly as a result. Globalization might cause cultures to look alike on the surface, but it would be dangerous to conclude from these disappearing clues that the fundamental cultural differences themselves, as manifested in people's values, beliefs, and attitudes, are also disappearing.

The Impact of Culture on Negotiations

Many definitions for the term *culture* have been given. Yet, none seems comprehensive enough to express its full meaning. We favor the very practical approach proposed by MIT professor Edgar H. Schein: "Culture is the way in which people solve problems." It captures the essence of why international negotiators need to understand cultural differences: the art of negotiation is the art of problem solving, which in itself is strongly influenced by the values, beliefs, attitudes, and behaviors that are shared, albeit to varying degrees, among the members of each cultural group. Disagreements over these factors often lead to cross-cultural conflicts that could seriously jeopardize the success of a negotiation. Adding to the challenge, we find upon closer inspection that *every* aspect of the negotiation process is subject to these influences and may take on a different meaning within the framework of a given culture:

- *Why negotiate?* In western business cultures, the primary purpose of negotiating is to 'make a deal.' Without the goal of engaging in a business agreement with clearly defined objectives, Westerners rarely consider negotiations meaningful. In contrast, many Asians may negotiate with the primary objective of building relationships and creating long-term alliances, even if the specific items being negotiated seem insignificant.

- *What to negotiate?* A wide range of different items can become the subject of negotiations. People from achievement-oriented cultures (refer to page 22), such as Americans or Canadians, tend to concentrate on tangible benefits when assessing the value of negotiated items or concessions, for example the price of a product or the cost of a service. Members of ascription-oriented cultures, for instance Indonesians or Colombians, may also be focusing on non-tangible benefits, such as the status that comes with forming a large partnership or the prestige of winning an important foreign customer. In order to obtain such benefits, they may be willing to accept terms outsiders to their cultures might view as unfavorable.

- **When to negotiate?** Timing and pace of negotiations can be a source of frustration for both sides. People from strongly relationship-oriented cultures, such as Venezuelans or the Japanese, may be unwilling to engage in serious business negotiations unless they already know their counterparts well and have had ample opportunity to develop relationships with them. If not, it could take several trips and many months before the core negotiation can begin. In contrast, negotiators from those task-oriented cultures whose members consider business relationships less critical, for instance Americans or Australians, may frequently attempt to speed up the process in order to 'get quick results.' These attitudes create conflicting objectives and often lead to tensions in the negotiation process. In extreme cases, talks may break down before the parties have even started conducting serious negotiations.

- **How to negotiate?** This is where approaches vary the most across cultures. There can be vastly different concepts of how a negotiation should be conducted. Protocol and formality, negotiation styles and tactics, bargaining and haggling exchanges, the way agreement is reached and documented, and many other rules and behaviors may differ in very fundamental ways. People in some cultures may insist on bargaining sequentially, going down a list item-by-item; others prefer a parallel multi-item bargaining approach that looks at the deal holistically. Some will openly share relevant information, willingly putting their cards on the table; others may play them close to the chest, revealing as little as possible about their motives and objectives. Some use logical reasoning to persuade their counterparts; others may prefer appeals to emotions and intuition. The list of potential issues is long. Many of these disagreements are hard to reconcile.

What makes these differences crucial is that most human beings hold a deep-founded belief that 'their' way of doing things, which is rooted in the preferred concepts of their culture, is the better one – or worse, the *only* acceptable one. The resulting spectrum of how people belonging to different cultures define 'proper' and 'improper' behaviors spawns an array of pitfalls that may be difficult to recognize even for very experienced negotiators.

Effectiveness in international negotiations requires a profound understanding of cultural influences, not a mere application of rules. A checklist of do's and don'ts alone, no matter how extensive, will not be enough to master tricky situations. Successful international negotiators have learned to leverage four essential competencies:

- They understand the values, beliefs, attitudes, and behaviors that are *relevant* in their counterpart's culture.

- They use, as well as recognize and counter as needed, negotiation techniques that are *effective* in the culture.

- They are familiar with culture-specific behaviors that are *important* since they stimulate a positive negotiation outcome.

- They know to avoid behaviors that could be *damaging* and might wreak havoc with the negotiation because of cultural incompatibilities.

There is much more to know about any of the world's cultures than this book has room to address. Our mission is more modest: we focus on those aspects that determine culture-specific relevance, impact, importance, and damage avoidance in international negotiations.

A few popular culture guides seem to imply that you must strictly follow local etiquette whenever you conduct business in another country. Experienced international negotiators know that this is untrue. In today's global world, people in all but the most rural places understand and often tolerate the fact that foreigners act and behave differently. In France, people may make fun of you behind your back if you use a fork with your right hand instead of with the left. Simply ignore it and focus on your business objectives instead. In Argentina, conversations may stop around you if you start chomping ice. Realize something is wrong and stop doing it, but do not worry about the impact the 'incident' might have on your business relationship. In Japan, you may cause a moment of embarrassment if you walk into a traditional restaurant with your shoes still on. Your local counterparts will be quick to stop you, politely asking that you take them off. Apologize, laugh with the Japanese group, then forget about it. This mishap will not affect your negotiation either. In each of these situations, people may be irritated at first but will quickly conclude that it was just an odd or funny incident. However, there is a critical line you must not cross: you must never speak or behave in ways that signal disrespect for people or culture.

Being odd will often be forgiven. Being rude, rarely.

Rudeness may lie in seemingly little things. Brazilians' feelings might be hurt if you gave them a brochure printed in Spanish rather than in Portuguese, the country's language. Indonesians may consider you aggressive and impolite if you keep frequent eye contact, which to them signals disrespect. Arabs may be seriously offended if you handed them something with your left hand, which Muslims consider unclean. Even though your perceived rudeness may reflect no bad intentions whatsoever, it could critically damage the progress of your negotiation. As an outsider to a culture, it is your responsibility to avoid behaviors its members define as offensive. Unfortunately, it can be difficult to distinguish between behaviors that may just be considered odd and those that are viewed as rude. Several factors influence this:

- Locals who are experienced in dealing with foreigners are usually more tolerant than those who have little or no cross-cultural experience.

- People living in big cities may be more relaxed about cultural faux pas than those living in rural areas.

- People in positions of high authority can be less forgiving than ordinary peasants usually are.

- Younger people may mostly ignore unusual behaviors, while older ones could be very strict.

- People in countries whose population is very diverse, such as the United States, usually tolerate a much wider spectrum of behaviors than those living in very homogeneous cultures, such as Japan.

- If your counterparts know that you are visiting the country for the first time, they may be much more forgiving than if you had many previous visits or if you actually lived there.

- In addition, individual beliefs and preferences unrelated to culture can also be strong influence factors.

Focusing on the essentials for business success, *Negotiating International Business* is a negotiator's compendium. It strives to provide relevant information on how to successfully conduct international business negotiations but cannot address all differences in manners and etiquette that are potential sources of conflict. If you are unsure whether the people you will be negotiating with are sufficiently experienced in interacting with other cultures and tolerant enough to forgive minor faux pas, we recommend that you familiarize yourself with the local etiquette of the country or countries you plan to visit. Several useful guides for this purpose are listed in the *References* and *Useful Websites* sections at the end of this book.

The Competent International Negotiator

Success in international negotiations is not limited to individuals with a specific personality or style. However, the following characteristics and behaviors, all of which can be learned and developed, are typical of highly effective cross-cultural negotiators:

- *Competent international negotiators know themselves.* Understanding one's values and preferences is critical when trying to bridge cultural gaps and reach agreement in foreign countries. Successful individuals know how directly or indirectly they communicate, how important business relationships are to them, to what extent they are willing to trust people with whom they have had only limited business interactions, how competitive they are, how they make decisions, and so on. Knowing themselves enables them to leverage their greatest strengths and overcome their shortcomings at critical junctures during the negotiation process.

- *Competent international negotiators realize that cross-cultural knowledge is vital to their success.* Looking beyond generalizations such as 'all humans are created equal,' they recognize how the historic, economic, social, and cultural environment in which members of a cultural group grow up affects values, behaviors, and practices. Accordingly, they familiarize themselves with relevant aspects of a potential business partner's culture before making initial contact. Having learned to recognize cultural differences, they are able to identify sensitivities and potential areas of cross-cultural conflict, which greatly improves their ability to negotiate productively and successfully.

- *Competent international negotiators understand the risks and benefits of stereotyping.* Generic cultural information is inevitably based on stereotypes, describing aspects that may be typical of a given culture but not necessarily of any of its individual members. Effective cross-cultural negotiators know that assumptions about their counterparts that are not based on first-hand experience can be dangerous and may cause substantial communication problems and disagreements. Individuals who believe that 'Arabs haggle all the time,' 'the Japanese never make individual decisions,' 'Russians are always aggressive when negotiating,' or that 'a German's word is as good as a contract' may rely on these assumptions when dealing with individuals from one of these cultures. However, they may find themselves in trouble when dealing with real Arabs, Japanese, Russians, or Germans, realizing too late that the people they are dealing with could have little in common with such stereotypical models.

Negotiators who have mastered the challenges of working across cultures avoid this mental trap. They realize that stereotypes can be valuable if based upon validated research and statistically relevant findings, but only when used as a collective description of typical values, preferences, practices, and behaviors within a society or group of people. No matter how accurate a stereotype about such a group may be, it might not apply at all to some of its individual members.

Competent negotiators therefore use stereotypical information only as a starting point when dealing with individuals from a given culture, as a set of assumptions that they are prepared to question and modify continually. They realize that adjusting their own behaviors to the cultural stereotypes may help initially since it will likely put their counterpart at ease and reduce the risk of cultural misunderstandings. At the same time, these effective negotiators remain open minded and frequently adjust their approach as they learn more about the other's individual characteristics and preferences.

Cultural stereotypes can be powerful tools helping negotiators prepare for cross-cultural interactions, but only if used right. Assuming that someone is indeed an 'average American' or 'average Chinese' is dangerous. Assuming that the person *is likely* to share practices and preferences with that fictitious 'average American' or 'average Chinese,' however, while remaining fully aware that the person could in fact turn out to be very different from the stereotype, is a sound use of cultural stereotyping.

- *Competent international negotiators continuously demonstrate respect.* Not shy in pursuing their interests and in remaining firm where appropriate, they will miss few opportunities to demonstrate that they respect their counterparts, never letting ego get in the way of negotiating. They know that negotiating is not about outsmarting or outmaneuvering the other party and understand that the end result is much more relevant than the way to get there. Most importantly, great cross-cultural negotiators are humble. They refuse to take themselves more seriously than they take the deal they are trying to close. Accordingly, they never dig in their heels and strive to show appreciation for the other party's beliefs and positions throughout the negotiation exchange.

Demonstrating respect for the other side includes acquiring knowledge and showing curiosity about the other's country and culture. Before meeting a foreign counterpart for the first time, effective cross-cultural negotiators might learn a few facts about the other country's history and cultural background. When applicable, they will learn some of the language, realizing that knowledge of at least some of its words and phrases will be greatly appreciated. Having no ambition to be 'cultural judges,' they never question the legitimacy of either side's values. In addition, they never openly criticize the other's country, even when counterparts may do so themselves.

- *Competent international negotiators are flexible and adaptable.* Knowing themselves and understanding their counterpart's cultures well, they are able to identify gaps and can decide how to bridge them effectively. Without having to blend perfectly into the other culture, successful individuals manage to expand their own cultural comfort zone enough to keep their counterparts at ease. They know when it is ok to follow their own preferred approaches, when it is better to play by the other side's cultural rulebook, and when to compromise somewhere between the extremes. They are also prepared to adjust to the numerous factors other than culture, such as socio-economic background, family, religion, schooling, and many others, that may influence others' values and practices. With counterparts who are less adaptable, this knowledge and attitude put them in control of the negotiation process and greatly improve their chances of achieving their objectives.

Smart negotiators always maintain credibility and integrity *as viewed by their counterparts*. In cross-cultural settings, this may require much flexibility, adjusting to the other side's standards and practices without sacrificing their own values. In some countries, it could mean negotiating in a straightforward style and staying away from deceitful and distractive tactics. In others, bargaining may be viewed as a game and negotiators might win the locals' respect by skillfully demonstrating their mastery of deceptive negotiation without losing their integrity. The key to success in international negotiations is adaptation, not transformation.

- *Competent international negotiators refuse to make assumptions about their counterparts' intentions.* They internalize the most important rule in international business, which is never to take anything personally. Instead of simply assuming that an apparently unfriendly remark or behavior reflects negative intentions, they go to great lengths to verify proper communication and identify cultural misunderstandings. In addition, they are unwilling to take things at face value. For example, they will not take a counterpart's poor grammar or pronunciation as an indication of limited intelligence, nor will they assume a lack of interest if a counterpart comes ill-prepared to a meeting. If in doubt about the other party's intentions, effective negotiators choose not to assume anything. Instead, they usually ask or otherwise try to learn more about their counterparts' true objectives.

- *Competent international negotiators are persistent and patient.* Different cultures may have vastly difference concepts of how much time to spend in each of the phases of negotiations. American's motto might be 'time is money' while their Arab counterparts may believe that 'haste is of the devil.' Successful negotiators are willing to allocate whatever time they need to accomplish their objectives, working through excessive bureaucracy, stalling tactics, slow decision cycles, and other obstacles as needed. Persistent enough to move the negotiation process as swiftly as possible, and patient enough to accept it to be as slow as necessary, they realize that both traits are equally valuable.

- *Competent international negotiators prepare well.* This includes all aspects of the negotiation process itself, but also factors peripheral to the negotiation that could become distractions and hindrances. Examples for this kind of preparation are obtaining proper travel documents and visas, preparing and aligning their negotiation team to ensure consistency and maximum impact, bringing information material and background documents that may prove useful during the negotiation exchange, and so on. Thus prepared, negotiators can focus all their energy on the success of the negotiation itself.

Chapter 2: Preparing for International Negotiations

Key Concepts: Negotiating, Bargaining, and Haggling

Negotiating includes all phases of an exchange designed to establish agreement between two or more parties over the provision of goods, services, financial incentives, or other benefits. The negotiation process ends when all related transactions between the parties have been completed. It could extend over a considerable time period, sometimes many years after the parties signed a contract.

Bargaining is a process of exchanging offers in order to negotiate the terms of a purchase, agreement, or contract. Accordingly, it represents one of the phases within the overall negotiation process. The offers made in the bargaining exchange constitute promises to provide tangible or intangible individual items, such as products, materials, properties, services, payments, warranties, or deadlines. Commonly referred to as concessions, these offers are usually contingent upon receiving certain benefits in return.

Haggling is defined as extreme bargaining and often includes repetitive patterns of small incremental requests or offers. Partners in international negotiations may unfortunately not agree on what the term 'extreme' means in this context. People in haggling-averse cultures such as Sweden may consider more than three subsequent offers for a particular item as excessive, even if each represents a significant improvement over the previous one. In contrast, cultures whose members enjoy haggling, such as Saudi Arabia, may consider ten or more such iterations as normal bargaining, even if each offers only a small improvement.

Phases of Negotiations

All domestic or international negotiations go through six major phases. As they move from one phase to the next, and often at major junctures in-between, experienced negotiators will track pre-defined milestones that serve as progress indicators, adjusting their tactics and concessions as necessary.

- *Preparation.* During this phase, both sides analyze context and boundaries of the negotiation, define their objectives and non-settlement alternatives, and plan their approach. This includes selecting strategies and tactics that support the negotiation objectives, planning timing and size of individual concessions, defining an exit strategy, and more. Throughout their preparation, effective negotiators also strive to learn as much about the other party as they possibly can.

- *Relationship Building.* Structure, duration, and relative importance of this phase are hugely culture-dependent. In some countries, the existence of close relationships is not a necessary precondition for doing business together, so this phase may include little more than brief introductions and some background checking. In other cultures, businesspeople may not be willing to enter into any serious bargaining without first getting to know their counterparts well and establishing strong links. Here, the relationship building process could take many months and require several meetings. This phase generally starts with the initial contact between the negotiating parties, which in many cultures can be critically important for their future interactions.

- *Information Gathering.* During this phase, negotiators seek to understand the other side's intentions, objectives, and goals. They will also strive to find out about the value their counterparts are assigning to the individual items being negotiated and the concessions they are prepared to make. Since objectives and value assessments are often poorly aligned between the parties, it is common for resistance and conflicts to emerge during the information gathering phase.

- *Bargaining and Decision-Making.* Depending on the negotiating parties' preferences and cultural practices, bargaining and decision making may represent separate phases or they might blend into one. Negotiations over multiple items are often characterized by iterative exchanges that move back and forth between bargaining and decision-making. The bargaining phase starts with one side making its opening offer, which is usually followed by alternating concessions, offers, and counteroffers between the parties. With some cultures, this exchange might include frequent haggling over single or multiple items.

  Decision making is also subject to strong cultural influences. They frequently determine who will be involved, which factors to consider, and how much time to spend in the decision-making process. Once both negotiating parties have indicated that they are close to reaching agreement, additional bargaining over remaining differences may be required in order to reach consensus and advance the negotiation to its final phases.

- *Closure.* The closure phase begins when both negotiating parties believe that they have reached agreement. It usually ends when they sign a formal contract. Depending on the parties' preferences, creating this document might already start during the bargaining exchange, using the draft contract as a protocol to keep track of interim agreements. Levels of detail included in its final version can range from high-level, capturing only the essential aspects of the agreement, to very detailed, with specific provisions for many cases and eventualities. The act of signing the contract may be a mere formality to some, while a very important step for others. Members of some cultures, for example Americans, distinguish strictly between the intentions of the final agreement and the provisions spelled out in the contract, often insisting that only the latter be considered binding. Others, for instance most Arabs, expect the spirit of the agreement to be upheld even when the contractual terms only loosely reflect it. Many such aspects are strongly influenced by cultural orientations.

- *Execution.* In the absence of other provisions, executing a contractual agreement normally starts shortly after its signature. This phase may include follow-up steps to exchange additional information, communicate progress, or clarify details. Both sides are then expected to implement their commitments as spelled out in the contract and/or agreed upon during closure. How accurately these commitments must be met in order to be considered satisfactory again varies across cultures.

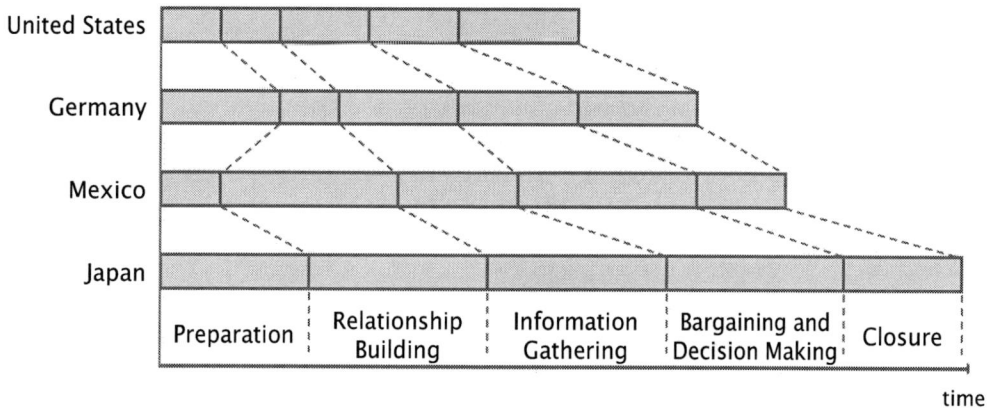

Figure 2.1 Comparison of negotiation phase durations in different cultures.

The overall length of the negotiation process and the time spent in each of its phases vary greatly. It is influenced by a number of factors, such as the parties' sense of urgency, how far apart their original objectives were, or how well their negotiation styles align. Cultural influences could also be substantial, as illustrated in Figure 2.1. It shows a qualitative analysis of how much time members of different cultures may be spending in each negotiation phase. This cross-cultural comparison is stereotypical and will not necessarily apply when actually negotiating with individual representatives from any of these cultures. It is interesting to note the variance in typical phase lengths, though. For instance, Americans, with their high sense of urgency, and Mexicans, with their relatively high acceptance of uncertainty, tend to spend much less time preparing for negotiations than German or Japanese businesspeople usually do. The latter commonly share a propensity for detailed analysis. On the other hand, Americans and Germans are usually willing to enter into serious negotiations without first getting to know the other party well, a concept that is frequently rejected by Mexican and Japanese businesspeople who allow substantially more time for relationship building. The Japanese may also spend extensive time gathering information before the bargaining exchange can begin.

We should emphasize that the structure of the negotiation process may not be as sequential as implied by the phase descriptions and by the segmentation shown in Figure 2.1. Many negotiators, especially members of highly polychronic cultures (see also page 47) who usually prefer a holistic approach to negotiating, may repeatedly move back and forth between the information gathering and bargaining phases before making any decisions. People from some countries may even re-open the bargaining exchange during the execution phase of a negotiation, when a contract has already been signed. Relationship building and information gathering tend to happen in parallel in many countries, for instance in Japan.

Context and Boundaries

Negotiating business deals with foreign counterparts requires a thorough understanding of the political, legal, economic, corporate, and cultural context and boundaries both parties are subjected to. Without such knowledge, there will be a substantial risk of missing aspects critical to the negotiation or even finding oneself in a 'mission impossible' after spending considerable time and effort. Let us take a look at each major factor:

- *Political environment.* Nowhere in the world are companies able to conduct international business independently of their countries' political situation. Governments frequently seek to influence large business deals in order to protect and enhance their country's political or economic strength, technological know-how, or infrastructure. Bureaucracies tend to present major hurdles even if a country's political climate is generally pro-business. They can become stifling when governments intend to keep strict control of local markets. Changes in political power may prove disruptive if existing business arrangements conflict with the new leaders' objectives. In addition, a lack of political stability may raise valid concerns over the long-term viability of business agreements, as is currently the case in countries such as Russia, Ukraine, Indonesia, or Thailand. Support from government offices, trade organizations, and independent consultants around the world often proves valuable when assessing these aspects.

- *Legal environment.* In countries where governments promote open business and free trade, legal regulations and restrictions can nonetheless represent serious impediments to business negotiations. Many an international negotiator has been taken by surprise when a counterpart informed them that what they proposed was actually illegal in the country. For instance, exclusive distributor agreements, common in many regions of the world, may be against the law in the European Union. Price discrimination across different groups of customers, another practice that is accepted in many countries, is unlawful in the United States, where companies are banned from using such business practices not only domestically but worldwide. Legal considerations often impact contractual aspects, too. A contract may be void if written in the wrong language, as is the case with English-only documents in the French-speaking Quebec province of Canada. Oral commitments could prove legally binding in Germany. Many such legal pitfalls exist. It is strongly advisable to work with legal experts who are well-familiar with applicable laws and regulations.

- *Economic environment.* Foreign exchange procedures, currency valuations, and general stability of markets are among the key factors to consider when assessing the potential value of an international business deal. Cross-border business arrangements regularly require financial transfers through foreign exchanges, which are typically controlled by central banks. It is vital to understand the procedures and commercial banking constraints governing this process. In addition, currency fluctuations, caused by inflation, general economic instability, or by outside factors such as shifts in the world's financial flows and systems frequently affect business arrangements. A deal that might have looked attractive at the time the contract was

signed could become very unfavorable should rates of exchange change significantly. It is essential to assess possible future currency fluctuations and consider
their implications for potential deals.

- *Corporate environment.* Strategic direction, market focus, level of international
experience, size and available resources, corporate values and attitudes, and many
other factors influence objectives, strategy, tactics, and styles of international business negotiators. Proper preparation for negotiations with another company includes finding out as much as possible about it, both at the strategic level and in
areas that relate directly to the negotiation process. It is crucial to understand the
type of agreement the potential partner is seeking: is the primary goal to close a
contract or to nurture a business relationship? Is the focus on short-term gains
or on long-term benefits? Similarly, it will be advantageous to identify the key
stakeholders in the negotiation that is about to begin: who is going to be at the
negotiation table, who will make important decisions, and who might be influencing them? In addition to direct company contacts, customers, suppliers, partners,
former employees, industry analysts, and others may be valuable sources for this
kind of information.

Understanding the ground rules the negotiating parties are willing to play by is
of equal importance. One such rule might address confidentiality requirements. If
sensitive information must be revealed over the course of the negotiation, the parties may prefer to close formal non-disclosure agreements (NDAs), or they could
choose to rely on verbal assurances of confidentiality. Either way, it will be important to clarify both sides' commitments upfront.

- *Cultural environment.* As we already saw in Chapter 1, the values, behaviors, and
practices that are unique to each country's culture wield powerful influences on all
aspects of the negotiation process. Their implications are usually harder to identify and prepare for than those of any other contextual negotiation factors. Before
familiarizing oneself with a specific culture, it is important to understand how
culturally homogeneous a country's population is. *Homogeneous* cultures, among
them many Asian, European, and Latin American countries, tend to tolerate a relatively narrow spectrum of 'acceptable' behaviors and practices. Cultural minorities
in these societies are often pressured to adjust to the majority's cultural rules. In
contrast, many culturally mixed countries exist. *Pluralistic* societies include population groups whose individual cultural norms differ in significant ways, which
may either be largely tolerated across the groups, as is the case between Belgium's
Flemings and Walloons, or which might be the cause of much friction and aggression, such as in Indonesia. *Heterogeneous* societies, whose cultural influences from
a variety of inhomogeneous population groups may be very diverse, usually tolerate a wide spectrum of styles and practices. Examples of the latter include Israel,
Switzerland, and the United States.

When preparing to negotiate with people in or from another country, it is important to know whether its culture is homogeneous, pluralistic, or heterogeneous as
this influences negotiation styles and tactics. Homogeneous and pluralistic cultures tend to impose several cultural taboos on their members. In pluralistic countries, these taboos may differ greatly between the individual cultural groups. That

could make it necessary to prepare for all of them, unless it is safe to assume that all counterparts all belong to the same cultural group. Heterogeneous cultures tend to tolerate a wider range of styles and behaviors. Nevertheless, these societies usually also hold up strong values that may impose stringent requirements which foreigners are expected to comply with.

Key Concepts: Corporate versus Cultural Influences

The corporate environment and the cultural context of a negotiation show several interdependencies. Policies, procedures, and practices of most companies are influenced by the cultures of their country of origin. Since multinational corporations frequently standardize their value systems and procedures on a worldwide basis, one might expect their employee base to be fairly homogeneous across national and cultural boundaries. However, it appears that **corporate influences** are able to moderate **cultural influences** only to a small degree, if at all. In fact, researchers have found that cultural influences tend to become more pronounced among employees working for companies of foreign, rather than domestic origin. One possible explanation for this phenomenon is that pressure on employees to conform with standardized organizational norms provokes a 'cultural resistance' aimed to protect local cultural values and practices.

This finding has significant consequences for international negotiators. For instance, if a negotiation with another company is set to include employees from different cultures, it will be vital to factor each counterpart's specific cultural influences into the preparation instead of assuming that a similar approach will work with all of them.

Essential Preparation Steps

To vary a famous quote by Thomas Alva Edison, "Success in international negotiations requires one percent inspiration and ninety-nine percent preparation." Indeed, the worst mistake anyone can make is to arrive at the negotiation table with no more than a perfunctory understanding of motives, objectives, expectations, and attitudes of both negotiating parties. Surprisingly, it is not uncommon to meet people who do just that: relying on their ability to 'figure things out as they go,' they spend little time preparing before engaging in international negotiations. Some of them may not realize that this makes them easy prey when dealing with competent counterparts.

As a smart negotiator, you know better than to make this mistake. Here are the six crucial steps that will get you ready for even the toughest international negotiation:

- *Identify your BATNA.* The *Best Alternative To Negotiated Agreement*, or BATNA, describes the most favorable non-settlement option that will still be available to you should you fail to reach agreement with your current counterparts. This could mean making a similar deal with another partner or otherwise engaging in business interactions that support your original strategic objectives. Few negotiations ever take place in which one side has no realistic alternative to reaching agreement, which tends to leave them in an extremely weak position.

Knowing your BATNA is important and becomes crucial in certain situations, for instance when a counterpart tries to exert strong pressure to close a deal. The BATNA will determine your options throughout the negotiation. For example, it will allow you to decide whether to accept the deal you are being offered or to walk away if those are your only alternatives. Identifying the BATNA requires brainstorming all available options, evaluating each of them, and selecting the one that is most attractive. Next, you should try to find ways to improve this option in order to identify your strongest possible BATNA. As a general rule, the more attractive it is, the stronger your overall negotiating position will be.

- *Define your objectives.* Business negotiators commonly pursue multiple objectives. These may include price targets, payment terms, warranty conditions, service arrangements, and many others. You must clearly define each of your objectives, setting your aspirations high and preparing to defend them through strong arguments if challenged by a counterpart.

Next, categorize your objectives. You may consider some of them essential, others as important, again others as desirable. There could also be some you might be indifferent about. Be realistic and honest when determining which is the case, since this matters when planning your approach. Items you consider essential tend to become strong negotiation levers for the other party if they learn about this fact, so do not make the mistake of classifying too many items in that category. Once your objectives are clear, consider substitutes. Would you be willing to trade one important item for another? If so, under what conditions? Having considered such aspects upfront may give you an edge during the bargaining exchange. Make sure to verify that your resulting objectives are indeed better than your BATNA. If not, why engage in the negotiation at all? You should also determine your Least Acceptable Result (LAR) which represents the minimum overall value of the deal you are willing to accept: is it the same as your BATNA, or will you only accept a deal that provides you with a higher value? If so, by how much?

- *Understand 'the other side.'* To maximize the success of your negotiation, you will need to learn everything you possibly can about your counterparts. What is the other party's BATNA? What are its objectives, strengths, and weaknesses? Which potential issues that could arise because of conflicting attitudes and objectives can you identify upfront? In addition, you should identify all of the stakeholders who will participate in your counterparts' decision process. Who will you be negotiating with directly, who will you be negotiating with indirectly, and who else might be influencing decisions? Is the final decision going to be made by a single person or by a group? If the latter, is it likely to require consensus? Knowing the answers to all of these questions will become relevant when defining your negotiation strategy.

The initial preparation phase is only the starting point to acquiring the necessary knowledge about the other side. You should continue this pursuit throughout the relationship-building, information gathering, and bargaining phases.

- *Plan your cultural approach.* Other important aspects are to verify your own understanding of the other side's culture and to carefully assess how 'locked into their culture' your counterparts are. Businesspeople in remote regions of underdeveloped countries may have very little experience with other cultures. With such counterparts, learning enough to command a working understanding of their culture may be your only promising option. While pulling in an advisor to close some of the cultural gap may help, this is rarely enough to achieve true collaboration. Your business partnership will likely remain frail in such a constellation.

In contrast, company employees who regularly deal with international partners or who work in a multinational environment may have adjusted to a more 'international' style of conducting business. While this will not eliminate principal cultural differences, the negotiation could include a mix of styles and practices, some of which may be reminiscent of local habits with others following widely practiced American or European business styles. Nevertheless, a general rule for international negotiations is that whoever is most 'conversant' in the other's culture will have a powerful advantage: their ability to influence decisions improves greatly, and they can employ styles and tactics from either side's cultural context. Negotiating from that position, you can continually modify and adjust your style as appropriate. While you may often find it advantageous to embrace the other's cultural script, you always retain the option to explain that 'things are done differently' in your own culture. As long as you avoid violating strict cultural taboos, you can thus introduce your own styles and practices and leverage them to your advantage.

Insisting on your own cultural style, either because you lack the required cross-cultural understanding or because you believe you are negotiating from a position of power, is a dangerous proposition. If you are lucky, your counterparts come better prepared than you and may therefore be able to close the cultural gap. This will give them a valuable advantage, though. Otherwise, it will be left to chance whether or not anything comes out of the negotiation at all. Either way, you are unlikely to walk away with the best deal you could possibly get.

- *Define your negotiation strategy.* The first step to defining your strategy is to analyze the strengths and weaknesses of each of your own objectives as well as those of the other side. Could your counterparts use some of your essential objectives as pressure points against you in order to obtain significant concessions? Such threats must be factored into your strategic approach. At the same time, you may be able to identify opportunities. For instance, can you leverage some of your counterparts' essential objectives in a similar fashion? In addition, can you identify items they will likely care about much more than you do?

  You must also consider many other factors that are often influenced by cultural aspects. For instance, you will need to carefully decide what negotiation styles to employ, how to use your main bargaining levers of power, information, and time most effectively, for example when sizing and timing concessions. We will discuss these aspects in greater detail in Chapter 6.

- *Define your exit strategy.* What are you going to do should the negotiation appear to lead nowhere? Will you be able to end the negotiation without leaving negative feelings on either side? If not, are you willing to burn your bridges with your counterparts, and have you considered the implications this fact may have on your ability to do business with others in the country? All of these questions need to be answered prior to making contact with a potential business partner. More often than not, asking them when you reach a standstill in the negotiation will be way too late – the damage could already be irreversible.

Team Negotiation

Preferences vary across cultures when it comes to team negotiation. For example, while Americans are often more inclined to 'go it alone,' arguing that this approach ensures consistency of strategy and is more efficient overall, the Chinese almost exclusively negotiate in teams and will usually employ groups of several negotiators. As a general rule, group-oriented cultures, among them most Asian and Latin American countries, tend to equate the size of the other side's team with the importance attributed to the negotiation. If a foreign party sends only a single individual or a small team to negotiate, their local counterparts may take this as a lack of interest in and commitment to building a dependable business partnership. Some may even refuse to enter into any serious negotiations under such circumstances.

Independent of cultural views, negotiating in teams in international settings has several other advantages. It allows bringing in and matching up different functional experts, ensuring that the right level of expertise is available when needed and fostering relationships between specialists on both sides who are usually quick to find common ground despite their cultural differences. In addition, well aligned teams are more likely to achieve their objectives since they can leverage greater experience and use a broader set of negotiation tactics to their advantage. Among others, the Chinese and the Taiwanese can be very effective team negotiators.

Team members need to be assigned specific roles to optimize their contributions to the negotiation process, such as:

- Team Leader or Facilitator
- Technical Expert
- Trade & Logistics Expert
- Legal Expert
- Cultural Expert / Relationship Builder

Selecting team members requires careful consideration of several factors. While functional expertise plays a role, other aspects are often more relevant when selecting team members for international negotiations. General negotiation experience and specific cultural understanding weigh strongly, as do the individuals' interpersonal skills, dependability, patience, persistence, and risk propensity. They also need to be focused on the negotiation objectives and willing to work hard to ensure alignment with their other team members. Shrewd negotiators tend to use disagreements among their counterparts to their own side's advantage.

Depending on their cultural background, some negotiators may also consider it important that rank, status, or age of team members on both sides match. Even if such expectations may seem irrelevant in one's own culture, it will be wise to address them when deciding how a team should be composed. Including an outsider on the team, for instance or independent consultant or someone from another part of the company, may also prove valuable. Such individuals often find it easier to keep a neutral and emotionally unbiased perspective of the status and progress of negotiations. In certain cultures, it may be beneficial to provide team members who do not belong to the same company with a business card designed to conceal that fact.

Executing a negotiation strategy as a team requires more than putting the right people in the right roles. It is of equal significance to prepare the team well, ensuring complete alignment between its members before the negotiation even starts. It is strongly recommended to practice different scenarios through role plays in order to prepare team members for tactics to use and for those that the other side is likely to employ. In the heat of the bargaining exchange, it will be much harder to reach this kind of alignment. However, it is best to interrupt negotiation in order to realign a team if disagreements surface among its members or if one of them is blundering. This is strongly preferable to bringing up such observations in front of the other party. Otherwise, its members might use the situation to play team members against each other.

In most settings, effective teams consistently achieve better negotiation results than effective individuals. The benefits of spending time upfront to prepare the team well are often significant and can be substantial.

Key Concepts: Individualistic versus Group-Oriented Cultures

Several intercultural researchers have conducted studies to analyze cultural preferences across a spectrum ranging from strong individualism to strong group orientation. They found that members of *individualistic cultures*, for instance Americans, Anglo-Canadians, Australians, or the Dutch, tend to place significant emphasis on individual interests and independence. While most of them value relationships with others, these are rarely viewed as an essential requirement for conducting business. People from these cultures usually also prefer individuals to make decisions. They may accept group decisions only if they view them to be in their own best interest.

In contrast, members of *group-oriented cultures*, for example the Chinese, Indians, Indonesians, Mexicans, or most Latin Americans, tend to value their group's collective beliefs and practices much more highly. Examples for such groups are the person's family, their social network, their work team, a larger organization they belong to, or the society they live in. To them, strong and dependable relationships are often critically important, both in their private lives and in business. Decision making in this culture is usually a collective process that may require reaching consensus among all group members.

Most cultures combine elements of both orientations, albeit to a varying degree. Preferences for individualism versus group orientation influence several aspects of the negotiation process, from team composure to relationship building, decision making, or general timing of phases and concessions.

Chapter 3: Relationships

Before we analyze the importance of relationships in business, let us define the term: in our context, 'relationship' describes interpersonal connections between two negotiating parties, which could be companies or individuals, that

- allow the individuals involved in the negotiation process to become familiar with each other,

- establish and nurture trust between them,

- promote win-win cooperation based on mutual benefit, and

- increase the parties' willingness to do business together, even if doing so involves significant risk and uncertainty.

How Relationships Impact Negotiations

It seems intuitively obvious that the strength of relationships between negotiating parties will significantly influence the outcome of negotiations between them. Human experience dictates being more careful when dealing with strangers with whom no relationship exists than with people we know and trust. Accordingly, strong relationships between the negotiating parties usually reduce the tension between them, bring balance and stability to the process, help both sides focus on the benefits of the exchange, and increase their dedication to overcome obstacles. The impact depends to no small degree on the negotiators' cultural background, though. When discussing country-specific aspects in Part III of this book, four different categories classify the importance of relationships for the negotiation process in a given culture:

- *Moderately important.* Members of cultures belonging to this group, which includes Americans, Australians, Austrians, Canadians, Germans, and a few others, rarely view strong relationships a necessary precondition for business interactions. Being task-oriented, they tend to focus on business objectives and contract clauses. Their primary motivators are often near-term financial or strategic benefits rather than long-term relationship aspects. Though they may expect to get to know the other party better while doing business together, they do not need to trust someone in order to make a deal with the person. Many in this group are reluctant to invest significant time and effort into relationship building during the early stages of business engagements. Negotiation styles and attitudes in these cultures do not depend much on relationship aspects. In addition, business ties exist mostly at the corporate level: if a new company representative is introduced into an existing business relationship, that person is usually soon accepted as a valid partner.

- *Important.* These cultures tend to value trust between business partners more highly than those in the previous category do. While they may also engage in negotiations without first getting to know their counterparts, members of this group will strive to learn much more about them over the course of the exchange. Once initial negotiations have been successful and trust has been established, a sense of loyalty may develop, facilitating future business engagements. Relationships still mostly exist at the corporate level with this group, but individual employees commonly also aim to strengthen personal ties with their business counterparts. These characteristics apply to many European cultures, among them Finland, France, Hungary, Northern Italy, Poland, Switzerland, the United Kingdom, and others.

- *Very important.* People in this group of cultures, which includes Indians, Hong Kong Chinese, Koreans, Mexicans, Pakistanis, Russians, Saudi Arabs, Southern Italians, Spaniards, most Latin Americans, and many others, value lasting and trusting business relationships. They strongly prefer to do business with those they know and like. Accordingly, they are prepared to spend significant time building and strengthening relationships. Usually not interested in near-term deals, they mostly focus on longer-term engagements and repeat business. Because potential business partners may first have to prove themselves trustworthy, initial engagements could be small, especially with foreigners. When members of this group engage in business interactions without first spending time to get to know their counterparts, this likely indicates that they are aiming for quick gains and are not interested in doing business with the other party in the long haul. The concept of corporate relationships does not mean much to this group. Since business is viewed as personal, individuals expect to spend considerable time and effort to develop close ties with their immediate counterparts even when their companies have a long history of doing business together.

- *Critically important.* Members of cultures belonging to this group, among them Asian countries such as China, Indonesia, Japan, Malaysia, the Philippines, and Taiwan, as well as countries such as Brazil, Egypt, or Greece, prefer to build deep and lasting relationships with prospective partners before entering into serious business engagements. They may expect to continue developing such relationships into true friendships as the business partnership continues. Both sympathy and trust are essential requirements for them to make deals with others.

In cultures where relationships are critically important, foreign negotiators often find it extremely difficult to reach business agreements if such agreements might adversely affect the other side's existing relationships with other parties. The prevalent business attitude in these cultures is that current partners must first be given opportunities and receive support that might allow them to win the deals the new party may be proposing. It may be only if these partners decline such an opportunity that the proposing party will be given serious consideration.

With this group, it is vital to be prepared to spend considerable time and effort building strong relationships throughout the negotiation process without appearing too focused on any agenda. With the exception of the Japanese, who seem equally focused on tasks and relationships, members of this group may appear less task-oriented than others may. They do not pay much attention to contracts, since most of them believe that the strength of business relationships matters much more than 'a piece of paper' does. Keeping in touch with them on a regular basis even after the negotiation exchange has ended will ensure that commitments are kept and opens doors for additional business. Since they mostly focus on long-term engagements and repeat business, decision makers may agree with initial deals that appear unfavorable for them, expecting their new partners to make up for this down the road. People in this group pay little attention to corporate-level connections, since few of them believe that business relationships can be successful without strong personal ties. While the more pragmatic among them may also engage in business interactions with relative strangers if the prospects are sufficiently attractive, members of this group will most likely focus on short-term benefits and might not shy away from taking unfair advantage of the other party when given a chance.

These characterizations provide several clues as to what to expect and where to focus when conducting business with people from foreign countries. However, these categorizations should never be taken at face value, since they apply mostly in business areas that do not critically depend on personal relationships. In some industries, such as banking, financial services, or legal counseling, the nature of business interactions requires strong trust between the parties irrespectively of their cultural background. Such a requirement may promote different practices in these industries. In any case, spending time and effort to build closer relationships in international interactions is always conducive to business and therefore strongly recommended, regardless of cultural background and type of business.

Westerners seeking to engage in international business in Africa, Asia, Latin America, and in Southern Europe often underestimate the impact of strong personal ties on the success or failure of negotiations. Experienced international negotiators realize that the number of countries where people view relationship building as very important or critically important far exceeds that of cultures who view them as less relevant. They adjust their behaviors and actions accordingly, realizing that failing to meet the expectations of a member of a strongly relationship-focused culture would make that counterpart unlikely to commit to any business deals.

Note that the categories we defined apply only to business relationships. Away from business, people may have different concepts of what constitutes relationships. For instance, Americans are often said to be 'easy to get to know, hard to get close to.' In business and elsewhere, they tend to be friendly but are often very selective when it comes to developing close friendships. In contrast, Austrians and Germans can be hard to get to know personally, especially in business situations. Away from business, though, many of them develop large networks of close friends with whom they may build strong and dependable relationships.

Showing Respect

Successful businesspeople know that showing respect for their negotiation partners is essential. In cross-cultural situations, the importance of demonstrating, by word and deed, esteem and regard for the other party only grows further. Counterparts who feel disrespected are likely to look for ways to 'make the other pay' for that, which tends to trigger emotional decisions and reduces the effectiveness of the negotiation. In strongly relationship-oriented cultures, seemingly small incidents might actually cause the negotiation process to break down completely if handled poorly.

Respect is expected at different levels. While all humans expect to be respected as individuals, most of them also want the organizations and institutions they represent, and their country and culture as a whole, to enjoy proper regard and appreciation. In individualistic culture, personal respect tends to be of utmost importance. In strongly group-oriented cultures, showing apparent disrespect for an organization or society may represent an even greater offense than treating individuals with less than the expected consideration and courtesy.

What people respect and what constitutes 'proper' respect are complex culture-specific concepts which are influenced by several factors. One of them is whether the respect members of a given culture are willing to pay another person more strongly depends on ascription or on the person's individual achievements.

Key Concepts: Ascription versus Achievement

In *ascription-oriented cultures*, for instance in most Asian and Latin American countries, people tend to focus on family background and hierarchical rank when assessing a person's importance and the respect he or she deserves. While those in positions of authority may be respected regardless of their personal shortcomings, individuals who have achieved significant personal successes but lack the 'right' background and rank might command little respect in these cultures.

In contrast, members of primarily *achievement-oriented cultures*, such as the United States, Canada, or Australia, much more appreciate individual accomplishments. They may respect business achievements, personal wealth, public recognition, and education irrespectively of a person's background and upbringing.

Another aspect that is specific to the cultural context is how much respect people expect to be shown. This depends largely on whether the culture's status orientation is primarily egalitarian or authoritarian.

Key Concepts: Egalitarian versus Authoritarian Cultures

People in strongly *egalitarian cultures*, among them Australians, the Dutch, Israelis, and Scandinavians, expect every person, regardless of his or her role, to be treated with respect and courtesy. They prefer flat hierarchies and may have little tolerance for individuals who think themselves superior to others. Authority is often informal, and respect depends much more on individual characteristics than on ranks or titles. Foreign senior executives may actually enjoy greater respect when downplaying their own role than if trying to signal status and importance.

Strongly *authoritarian cultures* view clear hierarchies as essential in business and elsewhere. Titles and degrees are generally respected in these cultures. Executives may enjoy enormous deference and tend to behave in paternalistic ways. They are expected to demonstrate their importance through status symbols and corresponding behaviors. Being overly friendly with people of lower rank can be counterproductive with this group of cultures, which includes Brazil, Greece, Indonesia, Malaysia, Pakistan, the Philippines, Saudi Arabia, Thailand, and others.

The concepts discussed so far are characterized by a focus on individual concerns. Violating any of the implied rules may disturb relationships with the affected individual but does not necessarily impact the interaction with others. However, respect often also represents a collective concept, especially when dealing with cultures that highly value group harmony.

Key Concepts: Harmony, the Concept of Face, and the Influence of Pride

Many cultures, especially group-oriented ones, are characterized by a strong preference for maintaining **harmony** across their members. This value is often reflected in the practice of individual embarrassment leading to collective shame. With some groups, corresponding behaviors may include wording concerns in positive and constructive ways or refraining from commenting on people in front of others. However, other societies, in particular many Asian ones, have little tolerance for any kind of negative communication and impose much stricter cultural rules. Symptoms of such strong harmony orientation may include evasive answers when people disagree with comments or requests, problems that are not openly confronted or even acknowledged, or statements that only reflect what the speaker believes a counterpart wants to hear, rather than what he or she really thinks. Members of these cultures often view direct communication as disrespectful.

Closely related to this orientation is the concept of **face**, which prevails in most Asian countries. *Face* is the external representation of a positive and harmonious self as viewed by others. The term's use is not limited to individuals; rather, families, groups, organizations, or even whole nations may have *face* in this sense. *Loss of face* can either be caused by own actions and behaviors deemed inappropriate within the culture, or by the actions of others. For instance, openly showing emotions may be viewed as a lack of self-control and can cause *loss of face* in some cultures, as can being treated disrespectfully by another person or group.

Pride is different from *face* inasmuch as it represents an internal value that depends on individuals' views of themselves. Nevertheless, since the perceptions of others strongly influence people's pride, this makes little difference in terms of cultural norms and accepted behaviors. Similar to the concept of *face*, pride may also be individual or collective. Expectations of proper actions and behaviors in countries where pride tends to play a significant role, such as in Spain, Mexico, or Latin America, resemble those of *face*-oriented cultures.

Causing an individual or a group to lose *face* or hurting someone's pride may have severe implications for relationships, even if done inadvertently. Since seemingly small infractions of cultural rules could jeopardize and even disrupt important negotiations, it is vital to respect these concepts, adjusting behaviors as necessary.

Effective Relationship Building

To feel closely connected with a business counterpart, most humans require three factors to come together: they need to know the individual well, like the person, and trust him or her to a comfortable degree. Accordingly, effective relationship building is stimulated by the following behaviors:

- *Allow your counterparts to get to know you.* As a general rule, the less your negotiation counterparts know about you, the more likely they will be to act cautiously, conceal their intentions, and slow the negotiation so they can gather further information. When considering the effectiveness of the immediate negotiation as well as its long-term implications, you will often find it to be in your best interest to share more information about yourself than you might otherwise view necessary. In fact, while negotiators in some countries only care to know about aspects that are immediately relevant to the negotiation exchange, members of many other cultures expect to learn seemingly immaterial details about their counterparts. They might seek to receive personal information, for example about your family background and education, understand your company's background and history, and get insight into your professional role and responsibilities. In some cultures, even highly personal questions, such as whether you are married or whether you have plans for children, are deemed acceptable. This interest is generally stimulated by your counterparts' desire to understand your values, beliefs, and preferred behaviors. It would be unwise to reject outright such questioning. In addition, your counterparts may inquire about your negotiation objectives and intentions. Whether or not they really expect you to share much of this information depends on the specific cultural context.

- *Nurture liking and empathy.* When dealing with cultures whose members strongly value relationships, whether or not your counterparts actually like you and feel good around you can make a substantial difference to their negotiation attitudes as well as their willingness to make concessions. Beyond showing respect, being open and sociable often promotes stronger liking. As with other cross-cultural aspects, playing by your counterparts' cultural 'rulebook' rather than by your own one will be vastly more effective. For example, some Westerners may be tempted to loosen up and show their personal side as a way to nurture liking. Members of other cultures, especially authoritarian ones, could view this approach as intrusive and disrespectful, even with close business partners. In many situations, it is wiser to maintain an air of restraint and formality around them while avoiding the appearance of being impersonal. Another example of culture-specific assumptions is that 'likeness creates liking,' which is not necessarily the case. For example, while most Americans value similarity and tend to bond more strongly with people with whom they share common interests, the French value difference and may warm up to people whose experiences and interests lie in different areas than their own ones. As a general rule, try to focus on what your counterparts value and enjoy, not on what might make yourself most comfortable.

Social events often create great opportunities to develop closer ties. Declining invitations to such events without giving *very* compelling reasons can be disastrous for the relationship building. A common way for people in many cultures to stimulate the process is to consume alcoholic drinks together. The Chinese, the Japanese, Koreans, Russians, and Ukrainians are somewhat notorious with this regard. No matter what your personal preference, it is generally recommended to participate in after-hours drinking in these cultures, since not joining in will be viewed as a sign that you are not interested in building closer relationships. However, avoid getting overly drunk, since this may again be held against you. If you are unwilling to drink alcohol, your best bet will be to claim medical reasons for this refusal. Doing so may nevertheless adversely affect your relationships.

- **Build trust.** Interpersonal trust depends on many influence factors. One of them is age: younger people are generally less mistrusting than older ones. Other factors depend on cultural context. Task-oriented people, among them many Americans, Australians, Austrians, Canadians, or Germans, base their trust mostly on competence and behavioral consistency. With them, you may establish and nurture trust by demonstrating that you are competent in your field, making realistic commitments, and consistently honoring such commitments or at least showing good intentions to do so.

Relationship-oriented people, on the other hand, focus more strongly on predictability. When negotiating with an unknown party, they value recommendations from others whom they already trust and will look for examples of past behavior that may indicate how dependable the potential new partner is. You will often find it easier to establish initial trust through third parties who can introduce you and give references. Regular communication and follow-up will be taken as indication of your continuous commitment to the business partnership. In addition, demonstrating your willingness to 'go the extra mile' by making unexpected efforts to support your counterparts will nurture their trust in you.

Levels of trust in unknown people differ substantially between cultures. In a cross-cultural survey, researchers have found that about two-thirds of people from Northern Europe or from China, and about half of the Americans surveyed, agreed with the statement that 'most people can be trusted.' In contrast, less than one in five Brazilians, Turks, or Romanians shared this belief. Accordingly, it may actually require substantially more effort and dedication to win people's trust and confidence in some cultures than in others.

Opportunities for relationship building abound around international negotiations. They include business meetings and conferences, lunches and dinners, business entertainment, social events, and many other occasions. Whether making small talk, meeting in formal settings, attending ceremonial banquets, or socializing at informal gatherings, always treat the event as an opportunity to deepen relationships with the other party. However, keep in mind that you will be more effective if you act in ways that are consistent with your counterparts' cultural expectations *in the particular setting*. Bringing up the wrong subjects during small talk, appearing too casual in meetings, failing to follow the rules of etiquette at banquets, or inappropriately bringing up business topics at social functions are all significant faux pas that could weaken the critical relationships you may be trying to build.

Gender-Specific Aspects of Relationship Building

In recent years, women's emancipation in business has fortunately made much progress in many countries around the world. Though a lot more may need to happen to achieve equal representation, it is unquestionable that more women than ever now fill professional roles and carry substantial responsibility. In spite of this general trend, building and nurturing effective business relationships across genders remains challenging in many countries and cultures. Two factors tend to get in the way:

- *Lack of concepts for business relationship building across genders.* Clear frameworks exist in all societies to determine how relationship building is conducted among men in business. However, such concepts often do not apply to males and females conducting business together, which complicates working across genders. Men in particular often behave differently when dealing with women, which tends to make the relationship building process harder and less effective.

- *Traditional expectations of female roles.* Men in several cultures may still hold on to traditional views of the roles women should fill and how women should behave around men. Western ways of doing business may clash with these beliefs. In countries such as Japan or Saudi Arabia, men may not be prepared to deal with women in business at all unless the women fill subordinate roles. Lacking a framework for dealing with women who hold substantial responsibility and make important decisions, they could behave awkwardly when dealing with such women. Chances are that some of them might avoid interactions altogether. In other authoritarian or patriarchic societies, for instance in Egypt, Indonesia, Greece, Spain, Turkey, or in many Latin American countries, men might be a bit more forthcoming. Nevertheless, many of them still openly or secretly disapprove of women filling what they view as 'male' roles. Accordingly, businesswomen often remain relative outsiders in these cultures. It can be difficult for them to win the trust and respect of their male counterparts. Paradoxically, relationship building can be particularly challenging for women in many of the cultures whose members value relationships most strongly.

As a result of these factors, building close relationships in international negotiations tends to be easier for male negotiators than for female ones. While this may appear –and indeed is– unfair, visiting businesswomen must realize and often accept that they might not be able to build close business relationships with some of their male counterparts in such countries, even if they are willing to make special efforts in order to prove themselves as likeable and trustworthy partners.

Chapter 4: Effective Communication

Language

In today's global environment, English has become the *lingua franca*, the almost universal language of the business world. By and large, the challenges presented by language differences are much less significant than they were only fifty years ago. Nonetheless, language barriers may still prove to be substantial obstacles in cross-cultural negotiations.

Even when interpreters are readily available, being able to speak the language of negotiation counterparts or teaming up with someone who does may create significant benefits. For one, speaking the same language strengthens relationships, since it tends to make people more comfortable with each other. On top of that, some of the information conveyed inevitably gets lost in translations. Languages commonly reflect concepts that are tied to their cultural context. Many of them lack certain words that could be important in another party's cultural framework. In addition, translations inevitably lose important clues, such as speech patterns and tone of voice that signal authority or indicate that someone is lying. Using interpreters should therefore be a last resort only if no viable alternative exists.

Even when one party is able to speak the other's language, one must remain aware of the risk of misunderstandings. Research has shown human communication to be ineffective even between native speakers of the same language. Translation inaccuracies, mispronunciation of words, and other lapses that are common when people communicate in a foreign language inevitably add further confusion and miscommunication.

Interacting with Non-native Speakers

Here are a few suggestions to help improve the communication across parties whose native languages are different:

- *Listen attentively.* Following the line of thought of a person speaking in a language that is foreign to the speaker can be hard, even if it happens to be your native language. You should generally pay closer attention in such situations than you might normally do when communicating with people in your own country.

- *Verify mutual understanding.* Because misunderstandings are frequent, giving and seeking feedback are very important in non-native language communication. Acknowledge frequently what is being said, and ask your counterparts to confirm their understanding whenever appropriate.

- *Use simple language, speak clearly, and slow down.* Unless you are talking in the listeners' native language, they may be struggling to identify and translate what you are saying. This process tends to be much slower than the speaker might assume. Choosing simple words, pronouncing them clearly, and slowing the speed of your speech will greatly improve the odds of being understood. If a foreign counterpart asks you to repeat something you said, do not conclude that they did not hear you. More likely, you may have used an expression unfamiliar to the person, or you may have talked too fast for the individual to cope with the required translation. Repeating what you said in a louder voice could only make the person uncomfortable without necessarily solving the problem. It will be more helpful if you repeat your message using different words and speaking more slowly.

- *Pause frequently.* Translating takes time. Even when counterparts seem reasonably fluent in a foreign language, they will be struggling to keep up with the message if you speak at normal speed in your native language. Pausing frequently will give them the time to understand and reflect on what is being said.

- *Repeat yourself and use visual aides.* You will frequently find that repeating important points is helpful in getting your messages across. Using visual aids is but one way to accomplish this: if what you say and what you show convey the same points, your chances of being understood improve considerably. For the same reason, provide handouts during your meetings and follow up with clear and easy-to-understand written summaries.

Non-Verbal Messages

Humans use gestures and other 'body language' to emphasize points or to send subtle messages. Some of these non-verbal messages may be intentional, while others are based on subconscious behaviors that are hard to control. The meaning of such messages is understood by most members of the person's cultural group, often also by others. For instance, most Westerners take smiles or nods of the head as indication of agreement, folded arms as disbelief or rejection, head scratching as a show of surprise or confusion, or fingers drumming on a table as a sign of impatience.

Unfortunately, only a few such clues are familiar to people all around the world, such as sitting straight, frequently blinking the eyes, or suddenly speaking in a higher pitched voice, which may all indicate that the person displaying the behavior is telling a lie. Most non-verbal messages are not universally understood, though. Greeks and Turks may read nods of the head as rejection. Asians tend to smile not only to express positive emotions, but also to conceal annoyance or anger. Other non-verbal messages may mean little or nothing to Westerners. For instance, some Asians inhale sharply when trying to indicate a serious problem. Others may look down while speaking with another person as a show of respect. Since gestures tend to be small and subtle in Asia, Westerners might miss some of them entirely.

Non-verbal communication can get even more complicated if gestures or behaviors take on different meanings across cultures. The American *OK* sign, with thumb and index finger forming a circle, is an obscene gesture in several countries. Slapping the open hand over a fist, which Americans and Canadians sometimes do to signal a passion for action, might be taken as a huge insult in Russia or Ukraine. Keeping frequent eye contact conveys sincerity in some cultures, while people in others may interpret the same behavior as rude and intrusive. Moving closer to another person in conversation may signal intimacy or mere friendliness. In contrast, moving away may be read as a sign of respect for a counterpart's personal space by some, while others could take it as an indication of discomfort that is caused by them.

Learning to use and interpret body language correctly is essential in any culture. Of equal importance is the ability to follow the other culture's implicit rules. For example, most Asians restrict their body language and disapprove of the extensive gestures that Italians, Spaniards, Mexicans, Latin Americans, and others may prefer. Asians also often consider touching others a major offense, even between people of the same gender. While the relevance of such non-verbal communication varies across cultures, getting it wrong can have disastrous consequences for relationships and negotiation outcomes alike.

Directness

A common cause of intercultural communication problems is how directly or indirectly people express themselves. Here are a few typical statements illustrating different styles:

Direct Communication	Indirect Communication
'We cannot do this.'	'This may be difficult.'
'Your proposal is unacceptable.'	'We need time to think about it.'
'This is not correct.'	'This is an interesting perspective.'
'This cannot be done today.'	'We will see.'
'I'm just calling things what they are.'	'We must be respectful of others.'
'Yes' means 'I agree.'	'Yes' means 'I heard what you said.'
'We will consider it' signals interest.	'We will consider it' signals skepticism or rejection.
'No' indicates rejection.	'No' is rarely used.

It is a popular misconception to believe that *indirect* represents the equivalent of *vague*. The contrary is true: it is possible to communicate very clear messages in a highly indirect fashion. However, most Westerners require extensive practice to learn this skill.

In addition to subtle verbal clues such as in the above examples, people in indirect cultures often use other ways to communicate their real message, making it important to 'read between the lines.' What is *not* being said often becomes more important than what *is*. For instance, if a person praises an insubstantial aspect of a proposal that has just been made, the real message may be that he or she dislikes essential parts of it. Silence is another, non-verbal way to communicate displeasure and rejection.

Several factors influence how directly people communicate, such as whether a culture is generally more individualistic or group-oriented, egalitarian or authoritarian, comfortable or uncomfortable with uncertainty. Typical levels of directness vary widely across cultures. The Dutch, Israelis, or people from the northeastern United States tend to be very direct, leaving little uncertainty in their statements. The British, Canadians, the French, or Americans from other parts of the country are usually fairly direct, though less so than the first group. Koreans, Mexicans, and most Latin Americans use more indirect communication and generally prefer subtlety over frankness and candor. The Chinese, Indonesians, Thais, and above all others, the Japanese tend to communicate in a very indirect manner that can be difficult for Westerners to interpret correctly.

It is characteristic of most societies that their members tend to view their own culturally preferred style as superior to others. People from direct cultures can get very frustrated with those communicating more indirectly, sometimes accusing them of being indecisive, evasive, or even sneaky. Similarly, members of cultural groups who value indirect communication may be shocked, feeling insulted or attacked by foreigners who communicate much more directly. As a general rule, it is usually easier for people from direct cultures, among them most Westerners, to adjust to more indirect ways of communication than the other way around. This is because they are generally familiar with the concept of diplomacy. In contrast, most Asians find it very difficult to be even nearly as blunt and outspoken as people in the West can be.

Levels of directness influence many aspects of international negotiations. Here are a few suggestions for Westerners preparing to interact with members of highly indirect cultures:

- *Do not force disagreement.* Always phrase offers and proposals in ways that will allow the other side to reject them without having to give a straight 'no' answer. Ask open questions and be prepared to propose alternatives rather than making take-it-or-leave-it statements.

- *Reject tactfully.* Respond with non-committal phrases if you dislike an offer or proposal. This is usually more effective than if you rejected it right away, since you will avoid offending your counterpart and also retain the option to change your mind later. Alternatively, make a counterproposal without commenting on the one your received, or simply ignore it altogether.

- *Be sensitive.* Listen carefully for subtle messages and watch your counterparts' body language for small clues.

- *Refrain from making assumptions.* Never assume that there is agreement because nobody said 'no.' Confirm agreement by asking the other side what they are willing to do.

- *Do not worry too much about the clarity of your message.* Westerners dealing with Asians, most of whom prefer indirect communication, often experience discomfort if things are 'left up in the air,' as they may see it. Fearing that subtle messages they previously conveyed may not have been properly understood, they often prefer to provide summaries at the end of meetings that clearly list issues and concerns. In reality, it is much likelier for Westerners' communication to lack the required subtlety than to be too indirect when dealing with Asians.

- *Avoid confrontation.* If the bargaining exchange becomes heated or when the negotiating parties get tied up in a dispute, it will be even more important to match your counterparts' communication style. Realize that in the heat of the argument you may be more inclined to communicate in a straightforward style while your counterparts will likely take this more negatively than they might do at other times.

Using Technology to Communicate

It should be obvious that using technology when communicating across cultures is intrinsically less efficient than speaking with a person face-to-face. Media such as e-mail, web conferencing, and various kinds of online collaboration tools come with significant shortcomings. They altogether block out body language and reduce opportunities for immediate feedback and clarification. In addition, they force what members of strongly relationship-oriented cultures usually view as impersonal communication: since they cannot see or hear their counterparts, they lose their sense of connectedness that affects communication and decision-making. Phone calls and conferences usually work better but still impose many restrictions. Even when using videoconferencing equipment, the only available technology that supports both verbal and non-verbal messages, subtle messages frequently get lost and participants tend to communicate more indirectly than they might in relaxed face-to-face settings.

As a general rule, how to use technology to communicate with a negotiation counterpart depends mostly on the importance and strength of the relationships. When communicating with people who highly value relationships, it is vital to find or create opportunities to meet with them whenever possible. Otherwise, it is best to use the phone. Until strong bonds have been established between both parties, the use of e-mail and other media should be restricted to exchanges of information or summaries of previous conversations. With members of cultures focusing less on relationship aspects, e-mail or web conferencing will generally prove effective. However, it will still be advisable to create opportunities to speak with counterparts face to face.

Making it Work

Communicating across cultures has been described as a minefield of practices, preferences, rules, and taboos that can be very difficult to cross. Nevertheless, anyone sensitive and flexible enough can make it work if they follow the right approach. Here are a few points to keep in mind for your next international negotiation:

- *Study the rules.* What members of a given culture consider appropriate or inappropriate may often appear arbitrary. Find enough information about your target culture's rulebook upfront to know what people expect.

- *Recognize communication preferences as cultural preferences.* How people in a given culture view the world determines to a large degree how they communicate. Learn enough about your counterparts' culture, and you will find it easy to communicate with them.

- *Realize that common language can be deceiving.* As Americans and the British have frequently discovered, speaking the same language does not mean that people share the same values and practices. In fact, meeting foreigners who are completely fluent in your own native language can mislead you to ignore cultural differences. Avoid falling into this mental trap by reminding yourself of the cultural differences if necessary.

- *Keep an open mind.* The hardest part of communicating across cultures can be to refrain from making assumptions about your counterparts' intentions. You will succeed if you make it a rule for yourself to verify any and all of your assumptions by seeking feedback and obtaining additional information before jumping to any conclusions.

Chapter 5: Initial Contacts and Meetings

Making Contact

Once you have assessed the environment you will be negotiating in, learned as much about the other party as you could, identified your BATNA, defined your negotiation strategy, and done everything else you needed to in order to be well prepared, the crucial next step will be to make initial contact. The most important decision at this point will be whether to contact the other party directly or through someone else. In some cases, there may be dependable existing contacts with the other side that could be leveraged. Otherwise, using third-party intermediaries is generally preferable, since such individuals could provide several valuable services:

- *Open doors.* Local intermediaries may be able to leverage existing relationships to make contact with a targeted company. In countries where relationships are critically important, it can be very difficult to get access to the right people without such contacts. In some cultures, for instance in Japan, it is also preferable to be introduced by an independent third party rather than by a representative of one's company.

- *Provide references.* As we established earlier, members of strongly relationship-oriented cultures often look for references from trusted sources to assess the predictability of a prospective new partner. Having local contacts who can serve as references can be invaluable.

- *Bridge cultural gaps.* A sufficiently experienced local intermediary will be able to bridge at least some of the gap between the cultures, allowing business to be conducted with greater effectiveness.

- *Improve the communication.* Assuming the person has the necessary skills, your intermediary may serve as an interpreter and help by clarifying subtle messages, body language, and other forms of indirect communication. If you work with the individual in a continual basis, he or she will also greatly improve the ongoing communication with your counterparts and reduce the risk of misunderstandings.

- *Establish continual local representation.* The right intermediary may serve as a representative throughout the negotiation, which can be advantageous in certain cultures. Having a local sponsor or agent may even be a legal requirement, as is the case in countries such as Egypt and Saudi Arabia.

Choosing the right intermediary can be crucial. In strongly relationship-oriented cultures, the reputation and respect a foreign party will enjoy depend to a large degree on the standing its local representative has or is able to develop with the other party. Companies lacking the necessary contacts to identify a respected intermediary in a targeted country should contact a local embassy, a trade organization, a chamber of commerce, or a local legal or accounting firm that may be able to provide a list of potential candidates.

Since the person must have the right contacts and reputation, choosing a representative requires careful selection. In countries where relationships are critically important, such as China, Indonesia, or Japan, such a third-party contact will be equally cautious before agreeing to represent a foreign company. Introducing a party to his or her local contacts that turns out to be unreliable or not trustworthy could have huge consequences for the individual's own reputation and relationships.

While intermediaries are often helpful, using one is not always necessary, especially in many Western cultures. Making direct contact with the other side may be more appropriate, in which case one needs to determine how best to do so. An initial letter introducing the company, outlining its proposal, and requesting a meeting is often the most promising approach. In authoritarian and status-oriented cultures, the overall impression such a letter gives may become a decisive factor, making it important its appearance and wording are impeccable.

Since decision processes may be complex, involving various hierarchical levels and requiring consultations across large groups of people, it is often difficult to determine how much time to allow for a response. In the United States, it is not unusual to receive a call from the recipient of a contact letter on the day it is received. A delay of more than a few weeks generally signals that the other party is not interested in the proposed deal. In contrast, many Arabs, Asians, or Latin Americans may require at least several weeks before responding to such a letter. Inquiring about it during this time can be counterproductive since these counterparts may take this as a lack of patience and long-term focus.

Setting Up the Initial Meeting

Once another party has signaled interest in negotiating, a number of aspects must be considered before setting up an initial meeting:

- *Preparation time*. Expectations of how much time to allow for upfront preparation vary greatly. In some countries, a week's notice may suffice, while people in others may consider three or even four weeks as too short. Showing too great a sense of urgency may be taken as a lack of patience and can be counterproductive.

- *Choice of location*. From a cross-cultural perspective, it makes little difference whether a negotiation takes place at a home location, in a counterparts' country, or elsewhere. The cultural distance between the parties, and thus the challenge to make the negotiation work, remains the same. Rules of etiquette may depend to a significant degree on the actual country where the negotiation takes place, though. Since unfamiliar settings tend to reduce people's comfort levels, it will generally be preferable to leverage the proverbial 'home advantage.' However, it is customary to let the party that has been contacted by the other choose the location.

- *Participants*. Which individuals need to attend an initial negotiation meeting depends to some degree on the cultural context. The core negotiation team (see also page 17) and any chosen intermediary, assuming that one is being used, will definitely be expected to attend. The Japanese, Mexicans, most Latin Americans, and others usually also expect a top executive on each side to attend the first meeting. This person will not be expected to attend subsequent meetings, though. Others, for instance the Chinese, Koreans, or Greeks, may expect continuous involvement of at least one senior executive throughout the negotiation. Members of a third cultural group, which includes Israel, the Nordics, Switzerland, the United States, and others, may not view the attendance of senior managers as essential. In any case, most counterparts will want to know upfront who will be attending the initial meeting, making it important to inform them in advance.

- *Agenda*. Setting an agenda ahead of the meeting is good practice. Doing so allows both parties to communicate upfront what they expect to cover in the meeting, giving them a chance to prepare and avoiding unwelcome surprises. If appropriate, one should propose an agenda and invite the other side to modify it as deemed necessary. The set agenda will not necessarily be followed, though, especially when meeting with members of highly polychronic cultures (see page 47).

The Critical First Meeting

As the old adage goes, "You will never get a second chance to make a first impression." When meeting foreign counterparts for the first time, chances are that the trust they are willing to place in a foreign visitor and the company he or she represent is much lower than if they were dealing with members of their own culture. The other party's representatives may initially remain cautious and reserved, sizing up the individual in order to determine whether the person is worthy of entertaining serious business discussions. First impressions become critically important at this point, as they are usually the basis for this decision.

Making matters even more challenging, people commonly tend to be less forgiving at first meetings than they may become down the road, when relationships have strengthened and trust has had a chance to develop. Comments or behaviors that may easily be forgiven in follow-on meetings could cause major issues at the critical initial one. It is vitally important to be 'on one's best behavior,' as viewed by the other party, when meeting for the first time. Below, we review aspects that require particular attention. The country-specific information in Part III of this book in most cases provides more detailed information.

- *Timeliness*. Cultural context to a large degree determines punctuality expectations. For example, people in countries like Germany, Switzerland, or Japan expect visitors to be right on time, while Greeks, Turks, Mexicans, or Latin Americans might tolerate delays of 15 minutes or more without viewing them as significant. As a general rule, foreigners are usually expected to be punctual while locals may not be, and people of lower status are often made to wait while those of high status might be received immediately. It is best never to show signs of impatience or anger if made to wait at an initial meeting.

- *Personal appearance*. Though people's expectations will again be dependent on their cultural background, it is generally preferable to err on the conservative side when it comes to dress codes. If in doubt, better risk being slightly overdressed rather than possibly appearing too casual. While body language and gestures also need to be adjusted to the specific culture, a few rules are universal. For instance, one should refrain from putting the hands on the hips, which is frequently interpreted as aggressive, or folding the arms, which many people interpret as defensive. Similarly, it is important not to stand too close to others or too far away, greet or talk to people with both hands in the pockets, or put the feet onto furniture. Any of these may insult some people.

- *Required protocol and formality*. The rules of what establishes 'proper' behavior at business meetings can be amazingly complex. They often include numerous aspects that members of a cultural group deem important, such as naming conventions and the use of titles, how to introduce or greet people, how to hand out and receive business cards, the order in which individuals should enter a room, or where to be seated. Once the meeting itself has started, protocol rules may dictate who leads discussions, who gets to speak when, how much time to spend on introductions and small talk before focusing on business aspects, which conversation topics to avoid, how to behave at the end of the meeting, and much more. While levels of formality vary considerably across cultures and some may generally be more forgiving than others, breaches of protocol at best create awkward situations and at worst could bring negotiations to a premature end.

- *Humor*. Culture guides often point out that 'humor does not travel,' which seems to imply that it is best to avoid telling jokes or making humorous remarks when traveling abroad. While this is sound advice at least with a few cultures, it ignores the important role that humor plays in business in many countries. This is most pronounced in the Anglo-Saxon world, for instance in Australia, Canada, Ireland, the United Kingdom, or the United States, where showing a strong sense of humor is important as it helps 'break the ice,' allowing meeting participants to quickly focus on the business at hand. In contrast, using humor in business situations is not advisable in Japan and may be rare in Germany, the Netherlands, the Nordics, and several other countries. Since definitions of what constitutes a proper sense of humor vary much across cultures, it is vital to keep jokes light and friendly, staying away from remarks that might be perceived as cynical, sarcastic, or depreciative, even if made with the best of intentions.

- *Presentations*. While one might assume that presentation styles are mostly homogeneous in business around the world, members of different cultures may actually disagree over what constitutes a well-delivered presentation. It pays to study these differences, modifying materials and delivery of presentations accordingly, as this tends to help in making a favorable initial impression. Members of some cultures may expect formal presentations that include much background information about presenter and company, while others may look for lengthy technical explanations with many facts and details. Again others may not want to receive any formal presentation at the first meeting. One group may expect to be given room for extensive questioning and discussion, while another might consider interruptions rude. Providing copies of presentations and other handouts is always appreciated, especially when translated to local languages. However, whether people prefer these materials to look simple or to have strong visual appeal is again influenced by their respective cultural background.

Chapter 6: Negotiating and the Bargaining Exchange

Negotiation Attitudes

Behaviors and practices of negotiators around the world are strongly influenced by individual views of 'how to negotiate right.' Three principal attitudes are prevalent in domestic and international negotiations. They are mostly determined by the individuals' preferred levels of assertiveness and cooperation:

- *Cooperative.* These negotiators believe in the value of working together with their counterparts in order to solve what they see as a joint problem between the parties. Negotiators who truly embrace this attitude intend to collaborate with their counterparts for collective gain, looking to 'expand the pie' and share benefits equitably. This is commonly referred to as *win-win* negotiating. While individuals with this mindset might remain firm when required, they rarely see a need to be highly assertive. Members of several cultures, among them Anglo-Canadians, the Dutch, the French, Germans, Northern Europeans, the Japanese, Thais, and many Latin Americans, prefer such a cooperative approach. A related, though less effective way to reach consensus with a negotiation partner is to compromise. This requires both sides to make meaningful concessions in order to stimulate mutually acceptable solutions. Compromising is frequent in certain highly relationship-oriented cultures, for instance in Thailand, where it helps minimize conflict and disagreement. In contrast, compromising may be viewed as 'not trying hard enough' and is often disliked by people from countries such as the Netherlands, France, or Germany.

- *Competitive.* Most competitive negotiators consider negotiating a zero-sum game. In their view, one side's gain will need to equal the other side's loss. Accordingly, such individuals tend to be more assertive and less cooperative than those in the first group. Their strategies and tactics focus on winning concessions of greater value than they are prepared to give up in return. Haggling, which often creates competitive advantages with counterparts who are uncomfortable with repetitive back-and-forth exchanges, can be extensive with some individuals in this group. Though competitive negotiators may become emotionally involved in the process, most of them consider negotiating a game and expect their counterparts not to take any of their behaviors personally. Countries where negotiators tend to be competitive include Argentina, Brazil, China, India, Indonesia, Italy, Mexico, South Korea, Spain, Taiwan, the United States, and others.

- *Adversarial.* Adversarial negotiators are typically characterized by he lowest levels of cooperation and the highest degrees of assertiveness among the three groups. Rather than tracking and celebrating their own gains, many of them appear focused on the other party's losses. Instead of collaborating with their counterparts, adversarial negotiators frequently employ uncooperative and even aggressive approaches and behaviors. Others use passive-aggressive tactics, refusing to participate or fully engage in the negotiation exchange and pretending to be disinterested in their counterparts' offerings. These behaviors are non-constructive and can make agreement between the parties very difficult to reach. Adversarial negotiators can be found anywhere in the world. They represent insignificant minorities in most countries. The small group of cultures where adversarial negotiating is more prevalent includes Russia and Ukraine. It is important to realize that this attitude does not necessarily reflect interpersonal animosity or hostile intentions. In fact, people who appear adversarial during the exchange may turn out to be friendly and sociable when away from the negotiation table.

While influenced by cultural context, negotiation attitudes mostly reflect individual preferences. Accordingly, none of the principal attitudes we describe is exclusive to any one culture, nor is any of them limited to a select group of countries. Highly adversarial negotiators may belong to cultures whose members generally prefer cooperative negotiating and vice versa. As a matter of fact, all three of these negotiation attitudes can be found anywhere around the world.

Conflicting attitudes can make it hard for negotiation parties to trust each other. However, it would be a mistake to assume that competitive or adversarial individuals invariably value relationships less than others do. It may seem counterintuitive that an apparently competitive or adversarial counterpart might belong to a strongly relationship-oriented society. However, members of such cultures might not necessarily consider these attitudes as inconsistent with their values. Some of them might view tough bargaining as a necessary precondition for lasting business engagements.

Bargaining Styles

Negotiation attitudes are mostly founded in individual negotiators' value systems. Such principal beliefs usually remain unchanged throughout negotiations. Nevertheless, experienced negotiators often employ multiple styles during the bargaining exchange, adjusting behaviors along the way as deemed necessary. The following bargaining styles are common:

- *Joint problem-solving.* This integrative bargaining style encourages the parties to work together constructively. Emphasizing a cooperative spirit, it relies on persuasion as the primary way to resolve disagreements. Though emotional pleas are not necessarily excluded, the use of rational arguments, supported by facts and figures, dominates the bargaining exchange between negotiators employing this style. Joint problem solving is common among cooperative negotiators and can be productive when dealing with highly competitive individuals as well. In contrast, adversarial negotiators rarely use this style.

- *Distributive bargaining.* If a party believes that the total value of the items being negotiated is fixed, it will likely adopt a distributive bargaining style. This commonly reflects competitive or adversarial negotiation attitudes. Such negotiators are rarely satisfied with both sides receiving equal benefits as a result of the bargaining exchange. Instead, many of them focus on winning as much as they possibly can. Common tactics indicating this style include bluffing and other deception tactics, threats and ultimatums, and general attempts to overpower or outsmart the other party.

- *Contingency bargaining*. A source of conflict and a frequent cause of disagreements between negotiating parties is that their assumptions about future trends and events may differ considerably. Contingency bargaining allows them to turn such a situation into a productive negotiation that focuses on credible scenarios. By introducing if-then clauses into the bargaining exchange, negotiators using this style can capture their own assumptions and those of their counterparts, stimulating constructive dialogues over how potential benefits will be distributed between the parties. Both cooperative or competitive negotiators may use this bargaining style. Since it requires a minimum level of collaboration between the parties, adversarial counterparts rarely adopt this style, though.

- *Debate*. Negotiators who prefer debating usually believe in the power of logical arguments, rhetoric, and intellectual capability. Debates tend to be less constructive than joint problem solving may be, where the parties focus on win-win results. Debates are normally stimulated by a negotiator's intent to persuade the other party to accept his or her position. Depending on the individual's objectivity and sense of fairness, either side might win such arguments. However, this bargaining style may lead to the parties 'digging in their heels' and getting stuck in non-constructive exchanges of positions. Debates are often initiated by strongly competitive or adversarial negotiators.

- *Non-directive discussion*. This explorative bargaining style aims to motivate negotiating parties to explore their assumptions and expectations. Since it is not necessarily designed to drive conclusions or to persuade others, this style is commonly employed in the information gathering phase and sometimes in the opening phase of the bargaining exchange. Negotiators using it are likely to switch to other styles when they believe that both sides are ready to work out their disagreements and identify acceptable settlement terms. Non-directive discussion requires cooperative attitudes on both sides of the negotiation table.

- *Relationship building*. This bargaining style can be valuable in strongly relationship-oriented cultures. It focuses on creating emotional bonds between the negotiating parties that are nurtured by mutual liking and trust. Negotiators using this style believe that trusting relationships are essential for successful business. They are often willing to compromise and make concessions as a way to indicate their commitment to a relationship. Though most popular among cooperative negotiators, this style is sometimes also employed by competitive ones.

Cultural factors significantly influence negotiators' choices of bargaining styles. Americans, Canadians, Dutch, Germans, Japanese, Northern Europeans, or Swiss people often prefer joint problem solving. The Chinese, Indians, Israelis, Russians, Taiwanese, Ukrainians, and many Latin Americans may favor distributive and contingency bargaining. Debating is a style frequently chosen by Australians, the French, French-Canadians, and Greeks. Building and leveraging relationships, while common across many cultures, may be particularly valued among Brazilians, Indonesians, Italians, Mexicans, Filipinos, Saudis, Spaniards, and Thais.

In any case, most negotiators will likely employ more than one of these styles during the bargaining exchange. For example, since smart negotiators pay attention to longer-term aspects of their business relationships, many of them combine competitive approaches with at least some cooperative elements. Generally competitive individuals may therefore compromise, make small concessions, or work with their counterparts in order to augment the mutual benefits of a proposed deal. This could reflect such individuals' realization that appearing competitive and unyielding throughout the exchange might cause their counterparts to become less cooperative. Nevertheless, such negotiators will likely continue to focus on coming out of the overall bargaining exchange ahead of their counterparts.

Another example for negotiators switching bargaining styles is that adversarial individuals often become more cooperative as the negotiation nears its end. Again, this aims to stimulate productive business relationships, even if the bargaining exchange itself was less constructive.

Being able to understand, recognize, and effectively deal with diverse negotiation attitudes and bargaining styles are vital skills for international negotiators. The most successful of them know how to control tone and atmosphere of the negotiation exchange independently of their counterparts' preferences. They do so by adjusting their own behaviors as appropriate, either by modifying attitudes and styles as appropriate or by employing negotiation techniques such as those described in Part II of this book, many of which serve to influence the other party's conduct and actions.

Bargaining Levers: Power, Information, and Time

The purpose of bargaining is to identify the terms under which the negotiating parties may reach agreement over a proposed deal. At its core, bargaining is a persuasion process designed to eliminate conflicting objectives, identify opportunities for mutual benefit, and find common ground between the parties. Persuasion mechanisms that might be employed during this exchange range from rational and logical reasoning to emotional, intuitive, and dogmatic appeals. While cultural preferences may drive certain preferences, people from all countries and cultures commonly employ any of these approaches.

In its most basic form, bargaining is the process that two negotiating parties use to identify an item's specific value that both of them consider attractive enough to agree with a transaction. For example, this could be the price for a product that one party intends to sell and the other intends to buy. Such an agreed value, or settling point, might lie anywhere within the settlement range shown in Figure 6.1.

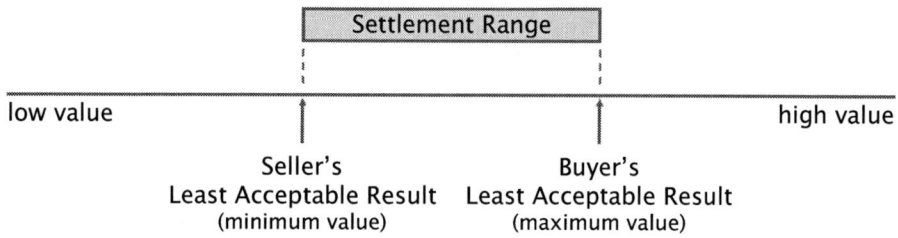

Figure 6.1 Settlement range.

The seller's and the buyer's respective Least Acceptable Result or LAR (see page 15) span the settlement range. Settlement might be impossible if the seller's LAR is higher than the buyer's LAR, that is, if the seller expects to receive more than the buyer is willing to give for the item under negotiation.

Being able to identify settlement ranges per Figure 6.1 is valuable in negotiations. However, real world business deals frequently show greater complexity and settling them may require reaching agreement over multiple items of tangible or intangible value. This could include identifying multiple settling points, accommodating both parties' assumptions about future events that could affect the negotiation outcome, and various other challenges.

The primary levers available to negotiators seeking to influence the other party's objectives, strategies, and decisions are power, information, and time. Skillful negotiators know how to advance their position and reduce the strength of their counterparts' position by utilizing all three of them:

• *Power.* Perceptions of power commonly influence most of the negotiating parties' decisions. How powerful a negotiator's position is perceived to be depends on a number of factors. Some of them, such as the size of the company represented and its available resources, are independent of the specific negotiation. Others may be situational. For example, if one side's BATNA is considerably more attractive than the other's, that party could strengthen its position by leveraging this knowledge as a pressure point during the bargaining exchange. Culture-specific factors may also have a significant impact on perceptions of power. They may be based on aspects such as status, rank, position, knowledge, experience, reputation, network and relationships, and more.

  Expectations of the distribution of power between buyers and sellers might also depend on the cultural context. Negotiators in countries such as Japan tend to attribute substantially more power to the buyer than to the seller, while members of egalitarian cultures, for instance the Dutch, may view both as equals.

  Smart negotiators realize that the concept of bargaining power is indeed subjective. They use this observation to their advantage, for instance by demonstrating attitudes, conveying expectations, and making demands that all signal a position of power. Such tactics might significantly improve a negotiator's position, even when dealing with counterparts whose bargaining power may seem superior. Effective countermeasures against such tactics include insisting on reciprocity in all exchanges of concessions, refusing to make repeat offers if an earlier one was rejected as 'not good enough,' and other behaviors that underline the equilibrium of power between the negotiating parties.

- *Information.* Any information that is available to a negotiating party might directly influence its strategies, tactics, and decisions. However, it is important to consider different categories. Information may be known, partially known, or unknown to either party. In addition, it might be real, presumed, or false. Information could be false because of misunderstandings between the parties, or because the party holding it was intentionally misled or even lied to. Such facets tend to complicate the exchange of information in international negotiations, which is often an intricate and convoluted process. In general, no strategy can be recommended universally for whether and when to share information. Negotiators facing such decisions must carefully consider a number of aspects. From a strategic standpoint, openly sharing all information about intentions, objectives, and goals is rarely in a negotiator's best interest. Not surprisingly, individuals taking this approach frequently find the results of negotiations to fall short of their expectations, especially when dealing with highly competitive counterparts. On the other hand, appearing to be hiding critical information is generally counterproductive. Members of several cultures, among them Americans, Australians, the British, Canadians, Indians, Northern Europeans, and others, view information sharing as a way to demonstrate good intentions and build trust. In contrast, most Russians, Turks, Ukrainians, and many others consider the same approach as naïve and foolish. These cultural preferences often correspond with preferred levels of uncertainty avoidance.

Key Concepts: High or Low Uncertainty Avoidance

Influential Dutch interculturalist Geert Hofstede identified a cultural characteristic he labeled ***uncertainty avoidance***, defined as 'the extent to which members of a culture feel threatened by unknown or uncertain situations.'

People from cultures whose uncertainty avoidance is ***high***, such as the French, the Japanese, South Koreans, Spaniards, and many Latin Americans, commonly prefer rules and structure over flexibility and 'creative chaos.' They may tolerate risk only if they are able to identify and analyze its components. Uncertain situations whose intrinsic risks remain unclear might cause high levels of anxiety. When negotiating, members of this group tend to dedicate substantial time and efforts to gathering and analyzing information about the other side. In addition, they often prefer contracts to be very detailed and explicit.

Conversely, people from ***low*** uncertainty avoidance cultures usually develop little anxiety over aspects which they cannot directly control. Often more curious and open to making changes than members of the first group are, they may be more willing to experiment and try out new ideas. This group of cultures includes Australia, Canada, India, Ireland, the United Kingdom, the United States, and others. Negotiators belonging to this group may consider extensive information gathering a waste of time, instead relying on their individual ability to navigate tricky situations and obtain information as needed.

Cultural preferences must be taken into account in all decisions about information sharing. In fact, failure to meet others' expectations could cause irritation and jeopardize relationships. In any case, certain practices are helpful regardless of the specific cultural context, as they commonly make the negotiation process more effective. One of them is to clarify technical and logistical requirements upfront, since failing to do so may delay negotiations and force unnecessary concessions later on. Another useful practice is to verify information through multiple sources whenever possible. As we discussed in Chapter 2, doing so is always advantageous. It can become crucial when dealing with people from cultures where lies and deceits are common when negotiating. Lastly, another good practice is to disclose alternative goals as a way to break up negotiation impasses if required.

- *Time*. Time constraints frequently create pressure in negotiations. There are two effective ways for negotiators to impose such time pressure and use it to their advantage. One is to leverage real or artificial deadlines, for instance by stating that a proposed deal will only be feasible if accepted by a certain date or time. By using this approach, negotiators may be able to instill fear in their counterparts that the deal might be off unless it is accepted as proposed. This could make the other party more conciliatory. However, this method of leveraging time tends to make negotiations less constructive, since it is often perceived as highly adversarial. It therefore requires careful planning and execution to avoid adversely impacting relationships between the parties.

  More promising, especially when dealing with people from fast-paced cultures where 'time is money,' such as the United States or Canada, is an alternate method of creating time pressure. It relies on using others' self-imposed deadlines or impatience against them and is frequently practiced by members of many cultures, among them most Asians, Latin Americans, and Southern Europeans. Upon learning that a counterpart is working against a deadline, such as a scheduled departure date or a time commitment made to someone else, members of these cultures may stall the bargaining exchange until shortly before this deadline, knowing that the other individual will likely become more inclined to make concessions in order to successfully close the deal in the remaining time. If no such deadline exists, procrastinating and generally slowing down the bargaining exchange may be effective as well, since doing so also creates a perceived incentive for the other party to make concessions in order to 'get things going again.' Because of such psychological pressure effects, time is commonly a more valuable lever for the negotiating party that is the most patient and persistent. Negotiators around the world use such tactics to offset differences in power or available information between the negotiating parties.

Making Offers and Concessions

When preparing to bargain, three highly interdependent aspects of concession making require careful consideration: pattern (number of bargaining rounds), timing (when to make offers and counteroffers), and magnitude (how small or large each concession should be). These decisions can be critical for the negotiation outcome.

Opening offers represent the first major challenge. They require implicit or explicit decisions between the parties as to which side will start the exchange. People from many cultures commonly expect the seller to open the bargaining. There may be reasons to ignore this practice, but in general, the importance of 'who goes first' tends to be overrated. Negotiators who are unsure of an item's real value usually have the option to start with an extreme opening offer, which frequently helps to obtain clues about the item's true value from the other party. As a matter of fact, research results suggest that negotiators starting with extreme openings on average achieve higher settlements than those making seemingly more realistic opening offers.

The message sent through the opening offer must be viewed as constructive by the other party and therefore requires considering culture-specific expectations. In the United States, such expectations may be that the offer is clear and positive, creates interest, stresses mutual benefits, and implies flexibility. Extreme opening offers only meet these expectations if not outrageously mismatched with the perceived value of the item or items being negotiated. In contrast, expectations in Arab countries may include that the opening offer leaves considerable room for haggling, stimulates negotiators' creativity, and signals interest in engaging in extensive bargaining exchanges with the other party.

Once an opening offer has been put on the table, a process of exchanging offers and counteroffers follows. The structure of this process is usually unpredictable. However, many aspects are influenced by cultural preferences. Researchers Donald Hendon and Rebecca Angeles Hendon conducted an interesting study regarding the timing and pattern of concession making. They presented negotiators from several countries with different patterns of sizing and timing concessions over subsequent bargaining rounds. The following table shows a few patterns used by the researchers and lists the strategy behind each of them:

Pattern	Round One	Two	Three	Four	Strategy
A	25	25	25	25	equivalent concessions
B	100	-	-	-	immediate submission
C	-	-	-	100	tough bargaining
D	10	20	30	40	protracted concessions
E	40	30	20	10	diminishing concessions

Members of several cultures were asked to identify the patterns they liked best and those they disliked the most. The results suggest strong cultural bias. While most participants neither liked nor disliked equivalent concessions (pattern A) and almost everyone disliked immediate submission (B), the other patterns triggered responses which depended significantly on the respondents' cultural background.

Tough bargaining (C) was generally favored by negotiators from competitive cultures, such as Americans and Brazilians. Israelis, Russians, or Ukrainians, none of whom were included in the study, might show similar preferences. In strongly harmony-oriented Asian cultures such as Indonesia or Malaysia, this pattern is generally not favored and may even be viewed as adversarial.

The strategy to make protracted concessions (D) generally creates incentives for persistent counterparts willing to spend considerable time negotiating. This pattern is favored by many Asians, for instance the Hong Kong Chinese, Filipinos, Indians, Indonesians, or Singaporeans, as well as others not included in the study, such as the Chinese. While many Americans also like this approach, they tend to increase concessions faster and will likely expect to go through fewer rounds of bargaining than Asians may. In cultures where bargaining is generally disliked, protracted concessions may be considered as uncooperative.

Diminishing concessions (E) are commonly preferred by Australians, Canadians, the Taiwanese, Thais, or Northern Europeans. This pattern is often well liked in cultures whose members expect the bargaining exchange to be short and mostly free of haggling. Around the world, making diminishing concessions is an acceptable strategy.

Patterns of individual concession making become even more complicated in negotiations that extend over multiple items. While a discussion of specific strategies would take us beyond the scope of this book, we should at least introduce one relevant characteristic that becomes important in this type of negotiations: the concept of *polychronicity*.

Key Concepts: Polychronic versus Monochronic Cultures

People who prefer *monochronic* work styles are used to pursuing actions and goals in a systematic fashion. Most of them tend to be punctual, value order and predictability, frequently use checklists, follow preset meeting agendas, and generally dislike interruptions or digressions. When negotiating, they often work their way down sequential lists of objectives, bargaining for each item separately. They may be unwilling to revisit aspects that had already been agreed upon. Monochronic people generally prefer to capture information in writing and may insist that written protocols and other papers be used to document interim agreements.

In contrast, people who prefer *polychronic* work styles are used to pursuing multiple actions and goals in parallel. They pay less attention to punctuality, value flexibility and spontaneity, enjoy changing concepts, ignore preset meeting agendas, and generally dislike routine work and bureaucracy. People with this preference often keep a holistic view of the overall negotiation process. They may jump back and forth between topics rather than addressing them in sequential order. In addition, they generally prefer to convey information orally so they can get immediate feedback or make changes on the fly.

Negotiators whose cultural and personal preferences are on opposite ends of this spectrum may struggle to tolerate the resulting differences. Members of strongly monochronic cultures, such as Americans, the British, Canadians, Germans, Northern Europeans, and the Swiss, tend to consider polychronic styles as confusing, irritating, and even annoying. In turn, members of strongly polychronic cultures, for example Brazilians, the Chinese, Egyptians, the French, Indians, Mexicans, Russians, Spaniards, and Venezuelans, often consider monochronic behaviors as closed-minded and overly restrictive. Both sides may view their own preferred styles as more effective. In any case, it is vital not to show irritation or anger when encountering behavior that conflicts with personal preferences.

Cultural influences are only one of the factors that determine such preferences. Although most cultures generally encourage one or the other, members of generally polychronic societies may prefer monochronic styles and vice versa.

Myths About Bargaining

As we have shown, bargaining exchanges are commonly shaped by a complex array of style preferences and strategic variants. That notwithstanding, a number of alleged 'truths' about bargaining are often brought up as guidance for inexperienced negotiators. Upon closer inspection, most such guidelines turn out to be culture-specific rather than universally applicable. Let us take a look at three popular myths:

- *"Tough wins."* This statement implies that negotiators who 'play hardball' and whose attitudes are generally highly competitive or adversarial have a greater chance of coming out ahead in negotiations. In actuality, this is rarely the case. Since humans commonly tend to 'fight fire with fire,' negotiations that are led in this spirit often escalate unnecessarily. In particular, negotiators in many strongly relationship-oriented cultures are less likely to cooperate with such tough negotiators. Their concessions during bargaining exchanges may therefore become smaller and less valuable, which is why tough negotiators rarely get the best deals possible.

  In contrast, a more universally valid statement is that 'firm wins.' Remaining firm at critical points during the negotiation exchange is respected by members of most cultures as long as the individual doing so demonstrates flexibility in other areas. Unlike being tough, firmness in select areas may be combined with highly collaborative behaviors in others, which can be a winning negotiation strategy.

- *"Winning makes people happy."* Although competitive individuals may strongly believe in its validity, this statement is not universally accepted either. People in many cultures tend to take an individual's passion for winning as indication of a win-lose mindset that is likely to leave one party with a less desirable outcome than the other. Highly cooperative negotiators, as well as members of strongly relationship-oriented cultures, are particularly likely to reject this attitude. Some in the latter group might even argue that it can be advantageous to be the 'loser' in a negotiation if making significant concessions paves the road to productive long-term business relationships. Even though the underlying intentions may be right, it is therefore generally not advisable to express a strong passion for winning when negotiating across cultures.

- *"It is important to keep the highest aspirations."* This piece of advice, which can be found in books about effective negotiation strategies, represents another popular myth. Keeping high aspirations throughout the negotiation process is unquestionably a sound strategy. Doing so encourages negotiators to explore ways to maximize the benefits of the business deal at hand, which often adds value for both parties. However, keeping the highest aspirations implies that a negotiator must focus on achieving the best possible outcome of the bargaining exchange rather than remaining cooperative and flexible. This may again violate the spirit of give-and-take that people in many cultures expect from their counterparts and could make the overall process less productive.

Decision Making

Key Concepts: Individualistic versus Group-Oriented Cultures

Members of strongly *individualistic cultures* value each person's preferences and desires. In these societies, individual decision making is generally encouraged and each individual may be held responsible for his or her own mistakes. The authority to make decisions either resides with top executives or it is delegated to lower levels in the organization. Those in charge do not necessarily have to consult with others before making decisions. Because of this, decision making can be quick. Consensus decision making is rare and is often considered too slow and ineffective by people in this category, which includes Americans, Australians, Canadians, the Dutch, Scandinavians, and others.

In strongly *group-oriented cultures*, individual preferences are generally considered less important than having a sense of belonging to the group, conforming to its norms, and maintaining harmony among its members. Such a group might be an individual's extended family, an organization, a social group, or the society as a whole. In group-oriented cultures, decision making usually requires involving everyone who may be affected. It could even require reaching consensus among all of the group's members. Since this can be very time consuming, decision making is often slow in such a cultural environment. The group as a whole is responsible for mistakes, even if individual members made them. Top executives supervise and coordinate the decision process. While their inputs often carry significant weight, they rarely act as sole decision makers. Most Asian cultures are strongly group-oriented, among them China, India, Indonesia, Japan, Malaysia, the Philippines, and Taiwan. Mexicans and most Latin Americans are also generally group-oriented, as are Greeks, the Portuguese, Turks, and numerous others.

Concepts of how decisions are made and who is involved in the process vary across organizations and cultures. Figure 6.2 explores possible structures of the negotiation exchange, assuming that decisions on the buyer's side are made by a single individual.

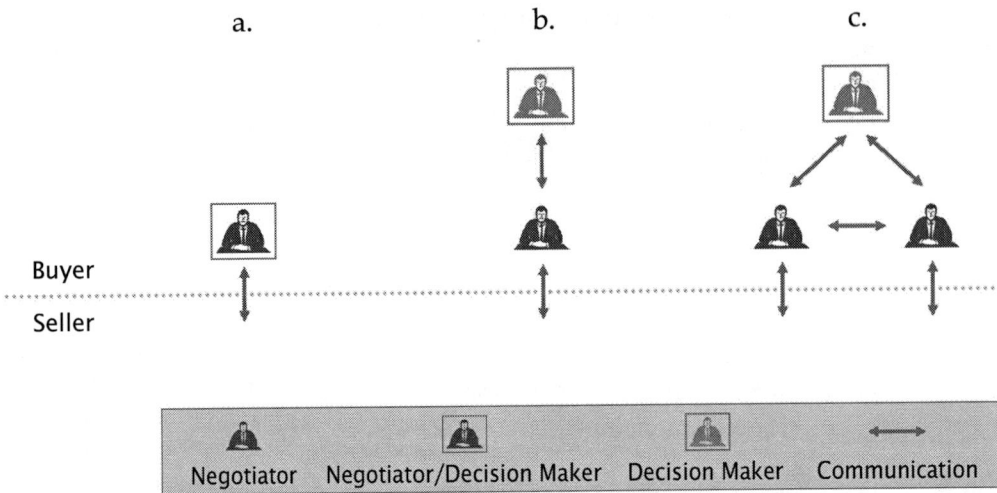

Figure 6.2 Individual decision making in negotiations.

- *Individual decision making - structure a.* Only one negotiator representing the buyer communicates with the seller. Though he or she may consult with others, this negotiator is the ultimate decision maker and does not require others' approval. In order to reach agreement, the seller needs to win the decision maker's support.

- *Individual decision making - structure b.* Only one negotiator representing the buyer communicates with the seller. However, the person acts as an intermediary. Decisions on the buyer's side are made by another individual, typically someone higher up in the hierarchy, who usually does not attend negotiation meetings. In order to reach agreement, the seller needs to get access to and win the support of the decision maker. Alternatively, the seller could try to win the intermediary's support, relying on that person's ability to influence the decision maker.

- *Individual decision making - structure c.* Several negotiators representing the buyer communicate with the seller, acting as intermediaries. Decisions on the buyer's side are made by another individual, typically someone higher up in the hierarchy, who usually does not attend negotiation meetings. In order to reach agreement, the seller needs to get access to and win the support of the decision maker. Alternatively, the seller could try to win the support of all or most of the intermediaries, relying on their ability to influence the decision maker.

All of these structures of individual decision making are predominantly found in individualistic cultures. The differences between them reflect two preferences: whether the negotiation meetings are attended by a single individual or by a group representing the buyer, and whether the decision maker is or is not directly involved in meetings and negotiation exchanges. If the decision maker does not attend meetings (structures b. or c.), this usually indicates either that the deal being negotiated is not viewed as important or that the status of the seller's most senior representative is perceived to be lower than that of the decision maker on the buyer's side. The choice of using more than one negotiator, as illustrated by structure c., may be influenced by a number of factors, which include individual participants' competencies and how the seller's team is composed, as well as corporate practices, legal aspects, and cultural orientations.

From the seller's perspective, the common denominator of the structures we have discussed so far is that the buyer's decisions are made by only one individual. While intermediaries might influence decisions to some degree, reaching agreement ultimately requires winning the support of the key person. In contrast, Figure 6.3 illustrates possible group decision-making structures, which often require more complex persuasion strategies.

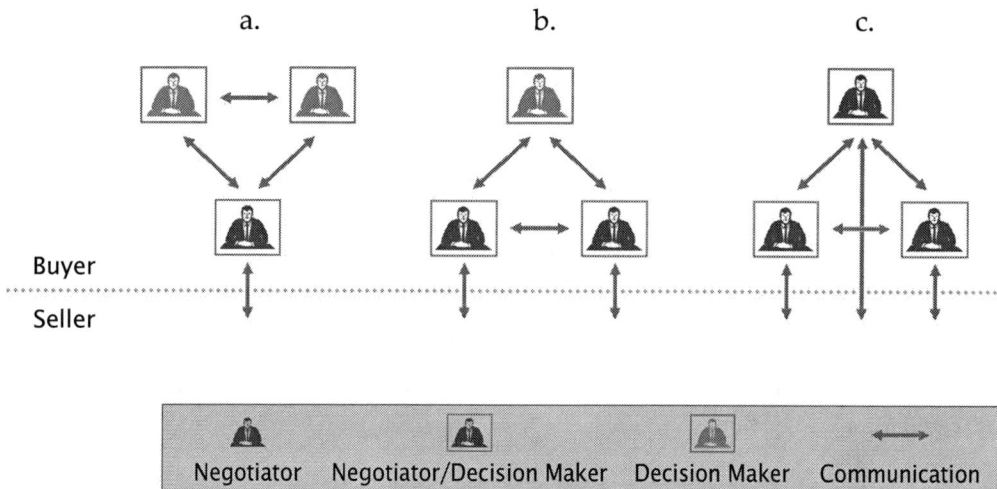

Figure 6.3 Group decision making in negotiations.

- *Group decision making - structure a.* Only one negotiator representing the buyer communicates with the seller, acting as an intermediary. The person also participates in making decisions. Others who usually do not attend negotiation meetings are also involved in the decision making process. Decisions might require reaching consensus among all involved or obtaining final approval by the most senior person. In order to reach agreement, the seller needs to win the support of most or all decision makers. Winning only the intermediary's support and relying on that person's ability to influence the other decision makers may not be a sufficient basis for reaching agreement.

- *Group decision making - structure b.* Two or more negotiators representing the buyer communicate with the seller. They are involved in the decision making process, as are others who usually do not attend negotiation meetings. Decisions might require reaching consensus among all involved or obtaining final approval by the most senior person. In order to reach agreement, the seller needs to win the support of most or all of the decision makers, including those absent from meetings. Alternatively, the seller could try to win the support of those attending the negotiation meetings, relying on their ability to influence the absent decision makers.

- *Group decision making - structure c.* Two or more negotiators representing the buyer communicate with the seller and jointly make decisions. Decision making might require reaching consensus among all involved. The representatives do not need to involve others when making decisions. In order to reach agreement, the seller needs to win the support of all or most of the decision makers. Winning only the support of the highest ranking person may not be a sufficient basis for reaching agreement.

Companies and organizations in group-oriented cultures commonly employ one of the decision making structures per Figure 6.3 when negotiating. Interactions that reflect structures a. or b. may indicate either that the deal being negotiated is not viewed as important or that the status of the seller's most senior representative is perceived to be lower than that of the highest ranking person on the buyer's side. The use of structure a. is rare, since most organizations in these cultures prefer to be represented by more than one individual.

We should emphasize that group decision making does not necessarily requires consensus. In cultures that are either highly egalitarian or strongly focused on preserving group harmony, establishing consensus among all team members may be the expected norm. In many other group-oriented cultures, though, decision making may only require that everyone is given a chance to express his or her opinion before final decisions are made.

Group-oriented decision making does not mean that every voice will carry equal weight. On the other hand, it can be dangerous to rely solely on the support of one or a few key influencers in a group, no matter how powerful they may appear to be within its hierarchy. A more promising strategy when dealing with such cultures is to invest the time and energy to build relationships with all or most of the group's members, especially those who may be key influencers, and with the final decision maker, assuming that such a role exists.

Decision making structures as presented in Figures 6.2 and 6.3 are obviously influenced by cultural preferences for individualism or group orientation, as well as those for egalitarianism or authoritarianism. A third culture-specific factor also warrants careful consideration in this context. It describes the propensity of members of a given culture to follow universalistic principles or to consider situational aspects when making decisions.

Key Concepts: Universalistic versus Particularistic Cultures

Members of strongly *universalistic cultures* prefer to follow established rules and practices when making decisions. For them, empirical evidence and other objective facts often weigh more strongly than personal feelings and experiences do. They dislike making exceptions, even if several facts speak in favor. In addition, they value contracts and usually expect them to be kept without exception. When confronted with new situations, people sharing this preference may concentrate on aspects of universal validity rather than looking for unique findings and observations. Typical representatives of this group of cultures are Americans, Australians, the British, Canadians, the Dutch, Germans, Northern Europeans, the Swiss, and others.

In strongly *particularistic cultures*, people making decisions will focus most of their attention onto the specific aspects of a situation and the people involved in it. Doubtful of absolute truths and convinced that the world around them is in constant motion, many of them are mistrustful of universal rules and norms. Most members of this group are highly relationship-oriented. They tend to consider legal contracts mere formalities, expecting partners to remain flexible and relying on the strength of relationships to ensure that agreements are kept. The group of particularistic cultures includes most Asian and Arab ones, as well as France, Greece, Italy, Mexico, Russia, Spain, Turkey, all of Latin America, and many other countries.

Successfully influencing decisions requires understanding and properly dealing with people's preferences. With members of universalistic cultures, it can be highly beneficial to identify established precedents which they might be able to follow, especially if a proposed deal requires them to consider unusual circumstances. In contrast, asking them to make a decision 'as a personal favor' may make these individuals suspicious and might be counterproductive. When dealing with people from particularistic cultures, on the other hand, it is often more advantageous to appeal to their intuition and to emphasize how a proposed deal will help strengthen relationships between the negotiating parties.

Chapter 7: Agreement, Closure, and Execution

Reaching Agreement

Key Concepts: Tentative Agreement – Agreement – Contract

Words which may seem clear within the framework of one country's cultural and legal context sometimes take on a different meaning in a different one. For example, the term *agreement* may be understood as final and dependable consent in one culture, while members of another culture may take it to mean little more than general intentions. Similarly, while people in one country may consider contracts irrevocable documents that must be followed to the letter, others may view them as summaries of past agreements that remain subject to change. Throughout this book, we take these terms to mean the following:

Tentative agreement is an intention shared by both sides to accept a negotiated condition in the future if certain expectations are met, for instance that the parties will reach consensus over items that are subject to further bargaining, that a proposed agreement will find the consent of decision makers who are not at the negotiation table, or that yet-to-be-verified information will prove correct. The negotiating parties usually acknowledge implicitly or explicitly that final agreement is contingent upon these and other factors. Tentative agreements may exist in oral form or in writing.

Agreement (sometimes referred to as *final agreement*) requires both parties to confirm their acceptance of a negotiated set of conditions with the intention to carry out all of the resulting obligations. Agreements can be closed orally or in writing. Depending on a country's legal system, agreements may or may not be legally binding.

Contract is a written document that confirms closure of an agreement between negotiating parties. Contracts commonly spell out all negotiated terms and conditions, as well as resulting obligations for both parties. Most such documents include provisions for cases such as modification, termination, or breach of contract. Contracts normally become binding when both parties accepted them through their signatures.

The process negotiators prefer to use in order to reach agreement may depend on their cultural background. Members of monochronic cultures, which includes Americans, Canadians, Germans, people from the Nordics, or the Swiss, tend to rely on iterative approaches. Since their propensity is commonly to work down lists of objectives in sequential order, bargaining for each item separately, they may seek to establish tentative agreement after each round. This is often documented through written protocols or meeting summaries. At major milestones, negotiators with this preference may request that tentative agreement be confirmed by the parties signing written documents such as Memorandums of Understanding (MoA) or Letters of Intent (LoI). These papers may have legal implications that need to be assessed. However, their primary role is usually to confirm mutual understanding and to reaffirm both parties' commitment to resolve remaining issues and disagreements. The dependability of tentative agreements, whether oral or in writing, might vary considerably across cultures.

Since members of polychronic cultures, for example the French, most Latin Americans, or Arabs from the Middle East, generally prefer a holistic approach that considers all aspects that are required in order to reach agreement, they are less inclined to work down itemized lists one by one. Accordingly, they may be reluctant to accept tentative agreements. When dealing with such negotiators, one should diligently track concessions on both sides as well as areas where consensus seems possible. However, it is best to remain open to revisiting individual aspects if requested by the other side.

Indicators that agreement is within reach and that a counterpart may be ready to close a deal depend to some degree on his or her cultural context. In countries where people enjoy bargaining and haggling, such as most Arab countries, Indonesia, Nigeria, Pakistan, the Philippines, or Turkey, a telling sign is often that subsequent concessions are getting smaller. With other negotiators, there could be a general shift in the focus of attention. For instance, when polychronic negotiators start addressing specific issues and details, this often indicates that they are ready to close. This applies especially to members of strongly relationship-oriented cultures, among them many Chinese, Egyptians, Greeks, Indonesians, Malaysians, or Singaporeans, but also to people from other polychronic cultures, for instance the French. In contrast, Americans, Germans, and others belonging to monochronic and task-oriented cultures may start to focus on bigger-picture aspects. Again, this is often a sign that they are ready to close the agreement. Several techniques to test and establish agreement are discussed in Part II of this book.

In previous chapters, we repeatedly mentioned the importance of patience and persistence for international negotiators. These qualities are imperative when trying to reach agreement and closure. In the eyes of many people around the world, impatience indicates a lack of commitment to and respect for the business relationship, a lack of personal discipline, or both. Either interpretation is prone to reduce a counterpart's comfort level and may complicate or delay closure.

Once agreement has been reached, symbolic acts commonly confirm the parties' intentions to honor it. This usually precedes the formal contract signature. One such act is the exchange of handshakes between the lead negotiators or between team members on both sides. Some Asians, for example the Japanese, usually confirm the mutual agreement by both parties stating precisely what it is they agree with. Written documents may serve for the same purpose and might be used in many cultures. In general, capturing agreements in writing is always recommended in international business, since this reduces the risk of communication failure and misunderstandings. It is usually not necessary –and sometimes unwise– to insist that such documents be signed. Doing so may be interpreted as a lack of trust. The same could be true if a negotiator demanded that the write-up include all details of the agreement. Some counterparts may be more comfortable with keeping this document high-level, capturing only the essential spirit of the agreement between the parties.

Closure: The Role of Contracts

Structure and content of contracts are commonly driven by company policies and practices, legal considerations, third-party requirements, and other factors. In addition, cultural preferences tend to have a significant influence on how businesspeople view the importance of a contract and how much detail they expect to be included. Four main categories can be identified:

- *Detailed contracts are preferred; they are viewed as important.* Cultures sharing this preference include Austria, Canada, Germany, the Netherlands, the Nordic countries, Switzerland, the United Kingdom, and the United States. Australians, the French, Hong Kong Chinese, and Israelis also often fall into this category, though they may be less obsessed over contractual details than others may. Generally, people in this group tend to view contracts as critical instruments, capturing all of the partners' resulting obligations, including provisions for many eventualities, and relying on legal enforcement if necessary to ensure that agreements be kept. Some of them may actually not believe that final agreement has been reached until the final version of the contract has been accepted by both parties. They might actually use the process of creating the contract as an opportunity to continue or re-open the bargaining exchange.

- *Detailed contracts are preferred; they are viewed as a formality.* A diverse group of cultures falls into this category, including Ireland, Italy, most Latin American countries, Pakistan, Philippines, Portugal, Singapore, South Korea, Spain, and others. Usually more strongly relationship-oriented than those in the first category, members of this group see contracts primarily as a communication tool. By capturing much detail, they verify both parties' understanding of the agreement. Nevertheless, they prefer to rely more on the relationship itself than on the disciplinary nature of the contract. The time it may take to complete a contract could be substantial in these cultures, though.

- *High-level contracts are preferred; they are viewed as important.* Cultures in this group, which includes India, Russia, South Africa, and Ukraine, tend to combine Western influences emphasizing the importance of written contracts with a relationship orientation that motivates people to focus on the essential aspects of the agreement rather than spelling out many details. Writing up a contract may still be time consuming in these countries as much attention may be given to its language and content.

- *High-level contracts are preferred; they are viewed as a formality.* This category includes countries such as China, Egypt, Greece, Indonesia, Malaysia, Mexico, Saudi Arabia, Taiwan, and Thailand. Since their cultures emphasize the importance of relationships, members of this group tend to pay little attention to contractual aspects unless legal circumstances force them to. Nevertheless, the final step of both parties formally signing the document may be highly ceremonial and is often celebrated with banquets and other events. The exchange of gifts is also common on these occasions. All of these practices commonly serve to strengthen relationships between the partners.

Note that a few cultures do not clearly fall into any of the above categories. For instance, while contracts are often a mere formality in underdeveloped countries like Nigeria, a wide range of styles may be found, reaching from those oriented at a high level to others which are very detailed. This sometimes reflects historic influences by foreign nations and individual companies.

Another exception is Japan: historically, this society had no use or need for contracts, since its strict system of honor and public enforcement provided the necessary checks and balances between business partners. Today, many Japanese still dislike closing written contracts, instead relying on written protocols and the strength of relationships.

Execution: After the Contract Has Been Signed

When conducting international business, it is crucial to recognize that negotiations do not end with the signing of the contract. Before the parties enter into the execution phase of a negotiation, three aspects require particular consideration:

- *Importance of commitments and deadlines.* What international partners view as commitments is not necessarily restricted to aspects that are clearly spelled out in contracts. Members of some cultures may also expect oral commitments or those captured in written exchanges and protocols to be dependable. The degree to which they expect such commitments to be met might vary considerably across cultures. While some partners may reject even a day's delay or a minor variation from an asserted product characteristic as unacceptable, others might remain casual about much more significant deviations. This emphasizes the importance of discussing and documenting such expectations during the closure phase of the negotiation, which can be extremely helpful should disagreements surface over such aspects later on.

- *Contract modifications and post-contract negotiation.* Around the world, business contracts commonly state that modifications require the consent of all contract partners. Such requests may actually lead to tensions between the parties. International partners, in particular members of strongly relationship-oriented cultures, often expect their counterparts to remain flexible should conditions change. This includes agreeing to modified contract terms and showing willingness to ignore some of them if necessary. Rejecting such requests could be detrimental to the relationship and tends to affect the other party's contract compliance. Moreover, businesspeople from China, South Korea, and several other countries frequently request contract changes, sometimes already a few weeks after the contract signing ceremony. Unlike Westerners, who often view contracts as continually binding documents designed to stand the test of time, members of these cultures tend to take them merely as reflections of both parties' intentions at the time they were signed. To them, the emergence of new facts or circumstances justifies requests to revisit aspects of the contract. When negotiating with such counterparts, it is therefore wise to consider the possibility of having to make additional concessions down the road.

- *Enforceability.* Few areas hold greater potential for culture clash than the legal enforcement of agreements and contracts. In countries with highly developed legal systems, business partners commonly rely on the framework they provide as a force to stimulate contract fulfillment. Whether or not contract partners are likely to take legal action against a counterpart who failed to fulfill contractual obligations often depends on the role relationships play in the country. For example, while litigation is a likely action in the United States or Canada in such a case, this option is rarely a choice in Japan. The Japanese and members of most other strongly relationship-oriented cultures prefer to resolve such issues through mediation or continued negotiation as required to restore full cooperation between the partners. In countries whose legal systems are less developed, the strength of relationships frequently determines whether and to what extent agreements are fulfilled. Regardless of the legal context, keeping in touch on a regular basis and continually nurturing close ties with partners who strongly focus on relationships is a powerful way to ensure that they will keep their commitments. Even in countries where legal systems are dependable, Alternative Dispute Resolution (ADR) through trained mediators is usually preferable over litigation. This approach often clears the path to maintaining or restoring business relationships.

Chapter 8: Why International Negotiations Fail

Attitudes

Below, we list a number of symptoms that commonly indicate company practices that may not be well tuned to the requirements of global business. These signs may be warning of an increased possibility of failing international negotiations and should therefore raise red flags for company management and negotiators alike. Some of the underlying issues may not necessarily be of consequence to the negotiation exchange itself. However, serious issues might surface once the negotiating parties have entered into the execution phase of an agreement between them.

- The company's leaders are unable to clearly communicate its reasons for seeking an international partner.

- Company management considers language, time zone differences, or trade laws and other legal implications the biggest obstacles to doing business globally.

- The company considers international business as secondary to its domestic goals and objectives.

- Executives believe that foreign business is little more than an extension of domestic business.

- Middle management feels that international partners cannot be trusted.

- Employees question the validity of the company going international, fearing job losses and reduced influence.

- Previous international business deals have fallen apart for reasons that are unclear, since they were not properly analyzed.

- International engagements are motivated by coincidences ("We happened to know a capable guy over there, so we established our office in Paris.") or based on subjective criteria ("Our boss likes visiting Japan, which is why we are looking for a partner there.")

Normally, these issues alone do not cause international deals to fail. However, they signal troublesome underlying attitudes that likely determine values, practices, and behaviors of negotiators directly involved in international deal making and others expected to support and execute the resulting agreements. If these individuals' attitudes clash with the required collaborative spirit, the chances of the cooperation being productive and sustainable will at best be slim.

A Few Case Studies

Case A: Americans in China

Attracted by the growing prosperity of the emerging middle class in China, Orange Corp., a successful U.S. brand of electronic entertainment products, decided to build a stronger presence in the country's consumer markets. The American team identified Chinese retail company Lucky Sun as a potential partner who appears to have the wherewithal required to support Orange's successful market entry.

Negotiations were intense and fierce. Committed to moving forward as quickly as possible, Orange Corp. wasted little time in preliminaries and kept a high sense of urgency throughout the negotiation. Realizing the market potential of Orange's products, Lucky Sun went along and, while negotiating fiercely, demonstrated its willingness to reach a mutually acceptable agreement. Because of the rapid pace, relationships between both sides remained somewhat perfunctory, which few among Orange's senior managers considered an issue.

After much back-and-forth bargaining, the parties put together a detailed contract and eventually signed it in a festive ceremony. Lucky Sun immediately started developing a marketing campaign designed to stimulate sales of Orange's products. However, a week before the planned release date of the campaign, Lucky Sun contacted Orange to request a higher retail margin than the contract between the companies provided for. Its management argued that the Chinese government had just released new regulations that would cause the cost of product returns, and thus Lucky Star's handling cost, to increase considerably. The contract included no provisions for such a case.

Orange's management immediately rejected the request. The company sent a corporate lawyer to China with the charter to remind Lucky Sun that the existing contract spelled out that margins would not be renegotiated during the first three years of the agreement. Lucky Sun appealed to Orange's chief executive, only to receive a harsh statement emphasizing that the partnership required both sides to honor their contractual agreements and adding that Orange considered the case closed.

A few days later, Lucky Sun decided to stop the marketing campaign. In fact, the retailer subsequently started actively promoting a competing South Korean brand, which eventually led to Orange filing a Civil Enforcement lawsuit against Lucky Sun in a local Chinese court. Today, more than three years after the original contract was signed, this lawsuit is still pending. After extensive market research and negotiations, Orange managed to sign up another retailer to support its Chinese market entry. It is paying that retailer a higher margin than it would have paid Lucky Sun.

This case presents a typical example of misaligned expectations and a lack of cross-cultural understanding on both sides. The American side failed to recognize the importance of relationship building and the different views the partners held of the role of contracts. The Chinese side may have failed to understand the pending changes in regulations. It also did not recognize that the American company expected its contract to be honored to the letter, not only in spirit. Accordingly, the Americans cried foul when the Chinese 'violated' the contract by requesting better terms after signature, while the Chinese took the apparent unwillingness to be flexible as indication that the Americans had no intentions to collaborate as trustworthy business partners. Had both parties understood each other's cultural framework better, they might have been able to identify a mutually acceptable solution to the situation.

Case B: Canadians in Turkey

Looking to expand its international sales, Canadian chemical company Chemron identified a sizable Turkish industrial conglomerate as a potential customer for industrial chemicals. Erkan Industries, the Turkish firm, was known to be dissatisfied with its current supplier.

Realizing the importance of relationship building and establishing local contacts, Chemron followed a suggestion by the Canadian chamber of commerce to hire a local representative in Turkey. Recruiting this individual indeed proved valuable, since he quickly managed to make contact with a senior manager at one of Erkan's numerous subsidiaries. After two meetings and a pleasant business dinner, relationships seemed to develop well between Chemron's negotiators and that manager. He promised to get the Canadians in touch with a key influencer within Erkan's extensive corporate hierarchy. Indeed, meeting with that executive seemed promising since he displayed sincere interest in Chemron's capabilities. In addition, he put its representatives in touch with another senior Erkan executive whose support he felt would be crucial.

Although the overall progress was slower than expected, Chemron was optimistic at becoming the Turkish company's primary vendor. After further efforts to strengthen relationships, its representatives submitted a formal offer outlining why Chemron was the right choice for Erkan and how it would be able to meet all of the customer's needs. This offer received much attention from Erkan's managers, some of whom pulled in others at the company who were asked to meet with the Canadians in order to further review and discuss the offer.

A week later, the Canadian team learned to its great surprise that Erkan had just awarded a large contract for the procurement of industrial chemicals to one of Chemron's competitors. This move would effectively shut out the Canadian company from most of the potential business with this customer. Neither its own contacts at Erkan nor the hired Turkish representative had given Chemron any indication that the negotiation was not going well.

In this case, most of the blame goes to the Canadian negotiators. Although they recognized cultural differences and tried to adjust to them, for instance by making efforts to build and strengthen relationships, they apparently failed to realize that they were in fact dealing with the wrong contacts. It is likely that the representatives of the Turkish company they were dealing with neither had the authority to make the required procurement decisions nor had any significant influence in the decision process. In cultures where personal pride is very important, such facts may not necessarily be revealed. The Turks may have dedicated their time because they were interested in exploring other opportunities or simply in learning more about the other party in general. This is not an unusual experience when doing business in Turkey, making it vital to identify the true decision makers before starting to negotiate with companies in the country. The local representative the Canadians had selected obviously lacked the insight and contacts required to recognize the situation.

Case C: Germans in Mexico

German carmaker ALV determined that its most promising option to establish a stronger presence in the important North American auto market was to set up an assembly plant in Mexico, with its low wages and good trade access to the United States. After assessing several alternatives, the company identified an existing plant in Guadalajara as the most suitable facility for the new assembly operation. Current owner Grupo Jalisco had put the plant up for sale. Negotiations appeared to be little more than a formality, since commercial real estate values seemed well established through other plants that had recently been sold in the Guadalajara area.

A middle manager representing ALV's worldwide facility management group set up a meeting with the current plant owner, prepared to spend no more than a day or two in the country. In spite of polite introductions and small talk, the initial meeting did not go well. Focused on reaching agreement quickly, ALV had previously submitted a detailed proposal in writing. However, Grupo Jalisco's negotiators had apparently not even read this proposal, since the sales price they demanded as the bargaining began was higher than the Germans' offer by a very substantial amount. The German negotiator sharply rejected the demand, stating that the Mexicans 'could not possibly be serious in asking for such an outrageous sum.' He reminded them of the offer ALV had already made, which he considered very reasonable.

What followed was a fierce competitive bargaining exchange. While Grupo Jalisco's negotiators successively lowered their demands, ALV's offer did not move by much. The company's representative repeatedly emphasized that his opening offer was fair and that he would not raise it unless the other side first provided a reasonable counteroffer. When Grupo Jalisco finally lowered its request by a sizeable amount, he started making small concessions in response, upon which the Mexican team responded with similarly small ones. Though the delta between bidding and asking price was no longer very substantial, subsequent concessions offered by either side were clearly becoming too small to support a mutually acceptable compromise.

More and more agitated over what he called the Mexicans' 'unreasonable behavior,' the German made what he announced as his final offer, suggesting that the Grupo Jalisco team 'take it or leave it.' Again, this did not seem to produce the desired response. The Mexican negotiators instead countered with another small concession. Determined to stay his course, the German threatened to end the meeting and return to his hotel unless Grupo Jalisco accepted his latest offer. Since this did not trigger a clear response either, he ultimately packed up his papers, rose, and left.

The following day, ALV's representative called Grupo Jalisco in order to reopen the negotiation. He was prepared to offer small additional concessions, which he was convinced was all it would take to seal the deal. To his surprise, his counterparts stated that they were no longer interested in negotiating with ALV. The plant later sold to another party for the exact same price the Germans had last offered. ALV's plans to assemble vehicles in Mexico were delayed by several months.

A number of cultural misunderstandings characterize this case. The most significant one may be the failure of both parties to respect each other's pride. The Mexican team might already have been offended when realizing that the German company sent a middle manager, rather than a top executive, to the negotiation. One of the Mexican representatives was probably a senior executive whose expectation was to interact with someone of similar rank. Calling the Mexicans' opening offer extreme and refusing to make meaningful concessions made matters worse. All of this, combined with the lack of opportunity for relationship building with their visitor, led the Mexican team to become increasingly uncooperative and combative. On the other hand, the Mexicans' disregard for the upfront written offer made the German doubt their professionalism. He took the other party's extreme opening offer as a provocation and may have felt that its failure to acknowledge his final offer as serious added insult to injury. Once both sides had dug in their heels, the negotiation exchange was bound to fail.

Recognizing Rules

Many negotiations that fail due to cultural conflict are characterized by a pattern of both sides starting with good intentions, increasingly becoming aggravated, and ultimately finding themselves in a downward spiral that can be very difficult to escape from. Ask international business negotiators about their worst foreign experiences and they may start telling horror stories, the implied message of which is usually that foreign counterparts 'broke the rules.'

Such rules usually represent unspoken expectations that others are required to meet. They may define right and wrong conduct, fair and unfair behavior, acceptable and unacceptable practices. For example, most American negotiators may have expectations of their counterparts such as these: 'never lie,' 'do not get emotional,' 'do not take anything personally,' 'be reasonable' (i.e., 'accept and respond to logical arguments and reasoning'), or 'honor the deals you make' (i.e., 'do not attempt to change or ignore agreements you closed'). While bending such rules might be tolerated to a certain degree, people may cry foul if one is broken. Few emotions change good intentions and positive attitudes faster than feelings of being cheated may. If that happens, the perpetrator is subsequently viewed with mistrust and suspicion. Repeated rule violations frequently tend to leave negotiations in a complete gridlock and often make it impossible for the parties to reach agreement.

The challenge in international negotiations is that there is more than one rulebook. The negotiating parties' views of what is acceptable and what is not may actually differ substantially. For instance, one party might view partial lying, cheating, or getting highly emotional as perfectly normal behaviors when negotiating, while the other may not. Herein lies the dilemma: in any such situation, the rules which negotiators on both sides expect to apply might differ considerably, while the negotiation exchange nevertheless requires the parties to establish and preserve reasonable levels of trust between them. The key to mastering this challenge lies in testing for and recognizing misaligned assumptions, understanding different rule sets, and finding or creating common ground that allows both sides to pursue their negotiation objectives while winning and maintaining each other's trust. Instead of assuming bad intentions or attitudes, negotiators may be able either to modify their behaviors or to openly discuss and resolve conflicting perceptions and expectations with their counterparts.

It's Not Always Culture

As motivational theorist Abraham Maslow once noted, "If the only tool you have is a hammer, you will see every problem as a nail." Even though cultural differences can be found at the heart of many conflicts in international negotiations, a similar caveat applies here.

Negotiation conflicts can be caused by opposing objectives, individual incompatibilities, cultural differences, and other factors. Assuming that learning enough about cultural differences is all it will take to make international negotiations productive and successful would be naïve. Worse, such a mindset could become a mental blindfold that might trigger poor decision-making. Competent negotiators remain aware of cultural stereotypes and use them only as a set of assumptions they question and modify continually when dealing with individual representatives of a given culture. Such individuals may hold values and beliefs that could deviate considerably from the norms of their cultural group. That does not render general observations about cultures useless. However, it explains how conflicts can be caused by individual styles rather than cultural differences. Adding further complexity, real-life experience suggests that cultural and personal values often both influence how individuals negotiate and which rules they expect themselves and others to follow.

All of this only amplifies the need to learn about a culture before engaging in negotiations with any of its members. Understanding cultural differences and preparing for another country's values and preferred styles is not a guarantee for success in international negotiations. Nevertheless, it greatly improves the odds of reaching agreement and builds a foundation for successful collaboration.

Part II: Negotiation Techniques Used Around the World

Unlike the basic concepts presented in Chapter 6, negotiation techniques are specific approaches that are applicable only within a certain negotiation style or in a specific situational context. Negotiators commonly use them to achieve progress towards their strategic objectives and to obtain tactical advantages. We include only those that are commonly used in many cultures, reviewing cultural implications and discussing caveats. We classify them into six different categories:

Chapter 9:	Deceptive Techniques
Chapter 10:	Pressure Techniques
Chapter 11:	Aggressive and Adversarial Techniques
Chapter 12:	Other Emotional Techniques
Chapter 13:	Defensive Techniques
Chapter 14:	Other Negotiation Techniques

In the country-specific information given in Part III of our book, we frequently refer to these techniques. This is not a comprehensive catalog, as many other options and variants exist.

Let us start with a few general notes and observations:

• Individual negotiation styles may influence a negotiator's choice of bargaining techniques as much as cultural preferences do. It would be a mistake to assume that all negotiators in a given country will or will not use certain techniques.

• Categories may overlap. For instance, some pressure techniques include deceitful elements, such as when a negotiator makes up artificial deadlines to create time pressure on a counterpart.

• Negotiation techniques are often combined for additional impact, which can make it hard to recognize them. For example, some negotiators employ fake nonverbal messages in order to make their act of showing disinterest in a deal more credible.

• Some of the techniques can be used to counter others. For instance, aggressive behavior often stops if a counterpart threatens in a calm and controlled fashion to walk out otherwise.

Chapter 9: Deceptive Techniques

The primary objective of using deceptive techniques is to conceal one's negotiation strategy and objectives, or to mislead the other side about the value one assigns to the items being negotiated. By withholding such information or by credibly communicating false information, negotiators intend to achieve agreements that favor their position.

Deceptive techniques are used in most cultures around the world. However, in societies where preserving *face* and maintaining strong relationships are important, deceiving a counterpart may jeopardize or destroy long-term business relationships if the party realizes that it is being deceived. In these countries, it is therefore strongly advisable either to refrain from using deceptive techniques or at least to employ only those your counterparts cannot identify as such.

Telling Lies

Negotiators may use outright or partial lies in order to mislead the other party about their strategy or to obtain bargaining advantages. For instance, they may claim that another party made them a better offer for the items being negotiated. This claim aims to make the other side believe that it might lose the deal to another bidder, putting pressure on it to improve its own offer. Another example is that a negotiator might invent reasons why concessions a counterpart is requesting cannot be granted. Lies only work if the other party finds them plausible and assumes that they actually represent the truth.

The first line of defense against lies is to prepare well upfront, collecting and thoroughly verifying relevant information about your counterpart's strategy, intentions, non-settlement options, constraints, and preferred negotiation styles. This will give you a strong foundation for decision making in situations where you think the other might be lying.

Should you suddenly be facing unexpected bargaining obstacles during a negotiation, it is usually best to test whether you are being lied to. In many cases, you can do this by attempting to break through the presumed lie. For example, follow up with several tough questions that challenge the allegation and watch for signs that your counterpart is indeed lying. There could be both verbal and nonverbal clues. Attempting to make their lies more credible, counterparts may use opening phrases such as 'To tell you the truth' or 'Let me be frank' which frequently indicate just the opposite of the intended message. Nonverbal clues include suddenly sitting straight, seeking eye contact where there was little of it before, frequently blinking the eyes, or speaking in a higher pitched voice than before. If you notice any of these clues, assume that you are being lied to. If verbal message and body language do not seem to match up, the nonverbal signals are generally better indicators. Follow up with probing questions if needed. The more pressure you can put on a liar, the more obvious his or her verbal and nonverbal signs will likely become.

Negotiators may use lies in all cultures and in all phases of negotiations. However, it is crucial to realize that definitions of what constitutes a lie and beliefs of when lying is acceptable during negotiations differ substantially across cultures. For example, most people in Northern Europe may agree with a definition of lying as 'not telling the truth.' In contrast, Americans may only agree with a much narrower definition of 'intentionally telling the untruth.' Many of them see nothing wrong with such tactics as omitting crucial information, putting unfavorable terms into easy-to-overlook fine print, making ambiguous statements that imply incorrect conclusions, or even intentionally misleading their counterparts. They might nevertheless be highly offended if another person referred to such behavior as lying.

In cultures where the concept of *face* is very important, such as China, India, Indonesia, Japan, Mexico, or in most Latin American countries, be very careful when asking probing questions in order to detect lies. Even if this makes it harder for you to decide whether someone is indeed lying, you will need to keep your questioning subtle and avoid exerting too much pressure. Unless you convincingly appear to be gathering further information rather than trying to expose a lie, you will risk causing a huge *loss of face* that could be very detrimental for the relationship. In addition, it can be difficult for Westerners to detect nonverbal clues in most Asian cultures, since their members tend to restrict their body language.

In cultures where people generally prefer aggressive negotiation styles, for instance in Israel, Russia, or Ukraine, it may sometimes be effective to directly confront the other party with your belief that its negotiators are lying. Doing so will usually not adversely affect the relationship unless it is done in an adversarial fashion.

Fake Nonverbal Messages

Experienced negotiators may fake nonverbal signals in order to mislead their counterparts about their intentions. Several facial expressions and gestures may help accomplish this. For instance, tightness around the mouth, running one's fingers through the hair, wringing one's hands, or gripping the armrests of a chair are behaviors that will likely be read as signs that the bargaining exchange is not going smoothly. Similarly, negotiators scratching the head, holding their hands together with the palms pointed outward, or folding their arms may send a message of disbelief or rejection. Others who continuously drum their fingers on the table or demonstratively check their watches signal their belief that they are wasting time. Nodding to indicate agreement and shaking the head to signal disagreement may also send strong messages.

Most of these nonverbal signals are designed to make the other side nervous about the state of the negotiation process, pushing it to make further concessions. To be effective, the signals need to follow shortly after the other party has made an offer or proposal.

Fake nonverbal messages may also be used as a distraction designed to confuse the other party. For example, a negotiator may make significantly more or a lot less frequent eye contact than people would normally do, which tends to make the other nervous. Sending a nonverbal message that indicates agreement, for instance by smiling, exhaling, or leaning back, and then unexpectedly stating a sharp 'no' could throw a counterpart off balance.

Deciding whether someone is faking nonverbal messages can be hard, especially if the person has been practicing the technique. It is often best to ask directly, for example by stating 'You seem displeased with my last offer. Please explain why.' Watch the body language when that person replies. If the nonverbal message was indeed a fake one, you will likely see indicators similar to those described under *Telling Lies* (see previous section). Since they have to concentrate on their verbal response, even experienced negotiators are usually unable to control all of their body language and gestures in such a situation.

Negotiators may use fake nonverbal messages in all cultures and in all phases of negotiations. Westerners with limited experience may find it difficult to detect nonverbal messages when dealing with people from many Asian countries. Members of these cultures tend to restrict their body language and may use subtle nonverbal clues, which Westerners may miss entirely.

When using fake nonverbal messages yourself, keep in mind that in some countries, such as Greece or Turkey, gestures and body language may commonly look different from how people in most cultures use them. The intended message may not always be received.

Appearing Weak or Playing Stupid

Negotiators may pretend to be unfamiliar with negotiating in general, new to the industry, or that they lack previous experience with deals like the one under negotiation. Attempting to make their claim more credible, they may wear cheap clothing or otherwise maintain an unprofessional appearance. Some may try to flatter counterparts with remarks such as 'Everybody tells me you are an experienced and fair negotiator' or 'I can clearly see what makes you so successful in everything you do.' Others again may fake illnesses or pretend that they have a weak heart.

Shrewd negotiators may use such tactics throughout all negotiation phases. They will continue to make 'stupid' mistakes if doing so strengthens their position. For instance, they might openly ask what a fair deal would look like, pretending they have no clue. They may frequently change subjects and use lies to instill confusion. When receiving concessions, 'stupid' negotiators may thank their counterparts and praise them for being fair. Next, they may go on to request further concessions, still pretending that they do not know what they are doing.

The technique's objective is to instill a false sense of security, leading a counterpart to let down his or her guard, and/or to win the other's sympathy. If successful, the other party might involuntarily release more information than intended or could become more lenient and collaborative. In some instances, a counterpart may even end up 'protecting' the allegedly inexperienced, weak negotiator, offering better conditions and making more concessions than he or she otherwise might do. Effective negotiators using this approach may be able to get away with very one-sided deals while still making the other party feel good about his or her generosity and fairness.

Executed right, the technique can be surprisingly effective. However, it is pivotal to keep up the act throughout the negotiation. Otherwise, counterparts tend to get suspicious and may react by keeping their information close to the chest and bargaining in more aggressive or adversarial ways.

Dealing with 'weak' or 'stupid' negotiators is often difficult, since they do not have to participate in the normal negotiation process. Unless you are certain that your counterpart is not just acting, you should never allow sympathy to affect your decision-making. Frequently remind yourself of what you consider a fair deal and ask why you would be willing to let the other get anything better than that. Also, realize that the 'stupid' negotiator in effect forces you do all the work during the negotiation exchange, which is anything but fair.

When suspecting that a counterpart is playing stupid, pay particular attention to the early phases of the negotiation. Clearly formulate your opening position. When the 'stupid' negotiator attempts to digress without responding to your offer, ask that person to state and justify his or her own position with equal clarity. The negotiator may attempt to deflect your request by claiming ignorance and switching topics. Do not let the person get away with that. Repeat your request and force him or her to participate in the negotiation exchange. Statements such as 'You must have some idea of what it is you want to get and what you are willing to give up for it' may help make the exchange more constructive.

Playing stupid is rare in cultures where the concept of *face* is very important, such as China, India, Indonesia, Japan, Mexico, or in most Latin American countries. However, negotiators in those countries who are experienced in working with Westerners may use the approach. In contrast, the Japanese will almost never use it. Negotiators from countries such as the Middle East, Turkey, or Russia, on the other hand, sometimes use it with great success, especially when dealing with Americans, Canadians, the British, or Australians.

Westerners, especially Americans, will hardly be successful with this technique. U.S. businesspeople have such a strong reputation around the world that such acting will not be perceived as credible.

Misrepresenting Value

Negotiators sometimes consciously overstate or understate the value of some or all of the items under negotiation. The objective of this technique is to receive more for what they have to offer and/or to give up less for what they want to obtain. Accordingly, such negotiators may either overstate the value of items they do not care about if they think that the other side is interested in them, or they may understate the value of items the other side has that they are interested in themselves.

The best defense against this technique is to conduct a thorough upfront assessment of the other side's objectives. In addition, watch carefully for verbal slips and non-verbal clues that may indicate their real intentions. This can be difficult, so you may have to trust your instincts if you were unable to obtain enough information prior to the bargaining exchange.

This technique may be used in many cultures and can be effective in the information gathering and bargaining phases of negotiations. However, consider that definitions of *good faith* vary greatly across cultures. In countries where honesty is strongly valued in negotiators, such as in the Nordics or in Switzerland, people may have little tolerance for such tactics. On the other hand, members of intense-bargaining cultures, for instance Russians, Turks, Ukrainians, or some Arabs, might be surprised if anyone took offense 'only' because they misrepresented the value of an item.

False Disinterest in Deal

If another party approaches them with a proposal, negotiators sometimes signal right away that they are not interested. If they agree to meet in order to discuss the proposal, they may state that they will do so only as a courtesy to the other, not to indicate that they are willing to make a deal.

Two possible motivations explain such behavior: for one, there might indeed not be much interest to negotiate, which means that reaching agreement may require considerable salesmanship. The more likely alternative, though, is that the party signaling a lack of interest does so only to achieve a favorable opening position. They could actually be quite interested but may be trying to force their counterparts to make an attractive offer. If successful, continuing to show little interest throughout the negotiation might repeatedly allow them to obtain one-sided concessions.

When dealing with a counterpart who pretends not to be interested, never open with an attractive offer. Instead, ask the person under which conditions he or she would be interested in making a deal. It may help to state that from your experience, whether a deal is of interest or not always depends on its terms and conditions. Wait until an answer is formulated and use it to open a more serious negotiation exchange. Alternatively, start with a low offer. Do not make it insultingly unattractive, but keep it below what you think the other party may find acceptable. When you receive an immediate rejection, ask what your counterpart would consider a realistic and attractive offer. Doing so usually allows the negotiation to become more constructive, even though the other side may continue pretending to be disinterested.

False disinterest can be most useful in the information gathering phase of a negotiation but may occasionally also be effective in the bargaining phase. The approach can be employed in any country. This includes cultures whose members generally enjoy bargaining, though they will usually just use it as a starting maneuver that may be quickly dropped. The technique is popular in France, where negotiators can be particularly good at making their counterparts feel like petitioners and may keep up this attitude throughout the negotiation.

False Disinterest in Concessions

This is a variant of the technique described in the previous section: negotiators who just received a major concession may pretend that they are not interested in it, even though they will secretly add it to their list of agreed items and terms. Unless the other party catches it, this gives them a bargaining advantage without having to reciprocate.

The best countermeasure against this tactic is to take back the concession you just made. A non-offensive way of doing so is to ask how much the concession is worth to the other side, stating that you will take it back and replace it with another offer instead if they do not care about it. The other will be quick to intervene in order to keep the concession if they indeed value it highly.

False disinterest in concessions may be shown in most cultures. The technique is applicable in the bargaining phase of a negotiation. In countries where people generally dislike haggling, such as Australia, Austria, Germany, Switzerland, or the Nordics, the approach is rare because it conflicts with their preference to keep the bargaining exchange as swift and short as possible.

False Demands

Negotiators sometimes request to receive items that they may not be seriously interested in. Such demands serve only as 'sacrifices' during the bargaining process. They are usually included in bundled requests for different concessions and designed in a way that makes them unacceptable to the other side. Accordingly, the other party will most likely shoot down such demands, creating opportunities for the originator to request other concessions 'instead.' For example, a negotiator aiming to get a lower price for a service agreement may request 'free training' from a potential supplier; when refused, he or she may then request to 'receive a 10 percent price reduction in lieu of the training.' Executed right, this approach is often more successful than directly requesting the desired concession.

A caveat is that negotiators must never admit that some of their demands were just tactical, since doing so could considerably weaken their negotiating position. Accordingly, it can be very difficult to backpedal should a counterpart actually agree with a false demand.

The best defense against this technique is to find out upfront what it is that the other side is seriously interested in. If you believe that your counterparts are making false demands, indicate that you are willing to give them what they request and watch their verbal and non-verbal reactions. To avoid locking yourself in, you should make it clear that you are only contemplating the concessions and not yet making them. If the other party suddenly changes topics or indicates that they are willing to accept an alternate arrangement, their demand was very likely a false one.

False demands, which may be brought up in many cultures, can be effective in the bargaining and closure phases of negotiations. Use the technique, and any countermeasures against it, with great caution in cultures where the concept of *face* is very important, for example in China, India, Indonesia, Japan, Mexico, or in most Latin American countries. The risk of causing (or suffering) *loss of face* is considerable. In addition, using the tactic may not help with aggressive/adversarial negotiators from cultures such as Russia or Ukraine. While they may enjoy rejecting your false demand, having done so will not necessarily make them more conciliatory.

False Concessions

In their initial proposals, skilled negotiators may include demands that serve only as 'bargaining material.' Such demands will be dropped later in the bargaining exchange as apparent concessions to stimulate counterparts to reciprocate with real concessions. This approach is often combined with **Written Offers** (see page 107): the initial written proposal may include clauses that impose 'processing fees,' 'rush delivery premiums,' 'legal fees,' and similar demands. Later, the negotiator may promise 'I will drop the processing fees if you give me [a desired concession] in return.' Such false concessions may mislead inexperienced negotiators into believing that their counterparts are acting fair, even when in reality the deal becomes one-sided.

If you believe that you may be offered a false concession, assess its value to yourself *and* the cost of what the other side is giving up. If your conclusion is that it will not cost the other much to drop the demand, point out that you were not prepared to accept it anyway and emphasize that give-and-take bargaining requires both sides to make true sacrifices.

False concessions are frequent in many countries. The technique can be effective in the bargaining phase of a negotiation, especially in cultures whose members dislike bargaining, such as Australia, Austria, Germany, Switzerland, or the Nordics. However, be careful in cultures where the concept of *face* is very important, such as China, India, Indonesia, Japan, Mexico, or most Latin American countries, as false concessions that are not credible could make you look bad and hurt the relationship.

Good Cop, Bad Cop

Widely known as a police interrogation method, this technique is also commonly used during business negotiations. It requires a team of negotiators to coordinate their roles. The objective of this approach is to soften up the other side and make its negotiators believe that they are getting the best possible deal, even when in reality they may end up with unfavorable conditions.

At least one person, the *bad cop*, needs to act in an aggressive or adversarial fashion. This person or group of people must appear influential and should ideally be positioned as the ultimate decision maker. The remaining team member(s) act in *good cop* roles, appearing to be reasonable and collaborative negotiators who sympathize with the other side's positions.

Throughout the negotiation process, the *bad cop* will put significant pressure on the other party, making unreasonable demands, rejecting concessions and insisting on getting better ones, threatening to cancel the whole deal, sometimes even acting irrationally to intimidate the other party. When the *bad cop* finally remains silent, the *good cop* will try to 'soften things up' while asking for further concessions. The two players may also perform acts when asked to reciprocate, with the *good cop* seemingly having to work hard to get the *bad cop* to agree even with small changes, which will then trigger new demands coming from their side. This cycle could be repeated many times during the bargaining exchange. Executed right, the *good cop* and the other party may end up collaborating to satisfy the *bad cop*, which inevitably favors the team using the technique. When they finally think that they are close to reaching a favorable agreement, the *bad cop* may leave the room for a while, giving the *good cop* an opportunity to propose to 'settle the deal now,' saying that they can agree with terms that represent the best the *bad cop* will ever accept.

The technique will only be effective if the main decision is expected to be made during the same meeting. Should a future negotiation round be required, or if the decision making follows after the meeting, the effectiveness of the tactic will be greatly reduced because the other party will likely analyze what happened and may reconsider their position.

If you are dealing with a party that you believe is employing 'good cop, bad cop,' do not confront them with that observation. Doing so will only deteriorate the overall meeting atmosphere, while it is highly unlikely that your counterparts will admit to using the tactic. Instead, focus your energy on not allowing the *bad cop* to control the negotiation. The easiest option is often simply to ignore the person, focus the interaction on the *good cop*. If the *bad cop* was presented to you as the highest-ranking person on the other team, use the countermeasures described under *Aggressive Behavior* (see page 91).

If the other party just rejected a proposal you made, ask the *good cop*, if necessary several times, whether your proposal was reasonable and acceptable. Should the *good cop* agree, you will find yourself in a much stronger negotiating position. Alternatively, if the *good cop* keeps evading and pointing to the *bad cop* as the reason your proposal cannot be accepted, the person will eventually lose credibility and find if hard to continue the act.

This negotiation technique is applicable in the bargaining phase of a negotiation. It could be used in many countries, among them cultures where negotiation styles can be competitive and relationships are only moderately important, such as the United States, Germany, Belgium, and the Netherlands, but also in some strongly relationship-oriented cultures, for instance in Brazil, Greece, the Philippines, or South Korea. Properly executed, the tactic will not necessarily affect the overall relationship between the negotiating companies. However, your side will need to exclude the *bad cop* from future negotiation rounds. In addition, your team needs to prepare well upfront to ensure full alignment, since the tactic can easily backfire if cracks show up between your team members' positions.

'Good cop, bad cop' is rare in most Arab and Asian countries, where people generally prefer to work with fully aligned negotiation teams. Do not use the approach in Japan, since it will only confuse your counterparts. They will most likely stall the negotiation until your team has 're-established harmony.'

Limited Authority

Negotiators may prefer to avoid the overt approach of *Good Cop, Bad Cop*, presented in the previous section, since it tends to put considerable strain on the relationship between the parties. A more subtle and therefore less offensive approach is to claim having limited authority to make decisions. Unlike *Good Cop, Bad Cop*, this variant also allows conducting negotiations individually rather than having to work in a team.

'Limited authority' implies that the person who has sufficient decision-making authority cannot or does not wish to attend the negotiation exchange itself, while the representatives who are at the negotiation table lack the necessary authority to decide major aspects. This creates opportunities to use the absent 'decision maker,' who in reality may not even exist at all, in a role similar to 'bad cop,' making tough demands and generally being uncooperative. In the simplest form of the tactic, negotiators may state 'I'll have to ask my boss for permission' whenever the other party requests a concession they are unwilling to make. Next, they might interrupt the meeting or leave the room temporarily in order to consult with the alleged 'decision maker,' upon which they might return to announce that 'the boss says he cannot agree with what you're asking for.'

Psychologically, this creates a situation in which the negotiation taking place in the meeting room itself may seem cooperative, even though the party using the technique continues to make tough demands and to refuse concessions. In the end, everyone in the room may be collaborating in order to satisfy the tough 'decision maker,' which favors the team using the tactic. Using it can be effective in the bargaining and closure phases of negotiations, and is usually employed late in the process, at a point when the other side is already emotionally committed to the deal. Skilled negotiators may combine it with *Nibbling* (see page 88) to obtain a series of last-minute concessions before they finally agree to close the deal.

When confronted with 'limited authority,' take into account that this does not necessarily represent an explicit negotiation tactic. You might be negotiating with representatives whose authority is indeed restricted, or your counterparts could be using a group process or a series of individual consultations to reach consensus decisions, in which case they will be unable to make major decisions at the negotiation table. The latter is common in many cultures and is very likely the case when negotiating in countries such as China, Japan, Malaysia, the Philippines, Singapore, or South Korea.

If you suspect that your counterparts are indeed using 'limited authority' as a tactic, insist that the person holding the authority to make final decisions join the negotiation. If necessary, threaten that you will otherwise terminate it. In many cases, either the decision maker will get directly involved, or the other representatives will suddenly have the necessary authority to continue the negotiation without needing further approval.

This countermeasure is risky to use in cultures where the concept of *face* is very important, such as China, India, Indonesia, Japan, Mexico, or most Latin American countries. Alternatively, ask the party rejecting your request what alternative it proposes instead. If you continuously demonstrate flexibility to change terms while keeping the value of the negotiated options the same, your counterparts may eventually stop using the technique since it will not be effective.

Lastly, keep in mind that you could sometimes find yourself in negotiation settings in which the final decision-maker refuses to attend while your counterparts at the negotiation table lack sufficient decision-making authority. In such cases, which may be frequent in countries like the Philippines, Russia, or Ukraine, your best option will be to negotiate in an equitable fashion while trying to win the support of your counterparts, whose inputs could and often will strongly influence the other party's final decision.

Crazy like a Fox

With this technique, negotiators may try to convince their counterparts that they are wholly irrational and unwilling (or unable) to follow logical arguments. This may include behaving in erratic ways, sending fake nonverbal messages, frequently switching between cooperative and hostile attitudes, using illogical arguments, or employing other behaviors that could be interpreted as insane. The tactic's objective is usually to confuse the other party and to stimulate them to agree with one-sided demands.

If a counterpart uses this approach with you, it will be best simply to ignore it, acting rationally yourself throughout the exchange. Remind yourself of your non-settlement options and prepare to walk away if necessary. Once the other party realizes that you are not willing to play their game, it may reconsider its strategy.

This negotiation technique, which can be employed throughout the negotiation process, is rare in all countries around the world. The reason we include it here is to emphasize that in a cross-cultural setting, what may seem irrational to you may not necessarily be viewed the same way by your foreign counterpart. Do not automatically assume that someone is irrational because you would act differently. Many cultural gaps can cause such misunderstandings, for instance if one side's primary focus is on financial gains while the other side's objective is to raise its status.

False Least Favorable Option

This technique is generally rare, since it is only effective with extremely adversarial opponents. Their attitude towards negotiating may be *win/lose*, and they may enjoy rejecting the other side's requests. Negotiators who have to deal with such counterparts could present two alternatives to them, asking for the less-favored option. The adversarial counterparts will probably reject this request, insisting on the remaining option. Since this is what it wanted in the first place, the party using the tactic has thus met its objectives. However, it should be careful not to show any triumph, since doing so would only further deteriorate the negotiation atmosphere.

Another version of the tactic consists of proposing a false worst case. Between several existing options, negotiators may state that any of them is good as long as it is not one they specifically point out, which in reality will be the one they desire. Extremely adversarial opponents may enjoy forcing them to choose that very option, again allowing them to achieve their objective.

This technique can be used in the bargaining and closure phases of negotiations. It may work well in countries where negotiations often become confrontational and very aggressive, such as in Russia or Ukraine. Elsewhere, it may be of some use when dealing with extreme negotiators. Never use it with cooperative negotiators who may agree with the proposed option. You will likely need to backpedal, which could considerably weaken your negotiating position.

Chapter 10: Pressure Techniques

The primary objective of using pressure techniques is to create a situation where the other side's negotiators accept an offer that is on the table, believing that neither their non-settlement options nor the expected outcome should they bargain any further are more favorable. It is sufficient to create a psychological perception for the technique to be effective; the members of the other side only have to *believe* that they have no better choice than to accept the offer.

It is unnecessary to employ an aggressive or adversarial negotiation style to apply pressure techniques effectively. Executed skillfully, they can be applied while continuing to negotiate in a cooperative style.

Opening with Best Offer

After making an initial offer, negotiators may attempt to skip the bargaining phase. They may state that they are disinterested in bargaining and that they are therefore putting their best offer on the table right away. To make the statement more convincing, they may add that they firmly believe that the offer reflects the true value of the item(s) under negotiation and that they are unwilling to pay more or receive less than the stated value.

This technique is most effective early in the bargaining phase of a negotiation since it aims to convince the other side that they will receive no concessions whatsoever. For it to work, the counterpart has to be convinced that it reflects a serious intention and not just a tactic. The less bargaining power counterparts have, the more likely they are to accept such an offer. This also assumes that they are sufficiently interested, believing that the offer is favorable over their non-settlement options. Prior to employing the tactic, negotiators using it therefore need to exploit the information gathering phase of the negotiation to ensure that they understand the value the other side attributes to the item(s) being negotiated. In international negotiations, this can be a risky approach since it is often hard to assess this value correctly.

People from many cultures use 'opening with best offer.' Note that the technique does not necessarily represent a conscious attempt to create pressure. In some cases, it may simply reflect a negotiator's honest preference. In particular, this may be the case with people who generally dislike bargaining, such as Australians, Austrians, Germans, Swiss, or people from Nordic countries. Generally, the less enthusiastic the members of a given culture are about bargaining, the more likely they are to accept. Some may actually like the approach since they appreciate the opportunity to cut the bargaining phase short.

Members of cultures where aggressive negotiating is generally preferred, for example Russians or Ukrainians, may also like this technique. They may use it only as a tactic to try out, quickly recovering if they find that it does not work with a given counterpart.

Because of these cultural variances, no single countermeasure exists that would work in all countries. If you believe that the other side uses the approach as a tactic and that it is willing to bargain if you refuse, it is best to simply ignore the offer, responding with an opening offer of your own instead. However, if you think that your counterparts might be serious about the approach, explain to them why you disagree with their value assessment and how this makes it impossible for you to accept their offer. Once you have done so, find a face-saving way to help them focus on further bargaining exchanges.

Do not assume that people have bad intentions when using the approach. Your counterparts may be inexperienced or uncomfortable with negotiating, or this technique may be viewed as perfectly ethical within their culture. Never take it personal if others use this approach.

Using this tactic may be perceived very negatively in cultures where people enjoy bargaining, for example in many Arab countries, Greece, Mexico, Nigeria, or Turkey. People in these countries may interpret the approach as an outright refusal to negotiate, which can be taken as a personal offense. Following emotional instinct rather than rational conclusion, they may decide to walk away even if your offer otherwise appears acceptable to them.

In a variant of 'opening with best offer,' a negotiator may try to apply it only to one of the items in a multi-item negotiation. The bargaining phase would still follow, only with a limited scope. For example, the negotiator could declare that the price of an item is inflexible but that related services, for example warranty terms or training offerings, are negotiable. This approach may have a higher chance of being accepted by the other side and will also be viewed as more cooperative.

Intransigence

This is a tactical variant of the *Best Offer* technique: if the other side refuses an initial offer, the negotiator who made it emphasizes that 'This is the maximum we pay' for the kind of product or services being offered, implying that he or she has made the best possible offer and is unable to make any further concessions.

This technique is most effective in the information gathering and bargaining phases of negotiations. Unlike *Best Offer*, intransigence may also work late in a negotiation when trying to draw a line, especially when negotiating from a position of strength. Large corporations, for example, often employ it when negotiating with individuals or smaller companies. The tactic creates pressure on the other side to accept whatever is on the table. However, it only works if the other side believes that it has no better alternative.

The most effective countermeasure is to emphasize that the offer made is not acceptable to you, threatening that you will walk away if you receive no further concessions. Once you announced this, remain silent and wait for a reaction. However, only use this response if you are indeed prepared to terminate the negotiation. Otherwise, your best option may be to accept what is being offered.

You will rarely encounter, and should not attempt to use, intransigence in cultures where people enjoy bargaining, such as Egypt, Greece, Iran, Mexico, Nigeria, or Turkey. People in these countries often view this approach as a refusal to negotiate, which many of them consider highly inappropriate. An intransigent approach may be received more favorably in countries where people generally dislike bargaining, such as Australia, Austria, Germany, the Nordics, or Switzerland. Members of these cultures may often use the tactic themselves.

Silence

As a way to reject a request for concessions or an offer, negotiators may sometimes remain completely silent. They will look serious, without grimacing, flinching, or otherwise sending non-verbal messages. In order for the technique to be effective, negotiators need to remain silent until their counterparts finally say something, even if this takes several minutes.

The objective of this tactic is to signal displeasure and create pressure on the other side to improve its offering. A negotiator using the technique attempts to advance his or her position, hoping that the other side either makes concessions in order to receive a more positive response or volunteers further information, giving in to an urge to 'justify' an apparently offensive position.

Never make additional concessions only because your negotiation counterpart remains silent. If you believe that others are using this technique with you, first, remain silent yourself. Keep in mind that you might be misreading their intentions; they could be contemplating your last offer or they might be distracted by something else. After an extensive period of silence, when you are certain that your counterparts use it as a tactic, calmly ask whether they plan to respond to your proposal. Avoid doing this too soon; let at least a minute or two pass before speaking again. If the silence continues, explain after a while that you are about to leave because they are apparently not interested in your proposal. Get up and walk towards the door. Assuming that your counterparts continue to be interested, they will stop you before you have left the room. At that point, the pressure is on them to explain their position and make a counterproposal.

Silence can be an effective technique in the bargaining and closure phases of negotiations. Shrewd negotiators in many cultures often use it. Since remaining silent rarely jeopardizes relationships, some may simply try the tactic to see whether it works with their negotiation counterparts. Worst case, it may temporarily affect the atmosphere of the negotiation, but it is usually easy to recover if necessary.

The tactic works well in communication-intense cultures where being silent is interpreted as sending a negative message. It can be an exceptionally powerful negotiation tool in the United States and Ireland, may be effective in countries like Argentina, Mexico, France, Italy, or Spain, and might work in Canada, Hong Kong, Singapore, Taiwan, and many other countries. However, members of some of these cultures can be very patient, so expect that it may take two minutes or more before your counterparts say something, realizing that the negotiation will otherwise come to a standstill. The technique does not have an impact in countries where silence is appreciated, for example in Finland. Keep in mind that silence is a normal part of conversations in many cultures, which may limit its usefulness as a tactic.

Final Offer

Attempting to convince their counterparts that they will receive no further concessions, negotiators may state something like 'This is my final offer' or 'This is the best I have to offer; take it or leave it.' The goal of this maneuver is to induce fear of losing the deal, thus creating pressure for the other to accept. Two important conditions must exist for this technique to work. For one, the other side has to be sufficiently interested in the offer. If its negotiators do not view it as preferable over their non-settlement options, they will decline, which either means that the deal is off or that the party making the 'final' offer has to make further concessions, leaving its representatives in a weakened negotiating position. In addition, final offers have to be credible, convincing the other side that its members will not get any better future offer. Otherwise, they may decide to 'call the bluff.'

It is best only to make final offers late in the game, especially when dealing with inexperienced negotiators. If the others are already mentally committed, their self-induced psychological pressure to 'not lose the deal' may lead them to believe that an offer is if it reflects no more than an attempt to bluff them.

Your best countermeasure when receiving a final offer is simply to ignore it. Re-state your own previous position, or make a different offer instead. If your counterparts are indeed serious, they will repeat several times that their offer is final. Otherwise, they will continue to bargain, realizing that they cannot pressure you into accepting their offer.

Final offers are frequent in many countries. The technique can be effective late in the bargaining phase, but also in the closure phase of a negotiation. In cultures where people enjoy extended bargaining, for instance in many Arab and Latin American countries, Indonesia, or Nigeria, one should not make a final offer until several rounds of bargaining have been completed. Otherwise, people may interpret the tactic as a refusal to negotiate in good faith. Strongly competitive or adversarial negotiators, for instance Israelis, Russians, or Ukrainians, are generally distrustful and reluctant to accept if your final offer comes too soon. Even if they consider it acceptable and think it may be the best one they will get, they might still not accept. In these cultures, many people believe that only extended, tough negotiations lead to good deals.

Generally, the less enthusiastic people within a given culture are about bargaining, the sooner they may accept final offers. Negotiators in countries such as Australia, Austria, Germany, the Nordics, or Switzerland may view final offers as opportunities to speed up the negotiation. Especially if they have only limited international experience, they may not believe that the other side could be bluffing, since they would only state final offers themselves if they were serious.

Final offers may often be bluffs in cultures where people either prefer an aggressive negotiation style, like Bulgaria, Israel, Russia, or Ukraine, or where they prefer tough bargaining, for instance in China, Korea, or in many countries in the Middle East. Never get upset because of this. Your counterparts may consider it a 'bargaining trick' and expect you not to take any of it personally.

If you are willing to 'play hardball,' another possible countermeasure when confronted with a final offer is to respond with a final offer of your own. It can be advantageous to combine this with a threat to walk out, linked to a time limit. For example, if a negotiator stated that his or her final offer is one million dollars, your response might be 'Your offer is completely unacceptable to me. I will not pay a cent more than $950,000. You have ten minutes to accept; otherwise, our negotiation is over.' Even experienced negotiators may sometimes be taken by surprise by such a response. It may convince them that it is best for them to offer further concessions rather than letting you walk out. Never use this approach if you are bluffing – it will ruin your negotiating position if you end up having to backpedal from such a confrontation. Since this maneuver is perceived as adversarial, you should also not use it when negotiating with members of strongly relationship-oriented cultures, such as China, Egypt, Greece, Indonesia, Malaysia, or Singapore.

Time Pressure

In task-oriented societies where people strongly value near-term achievements, such as the United States or Canada, time and deadlines can become important factors in negotiations. Since there is a high sense of urgency and a desire to 'close the deal' fast, many negotiators from these countries become more willing to make concessions when their deadline is approaching. Deadlines can either be self-imposed, for example if the person had planned to spend only a certain amount of time negotiating, or they may be dictated by external constraints. Examples for the latter are alternative offers that expire by a certain date, target dates imposed by management ('I need you to close this deal before the end of the quarter'), or conflicting arrangements, for instance if spending more time in the current negotiation means that the negotiator misses a subsequent meeting with another contact or a flight back home.

Shrewd negotiators in several cultures may exploit every opportunity to apply time pressure when negotiating with Americans or people from other fast-paced societies. Knowing about deadlines the other side is working against can give them a valuable advantage. One popular tactic in countries like Japan, South Korea, or China is for office staff to inquire about a foreign negotiator's or negotiation team's flight arrangements. The reason given may be to 'reconfirm travel arrangements in order to ensure that everything goes smoothly.' This is rarely the true motivation. Rather, the local negotiators now have an advantage, since they know when the other side will start feeling time pressure. They will not hesitate to leverage this knowledge, sometimes in drastic ways.

As an example, assume that you are arriving in China for a negotiation with a local company. You allowed two full days for the exchange, which should give both sides ample time to reach agreement. You plan to return home after the two days. Upon learning about your schedule, your Chinese negotiation partners may fill the first day with lengthy introductions of the company's history and explanations of its organization, operations, products, markets, and other presentations. They may take you out for a long lunch, give you an extensive factory tour, and arrange an evening banquet with numerous toasts and friendly conversations but no opportunity to discuss business. On the second day, they may suggest that you explain your proposal in depth, asking numerous questions and spending considerable time discussing minor aspects of terms and conditions that bear little or no relevance to the outcome of the negotiation. It may not be until late in the afternoon of the second day that they commence with the core negotiation. By that time, with only a few hours left before your scheduled departure, you will be under considerable time pressure and thus more likely to agree with less-than-favorable terms. While some cultures may view such an approach as unethical, the Chinese and others see nothing wrong with it. They use it often with great success.

Another approach that creates time pressure is to request changes to a pending agreement very late in the game. Russian, Ukrainian, Taiwanese, and negotiators from several other cultures often use this. Again, this variant requires that the negotiators using it know the other side's deadline. The requested changes will be more substantial than what they really hope to achieve, creating new bargaining room for them. The party that is under time pressure may be more amenable to making at least some concessions at this late point, since its only other options are now either to miss the deadline or to end the negotiation unsuccessfully.

Time pressure may not always be applied in order to exploit a counterpart's sense of urgency. Some negotiators use it primarily to determine how committed to a prospective deal the other party is. Either this could give them strategic advantages over the further course of the negotiation, or they might be testing the strength of the business relationship.

Your best defense against such time pressure techniques is patience and proper preparation. By setting aside ample time for the negotiation process, not allowing yourself to be pressured by deadlines, and being willing to return for a continuation of the negotiation if schedule conflicts get in the way, you can shield yourself from any time pressures the other side may attempt to apply. Your second best defense may be to avoid giving the other side opportunities to use deadlines against you. Either you may achieve this by not revealing details of your schedule or you may let your counterparts know, often more convincingly, that you have put aside plenty of time should the negotiation take longer than expected and that your travel arrangements can easily be changed. Using this approach, you will likely find the other side conducting the negotiation more swiftly.

This technique is most effective in the closure phase of negotiations. However, it works best when negotiating with people from fast-paced cultures where 'time is money,' such as the United States or Canada. In strongly relationship-oriented cultures where people allocate considerable time for negotiations, such as China, Egypt, Greece, Indonesia, Malaysia, or Singapore, one risks offending the other side's negotiators, since they may interpret the tactic as a lack of interest or as unwillingness to 'play by the rules.'

Expiring or Decreasing Offers

In addition to the time pressure techniques described in the previous section, there are a number of more overt approaches to put pressure on a negotiation party in order to obtain concessions or drive a deal to closure. One of them is to make an expiring offer that is valid only for a limited time, implying that otherwise the opportunity will be gone. Since this arrangement forces the buyer to make the seller's deadline the buyer's deadline also, the technique can be effective by stimulating quick decisions. As an example, many American companies add clauses to their formal offers that hold them to the offer for a given time period only. It is usually expected that the offering party continue to be interested in the arrangement beyond the expiration date of the offer. However, informing the other side that you will indeed not renew your offer can create time pressure if you convince them that you are serious. If done in an outright adversarial fashion, this technique is usually referred to as an *ultimatum*. Smart negotiators create counter-pressure by insisting that they will leave the negotiation unless the deadline is extended.

Decreasing offers employ hardball tactics that some negotiators may consider outright hostile. The basic principle is to offer the other party certain conditions only for a defined time period, after which the terms start getting worse. In its simplest version, this could be 'I offer you $10,000 for this item today, but I will only offer $9,500 tomorrow.' The fact that the 'clock is ticking' increases the pressure on the other side to accept the terms offered. There is no effective countermeasure to this tactic if the offering side indeed is willing to walk away from the deal. You can only hope that the technique represents a bluff. Since it is openly adversarial, you may encounter this technique in countries where aggressive negotiation styles prevail, such as Russia or Ukraine, but rarely in cultures that prefer a win-win approach to negotiating.

Using decreasing or expiring offers can be effective if you believe a buyer is generally attracted to your offer but still wants to 'shop around' for alternatives. Ideally, your offer will convince the buyer to make a fast decision in your favor. However, you have to be willing to walk away from the deal if that does not happen. Otherwise, the buyer will call your bluff, continuing the negotiation from a considerably stronger position.

Making decreasing or expiring offers can be useful in the closure phase of negotiations. Using them in international negotiations can be dangerous, though. Employ them only when negotiating with people from highly achievement-oriented cultures, such as Canada or the United States, from cultures that tolerate adversarial styles, such as Israelis, Russians, or Ukrainians, or in situations where you have attractive alternatives such that you do not want to pursue a deal with the current party unless it moves fast. When negotiating with members of strongly relationship-oriented cultures, such as China, Egypt, Greece, Indonesia, Malaysia, or Singapore, using such techniques can be disastrous and must be avoided.

Nibbling

When agreement seems close and both sides appear committed to making a deal, negotiators may attempt to gain further concessions by repeatedly demanding additional 'small' changes. They may say something like 'I could agree to close the deal if only you would accept this concession.' At times, they may combine the tactic with the *Limited Authority* technique, for instance by claiming that their boss will not let them close the deal unless they receive a particular commitment. Experienced negotiators may nibble repeatedly and can be surprisingly effective in doing so. Their effectiveness depends on whether the other side is mentally committed to making the deal. Since nibbling is done late in the game, usually in the closure phase of a negotiation, it also often creates time pressure, which may further increase the likelihood of getting additional concessions.

If a counterpart appears to be nibbling, ask yourself whether you really believe that the person will drop the deal if you refuse to agree with the requested changes. The answer is frequently 'no.' If you have reasons to make further concessions, for instance in order to nurture the relationship or to prevent loss of face, ask the other side to reciprocate.

Negotiators in cultures where people like bargaining and haggling frequently use this technique to gain advantages in the final phases of a negotiation. Some, for example Chinese or Koreans, may even do so after a contract has already been signed. Since nibbling generally does not affect the relationship, there is little risk associated with using the technique yourself. Avoid excessive nibbling in cultures where people strongly dislike haggling, such as Australia, Austria, Germany, Hungary, the Nordics, or Switzerland. You will rarely experience members of these cultures using this tactic.

Persistence

This technique requires being patient and persistent with a negotiation counterpart, while not making any significant concessions. Especially in the closure phase of a negotiation, when both sides are mentally committed to the deal and only seemingly small disagreements remain, the side that remains the most persistent usually ends up with the better deal. It is usually counterproductive to rush the end phase of a negotiation, and persistence often pays big rewards.

When using this technique, avoid getting obsessed over the risk of pushing the other side into second-guessing the deal. Once your counterparts are mentally committed to it, which assumes that all relevant obstacles have been removed, they may find the 'unnecessary' hold-ups over small issues annoying but will rarely walk away.

Persistence can have effects similar to *Time Pressure* on people from fast-paced cultures where 'time is money,' such as the United States or Canada. Members of most other cultures view it as less offensive, though, and the risk of offending your counterparts is low as long as you remain willing to make small concessions if necessary.

This technique is most effective in the closure phase of negotiations but may also work in other phases. There is no effective countermeasure other than being equally patient and persistent. Once the other side realizes that you are not likely to 'lose it' and give up something of significant value, its members usually become more cooperative.

Members of cultures where people typically have a low achievement orientation, for instance Russia, may not use this approach intentionally but may still make foreign negotiators feel pressured. Russians and others can sometimes wear out foreign negotiators simply through their seemingly unlimited patience and persistence, coupled with an apparent 'don't care' attitude. The only effective countermeasure is to allocate plenty of time for the negotiation, being equally patient and persistent.

Creating Physical Discomfort

Some negotiators seek to create pressure on their counterparts by making them physically uncomfortable. They may use conference rooms that are too warm, too cold, too small, or too noisy, serve no food or beverages during extended meetings, or find other ways to affect the physical well-being of their counterparts. They make sure that the unfavorable conditions come as a surprise, depriving the other party of its chances to prepare accordingly. The objective is similar to the *Time Pressure* technique: to stimulate the other party to end the negotiation as soon as possible by making greater concessions than its members might be willing to make otherwise.

Your best countermeasure if someone uses this approach is to ask in a non-aggressive way that the condition be changed. If your request is refused, either you can try to relax and ignore the issue, or you could state that you are too uncomfortable to continue the negotiation, suggesting to reconvene later at a place where you have some influence over the meeting atmosphere, such as a hotel conference room. It is essential to make this request in an apologetic manner and to avoid appearing aggressive or disrespectful.

Unlike *Time Pressure*, creating physical discomfort can be effective with people from many cultures. People from countries where negotiation styles are often somewhat aggressive, for instance Russians, Ukrainians, Israelis, the Chinese, or Koreans, are most likely to employ the technique. However, members of many other cultures may also use this approach.

Chapter 11: Aggressive and Adversarial Techniques

This chapter discusses negotiation techniques that members of many cultures may consider aggressive or adversarial. Depending on the cultural context, the word *aggressive* can take on multiple meanings. In the United States, it often has positive connotations, such as 'assertive, bold, and energetic.' However, Americans also understand another interpretation that is common in most other cultures and that we will use in this chapter: 'behaving in angry and violent ways.' The primary objective of using aggressive or adversarial techniques is to intimidate the other side, creating psychological pressure on its members to end the situation by agreeing with unfavorable terms.

In many cultures, for instance in Japan, Thailand, India, Mexico, or in most European and Latin America countries, the overt use of aggressive or adversarial negotiation techniques indicates that either the negotiating partners had no working relationship to begin with, or that it has broken down. However, it is important to realize that people in some cultures may see no contradiction in employing aggressive or adversarial techniques while maintaining and continuing to value strong relationships with the same counterparts. Countries where this attitude is frequent include Brazil, China, and South Korea. Somewhat surprisingly, members of cultures where negotiations tend to become confrontational, such as Russia or Ukraine, may also have this attitude. In the heat of a confrontation, it will be vital to remember that your counterparts are unlikely to have adversarial intentions, assuming that your relationship with them is strong.

Aggressive Behavior

Negotiators employing this technique may display a wide array of different behaviors that serve to seize control of the negotiation and dictate the agenda as well as terms of agreement. Negotiators behaving aggressively may attack personal integrity and professional competence of their counterparts, reject offers as unreasonable and insulting, shout and yell to instill fear, and so on. They often hope to intimidate weaker counterparts, with the goal of receiving additional concessions. To be credible, they have to use the tactic right from the start of the negotiation. Aggressive behavior may not always be a conscious tactic since it could also reflect a natural inclination.

When dealing with an aggressive negotiator, it is important to remain patient. Remember the old adage that 'dogs that bark do not bite.' Listen and watch carefully for leaks and non-verbal messages that may provide valuable information about your counterpart's objectives. It is usually best to remain quiet until he or she asks you to say something. When you finally do, calmly say that you are not finished in case you are interrupted. If necessary, point out that you did not talk while the other was speaking and that you now expect the same courtesy.

If your counterpart is behaving in an outright adversarial fashion, first try to calm things down. For example, you might use an excuse to call a short break. If the adversarial behavior continues after the break, which usually indicates the use of a technique rather than a state of emotion, state clearly that you will not participate in any further discussions unless conducted in a professional manner. If necessary, announce that you are taking another break and that you will terminate the negotiation if the person does not resume it in a professional manner afterwards. While it does create a risk of having to walk away, this approach will frequently make the negotiation more productive.

Russians and Ukrainians may employ aggressive behavior in all phases of negotiations. Negotiators in several other Central and Eastern European countries as well as Israel sometimes also resort to this technique. However, never use it in cultures where the concept of *face* is very important, such as China, India, Indonesia, Japan, Mexico, or most Latin American countries, even when your counterparts may seem to be employing it themselves. They will likely resume negotiating in a more cooperative fashion after a while.

A variant of this approach is referred to as 'passive-aggressive behavior.' Here, negotiators may completely refuse to cooperate with their counterparts. They may not actively engage in the process and show aggressive reactions to the other side's bargaining attempts. Unlike the **Fake Disinterest** technique discussed earlier, negotiators employing this approach, who usually have a distaste for bargaining, are not interested in the negotiation process and thus see no reason to participate in it. However, that does not mean that they will not be interested in reaching a deal.

The best way to deal with passive-aggressive behavior is often to propose a follow-up meeting, asking the person to prepare a contract proposal as a basis for discussion. Come to the next meeting equipped with your own written version. At that point, there are three possibilities: first, your counterpart may not have prepared any proposal, which gives you a chance to make your version the basis for discussion. Second, your counterpart may have a proposal that looks reasonable, in which case it is best to accept it. Third, your counterpart may have included clauses that you disagree with, in which case you could try to trade clauses between the two versions on the table where feasible. Either way, the fact that you now base the bargaining on written documents with clearly defined options makes the negotiation easier and likelier to proceed in a productive fashion.

Passive-aggressive negotiating, which affects all phases of the process, is not very culture-specific. People who generally dislike bargaining and do not view business relationships as very important are somewhat likely to take this approach. Generally, passive-aggressive behavior is rarely an effective negotiation technique unless the other side is very inexperienced.

Extreme Openings

Earlier in this book, we mentioned the importance of setting high aspirations, emphasizing that they must nevertheless be rationally defensible. Negotiators who use extreme openings, that is, initial offers that are difficult to defend rationally, do not intend to reveal their aspirations by doing so. They use the tactic to trigger reactions from the other side. For instance, they may start by offering one-fifth of the true value of an item they are interested to buy, hoping that their counterparts will react by stating that they 'expect at least $10,000' or 'ask for no less than 9,000,' for example. Extreme offers often provoke at least subtle reactions that can inadvertently provide valuable information and clues. Another motivation for the technique may be that the party using it does not have a clear idea of what a reasonable offer might be. Again, by making one that is 'unreasonable,' they hope to receive clues about their counterparts' expectations. The technique of using extreme openings may lead to one-sided deals if the other party has no idea of the true value of an item under negotiation. Antique dealers can make fortunes with this approach if clueless buyers accept their extreme initial offers.

If someone confronts you with an extreme opening, react first by showing complete shock, then point out that the offer you received is completely unrealistic. You might add that if the other party is indeed serious, you will be unable to make a deal with them. Insist on getting a *serious* offer instead. It is vital not to back off if this request is refused. If necessary, state that you are unwilling to enter into the negotiation process unless your counterpart makes a reasonable offer. If there is still no progress, make an equally unrealistic counteroffer that is extreme at the other end of the spectrum, then point out that both sides have made unrealistic offers and promise that you will respond in kind if you receive a realistic one. Another effective countermeasure may be to ask **Probing Questions** (see also page 104). This often works because your counterpart will be struggling to come up with a rational explanation to defend its offer.

Always dismiss extreme openings and consider your counterpart's second offer as his or her starting position. Otherwise, you might fall into the mental trap of feeling compelled to make big concessions yourself if the other moved far from their initial unrealistic position. When using extreme openings yourself, never offer a second bid because your counterpart rejected the initial opening as 'not good enough.' Instead, request to get a counteroffer.

The technique is only useful at the beginning of the bargaining phase. Its effectiveness depends hugely on the cultural context. In countries where relationships are critically important, for example in China, Indonesia, Malaysia, or Singapore, and in cultures where people generally dislike haggling, such as Australia, Austria, Germany, Switzerland, Hungary, or the Nordics, making extreme opening offers is often viewed as overly aggressive or adversarial. Members of these cultures may become very upset if someone uses the approach. In extreme cases, they may choose to terminate the negotiation. People in several other countries, for instance in Central Europe, also tend to dislike the approach but usually do not take it as negatively as the above group.

On the opposite end of the spectrum are cultures whose members enjoy haggling, such as most Arab countries, Indonesia, Nigeria, Pakistan, the Philippines, or Turkey. People in these cultures may think the technique perfectly acceptable and usually have no bad intentions when using it. Never interpret the tactic as an adversarial step. Instead, keep cool and try to maintain a positive attitude.

Anger

Negotiators using this technique may openly display angry behavior, for instance by raising voices or showing angry mimics and gestures, attempting to pressure the other side into making concessions. Rather than trying to create intimidation as *Aggressive Behavior* does, the purpose of this technique is to convince the other side of the seriousness of a position and to leverage most humans' inclination to compromise as a way to prevent conflicts from escalating. Competent negotiators use the tactic in a controlled manner, never losing their temper. However, for it to be effective, it is important to convince the other side that its members are indeed facing a serious outburst of temper. Some people may combine it with a *Walkout* (see page 95) for added psychological impact.

When confronted with angry behaviors, it is vital not to respond in kind. Stay calm and friendly, and remind yourself that you may be facing an intentional tactic, not an emotional reaction. Watching your counterpart's body language may help determine whether it is an act or not. In parallel, listen carefully for verbal leaks; even experienced negotiators may inadvertently reveal valuable information during this phase since few humans have the mental capacity to carefully choose their words while 'acting.' If you remain calm enough, it will become embarrassing for your counterpart at some point and he or she will be struggling to find a believable way to calm down. When the behavior finally stops, point to your recent concessions and ask how they could get so aggressive with someone who showed such a willingness to cooperate. You may be able to make them feel guilty and obtain concessions.

This technique is most effective in the bargaining and closure phases of negotiations. Russians and Ukrainians in particular use it often and may be masters at 'playing the act' in a convincing manner. The tactic can also be effective in many other European countries, the Middle East, the United States, or in Canada, even though members of these cultures will rarely use it themselves.

Generally, the effectiveness of this technique depends mostly on how important *face* and personal pride are in a given culture. People in the Nordics, for example, rarely use it and may become very uncomfortable if someone else does, though outbursts of anger will not necessarily damage the overall negotiation. In contrast, it is usually counterproductive to display anger openly in any of the South or East Asian countries, as well as in most of Latin America, where doing so can cause *loss of face* and respect.

Threats and Warnings

Negotiators trying to increase the pressure on their counterparts to accept proposals or make concessions may resort to open threats, informing them that any further refusal to concede certain points will have unfavorable consequences. Threats can be explicit ("We will terminate the negotiation if you do not accept") or implicit ("We will only be able to continue the negotiation if you accept"). They usually aim to convince the other party that the only alternative to accepting a demand is non-settlement.

Threats must be credible for the technique to work. When using the approach, give your counterparts enough information and paint a threatening yet realistic picture of the consequences of them being uncooperative. In addition, threats should reflect serious intentions. Should a threat you made turn out to have been a bluff, your negotiating position will be greatly weakened.

'Warnings' are threats of third-party consequences. Rather than threatening actions under the issuer's immediate control, they imply that others will affect the other side adversely unless they cooperate. For example, negotiators may warn that others will think badly of their counterparts should the proposed deal fall apart. Warnings are usually much less aggressive than threats are and may therefore be more effective.

When faced with a threat, two aspects are important to consider: whether you actually believe it, and whether you regard the consequences of the threat worse than your non-settlement alternatives. If either answer is 'no,' simply ignore the threat. This is almost always better than to challenge it, which bears the risk of hurting the other's pride or causing loss of face.

Threats and warnings may be used in many cultures and are most effective in the bargaining and closure phases of negotiations. Applied in a non-aggressive fashion, the technique is acceptable in most European countries, the United States, Canada, and many others. Never take threats or warnings personally. People in countries where negotiations may become confrontational and very aggressive, such as Israel, Russia, or Ukraine, often try to bluff when making threats without worrying about the potential loss of credibility.

How members of face-oriented cultures view the use of threats and warnings during negotiations can be confusing. On one hand, many, among them Indians, Indonesians, Japanese, and others, view them as inappropriate and often unacceptable. However, in other Asian countries such as China, South Korea, or Taiwan, as well as many Latin American countries, people may actually use the technique themselves, at least in indirect and more subtle ways. Even if they do, be cautious when using similar tactics yourself in these countries since the risk of damaging relationships can be significant.

Walking Out

Negotiators may use walkouts as an intimidation technique designed to convince the other party that no further concessions will be available to them. They usually do so by announcing that they see no value in negotiating any further, packing their briefcases, and leaving the room. 'Emotional' walkouts are accompanied by demonstrative behavior that may include yelling, making angry gestures, or slamming doors. They should come as a surprise to the other side. An alternative strategy is to use a 'calm' walkout, where the negotiator leaves the room quietly. This variant tells the other side that the behavior does not just reflect a temporary emotional outburst. It is often preceded by threats.

Walking out can be effective with risk-averse counterparts. However, it is always a gamble since the other side may end the negotiation. Smart negotiators never walk out unless they are happy with their non-settlement options.

A less aggressive variant can be used when negotiating as a team. Here, only one of the team members, usually an influential one, walks out at a critical junction of the negotiation exchange. The person remains calm while walking out, but facial expressions and body language convey that he or she is very displeased with the way the negotiation is going. The team members who remain in the room may be able to leverage the psychological pressure this created to obtain concessions from the other party.

If a negotiator walks out on you, never try to keep the person back or run after him or her. It may be effective to let him or her leave and go home yourself. Remain patient and let significant time pass, at least a few weeks. You will likely hear back from the person during that time, asking whether you want to resume the negotiation, in which case you will be in an advantaged position. There is a small risk that you may not hear back from him or her, which means that the negotiation is likely over. Getting in touch yourself inevitably puts you into a much weaker negotiating position, though.

If you do not want to take the risk of the negotiation being over, for instance because your non-settlement options are unfavorable, here is an alternate strategy: when the negotiator starts walking to the door, stop him or her by saying 'I'll give you one more chance.' Never say 'Stop,' 'Wait a minute,' or anything else that may sound like you are desperate for the other to stay. It is crucial to make it sound like you are doing *the other person* a favor by calling him or her back, not the other way around. Next, ask the person to return to the table and get settled again, and decide how you will try to break the impasse. This may include offering a different concession from what the other side has been requesting, which should re-engage both sides in the negotiation without either of them 'giving in.'

Walkouts can be employed in the bargaining and closure phases of negotiations. Russians and Ukrainians use them often, sometimes repeatedly during the same negotiation. People in other countries that are not strongly relationship focused, e.g. in Poland, the Czech Republic, the Netherlands, Germany, or Israel, may also use the tactic. Be cautious when using it with Americans, Canadians, or most Western Europeans, since there is a high probability of your negotiation being over.

Do not use this technique at all in strongly relationship-oriented cultures, which includes most countries in Asia and Latin America. It may be better to employ a 'friendly' walkout instead. If the negotiation seems to have reached a dead end and you are contemplating to end it unless the other side shows willingness to make concessions, start packing up your papers and announce something like this: 'I sense that we will not be able to reach agreement today. Rather than letting this affect our great relationship which I value very highly, I would prefer it if we ended our negotiation now. Let us please stay in touch and try to find a new opportunity in future that will allow us to work together.' The basic effect of this approach is similar to a 'calm' walkout: it forces your counterparts to decide whether to hold you back or let the negotiation end unsuccessfully. Nevertheless, this version usually does not damage the relationship and leaves doors open for a possible future cooperation.

Chapter 12: Other Emotional Techniques

This chapter discusses emotional negotiation techniques that members of most cultures view as neither aggressive nor adversarial. Most of them attempt to trigger emotional reactions as a way to obtain concessions or to motivate the other party to become more cooperative.

Attitudinal Bargaining

Negotiators use this technique to create or reestablish a constructive and cooperative negotiation atmosphere, especially with counterparts whose communication styles and negotiation attitudes are somewhat aggressive. They may smile frequently, subtly emphasize their interest in win-win outcomes of the negotiation, ask about the other side's concerns, and so on. Other actions may include choosing pleasant meeting venues and showing generally courteous behavior.

If none of these actions proves effective and the negotiation exchange becomes tense and aggressive, negotiators may state their belief that such a meeting atmosphere will adversely affect either side's ability to reach their objectives. They may ask directly what they can and what the other side is willing to do to make the exchange more productive, becoming quite forceful if needed. If a combative opponent's behavior still does not change, they may tell the other clearly that they will terminate the negotiation unless he or she returns to more civilized conduct.

Attitudinal bargaining can be effective in all phases of negotiations. Its impact may be small or negligible in cultures that promote adversarial negotiation styles, such as Russia or Ukraine. Nevertheless, the technique can be applied in all cultures with little risk of adversely affecting the meeting atmosphere. Concerns should be expressed very tactfully in cultures where the concept of *face* is important or where personal pride may be a strong factor, such as in China, India, Indonesia, Mexico, or in Latin America.

Dual Messages

Before or after making an offer, negotiators may sometimes send their counterparts dual messages, one that is overt and another that is more subtle and indirect. For instance, a car dealer may show a customer a more expensive car than he or she may be looking for, name the price, and then casually mention that the client probably could not afford this model. An IT service vendor may offer a more comprehensive solution than requested, mentioning to the prospective client that 'This one would give you much more value but probably exceeds your budget.' This approach can result in two effects: it often creates psychological pressure, playing to the other party's pride and challenging the person to opt for a bigger deal than was previously targeted. In addition, it can be an effective way to obtain information, since counterparts often react by revealing their bargaining objectives or limits.

When receiving dual messages, it is usually best to ignore the subtle part altogether. Remind yourself that if the negotiator bringing it up were serious with the comment, it would make no sense to send the message at all. Stick with your negotiating objectives and make it clear that you will not digress from them.

This technique can be useful in the information gathering and bargaining phases of negotiations. People in many countries may sometimes employ it. However, it is rare in cultures where the concept of *face* is very important, such as China, India, Indonesia, Japan, or Singapore, and in countries where relationships are critical, for instance in China, Indonesia, Malaysia, or Singapore. In these countries, the secondary message should be very subtle. Otherwise, you risk offending your counterparts and severely damaging the relationships.

Guilt and Embarrassment

Negotiators often try to make their counterparts feel guilty or embarrassed, hoping that this will stimulate them to make further concessions. Four variants can be effective:

- If the other party made an unreasonable demand, for instance by opening with an extreme offer, negotiators may explain calmly how unrealistic the proposal is. The effect can be intensified by pointing out how they had been looking forward to the negotiation or how disappointed they are by the unfair demand. They will then fall silent, which often increases the other's discomfort. When dealing with a cooperative counterpart, the negotiator using the technique may be able to exploit feelings of guilt or embarrassment by directly following with a request for a concession that the other may find difficult to decline. In such a situation, the concession becomes an apology for the behavior.

  If someone uses this technique with you, remind yourself that effective negotiations require that neither side take anything personal. It can be beneficial to point this out to your counterpart as well. However, doing so is risky in cultures where the concept of *face* is very important, such as China, India, Indonesia, Japan, or Singapore. People in these countries rarely use the tactic themselves, since such behavior may cause loss of face for both parties involved and jeopardizes existing relationships. Unless the ties with your counterparts are very strong, refrain from using the tactic in these cultures.

- Another way to execute this technique is for negotiators to make repeated demands they know the other side will reject. It is important to strike a careful balance, demanding concessions that go beyond what the other might accept but not so unreasonable that the other could justifiably get upset over them. Once a few such subsequent requests were rejected, they may remark something like 'Come on, you'll have to give me *something,*' attempting to make the other feel guilty for having rejected every one of the requests. This variant can be effective when bargaining with people from face-oriented cultures, some of whom may even respond to the initial demands with counterproposals of their own.

When confronted with this tactic, respond to the second round of demands with an observation that the parties must have different beliefs of the true value of the items being negotiated. Then, explain why you think the demand is unreasonable, and emphasize how much you are interested in finding a fair solution for both sides. This response will likely throw your counterpart off balance and may even create some embarrassment on his or her side.

- In an approach that is inverse to the previous one, negotiators may make several small concessions in a row. For example, they may successively drop their price in a series of apparently one-sided concessions from $1,000 to $980, then to $970, and then to $950. Next, they may suggest that they already made several price moves and that they will be unable to move down any further. The objective of this variant is to make the other party feel guilty about accepting several concessions without reciprocating, which could make them more likely to accept an unfavorable agreement.

  If someone makes such repeat concessions when negotiating with you, take them as a single move rather than several steps. What matters is how far overall your counterpart has moved, not how many steps it took to do so. Whether or not you consider the total significant should guide your response, but it will be important to point out that you are taking your counterpart's 'several moves' as only one.

- If a significant gap exists between both sides' latest proposals, negotiators may propose to 'split the difference,' suggesting that both agree instead to meet in the middle between their respective positions. On the surface, this may seem fair. However, more often than not, such a suggestion will come from the party that has more to gain, that is, whose position is farther away from the true value of the item or items being negotiated. Rejecting such a proposal can make the other party feel guilty even when they sense the imbalance.

  Should a counterpart use the approach with you, think carefully about both parties' previous moves and concessions. If you believe that you previously moved further toward a reasonable compromise than your counterpart did, meeting in the middle would give the other an unfair advantage, so reject the suggestion. Emphasize that you are very interested in making the deal fair and explain why you do not believe that splitting the difference would do both sides justice. Ask the other party to make a different suggestion, or make a counterproposal yourself.

Techniques to create guilt and embarrassment are most effective in the bargaining and closure phases of negotiations. In addition, they may occasionally help when trying to reach closure. In general, be careful when using them in cultures where the concept of *face* is very important, such as India, Indonesia, Japan, Mexico, or most Latin American countries. When rejecting a request, it will be important in these countries to send strong signals indicating that you value the relationship highly and that you are searching for a solution that both sides can feel good about. For instance, make counteroffers that include a concession (and ask for one in return).

Grimacing

Negotiators may grimace, flinch visibly, or look dejected as an indication that they are not in agreement with an offer or proposal they received. They usually remain silent afterwards, which serves to underline the message. The objective of this technique is to signal rejection in a not-too-aggressive way and to stimulate the other side to improve its offer. While this technique is similar to *Silence*, it includes an emotional component that can make some counterparts feel guilty.

If someone uses this behavior with you, ignore it and refuse to accept it in lieu of a response. Simply remain silent until the other person ultimately says something. If the silence continues for an extended time, use the same strategy as with the *Silence* pressure tactic: calmly ask whether the negotiator plans to respond to your proposal; if necessary, explain that you will leave because there is no apparent interest in it, get up, and start walking towards the door. If there is any interest in continuing the negotiation, your counterpart will stop you, at which point you will have gained the upper hand.

This technique is most effective in the bargaining phase of a negotiation and may be used in many countries. Members of cultures where the concept of *face* is very important, such as the Chinese, Indians, Indonesians, or the Japanese, expect gestures and body language to be very subtle. A dejected look on your face will still send them a clear message, while grimacing may reflect poorly upon you if done too demonstratively.

Appeals to Personal Relationships

Negotiators may appeal to personal relationships when trying to get the other side to agree with a proposal or to make a concession. This may include open hints such as 'You owe me this one for the sake of our friendship' or 'Show me that you value me by agreeing with this request.' They may sometimes use a future orientation by leveraging *Promises* (see also page 105), for instance in statements such as 'Accepting my request will affirm our relationship and give you great advantages in our future business relations.'

This technique attempts to put the other party in a psychological bind by equating rejection of a request with rejection of the overall relationship. This can create a serious dilemma, since the other's desire to obtain the best deal possible will conflict with the intention to build lasting and rewarding business relationships. Finding a constructive way out of this situation can be challenging.

Your best strategy when facing this dilemma is to take a realistic look at the situation. Rationally assess how strong your present relationship with the other party really is, and consider whether you believe that you owe the other side a concession or whether you trust your counterparts to reward you down the road if you agree with the request. As far as future rewards go, set the hurdle high; it is usually best to discard lofty promises and expectations as irrelevant.

Appeals to personal relationships can be effective in the bargaining and closure phases of negotiations. Curiously, this technique is most often employed by people whose culture does *not* value relationships very highly and by people using it only with others with whom they have *not* built strong relationships yet. Negotiators in the Middle East, in Central Europe, and elsewhere may try this approach frequently.

In contrast, the tactic is rare in most countries where relationships are critically important, for instance in China, Indonesia, Malaysia, or Singapore. People in these countries use such appeals only if strong relationships between the parties exist or are likely to emerge. If that is the case, such an appeal represents a promise that your counterparts will very likely live up to at some future point. In strongly relationship-focused cultures, do not appeal to personal relationships yourself unless you are fully committed to the future obligation such a request represents. In addition, be absolutely certain that you and your counterparts both feel good about the state of your relationship. If they reject your request because they feel differently, you lose *face* and are left in a weak negotiating position.

Chapter 13: Defensive Techniques

This chapter discusses effective countermeasures to some of the negotiation techniques described in previous chapters.

Changing the Subject

Negotiators may frequently digress or change subjects during the negotiation exchange in order to distract or confuse their counterparts. The technique's primary objective is to keep the other side from pursuing a systematic strategy and dictating the negotiation agenda. It can also be an effective way to accept concessions without reciprocating or to avoid releasing information.

When dealing with a negotiator using this style, carefully keep track of all commitments made on either side. If your counterpart changes subjects after you just made a concession, ask 'Does changing topics mean that you do not value the concession I just made?' Should the response you get be evasive, clearly state that you choose not to commit to the concession under the circumstances and continue with the new subject.

Changing the subject can be effective in all phases of negotiations. More often than not, the approach may reflect cultural differences rather than an intentional negotiation technique. People in polychronic cultures, for example in France, most of Latin America, the Middle East, and many other countries and regions, may naturally prefer this style and will have no bad intentions even when frequently changing subjects. Attempting to use the technique yourself will rarely be effective in these cultures.

On the other hand, it is not recommended to use the tactic with people from strongly monochronic cultures, such as the United States, Canada, Germany, Switzerland, or the Nordic countries. Priding themselves with being organized and systematic, they are unlikely to use it themselves and may get upset if you do.

Blocking

Negotiators who want to avoid answering sensitive questions often resort to blocking techniques. They may not like to respond if doing so would reveal their negotiation strategy, make it impossible to gain certain concessions, or otherwise give their counterparts a tactical advantage. Several blocking options can be effective. Negotiators may simply ignore questions as if they did not hear them, continuing the discussion. Done innocently enough, their counterparts may not even notice. With questions addressing several aspects, it is possible to focus on those that are easy to cover while ignoring others. Other options include responding to a different question from the one that was asked or giving general answers to specific questions. Politicians often use such tactics to deflect aggressive questions without appearing to be uncooperative.

Another alternative is to respond with a question, for instance by asking 'What would you suggest?' This might throw the other party off balance and put its negotiators on the defensive.

The best countermeasure against negotiators who block is to be very persistent. Asking the same questions over and over makes it hard to continue the approach. At some point, the other party will have to choose whether to give valid responses or to admit that it is unwilling to answer.

Blocking can be useful during the information gathering phase of a negotiation. It may take practicing before you will be able to use the technique effectively. In general, it is applicable in most countries. However, be prepared for people from strongly monochronic cultures, for instance Americans, Canadians, Germans, the Swiss, or anyone from the Nordics, to repeat their questions persistently. The technique is very unlikely to work in Japan, where most businesspeople will keep repeating their questions until they received satisfactory answers.

Blocking can be very effective in several other countries, especially in those where the concept of *face* is very important. Examples include China, India, Indonesia, Malaysia, and Singapore. For fear of causing loss of face, members of these cultures may refrain from repeating their questions. However, do not make your refusal to answer a question too obvious, since this might damage the relationship.

Probing Questions

Negotiators who are unwilling to accept their counterparts' offers may not want to reject them outright. Instead, they could respond by asking probing questions. The objective of this technique is to force the offering party's negotiators to explain the logic behind their proposal, which will ideally lead them to realizing that their offer was inadequate. Executed effectively, the approach is constructive and non-threatening, avoiding the risk of getting stuck because both sides 'dig in their heels.'

Asking probing questions can be an effective countermeasure against *Extreme Openings*. Negotiators using it start by stating their desire to understand the other's rationale, suggesting to jointly go through a detailed analysis of the value of the deal. Someone who just opened with an extreme offer will inevitably fail to find a rational explanation for it, especially if the deal includes several components that need to be explained individually. For instance, when interested in buying a business, the buyer may ask the potential seller who just requested an outrageous amount for it to assign specific values to each of the individual components of the deal, such as the company's buildings, equipment, inventories, and so on. When added up, the sum of these components will be significantly less than the total amount. While probably still exaggerated, these numbers represent a basis for discussing the true value in a more rational fashion.

This technique can be effective in the information gathering and bargaining phases of negotiations. Its value is not limited to situations where the other side used extreme openings. In fact, asking probing questions often helps the bargaining exchange become more rational. Negotiators in cultures who prefer rational problem-solving approaches, such as the United States and Canada, many European countries, or Japan, often resort to this tactic. Be careful when using it in cultures where the concept of *face* is very important, such as India, Indonesia, Japan, Mexico, or most Latin American countries. It could severely damage the negotiation if your questions make the other side look stupid or dishonest.

Directness

Asking very direct and candid questions can be an effective way to find out more about a negotiation party's intentions. For example, when a counterpart just rejected an offer as 'not good enough,' a skilled negotiator may respond by asking 'Ok, so how much are you willing to pay?' or 'What would you consider a fair agreement then?' The approach tends to work best if it comes as a surprise to the other party, since this may lead the other negotiators to openly sharing their intentions and objectives. Using the tactic can be especially valuable immediately after a counterpart has done some initial posturing or expressed a warning or threat. Even if the other party deflects the questioning, directness often helps focus the exchange on a realistic range.

If your counterpart in a negotiation asks you a very direct question that you do not want to answer, simply respond with a neutral statement that leaves enough further maneuvering room, such as 'I believe my previous proposal was fair but am willing to reconsider if you convince me that the value of the deal is higher than I think right now.'

Directness can be useful in the information gathering and bargaining phases of negotiations. It can be particularly effective in countries where people generally dislike bargaining but have a high sense of fairness, for instance in the Nordics. It is also applicable in many other cultures, though. Use it cautiously where the concept of *face* is very important, such as China, India, Indonesia, Japan, Mexico, or most Latin American countries, since directly rejecting the other party's objectives could lead to embarrassing situations. Avoid the tactic in cultures whose members enjoy and expect extended bargaining and haggling, such as in the Middle East, Indonesia, Mexico, or Nigeria, since asking direct questions may insult people who could view this as an outright refusal to bargain.

Promises

One of the most valuable negotiation techniques, making promises can be effective in both offensive and defensive situations. The basic approach is inverse to the **Threats and Warnings** technique described on page 94. Rather than implying a future negative reaction *unless* the other side agrees with a request or proposal, negotiators use the tactic by announcing a positive consequence *if* the other side agrees with their demands. In other words, promises reward affirmative behavior rather than punishing an adversarial one, which often contributes to creating a positive win-win atmosphere for the bargaining exchange. The underlying objective is to convince the other party that agreeing with the request is favorable over any non-settlement outcome.

Promises are normally specific, as in 'If you reduce your asking price by $1,000, I will improve my delivery terms by 2 weeks.' They must be credible and only work if the other party is confident that the promise will be kept. Unspecific promises, such as 'Trust me, you won't regret it if you agree with this,' are best ignored as they do not meet these criteria. It is vital for negotiators using the tactic to keep their promises. Otherwise, the other side may cry foul and could choose to terminate the negotiation.

Making promises can be effective in the bargaining and closure phases of negotiations. The technique can be used in all countries and is especially useful where the concept of *face* is very important, for example in China, India, Indonesia, Japan, Malaysia, and Singapore. However, it may be less effective in cultures where people are not motivated by future benefits, which includes Nigeria and several other African countries, some in the Middle East, and a few Asian countries such as Pakistan or Thailand. The technique may prove ineffective in cultures whose members view compromise as a sign of weakness, for instance Russia and Ukraine.

Dealing with Inflexible Positions

This technique can be useful when a negotiation has reached a standstill because members of one of the negotiating parties have 'dug in their heels,' refusing to compromise or change their position. Challenging them in such a situation is often of little help and may just add aggravation. Smart negotiators facing such counterparts may instead suggest to review the underlying objectives of the party causing the standstill. They will strive to find out what makes that particular position so important. Analyzing the other's needs and intentions is a constructive approach that can lead to the identification of alternative solutions while avoiding *loss of face* for either side.

For additional impact, it can be beneficial to emphasize areas of agreement between the parties rather than focusing only on areas of conflict. This step may foster the overall relationship and make the areas of conflict seem less critical. However, it is usually not sufficient by itself to eliminate the conflict.

The combined approach can be used in all cultures, including those who favor somewhat aggressive negotiation styles, such as Israel, Russia, or Ukraine. It is applicable in the bargaining and closure phases of negotiations.

Chapter 14: Other Negotiation Techniques

Range Offers

Negotiators who intend to signal their collaborative spirit and willingness to compromise may sometimes base an offer on a value range rather than on a specific number. For instance, they may state something like 'I think this would be worth between 9,000 and 10,000 to me, depending on your terms and conditions.' One scenario in which this approach might work well is if a negotiator does not know the true value of an item but is forced to make an early offer. Since they leave some bargaining room and are often perceived as conciliatory, range offers can be effective with competitive counterparts. An additional benefit is that the extremes of the range imply that this is the lowest or highest the offering party will go, promoting the idea that agreement can only be reached within this range.

Using this technique is not without risks, and experienced negotiators usually prefer to determine the exact amount they want to offer. Range offers tend to make the offering party look insecure, which could stimulate the other party to bargain more competitively. If you received a range offer yourself, focus on the end that is favorable for you and treat the situation as if the other side had offered this specific number. Furthermore, assume that the others will go beyond this end point if needed to reach agreement.

Range offers are usually ineffective with competitive or adversarial negotiators, which includes Russians and Ukrainians, but also many Americans, Israelis, and others. The tactic works better in cultures where the concept of *face* is very important, such as China, India, Indonesia, Japan, Malaysia, or Singapore, since settling the deal within the range that was offered is a face-saving and therefore favorable outcome in these countries.

Written Offers

Rather than starting the bargaining exchange with a verbal initial offer, negotiators may instead present one in writing. It is essential to create professional looking documents for this purpose. Because of the perceived seriousness and legitimacy of written documents, the other side may find it psychologically harder to demand changes to such offers. In rare cases, they may even accept them as presented.

Should you receive a written offer yourself, remember that it does not give you any advantage over a verbal one, so treat it as if it had been made orally. After all, the fact that someone typed it up alone does not make the proposal any more deserving.

Making written offers is acceptable in all cultures, though not always useful. The technique may not show much effect, if any, in polychronic cultures such as France, most of Latin America, or in the Middle East. Since people in these countries tend to pay little attention to written documents, you may find during your initial discussion that they have not even read the offer, instead asking you to explain what it says.

On the other hand, written offers can be surprisingly effective in monochronic cultures, especially those whose members generally dislike bargaining, such as Australia, Austria, Germany, the Nordics, or Switzerland. People from these countries often prepare such offers themselves. The approach is also common in other monochronic cultures, for example the United States and Canada.

Written Terms and Conditions

At a late state in the bargaining exchange, when closure seems within reach, negotiators may suddenly produce pre-printed documents or forms introducing additional terms and conditions, such as contract processing fees or shipping costs. Three factors can make this approach effective: for one, just as with other written offers, it leverages the authority of printed documents, which many people find psychologically hard to challenge. In addition, since the new documents usually introduce numerous conditions and requirements, some clauses favoring the initiating party may go undetected. On top of that, the tactic can become a variant of *Limited Authority* (see page 77): negotiators introducing additional terms and conditions often claim that these clauses are imposed on them, usually by some unnamed higher authority, and that they are unable to make any changes.

Car dealers and real estate agents frequently use written terms and conditions. However, the tactic is also common in many professional business situations, such as with outsourcing service providers, energy suppliers, and many others.

If you detect attempts to introduce non-negotiable written terms and conditions into the negotiation process, insist that both parties agree that everything remains negotiable. Should your counterparts insist that they do not have the authority to make changes, simply ask them to pull in someone who does. More often than not, they will find ways to work around such clauses if the alternative is that the deal may be off.

This technique can be effective in the bargaining and closure phases of negotiations. Its greatest potential exists when dealing with strongly monochronic cultures whose members generally dislike bargaining, such as Australia, Austria, Germany, the Nordics, or Switzerland. Many of them use written terms and conditions themselves whenever feasible. The tactic can also be effective in other monochronic cultures such as the United States and Canada. Because people in these cultures are often rushed, they may prefer accepting last-minute additions over further delaying closure of the negotiation.

The approach is usually ineffective in polychronic cultures such as France, most of Latin America, or many Arab countries. People in these countries generally pay less attention and assign less authority to written documents. They may therefore insist on negotiating all terms and conditions individually.

Stalling

Negotiators attempting to 'buy time' sometimes resort to stalling tactics. This includes becoming unresponsive, requesting additional documents or time-consuming 'clarifications,' repeatedly demanding insignificant changes to aspects that had previously been agreed upon, and other actions designed to slow the negotiation process. Unlike with *Time Pressure* (see page 85), the objective is usually not to make the other side more conciliatory. Instead, negotiators using the approach may hope that external circumstances will change in their favor, for instance if other potential partners emerge or if market conditions improve. They might also need the additional time to re-evaluate their negotiation strategy, to obtain additional information about their counterparts, or for some other reason.

Stalling negotiations can be risky in countries where business is generally fast-paced, such as the United States and Canada. Members of these cultures often hate wasting time and may have little patience if they feel that the other party is hiding or holding back something. Worst case, they could lose interest in the deal. While business is usually conducted at a slower pace in other monochronic cultures, for example in Australia, Austria, Germany, the Nordics, or Switzerland, people there also dislike stalling and may react with persistent attempts to accelerate the negotiation process.

Part III: Negotiate Right in Any of 50 Countries

For some of the countries listed in the following, short introductions provide special information, for example if a country's population includes people from different cultures. All numbers are taken from The World Factbook (see *References* at the end of this book).

Argentina

Partly owing to Argentina's location at the southern tip of Latin America, many businesspeople and officials in the country have only limited exposure to other cultures except for neighboring countries. Its culture is quite homogeneous. When negotiating business here, realize that people may expect things to be done 'their way.' However, many living in Buenos Aires, especially among younger generations, may have greater international experience and can be very open-minded.

Relationships and Respect

Argentina's culture is generally group-oriented. Asserting individual preferences may be seen as less important than having a sense of belonging to a group, conforming to its norms, and maintaining harmony among its members. Building lasting and trusting relationships is very important to most people in this country. However, unlike in many other Latin American countries, they are not always a necessary precondition for initial business interactions. Nevertheless, Argentines may want to do business only with those they know, like, and trust, so take the time needed to build and strengthen the relationship.

Business relationships in this country exist between people, not necessarily between companies. Even when you have won your local business partners' friendship and trust, they will not necessarily trust others from your company. That makes it very important to keep company interfaces unchanged. Changing a key contact may require the relationship building process to start over.

Establishing personal relationships with others in Argentina can create powerful networks and may help you a lot to achieve your business objectives. Whom you know may determine whether people want to get to know you. Similarly, whether people think you are worth knowing and trusting often weighs much more strongly than how competent you are or what proposals you may have to make. Personal networks rely mostly on strong friendships that also represent dependable mutual obligations. They may open doors and solve problems that would otherwise be difficult to master. Maintaining honest and cordial relations is crucial.

While Argentines are usually warm and friendly, they are also very proud and may be easily offended by comments that leave room for misunderstandings. 'Saving face' and respecting everyone's honor and personal pride are crucial requirements for doing business in the country, especially in rural areas and small cities. Causing embarrassment to another person or openly criticizing someone in front of others can have a devastating impact on your negotiation. Character and kindness towards others are very essential qualities. You will earn people's respect by showing empathy for others, treating everyone with dignity, and avoiding all aggressive behaviors.

In Argentina's business culture, the respect a person enjoys depends primarily on his or her status, rank, and education. The country's population is fairly young and age may not be respected as highly as in some other Latin American cultures. Showing status is important since people will take you more seriously. Carefully select your hotel and transportation. Use the services of others, such as a porter, to avoid being viewed as a low-ranking intermediary. The extreme differences that exist between the rich and the poor in this society are usually accepted and people believe that those in powerful positions are entitled to the privileges they enjoy. Accordingly, showing respect to those of higher status is very important. Admired personal traits include sincerity, integrity, and charisma.

Communication

The official language of Argentina is Spanish. It is notably different from the Spanish spoken in Spain, and it is unlike any other Spanish spoken in Latin America, owing to significant Italian influences. Many businesspeople speak at least some English, but being able to speak Spanish is a clear advantage. With high-ranking managers, it may otherwise be useful to engage an interpreter. To avoid offending the other side, ask beforehand whether an interpreter should be present at a meeting. When communicating in English, speak in short, simple sentences and avoid using jargon and slang. It will help people with a limited command of English if you speak slowly, summarize your key points often, and pause frequently to allow for interpretation. Even when the main meeting language is English, your counterparts may frequently speak Spanish among themselves, not necessarily to shut you out from the discussion but to reduce their discomfort and ensure a common understanding among them.

People in this country may speak louder than other Latin Americans may. In restaurants used for business, however, conversations should be kept at a quiet level. Interrupting others or speaking in parallel is acceptable. Emotions are usually shown very openly. Argentines generally converse in close proximity, standing only two feet or less apart. Never back away, even if this is much closer than your personal comfort zone allows. Doing so could be read as a sign that you are uncomfortable around them.

Communication in Argentina is generally quite direct. There is a tendency to use very pointed or exaggerated statements, so problems or disagreements may appear more severe than they really are. However, people may be reluctant to disagree openly with someone they like, in which case it can become difficult to know their true opinion. Silence is rare and usually indicates that there is a problem.

Gestures and body language can be very expressive, especially if they help underline what is being said. It is often not a good idea to imitate them, though. There may be frequent physical contact with others of the same gender. A pat on the shoulder is a sign of friendship. When pointing at people or objects, use your open hand rather than a finger. The American *OK* sign, with thumb and index finger forming a circle, can be read as an obscene gesture in Argentina. Non-verbal communication can be extensive, so watch carefully for small clues. Eye contact should be very frequent, almost to the point of staring. This conveys sincerity and helps build trust. Yawning in public is considered very rude.

Initial Contacts and Meetings

Choosing a local intermediary who can leverage existing relationships to make the initial contact is highly recommended. This person will help bridge the gap between cultures, allowing you to conduct business with greater effectiveness. Your embassy, a trade organization, a chamber of commerce, or a local legal or accounting firm may be able to provide a list of potential intermediaries. Without such a contact, it may be difficult to gain access to the right people.

Negotiations in the country can be conducted by individuals or teams of negotiators. It is vital that teams be well aligned, with roles clearly assigned to each member. Changing a team member may require the relationship building process to start over and should therefore be avoided.

Given the strong emphasis on hierarchy in the country's business culture, a senior executive should attend the initial meeting for your company and your negotiating team should include senior leaders who know your company well. There will not be an expectation that the executive attends future meetings. Similarly, the top executive on the Argentine side, who may also be the ultimate decision maker, may attend only initially. The most senior Argentine executive to attend throughout the negotiation will likely be at a similar level in the hierarchy as your own negotiation leader.

If possible, schedule meetings at least one to two weeks in advance. Since Argentines want to know whom they will be meeting, provide details on titles, positions, and responsibilities of attendees ahead of time. Agreeing on an agenda upfront can also be useful. Reconfirm your meeting, and be prepared for your counterparts to cancel or postpone meetings with little advance notice.

While meetings may start as much as 30 minutes late, people generally expect foreign visitors to be very punctual. Avoid being more than 5 to 10 minutes late, and call ahead if you will be. Displaying anger if you have to wait reflects very poorly on you. The most senior people usually arrive last. Otherwise, authority may sometimes be difficult to pick out, so watch for small hints of deference to identify the decision makers.

Names are usually given in the order of first name, then family name or names. Most Argentines have two family names, the first one from their father, and the second one from their mother. Use *Mr./Mrs./Miss* or *Señor/Señora/Señorita*, plus the family name (the first one if two family names are given). If a person has an academic title, such as *Doctor* or *Professor*, or a professional title such as *Ingeniero* or *Arquitecto*, use it instead, followed by the family name. Being respectful of such titles is very important. Do not react surprised if people address you as *Doctor*, as this is often a sign of respect or simply an indication that they are confused about your real title. Only close friends call each other by their first names. Introduce and greet older people first.

Third-party introductions are generally preferred. Introductions are accompanied by handshakes, often combined with a nod of the head. Men should wait for women to initiate handshakes.

The exchange of business cards is an essential step when meeting someone for the first time, so bring more than you need. It is strongly recommended to use cards with one side in English and the other in Spanish. Show doctorate degrees on your card and make sure that it clearly states your professional title, especially if you have the seniority to make decisions. When presenting your card, ensure that the Spanish side is facing the recipient. Smile and keep eye contact while accepting someone else's card, then carefully examine it. Next, place the card on the table in front of you.

Meetings start with small talk, which may be extensive. This may include personal questions about your background and family, allowing participants to become acquainted. It is important to be patient and let the other side set the pace. People appreciate a sense of humor, but keep it light and friendly, and be careful not to overdo it. Business is a serious matter in Argentina. Initial meetings may appear very formal, but the atmosphere usually is a bit more relaxed in subsequent meetings.

The primary purpose of the first meeting is to become acquainted and build relationships. Business may be discussed, but do not try to hurry along with your agenda. It is unrealistic to expect initial meetings to lead to straight decisions.

Presentation materials should be attractive, with good and clear visuals. Having your handout materials translated to Spanish is not a must, but it will be appreciated and helps in getting your messages across.

Negotiation

Attitudes and Styles - To Argentines, negotiating is usually a joint problem-solving process. While the buyer is in a superior position, both sides in a business deal own the responsibility to reach agreement. They expect long-term commitments from their business partners and will focus mostly on long-term benefits. Although the primary negotiation style is competitive, Argentines nevertheless value long-term relationships. While proposals should demonstrate the benefits to both negotiating parties, neither of them should take attempts to win competitive advantages negatively. It is crucial to remain non-confrontational and avoid direct conflict throughout the bargaining exchange. Ultimately, the culture promotes a win-win approach. You will earn your counterparts' respect by maintaining a positive, persistent attitude.

Should a dispute arise at any stage of a negotiation, you might be able to reach resolution by leveraging personal relationships and emphasizing long-term benefits. Patience and creativity will pay strong dividends. If you cannot resolve the situation, it is best to walk away without burning bridges. Since word often gets around in Argentina, you may otherwise affect your ability to do business with others in the country.

Sharing of Information – Even when personal relationships are strong, your Argentine counterparts may be reluctant to share information openly. Many believe that privileged information creates bargaining advantages. However, they are often very good at obtaining intelligence and information about their counterparts that puts them in an advantageous position. It is crucial to come well prepared with substantial background information about your potential business partner.

Pace of Negotiation – Expect negotiations to be slow and protracted. Argentines do not hurry and dislike people who do. They see impatience as a sign of weakness and may even think it rude. Be prepared to make several trips if necessary to achieve your objectives. Relationship building, information gathering, bargaining, and decision making may take considerable time. Attempts to rush the process are unlikely to produce better results and may be viewed as offensive. Throughout the negotiation, be patient, control your emotions, and accept the inevitable delays.

Most Argentines prefer a polychronic work style. They are used to pursuing multiple actions and goals in parallel. When negotiating, they often take a holistic approach and may seem to jump from one topic to another rather than addressing them in sequential order. Negotiators from strongly monochronic cultures, such as Germany, the United Kingdom, or the United States, may find this style confusing, irritating, and even annoying. In any case, do not show irritation or anger when encountering this behavior. Instead, keep track of the bargaining progress at all times, often emphasizing areas where agreement already exists.

If your counterparts appear to be stalling the negotiation, assess carefully whether their slowing down the process indicates that they are evaluating alternatives or that they are not interested in doing business with you. More likely, this behavior either represents an attempt to create time pressure in order to obtain concessions, which happens frequently, or it simply reflects the slow decision process in the country. Again, patience and persistence are vitally important.

Bargaining – While Argentines are not overly fond of bargaining and dislike haggling, they can be tough and often very competitive negotiators. The bargaining exchange can be extensive. Concessions never come easily, and requesting a compromise may become an issue of pride if presented in the wrong way. Rather than pushing for concessions, it may be better to re-address disagreements in follow-up meetings, which gives your counterparts the opportunity to reconsider their position without overtly losing face. Prices rarely move by more than 20 to 30 percent between initial offer and final agreement. Leave yourself sufficient room for concessions at different stages. After making one, always ask the other side to reciprocate. Throughout the process, remain cool and respectful, avoid confrontation, and frequently reaffirm the relationship.

During the bargaining exchange, keep in mind that intangible benefits such as increases in power and status may sometimes be more desirable to your counterparts than financial gains may. Offers to provide continuing service to an Argentine client, in spite of long distances, can also be valuable bargaining concessions. Businesspeople in the country often find it difficult to overcome the isolation imposed on them by geography. Dependency requires trust.

Deceptive techniques are frequent and can be effective. This includes tactics such as telling lies and sending fake non-verbal messages, pretending to be disinterested in the whole deal or in single concessions, misrepresenting an item's value, or making false demands and concessions. Your Argentine counterparts may make other attempts to mislead you in order to obtain bargaining advantages. Even when you can see right through a lie, it would be a grave personal insult to state or even hint that your counterpart is not telling the truth. It is advisable to verify information received from the local side through other channels. 'Good cop, bad cop' is a tactic that Argentines rarely use, though it could be effective on either side of the negotiation table. However, it could be devastating if the other side recognized this as a tactic, and your team will need to exclude any 'bad cop' member from future negotiation rounds. Businesspeople may claim limited authority, stating that they have to ask for their manager's approval. This could be a tactic or the truth.

Negotiators in the country use pressure techniques very carefully since there is always a risk of hurting someone's pride. Final offers and nibbling are rare and should be used with great caution. Never imply that your counterparts' only choices are 'take it or leave it' – they will very likely choose the latter. Be also careful when trying to open with your best offer. Argentines may consider this inappropriate or even insulting. Silence can be a very effective way to signal rejection of a proposal or to obtain further concessions. Do not use pressure tactics such as applying time pressure or making expiring offers as these may be taken as signs that you are not willing to build a long-term relationship. Your counterparts may even choose to terminate the negotiation.

Argentine negotiators avoid openly aggressive or adversarial techniques. While they may make indirect threats and warnings or subtly display anger, they will be careful not to appear aggressive when doing so. Extreme openings may be viewed as unfriendly and are best avoided. Never walk out or threaten to do so in an aggressive fashion as your counterparts will likely take this as a personal insult and may end all talks. However, threatening a 'friendly walkout' while strongly emphasizing the relationship may be very effective.

Emotional negotiation techniques, such as attitudinal bargaining or attempting to make you feel guilty, are very frequent and can be effective. Be cautious not to hurt someone's personal pride when employing any of these tactics, though. Pleas to personal relationships and other emotional appeals, such as emphasizing how your proposal will add to your counterparts' personal satisfaction or heighten their honor, can be very powerful. Your counterparts may use temperamental outbursts as a way to throw you off-balance. Keep your cool and do not respond in kind since this could become counterproductive.

Argentines may frequently employ defensive tactics such as blocking or changing the subject, asking probing or very direct questions, making promises, or keeping an inflexible position.

Corruption and bribery are quite common in Argentina's public and private sectors. However, people may draw the line differently, viewing minor payments as rewards for getting a job done rather than as bribes. Also, keep in mind that there is a fine line between giving gifts and bribing. What you may consider a bribe, an Argentine may view as only a nice gift. It may help if you introduce and explain your company's policies early on, but be careful not to moralize or appear to imply that local customs are unethical.

Decision Making – Most companies are hierarchical, and people expect to work within clearly established lines of authority. Decision makers are usually senior executives who will consider the best interest of the group or organization. They rarely delegate their authority, so it is important to deal with people at the top of the hierarchy. Gaining access to top managers can be difficult, though. You may have to deal with subordinates who could strongly influence the final decision, which may be made behind closed doors. Maintaining good relationships with these intermediaries is crucial to your success. Although the pace of business is accelerating, decision making can be a slow process that requires much patience. Attempts to rush or put pressure on the process are not likely to succeed.

When making decisions, businesspeople may not rely much on rules or laws. They usually consider the specific situation rather than applying universal principles. Personal feelings and experiences weigh more strongly than empirical evidence and other objective facts do, but people will consider all aspects. Argentines are often uneasy with change and reluctant to take risks. If you expect them to support a risky decision, you may need to find ways for them to become comfortable with it first, for instance by explaining contingency plans, outlining areas of additional support, or by offering guarantees and warranties.

Agreements and Contracts

Capturing and exchanging written understandings after meetings and at key negotiation stages is useful since oral statements and even handshakes are not always dependable. Do not rely on interim agreements to be final, even if they come in the form of written protocols. Any part of an agreement may still change significantly before both parties sign the final contract.

Written contracts tend to be lengthy and often spell out detailed terms and conditions for the core agreements as well as for many eventualities. Nevertheless, writing up and signing the contract is a formality. Argentines believe that the primary strength of an agreement lies in the partners' commitment rather than in its written documentation.

It is strongly advisable to consult a local legal expert before signing a contract. However, do not bring in your attorney until the negotiations have concluded. Argentines may read it as a sign of mistrust if you do.

Contracts are usually dependable, and the agreed terms are viewed as binding. Although partners are expected to remain somewhat flexible, requests to change contract details after signature may meet with strong resistance.

Women in Business

While *machismo* attitudes remain strong in this country, it has made a lot of progress towards gender equality over the last two decades. Women may be holding positions of similar income and authority as men. As a visiting businesswoman, emphasize your company's importance and your role in it. A personal introduction or at least a letter of support from a senior executive within your company may also help.

Female business travelers should graciously accept any chivalric gestures they receive, while exercising caution and acting professionally in business and social situations. Displaying confidence and some degree of assertiveness can be effective, but it is very important not to appear overly bold and aggressive.

Other Important Things to Know

Impeccable appearance is very important in Argentina. Dress conservatively and make sure shoes and suit are in excellent condition. First impressions can have a significant impact on how people view you.

Be prepared for long work hours. Meetings and conferences between companies may go well into the night before the social part begins.

While business dinners are common, lunches are not. Business is rarely discussed over meals. Wait to see whether your counterparts bring it up. If you can, avoid pouring wine, since there are several rituals and taboos around it that Argentines take very seriously.

Social events do not require strict punctuality. While it is best to arrive at dinners close to the agreed time, being late to a party by 30 minutes or more is perfectly acceptable.

Topics best avoided are the continuing tensions and conflicts between Argentina and Chile. Avoid making comparisons or talking about the similarities between the two countries. Similarly, do not talk about the conflict over the Malvinas (Falkland Islands) with Great Britain. In addition, do not refer to citizens of the United States as Americans. Most Latin Americans are sensitive to this point as they feel that the term includes them. They prefer to say *norteamericanos* or *North Americans*.

Australia

In spite of its geographic location, businesspeople and officials in Australia are usually experienced in interacting and doing business with visitors from other cultures. Though their business focus is mostly on Asia, Australians share more of their values and practices with Americans, Canadians, or the British than they do with any Asian group. The country's culture is quite homogeneous.

Relationships and Respect

While trust matters, business relationships are often only moderately important in this country. Their existence may not be a necessary precondition for initial interactions. Your counterparts' expectation may be to get to know you better as you do business together. *Mateship* is an important concept in Australia. Being called *mate* is a term of endearment among friends and can extend to business relationships as well. However, business can also be conducted on a continuous basis between parties who have never established such a personal relationship. In any case, it is helpful to let people see your personal side, as Australians often mistrust people who are 'all business.'

Business relationships in this country exist between companies as well as between individuals. If your company replaces you with someone else over the course of a negotiation, it will usually not be difficult for your replacement to take things over from where you left them. Likewise, if you introduce someone else from your company into an existing business relationship, that person may quickly be accepted as a valid business partner. This does not mean that Australians do not care about who they are dealing with. Personal integrity and dependability are important if you want to win their trust.

Australia is a very egalitarian society. While personal achievements enjoy respect, status and rank usually play only a small role. Australians tend to be distrustful of authority and may get very cynical with people who seem elitist or snobbish. There is usually much greater respect for the 'average person' than for those with great wealth or power. Refrain from praising or rewarding anyone in public. Unlike in many other cultures, it may raise suspicion about your motives. Admired personal traits include modesty, casualness, authenticity, and a sense of friendly humor.

Communication

Australian English is usually easy to understand for native English speakers, though it may represent a bit more of a challenge for others, especially since Australians tend to speak quickly and may use many colloquialisms. Brevity is often considered a virtue, so avoid using complicated or flowery language.

In discussions, Australians may use different styles and there are few rules. When someone is teasing you, this may be a sign that the relationship is going well, so try not to be offended. If you feel compelled to tease back, do so in an affable manner. Some people may show both positive and negative emotions openly, while others may believe that they have no place in business. Though conversations are usually animated, they may include moments of silence, which may not mean much. Australians generally converse standing around two to three feet apart.

Communication may be extremely direct. Australians do not find it difficult to say 'no.' Without any bad intentions, they may be frank to the point of bluntness, which sometimes feels rude to people from other cultures. At the same time, Australians respect people who have strong opinions, no matter whether they agree with them or not. However, be careful not to appear condescending when expressing such opinions. Australians rarely communicate 'between the lines,' so it is usually best to take what they say quite literally. Try to be equally clear in your own communication. Lastly, keep in mind that in spite of their preference for directness, most Australians are also trying to be polite and friendly. For that reason, a clear expectation may sometimes come disguised as a nice request.

Gestures and body language can be lively, but not overly so. Australians may make some physical contact, such as a backslap as a sign of friendship, but there is usually not a lot of it. The thumbs-up sign can be taken as a rude gesture in Australia if combined with an upward movement of the arm. Eye contact should be somewhat infrequent. While looking the other in the eye may convey sincerity, do not stare at people as this will likely make them uncomfortable.

Initial Contacts and Meetings

Having a local contact can be an advantage but is usually not a necessary precondition to doing business. Negotiations in the country can be conducted by individuals or teams of negotiators. Owing to the high degree of individualism that characterizes the culture, Australian teams are not always well aligned, which sometimes makes it easy to play one member against the other.

If possible, schedule meetings at least one week in advance. Though status is generally not important, bringing a top executive to the initial meeting underlines the importance you are assigning to the negotiation. Australians generally expect foreign visitors to be punctual. Being late by more than 10 to 15 minutes without having a valid and plausible excuse can be an offense. Call ahead if you are going to be more than 5 minutes late.

Names are usually given in the order of first name, family name. At least initially, use *Mr./Ms.* plus the family name. Titles are rarely used. Before calling Australians by their first name, wait until they offer it. This may happen quickly. Introductions are accompanied by handshakes. The standard greetings are 'pleased to meet you' or 'how do you do?' The latter is rhetorical and it is best to respond with 'pleased to meet you, too' or 'well, thank you, how are you?' Don't use 'G'day,' even if the locals do. They will likely think it superficial.

The exchange of business cards is not an essential step, but it is best to bring a sufficient supply. Offer your card to everyone present. You may not always get one in return. When presenting your card, smile and keep eye contact, then take a few moments to look at the card you received.

Meetings usually start with some small talk intended to establish personal rapport. People appreciate a sense of humor, but be careful not to overdo it. On the other hand, Australian humor can be ironic and sarcastic. They may use it to register disagreement or to ridicule an adversary. It is crucial not to take this style personally, even if some of it may feel like you are being attacked. One's private life is not a subject for discussion around meetings. The overall meeting atmosphere is usually very informal, though. While one purpose of the initial meeting is to get to know each other, its primary focus will be on business topics.

Presentation materials should be attractive, with good and clear visuals. Keep your presentation simple and straightforward. When introducing your product or service, it may work to your advantage if you openly talk about strong and weak points. A presentation full of excitement and hype will make your Australian audience suspicious and may become an object of ridicule. Digressing or giving excessive details will not be well-received by an Australian audience.

Negotiation

Attitudes and Styles – In Australia, negotiating often means engaging in a friendly debate aimed at reaching a mutually agreeable solution. Buyer and seller in a business deal are equal partners who both own the responsibility to reach agreement. They may focus equally on near-term and long-term benefits. The primary negotiation style is cooperative and people may be open to compromising if viewed helpful in order to move the negotiation forward. Since Australians believe in the concept of win-win, they expect you to reciprocate their respect and trust. While the negotiation exchange may include conflicts, both sides should keep a positive attitude and show willingness to work with the other in an effort to reach agreement.

Should a dispute arise at any stage of a negotiation, you might be able to reach resolution by taking the other side's concerns seriously and showing willingness to compromise if needed.

Sharing of Information – Australian negotiators believe in information sharing as a way to build trust. This does not mean that they will readily reveal everything you might want to know during your negotiation. However, negotiations may become difficult if one side appears to be hiding information from the other.

Pace of Negotiation – Negotiations can vary in speed, with larger organizations tending to take longer. Information gathering and bargaining usually move smoothly. Decision making can be rather slow, but it is usually faster than in most Asian countries. Be careful not to appear pushy during the process since this will often work against you.

Bargaining – Although Australians may employ some bargaining and haggling tactics, they are not overly fond of either. Prices rarely move by more than 20 to 30 percent between initial offer and final agreement. Substantial concessions may raise Australians' suspicion of being 'ripped off.' The profitability of a business deal may be valued higher than gains in market share or access to new markets may. Company policy is usually strictly followed, particularly in larger organizations, so be careful not to demand concessions that go against it.

Australians often prefer a straightforward negotiation style. They use deceptive techniques only infrequently, such as telling lies, sending fake non-verbal messages, pretending to be disinterested in the whole deal or in single concessions, or misrepresenting an item's value. 'Good cop, bad cop' is not advisable as the tactic may lead the Australian side to question your trustworthiness. Businesspeople may claim limited authority, stating that they have to ask for their manager's approval. More often than not, this will be the truth. Be cautious when using the techniques of making false demands or false concessions. Overt attempts to bluff your counterparts could backfire.

Australians dislike being pressured, so most pressure techniques are not advisable. Opening with your best offer may hurt their pride. Do not make a final offer too early in the bargaining process and avoid making one more than once. Silence may be perceived as cold and unfriendly, or as a sign that you are disinterested. Do not attempt to apply time pressure. Even though a few Australians may try doing this themselves, there is a risk that your counterpart may view it as inappropriate.

Australian negotiators avoid most aggressive or adversarial techniques. While they may make threats and warnings, or show anger, they will be careful not to appear aggressive when doing so. Using extreme openings may be effective, but some may view them as unfriendly, so use the technique with caution. Never walk out or threaten to do so in an aggressive fashion as your counterparts will likely take this as a personal insult and may end all talks.

Emotional negotiation techniques, such as attitudinal bargaining, attempting to make you feel guilty, grimacing, or appealing to personal relationships, may occasionally be employed. It is best to remain calm. Australian negotiators may frequently employ defensive tactics such as blocking or changing the subject, asking probing or very direct questions, or making promises.

Corruption and bribery are very rare in Australia. It is strongly advisable to stay away from giving gifts of significant value or making offers that could be read as bribery.

Decision Making – The decision maker is usually an individual who will consult with others and carefully consider their inputs. Top executives are often involved in the process, even if they do not attend meetings. This slows down the process and makes it important to win the support of top managers as well as influencers in subordinate roles.

When making decisions, businesspeople may apply universal principles rather than considering the specific situation. Empirical evidence and other objective facts weigh more strongly than personal feelings and experiences do, but they usually consider all aspects. Australians may be bold risk takers.

Agreements and Contracts

Capturing and exchanging meeting summaries can be an effective way to verify understanding and commitments. Although interim agreements are usually kept, do not consider them final. Only a final contract signed by both parties constitutes a binding agreement.

Written contracts tend to be lengthy. They often spell out detailed terms and conditions for the core agreements as well as for many eventualities. Signing the contract is important not only from a legal perspective, but also as a strong confirmation of your Australian partners' commitment. It is recommended to consult a local legal expert before signing a contract.

Contracts are usually dependable, and the agreed terms are viewed as binding. Requests to change contract details after signature may be considered as bad faith and will meet with strong resistance. It is important to maintain on-time deliveries.

Women in Business

Australian women are still struggling to attain positions of similar income and authority as men. However, many have attained influential business roles. Be sure to treat women with the same respect as men. A visiting businesswoman should have few problems in the country.

Other Important Things to Know

While business dinners are common, there may be little or no discussion of actual business aspects. Australians often prefer to keep business and pleasure separate.

Social events do not require strict punctuality. While it is best to arrive at dinners close to the agreed time, being late to a party by 15 minutes is acceptable.

Gift giving in business settings is rare. It is best not to bring a gift to an initial meeting in order to avoid raising suspicions about your motives.

Austria

Though the country's culture is quite homogeneous, Austrian businesspeople, especially those among younger generations, are usually experienced in interacting and doing business with visitors from other cultures. Austria's current political and economic role may seem modest on a world scale, but keep in mind that back in its days of being part of the Austro-Hungarian Empire it wielded huge power and influence. Austrians tend to be very proud of their country.

Relationships and Respect

Business relationships are often only moderately important in this country and may not be a necessary precondition for initial business interactions. Your counterparts' expectation may be to get to know you better as you do business together. Austrians may appear somewhat reserved even after you have had lengthy business interactions with them. Once the necessary trust has been established, though, there will be a sense of loyalty to you as a respected business partner, which can go a long way should a difficult situation arise. Most Austrian businesspeople expect their partners to make a long-term commitment to the engagement.

Business relationships in this country exist between companies as well as between individuals. If your company replaces you with someone else over the course of a negotiation, it may be easy for your replacement to take things over from where you left them. Likewise, if you introduce someone else from your company into an existing business relationship, that person may quickly be accepted as a valid business partner. This does not mean that Austrians do not care about who they are dealing with. Personal integrity and dependability are important if you want to win their trust.

In Austria's business culture, the respect a person enjoys depends primarily on his or her status, rank, and education. Admired personal traits include dependability, analytical thinking, and an ability to socialize.

Communication

Austria's official language is German. However, pronunciation and vocabulary are significantly different from German and also vary across the country's nine provinces. This tends to complicate the communication for those who learned German as a foreign language. Most businesspeople speak at least some English. With older high-ranking managers, it may be useful to engage an interpreter. Ask beforehand whether an interpreter should be present at a meeting. When communicating in English, speak in short, simple sentences and avoid using jargon and slang. It will help people with a limited command of English if you speak slowly, summarize your key points often, and pause frequently to allow for interpretation.

Businesspeople in this country usually speak in a controlled fashion, only occasionally raising their voices to make a point. At restaurants, especially those used for business lunches and dinners, keep conversations at a quiet level. Being loud may be regarded as bad manners. Emotions are not shown openly. People generally converse standing around three feet apart.

Communication is usually quite direct. Although Austrians may prefer a diplomatic style and could sometimes make vague statements, they are usually willing to share their opinions, concerns, and feelings with others. They do not find it difficult to say 'no' if they dislike a request or proposal. In situations where there is a strong conflict of opinions, people may even appear blunt and confrontational. Do not read too much into this.

Austrians use body language sparingly. They may make some physical contact, but there is usually not a lot of it. The American *OK* sign, with thumb and index finger forming a circle, can be read as an obscene gesture in Austria. The thumbs-up gesture is positive as it signals approval. Eye contact should be frequent, as this conveys sincerity and helps build trust. However, do not stare at people.

Initial Contacts and Meetings

Having a local contact can be an advantage but is usually not a necessary precondition to doing business in Austria. Letters of introduction by someone your local business counterpart knows and respects can be very powerful.

Negotiations in Austria can be conducted by individuals or teams of negotiators. A senior executive should attend the initial meeting for your company. There will not be an expectation that the executive attend future meetings.

If possible, schedule meetings at least three to four weeks in advance, and do not cancel one on short notice since that can be viewed as very rude. Since Austrians want to know whom they will be meeting, provide details on titles, positions, and responsibilities of attendees ahead of time. Agreeing on an agenda upfront can also be useful. That agenda is usually strictly followed. At any meeting, whether business or social, it is strongly advisable to be very punctual. The German term for being late, 'zu spät,' translates into 'too late' in English. Being more than 10 to 15 minutes late without having a valid and plausible excuse can be an offense.

Names are usually given in the order of first name, family name. Some Austrians may state their names in the opposite order, which can be confusing. Use *Mr./Ms.* or *Herr/Frau* plus the family name. If a person has a professional or academic title, it is very important to use it instead, followed by the family name. Only close friends call each other by their first names. Introductions are accompanied by firm handshakes.

Men should wait for women to initiate handshakes.

The exchange of business cards is an essential step when meeting someone for the first time, so bring more than you need. Most businesspeople in Austria read English, so there is no need to have your card translated. Show doctorate degrees on your card and make sure that it clearly states your professional title, especially if you have the seniority to make decisions. When presenting your card, smile and keep eye contact, then take a few moments to look at the card you received.

Meetings usually start with some small talk intended to establish personal rapport. People appreciate a sense of humor, but keep it light and friendly, and be careful not to overdo it. One's private life is usually not a subject for discussion around meetings. Business tends to be a serious matter in Austria. Most meetings are quite formal. The primary purpose of the first meeting is to become acquainted. However, most of it will focus on business topics. It is vital to come well prepared as Austrians hate wasting time. There may be no room to discuss anything that is not on the agenda.

Presentation materials should be attractive, with good and clear visuals. Keep your presentation succinct and methodically thought out. Since they value directness, be straightforward about both positive and negative aspects. Austrians are suspicious of hype and exaggerations. Having your English-language handout materials translated to German is not required, though it will be appreciated.

Negotiation

Attitudes and Styles – To Austrians, negotiating is usually a joint problem-solving process. While the buyer is in a superior position, both sides in a business deal own the responsibility to reach agreement. They may focus equally on near-term and long-term benefits. The primary negotiation style is cooperative, but people may be unwilling to agree with compromises unless it is their only option to keep the negotiation from getting stuck. Since Austrians believe in the concept of win-win, they expect you to reciprocate their respect and trust. It is strongly advisable to avoid any open confrontation and to remain calm, friendly, patient, and persistent.

Should a dispute arise at any stage of a negotiation, you might be able to reach resolution by focusing on logical arguments and facts while remaining open and constructive.

Sharing of Information – Austrian negotiators may spend considerable time gathering information and discussing details before the bargaining stage of a negotiation can begin. They usually share at least some information and rarely take it negatively if you ask about sensitive details, even if they may not want to answer.

Pace of Negotiation – Expect negotiations to be rather slow. Like their German neighbors, Austrians often follow a methodical and carefully planned approach in preparing for the negotiation and gathering information. Aspects of your proposals may be scrutinized repeatedly. Remain patient, control your emotions, and accept the inevitable delays. You may be able to speed up the process by sharing vital information upfront rather than 'keeping your cards close to your chest.'

Austrians generally prefer a monochronic work style. They are used to pursuing actions and goals systematically, and they dislike interruptions or digressions. When negotiating, they often work their way down a list of objectives in sequential order, bargaining for each item separately, and may be unwilling to revisit aspects that have already been agreed upon. This style may be difficult to tolerate for negotiators from highly polychronic cultures, such as most Asians, Arabs, some Southern Europeans, or most Latin Americans, who may view it as closed-minded and overly restrictive. In any case, do not show irritation or anger when encountering this behavior. Instead, be willing to bargain over some items individually. Otherwise, clearly indicate that your agreement is conditional and contingent on other items.

Bargaining – Austrians are not fond of bargaining and strongly dislike haggling. In addition, most of them do not appreciate aggressive sales techniques and view negotiations as a 'necessary evil' rather than a process to enjoy. Although the bargaining stage of a negotiation can be extensive, prices rarely move by more than 15 to 25 percent between initial offers and final agreement.

Austrians often prefer a straightforward negotiation style. They use deceptive techniques only infrequently, such as telling lies, sending fake non-verbal messages, pretending to be disinterested in the whole deal or in single concessions, misrepresenting an item's value, or making false demands and concessions. Carefully orchestrated, 'good cop, bad cop' may be an effective tactic to use in your own negotiation approach. Austrians may claim limited authority, stating that they have to ask for their manager's approval. More often than not, this will be the truth.

Negotiators in the country may use pressure techniques that include opening with their best offer or showing intransigence. When using similar tactics yourself, clearly explain your offer and avoid being aggressive. Austrians may make final offers quite early in the bargaining process; while this is not common practice, they could actually be serious. Periods of silence in conversations are normal and may not represent an attempt to use it as a negotiation technique. Be careful when using pressure tactics such as applying time pressure, making expiring offers, or nibbling. Your counterparts may consider these inappropriate unless they are strongly interested in your offer and clearly understand the rationale behind the approach. Otherwise, while the negotiation is not necessarily over, it may become less constructive.

Austrian negotiators avoid most aggressive or adversarial techniques since they dislike open confrontation. The risk of using such tactics yourself may not be worth the potential gain. While they may use threats and warnings, Austrians rarely openly display anger or walk out of the room. Extreme openings may be viewed as inappropriate and unfriendly and the tactic rarely works to your advantage. It is best to open with an offer that is already in the ballpark of what you really expect.

Emotional negotiation techniques, such as attitudinal bargaining, attempting to make you feel guilty, or grimacing, may occasionally be employed. It is best to remain calm. Appeals to personal relationships are rare. At times, Austrians may employ defensive tactics such as changing the subject, asking probing or very direct questions, making promises, or keeping an inflexible position.

Introducing written terms and conditions may be effective as this approach helps shorten the bargaining process, which your Austrian counterparts could find desirable.

Corruption and bribery are very rare in Austria. It is strongly advisable to stay away from giving gifts of significant value or making offers that could be read as bribery.

Decision Making – Companies are often hierarchical, even though they may initially not seem that way, and people expect to work within clearly established lines of authority. Decision makers are usually senior executives who will consider the best interest of the group or organization. They may sometimes delegate their authority to lower levels in the hierarchy. It is important to find or create opportunities to directly influence the decision maker rather than only meeting with subordinates. Because decision making is a methodical process that is conducted with great diligence and precision, it takes much time and requires patience.

When making decisions, businesspeople may apply universal principles rather than considering the specific situation. Personal feelings and experiences weigh less strongly than empirical evidence and other objective facts do, but they usually consider all aspects. Austrians are often uneasy with change and reluctant to take risks. If you expect them to support a risky decision, you may need to find ways for them to become comfortable with it first, for instance by explaining contingency plans, outlining areas of additional support, or by offering guarantees and warranties.

Agreements and Contracts

Capturing and exchanging meeting summaries can be an effective way to verify understanding and commitments. Actions that have been agreed upon are usually implemented immediately, even if a final contract is still pending. Although that contract is very important, interim agreements are usually kept.

Written contracts are serious matters in Austria and tend to be lengthy. They often spell out very detailed terms and conditions for the core agreements as well as for many eventualities. Legal aspects may be reviewed repeatedly. Signing the contract is important not only from a legal perspective, but also as a strong confirmation of your Austrian partners' commitment.

It is advisable to consult a local legal expert before signing a contract.

Contracts are usually dependable, and the agreed terms are viewed as binding. Requests to change contract details after signature may be considered as bad faith and will meet with strong resistance.

Women in Business

While Austrian society is making progress towards gender equality, few women have managed to attain positions of similar income and authority as men. As a visiting businesswoman, emphasize your company's importance and your role in it.

Female business travelers should graciously accept the old-fashioned courtesies that they will invariably encounter. Displaying confidence and assertiveness can be effective, but it is important not to appear overly bold and aggressive.

Other Important Things to Know

Conservative attire is important when doing business here. Male business visitors should wear suits with neckties on most occasions. First impressions can have a significant impact on how people view you.

Gift giving in business settings is rare. It is best not to bring a gift to an initial meeting in order to avoid raising suspicions about your motives.

Belgium

Most Belgian businesspeople, especially those among younger generations, are very experienced in interacting and doing business with visitors from other cultures. They are usually open-minded rather than forcing their ways upon you.

Belgium is a pluralistic country that is composed of two parts: Flanders in the Northeast, whose population is called Flemings and speaks Flemish, which is closely related to Dutch, and Wallonia in the Southwest, whose francophone population speaks a heavily-accented dialect of French. Flemings represent 58 percent of the population, Walloons, 31 percent. Most Belgians are very sensitive to their cultural and language differences. It is essential to be aware of and respect these differences. Never confuse the groups or imply that they are similar.

Relationships and Respect

Building lasting and trusting relationships is important for the success of your business interactions in Belgium. People may initially appear quite reserved. Generally, it is best to give your counterparts time to become comfortable with you. Mutual trust matters and you will likely have to prove yourself first. Once trust has been established, there will be a sense of loyalty to you as a respected business partner, which can go a long way should a difficult situation arise.

Business relationships in this country exist between companies as well as between individuals. If your company replaces you with someone else over the course of a negotiation, it may be easy for your replacement to take things over from where you left them. Likewise, if you introduce someone else from your company into an existing business relationship, that person may quickly be accepted as a valid business partner. However, personal integrity and dependability are important if you want to win their trust. Most Belgian businesspeople expect their partners to make a long-term commitment to the engagement.

In the country's business culture, the respect a person enjoys depends primarily on his or her achievements and education in Flanders, while status and family background may also play a strong role in Wallonia and in Brussels. Admired personal traits include discipline, intellectual capability, and resourcefulness.

Communication

Belgium has three official languages: Flemish, French, and English. Neither the Flemings nor the Walloons like being addressed in the other's language, so English is often the best choice. In Brussels, it is often best to ask which language people prefer if you speak more than one of them. Businesspeople usually speak English well, especially in the Flemish part of the country. When communicating in English, avoid using jargon and slang.

Belgians speak neither in quiet tones nor particularly loudly. At restaurants, especially those used for business lunches and dinners, keep conversations at a quiet level. Periods of silence do not necessarily convey a negative message. High levels of emotion are rarely shown in public, and self-control is seen as a virtue in Belgium. Flemings generally converse while standing around three feet apart, while Walloons may get a bit closer to each other.

Levels of directness in communication vary in this country. Whereas francophone Belgians tend to be formal and somewhat indirect, Flemings tend to be more informal and direct, though not as much as their Dutch neighbors. While most Belgians prefer subtlety to overt directness, you may hear a straight 'no' if someone dislikes a request or proposal.

Belgians use body language and gestures sparingly. They may make some physical contact, such as a backslap which only happens between close friends, but there is usually not a lot of it. The American *OK* sign, with thumb and index finger forming a circle, can be read as an obscene gesture in Belgium. The thumbs-up gesture is positive as it signals approval. Eye contact should be frequent, almost to the point of staring, as this conveys sincerity and helps build trust.

Initial Contacts and Meetings

Having a local contact can be an advantage, especially with Walloons, but it is usually not a necessary precondition to doing business. Negotiations in Belgium can be conducted by individuals or teams of negotiators.

Scheduling meetings in advance is required. However, you can sometimes do this on short notice if the parties had previous business interactions. Agreeing on an agenda upfront can be useful. It will usually be followed. Belgians generally expect foreign visitors to be punctual. Avoid being more than 15 minutes late, and call ahead if you will be.

Names are usually given in the order of first name, family name. With a Fleming, use *Mr./ Ms.* plus the person's family name. With a Walloon, use *Monsieur/ Madame* plus the person's family name. Only close friends call each other by their first names. Introductions are accompanied by light handshakes. Men should wait for women to initiate handshakes.

The exchange of business cards is standard practice when meeting someone for the first time. However, it is less of a ritual in Belgium than elsewhere. Almost all businesspeople read English, so there is no need to have your card translated. If you do, never present a Fleming with a card in French or a Walloon with a Flemish-language card. It is usually best to show doctorate degrees on your card and make sure that it clearly states your professional title, especially if you have the seniority to make decisions. However, your Belgian counterparts may not use any titles and degrees, and it can be hard to figure out who of the people you are meeting hold the most senior positions. When presenting your card, smile and keep eye contact, then take a few moments to look at the card you received.

Meetings either start with a few minutes of 'small talk' or get right down to business. One's private life has no place in meetings, and personal comments should be avoided. Business is a serious matter in Belgium, and meetings can be quite formal. However, humor is generally appreciated as long as it does not get too cynical or sarcastic. While the primary purpose of the first meeting is to become acquainted, the discussion will mostly focus on business topics. Belgians prefer meetings to be free of interruptions. Accepting phone calls or leaving a meeting for other inessential reasons is viewed with irritation as it may be taken as a sign of disrespect.

Presentation materials should be attractive, with good and clear visuals. Keep your presentation clear and concise. Belgians are generally suspicious of hype and exaggerations and may respond negatively to an aggressive sales approach that might be effective in other countries, such as the United States. Know your topic well, and use logical arguments and concrete examples to back up your proposals. Having your English-language handout materials translated to Flemish is not required, but it is advisable to have French translations when presenting in Wallonia.

Negotiation

Attitudes and Styles – To Belgians, negotiating is usually a joint problem-solving process. While the buyer is in a superior position, both sides in a business deal own the responsibility to reach agreement. They may focus equally on near-term and long-term benefits. The primary negotiation style is cooperative and people may be open to compromising if viewed helpful in order to move the negotiation forward. Since Belgians believe in the concept of win-win, they expect you to reciprocate their respect and trust. It is strongly advisable to avoid any open confrontation and to remain calm, friendly, patient, and persistent.

Should a dispute arise at any stage of a negotiation, you might be able to reach resolution by focusing on logical reasoning and facts while remaining open and constructive.

Sharing of Information – Belgian negotiators may spend considerable time gathering information and discussing details before the bargaining stage of a negotiation can begin. They usually share at least some information and rarely take it negatively if you ask about sensitive details, even if they may not want to answer. An exception is asking someone about salary, which the person may view as downright offensive.

Pace of Negotiation – Negotiations may be relatively fast in this country. However, Belgians often follow a methodical and carefully planned approach in preparing for the negotiation and gathering information. Aspects of your proposals may be scrutinized repeatedly.

Belgians, especially the Flemings, generally prefer a monochronic work style. They are used to pursuing actions and goals systematically, and they dislike interruptions or digressions. When negotiating, they often work their way down a list of objectives in sequential order, bargaining for each item separately, and may be unwilling to revisit aspects that have already been agreed upon. They may show little tolerance if a more polychronic counterpart challenges this approach, which they view as systematic and effective. This rigid style may be difficult to tolerate for negotiators from highly polychronic cultures, such as most Asians, Arabs, some Southern Europeans, or most Latin Americans, who may view it as closed-minded and overly restrictive. In any case, do not show irritation or anger when encountering this behavior. Instead, be willing to bargain over some items individually. Otherwise, clearly indicate that your agreement is conditional and contingent on other items. Walloons, on the other hand, tend to work in a more polychronic style that is more similar to that of the French.

Bargaining – Belgians are used to bargaining but dislike haggling. However, they can be tough negotiators and may be masters at finding common ground. The bargaining stage of a negotiation may take substantial time. Prices rarely move by more than 20 to 30 percent between initial offers and final agreement. Belgians usually show flexibility and 'common sense.' They are determined to find solutions both sides can live with and are often receptive to 'outside' ideas. Most aspects of the deal will be open to discussion. Focus your arguments on concrete facts and information. Exaggerated claims or bragging will not help your position.

Deceptive techniques might be used and it may be effective to use some of them yourself. This includes tactics such as telling lies and sending fake non-verbal messages, pretending to be disinterested in the whole deal or in single concessions, misrepresenting an item's value, or making false demands and concessions. Carefully orchestrated, 'good cop, bad cop' may be an effective tactic to use in your own negotiation approach. Belgians may claim limited authority, stating that they have to ask for their manager's approval. This could be a tactic or the truth.

Negotiators in the country may use pressure techniques that include opening with their best offer, showing intransigence, or making final offers. When using similar tactics yourself, clearly explain your offer and avoid being aggressive. Silence could simply be a part of the conversation, although it may also signal rejection of a proposal. Be careful when using pressure tactics such as applying time pressure, making expiring offers, or nibbling. Your counterparts may consider these inappropriate unless they are strongly interested in your offer and clearly understand the rationale behind the approach. Otherwise, while the negotiation is not necessarily over, it may become less constructive.

Avoid all aggressive tactics when negotiating with Belgians. They will not shy away from open confrontation if challenged, but this is almost guaranteed to deteriorate rather than strengthen your bargaining position. Opening with an extreme offer may be viewed as an unfriendly act. It is best to open with one that is already in the ballpark of what you really expect.

Emotional negotiation techniques, such as attitudinal bargaining, sending dual messages, attempting to make you feel guilty, or grimacing, may occasionally be employed. It is best to remain calm. Do not use appeals to personal relationships unless you have very strong ones with your negotiation counterparts.

Belgian businesspeople may employ defensive tactics such as changing the subject, blocking, asking probing or direct questions, making promises, or keeping an inflexible position.

Corruption and bribery are rare in Belgium, though not completely unheard of. Both legally and ethically, it is advisable to stay away from giving gifts of significant value or making offers that could be read as bribery.

Decision Making – Flemish companies are usually not very hierarchical. In Flanders, decision making is a consensus-oriented process during which many who are affected may get opportunities to voice their opinion. While senior managers are usually the ones making decisions, they will consider the best interest of the group or organization. They may sometimes delegate their authority to lower levels in the hierarchy. This process can take a long time and requires patience. It is important to win the support of people at all organizational levels who are involved in the negotiation, rather than focusing on upper management only. Once a decision has been made, it may be very difficult to change.

In the Wallonia part of Belgium, companies tend to be more hierarchical and decisions are usually made at the top of the organization. While the decision maker will still consider the best interest of the group or organization, he or she may not consult with others. Accordingly, it is important to identify and win the support of the final decision maker. Decision making is still slow with this group.

When making decisions, Flemish businesspeople may apply universal principles rather than considering the specific situation, while Walloons tend to look at each situation as a unique problem. With both, personal feelings and experiences often weigh more strongly than empirical evidence, logical arguments, and objective facts do. Belgians are often uneasy with change and reluctant to take risks. If you expect them to support a risky decision, you may need to find ways for them to become comfortable with it first, for instance by explaining contingency plans, outlining areas of additional support, or by offering guarantees and warranties.

Agreements and Contracts

Capturing and exchanging meeting summaries can be an effective way to verify understanding and commitments. Although interim agreements are usually kept, do not consider them final. Only a final contract signed by both parties constitutes a binding agreement.

Written contracts tend to be lengthy. They often spell out detailed terms and conditions for the core agreements as well as for many eventualities. Signing the contract is important not only from a legal perspective, but also as a strong confirmation of your Belgian partners' commitment.

Some documents will not even be legal unless they are written in both Flemish and French. It is recommended to consult a local legal expert before signing a contract. Belgian business law tends to be more protective of local companies than of foreign ones.

Contracts are usually dependable, and the agreed terms are viewed as binding. Your counterparts will make strong efforts to meet their commitments. Failure to meet the terms of a contract is likely to trigger legal action. However, your counterparts may occasionally ask you to reconsider aspects of the contract if conditions have changed.

Women in Business

While women enjoy similar rights as men, most Belgian women are still struggling to attain positions of similar income and authority. However, visiting businesswomen should have few problems in the country as long as they act professionally in business and social situations.

Other Important Things to Know

Business lunches, which may take a long time, and also dinners are common. Business may or may not be discussed. Wait to see whether your counterparts bring it up.

Social events do not require strict punctuality. While it is best to arrive at dinners close to the agreed time, being late to a party by 15 minutes, even more when meeting with Walloons, is perfectly acceptable.

Gift giving in business settings is rare. It is best not to bring a gift to an initial meeting in order to avoid raising suspicions about your motives.

The relationship between the Flemish and the Walloons is a sensitive topic. It may be best to avoid it in discussions.

Brazil

Businesspeople and officials in Brazil, especially older ones, usually have only limited experience with other cultures except for neighboring countries. When negotiating business here, realize that people may expect things to be done 'their way.' However, people living in large cities, especially those among younger generations, may have greater international experience and can be very open-minded.

Brazil's somewhat heterogeneous business world includes immigrants from several cultures, including Portuguese, Arabs, Germans, Italians, Polish, Japanese, Spaniards, and many others. They may not always share the values and preferences presented in this section.

Relationships and Respect

Brazil's culture is generally group-oriented. Asserting individual preferences may be seen as less important than having a sense of belonging to a group, conforming to its norms, and maintaining harmony among its members. Building lasting and trusting personal relationships is therefore critically important to most Brazilians, who often find it essential to establish strong bonds prior to closing any deals. People in this country usually want to do business only with those they know, like, and trust. If they initially seem suspicious and non-committal, you may be able to overcome this with consistent friendliness, dedication, and goodwill. Proceed with serious business discussions only after your counterparts have become very comfortable with you. This can be an extremely time-consuming process and often requires several trips to strengthen the bonds. You are unlikely to get anywhere without significant investments of both time and money.

People may base their trust in others on past experience. In order to establish productive business cooperation, it will be critically important to keep and demonstrate a long-term perspective and commitment. Brazilians may expect that you value people and relationships more strongly than your business objectives. They tend to distrust people who appear unwilling to spend the necessary time or whose motives for relationship building are unclear.

Business relationships in this country exist between people, not necessarily between companies. Even when you have won your local business partners' friendship and trust, they will not necessarily trust others from your company. That makes it very important to keep company interfaces unchanged. Changing a key contact may require the relationship building process to start over.

While Brazilians are usually warm and friendly, they are also very proud and may be easily offended by comments that leave room for misunderstandings. 'Saving face' and respecting everyone's honor and personal pride are crucial requirements for doing business in the country. Openly criticizing someone in front of others can have a devastating impact on your negotiation. Avoid open conflict, and know that politeness is crucial. In addition, showing genuine interest and compassion will win people's hearts.

In Brazil's business culture, the respect a person enjoys depends primarily on his or her status, rank, and education. Showing status is important since people will take you more seriously. Similarly, it is expected that everyone show respect to those of higher status. However, more and more people in the country, especially among younger generations, have started questioning whether those in powerful positions are entitled to special privileges. Admired personal traits include creativity, oratory skills, and bargaining skills.

Communication

The official language of Brazil is Portuguese. It is notably different from the Portuguese spoken in Portugal. Brazilians do not perceive themselves as Hispanics. They may take offense if addressed in Spanish. However, if you speak Spanish fluently, you may want to ask politely whether they would mind speaking it.

Many businesspeople speak at least some English. With some high-ranking managers, it may be useful to engage an interpreter. To avoid offending the other side, ask beforehand whether an interpreter should be present at a meeting. When communicating in English, speak in short, simple sentences and avoid using jargon and slang.

It will help people with a limited command of English if you speak slowly, summarize your key points often, and pause frequently to allow for interpretation. Even when the main meeting language is English, your counterparts may frequently speak Portuguese among themselves, not necessarily to shut you out from the discussion but to reduce their discomfort and ensure a common understanding among them.

While discussions may get very enthusiastic and lively, Brazilians generally dislike loud and boisterous behavior. However, it is crucial that you never lose your temper or appear impatient, as there is always a risk of hurting someone's pride. People may interrupt others or speak in parallel, but this is not recommended. Emotions are usually shown very openly. Brazilians generally converse in extremely close proximity, standing only one to two feet. Never back away, even if this is much closer than your personal comfort zone allows. Doing so could be read as a sign that you are uncomfortable around them.

Depending on the situation, communication in Brazil can be either direct or indirect. People usually avoid open conflict. In addition, they may be reluctant to disagree openly with someone they like, in which case it can become difficult to know their true opinion. However, in business settings they usually have no problem saying 'no' and may prefer frank messages to diplomatic ones. Brazilians can be direct and intense at the negotiation table, while polite and ambiguous in social settings. Silence likely signals embarrassment.

Gestures and body language can be very expressive. It is often not a good idea to imitate them, though. Physical contact with others of the same gender is ok. The American *OK* sign, with thumb and index finger forming a circle, is an obscene gesture in Brazil. Non-verbal communication can be very extensive, so watch for clues. If someone is flicking their fingertips underneath the chin, they are signaling that they do not know the answer to a question. Eye contact should be very frequent, almost to the point of staring. This conveys sincerity and helps build trust.

Initial Contacts and Meetings

Choosing a local intermediary, or *despachante*, who can leverage existing relationships to make the initial contact is highly recommended. This person will help bridge the gap between cultures, allowing you to conduct business with greater effectiveness. Your embassy, a trade organization, a chamber of commerce, or a local legal or accounting firm may be able to provide a list of potential *despachantes*.

It is often better to conduct negotiations in Brazil with a team of negotiators rather than to rely on a single individual. This signals importance, facilitates stronger relationship building, and may speed up the overall process. It is vital that teams be well aligned, with roles clearly assigned to each member. Brazilian negotiators may be very good at exploiting disagreements between members of the other team to their advantage. Changing a team member may require the relationship building process to start over and should therefore be avoided.

Given the strong emphasis on status and hierarchy in the country's business culture, a senior executive should attend the initial meeting for your company and your negotiating team should include senior leaders who know your company well. There will not be an expectation that the executive attends future meetings. Similarly, the top executive on the Brazilian side, who may also be the ultimate decision maker, may attend only initially.

If possible, schedule meetings at least one to two weeks in advance. Since people want to know whom they will be meeting, provide details on titles, positions, and responsibilities of attendees ahead of time. Agreeing on an agenda upfront can also be useful. Reconfirm your meeting, and be prepared for your counterparts to cancel or postpone meetings with little advance notice. While meetings may start considerably late, Brazilians generally expect foreign visitors to be punctual. Avoid being more than 10 to 15 minutes late, and call ahead if you will be. Displaying anger if you have to wait, which happens often, reflects very poorly on you.

Names are usually given in the order of first name, family name. Some Brazilians may also have a middle name. Initially, use *Mr. /Ms.* or *Senhor/Senhora* plus the family name. However, it is common to use these with the first same, such as in 'Senhor Eduardo.' If a person has a title, such as *Doctor* or *Professor*, use it instead. Before calling Brazilians by their first name, wait until they offer it. This may happen quickly. Introductions are accompanied by handshakes, which may be extensive.

The exchange of business cards is an essential step when meeting someone for the first time, so bring more than you need. It is strongly recommended to use cards with one side in English and the other in Portuguese. Do not offer a card that is in Spanish. Show doctorate degrees on your card and make sure that it clearly states your professional title, especially if you have the seniority to make decisions. When presenting your card, ensure that the Portuguese side is facing the recipient. Smile and keep eye contact while accepting someone else's card, then carefully examine it. Next, place the card on the table in front of you.

Meetings start with small talk, which may be extensive. This may include questions on a wide range of subjects. However, one's private life is not a subject for discussion around meetings. Most Brazilians dislike people who 'leap right into business.' It is important to be patient and let the other side set the pace. People appreciate a sense of humor, but keep it light and friendly, and be careful not to overdo it. Business is a serious matter in Brazil. While initial meetings may appear very formal, you may find the atmosphere at subsequent meetings to become much more relaxed. Overall, Brazilians tend to be less formal than most other Latin Americans may be.

The primary purpose of the first meeting is to become acquainted and build relationships. Business may be discussed, but do not try to hurry along with your agenda. It is unrealistic to expect initial meetings to lead to straight decisions.

Presentation materials should be attractive, with good and clear visuals. Having your handout materials translated to Portuguese is not a must, but it will be appreciated and helps in getting your messages across.

When the meeting is over, stay around and have some more small talk with your Brazilian counterparts. Leaving right away suggests that you have better things to do and may offend others.

Negotiation

Attitudes and Styles - Leveraging relationships is an important element when negotiating in Brazil. Nevertheless, Brazilians often employ distributive and contingency bargaining. While the buyer is in a superior position, both sides in a business deal own the responsibility to reach agreement. They expect long-term commitments from their business partners and will focus mostly on long-term benefits. The primary negotiation style is competitive and Brazilians can be very aggressive negotiators. While proposals should demonstrate the benefits to both negotiating parties, neither of them should take attempts to win competitive advantages negatively. It is crucial to remain non-confrontational and avoid direct conflict throughout the bargaining exchange. Ultimately, the culture promotes a win-win approach and people value long-term business relationships. You will earn your counterparts' respect by maintaining a positive, persistent attitude. Do not openly show aggression or frustration.

Should a dispute arise at any stage of a negotiation, you might be able to reach resolution by leveraging personal relationships.

Sharing of Information – Even when personal relationships are strong, your Brazilian counterparts may be reluctant to share information openly. Many believe that privileged information creates bargaining advantages. At the same time, information that may seem irrelevant may be reviewed over and over.

Pace of Negotiation – Expect negotiations to be slow and protracted. Brazilians do not hurry and dislike people who do. They see impatience as a sign of weakness and may even think it rude. Be prepared to make several trips if necessary to achieve your objectives. Relationship building, information gathering, bargaining, and decision making may take considerable time. Attempts to rush the process are unlikely to produce better results and may be viewed as offensive. Throughout the negotiation, be patient, control your emotions, and accept the inevitable delays.

Most Brazilians prefer a very polychronic work style. They are used to pursuing multiple actions and goals in parallel. When negotiating, they often take a holistic approach and may jump back and forth between topics rather than addressing them in sequential order. Negotiators from strongly monochronic cultures, such as Germany, the United Kingdom, or the United States, may find this style confusing, irritating, and even annoying. In any case, do not show irritation or anger when encountering this behavior. Instead, keep track of the bargaining progress at all times, often emphasizing areas where agreement already exists.

If your counterparts appear to be stalling the negotiation, assess carefully whether their slowing down the process indicates that they are evaluating alternatives or that they are not interested in doing business with you. More likely, this behavior either represents an attempt to create time pressure in order to obtain concessions, which happens frequently, or it simply reflects the slow decision process in the country. Again, patience and persistence are vitally important.

Bargaining – Brazilians are used to hard bargaining but are not overly fond of haggling. They can be tough and sometimes very aggressive negotiators. The bargaining exchange can be very extensive. While concessions never come easily, prices may move by 40 percent or more between initial offer and final agreement. Leave yourself sufficient room for concessions at different stages. After making one, always ask the other side to reciprocate. Throughout the process, remain cool and respectful, avoid confrontation, and frequently reaffirm the relationship.

During the bargaining exchange, keep in mind that intangible benefits such as increases in power and status may sometimes be more desirable to your counterparts than financial gains may.

Deceptive techniques are frequent and can be effective. This includes tactics such as telling lies and sending fake non-verbal messages, pretending to be disinterested in the whole deal or in single concessions, misrepresenting an item's value, or making false demands and concessions. Your Brazilian counterparts may make other attempts to mislead you in order to obtain bargaining advantages. Even when you can see right through a lie, it would be a grave personal insult to state or even hint that your counterpart is not telling the truth. It is advisable to verify information received from the local side through other channels. Brazilians sometimes use 'good cop, bad cop,' and it can be an effective tactic on either side of the negotiation table. However, it could be devastating if the other side recognized this as a tactic, and your team will need to exclude any 'bad cop' member from future negotiation rounds.

Negotiators in the country may frequently use pressure techniques that include making final offers, showing intransigence, or nibbling. Final offers may come more than once and are rarely final. Be careful when trying to open with your best offer. Brazilians may consider this inappropriate or even insulting. Silence can be a way to signal rejection of a proposal or to obtain further concessions. Do not use pressure tactics such as applying time pressure or making expiring offers as these may be taken as signs that you are not willing to build a long-term relationship. Your counterparts may even choose to terminate the negotiation.

Brazilian negotiators may sometimes appear aggressive or adversarial. Negotiations in the country could include confrontational elements. Using extreme openings is rare but can be effective to provoke an initial reaction. Negotiators may make threats and warnings, openly display anger, or even use walkouts. It is advisable not to respond in kind. There is always a huge risk to hurt your counterparts' pride and the margin for error is small. It will be best to remain firm and persistent, but also friendly and respectful.

Emotional negotiation techniques, such as attitudinal bargaining or attempting to make you feel guilty, are frequent and can be effective. Be cautious not to hurt someone's personal pride when employing any of these tactics, though. Pleas to personal relationships and other emotional appeals, such as emphasizing how your proposal will add to your counterparts' personal satisfaction or heighten their honor, can be very powerful. Your counterparts may use temperamental outbursts as a way to throw you off-balance. Keep your cool and do not respond in kind since this could become counterproductive.

Brazilians may frequently employ defensive tactics such as blocking or changing the subject, asking probing or very direct questions, making promises, or keeping an inflexible position.

Corruption and bribery are somewhat common in Brazil's public and private sectors. However, people may draw the line differently, viewing minor payments as rewards for getting a job done rather than as bribes. Also, keep in mind that there is a fine line between giving gifts and bribing. What you may consider a bribe, a Brazilian may view as only a nice gift.

Decision Making – Most companies are intensely hierarchical, and people expect to work with very clear lines of authority. Decision makers are usually top executives who will consider the best interest of the group or organization. They may or may not consult with others. Brazilian managers rarely delegate their authority. Gaining access to top managers can be difficult, though. You may have to deal with subordinates who have no decision-making authority but might nevertheless strongly influence the final decision, which may be made behind closed doors. Maintaining good relationships with these intermediaries is crucial to your success. Decision making can be a very slow process that requires much patience. Attempts to rush or put pressure on the process are not likely to succeed.

When making decisions, businesspeople may not rely much on rules or laws. They usually consider the specific situation rather than applying universal principles. Personal feelings and experiences, as well as intuition, weigh more strongly than empirical evidence and other objective facts do, but people will consider all aspects. Brazilians are often uneasy with change and reluctant to take risks. If you expect them to support a risky decision, you may need to find ways for them to become comfortable with it first, for instance by explaining contingency plans, outlining areas of additional support, or by offering guarantees and warranties.

Agreements and Contracts

Capturing and exchanging written understandings after meetings and at key negotiation stages is useful since oral statements are not always dependable. Signatures are not required to confirm commitments. Brazilians still mostly rely on handshakes and their word, which are usually dependable.

Written contracts tend to be lengthy and often spell out detailed terms and conditions for the core agreements as well as for many eventualities. Nevertheless, writing up and signing the contract is a formality. Brazilians believe that the primary strength of an agreement lies in the partners' relationship and commitment rather than in its written documentation.

It is recommended to consult a local legal expert before signing a contract. Local laws are often complex and difficult to understand. The Brazilian side may view it very unfavorably if you use a foreign lawyer. In addition, it may be best not to bring your attorney to the negotiation table as it could be read as a sign of mistrust.

Contracts are usually dependable, and the agreed terms are viewed as binding. However, business partners usually expect the other side to remain somewhat flexible if conditions change. Given the relatively unstable political and economic situation in the country, you should factor this possibility into your negotiation planning.

Women in Business

Machismo attitudes remain strong in this country. Women may be considered inferior, and they still have a hard time attaining positions of similar income and authority as men. As a visiting businesswoman, emphasize your company's importance and your role in it. A personal introduction or at least a letter of support from a senior executive within your company may help a lot.

Female business travelers should graciously accept any chivalric gestures they receive, while exercising caution and acting professionally in business and social situations. Displaying confidence and some degree of assertiveness can be effective, but it is very important not to appear overly bold and aggressive.

Other Important Things to Know

Social events do not require strict punctuality. While it is best to arrive at dinners close to the agreed time, being late to a party by 30 minutes or more is perfectly acceptable.

Business may be discussed during meals in Brazil.

Gift giving in business settings is rare, at least as long as no strong relationship exists. It is best not to bring a gift to an initial meeting in order to avoid raising suspicions about your motives.

A topic that is best avoided is the country's relationship with Argentina. In addition, do not refer to citizens of the United States as Americans. Brazilians are sensitive to this point as they feel that the term includes them.

Canada

Most Canadian businesspeople, especially those among younger generations, are experienced in interacting and doing business with visitors from other cultures. They often take a genuine interest in other countries and are usually open-minded rather than forcing their ways upon you.

Canada's heterogeneous population is composed of the English-speaking majority (Anglo-Canadians or *Anglophones* representing almost 60 percent), and the French-speaking minority (French-Canadians or *Francophones*, around 23 percent), most of whom live in the Quebec province. It is essential to be aware of and respect the significant cultural and language differences between them. There are also sizeable groups who have emigrated from other countries, including many of Asian or Arab heritages. Many of them live in Toronto or Vancouver. The information provided in this section pertains mostly to Anglo- and French-Canadians. In addition, it is important to recognize the many unique characteristics that make the country distinct from the United States.

Style differences across Canada's population can still be pronounced in smaller cities and rural areas. Western Canadians are usually open to doing business with people from many different countries and cultures, while people in Atlantic Canada can appear regionally focused and somewhat closed-minded. The pace of business may be the fastest around Toronto and Ottawa.

Relationships and Respect

Generally, business relationships are only moderately important in this country. They are usually not a necessary precondition for initial business interactions. Your counterparts' expectation may be to get to know you better as you do business together. This is especially true for Anglo-Canadians, while French-Canadians tend to place more emphasis on building stronger relationships before engaging in serious business interactions. Generally, people in the country may emphasize near-term results over long-range objectives but are usually also interested in building long-term relationships. However, many Canadians are competitive and may think it ok for partners in a productive business relationship to cooperate and compete at the same time, a view that others from strongly relationship-oriented cultures rarely share.

Business relationships in this country exist between companies as well as between individuals. If your company replaces you with someone else over the course of a negotiation, it may be easy for your replacement to take things over from where you left them. Likewise, if you introduce someone else from your company into an existing business relationship, that person may quickly be accepted as a valid business partner. This does not mean that the Canadians do not care about who they are dealing with. Personal integrity and dependability are important if you want to win their trust.

In the country's business culture, the respect a person enjoys depends primarily on his or her achievements and to a lesser degree, education. Rank and titles play a somewhat more important role here than they do in the United States. Admired personal traits include honesty, ambition paired with humility, tolerance, and reasonableness.

Communication

Canada is officially bilingual. The federal government works in the two official languages, English and French. Canadian English differs from both British and American English, though it is closer to the latter. There are distinct differences between French and Canadian French. Most French-Canadians also speak English.

Businesspeople in this country usually speak in a controlled fashion, only occasionally raising their voices to make a point. At restaurants, especially those used for business lunches and dinners, keep conversations at a quiet level. Being loud may be regarded as bad manners. Canadians are polite listeners and rarely interrupt others. Periods of silence do not necessarily convey a negative message. Anglo-Canadians usually do not openly show emotions, which is unlike French-Canadians, who tend to be more animated and expressive. People generally converse standing around two to three feet apart. French-Canadians will likely get closer than that.

While usually friendly and polite, communication in Canada is often quite direct. Canadians dislike vague statements and may openly share their opinions and concerns.

Too much diplomacy may confuse and irritate them and can give the impression of insincerity. They may ask for clarifications and rarely find it difficult to say 'no' if they dislike a request or proposal. If something is against company policy or cannot be done for other reasons, your counterpart will likely say so. They may view this as a simple statement of fact and might not understand that someone else could consider this directness insensitive.

Gestures and body language are usually subtle in Canada. Physical contact is rare and best avoided. Approval is shown by an upward pointing thumb or with the *OK* sign, with thumb and index finger forming a circle. Do not use your fingers to point at others. Instead, point with your head. Eye contact should be frequent, as this conveys sincerity and helps build trust. However, do not stare at people.

Initial Contacts and Meetings

Having a local contact can be an advantage, especially with French-Canadians, but it is usually not a necessary precondition to doing business.

Negotiations in Canada can be conducted by individuals or teams of negotiators. Both approaches have their distinct advantages. Since decisions are often made by individuals, meeting the decision-maker one-on-one may help get results quickly. On the other hand, a well-aligned team with clearly assigned roles can be quite effective when negotiating with a group of Canadians. Owing to the high degree of individualism that characterizes the culture, Canadian teams are not always well aligned, which sometimes makes it easy to play one member against the other.

Scheduling meetings in advance is required. However, you can sometimes do this on short notice, especially if the parties have had previous business interactions. Canadians generally expect visitors to be punctual. Avoid being more than 5 minutes late, and call ahead if you will be.

Names are usually given in the order of first name, family name. Use *Mr./Ms.* plus the family name. If a person has an academic title, such as *Doctor* or *Professor*, use it instead, followed by the family name. Before calling Canadians by their first name, wait until they offer it. This may happen quickly since the use of first names is not a sign of intimacy. However, do not use the other person's name as frequently as you might in the United States. Introductions are usually accompanied by handshakes. Men should wait for women to initiate handshakes. The standard greeting is 'how are you?' It is rhetorical, so it is best to respond with the same phrase or to say something like 'fine, thank you,' or 'I'm doing great, and you?'

The exchange of business cards is not a mandatory step, but it is best to bring a sufficient supply. They may sometimes be exchanged at the end rather than the beginning of the meeting. It is beneficial to include both French and English translations on your card. If you plan to conduct business in the province of Quebec, it is vital that your card is translated into French. Show doctorate degrees on your card and make sure that it clearly states your professional title, especially if you have the seniority to make decisions. Offer your card to everyone present. You may not always get one in return. When presenting your card, smile and keep eye contact, then take a few moments to look at the card you received. Next, place it on the table in front of you.

Meetings usually start with some polite small talk, which can be brief. Humor, which should be friendly and not overly ironic and sarcastic, is important and almost always appreciated. One's private life is not a subject for discussion around meetings. During the first meeting, it is best to preserve an air of formality while remaining polite and cordial, listening more than speaking.

While one purpose of the initial meeting is to get to know each other, the primary focus will be on business topics. Either the meeting leads to a straight decision or there will be a list of follow-up actions. Smaller deals may be decided and finalized at the first meeting. If the meeting concludes without next steps being defined, this may mean that there is no interest to continue the discussion.

Presentation materials should be very attractive, with good and clear visuals. Prepare thoroughly and make sure your key messages come across clearly. However, avoid delivering presentations full of excitement and hype since they will make your Canadian audience suspicious. Stringent French-language requirements exist in the province of Quebec, where you must provide a French translation for promotional material and other documents. Even in other provinces, Canadian organizations may require your material to be in both English and French, especially when dealing with government institutions. Make inquiries in advance if necessary.

Negotiation

Attitudes and Styles – To Canadians, negotiating is usually a joint problem-solving process. With French-Canadians, however, it may mean engaging in a somewhat more aggressive debate aimed at reaching a mutually agreeable solution. While the buyer is in a superior position, both sides in a business deal own the responsibility to reach agreement. They may focus equally on near-term and long-term benefits. The primary negotiation style is cooperative and people may be open to compromising if viewed helpful in order to move the negotiation forward. Since Canadians believe in the concept of win-win, they expect you to reciprocate their respect and trust. They are often very pragmatic and usually find compromises both sides can live with. While the negotiation exchange may include conflicts, you should keep a positive attitude and show willingness to work with the other side in an effort to reach agreement.

Should a dispute arise at any stage of a negotiation, you might be able to reach resolution by showing willingness to compromise and appealing to your counterparts' fairness.

Sharing of Information – Canadian negotiators usually spend time, sometimes a lot of it, gathering information and discussing details before the bargaining stage of a negotiation can begin. They may share a lot of information as a way to build trust. It can be very counterproductive to appear as if you are hiding facts from your Canadian counterparts. However, they will usually accept it if you state openly that you do not want to share certain information. They value information that is straightforward and to the point. Do not provide misleading information as your counterparts will likely consider this unfair and may try to 'get even.'

Canadians are generally suspicious of hype and exaggerations and may respond negatively to a 'hard sell' approach that might be effective in the United States.

Pace of Negotiation – Negotiations in Canada often move at a rapid pace. Though somewhat cautious, Canadians believe in the 'time is money' philosophy almost as strongly as Americans do. Accordingly, your counterparts will generally want to finish the negotiation in a timely manner and implement actions soon. Even complex negotiations may not require more than one trip, as follow-up negotiations are often conducted via phone and e-mail.

Canadians generally prefer a monochronic work style. They are used to pursuing actions and goals systematically, and they dislike interruptions or digressions. When negotiating, they often work their way down a list of objectives in sequential order, bargaining for each item separately, and may be unwilling to revisit aspects that have already been agreed upon. They may show little tolerance if a more polychronic counterpart challenges this approach, which they view as systematic and effective. This rigid style may be difficult to tolerate for negotiators from highly polychronic cultures, such as most Asians, Arabs, some Southern Europeans, or most Latin Americans, who may view it as closed-minded and overly restrictive. In any case, do not show irritation or anger when encountering this behavior. Instead, be willing to bargain over some items individually. Otherwise, clearly indicate that your agreement is conditional and contingent on other items.

Stalling a negotiation in an attempt to create time pressure in order to obtain concessions, or to gain the time needed to evaluate alternatives, may turn out to be a big mistake. Canadians hate wasting time and have little patience if they feel that the other side may be hiding or holding back something. Unlike in many other cultures, negotiators may actually become less inclined to make concessions if they feel that the overall bargaining exchange is taking too long. Worst case, your counterparts may lose interest in the deal.

Bargaining – Canadians are not overly fond of bargaining and dislike haggling. They can be tough negotiators but are usually less aggressive than Americans may be. Appearing confident and assertive is essential, though, since facing an apparently insecure counterpart may encourage Canadians to negotiate harder. State your position clearly and be willing to push for it as needed.

Negotiators in Canada may take firm positions at the beginning of the bargaining process. Once you convince them that you are intent on holding your own, they may become more willing to make concessions. However, prices rarely move by more than 10 to 20 percent between initial offer and final agreement.

Most people in this country expect to negotiate 'in good faith.' However, they may occasionally use deceptive negotiation techniques such as telling lies and sending fake non-verbal messages, pretending to be disinterested in the whole deal or in single concessions, misrepresenting an item's value, or making false demands and concessions. Since 'good cop, bad cop' requires strong alignment between the players, only experienced negotiators who have spent time practicing the tactic may be using it. Carefully orchestrated, it may be effective in your own negotiation approach.

Businesspeople may claim limited authority, stating that they have to ask for their manager's approval. This could be a tactic or the truth.

Canadian negotiators may use pressure techniques that include opening with their best offer, showing intransigence, making final or expiring offers, or nibbling. When using similar tactics yourself, clearly explain your offer and avoid being aggressive. Avoid making decreasing offers, as they will likely be viewed as inappropriate and offensive. Silence can sometimes be effective as a way to convey displeasure. Be careful when attempting to create time pressure. Although it can be very effective since the Canadians' sense of urgency usually works against them, their level of interest could drop and they might start considering alternatives to the deal at hand. Persistence is important, though, and you will frequently find your counterparts exploring all options to bring the negotiation to a successful close as quickly as they can.

Avoid aggressive tactics when negotiating with Canadians. They will not shy away from open confrontation if challenged, but this is likely to deteriorate rather than strengthen your bargaining position. French-Canadians may sometimes appear aggressive as the bargaining gets more heated. Remind yourself that they may not perceive it that way. Opening with an extreme offer may be viewed as an unfriendly act. It is best to open with one that is already in the ballpark of what you really expect.

Other emotional negotiation techniques may be more frequent. Canadians may employ attitudinal bargaining or send dual messages. It is often best simply to ignore these tactics. Attempts to make you feel guilty and appeals to personal relationships are rare since people believe that these have no place in business. However, using these tactics yourself may be surprisingly effective with some negotiators.

Canadian businesspeople may employ defensive tactics such as changing the subject, blocking, asking probing or direct questions, making promises, or keeping an inflexible position. Attempts to change the subject repeatedly in order to confuse your counterparts may meet with resistance, though.

Introducing written terms and conditions may be effective tactics that could help shorten the bargaining process, which most of your Canadian counterparts may find desirable. Similarly, they may frequently attempt to introduce pre-printed clauses. Unless these are based on company policies, which are usually non-negotiable, you should ignore such attempts and insist that all terms and conditions be discussed and agreed upon individually.

Corruption and bribery are very rare in Canada. It is strongly advisable to stay away from giving gifts of significant value or making offers that could be read as bribery.

Decision Making – Canadian companies are usually not overly hierarchical. Nevertheless, they usually have extensive policies and processes that may affect decision making. They are almost always followed. Decision makers are usually individuals who may or may not consult with others in the group or organization. Managers are expected to accept responsibility for their own as well as their employees' actions. Decision-making authority is often delegated to lower levels in the hierarchy and may not require any further approval from others. Generally, the size of a deal determines how high in the organization you need to go. Once the bargaining process has concluded, decisions are often made quickly.

When making decisions, businesspeople may apply universal principles rather than considering the specific situation. This is especially true for French-Canadians. Empirical evidence and other objective facts weigh much more strongly than personal feelings and experiences do. Canadians are medium risk takers who are often a bit more cautious than Americans may be.

Agreements and Contracts

Capturing and exchanging meeting summaries can be an effective way to verify understanding and commitments. Many Canadians pride themselves with being consistent, so they will likely keep their commitments, at least if they are sufficiently documented. While you should not consider interim agreements final, avoid the impression that you are not willing to hold up your commitments. Nevertheless, only a contract signed by both parties constitutes a binding agreement.

Written contracts tend to be lengthy and somewhat legalistic. They often spell out detailed terms and conditions for the core agreements as well as for many eventualities. They usually represent irrevocable commitments to the terms and conditions they define and can only be changed with both partners' consent.

Always consult a legal expert who has sufficient relevant experience before signing a contract. While the society is not quite as litigious as the one in the United States, Canadians are also quite willing to enforce contracts in court if necessary. Your legal counsel may also attend negotiations to provide legal advice throughout the bargaining process.

Contracts are usually dependable, and the agreed terms are viewed as binding. Requests to change contract details after signature may be considered as bad faith and will meet with strong resistance.

Women in Business

While women enjoy similar rights as men, many of them are still struggling to attain positions of similar income and authority. Nonetheless, Canadian women expect to be treated seriously and respectfully. A visiting businesswoman should have few problems in the country.

Other Important Things to Know

Business lunches and dinners are common. Canadians often discuss business during meals.

Punctuality is also valued in many social settings. It is best to be right on time for dinners, and to arrive at parties within 10 to 15 minutes of the agreed time.

Gift giving in business settings is rare, especially early in your engagement. It is best not to bring a gift to an initial meeting in order to avoid raising suspicions about your motives. However, partners may exchange small gifts when the contract is signed.

Chile

Partly owing to Chile's location at the southern tip of Latin America, most business-people and officials in the country have only limited exposure to other cultures except for neighboring countries. Its culture is quite homogeneous. When negotiating business here, realize that people may expect things to be done 'their way.' However, some among younger generations may have greater international experience and can be very open-minded.

Relationships and Respect

Chile's culture is generally group-oriented. Asserting individual preferences may be seen as less important than having a sense of belonging to a group, conforming to its norms, and maintaining harmony among its members. Building lasting and trusting relationships is very important to many Chileans, who often find it essential to establish strong bonds prior to closing any deals. People in this country usually want to do business only with those they know, like, and trust. Establishing productive business cooperation requires a long-term perspective and commitment. Proceed with serious business discussions only after your counterparts have become very comfortable with you. This can be a time-consuming process.

Business relationships in this country exist between people, not necessarily between companies. Even when you have won your local business partners' friendship and trust, they will not necessarily trust others from your company. That makes it very important to keep company interfaces unchanged. Changing a key contact may require the relationship building process to start over.

Establishing personal relationships with others in Chile can create powerful networks and may help you a lot to achieve your business objectives. Whether people think you are worth knowing and trusting often weighs much more strongly than how competent you are or what proposals you may have to make. Personal networks rely mostly on strong friendships that also represent dependable mutual obligations. They may open doors and solve problems that would otherwise be difficult to master. Maintaining honest and cordial relations is crucial.

While Chileans are usually warm and friendly, they are also very proud and may be easily offended by comments that leave room for misunderstandings. 'Saving face' and respecting everyone's honor and personal pride are crucial requirements for doing business in the country. Causing embarrassment to another person or openly criticizing someone in front of others can have a devastating impact on your negotiation. Character and kindness towards others are essential qualities. You will earn people's respect by showing empathy for others, treating everyone with dignity, and avoiding all aggressive behaviors.

In Chile's business culture, the respect a person enjoys depends primarily on his or her status, rank, and education. Admired personal traits include sincerity, honesty, and integrity.

Communication

While the official language of Chile is Spanish, it is notably different from the Spanish spoken in Spain. Many businesspeople speak at least some English, but being able to speak Spanish is a clear advantage. With high-ranking managers, it may otherwise be useful to engage an interpreter. To avoid offending the other side, ask beforehand whether an interpreter should be present at a meeting. When communicating in English, speak in short, simple sentences and avoid using jargon and slang. It will help people with a limited command of English if you speak slowly, summarize your key points often, and pause frequently to allow for interpretation. Even when the main meeting language is English, your counterparts may frequently speak Spanish among themselves, not necessarily to shut you out from the discussion but to reduce their discomfort and ensure a common understanding among them.

People in this country usually speak softly. While they may occasionally raise their voices to make a point, they dislike loud and boisterous behavior. At restaurants, keep conversations at a quiet level. In addition, avoid dominating the conversation. Emotions are usually not shown openly. People may converse in close proximity, standing only two feet or less apart. Never back away, even if this is much closer than your personal comfort zone allows. Doing so could be read as a sign that you are uncomfortable around them.

Communication in Chile is generally direct. However, people may sometimes tell you what they think you want to hear rather than what they really think. In addition, they may be reluctant to disagree openly with someone they like, in which case it can become difficult to know their true opinion. Silence may indicate that there is a problem.

Gestures and body language may be lively, but not overly so. There may be frequent physical contact with others of the same gender. This may include putting their hands on your shoulder while speaking to you. Slapping the open hand over a fist is a vulgar gesture. Eye contact should be very frequent, almost to the point of staring. This conveys sincerity and helps build trust.

Initial Contacts and Meetings

Choosing a local intermediary, or *enchufado*, who can leverage existing relationships to make the initial contact is highly recommended. This person will help bridge the gap between cultures, allowing you to conduct business with greater effectiveness. Your embassy, a trade organization, a chamber of commerce, or a local legal or accounting firm may be able to provide a list of potential *enchufados*. Alternatively, seek out the help of a local bank or consultant. Without such a contact, it may be difficult to gain access to the right people.

It is often better to conduct negotiations in Chile with a team of negotiators rather than to rely on a single individual. This signals importance, facilitates stronger relationship building, and may speed up the overall process. It is vital that teams be well aligned, with roles clearly assigned to each member. Changing a team member may require the relationship building process to start over and should therefore be avoided.

Given the strong emphasis on hierarchy in the country's business culture, a senior executive should attend the initial meeting for your company and your negotiating team should include senior leaders who know your company well. There will not be an expectation that the executive attends future meetings. Similarly, the top executive on the Chilean side, who may also be the ultimate decision maker, may attend only initially. The most senior Chilean executive to attend throughout the negotiation will likely be at a similar level in the hierarchy as your own negotiation leader.

If possible, schedule meetings at least two weeks in advance. Since Chileans want to know whom they will be meeting, provide details on titles, positions, and responsibilities of attendees ahead of time. While meetings may start late, Chileans generally expect foreign visitors to be punctual. Avoid being more than 10 to 15 minutes late, and call ahead if you will be. Displaying anger if you have to wait reflects very poorly on you. The most senior people usually arrive last. Otherwise, authority may sometimes be difficult to pick out, so watch for small hints of deference to identify the decision makers.

Names are usually given in the order of first name, then family name or names. Most Chileans have two family names, the first one from their father, and the second one from their mother. Use *Mr./Mrs./Miss* or *Señor/Señora/Señorita*, plus the family name (the first one if two family names are given). If a person has an academic title, use it instead, followed by the family name. Only close friends call each other by their first names. Introduce and greet older people first, then greet everyone else individually. Introductions are accompanied by handshakes. Men should wait for women to initiate handshakes.

The exchange of business cards is an essential step when meeting someone for the first time, so bring more than you need. It is strongly recommended to use cards with one side in English and the other in Spanish. Show doctorate degrees on your card and make sure that it clearly states your professional title, especially if you have the seniority to make decisions. When presenting your card, ensure that the Spanish side is facing the recipient. Smile and keep eye contact while accepting someone else's card, then carefully examine it. Next, place the card on the table in front of you. Never stuff someone's card into your back pocket or otherwise treat it disrespectfully. In addition, never write on a person's business card.

Meetings start with small talk, which may be extensive. This may include personal questions about your background and family, allowing participants to become acquainted. It is important to be patient and let the other side set the pace. People appreciate a sense of humor, but keep it light and friendly, and be careful not to overdo it. Business is a serious matter in Chile. Initial meetings may appear very formal, but the atmosphere usually is a bit more relaxed in subsequent meetings.

The primary purpose of the first meeting is to become acquainted and build relationships. Business may actually not be discussed at all. It is very unrealistic to expect initial meetings to lead to straight decisions.

Presentation materials should be attractive, with good and clear visuals. Use diagrams and pictures wherever feasible, cut down on words, and avoid complicated expressions. Having your handout materials translated to Spanish is not a must, but it will be appreciated and helps in getting your messages across.

Negotiation

Attitudes and Styles - To Chileans, negotiating is usually a joint problem-solving process. While the buyer is in a superior position, both sides in a business deal own the responsibility to reach agreement. They expect long-term commitments from their business partners and will focus mostly on long-term benefits. The primary negotiation style is cooperative and people may be open to compromising if viewed helpful in order to move the negotiation forward. Chileans are often very serious and straightforward negotiators. Since they believe in the concept of win-win, they expect you to reciprocate their respect and trust. It is strongly advisable to avoid aggressiveness and open confrontation, remaining calm, friendly, patient, and persistent.

Should a dispute arise at any stage of a negotiation, you might be able to reach resolution by showing flexibility and willingness to compromise. Emphasizing the long-term benefits of the deal may also help.

Sharing of Information – Even when personal relationships are strong, your Chilean counterparts may be reluctant to share information openly. Many believe that privileged information creates bargaining advantages.

Pace of Negotiation – While negotiations may be slow and protracted, Chileans are less bureaucratic and often move a bit faster than other Latin Americans may. On the other hand, they see impatience as a sign of weakness and may even think it rude. Be prepared to make several trips if necessary to achieve your objectives. Relationship building, information gathering, bargaining, and decision making may take considerable time. Throughout the negotiation, be patient, control your emotions, and accept the inevitable delays.

Most Chileans prefer a polychronic work style. They are used to pursuing multiple actions and goals in parallel. When negotiating, they often take a holistic approach and may jump back and forth between topics rather than addressing them in sequential order. Negotiators from strongly monochronic cultures, such as Germany, the United Kingdom, or the United States, may find this style confusing, irritating, and even annoying. In any case, do not show irritation or anger when encountering this behavior. Instead, keep track of the bargaining progress at all times, often emphasizing areas where agreement already exists.

Bargaining – Chileans are not fond of bargaining and strongly dislike haggling. Even in the country's street markets there is much less bargaining than in other countries in Latin America. Extensive negotiations may only lead to little movement. Prices rarely move by more than 15 to 25 percent between initial offer and final agreement. Throughout the exchange, remain cool and respectful, avoid confrontation, and frequently reaffirm the relationship. If needed, show willingness to compromise.

During the bargaining exchange, keep in mind that intangible benefits such as increases in power and status may sometimes be more desirable to your counterparts than financial gains may. Offers to provide continuing service to a Chilean client, in spite of long distances, can also be valuable bargaining concessions. Businesspeople in the country often find it difficult to overcome the isolation imposed on them by geography.

Deceptive techniques might be used and it may be effective to use some of them yourself. This includes tactics such as telling lies and sending fake non-verbal messages, pretending to be disinterested in the whole deal or in single concessions, or misrepresenting an item's value. None of these will be easy to see through. 'Good cop, bad cop' is a tactic that people rarely use, though it could be effective on either side of the negotiation table. However, it could be devastating if the other side recognized this as a tactic, and your team will need to exclude any 'bad cop' member from future negotiation rounds. Chileans may claim limited authority, stating that they have to ask for their manager's approval. This could be a tactic or the truth. Be cautious when using the techniques of making false demands or false concessions. Overt attempts to bluff your counterparts could backfire.

Negotiators in the country use pressure techniques very carefully since there is always a risk of hurting someone's pride. Opening with your best offer may work if presented right. Final offers and nibbling are rare and should be used with great caution. Never imply that your counterparts' only choices are 'take it or leave it' – they will very likely choose the latter. Silence can be a very effective way to signal rejection of a proposal or to obtain further concessions. Do not use pressure tactics such as applying time pressure or making expiring offers as these may be taken as signs that you are not willing to build a long-term relationship. Your counterparts may even choose to terminate the negotiation.

Chilean negotiators avoid openly aggressive or adversarial techniques. While they may make indirect threats and warnings or subtly display anger, they will be careful not to appear aggressive when doing so. Opening with an extreme offer could be viewed as an unfriendly act. It is best to open with one that is already in the ballpark of what you really expect. Never walk out or threaten to do so in an aggressive fashion as your counterparts will likely take this as a personal insult and may end all talks. However, threatening a 'friendly walkout' while strongly emphasizing the relationship may be very effective.

Emotional negotiation techniques, such as attitudinal bargaining, attempting to make you feel guilty, grimacing, or appealing to personal relationships, may occasionally be employed. It is best to remain calm. At times, Chileans may also employ defensive tactics such as changing the subject, asking probing or very direct questions, or making promises.

Corruption and bribery are rare in Chile, though not completely unheard of. Both legally and ethically, it is advisable to stay away from giving gifts of significant value or making offers that could be read as bribery.

Decision Making – Most companies tend to be very hierarchical, and people expect to work within clearly established lines of authority. Decision makers are usually top executives who will consider the best interest of the group or organization. In most cases, they will consult with others to reach greater consensus and support. They rarely delegate their authority, so it is important to deal with senior executives. Gaining access to top managers can be difficult, though. You may have to deal with subordinates who could strongly influence the final decision, which may be made behind closed doors. Maintaining good relationships with these intermediaries is crucial to your success. Decision making can be a slow process that requires much patience. Attempts to rush or put pressure on the process are not likely to succeed.

When making decisions, businesspeople may not rely much on rules or laws. They usually consider the specific situation rather than applying universal principles. Personal feelings and experiences weigh more strongly than empirical evidence and other objective facts do. Chileans are often uneasy with change and reluctant to take risks. If you expect them to support a risky decision, you may need to find ways for them to become comfortable with it first, for instance by explaining contingency plans, outlining areas of additional support, or by offering guarantees and warranties.

Agreements and Contracts

Capturing and exchanging written understandings after meetings and at key negotiation stages is useful since oral statements and even handshakes are not always dependable. Do not rely on interim agreements to be final, even if they come in the form of written protocols. Any part of an agreement may still change significantly before both parties sign the final contract.

Written contracts tend to be lengthy and often spell out detailed terms and conditions for the core agreements as well as for many eventualities. Nevertheless, writing up and signing the contract is a formality. Chileans believe that the primary strength of an agreement lies in the partners' commitment rather than in its written documentation.

It is strongly advisable to consult a local legal expert before signing a contract. However, do not bring in your attorney until the negotiations have concluded. Chileans may read it as a sign of mistrust if you do.

Contracts are usually dependable, and the agreed terms are viewed as binding. Although partners are expected to remain somewhat flexible, requests to change contract details after signature may meet with strong resistance.

Women in Business

Although many Chilean women are professionally advanced, *Machismo* attitudes remain strong in this country. Women may still be considered inferior, and they still rarely attain positions of similar income and authority as men. As a visiting businesswoman, emphasize your company's importance and your role in it. A personal introduction or at least a letter of support from a senior executive within your company may help a lot.

Female business travelers should graciously accept any chivalric gestures they receive, while exercising caution and acting professionally in business and social situations. Displaying confidence and some degree of assertiveness can be effective, but it is very important not to appear overly bold and aggressive.

Other Important Things to Know

Good posture and impeccable appearance are very important in Chile, as are proper etiquette and table manners. Dress conservatively and make sure shoes and suit are in excellent condition. First impressions can have a significant impact on how people view you.

Business lunches are common and can be extensive. They create good opportunities for business discussions.

Social events do not require strict punctuality. While it is best to arrive at dinners close to the agreed time, being late to a party by 30 minutes or more is perfectly acceptable.

Topics best avoided are the continuing tensions and conflicts between Chile and Argentina. Avoid making comparisons or talking about the similarities between the two countries. In addition, do not refer to citizens of the United States as Americans. Most Latin Americans are sensitive to this point as they feel that the term includes them. They prefer to say *norteamericanos* or *North Americans*.

China

The People's Republic of China is in the midst of a major transition from rigid communist country to a free-market society. Major style variances have evolved across the country's business population and must be considered when doing business here. For instance, significant cultural differences exist between rural and urban areas as well as between old people and younger ones. Generally, young people in major urban areas are more aggressive and willing to move faster than older ones in rural areas may be. Because of the highly competitive job markets in some of China's business hot spots, such as Shanghai or Shenzhen, employee turnover rates among the younger population is currently significant. This makes them more near-term oriented and less focused on relationships than other parts of the Chinese workforce. Nevertheless, the country's culture is quite homogeneous overall.

While most Chinese businesspeople and officials have only limited exposure to other cultures, some are very savvy in doing international business and may appear quite 'westernized.' Realize that people may expect things to be done 'their way,' though, and let them set the pace initially until you have had a chance to determine how your interaction can be most effective.

Owing to China's long period of isolation, there used to be a general bias against foreigners. This is gradually disappearing in many of the country's business centers. However, it is very important to show respect for the country's history and importance. While there is no problem with calling China a developing country, do not refer to it as a third-world country. After all, China's importance as a powerful nation reaches back some 5,000 years. It was the cradle for countless important inventions and has dominated the world as its economic center over the course of several centuries.

Relationships and Respect

China's culture is strongly group-oriented. Individual preferences are much less important than having a sense of belonging to a group, conforming to its norms, and maintaining harmony among its members. This is gradually changing among the younger generation, though. In any case, building lasting and trusting personal relationships is critically important. While members of other cultures may expect this to happen gradually over the course of a business engagement, many Chinese expect to establish strong bonds prior to closing any deals and to continue developing them into true friendships as the business partnership continues. Consequently, proceed with serious business discussions only after your counterparts have become comfortable with you, and keep in touch on a regular basis during negotiations and beyond. Since the Chinese orientation towards time is also different from most western countries, it is very important to remain patient and emphasize frequently the long-term benefits as well as your commitment to the business relationship you are seeking to build.

As in other Asian societies, relationships can create powerful networks. The Chinese concept, called *Guanxi*, is based on very strong commitments and mutual obligations. In western societies, people connected through close relationships expect certain favors of each other, but they are usually forgiving if circumstances get in the way. In China, such obligations are non-negotiable and must always be fulfilled. *Guanxi* can open doors and solve problems that would otherwise be very difficult to master. This makes relationship building vitally important when doing business in this culture. Being able to leverage *Guanxi* can be highly beneficial for a negotiator.

Relationships are based on familiarity, respect, and personal trust. Business relationships in this country exist between individuals or groups of people, not between companies. Even when you have won your local business partners' friendship and trust, they will not necessarily trust others from your company. That makes it very important to keep company interfaces unchanged. Changing a key contact may require the relationship building process to start over.

In Chinese culture, 'saving face' is very essential. Harmony must be maintained at all cost, and emotional restraint is held in high esteem. Causing embarrassment to another person may cause a *loss of face* for all parties involved and can be disastrous for business negotiations. Reputation and social standing strongly depend on a person's ability to control his or her emotions and remain friendly at all times. If you have to bring up an unpleasant topic with a person, never do so in public and always convey your message in ways that maintain the other's self-respect. The importance of diplomatic restraint and tact cannot be overestimated. Keep your cool and never show openly that you are upset. Also, consider that a person's *face* is a company's *face* – any individual employee's embarrassment may be felt by the whole company and could put you in a bad position.

Many Chinese, even among those with extensive international experience, consider the demanding and fast-paced western business style as arrogant or even rude. They are particularly critical of Westerners who appear to show off and 'blow their own horn.' Remaining modest and doing everything you can to maintain cordial relations is crucial to your success. When receiving praise, contrary to western practice, it is customary to insist that your are not worthy of it or to belittle your accomplishments. Thanking the other for the praise may be taken as arrogance since it signals that you accept the praise as valid. This should not stop you from complimenting others, though. While the Chinese view politeness and humility as essential ingredients for a successful relationship, these factors do not affect their determination to reach business goals. They are patient and persistent in pursuing their objectives. It is in your best interest to do the same.

In traditional Chinese business culture, the respect a person enjoys depends on age, rank, and, to a lesser degree, one's achievements. You will commonly find leaders in senior roles to be of advanced age. It is very important to treat elderly people with the greatest respect. Admired personal traits include patience, humility, and fine manners.

Communication

There are several related but different Chinese languages and dialects, the most important of which are Mandarin and Cantonese. While businesspeople may speak at least some English, their command of the language is often limited. It is usually best to use an interpreter, in which case it can be beneficial to employ your own one rather than relying on someone provided by your local counterparts. This will help you understand the subtleties of everything being said during your meetings. However, keep in mind that even professional interpreters may not always speak and understand English at a fully proficient level. When communicating in English, speak in short, simple sentences and avoid using slang and jargon. It will help people with a limited command of English if you speak slowly, summarize your key points often, and pause frequently to allow for interpretation.

Chinese businesspeople usually speak in quiet, gentle tones, and conversations may include periods of silence. At times, Chinese people talking among themselves may appear emotional, but this would be misleading. To the contrary, emotional restraint is held in high esteem. At restaurants, especially those used for business lunches and dinners, keep conversations at a quiet level. Loud and boisterous behavior is perceived as a lack of self-control. The Chinese generally converse while standing around three feet apart. However, it is also not unusual to encounter situations where a counterpart may seem to ignore one's personal space altogether.

Because the concept of 'saving face' is so important in this culture, communication is generally very indirect. When responding to a direct question, the Chinese may answer 'yes' only to signal that they heard what you said, not that they agree with it. Open disagreement should be avoided and any kind of direct confrontation is discouraged. People rarely respond to a question or request with a direct 'no.' Instead, they may give seemingly ambiguous answers such as 'I am not sure,' 'we will think about it,' or 'this will require further investigation.' Each of these could mean 'no.' It is beneficial to use a similarly indirect approach when dealing with the Chinese, as they may perceive you as rude and pushy if you are too direct. Only a person with whom you have no relationship yet may occasionally give you a straight 'no.' This is a bad sign since it could mean that your counterpart is not interested in engaging in business with you. If you have to convey bad news to the Chinese side, a face-saving way is to use a third party instead of communicating it yourself.

Gestures are usually very subtle in China. It is advisable to restrict your body language. Non-verbal communication is important, though, and you should carefully watch for others' small hints, just as they will be watching you. Avoid touching other people. Do not cross your legs if possible since this may be viewed as a lack of self-control. Also, do not use your hands when speaking since the Chinese will likely get distracted. When pointing at people or objects, use an open hand rather than a finger. Lightly tapping on the table using all fingers of one hand means 'thank you.' When referring to themselves, people put an index finger on their nose rather than pointing at their chest as Westerners do. It is considered improper to put your hand in your mouth or to cross your legs while seated. Eye contact should be infrequent. While it is beneficial to make some eye contact when meeting a person for the first time, the Chinese consider frequent eye contact intrusive and rude. It is generally considered respectful to look down when speaking with senior or elder people.

Do not take offense in the Chinese answering their mobile phones all the time, even in the middle of important discussions. In this polychronic culture, interrupting one conversation to have another one and then coming back to the first one is perfectly acceptable. It is not a sign of disrespect.

Initial Contacts and Meetings

Before initiating business negotiations in China, it is advantageous to identify and engage a local intermediary. This person will help bridge the cultural and communications gap, allowing you to conduct business with greater effectiveness. The person may be able to leverage existing relationships, which could significantly shorten the time it takes until your potential partner is ready to do business with you.

It is much better to conduct negotiations in China with a team of negotiators than to rely on a single individual. This signals importance, facilitates stronger relationship building, and may speed up the overall process. In addition, Chinese teams usually include highly skilled negotiators who know how to outmaneuver even well prepared individual counterparts. Facing them as a team will significantly strengthen your position. It is vital that teams be well aligned, with roles clearly assigned to each member. The Chinese may be very good at exploiting disagreements between members of the other team to their advantage. Changing a team member may require the relationship building process to start over and should therefore be avoided. Worst case, such a change can bring negotiations to a complete halt.

Given the strong emphasis on hierarchy in the country's business culture, a senior executive should lead major negotiations for your company and your negotiating team should include senior leaders who know your company well. In accordance with business protocol, people should enter the meeting room in hierarchical order. The Chinese may assume that the first foreigner to enter the room is the head of your delegation. The same is true on their side, allowing you to identify the most senior person. You may get other clues by observing who receives the highest amount of deference within a group of Chinese. That way, you may actually be able to identify the hierarchical structure across the whole group.

If possible, schedule meetings at least four weeks in advance. Since the Chinese want to know whom they will be meeting, provide details on titles, positions, and responsibilities of attendees ahead of time. Agreeing on an agenda upfront can also be useful. If you are trying to meet with company executives or high-ranking officials, be prepared for extensive back-and-forth communications until everything is finalized, and do not postpone or cancel meetings on short notice.

Punctuality expectations largely depend on the meeting participants' status and rank. The Chinese are careful not to waste a senior person's time. Being late to a meeting or social event without having a valid and plausible excuse can be a serious affront, so it is usually best to show up right on time. Meetings with lower-level managers are usually more flexible and may not even have a set time. In that case, arrive at your convenience and be prepared that you may be kept waiting for a while.

Chinese names are usually given in the order of family name, first name. The latter normally consists of two parts, the generational name and the given name. However, the two are often spoken and written as one. Some Chinese people use assumed western first names, in which case they give theirs in the order of first name followed by family name. When addressing people, use *Mr. /Ms.* plus the family name. Only close friends call each other by their first names, and you should never do so unless a person has explicitly asked you to. Furthermore, the Chinese are very status-conscious. If a person has a title or doctorate degree, use it to address him or her, for example, 'Doctor Yu' or 'Director Wang.' Introduce and greet older people first. Introductions are accompanied by handshakes and/or slight bows. Some people may not want to shake hands, so it is best to wait for your counterparts to initiate handshakes, which should be light and may last as long as ten seconds.

The exchange of business cards is an essential step when meeting someone for the first time, so bring more than you need. If someone presents you with his or her card and you do not offer one in return, the person will assume that you either do not want to make their acquaintance, that your status in your company's hierarchy is very low, or, quite to the contrary, that your status is very high. Since many people are unable to read English, it is better to use cards with one side in English and the other in Chinese. Show doctorate degrees on your card and make sure that it clearly states your professional title, especially if you have the seniority to make decisions. If any facts about your company are particularly noteworthy, for instance if it is the oldest or largest in your country or industry, mention this on your card since the Chinese view this very favorably. Also, consider having your company logo (but not the whole card) printed in gold ink. In Chinese culture, gold is the color of prosperity.

Present your business card with two hands, and ensure that the Chinese side is facing the recipient. Similarly, accept others' cards using both hands if possible. Smile and make eye contact while doing so, then examine the card carefully. Not reading someone's card can be an insult. Next, place the card on the table in front of you or into your card case. Never stuff someone's card into your back pocket or otherwise treat it disrespectfully. Do not write on a person's business card.

At the beginning of a meeting, there is normally some small talk. This allows participants to become personally acquainted. It is best to let the local side set the pace and follow along. People appreciate a sense of humor, but keep it light and friendly, and be careful not to overdo it. Business is a serious matter in China. While you will generally find the atmosphere to be pleasant at the first meeting, things may get more intense as the negotiation progresses.

The primary purpose of the first meeting is to get to know each other, start building relationships, and gather information about the other side's areas of interest, goals, and weak points for the upcoming negotiation. In general, meetings do not serve as events for decision-making. Instead, they are opportunities to indicate interest, intensify relationships, gather and exchange more information, or to communicate decisions. It would be unrealistic to expect a meeting to lead to a straight decision.

The most senior members of your group should lead the discussion. In Chinese business culture, it is inappropriate for subordinates to interrupt. It is good to make a presentation, but keep it simple and avoid over-designing it. Verify through diplomatic questions whether your audience understands you. Since saving *face* is so important, people will not openly admit it in front of others if they do not understand what you are presenting.

You will likely find the atmosphere of the first meeting to be pleasant and amicable. Do not take this to mean that your negotiation will be easy. People may turn tough and much more intense as soon as the real negotiation starts. In this culture of respecting each others' 'face,' the context of a situation often determines what behaviors are appropriate.

Most Chinese are comfortable with a high degree of initial vagueness. They may seem disinterested in clarifying many details until you have both come a long way with the business deal. Westerners may be uncomfortable with this perceived level of uncertainty. While it is acceptable and useful to try and clarify as much detail as possible even when your counterpart may not be eager to do so, do not read anything else into this style.

You should bring a sufficient number of copies of anything you present, such that each attendee gets one. The appearance of your presentation materials is not very important as long as you include good and easy-to-understand visuals. Use diagrams and pictures wherever feasible, cut down on words, and avoid complicated expressions. Because many colors have a special meaning in China, it is advisable to keep presentation copies, and even your actual slides, to black and white. Red is generally safe to use for illustrations and backgrounds since the Chinese consider it a happy color, but do not use it for text. Having your handout materials translated to Chinese is not a must, but it helps in getting your messages across.

You may have to make presentations to different levels of the organization in subsequent meetings; make sure that each is tailored to its audience. The Chinese side may also ask you at the end of the first meeting to sign a Letter of Intent. The role of this document is to confirm the seriousness of your intentions, not to serve as a legal contract. Check it carefully, though, since the Chinese may abruptly terminate the negotiation if you do not strictly follow your commitments.

When a meeting is over, you should leave before your Chinese counterparts.

Negotiation

Attitudes and Styles – In China, the primary approach to negotiating is to employ distributive and contingency bargaining. While the buyer is in a superior position, both sides in a business deal own the responsibility to reach agreement. They expect long-term commitments from their business partners and will focus mostly on long-term benefits. Although the primary negotiation style is competitive, the Chinese nevertheless value long-term relationships. Chinese negotiators may at times appear highly competitive or outright adversarial, fiercely bargaining for seemingly small gains. However, even when negotiating in a fairly direct and aggressive fashion, they ultimately maintain a long-term perspective and remain willing to compromise for the sake of the relationship. The culture promotes a win-win approach since this is the best way for everyone to save *face* throughout a negotiation. Do not confuse the sometimes-aggressive style with bad intentions. Keeping relationships intact throughout your negotiation is vital. It is best to remain calm, friendly, patient, and persistent, never taking anything personally. It will also be very important to maintain continuity in the objectives you pursue, the messages you deliver, and the people you include in the negotiation.

Should a dispute arise at any stage of a negotiation, you might be able to reach resolution through emphasizing the benefits to both sides, remaining flexible and showing willingness to compromise. Show your commitment to the relationship and refrain from using logical reasoning or becoming argumentative since this will only make matters worse. Patience and creativity will pay strong dividends. In extreme situations, leverage your local relationships (Guanxi) to influence your negotiation counterpart's decisions, or use a mediator, ideally the party who initially introduced you.

Sharing of Information – Chinese negotiators are willing to spend considerable time, sometimes many weeks or even months, gathering information and discussing various details before the bargaining stage of a negotiation can begin. Information is rarely shared freely, since the Chinese believe that privileged information creates bargaining advantages.

Be careful with what you are willing to share yourself and protect your intellectual property. In China, people may consider all information available to them a property they are entitled to use to their best interest.

Keep in mind that humility is a virtue in Chinese business culture. If you make exaggerated claims in an effort to impress the other side or to obtain concessions, they will likely investigate your claims before responding. This could prove very embarrassing.

Pace of Negotiation – Expect negotiations to be slow and protracted. Relationship building, information gathering, bargaining, and decision making may all take considerable time. Furthermore, negotiators often attempt to wear you down in an effort to obtain concessions. Be prepared to make several trips if necessary to achieve your objectives. Throughout the negotiation, be patient, show little emotion, and accept that delays occur.

The Chinese generally employ a polychronic work style. They are used to pursuing multiple actions and goals in parallel. When negotiating, they often take a holistic approach and may jump back and forth between topics rather than addressing them in sequential order. In multi-item negotiations, people may bargain and haggle over several aspects in parallel. It is not unusual for them to re-open a discussion over items that had already been agreed upon. In addition, they may take phone calls or interrupt meetings at critical points in a negotiation. While they may be doing some of this on purpose in order to confuse the other side, there are usually no bad intentions. Negotiators from strongly monochronic cultures, such as Germany, the United Kingdom, or the United States, may nonetheless find this style highly confusing and irritating. In any case, do not show irritation or anger when encountering this behavior. Instead, keep track of the bargaining progress at all times, often emphasizing areas where agreement already exists.

If your counterparts appear to be stalling the negotiation, assess carefully whether their slowing down the process indicates that they are evaluating alternatives or that they are not interested in doing business with you. While such behavior could represent attempts to create time pressure in order to obtain concessions, the slow decision process in the country is far more likely causing the lack of progress. People from fast-paced cultures tend to underestimate how much time this takes and often make the mistake of trying to 'speed things up.' Again, patience and persistence are vitally important.

Bargaining – Chinese businesspeople are often shrewd negotiators who should not be underestimated. Bargaining and haggling are aspects of everyday life, and people may use a wide array of negotiation techniques quite competently.

The bargaining stage of a negotiation can be extensive. Prices may move by 40 percent or more between initial offers and final agreement. Leave yourself sufficient room for concessions at many different levels and prepare several alternative options. This gives the Chinese negotiators room to refuse aspects of your proposal while preserving face. Ask the other side to reciprocate if you make concessions. It is not advisable to make significant early concessions since your counterparts expect further compromises as the bargaining continues. You can use the fact that aspects can be re-visited to your advantage, for instance by offering further concessions under the condition that the Chinese side reciprocate in areas that had already been agreed upon.

Deceptive techniques are frequently employed, and Chinese negotiators may expect you to use some of them as well. This includes tactics such as telling lies and sending fake non-verbal messages, pretending to be disinterested in the whole deal or in single concessions, misrepresenting an item's value, or making false demands and concessions. It is advisable to verify information received from the local side through other channels. Similarly, they treat 'outside' information with caution. Since negotiation teams must be well aligned and always have to preserve face, people rarely use 'good cop, bad cop.' It can sometimes be beneficial to use these tactics in your own negotiation approach. Carefully orchestrated, they may allow you to obtain valuable concessions without damaging the overall relationship. However, it could be devastating if the other side recognized this as a tactic, and any 'bad cop' member of your team also needs to be excluded from future negotiation rounds. The Chinese are not likely to use the 'limited authority' technique because groups rather than individuals normally make decisions. Be cautious when using the techniques of making false demands or false concessions. Since you must avoid causing loss of face, any overt attempts to bluff your counterparts could also backfire.

Negotiators may use pressure techniques that include keeping silent, making final or expiring offers, applying time pressure, or nibbling. Silence can sometimes be effective as a way to convey displeasure. Skilled Chinese negotiators may remain silent for a long time without showing any impatience. Don't let this fool you into thinking that they are not interested. Final offers may be made more than once and are almost never final. Do not announce any of your offers as 'final'– your counterparts will likely not believe that you are serious and may turn the tactic against you. Time pressure can be difficult to counter. If Chinese negotiators learn that you are working against a deadline, they may exploit this knowledge to increase the pressure on you to make concessions. Near the end of a negotiation, they may suddenly request large discounts, calling their request a 'compromise.' In extreme cases, they may try to renegotiate the whole deal on the final day of your visit. It is important never to take such techniques personally and to avoid open conflict. On the other hand, time pressure techniques rarely work against them since the Chinese are patient and persistent enough to overcome such challenges. However, you might be able to use these techniques should the negotiation take place on your home turf rather than in China. Nibbling may prove useful in the final phases of negotiations. None of this will take your counterparts by surprise, though. Avoid other common pressure tactics such as opening with your best offer or showing intransigence, since they cannot be applied effectively without running the risk of causing loss of face.

Chinese negotiators avoid most aggressive or adversarial techniques since they affect face. The risk of using any of them yourself is rarely worth the potential gain. Exceptions are extreme openings, which people use frequently, as well as threats and warnings. As long as extreme opening offers are not openly aggressive, this approach can be effective. Should your counterparts appear aggressive as the bargaining gets more heated, remind yourself that they may not perceive it that way. It might be wise to deflect the pressure, for example by explaining other arrangements you have accepted for similar deals in the past.

As in most strongly relationship-oriented cultures, negotiators may sometimes use emotional techniques such as attitudinal bargaining, attempting to make you feel guilty, grimacing, or appealing to personal relationships. Be cautious when doing this yourself. You might cause the other side to lose face, which could damage your negotiating position.

At times, defensive negotiation tactics may be used. The exception is directness, which is rare in China. People may be shocked if you are overly direct yourself, which can be counterproductive.

Note that opening with written offers and attempting to introduce written terms and conditions as a negotiation tactic is rarely successful. In most cases, businesspeople ignore or tactfully reject them and request that each aspect be negotiated individually.

Corruption and bribery are quite common in China's public and private sectors. However, people may draw the line differently, viewing minor payments as rewards for getting a job done rather than as bribes. Also, keep in mind that there is a fine line between giving gifts and bribing. What you may consider a bribe, a Chinese may view as only a nice gift. It may help if you introduce and explain your company's policies early on, but be careful not to moralize or appear to imply that local customs are unethical.

Decision Making – Organizations are usually very hierarchical. However, while you may sometimes encounter a western-style entrepreneur as the sole decision maker within their company, decision making is normally a consensus-oriented group process in China. This can be confusing for Westerners looking to identify the 'key decision maker' in an organization, while in reality such a role may not exist at all. Decisions are often made through a process involving many stakeholders who establish consensus through a series of deliberations and internal politics outsiders have very limited insight into. This process can take a long time and requires patience. Influencing the decision making requires understanding the Chinese side's intentions and building strong relationships with as many of the stakeholders as you possibly can. The role of the senior leaders is to orchestrate the process, not to make decisions themselves. Nevertheless, their input carries a lot of weight and they sometimes have the final say, so do everything you can to win their consent and support.

While the People's Republic has made significant strides to open its economy to global trade, do not underestimate the extent to which government bureaucrats still influence company decisions. It is wise to contact national, provincial, and local government representatives to fill them in upfront about your plans to negotiate with a local company. That way, you are more likely to receive preferential treatment from your desired partner as they do not want to displease their government. If your business interactions include a party or local government representative, it is essential to include the person in the negotiation and treat him or her as a senior decision maker, even if the person is or appears to be unfamiliar with the subject.

When making decisions, Chinese businesspeople may not rely much on rules or laws. They usually consider the specific situation rather than applying universal principles. Personal feelings and experiences weigh more strongly than empirical evidence and other objective facts do. Exceptions exist where party rules force them to be more dogmatic. The Chinese are often reluctant to take risks. If you expect them to support a risky decision, you may need to find ways for them to become comfortable with it first. You are much more likely to succeed if the relationship with your counterparts is strong and you managed to win their trust.

Agreements and Contracts

Capturing and exchanging written understandings after meetings and at key negotiation stages is useful since oral statements are not always dependable. While these serve as tools to improve the communication and strengthen commitments, they should not be taken for final agreements. Any part of an agreement may still change significantly before both parties sign the final contract.

It is important to realize that the Chinese have a very different view of written agreements and contracts from the one most Westerners have. While the People's Republic realizes that it needs to establish and enforce the necessary legal framework to participate in global trade, most businesspeople rely primarily on the strength of relationships rather than on written agreements when doing business. In the traditional Chinese view, agreements are just snapshots in time. They view contracts as papers that document the intent of a working relationship at the time they were written up and signed, not as final agreements that can stand the test of litigation.

Written contracts are usually kept high-level, capturing only the primary aspects, terms, and conditions of the agreement. Writing up and signing the contract is a formality. The Chinese believe that the primary strength of an agreement lies in the partners' commitment rather than in its written documentation. Before signing a contract, read it carefully. The local side may have made modifications without flagging them. While this could be perceived as bad-faith negotiation in other cultures, Chinese businesspeople may view the changes as clarifications.

Although your legal rights may not be enforceable, you should consult a local legal expert, ideally throughout the negotiation or at the very least before signing a contract. However, do not bring an attorney to the negotiation table, since this may be taken as a sign that you do not trust your counterparts.

Contracts alone are not dependable. Because of their view of the role that contracts play, the Chinese often continue to press for a better deal even after a contract has been signed. They may call 'clarification meetings' to re-discuss details. If you refuse to be flexible, allowing the relationship to deteriorate, contract terms may not be kept at all. Arbitration clauses often do little to resolve such a situation since arbitration can be very one-sided in China. Your best chance to ensure that your partners follow through on their commitments is to stay in regular contact and nurture the relationship throughout your business engagement.

Women in Business

Gender roles in China are clearly distinct. Although women officially have the same rights as men, they rarely manage to reach positions of similar income and authority. However, western-style equality is beginning to have an influence in urban areas.

As a visiting businesswoman, you will generally encounter few problems when visiting China, provided that you exercise caution and act professionally in business and social situations. Displaying confidence and some degree of assertiveness can be effective, but it is very important not to appear overly bold and aggressive. If you feel that your counterparts may be questioning your competence, it can be helpful to emphasize your company's importance and your role in it. A personal introduction or at least a letter of support from a senior executive within your company may help a lot. If a negotiating team includes women, it will be wise to let the Chinese side know about this up front so they can mentally prepare for it.

Other Important Things to Know

Business meals and entertainment, in particular banquets and other evening events, are very important as they help advance the vital process of building strong relationships. Refusing to participate in such activities is a signal that you are not seriously interested in doing business with your counterparts. Although business usually is not discussed during these events, there could be exceptions. Your Chinese counterparts may use them as opportunities to convey important messages or resolve disputes. Sometimes they may also try to obtain information from you that could strengthen their negotiating position. While you want to remain watchful, deflecting such inquiries if needed, never show signs of mistrust in your counterparts' intentions.

Especially with local companies that lack international expertise, business entertainment may sometimes include invitations Westerners may find highly inappropriate. In such cases, it will be very important to find a way to avoid the issue without openly rejecting the invitation, as this helps preserve *face* for all involved.

Gift giving is common in social and business settings in China. If you received one, it is best to reciprocate with an item of similar value that is typical of your home country. Giving a gift after signing a contract is viewed very favorably. Give and accept gifts using both hands. Do not open gifts in the presence of the giver unless your host did so first. There are numerous potential pitfalls in what to give and how to wrap it, so prepare upfront or ask someone from the country to avoid causing embarrassment.

Topics to avoid in discussions are China's relationship with Taiwan, Hong Kong's changing role, or negative aspects around the government, such as the censorship it exerts over the media and the Internet.

Colombia

Businesspeople and officials in Colombia usually have only limited exposure to other cultures except for neighboring countries. Its culture is quite homogeneous. When negotiating business here, people often expect things to be done 'their way.' However, some among younger generations may have greater international experience and can be more open-minded.

Relationships and Respect

Colombia's culture is generally group-oriented. Asserting individual preferences may be seen as less important than having a sense of belonging to a group, conforming to its norms, and maintaining harmony among its members. Building lasting and trusting personal relationships is very important to most Colombians, who often find it essential to establish strong bonds prior to closing any deals. People in this country usually want to do business only with those they know, like, and trust. If they initially seem suspicious and non-committal, you may be able to overcome this with consistent friendliness and goodwill. Establishing productive business cooperation requires a long-term perspective and commitment. Proceed with serious business discussions only after your counterparts have become very comfortable with you. This process can take even longer in Colombia than in other Latin American countries. It will probably require several trips to strengthen the bonds. Colombians tend to distrust people who appear unwilling to spend the time or whose motives for relationship building are unclear.

Business relationships in this country exist between people, not necessarily between companies. Even when you have won your local business partners' friendship and trust, they will not necessarily trust others from your company. That makes it very important to keep company interfaces unchanged. Changing a key contact may require the relationship building process to start over.

Establishing personal relationships with others in Colombia can create very powerful networks and may help you a lot to achieve your business objectives. Whom you know may determine whether people want to get to know you. Similarly, whether people think you are worth knowing and trusting often weighs much more strongly than how competent you are or what proposals you may have to make. Personal networks may open doors and solve problems that would otherwise be difficult to master. Maintaining honest and cordial relations is crucial. Third party introductions can be very helpful as a starting point to building a trusting relationship with a potential partner.

In Colombia's business culture, the respect a person enjoys depends primarily on his or her status, rank, and education. Admired personal traits include sincerity, integrity, and charisma.

Communication

While the country's official language is Spanish, it is notably different from the Spanish spoken in Spain. Many businesspeople speak at least some English, but being able to speak Spanish is a clear advantage. With high-ranking managers, it may otherwise be useful to engage an interpreter. To avoid offending the other side, ask beforehand whether an interpreter should be present at a meeting. When communicating in English, speak in short, simple sentences and avoid using jargon and slang. It will help people with a limited command of English if you speak slowly, summarize your key points often, and pause frequently to allow for interpretation. Even when the main meeting language is English, your counterparts may frequently speak Spanish among themselves, not necessarily to shut you out from the discussion but to reduce their discomfort and ensure a common understanding among them.

Colombians tend to be very formal. They usually speak softly. While they may occasionally raise their voices to make a point, they dislike loud and boisterous behavior. At restaurants, especially those used for business lunches and dinners, keep conversations at a quiet level. Emotions are usually not shown openly. People may converse in close proximity, standing only two feet or less apart. Never back away, even if this is much closer than your personal comfort zone allows. Doing so could be read as a sign that you are uncomfortable around them.

Communication in Colombia is usually not overly direct. People may not get straight to the point when trying to get a message across and you may have to read between the lines to understand what is being conveyed. They may tell you what they think you want to hear rather than what they really think. Silence may express embarrassment or otherwise communicate a negative message. It is beneficial to use a similarly indirect approach when dealing with Colombians, as they may perceive you as rude and pushy if you are too direct. The communication may become more direct and frank once a strong relationship has been established. However, Colombians may not find it difficult to say 'no' if they dislike a request or proposal.

Gestures and body language can be lively, especially if they help underline what is being said. There may be frequent physical contact with others of the same gender. This may include touching your arm while speaking to you. Friends may embrace while slapping each other's backs. The American *OK* sign, with thumb and index finger forming a circle, can be read as an obscene gesture in Colombia. Eye contact should be very frequent, almost to the point of staring. This conveys sincerity and helps build trust. Yawning in public is impolite.

Initial Contacts and Meetings

Choosing a local intermediary, or *enchufado,* who can leverage existing relationships to make the initial contact is highly recommended. This person will help bridge the gap between cultures, allowing you to conduct business with greater effectiveness.

It is often better to conduct negotiations in Colombia with a team of negotiators rather than to rely on a single individual. This signals importance, facilitates stronger relationship building, and may speed up the overall process. It is vital that teams be well aligned, with roles clearly assigned to each member. Colombian negotiators may be very good at exploiting disagreements between members of the other team to their advantage. Changing a team member may require the relationship building process to start over and should therefore be avoided.

Given the strong emphasis on hierarchy in the country's business culture, a senior executive should attend the initial meeting for your company and your negotiating team should include senior leaders who know your company well. There will not be an expectation that the executive attends future meetings. Similarly, the top executive on the Colombian side who is likely the ultimate decision maker may attend only initially. The most senior executive to attend throughout the negotiation on the Colombian side will likely be at a similar level in the hierarchy as your own negotiation leader.

If possible, schedule meetings at least two to three weeks in advance. Since Colombians want to know whom they will be meeting, provide details on titles, positions, and responsibilities of attendees ahead of time. While meetings may start considerably late, people generally expect foreign visitors to be punctual. Avoid being more than 10 to 15 minutes late, and call ahead if you will be. Displaying anger if you have to wait reflects very poorly on you.

Names are usually given in the order of first name, family names. Most Colombians have two family names, the first one from their father, and the second one from their mother. Use *Mr./Mrs./Miss* or *Señor/Señora/Señorita,* plus the father's family name, which is always the first one of the two family names given. If a person has an academic title, such as *Doctor* or *Professor,* use it instead, followed by the father's family name. Only close friends call each other by their first names. It is important to take your time with introductions and greetings, never appearing rushed. Introductions are accompanied by handshakes.

The exchange of business cards is an essential step when meeting someone for the first time, so bring more than you need. It is recommended to use cards with one side in English and the other in Spanish. Show doctorate degrees on your card and make sure that it clearly states your professional title, especially if you have the seniority to make decisions. When presenting your card, ensure that the Spanish side is facing the recipient. Smile and keep eye contact while accepting someone else's card, then carefully examine it. Next, place the card on the table in front of you.

Meetings start with small talk, which may be extensive. This may include personal questions about your background and family, allowing participants to become acquainted. It is important to be patient and let the other side set the pace. Initial meetings may appear formal, but the atmosphere usually is a bit more relaxed in subsequent meetings. People appreciate a sense of humor, but keep it light and friendly, and be careful not to overdo it. Business is a serious matter in Colombia. Meetings may appear somewhat chaotic, with frequent interruptions and several parallel conversations. Do not take this personally; it also does not indicate a lack of interest.

The purpose of the first meeting, maybe also the second one, is to become acquainted and build relationships. Business may be discussed, but do not try to hurry along with your agenda. Colombians dislike people who try to get to the point quickly. The goal should be to establish respect and trust between yourself and your counterparts. It is unrealistic to expect initial meetings to lead to straight decisions.

Presentation materials should be attractive, with good and clear visuals. Use diagrams and pictures wherever feasible, cut down on words, and avoid complicated expressions. Having your handout materials translated to Spanish is not a must, but it will be appreciated and helps in getting your messages across.

When the meeting is over, stay around and have some more small talk with your Colombian counterparts. Leaving right away suggests that you have better things to do and may offend others.

Negotiation

Attitudes and Styles - Leveraging relationships is an important element when negotiating in Colombia. Nevertheless, Colombians often employ distributive and contingency bargaining. While the buyer is in a superior position, both sides in a business deal own the responsibility to reach agreement. They expect long-term commitments from their business partners and will focus mostly on long-term benefits. Although the primary negotiation style is competitive, Colombians nevertheless value long-term relationships. While proposals should demonstrate the benefits to both negotiating parties, neither of them should take attempts to win competitive advantages negatively. It is critically important to remain non-confrontational and avoid direct conflict throughout the bargaining exchange. Ultimately, the culture promotes a win-win approach. You will earn your counterparts' respect by maintaining a positive, persistent attitude.

Should a dispute arise at any stage of a negotiation, you might be able to reach resolution by leveraging personal relationships and emphasizing long-term benefits. Patience and creativity will pay strong dividends.

Sharing of Information – Even when personal relationships are strong, your Colombian counterparts may be reluctant to share information openly. Many believe that privileged information creates bargaining advantages.

Pace of Negotiation – Expect negotiations to be slow and protracted. Colombians do not hurry and dislike people who do. Be prepared to make several trips if necessary to achieve your objectives. Relationship building, information gathering, bargaining, and decision making may take considerable time. Attempts to rush the process are unlikely to produce better results and may be viewed as offensive. Throughout the negotiation, be patient, control your emotions, and accept the inevitable delays.

Most Colombians prefer a polychronic work style. They are used to pursuing multiple actions and goals in parallel. When negotiating, they often take a holistic approach and may jump back and forth between topics rather than addressing them in sequential order. Negotiators from strongly monochronic cultures, such as Germany, the United Kingdom, or the United States, may find this style confusing, irritating, and even annoying. In any case, do not show irritation or anger when encountering this behavior. Instead, keep track of the bargaining progress at all times, often emphasizing areas where agreement already exists.

If your counterparts appear to be stalling the negotiation, assess carefully whether their slowing down the process indicates that they are evaluating alternatives or that they are not interested in doing business with you. More likely, this behavior either represents an attempt to create time pressure in order to obtain concessions, or it simply reflects the slow decision process in the country. Again, patience and persistence are vitally important.

Bargaining – Colombians are used to hard bargaining but generally dislike excessive haggling. They can be tough negotiators and the bargaining exchange is sometimes extensive. Although they may show interest in new ideas and concepts, Colombians often find it difficult to change their position. Since overly compromising is viewed as a sign of weakness, requesting a compromise may become an issue of pride if presented in the wrong way. Be respectful throughout the bargaining exchange. Rather than pushing for concessions, it may be better to re-address disagreements in follow-up meetings, which gives your counterparts the opportunity to reconsider their position without overtly losing face. Prices may move by about 25 to 35 percent between initial offer and final agreement. Leave yourself sufficient room for concessions at different stages. However, they will never come easily. After making concessions yourself, always ask the other side to reciprocate. Throughout the process, remain cool and respectful, avoid confrontation, and frequently reaffirm the relationship.

During the bargaining exchange, keep in mind that intangible benefits such as increases in power and status may sometimes be more desirable to your counterparts than financial gains may.

Deceptive techniques are frequent and can be effective. This includes tactics such as telling lies and sending fake non-verbal messages, pretending to be disinterested in the whole deal or in single concessions, misrepresenting an item's value, or making false demands and concessions. Your Colombian counterparts may play stupid or make other attempts to mislead you in order to obtain bargaining advantages. Even when you can see right through a lie, it would be a grave personal insult to state or even hint that your counterpart is not telling the truth. It is advisable to verify information received from the local side through other channels. 'Good cop, bad cop' may be used and could prove effective on either side of the negotiation table. However, it could be devastating if the other side recognized this as a tactic, and your team will need to exclude any 'bad cop' member from future negotiation rounds. Colombians may claim limited authority, stating that they have to ask for their manager's approval. This is usually the truth.

Negotiators in the country may use pressure techniques that include making final offers, showing intransigence, or nibbling. Final offers may come more than once and are rarely final. Be careful when trying to open with your best offer. Colombians may consider this inappropriate or even insulting. Silence can be an effective way to signal rejection of a proposal or to obtain further concessions. Do not use pressure tactics such as applying time pressure or making expiring offers as these may be taken as signs that you are not willing to build a long-term relationship. Your counterparts may even choose to terminate the negotiation.

Colombian negotiators avoid openly aggressive or adversarial techniques. While they may make indirect threats and warnings or subtly display anger, they will be careful not to appear aggressive when doing so. Extreme openings are not frequently used since they may adversely affect the relationship, so be very cautious when using the tactic yourself. Never walk out or threaten to do so in an aggressive fashion as your counterparts will likely take this as a personal insult and may end all talks. However, threatening a 'friendly walkout' while strongly emphasizing the relationship may be very effective.

Emotional negotiation techniques, such as attitudinal bargaining or attempting to make you feel guilty, are frequent and can be effective. Be cautious not to hurt someone's personal pride when employing any of these tactics, though. Pleas to personal relationships and other emotional appeals, such as emphasizing how your proposal will add to your counterparts' personal satisfaction or heighten their honor, can be very powerful. Colombians may frequently employ defensive tactics such as blocking or changing the subject, asking probing or very direct questions, making promises, or keeping an inflexible position.

Corruption and bribery are somewhat common in Colombia's public and private sectors. However, people may draw the line differently, viewing minor payments as rewards for getting a job done rather than as bribes. Also, keep in mind that there is a fine line between giving gifts and bribing. What you may consider a bribe, a Colombian may view as only a nice gift.

Decision Making – Most companies tend to be very hierarchical, and people expect to work within clearly established lines of authority. Many businesses in Colombia are still family-owned. Decision makers are usually heads of family or senior executives who will consider the best interest of the group or organization. While they may consult with others and prefer to reach consensus before making the final call, bosses accept all of the responsibility. Authority is rarely delegated, so it is important to deal with senior executives. At the same time, subordinates may strongly influence the final decision and maintaining good relationships with them can be crucial to your success. Although the pace of business is accelerating, decision making can be a slow process that requires much patience. Attempts to rush or put pressure on the process are not likely to succeed.

When making decisions, businesspeople may not rely much on rules or laws. They usually consider the specific situation rather than applying universal principles. Personal feelings and experiences weigh much more strongly than empirical evidence and other objective facts do. Colombians are often uneasy with change and reluctant to take risks. If you expect them to support a risky decision, you may need to find ways for them to become comfortable with it first, for instance by explaining contingency plans, outlining areas of additional support, or by offering guarantees and warranties.

Agreements and Contracts

Capturing and exchanging written understandings after meetings and at key negotiation stages is useful. Oral commitments may sound stronger than what your Colombian counterparts may be willing to put in writing. Do not rely on interim agreements to be final, even if they come in the form of written protocols. Any part of an agreement may still change significantly before both parties sign the final contract.

Written contracts tend to be lengthy and often spell out detailed terms and conditions for the core agreements as well as for many eventualities. Nevertheless, writing up and signing the contract is a formality. Colombians believe that the primary strength of an agreement lies in the partners' commitment rather than in its written documentation.

It is advisable to consult a local legal expert before signing a contract. However, do not bring in your attorney until the negotiations have concluded. Colombians may read it as a sign of mistrust if you do.

Signed contracts may not always be honored. This depends to no small degree on the strength of the continuing relationship between the contract partners. It is strongly advisable to continue staying in touch and maintaining the trust of your Colombian business partner. Business partners usually expect the other side to remain somewhat flexible if conditions change, which may include agreeing to modify contract terms. Given the relatively unstable political and economic situation in the country, you should factor this possibility into your negotiation planning.

Women in Business

Machismo attitudes remain strong in this country. However, women are more involved in business life than elsewhere in Latin America, although they rarely attain positions of similar income and authority as men. As a visiting businesswoman, it is often effective to emphasize your company's importance and your role in it.

Female business travelers should graciously accept any chivalric gestures they receive, while exercising caution and acting professionally in business and social situations. Displaying confidence and some degree of assertiveness can be effective, but it is very important not to appear overly bold and aggressive.

Other Important Things to Know

Social events do not require strict punctuality. While it is best to arrive at dinners close to the agreed time, being late to a party by 30 minutes or more is perfectly acceptable.

Do not refer to citizens of the United States as Americans. Most Latin Americans are sensitive to this point as they feel that the term includes them. They prefer to say *norteamericanos* or *North Americans*.

Colombia is a high-crime country. International visitors potentially face mugging, burglary, and even kidnapping. It is strongly advisable to dress inconspicuously and leave status symbols such as expensive watches or briefcases at home.

Czech Republic

The western part of former Czechoslovakia, the Czech Republic became an independent political entity when the country and Slovakia separated in 1993. Culturally and ethnically, it is very homogenous. Owing to its history within the former Eastern Bloc until 1989, some businesspeople and officials in the Czech Republic may have only limited exposure to other cultures except for neighboring countries. However, many Czechs, especially those among younger generations and people living in Prague, have gained greater international experience since then and are open-minded.

Relationships and Respect

While building trust matters, business relationships are only moderately important in this country. They are usually not a necessary precondition for initial business interactions. Your Czech counterparts may appear friendly but somewhat reserved even after they have had several business interactions with you. However, most of them will eventually open up, so take the time needed to strengthen the relationship. Asking personal questions is acceptable and may help you get closer to your counterparts.

Business relationships in this country exist both at the individual and company level. However, if your company replaces you with someone else over the course of a negotiation, it may be easy for your replacement to take things over from where you left them. Likewise, if you introduce someone else from your company into an existing business relationship, that person may quickly be accepted as a valid business partner.

In the Czech Republic's business culture, the respect a person enjoys depends primarily on his or her experience and achievements, though the Czechs are generally not as result-driven as Americans are. Admired personal traits include creativity, flexibility, and analytical thinking.

Communication

The country's official language, Czech, is closely related with Polish. Many people also speak Russian. Most younger businesspeople speak English at a conversational level. With older people, among them some high-ranking managers, it may occasionally be useful to engage an interpreter. To avoid offending the other side, ask beforehand whether an interpreter should be present at a meeting. When communicating in English, speak in short, simple sentences and avoid using slang and jargon. It will help people with a limited command of English if you speak slowly, summarize your key points often, and pause frequently to allow for interpretation.

People in this country usually speak softly. While they may occasionally raise their voices to make a point, they dislike loud and boisterous behavior. At restaurants, keep conversations at a quiet level. Emotions are not shown openly. People generally converse while standing around three feet apart.

While the communication may initially be somewhat indirect, it will likely become more direct, though never blunt, once a Czech knows and trusts you. At that point, people will not find it difficult to say 'no' if they dislike a request or proposal. Silence could signal that there is a problem, especially when they also lower their eyes.

Czechs tend to use body language sparingly, and there is little physical contact between people. They may not understand the American *OK* sign, with thumb and index finger forming a circle. Eye contact should be frequent, almost to the point of staring. This conveys sincerity and helps build trust.

Initial Contacts and Meetings

Having a local contact can be an advantage but is usually not a necessary precondition to doing business. Negotiations in the Czech Republic can be conducted by individuals or teams of negotiators.

Scheduling meetings in advance is required. However, you can sometimes do this on short notice if the parties had previous business interactions. You may be unable to meet the top executive of an organization at the first meeting, so be prepared to deal with subordinates. They may have significant influence over the final decision. While meetings may not always start on time, Czechs generally expect foreign visitors to be punctual. Avoid being more than 10 to 15 minutes late, and call ahead if you will be.

Names are usually given in the order of first name, family name. Use *Mr./Ms./Miss* plus the family name. If a person has an academic title, always use it instead, followed by the family name. Among Czechs, only close friends call each other by their first names. However, many have grown accustomed to foreigners and use first names when communicating with them. Introduce or greet the most senior person first. Thereafter, greet everyone else individually. Introductions are accompanied by firm and brief handshakes.

The exchange of business cards is an essential step when meeting someone for the first time, so bring more than you need. You may not always get one in return, though. Most businesspeople in the Czech Republic read English, so there is no need to have your card translated. Show doctorate degrees on your card, since Czechs highly value formal education. Also, make sure that it clearly states your professional title, especially if you have the seniority to make decisions. When presenting your card, smile and keep eye contact, then take a few moments to look at the card you received.

Meetings usually start with some small talk intended to establish personal rapport, which could be brief. People appreciate a sense of humor, but keep it light and friendly, and be careful not to overdo it. Business is a serious matter in this country. The first meeting may be quite formal, but this usually gets more relaxed down the road. Its primary purpose is to become acquainted. Business will be discussed, but do not try to hurry along with your agenda.

Presentation materials can be simple without colorful backgrounds and fancy graphs. However, good and easy-to-understand visuals are important. Having your handout materials translated to Czech is not a must, but it will be noted favorably.

Negotiation

Attitudes and Styles – To the Czechs, negotiating is usually a joint problem-solving process. While the buyer is in a superior position, both sides in a business deal own the responsibility to reach agreement. They may focus equally on near-term and long-term benefits. Although the primary negotiation style is competitive, Czechs nevertheless value long-term relationships and look for win-win solutions. Negotiators may at times appear stubborn and unwilling to compromise. It is best to avoid any open confrontation and to remain calm, friendly, patient, and persistent, never taking anything personally.

Should a dispute arise at any stage of a negotiation, you might be able to reach resolution by focusing on logical arguments and facts while remaining open and constructive.

Sharing of Information - Czechs usually play their cards close to the chest, although some may share information as a way to build trust. Like their German neighbors, Czechs often follow a methodical and carefully planned approach in preparing for the negotiation and gathering information. Aspects of your proposals may be scrutinized repeatedly.

Pace of Negotiation – Although the pace of business is increasing, expect negotiations to be slow and protracted. Be prepared to make several trips if necessary to achieve your objectives. Remain patient, control your emotions, and accept that delays may occur.

Bargaining – While businesspeople in the country may have learned the ground rules of international negotiations, their experience is usually limited. Most of them are not fond of bargaining and strongly dislike haggling. However, Czechs may be very persistent negotiators and it can be very difficult to obtain concessions from them. Although the bargaining stage of a negotiation can be extensive, prices rarely move by more than 15 to 25 percent between initial offers and final agreement. It can be hard to get a Czech to change an offer already made, so even seemingly small concessions may take some tough bargaining. In addition, local negotiators may make last-minute attempts to change agreed pricing, sometimes pretending they 'forgot' what had previously been discussed.

Czechs often prefer a straightforward negotiation style. They use deceptive techniques only infrequently, such as telling lies, pretending to be disinterested in the whole deal or in single concessions, misrepresenting an item's value, or making false demands and concessions. Carefully orchestrated, 'good cop, bad cop' may be an effective tactic to use in your own negotiation approach. Czechs may claim limited authority, stating that they have to ask for their manager's approval. More often than not, this will be the truth.

Negotiators in the country can appear very intransigent, which may not be a conscious tactic but could nonetheless increase the pressure on you. If they announce an offer as final, they likely mean it, even if this is done early in the bargaining process. If Czechs appear to be creating time pressure, their primary motivation may be to shorten the negotiation process. Silence could simply be a part of the conversation, although it may also signal rejection of a proposal. Nibbling and making expiring offers is rare. Either of these tactics may be viewed as overly aggressive. Be careful when using pressure tactics such as applying time pressure or making expiring offers. Czechs may consider these inappropriate unless they are strongly interested in your offer and clearly understand the rationale behind the approach. Otherwise, while the negotiation is not necessarily over, it may become less constructive.

Czech negotiators avoid most aggressive or adversarial techniques since they dislike open confrontation. The risk of using such tactics yourself may not be worth the potential gain. While they may use subtle threats and warnings, Czechs rarely openly display anger or walk out of the room. Extreme openings may be viewed as unfriendly. It is best to open with an offer that is already in the ballpark of what you really expect.

Emotional negotiation techniques, such as attitudinal bargaining, attempting to make you feel guilty, or grimacing, may occasionally be employed. It is best to remain calm. At times, Czechs may also employ defensive tactics such as changing the subject, asking probing or very direct questions, or making promises. They may often keep an inflexible position.

Introducing written terms and conditions may be effective as this approach helps shorten the bargaining process, which your Czech counterparts might find desirable.

As the country is moving from a socialist country to a free-market economy, corruption and bribery have become somewhat common in the Czech Republic's public and private sectors. However, people may draw the line differently, viewing minor payments as rewards for getting a job done rather than as bribes. Also, keep in mind that there is a fine line between giving gifts and bribing. What you may consider a bribe, a Czech may view as only a nice gift.

Decision Making – Companies are often hierarchical, and people may expect to work within clearly established lines of authority. However, others prefer a greater degree of independence. Decision makers are primarily senior managers who consider the best interest of the group or organization. They may sometimes delegate their authority to lower levels in the hierarchy. Others are often consulted in a committee-style process in order to reach greater consensus over and support of the decision. This slow and methodical process can take time and requires patience.

When making decisions, businesspeople usually consider the specific situation rather than applying universal principles. Personal feelings and experiences weigh as strongly as empirical evidence and other objective facts, and they usually consider all aspects. Czechs are often reluctant to take risks. If you expect them to support a risky decision, you may need to find ways for them to become comfortable with it first, for instance by explaining contingency plans, outlining areas of additional support, or by offering guarantees and warranties.

Agreements and Contracts

Capturing and exchanging meeting summaries can be an effective way to verify understanding and commitments. However, Czechs may consider verbal agreements as sufficient. It is best not to consider either of them final. Only a contract signed by both parties constitutes a confirmed agreement.

Written contracts tend to be lengthy. They often spell out detailed terms and conditions for the core agreements as well as for many eventualities. Signing the contract is important as a confirmation of your Czech partners' commitment.

It is strongly advisable to consult a local legal expert before signing a contract. The Czech Republic has established many complicated laws and regulations. However, do not bring your attorney to the negotiation table, as this may be taken as a sign that you do not trust your counterparts.

Signed contracts may not always be honored. They can also be hard to enforce, especially for foreigners. In the Czech view, they may represent little more than statements of intent. They expect both sides to remain somewhat flexible if conditions change, which may include agreeing to modify contract terms.

Women in Business

Women enjoy the same rights as men and are treated almost the same at work, although many Czech women are still struggling to attain positions of similar income and authority. Visiting businesswomen should have few problems in the country as long as they act professionally in business and social situations.

Other Important Things to Know

Business meals, especially dinners, play less of a role than in most other countries. If you get to attend one, expect to discuss business only before or after, but not during the meal.

Social events do not require strict punctuality. While it is best to arrive at dinners close to the agreed time, being late to a party by 10 to 15 minutes is perfectly acceptable.

Gift giving in business settings is rare. It is best not to bring a gift to an initial meeting in order to avoid raising suspicions about your motives.

Denmark

Danish businesspeople, especially those among younger generations, are usually experienced in interacting and doing business with visitors from other cultures. Culturally and ethnically, the country is very homogenous. Danes tend to be proud people who may not be very open to information or assistance from outside. Though in close proximity, the Danish culture is substantially different from Germany's. Do not remark or even assume that they are similar.

Relationships and Respect

Although Danes can be strong individualists, in general they may be more concerned about group interests than individuals' desires. Business relationships are often only moderately important in this country and are usually not a necessary precondition for initial business interactions. Your counterparts' expectation may be to get to know you better as you do business together. Unless past business interactions have already met their approval, Danes may be cautious, appearing reserved and proceeding slowly. Once the necessary trust has been established, though, there will be a sense of loyalty to you as a respected business partner, which can go a long way should a difficult situation arise.

Business relationships in this country exist between companies as well as between individuals. If your company replaces you with someone else over the course of a negotiation, it may be easy for your replacement to take things over from where you left them. Likewise, if you introduce someone else from your company into an existing business relationship, that person may quickly be accepted as a valid business partner. This does not mean that the Danes do not care about who they are dealing with.

Denmark is an egalitarian and tolerant society. It can be offensive to criticize other people or systems. Treating someone preferentially is generally discouraged. Bosses are expected to be team leaders rather than solitary decision-makers, and autocratic behavior may meet with strong disapproval. In the country's business culture, the respect a person enjoys depends primarily on his or her achievements. Admired personal traits include individual initiative, knowledge, and expertise.

Communication

While Danish, the country's official language, resembles Swedish and Norwegian, it has only few commonalities with German. Most businesspeople in Denmark speak English well. However, avoid using jargon and slang.

Danes usually speak in quiet, gentle tones. Interrupting others may be considered rude. At restaurants, especially those used for business lunches and dinners, keep conversations at a quiet level. Emotions are not shown openly and periods of silence do not necessarily convey a negative message. People generally converse standing about three to four feet apart.

Danish communication is usually very direct. Danes dislike vague statements and openly share opinions, concerns, and feelings with others. In fact, too much diplomacy may confuse and irritate Danes and can give the impression of insincerity. They may ask for clarifications and do not find it difficult to say 'no' if they dislike a request or proposal. If something is against company policy or cannot be done for other reasons, your counterpart will likely say so. They may view this as a simple statement of fact and might not understand that someone else could consider this directness insensitive. When communicating via letters or e-mail, do not waste time looking for messages 'between the lines.' Since the communication is mostly straightforward, there may not be any.

Danes use body language sparingly, although facial expressions may provide clues if they dislike an idea or proposal. Physical contact is rare and best avoided. The American *OK* sign, with thumb and index finger forming a circle, can be read as an obscene gesture in Denmark. The thumbs-up gesture is positive as it signals approval. Eye contact should be frequent, almost to the point of staring, as this conveys sincerity and helps build trust.

Initial Contacts and Meetings

Having a local contact can be an advantage but is usually not a necessary precondition to doing business in Denmark. Negotiations in Denmark can be conducted by individuals or teams of negotiators.

Scheduling meetings in advance is required. However, you can sometimes do this on short notice, especially if the parties have had previous business interactions. Danes generally expect visitors to be punctual. Being late by more than 10 to 15 minutes without having a valid and plausible excuse can be an offense. Call ahead if you are going to be more than 5 minutes late.

Names are usually given in the order of first name, family name. Some Danes may have two first names. Use *Mr./Ms.* plus the family name. If a person has an academic title, such as *Doctor* or *Professor*, use it instead, followed by the family name. Before calling Danes by their first name, wait until they offer it unless they introduced themselves using their first name only. Introduce and greet high-ranking and senior people first. Introductions are accompanied by firm and brief handshakes.

The exchange of business cards is an essential step when meeting someone for the first time, so bring more than you need. Almost all businesspeople in Denmark read English, so there is no need to have your card translated. Do not show advanced degrees on your card, but make sure that it clearly states your professional title, especially if you have the seniority to make decisions. If any facts about your company are particularly noteworthy, for instance if it is very old or the largest in your country or industry, mention this on your card since the Danes view this favorably. When presenting your card, smile and keep eye contact, then take a few moments to look at the card you received.

Meetings either start with a few minutes of 'small talk' or get right down to business. A sense of humor is appreciated, but know that Danish humor is often quite reserved and dry. One's private life has no place in meetings, and personal comments should be avoided. Business is mostly a serious matter in Denmark, and meetings can be quite formal. While the primary purpose of the first meeting is to become acquainted, the discussion will mostly focus on business topics. It is vital to come well prepared as the Danes hate wasting time.

Presentation materials can be simple without colorful backgrounds and fancy graphs. However, good and easy-to-understand visuals are important. Having your English-language handout materials translated to Danish is not required. Keep your presentation succinct and to the point. While details matter, Danes prefer to discuss issues in short meetings and make the decision right there. Information overload, written protocols, and so on may therefore work against you.

Negotiation

Attitudes and Styles – To the Danes, negotiating is usually a joint problem-solving process. Buyer and seller in a business deal are equal partners who both own the responsibility to reach agreement. They may focus equally on near-term and long-term benefits. The primary negotiation style is cooperative and people may be open to compromising if viewed helpful in order to move the negotiation forward. Since the Danes believe in the concept of win-win, they expect you to reciprocate their respect and trust. It is strongly advisable to avoid any open confrontation and to remain calm, friendly, patient, and persistent.

Should a dispute arise at any stage of a negotiation, you might be able to reach resolution by focusing on logical reasoning and facts while remaining open and constructive.

Sharing of Information – Danish negotiators believe in information sharing as a way to build trust. This does not mean that they will readily reveal everything you might want to know during your negotiation. However, negotiations can become very difficult if one side appears to be hiding information from the other. A good part of the communication may be in writing, which Danes often prefer.

Pace of Negotiation – Expect negotiations to be fairly swift. While diligent, Danish businesspeople are less obsessive over details than Germans are and strive to conclude negotiations quickly if possible. This does not mean that they will readily accept unfavorable terms.

The Danes generally prefer a monochronic work style. They are used to pursuing actions and goals systematically, and they dislike interruptions or digressions. When negotiating, they often work their way down a list of objectives in sequential order, bargaining for each item separately, and may be unwilling to revisit aspects that have already been agreed upon. They may show little tolerance if a more polychronic counterpart challenges this approach, which they view as systematic and effective. This rigid style may be difficult to tolerate for negotiators from highly polychronic cultures, such as most Asians, Arabs, some Southern Europeans, or most Latin Americans, who may view it as closed-minded and overly restrictive. In any case, do not show irritation or anger when encountering this behavior. Instead, be willing to bargain over some items individually. Otherwise, clearly indicate that your agreement is conditional and contingent on other items.

Bargaining – Danes are not fond of bargaining and strongly dislike haggling. They do not appreciate aggressive sales techniques. The bargaining stage of a negotiation is usually relatively short and prices rarely move by more than 10 to 20 percent between initial offers and final agreement. The concept of fairness is very important to Danes, so while it is not difficult to obtain concessions, your counterparts will expect reciprocity and may take it very negatively if the bargaining exchange is too one-sided.

Danes prefer to negotiate in a straightforward and honest style. They use few deceptive negotiation techniques, such as pretending to be disinterested in the whole deal or in single concessions. Realize that using most other tactics in this category yourself, whether it is telling lies, sending fake non-verbal messages, misrepresenting an item's value, making false demands and concessions, or claiming 'limited authority,' could jeopardize the trust between the parties and damage the negotiation. Carefully orchestrated, 'good cop, bad cop' may be an effective tactic to use, though.

Negotiators in the country may use pressure techniques that include opening with their best offer, showing intransigence, or making final offers. When using similar tactics yourself, clearly explain your offer and avoid being aggressive. Danish negotiators may make a final offer quite early in the bargaining process. While this is not common practice, it could actually be a serious attempt to speed up the negotiation. Periods of silence in conversations are normal and may not represent an attempt to use it as a negotiation technique. Be very careful when using pressure tactics such as applying time pressure, making expiring offers, or nibbling. Your counterparts may consider these inappropriate unless they are strongly interested in your offer and clearly understand the rationale behind the approach. Otherwise, while the negotiation will not necessarily be over because of this, the Danish side may become very reserved and cautious.

Avoid all aggressive tactics when negotiating with Danes. They will not shy away from open confrontation if challenged, but this is almost guaranteed to deteriorate rather than strengthen your bargaining position. Opening with an extreme offer could be viewed as an unfriendly act. It is best to open with one that is already in the ballpark of what you really expect.

Other emotional negotiation techniques are also rare and should be avoided when negotiating in Denmark, and appeals to personal relationships not only rarely work but also may be counterproductive. Danes often employ defensive tactics such as asking probing or very direct questions, making promises, or keeping an inflexible position.

Opening with written offers and introducing written terms and conditions may be effective tactics that could help shorten the bargaining process, which your Danish counterparts often find desirable.

Corruption and bribery are very rare in Denmark. It is strongly advisable to stay away from giving gifts of significant value or making offers that could be read as bribery.

Decision Making – This is a bit faster in Denmark than in most other European countries. The decision maker is often the most senior manager participating in the negotiation, unless the size of the deal dictates that the company's top management needs to approve it. Managers usually encourage their team members to express their opinions and always consider the best interest of the group or organization when making decisions. They may also delegate their authority to lower levels. Decisions are often made by consensus of a group of managers. Once a decision has been made, it may be difficult to change.

When making decisions, businesspeople may apply universal principles rather than considering the specific situation. They often dislike 'making exceptions,' even when arguments speak in favor of doing so. Personal feelings and experiences are considered irrelevant in business negotiations, so people focus on empirical evidence, logical arguments, and objective facts. Most Danes are moderate risk takers.

Agreements and Contracts

Capturing and exchanging meeting summaries can be an effective way to verify understanding and commitments. Although verbal agreements are already considered binding and will likely be kept, do not consider them final. Only a final contract signed by both parties constitutes a binding agreement.

Although written contracts are serious matters in Denmark, it is best to keep them concise without including too many legalistic details. Signing the contract is important not only from a legal perspective, but also as a strong confirmation of your Danish partners' commitment.

It is recommended to consult a local legal expert before signing a contract.

Contracts are almost always dependable, and the agreed terms are viewed as binding. Requests to change contract details after signature may be considered as bad faith and will meet with strong resistance.

Women in Business

Denmark is one of the most progressive countries in the world when it comes to equality between men and women. Most women are working, and many hold business leadership positions. A visiting businesswoman will find it very easy to do business in the country. She can initiate meetings and even social engagements with men without restrictions.

Other Important Things to Know

Punctuality is also valued in most social settings. It is best to be right on time for dinners, and to arrive at parties within 10 to 15 minutes of the agreed time.

Gift giving in business settings is rare. It is best not to bring a gift to an initial meeting in order to avoid raising suspicions about your motives.

Egypt

Though the country's culture is quite homogeneous, Egyptian businesspeople are usually experienced in interacting and doing business with visitors from other cultures. However, that does not always mean that they are open-minded. When negotiating business here, realize that people may expect things to be done 'their way.' Business practices may show European and Arab influences.

Although many Egyptians are not practicing Muslims and some are Christians, keep in mind that this is an Islamic country. Showing any disrespect for the religion could have disastrous consequences.

Relationships and Respect

Egypt's culture expects its members to have a sense of belonging to and conforming with their group. At the same time, it leaves room for individual preferences. Building lasting and trusting personal relationships is critically important to most Egyptians, who often expect to establish strong bonds prior to closing any deals. People in this country may do business only with those they know and like. Establishing productive business cooperation requires a long-term perspective and commitment. Social interactions may be just as important as business contacts, if not more. Consequently, proceed with serious business discussions only after your counterparts have become very comfortable with you. This is usually a slow process.

Business relationships in this country exist between people, not necessarily between companies. Even when you have won your local business partners' friendship and trust, they will not necessarily trust others from your company. That makes it very important to keep company interfaces unchanged. Changing a key contact may require the relationship building process to start over. Worst case, such a change may bring negotiations to a complete halt.

Establishing relationships with others in Egypt can create powerful networks, and whom you know may determine whether people want to get to know you. Maintaining cordial relations is crucial. Third party introductions can be very helpful as a starting point to building a trusting relationship with a potential partner.

'Saving face' is very essential. Causing embarrassment to another person may cause a *loss of face* for all parties involved and can be disastrous for business negotiations. The importance of diplomatic restraint and tact cannot be overestimated. Keep your cool and never show openly that you are upset. It may be better to accept a compromise, even an unfavorable one, if the alternative means that your counterpart loses face.

In Egyptian business culture, the respect a person enjoys depends primarily on his or her age, rank, and status. It is crucial to treat elderly people with the greatest respect. Showing status is important since people will take you more seriously. Carefully select your hotel and transportation. Use the services of others, such as a porter, to avoid being viewed as a low-ranking intermediary.

Communication

The official language of Egypt is Arabic. Most businesspeople speak at least some English. Since you are required to have a local agent when doing business in this country, select someone who can also assist with translations. When communicating in English, speak in short, simple sentences and avoid using jargon and slang. Never use a language to communicate within your team that your Egyptian counterparts cannot understand, since they will likely take this very negatively.

Egyptians usually speak in quiet, gentle tones. They may occasionally raise their voices to make a point. A raised voice may also indicate anger, which would be a very bad signal. People in the country generally converse in close proximity, standing only two feet or less apart. Never back away, even if this is much closer than your personal comfort zone allows. Doing so could be read as a sign that you are uncomfortable around them.

Communication is generally rather indirect. Egyptians often use circuitous language, which can make it difficult for Westerners to figure out the exact message. They love flowery phrases, exaggerations, and other rhetoric. Open disagreement and confrontation are rare, so you usually do not hear a direct 'no.' When an Egyptian says 'yes,' he or she may actually mean 'possibly.' Ambiguous answers such as 'we must look into this' or 'we will think about it' usually mean 'no.' Silence is another way to communicate a negative message. It is beneficial to use a similarly indirect approach when dealing with Egyptians, as they may perceive you as rude and pushy if you are too direct.

Gestures and body language can be extensive. It is often not a good idea to imitate them, though. People tend to make frequent physical contact. Men may greet each other by hugging and kissing as a sign of friendship. However, never touch someone's head, not even that of a child. Since Muslims consider the left hand unclean, use it only if inevitable. Pointing at people or objects is impolite. Instead, wave your open hand toward the object. The thumbs-up gesture is an offensive gesture throughout the Arab world. Tapping your index fingers together is also improper. Eye contact should be frequent, almost to the point of staring. This conveys sincerity and helps build trust. However, keep it less frequent when dealing with a superior.

Egyptians enjoy showing positive emotions. They smile frequently, though this does not always indicate amusement or approval. Instead, a smile may hide feelings of distress or even anger.

Initial Contacts and Meetings

Egyptian law requires a local agent to do business in the country. Your agent will also help bridge the cultural and communications gap, allowing you to conduct business with greater effectiveness. Without an agent who is knowledgeable and extremely well-connected, doing business in the country will be very difficult and frustrating. Choose your representation carefully to ensure that they can accomplish what you expect them to do.

Negotiations in Egypt can be conducted by individuals or teams of negotiators. Changing a team member may require the relationship building process to start over and should therefore be avoided. Given the strong emphasis on hierarchy in the country's business culture, a senior executive should attend the initial meeting for your company and your negotiating team should include senior leaders who know your company well. There will not be an expectation that the executive attends future meetings.

Scheduling meetings in advance is required. However, you can do this on short notice if the parties had previous business interactions. Schedules are usually loose and flexible. However, some Egyptians may appear surprisingly focused on punctuality. It is best not to be more than 10 to 15 minutes late. Displaying anger if you have to wait, which happens often, reflects very poorly on you. The most senior meeting participants usually often arrive last.

Egyptian names can have several parts and may be difficult to identify. It may be best to inquire from someone upfront or politely ask the person how to address him or her correctly. In that case, make sure you do the same for your own name. Titles, such as *Doctor* or *Professor*, are highly valued. Always use them when addressing a person who carries one. Do not call Egyptians by their first name unless they offered it, which is rare. Introduce and greet the most senior person first. Introductions are accompanied by handshakes using the right hand. Men should wait for women to initiate a handshake. If they do not, just smile and nod.

After the introductions, offer your business card to everyone present. Cards should be in English on one side and in Arabic on the reverse. Show doctorate degrees on your card and make sure that it clearly states your professional title, especially if you have the seniority to make decisions. Present your card with your right hand, with the Arabic side facing the recipient. Similarly, accept others' cards using only the right hand. Smile and keep eye contact while doing so, then examine the card carefully. Next, place it on the table in front of you or into your card case.

Meetings start with extensive small talk, which may include prolonged inquiries about your health, family, and so on. This may include very personal questions. It is important to be patient and let the other side set the pace. Frequent meeting interruptions are normal and do not signal a lack of interest.

The primary purpose of the first meeting is to get to know each other. Business may be discussed, but do not try to hurry along with your agenda. It is unrealistic to expect initial meetings to lead to straight decisions.

Presentations should be short and concise. Your presentation materials should be attractive, with good and clear visuals. Having your handout materials translated to Arabic is not a must, but it helps in getting your messages across and is thus preferable.

Negotiation

Attitudes and Styles - Leveraging relationships is an important element when negotiating in Egypt. Nevertheless, Egyptians often employ distributive and contingency bargaining. While the buyer is in a superior position, both sides in a business deal own the responsibility to reach agreement. They expect long-term commitments from their business partners and will focus mostly on long-term benefits. Although the primary negotiation style is competitive, Egyptians nevertheless value long-term relationships and look for win-win solutions. Hard bargainers are respected as long as they avoid creating direct conflict. Attempts to win competitive advantages should not be taken negatively. You will earn your counterparts' respect by maintaining a positive, persistent attitude.

Should a dispute arise at any stage of a negotiation, you might be able to reach resolution through using logical arguments and showing willingness to compromise. Patience and creativity will pay strong dividends. In extreme situations, use a mediator with whom both sides have a good relationship.

Sharing of Information - Information is rarely shared freely, since Egyptians believe that privileged information creates bargaining advantages.

Pace of Negotiation – Expect negotiations to be slow and protracted, and be prepared to make several trips if necessary to achieve your objectives. Decisions are usually made between negotiation rounds rather than at the table. Throughout the negotiation, be patient, control your emotions, and accept that delays occur. Attempts to rush the process are unlikely to produce better results and may be viewed as offensive.

Egyptians generally employ a polychronic work style. They are used to pursuing multiple actions and goals in parallel. When negotiating, they often take a holistic approach and may jump back and forth between topics rather than addressing them in sequential order. Negotiators from strongly monochronic cultures, such as Germany, the United Kingdom, or the United States, may find this style confusing, irritating, and even annoying. In any case, do not show irritation or anger when encountering this behavior. Instead, keep track of the bargaining progress at all times, often emphasizing areas where agreement already exists.

If your counterparts appear to be stalling the negotiation, assess carefully whether their slowing down the process indicates that they are evaluating alternatives or that they are not interested in doing business with you. While such behavior could represent attempts to create time pressure in order to obtain concessions, the slow decision process in the country is far more likely causing the lack of progress. People from fast-paced cultures tend to underestimate how much time this takes and often make the mistake of trying to 'speed things up.' Again, patience and persistence are vitally important.

Bargaining – Egyptian businesspeople are often shrewd negotiators who should not be underestimated. Most of them are influenced by 'bazaar trader' mentalities and love bargaining and haggling. They expect to do a lot of it during a negotiation and may be seriously offended if you refuse to play along. The bargaining stage of a negotiation can be extensive. Prices often move more than 50 percent between initial offers and final agreement. Leave yourself a lot of room for concessions at many different stages. Ask the other side to reciprocate if you made one. It is not advisable to make significant early concessions since your counterparts expect further compromises as the bargaining continues. You can use the fact that aspects can be re-visited to your advantage, for instance by offering further concessions under the condition that the Egyptian side reciprocate in areas that had already been agreed upon.

Deceptive techniques are frequent and can be effective. This includes tactics such as telling lies and sending fake non-verbal messages, pretending to be disinterested in the whole deal or in single concessions, misrepresenting an item's value, or making false demands and concessions. Expect your Egyptian counterparts to be masters at this game. They may occasionally play stupid or otherwise attempt to mislead you in order to obtain bargaining advantages. Lies will be difficult to detect. It is advisable to verify information received from the local side through other channels. Similarly, they treat 'outside' information with caution. Egyptians may claim limited authority, stating that they have to ask for their manager's approval. This could be a tactic or the truth. Be cautious when using the techniques of making false demands or false concessions. Overt attempts to bluff your counterparts could backfire.

Negotiators in the country may use pressure techniques that include making final offers or nibbling. Final offers may come more than once and are rarely final. Do not use tactics such as applying time pressure, opening with your best offer, or making expiring offers, since Egyptians could view these as signs that you are not willing to build a long-term relationship. They may choose to terminate the negotiation. Silence can be an effective way to signal rejection of a proposal.

Egyptian negotiators will avoid openly aggressive or adversarial techniques but may use more subtle versions. Making an extreme opening offer is a standard practice to start the bargaining process. Negotiators may also make indirect threats and warnings, or subtly display anger. Use these tactics with caution yourself since they may adversely affect the relationship if employed too aggressively. Do not walk out or threaten to do so as your counterpart may take this as a personal insult.

Emotional negotiation techniques, such as attitudinal bargaining, sending dual messages, attempting to make you feel guilty, grimacing, or appealing to personal relationships, are frequent and can be effective. Be cautious not to cause *loss of face* when employing any of them yourself. Also, know that Egyptians can become quite emotional during fierce bargaining. It is best to remain calm. At times, defensive tactics such as blocking or changing the subject, asking probing or very direct questions, or making promises may be used.

Corruption and bribery are quite common in Egypt's public and private sectors. However, people may draw the line differently, viewing minor payments as rewards for getting a job done rather than as bribes. Also, keep in mind that there is a fine line between giving gifts and bribing. What you may consider a bribe, an Egyptian may view as only a nice gift. It may help if you introduce and explain your company's policies early on, but be careful not to moralize or appear to imply that local customs are unethical. When in doubt, get your agent's advice and be willing to follow it.

Decision Making – Most companies tend to be very hierarchical, and people expect to work within clearly established lines of authority. Although the pace of business is accelerating, decision making can be a very slow and deliberate process in Egypt. Decision makers are usually individuals who consider the best interest of the group or organization. They may consult with others before making the call. Subordinates may be reluctant to accept responsibility. Decision makers also rarely delegate their authority, so it is important to deal with senior executives.

When making decisions, businesspeople may consider the specific situation or follow universal principles. Personal feelings and experiences weigh more strongly than empirical evidence and other objective facts do, but they will consider all aspects. Egypt is a fatalistic culture. Since faith dictates that one's destiny lies in the hands of God, accepting the status quo is the norm. Egyptians are therefore often reluctant to take risks. If you expect them to support a risky decision, you may need to find ways for them to become comfortable with it first. You are much more likely to succeed if the relationship with your counterparts is strong and you managed to win their trust.

Agreements and Contracts

Capturing and exchanging meeting summaries can be an effective way to verify understanding and commitments. Agreements are only final when the participants part. Until then, the Egyptian side may unilaterally abrogate them, possibly even if they were already signed.

Although businesspeople in the country understand the role of contracts well, they may view them only as general guides for conducting business, expecting that both parties are willing to change terms if there is a change of conditions. Written contracts are usually kept high-level, capturing only the primary aspects, terms, and conditions of the agreement. Writing up and signing the contract is a formality. Egyptians believe that the primary strength of an agreement lies in the partners' commitment rather than in its written documentation. Accordingly, do not propose an overly detailed contract since that may cause hurt feelings.

It is strongly advisable to consult a local legal and taxation expert before signing a contract. However, do not bring your attorney to the negotiation table. Some Egyptians may read it as a sign of mistrust if you do.

Since personal honor is highly valued in Egypt, contracts are usually dependable and your partners will strive to keep their commitments. However, business partners usually expect the other side to remain flexible if conditions change, which may include agreeing to modify contract terms.

Women in Business

Many Egyptian women are working and a few have made it into leadership positions. Visiting businesswomen should have few problems in the country as long as they act professionally in business and social situations. Female business travelers need to dress in accordance with local customs, which means that collarbones and knees need to be covered at all times and that clothes should not be form-fitting.

Men should not bring up the subject of women with male business partners. Do not even inquire about a wife's or daughter's health.

Other Important Things to Know

Impeccable appearance is very important when doing business here. Male business visitors should wear conservative suits with neckties on most occasions. Make sure shoes and suit are in excellent condition.

Avoid setting up meetings during Ramadan. During this month-long fasting period, Muslims neither eat nor drink from dawn to dusk, which often results in a lack of concentration. If you attend meetings during Ramadan, do not eat, drink, or smoke in the presence of others.

Topics to avoid in conversations include all aspects of Egyptian domestic and foreign politics. Should your local counterparts bring them up, respond in a very diplomatic fashion.

Social events do not require strict punctuality. While it is best to arrive at dinners close to the agreed time, being late to a party by 30 minutes or more is advisable. You should follow your host's lead when deciding whether to drink alcohol.

Finland

Finnish businesspeople, especially those among younger generations, are usually experienced in interacting and doing business with visitors from other cultures. Culturally and ethnically, the country is quite homogenous, though there is a Swedish minority of around six percent of the population.

The Finns tend to be proud people who may not be very open to information or assistance from outside. Though relations are generally good across all Nordic countries, the Finnish culture is quite different from those of Sweden, Norway, or Denmark. Be careful not to appear to be lumping them all into the same category. In fact, it is a popular misperception that Finland is a Scandinavian country, which it is not.

Relationships and Respect

The Finnish culture is not one of strong individualists, at least not in the workplace. There are few elements of competition across business teams, and people may not want to stand out in the group. Building lasting and trusting relationships is important to most people in this country. However, they are usually not a necessary precondition for initial business interactions. Your counterparts' expectation may be to get to know you better as you do business together. Over time, such relationships can become very strong and may be crucial should a difficult situation arise, but this takes a long time. Until then, Finns may be cautious, appearing reserved and proceeding very slowly.

Business relationships in this country exist between companies as well as between individuals. If your company replaces you with someone else over the course of a negotiation, it may be easy for your replacement to take things over from where you left them. Likewise, if you introduce someone else from your company into an existing business relationship, that person may quickly be accepted as a valid business partner. However, building closer relationships will again require a long time. Personal integrity and dependability along the way are very important.

Finland is an egalitarian society. Treating someone preferentially is generally discouraged. Although Finnish companies tend to be somewhat hierarchical, superiors are not necessarily considered superior. Bosses are usually easily accessible and are expected to be team members and leaders at the same time. Autocratic behavior may meet with strong disapproval. In the country's business culture, the respect a person enjoys depends primarily on his or her achievements. Admired personal traits include sincerity and seriousness, humility, knowledge, and expertise.

Communication

Finland has two official languages, Finnish and Swedish. Finnish is fundamentally different from the other Nordic languages. Most businesspeople speak English well. However, avoid using jargon and slang.

Conversations among Finns may seem less animated than in most other cultures around the world. People in this country usually speak softly. Never be loud and forceful – to the contrary, remaining reserved and appearing somewhat shy may leave a favorable impression. Silence is almost a form of communication for the Finns, and they may pause in the middle of a conversation for a much longer time than a foreigner may find comfortable. Do not rush to fill in these pauses since your counterparts may only be taking time to think or formulate their thoughts. Never assume that extensive silence conveys a negative message – in Finland, this is rarely the case. Interrupting others is considered rude. Emotions are rarely shown in public, and the lively exuberance Americans often display can make Finns very uncomfortable. People generally converse standing about three to four feet apart.

Since confrontation is mostly avoided, Finnish communication is usually quite indirect. When rejecting an offer or proposal, they may resort to polite phrases that may not always clearly convey the message, trying to preserve the harmony instead. On the other hand, Finns strive to keep business conversations focused on facts and objectives. By listening carefully, you will be able to pick out the key messages. Once your counterparts have become very comfortable with you, the communication often becomes more direct.

Finns use body language sparingly, and their facial expressions may be hard to read. Avoid talking with your hands or making physical contact. Do not fold your arms since this may be interpreted as arrogant. Eye contact should be frequent, especially when you are talking, as this conveys sincerity and helps build trust.

Initial Contacts and Meetings

Having a local contact can be an advantage but is usually not a necessary precondition to doing business in Finland. Negotiations in Finland can be conducted by individuals or teams of negotiators. It is beneficial to make sure that your team is well aligned in order to avoid confusing and irritating your counterparts.

Scheduling meetings in advance is required. However, you can sometimes do this on short notice, especially if the parties have had previous business interactions. Avoid rescheduling meetings if you can. Finns value punctuality. At any meeting, whether business or social, it is therefore best to be right on time. Arriving late, and also being early, may be taken as a sign of disrespect. Expect meetings to end on or close to the scheduled time.

Names are usually given in the order of first name, family name. Using *Mr./Mrs./Miss* plus the family name is acceptable, but people are also commonly addressed only with their professional title, especially if they hold a senior position. Academic titles are less important and do not need to be used unless someone introduces themselves with one. Before calling Finns by their first name, wait until they offer it. Introductions are accompanied by firm handshakes.

The exchange of business cards is common practice. Most businesspeople in Finland read English, so there is no need to have your card translated. Showing academic degrees on your card is not important. When presenting your card, smile and keep eye contact, then take a few moments to look at the card you received.

Meetings usually get right down to business with little or no small talk. Keep in mind that Finns are sincere people who dislike superficiality in conversation. Humor rarely has a place in business discussions, one's private life should not be discussed there at all, and personal comments should also be avoided. Business is a serious matter in Finland, and meetings can be quite formal. While the primary purpose of the first meeting is to become acquainted, the discussion will mostly focus on business topics. It is unrealistic to expect initial meetings to lead to straight decisions.

Presentations should be short, concise, and clearly structured. Include facts and figures wherever appropriate. Your audience may not interrupt you to ask questions, so allow sufficient time for questions and clarifications at the end. Exaggerations and hype are often counterproductive since people will not believe them and may question your integrity. The appearance of your presentation materials is not very important as long as you include good and easy-to-understand visuals. Having your English-language handout materials translated to Finnish is not required, though it will be appreciated.

Negotiation

Attitudes and Styles – To Finns, negotiating is usually a joint problem-solving process. Buyer and seller in a business deal are equal partners who both own the responsibility to reach agreement. They may focus equally on near-term and long-term benefits. The primary negotiation style is cooperative and people may be open to compromising if viewed helpful in order to move the negotiation forward. Since the Finns believe in the concept of win-win, they expect you to reciprocate their respect and trust. It is strongly advisable to avoid any open confrontation or conflict, and to remain calm, unemotional, patient, and persistent.

Should a dispute arise at any stage of a negotiation, you might be able to reach resolution by focusing on logical reasoning and facts while remaining open and constructive.

Sharing of Information – Finnish negotiators believe in information sharing as a way to build trust. This does not mean that they will readily reveal everything you might want to know during your negotiation. However, negotiations can become very difficult if one side appears to be hiding information from the other.

Pace of Negotiation – Expect negotiations to be slow. The methodical and carefully planned approach the Finns use in preparing for the negotiation and gathering information takes considerable time, as does the effort needed to work out details of an agreement. Remain patient, control your emotions, and accept the inevitable delays.

The Finns generally prefer a monochronic work style. They are used to pursuing actions and goals systematically, and they dislike interruptions or digressions. When negotiating, they often work their way down a list of objectives in sequential order, bargaining for each item separately, and may be unwilling to revisit aspects that have already been agreed upon. They may show little tolerance if a more polychronic counterpart challenges this approach, which they view as systematic and effective. This rigid style may be difficult to tolerate for negotiators from highly polychronic cultures, such as most Asians, Arabs, some Southern Europeans, or most Latin Americans, who may view it as closed-minded and overly restrictive. In any case, do not show irritation or anger when encountering this behavior. Instead, be willing to bargain over some items individually. Otherwise, clearly indicate that your agreement is conditional and contingent on other items.

Bargaining – Finns are not fond of bargaining and strongly dislike haggling. They also do not appreciate aggressive sales techniques. While the bargaining stage of a negotiation may take time and require several meetings, prices rarely move by more than 15 to 25 percent between initial offers and final agreement. The concept of fairness is very important to the Finns, so while it is not difficult to obtain small concessions, your counterparts expect reciprocity and may take it very negatively if the bargaining exchange is too one-sided.

Finns prefer to negotiate in a straightforward and honest style. They use few deceptive negotiation techniques, such as pretending to be disinterested in the whole deal or in single concessions. Realize that using most other tactics in this category yourself, whether it is telling lies, sending fake non-verbal messages, misrepresenting an item's value, making false demands and concessions, or claiming 'limited authority,' could jeopardize the trust between the parties and damage the negotiation. 'Good cop, bad cop' is also not advisable as the tactic may lead the Finnish side to question your trustworthiness.

Negotiators in the country use pressure techniques only as long as they can be applied in a non-confrontational fashion. They may open with their best offer, show some intransigence, or make a final offer, but often remain willing to make small compromises. Finnish negotiators may make their final offer quite early in the bargaining process, attempting to speed up the negotiation. Silence is never a negotiation technique in Finland. Be very careful when using pressure tactics such as applying time pressure, making expiring offers, or nibbling. Your counterparts likely consider these inappropriate. While the negotiation will not necessarily be over because of this, the Finnish side may become very reserved and cautious.

Avoid all aggressive tactics when negotiating with Finns. They will not shy away from open confrontation if challenged, but this is almost guaranteed to deteriorate rather than strengthen your bargaining position. Opening with an extreme offer could be viewed as an unfriendly act. It is best to open with one that is already in the ballpark of what you really expect.

All emotional negotiation techniques should be avoided when negotiating in Finland. Appeals to a personal relationship may work only if it is long-standing and very strong. Finns may employ defensive tactics such as asking direct or probing questions, or making promises.

Opening with written offers and introducing written terms and conditions may be effective tactics that could help shorten the bargaining process, which your Finnish counterparts may find desirable.

Corruption and bribery are very rare in Finland. It is strongly advisable to stay away from giving gifts of significant value or making offers that could be read as bribery.

Decision Making – Finnish companies are somewhat more hierarchical than in other Nordic countries. Decision makers are usually individuals, with the size of the deal determining which level in the hierarchy he or she needs to hold. However, there is a strong consensus orientation, so others are usually consulted to reach greater group support. Influencing the decision thus requires winning the support of others involved in the decision process, not only that of the most senior manager. Decision making takes some time but is usually faster than in Sweden or Norway.

When making decisions, businesspeople may apply universal principles rather than considering the specific situation. They dislike 'making exceptions' even when arguments speak in favor of doing so. Personal feelings and experiences are considered irrelevant in business negotiations, so people focus on empirical evidence, logical arguments, and objective facts. The Finns are often reluctant to take risks. If you expect them to support a risky decision, you may need to find ways for them to become comfortable with it first, for instance by explaining contingency plans, outlining areas of additional support, or by offering guarantees and warranties.

Agreements and Contracts

Capturing and exchanging meeting summaries can be an effective way to verify understanding and commitments. Although interim agreements are usually kept, do not consider them final. Only a final contract signed by both parties constitutes a binding agreement.

Written contracts tend to be lengthy. They often spell out detailed terms and conditions for the core agreements as well as for many eventualities. Signing the contract is very important not only from a legal perspective, but also as a strong confirmation of your Finnish partners' commitment.

It is recommended to consult a local legal expert before signing a contract. However, it is better not to bring your attorney to the negotiation table.

Contracts are almost always dependable, and the agreed terms are viewed as binding. Requests to change contract details after signature may meet with strong resistance and may be considered as bad faith unless the environment has changed considerably.

Women in Business

Gender equality is very high in Finland. Most women are working, and many hold leadership positions that are similar in income and authority to those of men. Quite a few Finnish women have made it into top business positions. Visiting businesswomen should have few problems in the country as long as they act professionally in business and social situations.

Other Important Things to Know

Punctuality is also highly valued in all social settings. It is best to be right on time for dinners and parties.

Gift giving in business settings is rare. It is best not to bring a gift to an initial meeting in order to avoid raising suspicions about your motives.

When dealing with smaller companies that have little international experience, be prepared that your counterparts may invite you to continue a business discussion in a sauna, though usually not at the first meeting. If you are unwilling to join them, it is better to claim health reasons than to directly reject the invitation.

France

Though the country's culture is relatively homogeneous, French businesspeople, especially those among younger generations, are usually experienced in interacting and doing business with visitors from other cultures. However, that does not always mean that they are open-minded. When negotiating business here, realize that some people may expect things to be done 'their way.'

It is very important to show respect for the country's history and importance. The French attitude may sometimes appear arrogant or egoistical to foreigners. However, any sign of disrespect or a refusal to endorse it as a great and important nation can have a substantial impact on your business relationship.

Relationships and Respect

Building lasting and trusting relationships is important and can be vital for the success of your business engagements in France. However, they are usually not a necessary precondition for initial business interactions. The French often focus on long-term objectives and expect to establish strong relationships over the course of their business engagements. This takes time and effort. People tend to be suspicious of early friendliness, and an overly casual approach can be viewed as intrusiveness. Early in the relationship building process, proper behavior is key and it is best to appear somewhat reserved. Personal questions should not be asked until the relationship has become stronger.

Business relationships in this country exist both at the individual and company level. The French usually want to do business only with those they like and trust. However, if your company replaces you with someone else over the course of a negotiation, it may be easy for your replacement to take things over from where you left them. Likewise, if you introduce someone else from your company into an existing business relationship, that person may quickly be accepted as a valid business partner.

In the country's business culture, the respect a person enjoys depends primarily on his or her education, status, and achievements. Admired personal traits include intellectual capability and wit, resourcefulness, dignity, poise, and tact. More than members of most other cultures, the French value difference and may enjoy building relationships with people whose experiences and interests are different from their own ones.

Communication

The country's official language is French. However, several other languages and dialects exist. Most younger businesspeople speak English, many of them well. On rare occasions, it may be useful to engage an interpreter. To avoid offending the other side, ask beforehand whether an interpreter should be present at a meeting. When communicating in English, speak in short, simple sentences and avoid using jargon and slang. It will help people with a limited command of English if you speak slowly, summarize your key points often, and pause frequently to allow for interpretation.

The French consider strong oratory skills an expression of a superior mind. Many of them are therefore uncomfortable and feel clumsy when speaking in a foreign language. Even when the main meeting language is English, your counterparts will frequently speak French among themselves, not necessarily to shut you out from the discussion but to reduce their discomfort and to ensure that everyone on the local side shares the same understanding. People will appreciate and remember if you learn a few basic French phrases. When you speak their language, they may frequently correct your mistakes in grammar or pronunciation. Do not take this personally, since their motivation will only be to help you speak their language effectively and 'look good.' If you do not speak any French, it will be viewed favorably if you expressed regret for that fact.

While they often have heated debates and occasionally raise their voices to make a point, the French dislike loud and boisterous behavior. They may interrupt each other frequently during their passionate disputes, though. People's sometimes-intense outbursts are not necessarily signs of irritation or anger, and it is often hard to tell when they indeed are. At restaurants, especially those used for business lunches and dinners, keep conversations at a quiet level. Emotions other than passion are rarely shown in public, and self-control is seen as a virtue. Periods of silence do not necessarily convey a negative message. People in France generally converse in relatively close proximity of around two to three feet apart.

Although the French also value tact or diplomacy, communication can be very direct and people may frequently question and probe into others' arguments. Logic dominates most disputes, and few things may anger a French businessperson more than an ill-conceived or illogical argument. Note that it matters little whether they agree with your point or not. You may actually be able to earn their respect by presenting confrontational ideas and defending them well in the inevitable debate that follows. Your counterparts will admire your ability to justify your position, demonstrate that you are well informed, and maintain your composure. The concept of 'saving face' is not very important in this country. While you want to remain respectful, pointing out mistakes is accepted and often appreciated. Being direct is better than appearing evasive or deceptive. Avoid giving ambiguous answers such as 'We will consider it,' 'This will take further investigation,' or 'Perhaps' if your real answer is 'no.'

Gestures and body language can be extensive, especially if they help underline what is being said. It is often not a good idea to imitate them, though. The French may make some physical contact, but there is usually not a lot of it. The American *OK* sign, with thumb and index finger forming a circle, means *zero* in France. The thumbs-up gesture is positive as it signals approval. Slapping the open hand over a fist is a vulgar gesture. Eye contact should be frequent, almost to the point of staring, as this conveys sincerity and helps build trust.

Initial Contacts and Meetings

Having a local contact can be an advantage but is usually not a necessary precondition to doing business. Negotiations in France can be conducted by individuals or teams of negotiators.

If possible, schedule meetings at least two weeks in advance. Since the French want to know whom they will be meeting, provide details on titles, positions, and responsibilities of attendees ahead of time. Setting an agenda upfront is recommended but not always necessary. While meetings may not always start on time, the French generally expect foreign visitors to be punctual. Avoid being more than 10 to 15 minutes late, and call ahead if you will be.

Names are usually given in the order of first name, family name. However, do not be confused if someone does it the other way around. Some French people have two first names, which are often hyphenated. Use *Monsieur/Madame* plus the family name. Do not use *Mr./Ms.* Titles are very important. If a person has one, use it instead, followed by the family name. Only close friends call each other by their first names, and the French may respond very negatively if you violate this rule. Introductions are accompanied by light handshakes. Men should wait for women to initiate handshakes. Some people may not smile during a handshake – do not read much into it.

The exchange of business cards is not an essential step, but it is best to bring a sufficient supply. Most businesspeople in France read English, so there is no need to have your card translated. If you do, indicate your position in French and include Ph.D.-level degrees if you have any. In addition, make sure that your card clearly states your professional title, especially if you have the seniority to make decisions. When presenting your card, smile and keep eye contact, then take a few moments to look at the card you received. Next, place it on the table in front of you.

Meetings either start with a few minutes of 'small talk' or get right down to business. French humor can be ironic and cynical. Do not respond in kind since you will risk inadvertently offending your counterparts. One's private life has no place in meetings, and personal comments should be avoided. Business is a serious matter in France. During the first meeting, it is best to preserve an air of formality while remaining polite and cordial. While the primary purpose of the first meeting is to become acquainted, the discussion will mostly focus on business topics. It is unrealistic to expect initial meetings to lead to straight decisions.

Presentation materials should be attractive, with good and clear visuals, but not too colorful or flashy. Keep your presentation clear and concise. The French are generally suspicious of hype and exaggerations and may respond negatively to a 'hard sell' approach that might be effective in the United States. They often seem to treat business discussions as intellectual exercises and can get carried away with passionate debates over seemingly small issues. Know your topic well, and use logical arguments and concrete examples to back up your proposals. Having your English-language hand-out materials translated to French is not a must, but it will be noted very favorably.

Negotiation

Attitudes and Styles - In France, the primary approach to negotiating is to engage in a debate aimed at reaching a mutually agreeable solution. While the buyer is in a superior position, both sides in a business deal own the responsibility to reach agreement. They may focus equally on near-term and long-term benefits. The primary negotiation style is cooperative, but people may be unwilling to agree with compromises unless it is their only option to keep the negotiation from getting stuck. In addition, negotiators in this country may be very passionate and can appear outright aggressive. The French may not always show a win-win attitude, especially if they believe that 'logical' reasons support their position. While the exchange of facts and arguments may get heated, it is vital to avoid any open confrontation and to remain calm, composed, patient, and persistent.

Sharing of Information – French negotiators may spend significant time gathering information and discussing details before the bargaining stage of a negotiation can begin. They usually share at least some information and rarely take it negatively if you ask about sensitive details, even if they may not want to answer. However, you may have to find critical bits of information yourself. It can be highly valuable to leverage other contacts with the French side if you have any.

The French value Cartesian logic. Accordingly, they will take nothing for granted until it is demonstrated.

Pace of Negotiation – Expect negotiations to be slow. While the French may not always spend a lot of time in preparing for the negotiation, bargaining and decision making can take a long time. Aspects of your proposals may be analyzed and scrutinized repeatedly. Remain patient, control your emotions, and accept the inevitable delays.

The French, especially in the South, generally employ a polychronic work style. They are used to pursuing multiple actions and goals in parallel. When negotiating, they often take a holistic approach and may jump back and forth between topics rather than addressing them in sequential order. In multi-item negotiations, people may bargain and haggle over several aspects in parallel. In the middle of an argument, the focus may change away from the immediate issue. It is not unusual for the French to re-open a discussion over items that had already been agreed upon. In addition, they may take phone calls or interrupt meetings at critical points in a negotiation. While they may be doing some of this on purpose in order to confuse the other side, there are usually no bad intentions. Negotiators from strongly monochronic cultures, such as Germany, the United Kingdom, or the United States, may nonetheless find this style confusing and irritating. In any case, do not show irritation or anger when encountering this behavior. Instead, keep track of the bargaining progress at all times, often emphasizing areas where agreement already exists.

Bargaining – The French are not fond of bargaining and strongly dislike haggling. The bargaining stage of a negotiation may take substantial time, though, with significant time spent discussing proposals and debating the merits of specific terms and conditions. Prices rarely move by more than 25 to 30 percent between initial offers and final agreement. Businesspeople in this country may only make concessions if the logic of their arguments has been defeated. Exaggerated claims or bragging will not help your position. However, the French will remain open to any new information.

Deceptive techniques might be used and it may be effective to use some of them yourself. This includes tactics such as telling lies and sending fake non-verbal messages, misrepresenting an item's value, or making false demands and concessions. The French are very good at pretending to be disinterested in the whole deal or in single concessions, making you feel like a petitioner. Carefully orchestrated, 'good cop, bad cop' may be an effective tactic to use in your own negotiation approach. Businesspeople may claim limited authority, stating that they have to ask for their manager's approval. This could be a tactic or the truth.

Negotiators in the country may use pressure techniques that include opening with their best offer, showing intransigence, applying time pressure, or making final or expiring offers. Some of these may be done very compellingly and can only be countered by 'calling the bluff.' When using similar tactics yourself, avoid being overly aggressive. Silence is rarely used as a negotiation technique. Avoid using decreasing offers as they will likely be viewed as offensive and inappropriate.

Though they may appear aggressive, French negotiators are rarely openly adversarial. Threats and warnings may be used, but negotiators in the country rarely openly display anger or walk out of the room. Using extreme openings may sometimes help in obtaining information since the French may view it as an intellectual challenge. However, since it could also be viewed as unfriendly, use the technique with caution. Persistence alone rarely helps in making progress unless it is paired with new ideas and arguments.

Negotiators may sometimes use emotional techniques such as attitudinal bargaining, sending dual messages, attempting to make you feel guilty, grimacing, or appealing to personal relationships. It is best to remain calm and composed, repeating the arguments that support your position.

French businesspeople may employ defensive tactics such as changing the subject, blocking, asking probing or direct questions, making promises, or keeping an inflexible position. All of these are ok to use against them as well.

Corruption and bribery are rare in France, though not completely unheard of. Both legally and ethically, it is advisable to stay away from giving gifts of significant value or making offers that could be read as bribery.

Should a negotiation stall, the French will often keep restating their position. It takes a new fact or aspect to break the impasse. Disputes are resolved by focusing on logical reasoning and facts. Generally, it can be effective to use surprise or distraction tactics in case of conflicts as a way to get your counterparts to take a different look at the situation.

Decision Making – The country's business culture is quite hierarchical. Decision makers are usually senior executives who consider the best interest of the group or organization. While they are likely to consult with others, bosses accept all of the responsibility. The people you are dealing with may only be intermediaries. Nevertheless, they could strongly influence the final decision, so try to win their support. Gaining access to top managers can be difficult. The French may examine every minute detail before arriving at a decision. Consequently, decision making is a very slow and deliberate process in France. On the other hand, it is an accepted practice to work around rules and regulations if needed. This often requires the support of an influential contact that is willing to help.

When making decisions, French businesspeople usually consider the specific situation rather than applying universal principles. Empirical evidence, logical arguments, and objective facts weigh much more strongly than personal feelings and experiences do. The French are often uneasy with change and reluctant to take risks. If you expect them to support a risky decision, you may need to find ways for them to become comfortable with it first, for instance by explaining contingency plans, outlining areas of additional support, or by offering guarantees and warranties.

Agreements and Contracts

Capturing and exchanging written understandings after meetings and at key negotiation stages is useful since oral statements are not always dependable. Although interim agreements are usually kept, do not consider them final. Only a final contract signed by both parties constitutes a binding agreement.

Written contracts tend to be lengthy. They often spell out detailed terms and conditions for the core agreements as well as for many eventualities. Signing the contract is important not only from a legal perspective, but also as a strong confirmation of your French partners' commitment.

It is recommended to consult a local legal expert before signing a contract. However, do not bring your attorney to the negotiation table.

Contracts are usually dependable, and the agreed terms are viewed as binding. Requests to change contract details after signature may be considered as bad faith and will meet with strong resistance. While your counterparts will expect you to keep all your commitments and respond harshly if you fail to do so, they may not always fulfill their own obligations to the letter.

Women in Business

While French society is making progress towards gender equality and some women hold important positions, most of them are still struggling to attain positions of similar income and authority as men. As a visiting businesswoman, emphasize your company's importance and your role in it.

Female business travelers should graciously accept any chivalric gestures they receive. Displaying confidence and assertiveness can be effective, but it is important not to appear overly bold and aggressive.

Other Important Things to Know

Conservative attire is important when doing business here. Businesspeople dress less fashionably than you may expect, given the country's reputation. Male business visitors should wear dark suits with neckties on most occasions, a bit more fashionable clothing for evening events. First impressions can have a significant impact on how people view you.

Business discussions are frequent during lunches, but don't suggest to 'work through lunch.' In addition, do not expect to discuss business during a dinner. The topic may and often will come up at the end of the meal, but you should wait for your host to bring it up.

Etiquette in eating is important. Be on your best behavior during all meals in France.

Social events do not require strict punctuality. While it is best to arrive at dinners close to the agreed time, being to a party by 10-15 minutes late is acceptable. This is more relaxed in the South.

Gift giving in business settings is rare. It is best not to bring a gift to an initial meeting in order to avoid raising suspicions about your motives.

The French have great respect for privacy. A person's home is usually off limits. Even when someone invited you to a dinner at his or her home, do not expect to see much of it.

Germany

German businesspeople, especially those among younger generations, are usually very experienced in interacting and doing business with visitors from other cultures. However, that does not always mean that they are open-minded. When negotiating business here, realize that some people may expect things to be done 'their way.'

While German culture is still relatively homogeneous, the reunification of the eastern part of the country in 1990 introduced new aspects as the East Germans had adopted some differing values during two generations of communist rule. However, West German influences tend to prevail in the country's business life, even in the East of the country.

Relationships and Respect

Business relationships are often only moderately important in this country and are usually not a necessary precondition for initial business interactions. Your counterparts' expectation may be to get to know you better as you do business together. Until business interactions that have met their approval have been conducted, most Germans will be very cautious, appear quite reserved, and proceed slowly. Once the necessary trust has been established, though, there will be a sense of loyalty to you as a respected business partner, which can go a long way should a difficult situation arise. Most German businesspeople expect their partners to make a long-term commitment to the engagement.

Business relationships in this country exist between companies as well as between individuals. If your company replaces you with someone else over the course of a negotiation, it may be easy for your replacement to take things over from where you left them. Likewise, if you introduce someone else from your company into an existing business relationship, that person may quickly be accepted as a valid business partner. This does not mean that the Germans do not care about who they are dealing with. Personal integrity and dependability are important if you want to win their trust.

Although they prefer to keep business and private life separate, it is possible to build strong personal relationships with your German business partners. This will take time, usually months or even years. Attempts to accelerate this process may only raise suspicion. Honesty is a key factor and trust is much more easily lost than gained in this country. Paradoxically, if your German counterparts tell you some unpleasant truths, that may actually indicate that they feel good about the relationship with you. They may expect you to be equally candid once close ties have been established. Nevertheless, Germans can be very sensitive to criticism. Be careful not to embarrass them publicly. If in doubt, it is usually better to phrase your inputs more subtly than your German counterparts themselves might do. For example, people may be quick to blame others when problems occur, but they may take it very negatively if a foreigner does the same with them.

In Germany's business culture, the respect a person enjoys depends primarily on his or her achievements, status and rank, and education. Admired personal traits include dependability, analytical thinking, knowledge, and experience.

Most Germans believe that their country's workers are more effective than others. This is a matter of great pride, so even if you have evidence to the contrary, it is best not to challenge this belief.

Communication

The country's official language is German. However, pronunciation and vocabulary vary greatly across different regions, which may complicate the communication for someone who learned German as a foreign language. Many businesspeople speak English, often well, and interpreters are rarely needed. However, many Germans prefer and are more familiar with British English. Since it is different from American English to the point where misunderstandings may happen easily, familiarize yourself with the differences upfront if necessary. Speaking in short, simple sentences and avoiding jargon and slang are helpful.

Businesspeople may speak a bit louder than those in most other cultures, though usually not as loud as Americans. However, speaking slowly and clearly is a sign of authority. At restaurants, especially those used for business lunches and dinners, keep conversations at a quiet level. Being loud may be regarded as bad manners. People generally converse standing about three to four feet apart.

German communication is usually very direct. Germans dislike vague statements and may openly share opinions, concerns, and feelings with others. In fact, too much diplomacy may confuse and irritate Germans and can give the impression of insincerity. They may ask for clarifications and do not find it difficult to say 'no' if they dislike a request or proposal. If something is against company policy or cannot be done for other reasons, your counterpart will likely say so or reject the proposition without explanation. They may view this as a simple statement of fact and might not understand that someone else could consider this directness insensitive. When communicating via letters or e-mail, do not waste time looking for messages 'between the lines.' Since the communication is mostly straightforward, there may not be any.

At times, people may appear overly blunt and confrontational. Discussions among Germans may appear heated or even combative to the outsider. Do not read too much into this – they could actually be close friends. However, while they are generally quite formal and controlled, people can become highly emotional and show little restraint if their sense of order is challenged.

The American habit of first highlighting the positives before addressing issues may confuse Germans. In this culture, each has to stand on its own, so when raising a concern, do so without 'softening' the message.

Germans use body language sparingly, although facial expressions and other clues can be quite telling, especially if they dislike an idea or proposal. They may make some physical contact, such as a backslap as a sign of friendship, but such contacts are rare. The American *OK* sign, with thumb and index finger forming a circle, is an obscene gesture in Germany, as is putting the thumb between index and middle finger in a fist. The thumbs-up gesture is positive as it signals approval. Eye contact should be frequent, almost to the point of staring, as this conveys sincerity and helps build trust.

Initial Contacts and Meetings

Having a local contact can be an advantage but is usually not a necessary precondition to doing business in Germany. Negotiations can be conducted by individuals or teams of negotiators. You may find a German team compartmentalizing their arguments, with each member focusing on a specific area.

If possible, schedule meetings at least one to two weeks in advance, and do not cancel one on short notice since that can be viewed as rude. Germans may want to know whom they will be meeting, so provide details on titles, positions, and responsibilities of attendees ahead of time. It is common practice to agree on an agenda upfront. As that agenda is usually strictly followed, it is advisable to put the most important subject at the top. Germans may remind others of the agreed-upon agenda and may interrupt if they feel someone is getting off topic or addressing secondary points they do not consider important. This may be very uncomfortable for visitors from strongly relationship-oriented cultures where the concept of *face* is important.

If you are unsure about company style and procedures when preparing for a meeting, do not hesitate to ask your German counterpart in private what to expect. Doing so does not leave your counterpart in any uncomfortable position. If anything, this person may take your question as a sign that you are making a serious effort to re-spect German habits and will not hesitate to give you advice.

At any meeting, whether business or social, it is strongly advisable to be very punc-tual. The German term for being late, 'zu spät,' translates into 'too late' in English. Being more than 10 to 15 minutes late without having a valid and plausible excuse can be a serious offense.

Names are usually given in the order of first name, family name. Note that Southern Germans may state their names in the opposite order, which can be confusing. Some Germans have two first names, often with a hyphen between them. In any case, use *Mr./Ms.* or *Herr/Frau* plus the family name to address someone. If a person has an academic title, such as *Doktor* or *Professor*, it is important to use it in addition, fol-lowed by the family name, as in 'Herr Doktor Meier.' Including professional titles as well, such as in 'Herr Direktor Doktor,' is now considered old-fashioned. Only close friends call each other by their first names. You may never get to that point in a business relationship, although it is becoming more common among young people. Introduce and greet high-ranking and senior people first. If possible, wait to be in-troduced rather than doing it yourself. Introductions are accompanied by firm hand-shakes. Men should wait for women to initiate handshakes.

The exchange of business cards is an essential step when meeting someone for the first time, so bring more than you need. Most businesspeople in Germany read Eng-lish, so there is no need to have your card translated. However, it will be appreciated if you do. Show advanced degrees on your card and make sure that it clearly states your professional title, especially if you have the seniority to make decisions. When presenting your card, smile and keep eye contact, then take a few moments to look at the card you received. Next, place it on the table in front of you.

Meetings may start with little or no small talk. Most of the interactions will focus on business topics. People appreciate a sense of humor, but be very careful not to overdo it. One's private life is not a subject for discussion around meetings. Business is a seri-ous matter in Germany.

Most meetings are quite formal. While the primary purpose of the first meeting is to become acquainted, the discussion will quickly focus on technical aspects of the business. It is vital to come well prepared as Germans hate wasting time. They may launch into what could feel like an academic oral examination, with many hard-and-fast questions. While this can be very uncomfortable for the foreign visitor, a high intensity of such questioning signals that the German side is seriously interested. Before they feel they can make any commitments, they seek to understand risks and eliminate uncertainties, so it is in your best interest to play along.

Presentation materials should be attractive, with good and clear visuals, but not too flashy. Keep your presentation succinct and methodically thought out, but make sure it includes all details your counterparts may consider important. Since Ger-mans value directness, be straightforward about both positive and negative aspects of your proposal. Germans are generally suspicious of hype and exaggerations and may respond negatively to an aggressive sales approach that might be effective in the United States. Throughout the meeting, remain positive even if your audience seems overly critical. Germans often look for deficiencies in your products or services and may openly draw your attention to them. This does not mean that they do not like what you are presenting. Know your topic well, and use logical arguments and concrete examples to back up your proposals. At the end of a presentation, Germans may signal their approval by rapping their knuckles on the tabletop instead of applauding. Other indicators of sincere interest include in-depth technical discussions and requests for further technical information.

Having your English-language handout materials translated is not required, though it will be appreciated. Germans are usually not impressed by high-gloss brochures and catchy slogans. Informational brochures should be serious in tone, providing a substantial amount of technical data and other hard facts. Your products are expected to conform exactly to the descriptions given.

Negotiation

Attitudes and Styles – To Germans, negotiating is usually a joint problem-solving process. While the buyer is in a superior position, both sides in a business deal own the responsibility to reach agreement. They may focus equally on near-term and long-term benefits. The primary negotiation style is cooperative, but people may be unwilling to agree with compromises unless it is their only option to keep the negotiation from getting stuck. Since Germans believe in the concept of win-win, they expect you to reciprocate their respect and trust. It is strongly advisable to avoid any open confrontation and to remain calm, friendly, patient, and persistent.

Should a dispute arise at any stage of a negotiation, you might be able to reach resolution by focusing on logical arguments and additional data. Try to find some common ground with your counterparts. At times, apologies may help make Germans more conciliatory.

Sharing of Information – German negotiators may spend considerable time gathering information and discussing details before the bargaining stage of a negotiation can begin. They may ask numerous questions to obtain additional information. They will not take it negatively if you ask about sensitive details, even if they may not want to answer, though they usually share at least some of their information. While it can be counterproductive to appear as if you are hiding facts from your German counterparts, they will be accepting if you state openly that you do not want to share certain information.

Pace of Negotiation – Expect negotiations to be slow. The methodical and carefully planned approach Germans use in preparing for the negotiation and gathering information takes considerable time, as does the effort needed to work out details of an agreement. Remain patient, control your emotions, and accept the inevitable delays.

Germans generally prefer a monochronic work style. They are used to pursuing actions and goals systematically, and they dislike interruptions or digressions. When negotiating, they often work their way down a list of objectives in sequential order, bargaining for each item separately, and may be unwilling to revisit aspects that have already been agreed upon. They can get highly agitated or even emotional if a more polychronic counterpart challenges this approach, which they view as systematic and effective. This rigid style may be difficult to tolerate for negotiators from highly polychronic cultures, such as most Asians, Arabs, some Southern Europeans, or most Latin Americans, who may view it as closed-minded and overly restrictive. In any case, do not show irritation or anger when encountering this behavior. Instead, be willing to bargain over some items individually. Otherwise, clearly indicate that your agreement is conditional and contingent on other items.

Bargaining – Germans are not fond of bargaining and strongly dislike haggling. Many of them do not appreciate aggressive sales techniques and view negotiations as a 'necessary evil' rather than a process to enjoy. Although the bargaining stage of a negotiation can be extensive, prices rarely move by more than 15 to 25 percent between initial offers and final agreement. Businesspeople in this country do not make concessions easily.

Germans prefer to negotiate in a very straightforward style. They use deceptive techniques only infrequently, such as telling lies, sending fake non-verbal messages, pretending to be disinterested in the whole deal or in single concessions, misrepresenting an item's value, or making false demands and concessions. Carefully orchestrated, 'good cop, bad cop' may be an effective tactic to use in your own negotiation approach. Germans may claim limited authority, stating that they have to ask for their manager's approval. More often than not, this will be the truth.

Negotiators in the country may use pressure techniques that include opening with their best offer or showing intransigence. When using similar tactics yourself, clearly explain your offer and avoid being overly aggressive. Germans may make final offers quite early in the bargaining process; while this is not common practice, they could actually be serious. Periods of silence in conversations are normal and may not represent an attempt to use it as a negotiation technique. Be careful when using pressure tactics such as applying time pressure, making expiring offers, or nibbling. Your counterparts may consider these inappropriate unless they are strongly interested in your offer and clearly understand the rationale behind the approach. Otherwise, while the negotiation is not necessarily over, it may become less constructive.

While German negotiators may occasionally appear aggressive, they rarely view it that way themselves and usually do not employ such behavior for tactical reasons. They will not shy away from open confrontation if challenged, though. Attempts to gain advantages by being aggressive with a large German company will likely work against you. Threats and warnings, openly displayed anger, or walkouts may be used to some degree, but they are normally based upon calculated negotiation strategies rather than aggressive attitudes. Extreme openings are viewed as inappropriate and may upset your German counterparts. It is best to open with an offer that is already in the ballpark of what you really expect.

Emotional negotiation techniques, such as attitudinal bargaining, attempting to make you feel guilty, or grimacing, may occasionally be employed. It is best to remain calm. Appeals to personal relationships are rare. Germans often employ defensive tactics such as blocking, asking probing or very direct questions, or keeping an inflexible position.

Opening with written offers and introducing written terms and conditions may be effective as doing so allows for proper preparation and could help shorten the bargaining process. Your German counterparts will likely find both benefits desirable.

Corruption and bribery are very rare in Germany. It is strongly advisable to stay away from giving gifts of significant value or making offers that could be read as bribery.

Decision Making – Companies are often very hierarchical, even though they initially may not seem that way, and people expect to work within clearly established lines of authority. Nevertheless, Germans do not accept authority as readily as others might assume; in the German view, hierarchies are effective since they help establish order, not because bosses are 'better' than those they manage.

Decision makers are usually senior executives who consider the best interest of the group or organization. They may delegate their authority to lower levels, which is often done in a formal process that includes written approvals. Decisions are often made by consensus of a group of senior managers. It is important to find or create opportunities to directly influence the decision makers rather than only meeting with subordinates. Because decision making is a methodical process that is conducted with great diligence and precision, it takes much time and requires patience. Once a decision has been made, it is extremely difficult to change.

When making decisions, businesspeople may apply universal principles rather than considering the specific situation. They often dislike 'making exceptions,' even when arguments speak in favor of doing so. Personal feelings and experiences are considered irrelevant in business negotiations, so people focus on empirical evidence, logical arguments, and objective facts. Germans are often uneasy with change and reluctant to take risks. If you expect them to support a risky decision, you may need to find ways for them to become comfortable with it first, for instance by explaining contingency plans, outlining areas of additional support, or by offering guarantees and warranties.

Agreements and Contracts

Capturing and exchanging meeting summaries can be an effective way to verify understanding and commitments. Oral agreements and statements of intent may already be legally binding and are usually dependable, though they do not substitute for written contracts. Actions that have been agreed upon are usually implemented immediately, even if a final contract is still pending.

Know that German law makes offers binding unless otherwise noted. It is best to mark your offers with 'good until …' or to add a 'subject to change' clause.

Written contracts are serious matters in Germany and tend to be lengthy. They often spell out very detailed terms and conditions for the core agreements as well as for many eventualities. Legal aspects may be reviewed repeatedly. Signing the contract is important not only from a legal perspective, but also as a strong confirmation of your partners' commitment. In most German companies, only high-ranking managers have signature authority. They will sign *i.V.* ('in Vertretung,' meaning that they have full authority to represent their company) or *p.p.* ('per procura,' which means that their authority is limited).

It is recommended to consult a local legal expert before signing a contract. However, do not bring your attorney to the negotiation table as it may be viewed as a sign of mistrust.

Contracts are usually dependable, and the agreed terms are viewed as binding. Requests to change contract details after signature may be considered as bad faith and will meet with strong resistance. Failure to meet the terms and conditions of a signed contract may trigger legal action against you. However, German punctuality does not always extend to deadlines and delivery commitments. Significant delays may happen without explanation or apology.

Women in Business

While German society is making progress towards gender equality, few women have managed to attain positions of similar income and authority as men. As a visiting businesswoman, emphasize your company's importance and your role in it. A personal introduction or a letter of support from a senior executive within your company may also help.

As a female business traveler, displaying confidence and assertiveness can be effective, but it is important not to appear overly bold and aggressive.

Other Important Things to Know

While wearing conservative attire is always a safe choice when doing business here, do not show surprise or make any comments if your German counterparts show up in outfits that combine unusual colors or include unorthodox fashion accessories. In any case, posture is important in this country. An overly laid-back attitude may be viewed as impolite or even disrespectful.

Business lunches and dinners are common. However, business is rarely discussed over dinner. Wait to see whether your counterparts bring it up.

Gift giving in business settings is rare. It is best not to bring a gift to an initial meeting in order to avoid raising suspicions about your motives.

Greece

Though the country's culture is quite homogeneous, Greek businesspeople, especially those among younger generations, are usually experienced in interacting and doing business with visitors from other cultures. However, that does not always mean that they are open-minded. When negotiating business here, realize that people may expect things to be done 'their way.' Greeks tend to be very proud of their country and may strongly reject any critique of its ways.

Relationships and Respect

Building lasting and trusting personal relationships is critically important to most Greeks, who may expect to establish strong bonds prior to closing any deals. People in this country usually want to do business only with those they know and like. Establishing productive business cooperation requires a long-term perspective and commitment. Consequently, proceed with serious business discussions only after your counterparts have become very comfortable with you. This is usually a slow process. Greeks tend to distrust people who appear unwilling to spend the time or whose motives for relationship building are unclear.

Business relationships in this country exist between people, not necessarily between companies. Even when you have won your local business partners' friendship and trust, they will not necessarily trust others from your company. That makes it very important to keep company interfaces unchanged. Changing a key contact may require the relationship building process to start over.

Establishing personal relationships with others in Greece can create powerful networks and is vital to doing business. Whom you know may determine whether people want to get to know you. Personal networks rely mostly on strong friendships that also represent dependable mutual obligations. They may open doors and solve problems that would otherwise be very difficult to master. Maintaining honest and cordial relations is crucial. Third party introductions can be very helpful as a starting point to building a trusting relationship with a potential partner.

'Saving face' is very essential in Greece. Causing embarrassment to another person may cause a *loss of face* for all parties involved and can be disastrous for business negotiations. The importance of diplomatic restraint and tact cannot be overestimated. Keep your cool and never show openly that you are upset. Avoid open conflict, and know that politeness is crucial. While Greeks are usually very friendly, they are very proud and may be easily offended.

In the Greek business culture, the respect a person enjoys depends primarily on his or her age, rank, and status. However, personal achievements are now playing a bigger role than they used to. It is important to treat elderly people with the greatest respect. Admired personal traits include personal warmth and sociability.

Communication

Greek is the country's official language. Many businesspeople speak at least some English. It may occasionally be beneficial to use an interpreter, though. To avoid offending the other side, ask beforehand whether an interpreter should be present at a meeting. When communicating in English, speak in short, simple sentences and avoid using jargon and slang. It will help people with a limited command of English if you speak slowly, summarize your key points often, and pause frequently to allow for interpretation.

Since they respect assertiveness, Greeks usually speak forcefully. Conversations may get loud and passionate. Greeks usually show their emotions openly. However, never lose your temper or appear impatient. People in the country generally converse in close proximity, standing only two feet or less apart. Never back away, even if this is much closer than your personal comfort zone allows. Doing so could be read as a sign that you are uncomfortable around them.

Communication in Greece can be direct and straightforward, especially among friends and close business partners. Early in the business relationship, people may communicate more indirectly, appearing vague and non-committal. If in doubt, watch for subtle messages that may signal issues and concerns. Silence is often a way to communicate a negative message.

Gestures and body language can be extensive. It is often not a good idea to imitate them, though. There may be frequent physical contact with others of the same gender. The American *OK* sign, with thumb and index finger forming a circle, may be taken as an obscene gesture in Greece. It is also rude to cross your arms while facing a person. Eye contact should be frequent, almost to the point of staring. This conveys sincerity and helps build trust. It is best to mask anger with a smile.

The Greek way to signal 'no' is by raising the eyebrows, sometimes together with a backward tilt of the head. Tilting the head to the side may signal 'yes.' However, many Greeks have adopted the western way of nodding or shaking the head.

Initial Contacts and Meetings

Before initiating business negotiations in Greece, it is advantageous to identify and engage a local intermediary. This person will help bridge the cultural and communications gap, allowing you to conduct business with greater effectiveness.

Negotiations in Greece can be conducted by individuals or teams of negotiators. Changing a team member may require the relationship building process to start over and should therefore be avoided. The most senior executive on your side should have the necessary authority and clearly act as the leader of your team. Similarly, the highest-ranking person on the Greek side will likely attend and will be the decision maker.

If possible, schedule meetings at least one to two weeks in advance. Since Greeks want to know whom they will be meeting, provide details on titles, positions, and responsibilities of attendees ahead of time. They will expect to do business with the most important person in your organization. Setting an agenda upfront is usually not necessary. It would likely not be followed anyway. Although Greeks may not be very punctual, foreign visitors are generally expected to be on time. Avoid being more than 10 to 15 minutes late, and call ahead if you will be. Displaying anger if you have to wait reflects very poorly on you.

Names are usually given in the order of first name, family name. Use *Mr./Mrs./Miss* plus the family name. If a person has a professional or academic title, use it instead, followed by the family name. Before calling Greeks by their first name, wait until they offer it. Greet the most senior person first, and then greet everyone else in the room individually. Introductions are accompanied by firm handshakes.

After the introductions, offer your business card to everyone present. The process of exchanging cards is usually quite relaxed. There is no need to have them translated to Greek, but it will be preferably noted if you do. When presenting your card, smile and keep eye contact, then take a few moments to look at the card you received. Next, place it on the table in front of you.

Meetings start with small talk, which can be extensive. It is important to be patient and let the other side set the pace. Initial meetings can be quite formal, but this usually gets more relaxed as the relationship develops. Some humor is welcome, but always keep it light and friendly. Meetings in Greece may appear somewhat chaotic, with frequent interruptions and several parallel conversations. Do not take this personally; it also does not indicate a lack of interest.

The primary purpose of the first meeting is to become acquainted and build relationships. Little else may happen, and you may actually not get to talk about business at all. It is unrealistic to expect initial meetings to lead to straight decisions.

Presentation materials should be attractively designed, with good and clear visuals. Greeks communicate primarily orally and visually, so avoid using too much text. Having your handout materials translated to Greek is not a must, but it helps in getting your messages across.

Negotiation

Attitudes and Styles - Leveraging relationships is an important element when negotiating in Greece. Greeks often engage in debates aimed at reaching a mutually agreeable solution. However, negotiating in the country may also include tough bargaining at many levels. While the buyer is in a superior position, both sides in a business deal own the responsibility to reach agreement. They expect long-term commitments from their business partners and will focus mostly on long-term benefits. Although the primary negotiation style is competitive, the Greek nevertheless value long-term relationships and look for win-win solutions. While proposals should demonstrate the benefits to both negotiating parties, attempts to win competitive advantages should not be taken negatively. You earn your counterparts' respect by maintaining a positive, persistent attitude.

Should a dispute arise at any stage of a negotiation, you might be able to reach resolution or an acceptable compromise by leveraging personal relationships, assuming that they are strong enough.

Sharing of Information – The level of information sharing depends largely on the strength of the relationship. During initial negotiations, the Greeks often play their cards close to the chest.

Pace of Negotiation – Expect negotiations to be slow and protracted, and be prepared to make several trips if necessary to achieve your objectives. Initial exchanges that precede the bargaining stage of the negotiation may be lengthy. Decisions are usually made between meetings rather than at the table. Throughout the negotiation, be patient, control your emotions, and accept that delays occur. Attempts to rush the process are unlikely to produce better results and may be viewed as offensive.

Greeks generally employ a polychronic work style. They are used to pursuing multiple actions and goals in parallel. When negotiating, they often take a holistic approach and may jump back and forth between topics rather than addressing them in sequential order. Negotiators from strongly monochronic cultures, such as Germany, the United Kingdom, or the United States, may find this style confusing, irritating, and even annoying. In any case, do not show irritation or anger when encountering this behavior. Instead, keep track of the bargaining progress at all times, often emphasizing areas where agreement already exists.

If your counterparts appear to be stalling the negotiation, assess carefully whether their slowing down the process indicates that they are evaluating alternatives or that they are not interested in doing business with you. While such behavior could represent attempts to create time pressure in order to obtain concessions, the slow decision process in the country is far more likely causing the lack of progress. People from fast-paced cultures tend to underestimate how much time this takes and often make the mistake of trying to 'speed things up.' Again, patience and persistence are vitally important.

Bargaining – Most Greeks enjoy bargaining and haggling. They expect to do a lot of it during a negotiation. This may include a lot of drama, exaggerations, and bragging. Your counterparts may be offended if you refuse to play along.

The bargaining exchange of a negotiation can be very extensive. Opening stage and initial offers on both sides are critically important when negotiating with Greeks. Many believe that the first person to quote a price will end up getting the worse part of the deal, and that initial proposals should never be accepted. Accordingly, either they may wait for you to make an initial offer and then reject it right away, or they open with an extreme offer that is far from realistic, carefully watching your response. Know your objectives, and work slowly and persistently towards them. At the same time, remain professional and keep a positive attitude throughout the exchange.

Prices often move 40 percent or more between initial offers and final agreement. Leave yourself a lot of room for concessions at different stages. However, concessions will never come easily, and Greeks sometimes find it difficult to change their position. When conceding yourself, present this as a decision you made because you like and respect your counterpart. Always ask the other side to reciprocate. You can use the fact that aspects can be re-visited to your advantage, for instance by offering further concessions under the condition that the Greek side reciprocate in areas that had already been agreed upon.

Deceptive techniques are frequent and can be effective. This includes tactics such as telling lies and sending fake non-verbal messages, pretending to be disinterested in the whole deal or in single concessions, misrepresenting an item's value, or making false demands and concessions. Expect your Greek counterparts to be good at this game. They may occasionally play stupid or otherwise attempt to mislead you in order to obtain bargaining advantages. Lies will be difficult to detect. It is advisable to verify information received from the local side through other channels. Even when you can see right through a lie, it would be a grave personal insult to state or even hint that your counterpart is not telling the truth. Greeks rarely claim limited authority since you will usually be dealing directly with the decision maker.

Negotiators in the country may use pressure techniques that include making final offers or nibbling. Final offers may come more than once and are rarely final. Do not use tactics such as applying time pressure, opening with your best offer, or making decreasing or expiring offers, since your Greek counterparts could view these as signs that you are not willing to build a long-term relationship. They may choose to terminate the negotiation. Silence can be an effective way to signal rejection of a proposal.

Greek negotiators avoid openly aggressive or adversarial techniques but may use more subtle versions. Extreme openings are frequently employed as a way to start the bargaining process. In addition, they may make indirect threats and warnings or subtly display anger. Use these tactics with caution yourself since they may adversely affect the relationship if employed too aggressively. Do not walk out or threaten to do so as your counterparts will likely take this as a personal insult and may end all talks.

Emotional negotiation techniques, such as attitudinal bargaining, sending dual messages, attempting to make you feel guilty, grimacing, or appealing to personal relationships, are frequent and can be effective. Be cautious not to cause *loss of face* when employing any of them yourself. Also, know that Greeks tend to exaggerate situations and can become quite emotional during fierce bargaining. It is best to remain calm. At times, defensive tactics such as blocking or changing the subject, asking probing or very direct questions, making promises, or keeping an inflexible position may be used.

Corruption and bribery are somewhat common in Greece's public and private sectors. However, people may draw the line differently, viewing minor payments as rewards for getting a job done rather than as bribes. Also, keep in mind that there is a fine line between giving gifts and bribing. What you may consider a bribe, a Greek may view as only a nice gift.

Decision Making – Most companies are hierarchical, and people expect to work within clearly established lines of authority. Many businesses in Greece are still family-owned. Although the pace of business is accelerating, decision making can be a slow process. Decision makers are usually senior executives who consider the best interest of the group or organization. They may consult with others and often prefer to reach consensus before making the final call. Subordinates may be reluctant to accept responsibility. Decision makers also rarely delegate their authority, so it is important to deal with senior executives.

When making decisions, businesspeople usually consider the specific situation rather than applying universal principles. Personal feelings and experiences weigh much more strongly than empirical evidence and other objective facts do. Greeks are often uneasy with change and reluctant to take risks. If you expect them to support a risky decision, you may need to find ways for them to become comfortable with it first, for instance by explaining contingency plans, outlining areas of additional support, or by offering guarantees and warranties.

Agreements and Contracts

Capturing and exchanging written understandings after meetings and at key negotiation stages is useful since oral statements are not always dependable. It may be helpful to ask your counterparts to initial these write-ups as a way to document consensus. However, do not mistake them for final agreements. Any part of an agreement may still change significantly before both parties sign the contract.

Written contracts are usually kept high-level, capturing only the primary aspects, terms, and conditions of the agreement. Writing up and signing the contract is a formality. Greeks believe that the primary strength of an agreement lies in the partners' commitment rather than in its written documentation.

It is advisable to consult a local legal expert before signing a contract. However, do not bring your attorney to the negotiation table. Greeks may read it as a sign of mistrust if you do.

Signed contracts may not always be honored. This depends to no small degree on the strength of the continuing relationship between the contract partners. It is strongly advisable to continue staying in touch and maintaining the trust of your Greek business partner. Business partners usually expect the other side to remain somewhat flexible if conditions change, which may include agreeing to modify contract terms.

Women in Business

Greece remains a male-dominated society. Women may still be considered inferior and rarely attain important positions. As a visiting businesswoman, emphasize your company's importance and your role in it. A personal introduction or at least a letter of support from a senior executive within your company may help a lot.

Female business travelers should graciously accept any chivalric gestures they receive. While you should acknowledge compliments with a brief short smile, it is best to exercise caution and act professionally in business and social situations. Displaying confidence and some degree of assertiveness can be effective, but it is very important not to appear overly bold and aggressive.

Other Important Things to Know

Conservative attire is important when doing business here. Male business visitors should wear dark suits with neckties on most occasions. First impressions can have a significant impact on how people view you.

Social events do not require strict punctuality. While it is best to arrive at dinners close to the agreed time, being late to a party by 20 to 30 minutes is perfectly acceptable.

Greeks enjoys discussing politics and are often well informed. They may be very outspoken, openly sharing their opinion. It is best to take a neutral or positive stance in such discussions. The same applies if the topic of religion comes up in a conversation. Topics to avoid in discussions are Greece's relationship with Turkey, the tensions over Cyprus, as well as issues around the former Yugoslavian neighbors to the north. Greeks also dislike being stereotyped the way you may find in Hollywood movies. The culture is indeed quite diverse and complex.

Gift giving in business settings is rare. It is best not to bring a gift to an initial meeting in order to avoid raising suspicions about your motives. Never overly praise something your host owns. He may feel obliged to give it to you, which could create a very difficult situation.

Hong Kong

Reunited with China since the British rule ended in 1997, Hong Kong is technically a Chinese Special Administration Region, not a separate country. However, its quite homogeneous culture remains distinctly different from China's in several important areas. It would be a mistake to assume that Hong Kong and China are practically the same. One needs to prepare separately for negotiations in Hong Kong. With its entrepreneurial and intensely fast-paced business culture, Hong Kong in some ways stands in closer comparison with the United States than with China. Businesspeople in Hong Kong are generally less long-term oriented than their brethren in the People's Republic.

Hong Kong's businesspeople, especially those among younger generations, are usually experienced in interacting and doing business with visitors from other cultures. When negotiating business here, expect most people to be flexible and open-minded as they are eager to do business with others.

Relationships and Respect

Hong Kong's culture is generally group-oriented. Asserting individual preferences may be seen as less important than having a sense of belonging to a group, conforming to its norms, and maintaining harmony among its members. Building lasting and trusting personal relationships is therefore very important. While members of other cultures may expect this to happen gradually over the course of a business engagement, many Hong Kong Chinese expect to establish some level of relationship prior to closing any deals. Although this is gradually changing, it is still advantageous to proceed with serious business discussions only after you allowed your counterparts to become comfortable with you as a person. Once you have proven yourself a trustworthy partner, making the next deal will become much easier.

Relationships are based on familiarity, respect, and personal trust. Unlike in most western countries, business relationships in Hong Kong exist mostly between individuals or groups of people rather than between companies. Accordingly, if your company replaces you with another representative, relationships need to be built anew.

In Hong Kong's culture, 'saving face' is also critical. Harmony must be maintained at all cost, and emotional restraint is held in high esteem. Causing embarrassment to another person may cause a *loss of face* for all parties involved and can be disastrous for business negotiations. Reputation and social standing strongly depend on a person's ability to control one's emotions and remain friendly at all times. If you have to bring up an unpleasant topic with a person, never do so in public and always convey your message in ways that maintain the other's self-respect. The importance of diplomatic restraint and tact cannot be overestimated. Keep your cool and never show openly that you are upset.

Remaining modest and doing everything you can to maintain cordial relations is crucial to your success. When receiving praise, insist that you are not worthy of it or belittle your accomplishments, but thank the other for the compliment. This should not stop you from complimenting others. While the Hong Kong Chinese view politeness and humility as essential ingredients for a successful relationship, these factors do not affect their determination to reach business goals. They are patient and persistent in pursuing their objectives. It is in your best interest to do the same.

In Hong Kong's business culture, the respect a person enjoys depends primarily on his or her status, rank, achievements, and education. It is also important to treat elderly people with great respect. Admired personal traits include humility, sincerity, and fine manners.

Communication

Hong Kong's official languages are Chinese and English. Cantonese is the most widely spoken Chinese dialect here. Many businesspeople speak English, often quite well. However, it may occasionally be useful to have an interpreter. To avoid offending the other side, ask beforehand whether an interpreter should be present at a meeting. When communicating in English, speak in short, simple sentences and avoid using slang and jargon.

Businesspeople in Hong Kong usually speak in quiet, gentle tones. Conversations may occasionally include extended periods of silence. This does not necessarily convey a negative message. At times, Hong Kong Chinese people talking among themselves may appear emotional, but this would be misleading. To the contrary, emotional restraint is held in high esteem. At restaurants, especially those used for business lunches and dinners, keep conversations at a quiet level. Loud and boisterous behavior is perceived as a lack of self-control. People generally converse while standing around two to three feet apart.

Because the concept of 'saving face' is so important in this culture, communication is generally very indirect. When responding to a direct question, Hong Kong Chinese may answer 'yes' only to signal that they heard what you said, not that they agree with it. Open disagreement should be avoided and any kind of direct confrontation is discouraged. People rarely respond to a question or request with a direct 'no.' Instead, they may give seemingly ambiguous answers such as 'I am not sure,' 'we will think about it,' or 'this will require further investigation.' Each of these could mean 'no.' It is beneficial to use a similarly indirect approach when dealing with Hong Kong Chinese, as they may perceive you as rude and pushy if you are too direct. Only a person with whom you have no relationship yet may occasionally give you a straight 'no.' This is a bad sign since it could mean that your counterpart is not interested in engaging in business with you. If you have to convey bad news to the Chinese side, a face-saving way is to use a third party instead of communicating it yourself.

Gestures can be very subtle in Hong Kong. Non-verbal communication is important, though, and you should carefully watch for others' small hints, just as they will be watching you. Avoid touching other people except for handshakes. When pointing at people or objects, use your open hand rather than a finger. When referring to themselves, people put an index finger on their nose rather than pointing at their chest as

Westerners do. Eye contact should be infrequent. While it is beneficial to make some eye contact when meeting a person for the first time, the Hong Kong Chinese consider frequent eye contact intrusive and rude.

Do not take offense in Hong Kong businesspeople answering their mobile phones all the time, even in the middle of important discussions. In this polychronic culture, interrupting one conversation to have another one and then coming back to the first one is perfectly acceptable. It is not a sign of disrespect.

Initial Contacts and Meetings

Having a local contact can be an advantage but is usually not a necessary precondition to doing business. Most Hong Kong Chinese are experienced in doing international business.

It is often better to conduct negotiations in Hong Kong with a team of negotiators than to rely on a single individual. This signals importance, facilitates stronger relationship building, and may speed up the overall process. In addition, Hong Kong teams usually include highly skilled negotiators who know how to outmaneuver even well prepared individual counterparts. Facing them as a team will significantly strengthen your position. It is vital that teams be well aligned, with roles clearly assigned to each member. Local negotiators may be very good at exploiting disagreements between members of the other team to their advantage. Changing a team member may require the relationship building process to start over and should therefore be avoided.

If possible, schedule meetings at least three weeks in advance. Since the Chinese want to know whom they will be meeting, provide details on titles, positions, and responsibilities of attendees ahead of time. Agreeing on an agenda upfront can also be useful. Given the strong emphasis on hierarchy, a senior executive should lead the negotiations for your company and your negotiating team should include senior leaders who know your company well.

People are careful not to waste others' time. Being late to a meeting or social event without having a valid and plausible excuse can be an affront. Call ahead if you are going to be more than five minutes late. If a delay happened, which given the sometimes chaotic traffic is sometimes inevitable, apologize profoundly even if it was not your fault. The most senior person on your team should enter the meeting room first.

Chinese names are traditionally given in the order of family name, first name, where the latter may consist of two names, the generational name and the given name. These two are usually hyphenated but may be spoken and written as one. Many people use assumed western first names, in which case they give theirs in the order of first name followed by family name. Like their mainland neighbors, the Hong Kong Chinese are very status-conscious. If a person has a title or doctorate degree, use it to address that person, for example, 'Doctor Ng' or 'Director Chan.' Otherwise, use *Mr. / Ms.* plus the family name. Introduce and greet older people first. Before calling Hong Kong Chinese by their first name, wait until they offer it. Greetings are accompanied by slight bows and/or handshakes, which are light and may last as long as ten seconds.

The exchange of business cards is an essential step when meeting someone for the first time, so bring more than you need. If someone presents you with his or her card and you do not offer one in return, the person will assume that you either do not want to make their acquaintance, that your status in your company's hierarchy is very low, or, quite to the contrary, that your status is very high. Although many people are able to read English, it is preferable to use cards with one side in English and the other in Chinese. Show doctorate degrees on your card and make sure that it clearly states your professional title, especially if you have the seniority to make decisions. If any facts about your company are particularly noteworthy, for instance if it is the oldest or largest in your country or industry, mention this on your card since Hong Kong businesspeople may view it very favorably. Also, consider having your company logo (but not the whole card) printed in gold ink. In Chinese culture, gold is the color of prosperity.

Present your card with two hands, and ensure that the Chinese side is facing the recipient. Similarly, accept others' cards using both hands if possible. Smile and make eye contact while doing so, then examine the card carefully. Not reading someone's card can be an insult. Next, place the card on the table in front of you or into your card case. Never stuff someone's card into your back pocket or otherwise treat it disrespectfully.

At the beginning of a meeting, there may or may not be some small talk. It is best to let the local side set the pace and follow along. People appreciate a sense of humor, but keep it light and friendly, and be careful not to overdo it. Business is usually a serious matter in Hong Kong. While you will generally find the atmosphere to be pleasant at the first meeting, things may get very intense as the negotiation progresses.

The primary purpose of the first meeting is to get to know each other, start building relationships, and gather information about the other side's areas of interest, goals, and weak points for the upcoming negotiation. The most senior members of your group should lead the discussion. It is inappropriate for subordinates to interrupt. It is good to make a presentation, but keep it simple and avoid over-designing it. Verify through diplomatic questions whether your audience understands you. Since saving *face* is so important to the Chinese, people will not openly admit it in front of others if they do not understand what you are presenting.

You will likely find the atmosphere of the first meeting to be pleasant and amicable. Do not take this to mean that your negotiation will be easy. People may turn tough and much more intense as soon as the real negotiation starts. In this culture of respecting each others' *face*, the context of a situation often determines what behaviors are appropriate.

Most Chinese are comfortable with a high degree of initial vagueness. They may seem disinterested in clarifying many details until you have both come a long way with the business deal. Westerners may be uncomfortable with this perceived level of uncertainty. While it is acceptable and useful to try and clarify as much detail as possible even when your counterpart may not be eager to do so, do not read anything else into this style.

You should bring a sufficient number of copies of anything you present, such that each attendee gets one. The appearance of your presentation materials is not very important as long as you include good and easy-to-understand visuals. Because many colors have a special meaning for the Chinese, it is advisable to keep presentation copies, and even your actual slides, to black and white. Red is generally safe to use for illustrations and backgrounds since the Chinese consider it a happy color, but do not use it for text. Having your handout materials translated to Chinese is not a must, but it helps in getting your messages across. Bring a sufficient number of copies such that each attendee gets one. You may have to make presentations to different levels of the organization in subsequent meetings; make sure that each is tailored to its audience.

Negotiation

Attitudes and Styles - In Hong Kong, the primary approach to negotiating is to employ distributive and contingency bargaining. While the buyer is in a superior position, both sides in a business deal own the responsibility to reach agreement. They expect long-term commitments from their business partners and will focus mostly on long-term benefits. Although the primary negotiation style is competitive, the Hong Kong Chinese nevertheless value long-term relationships. Negotiators may at times appear highly competitive, though rarely adversarial. However, even when negotiating in a fairly direct and aggressive fashion, they ultimately maintain a long-term perspective and remain willing to compromise for the sake of the relationship. The culture promotes a win-win approach since this is the best way for everyone to save *face* throughout a negotiation. Do not confuse the sometimes-aggressive style with bad intentions. Keeping relationships intact throughout your negotiation is vital. It is therefore best to remain calm, friendly, patient, and persistent, never taking anything personally. It will also be very important to maintain continuity in the objectives you pursue, the messages you deliver, and the people you include in the negotiation.

Should a dispute arise at any stage of a negotiation, you might be able to reach resolution through emphasizing the benefits to both sides, remaining flexible and showing willingness to compromise. Show your commitment to the relationship and refrain from using logical reasoning or becoming argumentative since this will only make matters worse. Patience and creativity will pay strong dividends. In extreme situations, a mediator, ideally the party who initially introduced you, may help move the negotiation forward.

Sharing of Information – Hong Kong negotiators may be willing to spend considerable time gathering information and discussing various details before the bargaining stage of a negotiation can begin. Information is shared more openly than in China as Hong Kong's businesspeople believe in the value of give-and-take. However, expecting your counterpart to reveal everything you might want to know during your negotiation would be naïve.

Keep in mind that humility is a virtue in Hong Kong's business culture. If you make exaggerated claims in an effort to impress the other side or to obtain concessions, they will likely investigate your claims before responding.

Pace of Negotiation – While the implementation of agreements will be fast and swift, negotiations can be slow and protracted, with extensive attention paid to small details. Relationship building, information gathering, bargaining, and decision making all take time. Furthermore, negotiators often attempt to wear you down in an effort to obtain concessions. Be prepared to make several trips if necessary to achieve your objectives. Throughout the negotiation, be patient, show little emotion, and accept that delays may occur.

The Hong Kong Chinese generally employ a polychronic work style. They are used to pursuing multiple actions and goals in parallel. When negotiating, they often take a holistic approach and may jump back and forth between topics rather than ad-dressing them in sequential order. In multi-item negotiations, they may bargain and haggle over several items. It is not unusual for them to re-open a discussion over items that had already been agreed upon. In addition, they may take phone calls or interrupt meetings at critical points in a negotiation. While they may be doing some of this on purpose in order to confuse the other side, there are usually no bad inten-tions. Negotiators from strongly monochronic cultures, such as Germany, the United Kingdom, or the United States, may nonetheless find this style highly confusing and irritating. In any case, do not show irritation or anger when encountering this be-havior. Instead, keep track of the bargaining progress at all times, often emphasizing areas where agreement already exists.

If your counterparts appear to be stalling the negotiation, assess carefully whether their slowing down the process indicates that they are evaluating alternatives or that they are not interested in doing business with you. While such behavior could repre-sent attempts to create time pressure in order to obtain concessions, the slow decision process in the country is far more likely causing the lack of progress. People from fast-paced cultures tend to underestimate how much time this takes and often make the mistake of trying to 'speed things up.' Again, patience and persistence are vitally important.

Bargaining – Many Hong Kong businesspeople are shrewd negotiators who should not be underestimated. Although tactics may not be as extreme as those of their mainland neighbors, bargaining and haggling are aspects of everyday life in Hong Kong and its people are often skilled in using a wide array of negotiation techniques. The bargaining stage of a negotiation can be extensive. Prices may move by about 25 to 35 percent between initial offers and final agreement, sometimes even more. Leave yourself sufficient room for concessions at many different levels and prepare several alternative options. This gives the local negotiators room to refuse aspects of your proposal while preserving face. Ask the other side to reciprocate if you make concessions. It is not advisable to make significant early concessions since your coun-terparts expect further compromises as the bargaining continues. You can use the fact that aspects can be re-visited to your advantage, for instance by offering further concessions under the condition that the other side reciprocate in areas that had al-ready been agreed upon.

Deceptive techniques are frequent, and Hong Kong negotiators may expect you to use some of them as well. This includes tactics such as telling lies and sending fake non-verbal messages, pretending to be disinterested in the whole deal or in single concessions, misrepresenting an item's value, or making false demands and conces-sions. It is advisable to verify information received from the other side through other channels if you have a chance. Similarly, they treat 'outside' information with cau-tion. Since negotiation teams must be well aligned and always have to preserve face, businesspeople rarely use 'good cop, bad cop.' It can sometimes be beneficial to use this tactic in your own negotiation approach. Carefully orchestrated, they may allow you to obtain valuable concessions without damaging the overall relationship. However, it could be devastating if the other side recognized this as a tactic, and any 'bad cop' member of your team also needs to be excluded from future negotiation rounds. Depending on the decision structures within their company, the Hong Kong Chinese may or may not use the 'limited authority' technique. Be cautious when using the techniques of making false demands or false concessions. Since you must avoid causing loss of face, any overt attempts to bluff your counterparts could also backfire.

Negotiators may use pressure techniques that include keeping silent, making final or expiring offers, applying time pressure, or nibbling. Final offers may be made more than once and are almost never final. Do not announce any of your offers as 'final'– your counterparts will likely not believe that you are serious and may turn the tactic against you. Time pressure can be difficult to counter. If negotiators learn that you are working against a deadline, they may exploit this knowledge to increase the pressure on you to make concessions. Near the end of a negotiation, they may suddenly request large discounts, calling their request a 'compromise.' In extreme cases, they may try to renegotiate the whole deal on the final day of your visit. It is important never to take such techniques personally and to avoid open conflict. On the other hand, time pressure techniques rarely work against them since businesspeople in Hong Kong are patient and persistent enough to overcome such challenges. However, you might be able to use these techniques should the negotiation take place on your home turf rather than in Hong Kong. Silence can sometimes be effective as a way to convey displeasure, and nibbling may prove useful in the final phases of negotiations. None of this will take your counterparts by surprise, though. Avoid other common pressure tactics such as opening with your best offer or showing intransigence, since they cannot be applied effectively without running the risk of causing loss of face.

Hong Kong negotiators avoid most aggressive or adversarial techniques since they affect face. The risk of using any of them yourself is rarely worth the potential gain. Exceptions are extreme openings, which the Hong Kong Chinese use frequently, as well as threats and warnings. As long as an extreme opening offer is not openly aggressive, this approach can be effective. Should your counterparts appear aggressive as the bargaining gets more heated, remind yourself that they may not perceive it that way. It might be wise to deflect the pressure, for example by explaining other arrangements you have accepted for similar deals in the past.

As in most strongly relationship-oriented cultures, negotiators may sometimes use emotional techniques such as attitudinal bargaining, attempting to make you feel guilty, grimacing, or appealing to personal relationships. Be cautious when doing this yourself. You might cause the other side to lose face, which could in turn damage your negotiating position. Another emotional tactic you may encounter is if your counterpart proposes to 'split the difference.' You may often find that it is not in your best interest to accept. Politely explain why you cannot agree and make a counterproposal.

At times, defensive negotiation tactics may be used. The exception is directness, which is rare in Hong Kong. People may be shocked if you are overly direct yourself, which can be counterproductive.

Note that opening with written offers and attempting to introduce written terms and conditions as a negotiation tactic is rarely successful. In most cases, businesspeople ignore or tactfully reject them and request that each aspect be negotiated individually.

Corruption and bribery are rare in Hong Kong. It is strongly advisable to stay away from giving gifts of significant value to individuals or making offers that could be read as bribery.

Decision Making – Most of Hong Kong's companies tend to be very hierarchical, and people expect to work within clearly established lines of authority. While decision making can be a consensus-oriented group process as is usually the case in mainland China, there are also many western-style entrepreneurs in Hong Kong who act as the sole decision makers within their companies. In any case, it is important for the decision maker to consider the group interests and consult with others. Decision making can be fast, or it may take a long time and require a lot of patience.

When making decisions, businesspeople usually consider the specific situation rather than applying universal principles. Personal feelings and experiences may weigh more strongly than empirical evidence, but they also consider objective facts. The Hong Kong Chinese are more likely to take risks than their mainland siblings are, but they also need to become comfortable with them first.

Agreements and Contracts

Capturing and exchanging meeting summaries can be an effective way to verify understanding and commitments. Although interim agreements are usually kept, do not consider them final. Only a final contract signed by both parties constitutes a binding agreement.

The Hong Kong Chinese are influenced by two very different views of the roles of agreements and contracts. On one hand, the traditional Chinese position is that agreements are just snapshots in time. They view contracts as papers that document the intent of a working relationship at the time they were written up and signed, not as final agreements that can stand the test of litigation. On the other hand, there is the British influence, which dictates that contracts be taken seriously and followed to the letter. As a result, final written contracts are usually dependable, although it is always wise to nurture your relationship with a Hong Kong partner on a continuous basis.

Written contracts tend to be lengthy. They often spell out detailed terms and conditions for the core agreements as well as for many eventualities. Signing the contract is important not only from a legal perspective, but also as a strong confirmation of your partners' commitment. Before signing one, read it carefully. The Hong Kong side may have made modifications without flagging them. While this could be perceived as bad-faith negotiation in other cultures, local businesspeople may view the changes as clarifications.

Your legal rights are usually enforceable. It is recommended that you consult a local legal expert before signing a contract. Also, ensure that your products are patented or registered in Hong Kong to protect them against imitation. However, do not bring an attorney to the negotiation table, as this may be taken as a sign that you do not trust your counterparts.

Contracts are usually dependable, and the agreed terms are viewed as binding. Nevertheless, businesspeople may continue to press for a better deal even after a contract has been signed. They may call 'clarification meetings' to re-discuss or further work out details. Never view the contract signature as the end point of the negotiation. Your best chance to ensure that your partners follow through on their commitments is to stay in regular contact and nurture the relationship throughout your business engagement.

Women in Business

Gender roles in Hong Kong are clearly distinct. However, western-style equality is having some influence, and women may be found in senior positions.

As a visiting businesswoman, you will generally encounter few problems when visiting Hong Kong, provided that you exercise caution and act professionally in business and social situations. Displaying confidence and some degree of assertiveness sometimes impresses male Chinese counterparts, but it is important not to appear overly bold and aggressive. If you feel that your counterparts may be questioning your competence, it can be helpful to emphasize your company's importance and your role in it. A personal introduction or at least a letter of support from a senior executive within your company may help a lot.

Other Important Things to Know

Business meals and entertainment, in particular banquets and other evening events, are important as they help advance the vital process of building strong relationships. Refusing to participate in these activities is a signal that you are not seriously interested in doing business with your counterparts. Business may be discussed during these events. Your counterparts may use them as opportunities to convey important messages or resolve disputes. Sometimes they may also try to obtain information from you that could strengthen their negotiating position. While you want to remain watchful, deflecting such inquiries if needed, never show signs of mistrust in your counterparts' intentions.

Especially with local companies that lack international expertise, business entertainment may sometimes include invitations Westerners may find highly inappropriate. In such cases, it will be very important to find a way to avoid the issue without openly rejecting the invitation, as this helps preserve *face* for all involved.

The Hong Kong Chinese value punctuality in most social settings. It is best to be right on time for dinners and banquets, and to arrive at parties within 10 to 15 minutes of the agreed time.

Gift giving is common in social and business settings in Hong Kong. If you received one, it is best to reciprocate with an item of similar value that is typical of your home country. Giving a gift after signing a contract is viewed very favorably. However, while gifts of significant value will be accepted to save face, the recipient company would likely give them to charity or use them in a raffle later. Give and accept gifts using both hands. Do not open gifts in the presence of the giver unless your host did so first. There are numerous potential pitfalls in what to give and how to wrap it, so prepare upfront or ask someone from the country to avoid causing embarrassment.

The ancient Chinese astrology of *fengshui* plays a significant role in Hong Kong's business life and must be respected. It is wise to include a *fengshui* consultation when preparing for celebrations, opening an office, signing a contract, or similar events.

Hungary

Owing to its history within the former Eastern Bloc until 1990, when it held its first multi-party elections and started to become a free-market economy, businesspeople and officials in Hungary may have only limited exposure to other cultures except for neighboring countries. Its culture is quite homogeneous. However, many, especially among younger generations, have gained greater international experience after the reforms and can be very open-minded.

Though the country's current political and economic role may be modest on a world scale, keep in mind that back in its days of being part of the Austro-Hungarian Empire it wielded huge power and influence. Hungarians tend to be very proud of their country.

Relationships and Respect

Building lasting and trusting personal relationships is important to most people in this country. Such relationships are not necessarily a prerequisite to doing business, as Hungarians may be interested in quick deal making with foreigners. However, you will have to prove yourself as a trustworthy partner before they may be agreeable with any extended engagements. This may include asking and answering very personal questions since people expect to get to know you well. Holding back would be viewed very negatively. People in the country are very sensitive to being treated disrespectfully. In addition, they are generally suspicious of outsiders, especially foreigners. Establishing productive business relationships is therefore a slow process that requires a long-term perspective and commitment. As a reward, they may last forever.

Business relationships in this country exist between individuals or groups of people, not between companies. Even when you have won your local business partners' friendship and trust, they will not necessarily trust others from your company. That makes it important to keep company interfaces unchanged. Changing a key contact may require the relationship building process to start over.

In Hungary's business culture, the respect a person enjoys depends primarily on his or her status, education, and achievements. Admired personal traits include eloquence, poise, and an ability to socialize.

Communication

The country's official language, Hungarian, is not related to any Slavic language. Many businesspeople speak at least some English. With older people, it may be useful to engage an interpreter. To avoid offending the other side, ask beforehand whether an interpreter should be present at a meeting. When communicating in English, speak in short, simple sentences and avoid using slang and jargon. It will help people with a limited command of English if you speak slowly, summarize your key points often, and pause frequently to allow for interpretation.

People in this country usually speak softly. While they may occasionally raise their voices to make a point, they dislike loud and boisterous behavior. At restaurants, especially those used for business lunches and dinners, keep conversations at a quiet level. Being loud may be regarded as bad manners. Emotions may be shown openly, though, and discussions may stimulate much passion and excitement. People generally converse standing around two to three feet apart.

Communication is usually quite direct. Hungarians dislike vague statements and openly share opinions, concerns, and feelings with others. They do not find it difficult to say 'no' if they dislike a request or proposal.

Hungarians use body language sparingly, and there is little physical contact between them. They may not understand the American *OK* sign, with thumb and index finger forming a circle. The thumbs-up gesture is positive as it signals approval. Eye contact should be frequent, almost to the point of staring. This conveys sincerity and helps build trust.

Initial Contacts and Meetings

Choosing a third party intermediary is important, since having a local contact is advantageous for doing business in this country. This could be a business consultant or lawyer who effectively bridges the gap between cultures, allowing you to conduct business with greater effectiveness. This person will be expected to represent you on a continuing basis rather than just being an initial 'door-opener.'

Negotiations in Hungary can be conducted by individuals or teams of negotiators. You may not be able to meet the senior executives of an organization at the first meeting, so be prepared to deal with subordinates. They may have significant influence over the final decision.

If possible, schedule meetings at least two weeks in advance, and do not cancel one on short notice since that can be viewed as very rude. Since Hungarians want to know whom they will be meeting, provide details on titles, positions, and responsibilities of attendees ahead of time. People generally expect visitors to be punctual. Avoid being more than 5 to 10 minutes late, and call ahead if you will be. Allow ample time since your meetings may run over considerably.

Names are usually given in the order of family name, first name. Use them in that order, or *Mr./Ms.* plus the family name. If a person has a professional or academic title, it is important to use it instead, followed by the family name. Only close friends call each other by their first names, though this is gradually changing among the younger generation. Introductions are accompanied by handshakes. Men should wait for women to initiate handshakes.

The exchange of business cards is an essential step when meeting someone for the first time, so bring more than you need. You may not always get one in return, though. Most businesspeople in Hungary read English, so there is no need to have your card translated. However, it is very much appreciated if you do. Show doctorate degrees on your card and make sure that it clearly states your professional title, especially if you have the seniority to make decisions. When presenting your card, smile and keep eye contact, then take a few moments to look at the card you received.

Meetings may or may not start with some small talk intended to establish personal rapport. People appreciate a sense of humor, but keep it light and friendly. The first meeting may be quite formal, but this usually gets more relaxed down the road. Its primary purpose is to become acquainted. Business will be discussed, but do not try to hurry along with your agenda.

Hungarian negotiators may try to convince you that they have the background and experience required to be successful. Businesspeople may exaggerate their capabilities or make questionable promises in order to maintain foreign contacts.

Presentation materials should be attractive, with good and clear visuals. Avoid too much text and limit graphs unless they are interesting to look at. It is characteristic of Hungarians to be somewhat pessimistic, so a lack of enthusiastic responses should not discourage you. Having your handout materials translated to Hungarian is not a must, but it will be noted favorably.

Negotiation

Attitudes and Styles – To Hungarians, negotiating is usually a joint problem-solving process. While the buyer is in a superior position, both sides in a business deal own the responsibility to reach agreement. They may focus equally on near-term and long-term benefits. The primary negotiation style is cooperative, but people may be unwilling to agree with compromises unless it is their only option to keep the negotiation from getting stuck. The culture promotes a win-win approach to negotiating. While people respect a strong achievement orientation, avoid appearing overly pushy and aggressive.

Should a dispute arise at any stage of a negotiation, you might be able to reach resolution by focusing on logical arguments and facts. However, this may not get you anywhere as long as the relationship with your counterparts is still weak. In extreme situations, try to find a mediator whom both sides respect.

Sharing of Information – Hungarians are very detail-oriented and may spend considerable time gathering information before the bargaining stage of a negotiation can begin. At the same time, they usually play their cards close to the chest, although some may share information as a way to build trust.

Pace of Negotiation – Although the pace of business is increasing, negotiations can be slow and protracted. Be patient, control your emotions, and accept that delays may occur.

Bargaining – While Hungarians are generally not overly fond of bargaining and somewhat dislike haggling, they can be quite good at both. The bargaining stage of a negotiation may take less time than in other Eastern European countries. Though repeated concessions will be made and expected on both sides, prices rarely move by more than 20 to 30 percent between initial offers and final agreement.

Deceptive techniques might be used and it may be effective to use some of them yourself. This includes tactics such as telling lies and sending fake non-verbal messages, pretending to be disinterested in the whole deal or in single concessions, or misrepresenting an item's value. None of these will be easy to see through. Hungarians rarely use 'good cop, bad cop;' however, it can sometimes be beneficial to use this tactic in your own negotiation approach. Carefully orchestrated, it may allow you to obtain valuable concessions without damaging the overall relationship. Businesspeople may claim limited authority, stating that they have to ask for their manager's approval. This could be a tactic or the truth. Be cautious when using the techniques of making false demands or false concessions. Overt attempts to bluff your counterparts could backfire.

Negotiators in the country may use pressure techniques that include opening with their best offer or making final offers. When using similar tactics yourself, clearly explain your offer and avoid being aggressive. Silence can be an effective way to signal rejection of a proposal. Be careful when using pressure tactics such as showing intransigence, applying time pressure, or nibbling. Hungarians may consider these inappropriate unless they are strongly interested in your offer and clearly understand the rationale behind the approach. Otherwise, while the negotiation is not necessarily over, it may become less constructive.

Hungarian negotiators avoid most aggressive or adversarial techniques. The risk of using any of them yourself is rarely worth the potential gain. Extreme openings may be viewed as unfriendly. It is best to open with an offer that is already in the ballpark of what you really expect.

Emotional negotiation techniques, such as attitudinal bargaining, attempting to make you feel guilty, grimacing, or appealing to personal relationships, may occasionally be employed. It is best to remain calm. At times, Hungarians may also employ defensive tactics such as changing the subject, asking probing or very direct questions, or making promises.

Introducing written terms and conditions may be effective as this approach could lend credibility to your position.

As the country is moving from a socialist country to a free-market economy, corruption and bribery have become somewhat common in Hungary's public and private sectors. However, people may draw the line differently, viewing minor payments as rewards for getting a job done rather than as bribes. Also, keep in mind that there is a fine line between giving gifts and bribing. What you may consider a bribe, a Hungarian may view as only a nice gift.

Decision Making – Companies are often hierarchical, and people may expect to work within clearly established lines of authority. Decision makers are usually senior executives who consider the best interest of the group or organization. Others may be consulted in order to reach greater consensus and support. This process takes time and requires patience. Hungarians usually indicate it if they are not interested in doing business.

When making decisions, businesspeople may not rely much on rules or laws. They usually consider the specific situation rather than applying universal principles. Personal feelings and experiences weigh as strongly as empirical evidence and other objective facts, and they usually consider all aspects. Hungarians are often reluctant to take risks. If you expect them to support a risky decision, you may need to find ways for them to become comfortable with it first, for instance by explaining contingency plans, outlining areas of additional support, or by offering guarantees and warranties.

Agreements and Contracts

Capturing and exchanging meeting summaries can be an effective way to verify understanding and commitments. Although Hungarians usually keep interim agreements, do not consider these final. Only a contract signed by both parties constitutes a binding agreement.

Written contracts are serious matters in Hungary and tend to be lengthy. They often spell out very detailed terms and conditions for the core agreements as well as for many eventualities. Legal aspects may be checked over and over. Signing the contract is important not only from a legal perspective, but also as a strong confirmation of your Hungarian partners' commitment.

It is strongly advisable to consult a local legal expert before signing a contract. However, do not bring your attorney to the negotiation table, as this may be taken as a sign that you do not trust your counterparts.

Contracts are usually dependable. Your partners expect you to meet all your committed deadlines and delivery dates. If delays are foreseeable, it is much better to contact your Hungarian counterparts upfront and work out a solution together with them.

Women in Business

While Hungarian society is making progress towards gender equality and some women hold important positions, most of them are still struggling to attain positions of similar income and authority as men. As a visiting businesswoman, emphasize your company's importance and your role in it. A personal introduction or a letter of support from a senior executive within your company may also help.

Female business travelers should graciously accept any chivalric gestures they receive. Displaying confidence and assertiveness can be effective, but it is important not to appear overly bold and aggressive.

Other Important Things to Know

Business meals and entertainment are very important as they help advance your relationships. Refusing to participate in these activities is a signal that you are not seriously interested in doing business with your counterparts. Business may or may not be discussed during these events. Wait to see whether your counterparts bring it up.

Punctuality is valued in most social settings. It is best to be right on time for dinners, and to arrive at parties within 5 to 10 minutes of the agreed time.

Gift giving in business settings is rare. It is best not to bring a gift to an initial meeting in order to avoid raising suspicions about your motives.

India

India's pluralistic population consists of about 80 percent Hindus, 12 percent Muslims, and 8 percent members of other ethnic groups. Among the Hindus, the oft-quoted caste system plays only a small role in business. The business culture can be quite diverse and regional style differences may be significant. While Southern Indian companies, especially those around Bangalore and Hyderabad, tend to be progressive in some ways, southern Indians are often more sober and conservative than the more extroverted Northerners. Another factor that influences styles is whether people work in the government or traditional manufacturing sectors, versus the more flexible and faster-moving technology and service sectors. Business practices may sometimes differ from what we describe in this section.

Outside of the country's business centers, such as Bangalore, Chennai, Hyderabad, Mumbai, New Delhi, or Kolkatta, businesspeople and officials in India usually have only limited exposure to other cultures. When negotiating business here, realize that people may expect things to be done 'their way.'

Most Indians are proud of their country's progress, its achievements, and its dynamism. Your partners would like to see you acknowledge and respect this.

Relationships and Respect

India's culture is generally group-oriented. Asserting individual preferences may be seen as less important than having a sense of belonging to a group, conforming to its norms, and maintaining harmony among its members. Building lasting and trusting personal relationships is therefore very important, though to a lesser degree than in several other Asian countries. Some Indians may engage in business while the relationship building process is still ongoing. This is especially the case with internet-based businesses. Others in the country may expect to establish strong relationships prior to closing any deals, though. Generally, it is beneficial to allow some time for your Indian counterparts to get to know and become comfortable with you prior to proceeding with serious business discussions. Talking about your friends and family is an important part of establishing a relationship with those involved in the negotiating process. Many Indian companies are still family businesses. In any case, your local partners will expect you to be committed to the business relationship for many years.

Relationships are based on mutual trust and respect, which can take a long time to establish. Business relationships in this country exist both at the individual and company level. Indians usually want to do business only with those they like and trust. However, if your company replaces you with someone else over the course of a negotiation, it may not be overly difficult for your replacement to take things over from where you left them. Likewise, if you introduce someone else from your company into an existing business relationship, that person may quickly be accepted as a valid business partner when investing time and energy into nurturing his or her relationships.

Though not quite as critical as in most Far East countries, 'saving face' is very important in India's culture. Showing respect for others is essential. Causing embarrassment to another person may cause a *loss of face* for all parties involved and can be detrimental for business negotiations. It is best to control your emotions and remain friendly at all times. If you have to bring up an unpleasant topic with an Indian, never do so in public and always convey your message in ways that maintain the other's self-respect.

Indians are usually very friendly and polite. They prefer to do business with others who treat them with deference and genuinely like them, and it is important to demonstrate similar behaviors yourself. These factors do not affect anybody's determination to reach business goals, though, and your counterparts will patiently and persistently pursue their objectives. It is in your best interest to do the same.

In Indian business culture, the respect a person enjoys depends primarily on his or her age, status, and rank. There is also a deep respect for university degrees. Within family-run businesses, there is a common belief that 'outsiders' are not to be trusted. The head of the family may even keep information from family members. Admired personal traits include friendliness and sociability, flexibility, humility, compassion, resilience, and an ability to find common ground between opposing positions.

Communication

Although Hindi is the official language across all of India, many of its states have different local languages, some more than one. Almost all businesspeople speak English well. However, it is advisable to speak in short, simple sentences and avoid using jargon and slang.

Indians, especially those in the southern and western parts of the country, usually speak in quiet, gentle tones. At times, they may even appear shy. Do not mistake this for a lack of confidence. Their reticence and humility only reflect their politeness and respect for others. Loud and boisterous behavior is often perceived as a lack of self-control. Loudness may also be equated with dishonesty. However, positive emotions may be shown openly. Indians generally converse while standing around three feet apart.

Because being friendly is so important in this culture, communication is generally indirect. When responding to a direct question, Indians may answer 'yes' only to signal that they heard what you said, not that they agree with it. Open disagreement and confrontation are best avoided, so you may not hear a direct 'no.' Instead, they may give seemingly ambiguous answers such as 'I am not sure,' 'we will think about it,' 'this will require further investigation,' or 'yes, but...' Each of these could mean 'no,' as does a 'yes' that sounds hesitant or weak. It is beneficial to use a similarly indirect approach when dealing with Indians, as they may perceive you as rude and pushy if you are too direct. Polite nods and smiles do not always signal agreement. Instead, they help preserve a friendly atmosphere. It is in your best interest to give feedback in a positive and constructive spirit while masking any negative feelings with a smile.

An Indian who considers you a superior may hesitate to give you direct feedback. Instead, the person may tell you what he or she thinks you want to hear, especially when others are around. This is a way to save *face* for you and the individual. Similarly, if asked to give constructive feedback, people may resort to highlighting only the positives, in which case you should listen carefully for what is *not* being said. Candid comments and criticism may only be conveyed in private, and often indirectly through a third party. Similarly, it can be effective to deliver negative responses to your negotiation counterparts through a third party, which is a more face-saving way. Respect levels of hierarchy when doing so, since Indians may take it very negatively if you seem to be going around the chain of command.

Gestures and body language are usually much more extensive in India than in most other Asian countries. However, avoiding any physical contact with other people except for handshakes is crucial. Though elderly people may sometimes do so as a blessing, you should avoid touching someone's head, even with children. Hindus and Muslims consider the left hand unclean, so use it only if inevitable. When pointing at people, use your chin rather than a finger or your whole hand. Southern Indians may shake their head in a movement similar to the western 'no' when they are signaling 'yes.' While Indians may make frequent eye contact with peers, looking away is generally a sign of respect and does not convey insincerity or dishonesty.

Initial Contacts and Meetings

Before initiating business negotiations in India, it is highly advantageous to identify and engage a local intermediary, especially if you represent a small company. This person will help bridge the cultural and communications gap and maneuver within India's intricate bureaucracy, getting the necessary papers signed and stamped.

Negotiations in India can be conducted by individuals or teams of negotiators. Teams should be well aligned, with roles clearly assigned to each member. Changing a team member may require the relationship building process to start over and should be avoided.

If possible, schedule meetings at least four weeks in advance. Agreeing on an agenda upfront is useful, even though it may not be strictly followed. While meetings may start considerably late, Indians generally expect foreign visitors to be punctual. Avoid being more than 10 to 15 minutes late. It is best to be on time, as Indians are generally impressed with punctuality.

Many Southern Indians do not use family names. Use *Mr./Ms.* plus their first name. Muslims, Sikhs, and others have many variations of naming patterns. It is often best to ask people politely how to address them correctly. In that case, make sure you do the same for your own name. Academic and professional titles are very important and highly valued by Indians. Always use them when addressing a person who carries one. Introduce and greet older people first. The traditional Indian greeting is the *namaste* (putting both hands together in a prayer-like gesture). Foreigners are not expected to follow this custom, though, so accompany your introductions by light handshakes using the right hand. Men should wait for women to initiate handshakes. Some Indian women may not want to make physical contact with men, in which case it is best to just nod and smile or join your hands together in a *namaste*.

After the introductions, offer your business card to everyone present. It is not necessary to have it translated into an Indian language. Show advanced degrees on your card and make sure that it clearly states your professional title, especially if you have the seniority to make decisions. Present your card with your right hand, with the print facing the recipient. Similarly, accept others' cards using only the right hand. When presenting your card, ensure that it faces the recipient. Smile and keep eye contact, then take a few moments to look at the card you received. Next, place it on the table in front of you or into your card case.

Meetings start with some small talk intended to establish personal rapport. This may include some personal questions about your family and allows participants to become personally acquainted. It is important to be patient and let the Indian side set the pace. People enjoy some friendly humor, but avoid appearing sarcastic or cynical.

The primary purpose of the first meeting is to get to know each other. Business may be discussed, but do not try to hurry along with your agenda. It is unrealistic to expect initial meetings to lead to straight decisions.

Presentation materials should be attractive, with good and clear visuals. Indians are often impressed with technical expertise. Having your English-language handout materials translated to Hindi or another Indian language is usually not required.

Negotiation

Attitudes and Styles - In India, the primary approach to negotiating is to employ distributive and contingency bargaining. While the buyer is in a superior position, both sides in a business deal own the responsibility to reach agreement. They expect long-term commitments from their business partners and will focus mostly on long-term benefits. Although the primary negotiation style is somewhat competitive, Indians nevertheless value long-term relationships and look for win-win solutions. They may occasionally appear to be pursuing a win-lose approach, in which case it pays to help them focus on mutual benefit. However, avoid being confrontational.

Should a dispute arise at any stage of a negotiation, you might be able to reach resolution through showing friendliness, respect, and willingness to compromise. Show your commitment to the relationship and refrain from using logical reasoning or becoming argumentative since this will only make matters worse. As long as you remain friendly, this likely opens new paths to obtaining agreement.

Sharing of Information – Indian negotiators will first spend some time gathering information and discussing various details before the bargaining stage of a negotiation can begin. People may share information quite openly in an effort to build trust. This does not mean that they will readily reveal everything you might want to know during your negotiation. However, negotiations can become very difficult if one side appears to be hiding information from the other, which may result in attempts to outsmart each other.

Pace of Negotiation – Expect negotiations to be slow and protracted. Delays are often inevitable, particularly when dealing with government bureaucracy. Be prepared to make several trips if necessary to achieve your objectives. Throughout the negotiation, be patient, control your emotions, and accept that delays occur. Indians view impatience or pushiness as rude.

Indians generally employ a polychronic work style. They are used to pursuing multiple actions and goals in parallel. When negotiating, they often take a holistic approach and may jump back and forth between topics rather than addressing them in sequential order. Negotiators from strongly monochronic cultures, such as Germany, the United Kingdom, or the United States, may find this style confusing, irritating, and even annoying. In any case, do not show irritation or anger when encountering this behavior. Instead, keep track of the bargaining progress at all times, often emphasizing areas where agreement already exists.

If your counterparts appear to be stalling the negotiation, assess carefully whether their slowing down the process indicates that they are evaluating alternatives or that they are not interested in doing business with you. While such behavior could represent attempts to create time pressure in order to obtain concessions, a desire first to get to know you better or the slow decision process in the country are far more likely causing the lack of progress. People from fast-paced cultures tend to underestimate how much time this takes and often make the mistake of trying to 'speed things up.' Again, patience and persistence are vitally important.

Bargaining – Indian businesspeople are often shrewd negotiators who should not be underestimated. Most of them love bargaining and haggling, although they may not do it as extensively as other Asians. The bargaining stage of a negotiation can be extensive. Prices often move more than 40 percent between initial offers and final agreement. However, technical assistance, training, and other costs may also be important bargaining factors and Indians remain flexible throughout most of the bargaining. Leave yourself a lot of room for concessions at different stages. Ask the other side to reciprocate if you made one. You can use the fact that aspects can be re-visited to your advantage, for instance by offering further concessions under the condition that the Indian side reciprocate in areas that had already been agreed upon.

Deceptive techniques might be used and it may be effective to use some of them yourself. This includes tactics such as telling lies and sending fake non-verbal messages, pretending to be disinterested in the whole deal or in single concessions, or making false demands and concessions. Indians rarely use 'good cop, bad cop;' however, it can sometimes be beneficial to use this tactic in your own negotiation approach. Carefully orchestrated, it may allow you to obtain valuable concessions without damaging the overall relationship. However, your team will need to exclude any 'bad cop' member from future negotiation rounds. Businesspeople may claim limited authority, stating that they have to ask for their manager's approval. This could be a tactic or the truth. Be cautious when using the techniques of making false demands or false concessions. Overt attempts to bluff your counterparts could backfire.

Negotiators in the country may occasionally use pressure techniques that include making final offers or nibbling. Final offers should not be made too soon since your counterpart may not believe that you are serious. Do not use tactics such as applying time pressure or making expiring offers, since Indians could view these as signs that you are not willing to build a long-term relationship. They may choose to terminate the negotiation. Periods of silence in conversations are normal and may not represent an attempt to use it as a negotiation technique. Avoid pressure tactics such as opening with your best offer or showing intransigence, since they cannot be applied effectively without running the risk of causing loss of face.

Indian negotiators avoid most aggressive or adversarial techniques since they affect respect and trust. The risk of using any of them yourself is rarely worth the potential gain. As in most strongly relationship-oriented cultures, negotiators may sometimes use emotional techniques such as attitudinal bargaining, attempting to make you feel guilty, grimacing, or appealing to personal relationships. Be cautious when doing this yourself. You might cause the other side to lose face, which could damage your negotiating position.

At times, defensive tactics such as blocking or changing the subject, asking probing questions, or making promises may be used by Indians. Unlike many other Asians, Indians may sometimes ask direct questions in order to obtain information. Be cautious not to overdo this yourself, though.

Corruption and bribery are quite common in India's public and private sectors. However, Indians respect companies that have high ethical standards. People may draw the line differently, though, viewing minor payments as rewards for getting a job done rather than as bribes. Also, keep in mind that there is a fine line between giving gifts and bribing. What you may consider a bribe, an Indian may view as only a nice gift. It may help if you introduce and explain your company's policies early on, but be careful not to moralize or appear to imply that local customs are unethical.

Decision Making – Most companies tend to be very hierarchical, and people expect to work within clearly established lines of authority. Disagreeing with or criticizing superiors is often viewed as unacceptable. Decision making is a slow and deliberate process in India. Decision makers are usually top executives who consider the best interest of the group or organization. They may consult with others before making the call. Subordinates may be reluctant to accept responsibility. Decision makers also rarely delegate their authority, so it is important to deal with senior executives. They expect to deal with equals. People may not always be open to new ideas. You best chance for success is to give the decider time and do some lobbying with key influencers.

When making decisions, Indian businesspeople usually consider not only universal principles, but also the specific situation. Personal feelings and experiences weigh more strongly than empirical evidence and other objective facts do, but they will consider all aspects. An argument appealing to both feelings and faith is often more convincing to an Indian than one using only objective facts and practical reasons.

Indians are willing to take calculated risks if they believe that the rewards are worth it. However, they may frequently attribute both success and failure to environmental factors rather than to individual reasons.

Agreements and Contracts

Capturing and exchanging meeting summaries can be an effective way to verify understanding and commitments. Indians may signal consensus through enthusiastic statements that phrase the agreement in their own words. Interim agreements, even oral ones, are considered binding and usually kept. Nevertheless, it is best to consider only a final contract that has been signed by both parties a binding agreement.

Written contracts should be clear and concise, without too many detailed terms and conditions. Signing the contract is important not only from a legal perspective, but also as a strong confirmation of your Indian partners' commitment.

Legal rights are generally enforceable in India, though the process can be lengthy and cumbersome. You should consult a local legal expert throughout the negotiation or, at the very least, before signing a contract. However, it is best not to appear overly legalistic. Do not bring an attorney to the negotiation table, since this may be taken as a sign that you do not trust your counterparts.

Signed contracts may not always be honored. This depends to no small degree on the strength of the continuing relationship between the contract partners. It is strongly advisable to continue staying in touch and maintaining the trust of your Indian business partner. Business partners usually expect the other side to remain somewhat flexible if conditions change, which may include agreeing to modify contract terms.

Do not expect your Indian business partners to follow commitments to the letter. While deadlines are viewed as important, many businesspeople claim that they have met their commitments even if they were a week or more late. Remain flexible and try to accommodate this in your own plans.

Women in Business

While India is still a male-dominated society, there are many women in professional positions, some with significant authority and influence. At the same time, women are still struggling to attain positions of similar income and authority as men. Nevertheless, visiting businesswomen should have few problems in the country as long as they act professionally in business and social situations.

Other Important Things to Know

Business lunches are more common than business dinners, but the latter may create good opportunities to strengthen relationships. Business may not get discussed. Always keep in mind that Hindus eat no beef, Muslims do not eat pork, and many Indians are vegetarians. At restaurants, especially those used for business lunches and dinners, keep conversations at a quiet level, since being loud may be regarded as bad manners. It is best to avoid drinking alcohol since some Indians may take offense.

Social events do not require strict punctuality. While it is best to arrive at dinners close to the agreed time, being late to a party by 15 to 20 minutes is perfectly acceptable.

Gift giving is fairly common in social and business settings in India, including initial meetings. If you received one, it is best to reciprocate with an item of similar value that is typical of your home country.

Topics to avoid in conversations are India's role as a nuclear power, its relationship with Pakistan, and the tensions over Kashmir.

Indonesia

Although a small minority in this pluralistic country, many Indonesian businesspeople are Chinese and may have strong family connections back to China. As a country, Indonesia consists of countless islands that are quite heterogeneous in history and culture. The information given in this section applies to all of them to some degree, but may not always be comprehensive. Always keep in mind that this is essentially an Islamic country. Showing any disrespect for the religion could have disastrous consequences.

Businesspeople and officials in Indonesia usually have only limited exposure to other cultures except for neighboring countries. When negotiating business here, realize that people may expect things to be done 'their way,' and let them set the pace initially until you have had a chance to determine how your interactions are most effective.

Relationships and Respect

Indonesia's culture is strongly group-oriented. Asserting individual preferences may be seen as less important than having a sense of belonging to a group, conforming to its norms, and maintaining harmony among its members. Building lasting and trusting personal relationships is therefore critically important to most Indonesians, who expect to establish strong bonds prior to closing any deals. People in this country usually do business only with those they know and like. Establishing productive business cooperation requires a long-term perspective and commitment. Consequently, proceed with serious business discussions only after your counterparts have become comfortable with you.

Relationships are based on familiarity, respect, and personal trust, which can take a long time to establish. Business relationships in this country exist between people, not necessarily between companies. Even when you have won your local business partners' friendship and trust, they will not necessarily trust others from your company. That makes it very important to keep company interfaces unchanged. Changing a key contact may require the relationship building process to start over.

In Indonesia's culture, 'saving face' is very essential. Every person's reputation and social standing rests on this concept. Causing embarrassment to another person may cause a *loss of face* for all parties involved and can be disastrous for business negotiations. Reputation and social standing strongly depend on a person's ability to control emotions and remain friendly at all times. If you have to bring up an unpleasant topic with an Indonesian, never do so in public and always convey your message in ways that maintain the other's self-respect. The importance of diplomatic restraint and tact cannot be overestimated. Keep your cool and never show openly that you are upset.

Indonesians are usually very friendly and polite. Since they prefer to do business with others who treat them with deference and genuinely like them, it is important to demonstrate similar behaviors yourself. These factors do not affect anybody's determination to reach business goals, though, and your counterparts will patiently and persistently pursue their objectives. It is in your best interest to do the same.

In Indonesian business culture, the respect a person enjoys depends primarily on his or her status, rank, and age. Showing status is important since people will take you more seriously. Carefully select your hotel and transportation. Use the services of others, such as a porter, to avoid being viewed as a low-ranking intermediary. Admired personal traits include patience, good listening skills, experience, and wealth.

It is very difficult for Indonesians to have a conversation with a person whose status is unclear, since knowing whether someone is a superior, inferior, or equal strongly influences behaviors. Important business leaders often have a military background. However, top executives can be surprisingly accessible and willing to meet with foreign business visitors.

Communication

The official language is Bahasa Indonesia, which is a modified form of Malay. Younger businesspeople may speak English fluently. Older people, among them most high-ranking managers, rarely speak English well. It may be useful to engage an interpreter. To avoid offending the other side, ask beforehand whether an interpreter should be present at a meeting. When communicating in English, speak in short, simple sentences and avoid using slang and jargon. It will help people with a limited command of English if you speak slowly, summarize your key points often, and pause frequently to allow for interpretation. Do not assume that your audience readily understands you. Since saving *face* is so important in this culture, people will not admit in front of others that they are having difficulties.

Indonesians usually speak in quiet, gentle tones. At times, they may even appear shy. However, this only reflects their politeness and respect for others. Conversations may include extended periods of silence, sometimes as long as ten seconds or more. In restaurants, especially in those used for business, keep conversations at a quiet level. Loud and boisterous behavior is perceived as a lack of self-control. Indonesians generally converse while standing around three feet apart.

Because being friendly and saving *face* are so important in this culture, communication is generally very indirect. Indonesians may allow someone to proceed incorrectly, even if the result could be disastrous, since correcting him or her might cause embarrassment for the person. Similarly, people may be reluctant to admit if they do not know the answer to a question. When responding to a direct question, Indonesians may answer 'yes' only to signal that they heard what you said, not that they agree with it. Open disagreement and confrontation must be avoided, so you rarely hear a direct 'no.' Instead, they may give seemingly ambiguous answers such as 'I am not sure,' 'we will think about it,' 'this will require further investigation,' or 'yes, but...' Each of these could mean 'no,' as does a 'yes' that sounds hesitant or weak. Alternatively, a respondent may deliberately ignore your question. It is beneficial to use a similarly indirect approach when dealing with Indonesians, as they may perceive you as rude and pushy if you are too direct.

An Indonesian who considers you a superior may tell you what he or she thinks you want to hear, especially when others are around. This is a way to save *face* and preserve honor, known as 'keeping father happy.' Similarly, if asked to give constructive feedback, Indonesians may resort to highlighting only positives, in which case you should listen carefully for what is *not* being said. Candid comments and criticism may only be conveyed in private, often through a third party. Similarly, it can be effective to deliver negative responses to your negotiation counterparts through a third party, which is a more face-saving way.

Indonesian Chinese consider it polite to offer both the positive and negative possibilities when asking a question that requires a decision. For example, they may ask 'Do you want to go back to your hotel or not?'

Gestures are usually subtle. It is advisable to restrict your body language. Non-verbal communication is important, though, and you should carefully watch for others' small hints, just as they will be watching you. Avoid any physical contact with Indonesians except for handshakes. Do not stand with your back to a senior or high-ranking person. Hindus and Muslims consider the left hand unclean, so use it only if inevitable. Avoid showing the soles of your shoes when seated as this is considered disrespectful. Pointing at other people is generally considered rude. If you absolutely have to, use your thumb while keeping the fist closed rather than pointing with your index finger. Slapping the open hand over a fist can be read as a vulgar gesture. Sucking in air through the teeth indicates that there is a serious problem. Eye contact should be infrequent. While it is beneficial to make some eye contact when meeting a person for the first time, Indonesians consider frequent eye contact intrusive and rude. It is generally considered respectful to look down when speaking with senior or elder people. Avoid any facial expressions that may suggest disagreement, such as grimacing or shaking your head.

Smiles do not always indicate amusement or approval. Frequently, smiling masks embarrassment, shyness, disapproval, and other feelings of distress. Accordingly, Westerners may sometimes observe Indonesians smiling or laughing at what they might consider inappropriate moments.

Initial Contacts and Meetings

Before initiating business negotiations in Indonesia, it is highly advantageous to identify and engage a local intermediary. This person will help bridge the cultural and communications gap, allowing you to conduct business with greater effectiveness.

Negotiations in Indonesia can be conducted by individuals or teams of negotiators. The latter is preferable when dealing with Chinese Indonesians, as functional specialists on both sides can build the all-important relationships between themselves faster and more effectively, your team will bring broader functional expertise to the table, and you will be able to assign different roles to each team member, maximizing the team's impact. Each of these factors speeds up the negotiation process. It is vital that teams be well aligned, with roles clearly assigned to each member. Changing a team member may require the relationship building process to start over and should therefore be avoided.

If possible, schedule meetings at least four weeks in advance. Since Indonesians want to know whom they will be meeting, provide details on titles, positions, and responsibilities of attendees ahead of time. Agreeing on an agenda upfront can also be useful, even though it may not be strictly followed. Indonesians have little sense of urgency about time and dislike being hurried. Meetings may therefore start considerably late. However, Indonesians generally expect foreign visitors to be punctual. Avoid being more than 10 to 15 minutes late. If meeting a Chinese or anyone of higher rank, it is best to be right on time as a sign of respect. Displaying anger if you have to wait, which happens often, reflects very poorly on you.

Meetings tend to be very formal. In accordance with business protocol, the Indonesian participants enter the meeting room in hierarchical order.

Many variations of naming patterns exist in Indonesia. It is often best to ask people politely how to address them correctly. In that case, make sure you do the same for your own name. Properly pronouncing your counterparts' names is very important. Academic and professional titles are highly valued and must always be used. Negotiating teams should line up so that the most important individuals are introduced first. If introducing two people, it is important to state the name of the most important person first. Introductions are accompanied by handshakes using the right hand. Handshakes should be light and may last as long as ten seconds. Men should wait for women to initiate handshakes. Some Indonesian women may not want to make physical contact with men, in which case it is best to just nod and smile.

After the introductions, offering your business card to everyone present is very important. Business cards should be printed or –preferably– embossed in English. It is recommended to have the other side of your card translated into Bahasa Indonesia. Show advanced degrees on your card and make sure that it clearly states your professional title, especially if you have the seniority to make decisions. Present your card with your right hand, with the Bahasa Indonesian side facing the recipient. Similarly, accept others' cards using only the right hand. Smile and make eye contact while doing so, then examine the card carefully. Not reading someone's card can be an insult. Next, remark upon the card and then place it on the table in front of you or into your card case. Never stuff someone's card into your back pocket or otherwise treat it disrespectfully. Never write on a person's business card.

Meetings start with a lot of small talk, which can be extensive, occasionally lasting more than an hour. This allows participants to become personally acquainted. It is important to be patient and let the Indonesian side set the pace. People appreciate a sense of humor, but keep it light and friendly, and be careful not to overdo it. Business is a serious matter in Indonesia.

The primary purpose of the first meeting is to become acquainted and build relationships. Little else may happen, and you may actually not get to talk about business at all. It is unrealistic to expect initial meetings to lead to straight decisions. Occasionally, participants may say very little during an initial meeting. This should not be interpreted negatively. Participants often remain indifferent until they have had a chance to convene with their group to gather consensus.

Presentation materials should be attractive, with good and clear visuals. Use diagrams and pictures wherever feasible, cut down on words, and avoid complicated expressions. Having your handout materials translated to Bahasa Indonesia is not a must, but it helps in getting your messages across. Correspondence with government officials must be in Bahasa Indonesia.

Negotiation

Attitudes and Styles – Leveraging relationships is an important element when negotiating in Indonesia. Nevertheless, Indonesians often employ distributive and contingency bargaining. While the buyer is in a superior position, both sides in a business deal own the responsibility to reach agreement. They expect long-term commitments from their business partners and will focus mostly on long-term benefits. Although the primary negotiation style is competitive, Indonesians nevertheless value long-term relationships. While the communication style is deferential and quiet, they respect hard bargainers. Nevertheless, both sides will remain friendly throughout the negotiation, and attempts to win competitive advantages should not be taken negatively. The culture promotes a win-win approach since this is the best way for everyone to save *face* throughout a negotiation. You earn your counterparts' respect by maintaining a positive, persistent attitude.

Sharing of Information – Indonesian negotiators will spend some time gathering information and discussing various details before the bargaining stage of a negotiation can begin. They rarely share their information freely.

Pace of Negotiation – Expect negotiations to be slow and protracted. Relationship building, information gathering, bargaining, and decision making all take considerable time. Be prepared to make several trips if necessary to achieve your objectives. Throughout the negotiation, be patient, control your emotions, and accept that delays occur.

Indonesians generally employ a polychronic work style. They are used to pursuing multiple actions and goals in parallel. When negotiating, they often take a holistic approach and may jump back and forth between topics rather than addressing them in sequential order. Negotiators from strongly monochronic cultures, such as Germany, the United Kingdom, or the United States, may find this style confusing, irritating, and even annoying. In any case, do not show irritation or anger when encountering this behavior. Instead, keep track of the bargaining progress at all times, often emphasizing areas where agreement already exists.

If your counterparts appear to be stalling the negotiation, assess carefully whether their slowing down the process indicates that they are evaluating alternatives or that they are not interested in doing business with you. While such behavior could represent attempts to create time pressure in order to obtain concessions, the slow decision process in the country is far more likely causing the lack of progress. People from fast-paced cultures tend to underestimate how much time this takes and often make the mistake of trying to 'speed things up.' Again, patience and persistence are vitally important.

Bargaining – Indonesian businesspeople are often shrewd negotiators who should not be underestimated. Most of them love bargaining and haggling. They expect to do a lot of it during a negotiation and may be offended if you refuse to play along. However, they are more likely to focus on the big picture rather than negotiating point-by-point. The bargaining stage of a negotiation can nevertheless be extensive. Prices may move by 40 percent or more between initial offers and final agreement. Leave yourself a lot of room for concessions at different stages. Ask the other side to reciprocate if you made one. You can use the fact that aspects can be re-visited to your advantage, for instance by offering further concessions under the condition that the Indonesian side reciprocate in areas that had already been agreed upon.

Deceptive techniques might be used and it may be effective to use some of them yourself. This includes tactics such as telling lies and sending fake non-verbal messages, initially pretending to be disinterested in the whole deal or in single concessions, misrepresenting an item's value, or making false demands and concessions. It is advisable to verify information received from the Indonesian side through other channels if you have a chance. Similarly, they treat 'outside' information with caution. Indonesians do not use 'good cop, bad cop' and it is best to avoid the tactic since the implications for relationships can be significant. They may claim limited authority, stating that they have to ask for their manager's approval. This could be a tactic or the truth. Since you must avoid causing loss of face, be cautious when using the techniques of making false demands or false concessions. Any overt attempts to bluff your counterparts could backfire.

Negotiators in the country may occasionally use pressure techniques that include making final offers or nibbling. Final offers may come more than once and are rarely final. Do not use tactics such as applying time pressure or making expiring offers, since Indonesians could view these as signs that you are not willing to build a long-term relationship. They may choose to terminate the negotiation. Periods of silence are frequent and usually reflect a natural inclination rather than the intentional use of a negotiation technique. Avoid pressure tactics such as opening with your best offer or showing intransigence, since they cannot be applied effectively without running the risk of causing loss of face.

Indonesian negotiators avoid most aggressive or adversarial techniques since they affect face. The risk of using any of them yourself is rarely worth the potential gain. As an exception, extreme openings may be used as a way to start the bargaining process. However, use the tactic with caution since it may adversely affect the relationship if employed too aggressively.

As in most strongly relationship-oriented cultures, negotiators may sometimes use emotional techniques such as attitudinal bargaining, attempting to make you feel guilty, grimacing, or appealing to personal relationships. Be cautious when doing this yourself. You might cause the other side to lose face, which could damage your negotiating position.

At times, defensive tactics such as blocking or changing the subject, asking probing questions, or making promises may be used by Indonesians. The exception is directness, which is very rare in this society. They may be shocked if you are overly direct yourself, which can be counterproductive.

Note that opening with written offers and attempting to introduce written terms and conditions as a negotiation tactic is rarely successful. In most cases, businesspeople ignore or tactfully reject them and request that each aspect be negotiated individually.

Corruption and bribery are common in Indonesia's public and private sectors. However, people may draw the line differently, viewing minor payments as rewards for getting a job done rather than as bribes. Also, keep in mind that there is a fine line between giving gifts and bribing. What you may consider a bribe, an Indonesian may view as only a nice gift. It may help if you introduce and explain your company's policies early on, but be careful not to moralize or appear to imply that local customs are unethical. Alternatively, let your local representative handle such aspects.

Conflicts and disputes that may arise during a negotiation can be difficult to resolve because Indonesians prefer to ignore or deny them. Patience and continuous friendliness pay strong dividends. In extreme situations, use a mediator, ideally the party who initially introduced you.

Decision Making – The country's business culture is extremely hierarchical and superiors enjoy enormous deference. Decision making is a very slow and deliberate process in Indonesia. Superiors tend to behave in paternalistic ways. However, they normally seek the consensus of the group. Decision makers are usually senior executives who consult with others and carefully consider their inputs. Be sure that you are meeting with managers who have sufficient decision-making authority, especially in the final stages of your negotiation.

When making decisions, Indonesian businesspeople may not rely much on rules or laws. They usually consider the specific situation rather than applying universal principles. Personal feelings and experiences weigh as strongly as do empirical evidence and other objective facts. Most Indonesians are moderate risk takers.

Agreements and Contracts

Capturing and exchanging meeting summaries can be an effective way to verify understanding and commitments. Never take interim commitments for final agreements. Any part of an agreement may still change significantly before both parties sign the final contract.

Businesspeople in the country may view contracts only as general guides for conducting business, expecting that both parties are willing to change terms if there is a change of conditions. Written contracts are usually kept high-level, capturing only the primary aspects, terms, and conditions of the agreement. Writing up and signing the contract is a formality. Indonesians believe that the primary strength of an agreement lies in the partners' commitment rather than in its written documentation. Chinese Indonesians often consult astrologers and may prefer to delay signature of a contract until a 'lucky' day arrives.

Although your legal rights are difficult to enforce legally, you should consult a local legal expert, ideally throughout the negotiation or at the very least before signing a contract. However, do not bring an attorney to the negotiation table, since this may be taken as a sign that you do not trust your counterparts.

Doing business in Indonesia still can be a high-risk undertaking. Contracts are often not considered final agreements and may not be honored at all. It is commonplace for negotiations to continue after a contract has already been signed. Both sides are expected to remain flexible. Your best chance to ensure that your local partners follow their commitments is to stay in regular contact and nurture the relationship throughout your business engagement.

Women in Business

While Indonesia is still a male-dominated society, the position of women is quite different from other Muslim countries. They are allowed to vote, have full civil rights, and quite a few can be found in leadership positions. At the same time, most women are still struggling to attain positions of similar income and authority as men. Visiting businesswomen should have few problems in the country as long as they act professionally in business and social situations.

Other Important Things to Know

Business might get discussed over lunch and dinner. During small talk and other social conversations, you may be asked very personal questions. If you do not want to answer, smile or politely explain that such topics are not discussed openly in your culture.

Social events do not require strict punctuality. While it is best to arrive at dinners close to the agreed time, being late to a party by 30 minutes is usually acceptable. With people of high rank, however, it is best to be punctual.

Gift giving is common in social settings in Indonesia, though less so in business. If you received one, it is best to reciprocate with an item of similar value that is typical of your home country. Giving a gift after signing a contract is viewed very favorably. Give and accept gifts using only the right hand. Do not open gifts in the presence of the giver unless your host did so first. There are numerous potential pitfalls in what to give and how to wrap it, so prepare upfront to avoid causing embarrassment.

Ireland

Though the country's culture is quite homogeneous, Irish businesspeople, especially those among younger generations, are usually experienced in interacting and doing business with visitors from other cultures. However, that does not always mean that they are open-minded. When negotiating business here, realize that some people may expect things to be done 'their way.' In addition, many prefer to deal with other Irish people rather than with foreigners. Unless you have a valuable proposition to make, it may prove difficult to be accepted as a business partner.

Most Irish people are very proud of their country and expect others to show appreciation for its history and accomplishments.

Relationships and Respect

Building lasting and trusting relationships is very important in Ireland and can be crucial for your business success. People in this country usually want to do business only with those they know, like, and trust. If they initially seem suspicious and non-committal, you may be able to overcome this with consistent friendliness and goodwill. Proceed with serious business discussions only after your counterparts have become very comfortable with you. This includes letting them see your personal side, as the Irish often mistrust people who are 'all business.' Relationship building can be a very time-consuming process that may require several trips to strengthen the bonds. You may be able to establish trust by emphasizing common ground. For example, express your own distrust of authority or bureaucracy whenever there is an opportunity for it. While compliments are generally appreciated, you should refrain from praising or rewarding anyone in public. Unlike in many other cultures, it may raise suspicion about your motives.

Business relationships in this country exist both at the individual and company level. If your company replaces you with someone else over the course of a negotiation, it may be easy for your replacement to take things over from where you left them. Likewise, if you introduce someone else from your company into an existing business relationship, that person may quickly be accepted as a valid business partner.

Families play an important role in Ireland's society and business life. Many companies are family-owned or controlled. Families often extend into powerful networks that include friends, business partners, and others. Becoming integrated into such networks through personal relationships is vital to doing business in the country. Whom you know may determine whether people want to get to know you. Similarly, whether people think you are worth knowing and trusting may weigh more strongly than how competent you are or what proposals you may have to make. As a trusted business partner, you may be expected to attend family events such as weddings or funerals.

While the Irish are usually warm and friendly, they are also very proud and may be easily offended by comments that leave room for misunderstandings. 'Saving face' and respecting everyone's honor and personal pride are crucial requirements for doing business in the country. Openly criticizing someone in front of others can have a devastating impact on your negotiation. Avoid open conflict, and know that politeness is crucial. In addition, showing genuine interest and compassion will win people's hearts.

In Ireland's business culture, the respect a person enjoys depends primarily on his or her education and achievements. Status and rank usually play only a small role.

The Irish tend to be distrustful of authority and may become very cynical with people who seem elitist or snobbish. There is usually much greater respect for the 'underdog' than for those with great wealth or power. Admired personal traits include modesty, a sense of humor, and sociability.

Communication

Irish English is usually easy to understand for native English speakers, but may represent a challenge for others. Some people in Ireland have a tendency to talk very fast when excited. At times, you may have to ask them to slow down.

While discussions may get animated and emotional, the Irish generally dislike loud and boisterous behavior. They may show their emotions openly. When someone is teasing you, try not to be offended. If you feel compelled to tease back, do so in an affable manner. Silence is rare and may make people uncomfortable. The Irish generally converse standing around two to three feet apart.

Communication is usually quite direct, but almost never confrontational. For that reason, some Irish may find it difficult to say 'no.' If you do not get a clear 'yes' right away, do not assume that you have won them over. People rarely communicate 'between the lines,' so it is usually best to take what they say quite literally. Try to be equally clear in your own communication.

Gestures and body language can be lively, but not overly so. There may be some physical contact with others of the same gender. Eye contact should be frequent, but do not stare at others.

Initial Contacts and Meetings

Having a local contact can be an advantage but is usually not a necessary precondition to doing business. Negotiations in Ireland can be conducted by individuals or teams of negotiators.

Scheduling meetings in advance is required. However, you can sometimes do this on short notice, especially if the parties have had previous business interactions. One good way of getting to know people is to meet for coffee in a good hotel. This does not require a formal request; the prospect of discussing the possibility to do business together is usually all it will take. While meetings may start considerably late, the Irish generally expect foreign visitors to be punctual. Avoid being more than 10 to 15 minutes late, and call ahead if you will be.

Names are usually given in the order of first name, family name. Use *Mr./Mrs./Miss* plus the family name. If a person has a title, such as *Doctor* or *Professor*, use it instead, followed by the family name. Before calling Irish people by their first name, wait until they offer it. Introductions are accompanied by handshakes. The standard greetings are 'Pleased to meet you' or 'How are you?'

The exchange of business cards is not an essential step, but it is best to bring a sufficient supply. Offer your card to everyone present. You may not always get one in return. When presenting your card, smile and keep eye contact, then take a few moments to look at the card you received. Next, place it on the table in front of you.

Meetings start with small talk, which may be extensive. This may include personal questions about your background and family, allowing participants to become acquainted. Let the other side set the pace. However, you may find that the overall pace of the meeting can be faster than you might have expected. Meetings are often relaxed and informal. People appreciate a sense of friendly humor, but avoid being sarcastic or cynical. While the primary purpose of the first meeting is to become acquainted, the discussion will mostly focus on business topics. Be prepared for your counterparts to 'size you up' during the initial encounter.

Presentation materials should be attractive, with good and clear visuals. Keep your presentation simple and straightforward. However, be prepared that people may be easily distracted and willing to digress if they think an idea is interesting. There can be a lot of superficiality early in the business interaction, so take premature promises with a grain of salt.

Negotiation

Attitudes and Styles – In Ireland, negotiating is usually viewed as a joint problem-solving process. While the buyer is in a superior position, both sides in a business deal own the responsibility to reach agreement. They expect long-term commitments from their business partners and will focus more on long-term benefits than on short-term gains. The primary negotiation style is cooperative and people may be open to compromising if viewed helpful in order to move the negotiation forward. Since the Irish believe in the concept of win-win, they expect you to reciprocate their respect and trust. While people respect a strong achievement orientation, avoid appearing overly pushy and aggressive.

Should a dispute arise at any stage of a negotiation, you might be able to reach resolution through give-and-take compromising and appeals to your counterparts' fairness.

Sharing of Information – Irish negotiators may share some information as a way to build trust. Be careful with what you are willing to share yourself and protect your intellectual property.

Pace of Negotiation – Negotiations are usually swift. While the upfront relationship building may take some time, information gathering and bargaining usually move smoothly, and decision making can be very fast if you are dealing with the right people.

Bargaining – Irish businesspeople are used to hard bargaining and may employ some haggling. However, they do not appreciate aggressive sales techniques. Prices may move by about 25 to 35 percent between initial offer and final agreement. However, the profitability of a business deal may be valued higher than gains in market share or access to new markets. Company policy is usually strictly followed, particularly in larger organizations, so be careful not to demand concessions that go against it.

The Irish often prefer a straightforward negotiation style. They use deceptive techniques only infrequently, such as telling lies, sending fake non-verbal messages, pretending to be disinterested in the whole deal or in single concessions, or misrepresenting an item's value. 'Good cop, bad cop' is not advisable as the tactic may lead the Irish side to question your trustworthiness. Businesspeople may claim limited authority, stating that they have to ask for their manager's approval. More often than not, this will be the truth. Be cautious when using the techniques of making false demands or false concessions. Overt attempts to bluff your counterparts could back-fire.

The Irish dislike being pressured, so most pressure techniques are not advisable. Opening with your best offer may hurt their pride. Do not make a final offer too early in the bargaining process and avoid making one more than once. Silence may be perceived as cold and unfriendly. Do not use pressure tactics such as applying time pressure or making expiring offers. The Irish could view these as signs that you are not willing to build a long-term relationship and may choose to terminate the negotiation.

Irish negotiators avoid most aggressive or adversarial techniques. While they may make indirect threats and warnings, they will be careful not to appear aggressive when doing so. Extreme openings may be viewed as unfriendly and are best avoid-ed. Never walk out or threaten to do so in an aggressive fashion as your counterparts will likely take this as a personal insult and may end all talks. However, threatening a 'friendly walkout' while strongly emphasizing the relationship may be very effec-tive.

Emotional negotiation techniques, such as attitudinal bargaining, attempting to make you feel guilty, grimacing, or appealing to personal relationships, may occasionally be employed. It is best to remain calm. Irish negotiators may frequently employ de-fensive tactics such as blocking or changing the subject, asking probing or very direct questions, or making promises.

Corruption and bribery are rare in Ireland, though not completely unheard of. Both legally and ethically, it is advisable to stay away from giving gifts of significant value or making offers that could be read as bribery.

Decision Making – Two different styles exist in Ireland: Some companies, especially family-owned businesses, may be quite hierarchical, with the person at the top be-ing the sole decision maker. Here, decisions can be very fast. Many other companies, however, are less hierarchical and involve people at several levels of the organization in the decision process. While it will inevitably be a bit slower, this approach can still be fairly swift and effective in Ireland. In any case, it will be beneficial to win the sup-port of the top executive of the organization.

When making decisions, businesspeople usually consider the specific situation rath-er than applying universal principles. Empirical evidence and other objective facts weigh more strongly than personal feelings and experiences do. Most Irish are mod-erate risk takers.

Agreements and Contracts

Capturing and exchanging meeting summaries can be an effective way to verify un-derstanding and commitments. Deals may still be sealed with a handshake, though this is becoming less common. It is vital to keep all commitments as failing to do so may lock you out not only from this partner but also from many potential others in Ireland.

Written contracts tend to be lengthy and often spell out detailed terms and conditions for the core agreements as well as for many eventualities. Nevertheless, writing up and signing the contract is a formality. The Irish believe that the primary strength of an agreement lies in the partners' commitment rather than in its written documentation.

It is recommended to consult a local legal expert before signing a contract. However, do not bring in your attorney until the negotiations have concluded. Irish people may read it as a sign of mistrust if you do.

Contracts are usually dependable, and the agreed terms are viewed as binding. Requests to change contract details after signature may be considered as bad faith and will meet with strong resistance. It is important to maintain on-time deliveries.

Women in Business

While women enjoy similar rights as men, most Irish women are still struggling to attain positions of similar income and authority. However, visiting businesswomen should have few problems in the country as long as they act professionally in business and social situations.

Other Important Things to Know

Business attire is less important in Ireland than elsewhere. However, men should wear a suit and tie at initial meetings.

Social events do not require strict punctuality. While it is best to arrive at dinners close to the agreed time, being late to a party by 15 to 30 minutes or more is perfectly acceptable.

If you are offered a beer in a pub, you will be expected to pay for the next round. Not living up to this expectation is a major faux pas.

Gift giving in business settings is rare. It is best not to bring a gift to an initial meeting in order to avoid raising suspicions about your motives. Later on, small gifts will be appreciated on special occasions, such as Christmas.

Israel

Most Israeli businesspeople, especially those among younger generations, are experienced in interacting with other cultures.

Eighty percent of this heterogeneous culture's population is Jewish. The remaining twenty percent are mostly Arabic Muslims and Christians. Among the Jews, the primary groups are Ashkenazim (Europe- or American-born), Sephardim (mostly born in the Arabic Middle East or around the Mediterranean), and Sabras (Hebrew: *Tza-*

bars, indicating those born in Israel). Given the diverse nature of the population, business practices may reflect a diverse mix of North American, European, Russian, or other cultural influences. About 20 percent of the population is practicing, religious, or orthodox Jews. The information given in this section represents general guidelines but may not always apply in full.

Most Israelis are very proud of their country and expect others to show some appreciation for its challenging political environment. It can be disastrous for your business if you openly critique the country's current policies. Instead, familiarize yourself with some of the country's history or at least show some interest in learning more about it.

Relationships and Respect

Israel's culture expects its members to have a sense of belonging to and conforming with their group. At the same time, it leaves a lot of room for individual preferences. Building lasting and trusting personal relationships is important to most people in this country, although the degree to which that applies may vary widely depending on where they grew up. Israeli Arabs usually expect to establish strong bonds prior to closing any deals and often prefer to do business only with those they know and like. This may be a slow process. Other Israelis, especially Sabras, may be willing to move faster and engage in business much sooner, since they usually may care much less about rapport and the social aspects of conducting business. Generally, it is always helpful to give your Israeli counterparts time to become at least somewhat comfortable with you. In addition, mention other contacts in the country if you have any.

Business relationships in this country exist between companies as well as between individuals. If your company replaces you with someone else over the course of a negotiation, it may be easy for your replacement to take things over from where you left them. Likewise, if you introduce someone else from your company into an existing business relationship, that person may quickly be accepted as a valid business partner. This does not mean that the Israelis do not care about who they are dealing with. Israeli Arabs focus much more on personal relationship aspects than others in the country.

In Israel's business culture, the respect a person enjoys depends primarily on his or her achievements and education. Status and age are less important than in most other countries in this democratic and egalitarian country. Initial impressions may last a long time, especially when dealing with Jewish Israelis, so it is vital to focus on creating the right ones early on.

Communication

While Hebrew is the official language and many people speak Arabic, English is widely used as well. Having come from anywhere around the world, some Israelis may not speak English well. Nevertheless, most businesspeople have a good understanding of it, and interpreters are rarely needed. In spite of that, side discussions in Hebrew are frequent and should be given sufficient room. Their purpose is usually to make internal discussions more effective, not to shut you out from the discussion.

Israelis normally speak in loud, enthusiastic tones. Interrupting others or speaking in parallel is acceptable. They may appear aggressive even when they do not mean to. Silence has little use in conversations, where long pauses are very rare. People in the country generally converse in close proximity, standing only two feet or less apart. Never back away, even if this is much closer than your personal comfort zone allows. Doing so could be read as a sign that you are uncomfortable around them.

Communicating with Jewish Israelis tends to be extremely direct. They have no problem saying 'no,' and generally prefer frank and unmistakable messages to diplomatic and ambiguous ones. Words like 'want,' 'need,' 'must' may be used more often than 'wish,' 'would like,' or 'should.' Even adversarial-sounding statements such as 'you're wrong' or 'you don't understand' are probably only meant as factual statements. Try not to take any of them personally. Israelis often delight in argument and may appear very opinionated. Although this may seem confrontational, they usually value receiving equally candid messages, even when they disagree. Discussions among Jewish Israelis may appear heated or even combative to the outsider. Do not read too much into this – they could actually be close friends.

Israeli Arabs may be less direct, even if they insist that they are telling the truth or giving you the facts. When they say 'yes,' it may actually mean 'possibly.' Ambiguous answers such as 'we must look into this' or 'we will think about it' may mean 'no.' Overall, the range of communication preferences can be very wide and the actual style may strongly depend on who it is you are dealing with.

Gestures and body language can be extensive, and Israelis tend to make frequent physical contact. Israeli Arabs consider the left hand unclean, so use it only if inevitable. Pointing at people or objects is impolite. Instead, wave your open hand toward the object. The thumbs-up gesture and pointing your thumb sideways can be taken as offensive gestures in Israel. Eye contact should be frequent, almost to the point of staring. This conveys sincerity and helps build trust.

Initial Contacts and Meetings

Choosing a third party intermediary may be helpful, especially with Israeli Arabs. This could be a consultant or lawyer who effectively bridges the gap between cultures, allowing you to conduct business with greater effectiveness. The rank of visitors does not matter as long as they are knowledgeable and have sufficient decision authority. Negotiations in Israel can be conducted by individuals or teams of negotiators. Changing team members is usually not a problem, though it may slow the negotiation progress. If you are negotiating with Israeli Arabs, it is best to keep the team unchanged since otherwise relationship building will have to start over. There is no need for a senior executive to attend the initial meeting for your company.

Scheduling meetings in advance is required. However, you can sometimes do this on short notice, especially if the parties have had previous business interactions. Israelis tend to find ways to make things happen as long as they are interested in what the other party has to offer. Depending on your counterparts' cultural background, punctuality expectations can range from right on time to very flexible. It is best to avoid being more than 10 to 15 minutes late; call ahead if you will be. Displaying anger if you have to wait only reflects poorly on you.

Reflecting the fact that people move to Israel from all around the world, every variation of naming patterns can be found. Unless you recognize the elements of a name, in which case you should address them as *Mr./Ms.* followed by their family name, it is best to ask people politely how to address them correctly. In that case, make sure you do the same for your own name. If a person has an academic title, use it together with their family name. Before calling Israelis by their first name, wait until they offer it unless they introduced themselves using their first name only. Introductions are accompanied by firm handshakes.

After the introductions, offer your business card to everyone present. The process of exchanging cards is usually quite relaxed. Cards should be in English; there is no need to have them translated to Hebrew. Present your card with your right hand. Similarly, accept others' cards using only the right hand. Smile and keep eye contact while doing so, then examine the card.

Meetings usually start with small talk. With Israeli Arabs, it may be extensive and include prolonged inquiries about your health, family, and so on. While Jewish Israelis may not want to discuss family matters, they might enjoy talking about other personal and professional subjects. It is important to be patient and let your local counterparts set the pace. Meeting interruptions are normal and do not signal a lack of interest or respect.

While one purpose of the first meeting is to get to know each other, most of it will focus on business topics. Israelis prefer discussions that are straightforward and emphasize the 'bottom line.' Nevertheless, digressions are likely if a side topic is of interest to the group. Some humor, which can be ironic and cynical, may be appreciated, but business is mostly a serious matter in Israel.

Presentations should be short and concise. Your materials should be attractive, with good and clear visuals. Having your English-language handout materials translated to Hebrew is not required, though it will be appreciated.

Negotiation

Attitudes and Styles - In Israel, the primary approach to negotiating is to employ distributive and contingency bargaining. While the buyer is in a superior position, both sides in a business deal own the responsibility to reach agreement. Israeli Arabs expect everyone to make a long-term commitment to their business engagement and will mostly focus on its long-term benefits. Jewish Israelis, on the other hand, may pay more attention to the near-term benefits of the deal. Although the primary negotiation style is somewhat competitive, Israelis nevertheless value long-term relationships and look for win-win solutions. Attempts to win competitive advantages should not be taken negatively. You earn your counterparts' respect by maintaining a positive, persistent attitude.

Israelis may start negotiations with Westerners from an initial standpoint of respect and appreciation. That will not keep them from becoming tough and competitive as the negotiation process unfolds.

Should a dispute arise at any stage of a negotiation, you might be able to reach resolution through using logical arguments and showing willingness to compromise. Patience and creativity will pay strong dividends.

Sharing of Information - Information is rarely shared freely, since the locals believe that privileged information creates bargaining advantages.

Pace of Negotiation – Expect negotiations to be slow and protracted. Even though decision making itself may be fast, the time spent to exchange information and bargain can be much longer than you may expect. Be patient, control your emotions, and accept that delays may occur.

Bargaining – Israeli businesspeople are often shrewd negotiators who should not be underestimated. They are used to, and may even enjoy, hard bargaining but usually haggle less than their Arab neighbors may. The bargaining stage of a negotiation can be extensive. Prices may move by 40 percent or more between initial offers and final agreement. Leave yourself a lot of room for concessions at different stages. However, since overly compromising is viewed as a sign of weakness, concessions never come easily. It is not advisable to make significant early concessions, since your counterparts expect further compromises as the bargaining continues.

Deceptive techniques are frequent and can be effective. This includes tactics such as telling lies and sending fake non-verbal messages, pretending to be disinterested in the whole deal or in single concessions, misrepresenting an item's value, or making false demands and concessions. Expect your Israeli counterparts to be good at this game. They may occasionally play stupid or otherwise attempt to mislead you in order to obtain bargaining advantages. Lies will be difficult to detect. It is advisable to verify information received from the local side through other channels. Similarly, they treat 'outside' information with caution. Israelis may use 'good cop, bad cop' as a way to obtain concessions. It can sometimes be beneficial to use this tactic in your own negotiation approach. 'Limited authority' is a rare tactic which is best avoided.

Negotiators in the country may use pressure techniques that include intransigence, making final or expiring offers, applying time pressure, or nibbling. When using similar tactics yourself, clearly explain your offer and avoid being overly aggressive. Final offers may come more than once and are rarely final. In general, attempts to rush the bargaining process are rarely successful and may be viewed very negatively. Israelis Arabs may be offended if you make a final offer too soon. They usually expect to go through extensive rounds of bargaining with several 'final' offers before reaching agreement. Silence can be an effective way to signal rejection of a proposal.

Israeli negotiators may sometimes appear aggressive or adversarial. Negotiations in the country tend to include confrontational elements. Extreme openings are frequent as a way to start the bargaining process. Negotiators may also make threats and warnings, openly display anger, or even use walkouts. It is ok to respond in kind, although you should be careful not to outdo your counterparts.

Emotional negotiation techniques, such as attitudinal bargaining, sending dual messages, attempting to make you feel guilty, grimacing, or appealing to personal relationships, are frequent and can be effective. Israelis can become very emotional during fierce bargaining. It is best to remain calm. At times, defensive tactics such as blocking or changing the subject, asking probing or very direct questions, or making promises may be used.

Corruption and bribery are rare in Israel, though not completely unheard of. Both legally and ethically, it is advisable to stay away from giving gifts of significant value or making offers that could be read as bribery.

Decision Making – Hierarchies do not play a very strong role in Israeli companies. Decision makers are usually individuals who consider the best interest of the group or organization. Their authority is often delegated to lower management levels. Independent decision making is encouraged, since personal initiative and achievement are strong values. Nevertheless, many Israelis will consult with others to reach greater consensus and support. Consequently, some may make quick decisions, while with others it can take a long time to arrive at a final decision.

When making decisions, businesspeople usually consider the specific situation rather than follow universal principles. Personal feelings and experiences weigh more strongly than empirical evidence and other objective facts do, but they will consider all aspects. While some Israelis enjoy risk-taking, others may be fatalistic and risk-averse. You may first need to find ways for them to become comfortable with high risks.

Agreements and Contracts

Capturing and exchanging written understandings after meetings and at key negotiation stages is both common and useful. Oral statements may not always be dependable. However, do not mistake them for final agreements. Any part of an agreement may still change significantly before both parties sign the contract, even when you believe a decision was made.

Written contracts tend to be lengthy. They often spell out detailed terms and conditions for the core agreements as well as for many eventualities. Signing the contract is important not only from a legal perspective, but also as a strong confirmation of your Israeli partners' commitment. It is strongly advisable to consult a local legal expert before signing a contract.

Contracts are usually dependable, and the agreed terms are viewed as binding. Requests to change contract details after signature may meet with strong resistance.

Women in Business

Although the country is still male-dominated, this society promotes equality between the genders, and Israeli women can be found in positions of authority. Visiting businesswomen should have few problems in the country as long as they act professionally in business and social situations.

Strictly observant Orthodox Jews may not want to touch any woman. If a woman wants to pass something to such a man, she should place it on a table. Female visitors are expected to follow this practice when presenting their business cards to Orthodox men, who can be identified by their skullcaps, or hats and black clothing.

Other Important Things to Know

Compared with other countries, personal appearance and attire are somewhat less important when doing business here. In many industries and business sectors, appearing rather casual can be a better choice than being 'over-dressed.'

Lunches and dinners are great opportunities to get to know your counterparts better and discuss business.

Punctuality rules in social settings may again depend on your Israeli counterparts' cultural heritage. It is best to arrive at dinners close to the agreed time. Being late to a party by 15 minutes is almost always acceptable; with many Israelis, arriving more than an hour later may still be ok.

Gift giving in business settings is rare. It is best not to bring a gift to an initial meeting in order to avoid raising suspicions about your motives.

Topics to avoid in discussions are the tensions over Palestine and with the country's other Arabic neighbors.

Lastly, keep in mind that the Israeli workweek starts on Sunday and ends on Thursday. Never try to pressure a practicing, religious, or orthodox Jew into working during Sabbath (Friday evening through Saturday night). Similarly, the Friday is a holy day for Muslims.

Italy

Italian businesspeople, especially those among younger generations, are often experienced in interacting and doing business with visitors from other cultures. However, that does not always mean that they are open-minded. When negotiating business here, realize that people may expect things to be done 'their way.'

Though the country's culture is relatively homogeneous, business cultures are considerably different between the North and the South. People in the North tend to be business-focused, serious, and somewhat reserved. South of Bologna, and much more so south of Rome, business and negotiation styles get much more relaxed and people are often more personable. These variances affect many aspects of negotiations in Italy.

Relationships and Respect

Building lasting and trusting relationships is important to most people in this country. However, they are not a necessary precondition for initial business interactions, at least in the northern parts of the country. Southern Italians may expect to establish strong bonds prior to closing any deals. Generally, Italians tend to follow their feelings and intuition. Many of them prefer to do business only with people they know and like. Consequently, proceed with serious business discussions only after your counterparts have become very comfortable with you. Italians tend to distrust people who appear unwilling to spend the time or whose motives for relationship building are unclear.

Business relationships in this country exist both at the individual and company level. If your company replaces you with someone else over the course of a negotiation, it may be easy for your replacement to take things over from where you left them. Likewise, if you introduce someone else from your company into an existing business relationship, that person may quickly be accepted as a valid business partner. Again, this may take longer in the South.

Establishing personal relationships with others in Italy can create powerful networks and may help you a lot to achieve your business objectives. Whom you know may determine whether people want to get to know you. Similarly, whether people think you are worth knowing may weigh more strongly than what proposals you have to make. Maintaining honest and cordial relations is crucial. Third party introductions can be very helpful as a starting point to building a trusting relationship with a potential partner.

When dealing with Italians, especially those in the South, nothing matters more than a concept known as *bella figura* (beautiful posture). It means maintaining the right sense of civility and formality at all times. This includes a person's sense of honor, the ability to be assertive without appearing arrogant, how well he or she presents and expresses himself or herself, and many other actions and behaviors that are expected to contribute to the beauty and sense of order in the world. Personal pride is very critical. It can be catastrophic to your business relationship should you ever insult the honor or personal pride of your Italian counterparts or their families and friends, even if done inadvertently. Never show disrespect to the country as a whole, to your counterparts' friends and family, or to their personal accomplishments and possessions.

In Italy's business culture, the respect a person enjoys depends primarily on his or her status, rank, and age. It is important to treat elderly people with the greatest respect. Admired personal traits include assertiveness and poise, but also personal warmth and sociability.

Communication

The country's official language is Italian. There are also German-, French-, and Slovene-speaking minorities in the country. Many Italians, especially in the South, do not speak English well, so you may sometimes need a translator. When communicating in English, speak in short, simple sentences and avoid using jargon and slang. It will help people with a limited command of English if you speak slowly, summarize your key points often, and pause frequently to allow for interpretation. Italians will rarely admit it if they do not understand parts of the conversation. Even when the main meeting language is English, your counterparts will frequently speak Italian among themselves, not necessarily to shut you out from the discussion but to reduce their discomfort and ensure a common understanding among them.

Southern Italians often speak loudly and passionately. They enjoy eloquent and elaborate discussions, which may sometimes become heated and emotional debates. In addition, they may interrupt each other frequently. People may show their emotions very openly. However, it is crucial that you never lose your temper or appear impatient, as there is always a risk of hurting someone's pride. Italians in the South generally converse in close proximity, standing only two feet or less apart. Never back away, even if this is much closer than your personal comfort zone allows. Doing so could be read as a sign that you are uncomfortable around them.

While Northern Italians also appreciate animated discussions, business meetings are usually quieter affairs here. They are mostly conducted in a controlled atmosphere, and the person with the highest authority rarely has to raise his or her voice. Emotions may still be shown, though, and silence likely delivers a negative message. In conversations, Northern Italians may stand a little further apart than their compatriots in the South, but this may still be closer than what people from North America or Northern Europe may be comfortable with.

Communication in Italy is usually not overly direct. People may not get straight to the point when trying to get a message across, and you may have to read between the lines to understand what is being conveyed. Especially in the South, they may tell you what they think you want to hear rather than what they really think. However, Italians will not find it difficult to say 'no' if they dislike a request or proposal. They will appreciate constructive criticism if made in a respectful and not overly blunt manner. Silence is again rare and usually signals that there is a problem.

Gestures and body language can be extensive. It is often not a good idea to imitate them, though. Italians tend to gesticulate a lot. Do not read too much into it. There may be frequent physical contact with others of the same gender. Eye contact should be frequent, almost to the point of staring. This conveys sincerity and helps build trust. Anger may sometimes be masked with a smile.

Initial Contacts and Meetings

Choosing a local intermediary who can leverage existing relationships to make the initial contact is important, since having a contact is advantageous for doing business in this country. This person will help bridge the gap between cultures, allowing you to conduct business with greater effectiveness.

Negotiations in Italy can be conducted by individuals or teams of negotiators. The most senior executive on your side should have the necessary authority and clearly act as the leader of your team. Similarly, the highest-ranking person on the Italian side will likely attend and will be the decision maker.

If possible, schedule meetings at least two to three weeks in advance. Since Italians want to know whom they will be meeting, provide details on titles, positions, and responsibilities of attendees ahead of time. They will expect to do business with the most important person in your organization. An agenda may be set upfront, but this is only a formality. It will likely not be followed. While meetings may start considerably late, Italians generally expect foreign visitors to be punctual. Avoid being more than 10 to 15 minutes late, and call ahead if you will be. This is less critical in the South of the country. Displaying anger if you have to wait only reflects poorly on you.

Names are usually given in the order of first name, family name. However, some Italians may do it the other way around. Use *Mr./Ms.* or *Signor/Signora* followed by the family name. If a person has a title, such as *Doctor* (*Dottore/Dottoressa*, frequently used for people with any advanced degree) or *Professor* (*Professore/Professoressa*), use it instead, followed by the family name. Many other professional titles may be used. Only close friends call each other by their first names. Introduce or greet the most senior person first. Thereafter, greet everyone else individually. Introductions are accompanied by handshakes. Men should wait for women to initiate handshakes.

The exchange of business cards is an essential step when meeting someone for the first time, so bring more than you need. There is no need to have them translated to Italian, but it will be preferably noted if you do. Show advanced degrees on your card and make sure that it clearly states your professional title, especially if you have the seniority to make decisions. When presenting your card, smile and keep eye contact, then take a few moments to look at the card you received. Next, place it on the table in front of you.

Meetings start with small talk, which can be extensive. It is important to be patient and let the other side set the pace. Initial meetings can be quite formal, but this usually gets more relaxed as the relationship develops. Humor will be appreciated as long as it is not sarcastic or cynical. Meetings in Italy may appear somewhat chaotic, with frequent interruptions and several parallel conversations. Do not take this personally; it also does not indicate a lack of interest.

The primary purpose of the first meeting is to become acquainted and build relationships. Business may be discussed, but do not try to hurry along with your agenda. The goal should be to establish respect and trust between yourself and your counterparts. It is unrealistic to expect initial meetings to lead to straight decisions.

Presentation materials should be attractive and aesthetically pleasing, with good and clear visuals. Remember to maintain your *bella figura* throughout your presentation. Come to the meeting with a carefully planned and logically organized proposal. Leave additional information that supports your proposal. Having your handout materials translated to Italian is not a must, but it helps in getting your messages across.

Negotiation

Attitudes and Styles - Leveraging relationships is an important element when negotiating in Italy. Nevertheless, Italians often employ distributive and contingency bargaining. While the buyer is in a superior position, both sides in a business deal own the responsibility to reach agreement. They expect long-term commitments from their business partners and will focus mostly on long-term benefits. Although the primary negotiation style is competitive, Italians nevertheless value long-term relationships and look for win-win solutions. While proposals should demonstrate the benefits to both negotiating parties, neither of them should take attempts to win competitive advantages negatively. It is important to remain non-confrontational throughout the bargaining exchange. Demanding that strict rules be followed during the negotiation process conflicts with the Italians' casual attitude and will likely not get you anywhere either. You will earn your counterparts' respect by remaining relaxed while maintaining a positive, persistent attitude.

Should a dispute arise at any stage of a negotiation, you might be able to reach resolution or an acceptable compromise by leveraging personal relationships, assuming that they are strong enough.

Sharing of Information – The level of information sharing depends on the strength of the relationship. During initial negotiations, Italians may play their cards close to the chest. Most of them believe in information sharing as a way to build trust, though.

Pace of Negotiation – Expect negotiations to be slow and protracted, and be prepared to make several trips if necessary to achieve your objectives. Information gathering, bargaining, and decision making may take considerable time. Decisions are usually made between meetings rather than at the table. Throughout the negotiation, be patient, control your emotions, and accept that delays occur. Attempts to rush the process are unlikely to produce better results and may be viewed as offensive.

If your counterparts appear to be stalling the negotiation, assess carefully whether their slowing down the process indicates that they are evaluating alternatives or that they are not interested in doing business with you. While such behavior could represent attempts to create time pressure in order to obtain concessions, the slow decision process in the country is far more likely causing the lack of progress. People from fast-paced cultures tend to underestimate how much time this takes and often make the mistake of trying to 'speed things up.' Again, patience and persistence are important.

Bargaining – Italians, especially in the South, are used to hard bargaining and haggling. They may expect to do a lot of it during a negotiation. Strong emotions and much drama may accompany the process, with a wide spectrum reaching from flattery to bitter complaints, but never open aggression. Spend time to understand your counterparts' objectives and prepare for unexpected moves or changes.

The bargaining exchange can be extensive. Prices may move by 40 percent or more between initial offers and final agreement. Leave yourself a lot of room for concessions at different stages. If needed, show willingness to compromise as a way to preserve the honor of both parties. After making concessions, always ask the other side to reciprocate.

Deceptive techniques are frequent and can be effective. This includes tactics such as telling lies and sending fake non-verbal messages, pretending to be disinterested in the whole deal or in single concessions, misrepresenting an item's value, or making false demands and concessions. Expect your Italian counterparts to be good at this game. They may occasionally play stupid or otherwise attempt to mislead you in order to obtain bargaining advantages. Lies will be difficult to detect. It is advisable to verify information received from the local side through other channels. 'Good cop, bad cop' may be used on either side of the negotiation table. Italians may claim limited authority, stating that they have to ask for their manager's approval. This could be a tactic or the truth.

Negotiators in the country may use pressure techniques that include making final offers or nibbling. Final offers may come more than once and are rarely final. Italians may also sometimes make surprise demands in a similar 'take it or leave it' style. In these cases, they may be testing your limits to see how far you will go. Be careful when using tactics such as opening with your best offer, showing intransigence, applying time pressure, or making decreasing or expiring offers. Italians may consider these inappropriate unless they are strongly interested in your offer and clearly understand the rationale behind the approach. Otherwise, while the negotiation is not necessarily over, it may become less constructive. Silence can be an effective way to signal rejection of a proposal.

Italian negotiators avoid openly aggressive or adversarial techniques. While they may make indirect threats and warnings or subtly display anger, they will be careful not to appear aggressive when doing so. Although extreme openings are rare, the tactic may be effective for you as a way to start the bargaining process. Do not walk out or threaten to do so as your counterparts will likely take this as a personal insult and may end all talks.

Emotional negotiation techniques, such as attitudinal bargaining, sending dual messages, attempting to make you feel guilty, grimacing, or appealing to personal relationships, are frequent and can be effective. Be cautious not to hurt someone's personal pride when employing any of these yourself, though. At times, defensive tactics such as blocking or changing the subject, asking probing or very direct questions, making promises, or keeping an inflexible position may be used.

Note that opening with written offers and attempting to introduce written terms and conditions as a negotiation tactic is rarely successful. In most cases, businesspeople ignore or tactfully reject them and request that each aspect be negotiated individually.

Corruption and bribery are somewhat common in Italy's public and private sectors, especially in the South. However, people may draw the line differently, viewing minor payments as rewards for getting a job done rather than as bribes. Also, keep in mind that there is a fine line between giving gifts and bribing. What you may consider a bribe, an Italian may view as only a nice gift.

Decision Making – Most companies are hierarchical, and people expect to work within clearly established lines of authority. Decision makers are primarily senior managers who consider the best interest of the group or organization. Others are often consulted in a committee-style process in order to reach greater consensus over and support of the decision. This process can take a very long time and requires patience. Attempts to rush or put pressure on the decision making process is an affront to Italian business protocol. It may sometimes be difficult to identify the primary decision maker. In family businesses, it is always the head of the family, though. In other companies, it is strongly advisable to make contact with the most senior manager, seeking to get his or her support even if the person may not be the sole decision maker.

When making decisions, businesspeople usually consider the specific situation rather than applying universal principles. Personal feelings and experiences weigh more strongly than empirical evidence and other objective facts do, but all aspects are considered. Italians are often uneasy with change and reluctant to take risks. If you expect them to support a risky decision, you may need to find ways for them to become comfortable with it first, for instance by explaining contingency plans, outlining areas of additional support, or by offering guarantees and warranties.

Agreements and Contracts

Capturing and exchanging meeting summaries can be an effective way to verify understanding and commitments. Most Italians expect that verbal commitments be honored, although they may not be fully dependable themselves. Do not mistake interim agreements for final ones. Any part of an agreement may still change significantly before both parties sign the contract.

Written contracts tend to be lengthy and often spell out very detailed terms and conditions for the core agreements as well as for many eventualities. Nevertheless, writing up and signing the contract is a formality. Italians believe that the primary strength of an agreement lies in the partners' commitment rather than in its written documentation.

It is advisable to consult a local legal expert before signing a contract. However, do not bring your attorney to the negotiation table. Italians may read it as a sign of mistrust if you do.

While contracts are usually dependable, their terms are not always strictly met. Business partners usually expect the other side to remain somewhat flexible if conditions change, which may include agreeing to modify contract terms.

Women in Business

While Italian society is making progress towards gender equality and some women hold important positions, most of them are still struggling to attain positions of similar income and authority as men. As a visiting businesswoman, emphasize your company's importance and your role in it. A personal introduction or a letter of support from a senior executive within your company may also help.

Female business travelers should graciously accept any chivalric gestures they receive. Complimenting women on their appearance is common and viewed as perfectly acceptable. Should someone making such a compliment go too far, it is best simply to ignore the person. Generally, displaying confidence and assertiveness can be effective, but it is important not to appear overly bold and aggressive.

Other Important Things to Know

Good and fashionable attire is very important when doing business here. Male business visitors should wear dark suits with neckties on most occasions. First impressions can have a significant impact on how people view you.

Business dinners are common and present great opportunities to strengthen relationships. However, business itself is rarely discussed over meals.

Social events do not require strict punctuality. While it is best to arrive at dinners close to the agreed time, being late to a party by 15 to 30 minutes or more is perfectly acceptable.

Do not ask people you meet in a social setting about 'what they do.' They will likely view it inappropriate and may even take your seemingly harmless question as an insult.

Gift giving in business settings is rare, especially in Northern Italy. It is best not to bring a gift to an initial meeting in order to avoid raising suspicions about your motives.

Japan

Many Japanese businesspeople are experienced in interacting with other cultures. However, that does not mean that they are open-minded. When negotiating business here, people expect that you understand and follow the Japanese way of doing things. After all, this country, with its history as an isolated 'Island Nation,' is culturally very homogeneous, and commonality of customs is considered very desirable.

Relationships and Respect

Japan's culture is strongly group-oriented. Individual preferences are less important than having a sense of belonging to a group, conforming to its norms, and maintaining harmony among its members, who are expected to develop an intense loyalty to the group as a whole. Building lasting and trusting personal relationships is therefore critically important. While members of other cultures may expect this to happen gradually over the course of a business engagement, most Japanese expect to establish strong relationships prior to closing any deals. Your local partner wants to know that you and your company are strongly committed to this relationship and that they can depend on you. Proceed with serious business negotiations only after your counterparts have become comfortable with you. Since people are generally suspicious of foreigners, gaining their trust and establishing good will is going to take time.

Once you have reached that point, the Japanese may still prefer to keep the initial engagement small and low-risk. They view this as an opportunity for you to prove yourself. Larger-scale business engagements require time to build. Since the Japanese are very long-term oriented, they usually prefer this slow approach. It is very important to emphasize frequently the long-term benefits and your commitment to them and to the business relationship you are seeking to build. Keep in touch on a regular basis throughout all stages of your business engagement, but realize that the strength of a relationship in this country depends much less on whether someone likes you than on whether they consider you trustworthy and dependable.

Business relationships in Japan may exist both at the individual and at the company level. However, the former weighs more strongly. You need to build corporate relationships at all levels of the organization, not just at the top. It is critically important for most Japanese to deal with others they know, respect, and trust. However, if your company replaces you with someone else over the course of a negotiation, it may be somewhat easier for your replacement to take things over from where you left them if your company is already considered dependable. To ease the transition, the person who enjoys your Japanese counterparts' strongest trust must endorse the new team member as an influential and dependable person.

In Japan, the concept of *face* is possibly even more important than in other Asian societies. Reputation and social standing strongly depend on a person's ability to control emotions and preserve group harmony. The importance of diplomatic restraint and tact cannot be overestimated. Always keep your cool and never lose your composure. Causing embarrassment to another person may cause a *loss of face* for all parties involved and can be disastrous for business negotiations. If you have to bring up an unpleasant personal topic with someone, never do so in public and always convey your message in ways that maintain the other's self-respect.

'Giving face' is crucial to develop relationships. Showing great respect for and genuinely praising the group or organization will be favorably noted. However, never single out a Japanese person, whether for praise or criticism, in front of the group. Doing so embarrasses him or her and may cause the person as well as the group to lose face. The group identity always prevails. However, privately complimenting a person is appreciated.

It is polite to apologize often. A person may express profound apologies for being a few minutes late, having a cold, taking you out for dinner to a place where the food turns out to be only average, and for virtually any other aspect of daily life you may not even consider worth mentioning. Humility is valued very highly in this country, and foreigners are encouraged to show a similar attitude.

Requesting a favor from someone in Japan you do not have an existing relationship with is considered inappropriate and may be ignored altogether. Once relationships exist, they are bound by a rigid concept of mutual obligations. In western societies, people connected through close relationships may expect certain favors of each other, but they are usually forgiving if circumstances get in the way. In Japan, such obligations are non-negotiable and must be fulfilled without exception. Even small favors can create such obligations. For example, if you ask someone to introduce you to someone else, the intermediary has an obligation to the other party if he or she does so. Should you later prove unworthy of this connection, for instance by failing to meet your commitments, the intermediary loses face. Since this can have significant consequences for these intermediaries, they will only make such introductions if they are convinced that they can trust you.

In Japanese business culture, the respect a person enjoys depends primarily on his or her age, status, and rank. You will commonly find leaders in senior roles to be of advanced age. It is very important to treat elderly people with the greatest respect. Japan is not an egalitarian society. Nevertheless, humility is highly valued, and the Japanese are masters of subtlety. Other admired personal traits include loyalty, team orientation, and sociability.

Communication

The country's official language is Japanese. Most local businesspersons, even younger ones, do not speak and understand English well. The understanding of written text is better than that of spoken English, so it is always a good idea to bring written proposals and confirm key points of oral communications in writing. Pause frequently and give the Japanese side time for translation and discussion. Verify through diplomatic questions whether your counterparts understood you. Since saving *face* is so important, people will not openly admit it in front of others if they do not understand what you are saying. If in doubt, try writing down key points on paper or on a white board.

In some cases, it is necessary to have an interpreter. Politely inquire beforehand whether an interpreter should be present at a meeting. However, keep in mind that even interpreters may not always speak and understand English at a fully proficient level. Also, realize that in this strongly relationship-oriented culture, an independent interpreter hired by you for a meeting is viewed an as outsider by the Japanese side, so your counterparts may be reluctant to speak openly. At the same time, interpreters may feel no allegiance with you, so they may be telling you what they think you want to hear rather than what the other side said. It is highly recommended to use someone from within your company as a negotiation team member who can translate, or correct the translator on missed key points. If that is not an option, it is better to ask the Japanese side whether they can provide someone within their team to handle translations. When communicating in English, speak in short, simple sentences free of jargon and slang. Pausing as often as you can gives people a better chance to translate and understand what you said. Also, allow for frequent side discussions in Japanese.

Japanese businesspeople usually speak in quiet, gentle tones. Maintaining a low-key and polite manner is important, and showing emotional restraint at all times is essential. Do not show anger or other negative emotions. Instead, mask these feelings with a smile. Conversations may include extended periods of silence, sometimes as long as ten seconds or more. This signals neither agreement nor rejection. At restaurants, especially those used for business lunches and dinners, keep conversations at a quiet level. Loud and boisterous behavior may be perceived as a lack of self-control. People generally converse while standing around three to four feet apart.

Because the concept of *face* is pivotal in this culture, communication is generally extremely indirect, even more so than in other Asian countries. When responding to a direct question, the Japanese may answer 'yes' only to signal that they heard what you said, not that they agree with it. Responding to a question or request with a direct 'no' is rarely an option in Japan. The strongest expression you may hear is 'that may be very difficult,' which is a clear-cut 'no.' Alternatively, they may give seemingly ambiguous answers such as 'I am not sure,' 'we will think about it,' or 'this will require further investigation.' Each of these indicate serious problems that need to be resolved. In your own communication, try to be equally polite and indirect. Avoid open refusals, disagreement, or confrontations at all cost. If you have to convey bad news to the Japanese side, the face-saving way is to also combine it with some good news or an acceptable solution.

In many societies, the sender is responsible for getting the message. In Japan, it is the receiver. Asking for clarification if something was too ambiguous is therefore acceptable. In addition, asking questions more than once is a way to get a complete answer. Saying 'Yes,' which you hear all the time, only means 'I heard what you said' – it does not signal understanding or agreement. A way to get a clear statement even if it might be negative is to phrase your questions such that the respondent can answer with 'yes.' An example would be 'do you have concerns?'

Gestures are usually very subtle in Japan. It is strongly advisable to restrict your body language. Non-verbal communication is very important, though, and you should carefully watch for others' small hints, just as they will be watching you. Do not make physical contact with other people except for handshakes. Do not use your hands when speaking since it may distract the Japanese. The American *OK* sign, with thumb and index finger forming a circle, means *money* in Japan. Pointing at people or objects is very impolite. Instead, wave your open hand toward the object. When referring to themselves, people put an index finger on their nose rather than pointing at their chest as Westerners do. Sucking in air through the teeth indicates that there is a serious problem. If the person puts a hand on the back of the neck at the same time, it signals, 'This is impossible.' Scratching the back of one's head, frowning, or scratching the eyebrow indicate apprehension or rejection. Moving the open hand in front of the face in a fanning motion, with the palm facing left again signals a negative response. Do not blow your nose in public since people find this repelling.

Unless strong personal relationships exist with a person, eye contact should be infrequent. Lowering one's eyes is a sign of respect. However, there may be intensive eye contact between friends or long-term business partners. If someone closes his or her eyes during a discussion, presentation, or speech, the Japanese assume that the person is listening attentively, while Westerners may erroneously assume that he or she is taking a nap. Smiles and laughter do not always indicate friendliness, amusement, or approval. They may mask a lack of understanding, embarrassment, disapproval, and other feelings of distress. Accordingly, Westerners may sometimes observe Japanese people smiling or laughing at what they might consider inappropriate moments.

Initial Contacts and Meetings

Before initiating business negotiations in Japan, identify a highly respected local person with whom you have or can establish a good relationship. Then, ask for this person's endorsement and connection to the potential Japanese partner you are targeting. Choose the intermediary carefully and consider the *face* issues for everyone involved. An intermediary should not be part of either one of the parties involved in the business interaction.

Negotiations in Japan require a team of negotiators instead of relying on a single individual. Always select your team members carefully. A negotiation team should be composed of people filling several functional roles, including both subject experts and specialized negotiators. It is vital that your team is well aligned. Disagreeing with each other in front of the Japanese can be disastrous. The size of your team conveys the level of seriousness, so larger is better. If possible, find out who will participate on the Japanese side, and match your team members up with them for closer relationship building. Status matters a lot, and a mismatch could be embarrassing for everyone. Changing a team member may require the process of building relationships to start over. However, if you introduce a new person from your company into an existing business relationship, that person will become a valid negotiation partner more quickly than if your company has no previous history with the Japanese side.

Given the strong emphasis on hierarchy in the country's business culture, a senior executive should attend the initial meeting for your company and your negotiating team should include senior leaders who know your company well. There will not be an expectation that the executive attends future meetings.

If possible, schedule meetings at least three weeks in advance. The Japanese do not like surprises. Since they want to know whom they will be meeting, provide details on titles, positions, and responsibilities of attendees ahead of time. One-on-one meetings are very rare and require strong existing relationships and trust. Communicate the meeting purpose and agree on an agenda with your counterparts ahead of the meeting. The agenda is usually strictly followed. At any meeting, whether business or social, it is strongly advisable to be very punctual. If a delay is inevitable, call ahead and apologize profoundly even if it was not your fault.

Names are usually given in the order of first name, family name. It is possible to use *Mr./Ms.* plus the family name. However, it is more respectful to address a male Japanese person in the traditional way, with the family name followed by '-san.' A person named Hiroshi Watanabe thus becomes 'Watanabe-san,' which roughly means 'honorable Mr. Watanabe.' If the person has an academic title, you can use it, again followed by family name and '-san.' Never call Japanese people by their first name unless they insist on it. Wait to be introduced rather than introducing yourself. Introduce and greet older people first. Japanese-style introductions are accompanied by bowing, following a complicated ritual which foreigners are not expected to know or comply with. Instead of trying to bow at the risk of getting it wrong, respond with a nod of the head if someone bows at you, and then follow through with a handshake.

The exchange of business cards is an essential step when meeting someone for the first time, so bring a lot more than you need. Under no circumstances should you use paper copies because you ran out of cards. Business cards are symbols of 'personal identity.' If someone presents you with his or her card and you do not offer one in return, the person will assume that you either do not want to make their acquaintance, that your status in your company's hierarchy is very low, or, quite to the contrary, that your status is very high. Use cards where one side is in English and the other in Japanese. Show any advanced degrees as well as memberships in professional associations on your card. Also, make sure that it clearly states your professional title, especially if you have the seniority to make decisions. Present your card with two hands, and ensure that the Japanese side is facing the recipient. Similarly, accept others' cards using both hands if possible. Smile and keep eye contact while doing so, then examine the card carefully. Not reading someone's card can be an insult. Next, place the card on the table in front of you or into your card case. Never stuff someone's card into your back pocket or otherwise treat it disrespectfully. In addition, never write on a person's business card. People of high rank may have their card presented by subordinates.

At the beginning of a meeting, there is normally some small talk. This allows participants to slowly become personally acquainted. Light humor may be welcome, although you should avoid western-style jokes. It is best to let the local side set the pace and follow along. Overall, negotiations are generally very formal and serious. The primary purpose of the first meeting is to get to know each other and start building relationships and mutual trust. It would be very unrealistic to expect a meeting to lead to a straight decision.

The highest-ranking person in a Japanese group may be difficult to pick out. It could be the one who says the least. To know for sure, look at their business cards. In addition, the person with most authority enjoys the middle position at the table. However, do not just speak to the person with the most authority. Always respond to the person who is doing the talking or asking the questions. Be respectful to everyone in the meeting.

Begin your part of the meeting with remarks about individual and company relationships, even if there is just a short history. Also, emphasize the status, size, and accomplishments of your company if possible. It is good to make a presentation, but keep it simple and avoid over-designing it. Refrain from discussing the pros and cons of an aspect in the same context, as this might confuse your counterparts and could raise mistrust.

You should bring a sufficient number of copies of anything you present, such that each attendee gets one. Presentation materials can be simple without colorful backgrounds and fancy graphs. However, good and easy-to-understand visuals are important. A persuasive presentation describes how your product or service can enhance the prosperity and reputation of the Japanese side. Presentations can be very long. The Japanese expect to discuss many details, so come well prepared, and bring enough background information. Having your handout materials translated to Japanese is not a must, but it helps in getting your messages across.

Negotiation

Attitudes and Styles – To the Japanese, negotiating is usually a joint problem-solving process. The buyer clearly has a dominant role and the seller carries a stronger burden to support that buyer than in most other societies. Vendors are expected to do whatever it takes to satisfy their customer's needs, and salespeople may receive harsh treatment from unhappy clients. In extreme cases, Japanese customers may demand to receive details of their vendors' cost structure and expect to receive prices at some margin above that. At the same time, both sides are expected to 'take care of each other.' The buyer will therefore ensure that the seller makes a profit in the deal, though what they may consider acceptable is often lower than in many other countries. Ultimately, both sides are partners in a mutual dependency that is bound by their relationship. Both are expected to make a long-term commitment to their business engagement and will mostly focus on its long-term benefits. Sellers may be expected to accept short-term losses for longer-term gains. A Japanese buyer is interested in what the vendor will do to reduce costs in the future, expecting that most of the savings are passed on so that both buyer and seller can enjoy more business through reducing the cost of their product or service. The primary negotiation style is cooperative and people may be open to compromising if viewed as helpful in order to move the negotiation forward. It is important to be flexible and creative to get a deal that both sides are pleased to have.

Should a dispute arise at any stage of a negotiation, resolving it may require the help of an external mediator, ideally the party who initially introduced you.

Sharing of Information - The time spent to gather information and discuss various details before the bargaining stage of a negotiation can begin is usually extensive. In this phase, the Japanese seek to find the other side's weaknesses. They rarely share information freely, since the Japanese view is that having privileged information creates bargaining advantages. Your counterparts consider putting all your cards on the table foolish. However, it is unwise to surprise the Japanese. If you have new information that is significant, share it with your counterparts prior to your next negotiation round.

Keep in mind that the Japanese are very detail-oriented. If you make exaggerated claims in an effort to impress the other side or to obtain concessions, they will likely investigate your claims before responding. This could become very embarrassing and may ruin the trust that has been built.

Pace of Negotiation - Expect negotiations to be slow and protracted, with immense attention paid to details throughout all stages. Relationship building, information gathering, bargaining, and decision making all take considerable time. The opening game may be slow since your Japanese counterparts are often unspecific about what they expect from you. Negotiators often attempt to wear you down in an effort to obtain concessions. It is not advisable to make significant early concessions since that may be interpreted as a lack of preparation or interest. Be prepared to make several trips if necessary to achieve your objectives. Throughout the negotiation, remain calm, friendly, patient, and persistent. Never allow issues during the negotiation process to create personal conflicts with your counterparts. Delays will be inevitable, making patience extremely important if you want to get anywhere in Japan.

If your counterparts appear to be stalling the negotiation, assess carefully whether their slowing down the process could indicate that they are not interested in doing business with you. More often than not, though, this behavior indicates either that they need time for internal discussions, or that they are trying to put you under time pressure in order to obtain concessions.

Bargaining - The Japanese negotiation style is very formal and tolerates only a restricted set of negotiation tactics. Many techniques that may be accepted or even admired elsewhere could jeopardize the success of a negotiation in this country. The Japanese are used to bargaining but often frown upon haggling. The bargaining stage of a negotiation can be extensive. When making new proposals, a negotiating party should explain the rationale behind them. However, some Japanese may have a dislike for making concessions, expecting both sides to come to the table with their best offer. If you sense this to be the case, quickly moving to a range you are willing to accept is your best strategy. Though concessions never come easily, prices may move by about 25 to 40 percent between initial offers and final agreement. Leave yourself sufficient room for concessions at different levels and prepare alternative options. This gives the Japanese negotiators room to refuse aspects of your proposal while preserving face. Japanese concessions typically come late in the bargaining, typically after a break that gave them a chance to establish consensus. Aspects can be re-visited. You can use this to your advantage, for instance by offering further concessions under the condition that the Japanese side reciprocate in areas that had already been agreed upon.

Deceptive techniques may sometimes be employed, and Japanese negotiators may expect you to use some of them as well. This could include tactics such as pretending to be disinterested in the whole deal or in single concessions, misrepresenting the value of some items, or making false demands and concessions. It is advisable to verify information received from the Japanese side through other channels if you have a chance. Similarly, they treat 'outside' information with caution. Another approach is to ask further questions in order to understand underlying assumptions or data. Since negotiation teams must act in consensus and preserve face, the Japanese do not use 'good cop, bad cop.' It is not a good idea to use this tactic in your own negotiation approach. The Japanese will also not claim 'limited authority' because the group makes all decisions. Be cautious when using the techniques of making false demands or false concessions. Since avoiding *loss of face* is critical, any overt attempts to bluff your counterparts could backfire, killing any trust that may have been established. For the same reason, refrain from telling lies to your counterparts under all circumstances.

Negotiators may use pressure techniques that include opening with a written offer, keeping silent, or applying time pressure. The Japanese may remain silent, possibly for a minute or more, as a way to pressure you into making a concession. Sometimes, silence may be a way to convey displeasure. This tactic works in both directions. Time pressure can be difficult to counter. If Japanese negotiators learn that you are working against a deadline, they may exploit this knowledge to increase the pressure on you to make concessions. Near the end of a negotiation, they may suddenly request last-minute concessions and 'compromises.' In extreme cases, they may try to renegotiate the whole deal on the final day of your visit. It is important never to take such techniques personally and to avoid open conflict. Know what concessions you are willing to make. On the other hand, time pressure techniques rarely work against them since the Japanese are patient and persistent enough to overcome such challenges. Final offers and nibbling are rare and should be used with great caution since they may cause a loss of face. Avoid other common pressure tactics such as opening with your best offer, showing intransigence, or making expiring offers.

Japanese negotiators avoid aggressive or adversarial techniques since these again affect face. On rare occasions, they may use extreme openings, in which case it should not be difficult to motivate them to move to more reasonable levels. Subtle warnings may be used on occasion, but never openly threaten the other side in any way. Respond in kind if necessary, but do not openly discuss your non-settlement options and alternatives.

Unlike in other strongly relationship-oriented cultures, Japanese negotiators rarely use emotional techniques such as attitudinal bargaining, grimacing, guilt and embarrassment, or appeals to personal relationships. They believe that emotions have no place in business negotiations in this country.

Defensive tactics such as changing the subject, asking probing questions, making promises, or keeping an inflexible position may be used. The exception is directness, which is very rare in this society. They may be shocked if you are overly direct yourself, which can be counterproductive. Attempts to use blocking techniques to keep the Japanese side from obtaining certain information may be ignored; they will persistently repeat similar questions until they get a satisfactory answer. Making promises as an incentive for the Japanese to reconsider their position may sometimes work well.

It can be effective to introduce written terms and conditions as a negotiation tactic. However, be careful and continue to show flexibility if needed to allow the Japanese side to save face.

Decision Making – Most of Japan's companies tend to be very hierarchical, and people expect to work within clearly established lines of authority. While Japanese decision making is a group process through which consensus is established, an individual manager, rather than a team, is the one making the final decision. Westerners may mistakenly assume that this manager is the 'key decision maker' in an organization, while in reality such a role usually does not exist at all. The process the Japanese use to reach decisions involves many stakeholders who establish consensus through a series of deliberations. Since uncertainty and change cause distress in Japanese culture, they will go over your proposal in painstaking detail, dissecting every sentence and asking for more detail until they understand the exact meaning. Many factors that affect their decision are carefully analyzed, considered, and discussed along the way. In addition, the exact impact of a change on everyone in the group and beyond is analyzed as part of the group consensus process. This can take a very long time and requires a great deal of patience. To influence the decision process, build strong relationships with as many of the stakeholders as you possibly can. The role of the senior leaders is to orchestrate the process, help establish consensus, and formulate the ultimate decision.

When making decisions, businesspeople in the country usually consider the specific situation rather than applying universal principles. Personal feelings and experiences may weigh more strongly than empirical evidence, but they will also consider and analyze objective facts. The Japanese are often very reluctant to take risks or make changes. If you expect them to support a risky decision, you need to find ways for them to reduce the risk first.

Agreements and Contracts

Written meeting protocols are frequently used. They may get signed by both sides to indicate agreement. Their purpose is to ensure error-proof communication, not to introduce any legalities. If time ran out, then a follow up e-mail should be sent quickly after the meeting by one of the parties, asking the other side to confirm or modify. Make sure to put every important assumption you are making into that protocol to avoid surprises down the road.

The way the Japanese communicate agreement is by clearly stating all terms and conditions they agree with. An agreement exists only if both parties have done this, so do not simply respond with 'yes' instead of following this approach. Agreements may be acknowledged by nods or slight bows rather than handshakes. Do not pressure the Japanese into signing contracts.

If used at all, written contracts are normally kept high-level, capturing only the primary aspects, terms, and conditions of the agreement. The Japanese believe that the primary strength of an agreement lies in the partners' commitment rather than in its written documentation. Carefully explain and document confidentiality agreements. However, the Japanese may still distribute information within their company even if you are trying to restrict that.

Using a local attorney, rather than a western one, is viewed favorably. Their primary role is to function as notaries. Lawsuits are extremely rare in Japan, and filing one will likely destroy your business relationship for good.

Signed contracts will be honored. However, the Japanese do not view them as final agreements since their expectation is that both sides remain flexible if conditions change, which may include agreeing to modify contract terms.

Women in Business

Japan is still a strictly male-dominated society, and although roles have started to change some, the concept of gender equality is foreign to the country. Some companies retain very traditional views, while others try to be more accommodating to women. Many women do not work, though, and those who do still have little opportunity to attain positions of similar income and authority as men.

Japanese men who have not been abroad may not be used to dealing with women in business settings. The most promising way to overcome this is to make a concentrated effort to demonstrate skills and professional competence. As a visiting businesswoman, emphasize your company's importance and your role in it. A personal introduction or at least a letter of support from a senior executive within your company may also help. In addition, dress very conservatively and professionally.

Japanese men are not accustomed to working with business women. This creates some advantages and some disadvantages. A business women will probably be treated better and get more information, since that is the polite way to treat a woman guest. Social situations present a challenge to both sides, though. Japanese men are usually unaccustomed to socializing with women on an equal level. Female business travelers cannot participate in the same way as a man in the Karaoke sessions or golfing events. They should exercise caution and act professionally in business and social situations. Displaying confidence and assertiveness can be advantageous, but being overly aggressive could create major issues.

Other Important Things to Know

Formal, conservative attire is important when doing business here. Male business visitors should wear dark suits with neckties on most occasions.

Business meals and entertainment, in particular dinners, Karaoke evenings, and other evening events that may include heavy alcohol consumption are very important as they help advance the vital process of building strong relationships. Refusing to participate in these activities may be taken as a clear signal that you are not seriously interested in doing business with your counterparts. Although these are primarily social functions, business is often discussed informally in smaller groups, many times one-on-one. Your Japanese counterparts may use these discussions as opportunities to convey important messages or resolve disputes. Sometimes they may also try to obtain information from you that could strengthen their negotiating position. While you want to remain watchful, deflecting such inquiries if needed, never show signs of mistrust in your counterparts' intentions.

Topics to avoid in conversation are Japan's relationships with South Korea and especially with China.

Gift giving is common in social and business settings in Japan, including initial meetings. If you received one, it is best to reciprocate with an item of similar value that is typical of your home country. Giving a gift after signing a contract is also viewed very favorably. Give and accept gifts using both hands. Do not open gifts in the presence of the giver unless your host did so first. There are numerous potential pitfalls in what to give and how to wrap it, so prepare upfront or ask someone from the country to avoid causing embarrassment.

Cigarette smoking is very common in Japan. Do not comment on it, and allow for cigarette breaks during meetings and negotiation sessions.

Be prepared for work hours that may be extreme even to U.S. standards. Office meetings within the company may last until well past midnight, and other meetings and conferences between companies may still go well into the night before the social part begins.

Malaysia

Malaysia's population represents a pluralistic mix of several cultures. While ethnic Malays are in the majority, representing 58 percent of the population, Chinese (24 percent) and Indians (8 percent), whose perspectives and customs are significantly different, largely dominate the business culture. Businesspeople and officials in Malaysia usually have only limited exposure to other cultures except for neighboring countries. When negotiating business here, realize that people may expect things to be done 'their way,' and let them set the pace initially until you have had a chance to determine how your interactions are most effective.

Relationships and Respect

Malaysia's culture is strongly group-oriented. Asserting individual preferences may be seen as less important than having a sense of belonging to a group, conforming to its norms, and maintaining harmony among its members. Building lasting and trusting personal relationships is therefore critically important to most Malaysians, who often expect to establish strong bonds prior to closing any deals. Regardless of ethnicity, people in this country usually do business only with those they know and like. Establishing productive business cooperation requires a long-term perspective and commitment. Consequently, proceed with serious business discussions only after your counterparts have become comfortable with you.

Relationships are based on familiarity, respect, and personal trust. Business relationships in this country exist between people, not necessarily between companies. Even when you have won your local business partners' friendship and trust, they will not necessarily trust others from your company. That makes it very important to keep company interfaces unchanged. Changing a key contact may require the relationship building process to start over.

In Malaysian culture, 'saving face' is very essential. Causing embarrassment to another person may cause a *loss of face* for all parties involved and can be disastrous for business negotiations. Reputation and social standing strongly depend on a person's ability to control emotions and remain friendly at all times. If you have to bring up an unpleasant topic with a Malaysian, never do so in public and always convey your message in ways that maintain the other's self-respect. The importance of diplomatic restraint and tact cannot be overestimated. Keep your cool and never show openly that you are upset. Remaining modest and doing everything you can to maintain cordial relations is crucial to your success.

While Malaysians view politeness and humility as essential ingredients for a successful relationship, these factors do not affect their determination to reach business goals. They are patient and persistent in pursuing their objectives. It is in your best interest to do the same.

In Malaysian business culture, the respect a person enjoys depends primarily on his or her status, rank, and age. You will commonly find leaders in senior roles to be of advanced age. It is important to treat elderly people with the greatest respect, which includes refraining from smoking and not wearing sunglasses in their presence.

Communication

Bahasa Melayu is the official language of Malaysia. Although most government officials speak at least some English, their command of the language may be limited and they may prefer to use their own one. An interpreter may be provided, though. Note that the English spoken in Malaysia often has unique pronunciations, syntax, and grammar, which can lead to misunderstandings. When communicating in English, speak in short, simple sentences and avoid using slang and jargon. It will help people with a limited command of English if you speak slowly, summarize your key points often, and pause frequently to allow for interpretation. Correspondence with government officials must be in Bahasa Melayu.

Malaysian businesspeople usually speak in quiet, gentle tones, and conversations may include extended periods of silence. Before answering a question, business protocol requires making a respectful pause, taking the time to collect one's thoughts. Such a period of extended silence, which may last as long as 10 seconds or more, signals neither agreement nor rejection. In any case, loud and boisterous behavior is perceived as a lack of self-control, and emotions are not shown openly. Malaysians generally converse while standing around two to three feet apart.

Because the concept of saving *face* is so important in this culture, communication is generally very indirect. When answering a direct question, people may answer 'yes' without meaning it. When responding to a direct question, Malaysians may answer 'yes' only to signal that they heard what you said, not that they agree with it. Open disagreement and confrontation must be avoided, so you rarely hear a direct 'no.'

Instead, they may give seemingly ambiguous answers such as 'I am not sure,' 'we will think about it,' 'this will require further investigation,' or 'yes, but....' Each of these could mean 'no,' as does a 'yes' that sounds hesitant or weak. Alternatively, a respondent may deliberately ignore your question. It is beneficial to use a similarly indirect approach when dealing with Malaysians, as they may perceive you as rude and pushy if you are too direct. Only a person with whom you have no relationship yet may occasionally give you a straight 'no.' This is a bad sign since it could mean that your counterpart is not interested in engaging in business with you. Sometimes, a negative response may be delivered through a third party, which is a more face-saving way.

Malaysian Chinese consider it polite to offer both the positive and negative possibilities when asking a question that requires a decision. For example, they may ask 'Do you want to go back to your hotel or not?'

Gestures and body language are usually subtle. Non-verbal communication is important, though, and you should carefully watch for others' small hints, just as they will be watching you. Avoid any physical contact with Malaysians except for handshakes. Most importantly, never touch someone's head, not even that of a child. Hindus and Muslims consider the left hand unclean, so use it only if inevitable. When pointing at people or objects, use your open hand or point with your right thumb rather than using your index finger. When referring to themselves, Chinese Malaysians put their right index finger on their nose rather than pointing at their chest as Westerners do. Sucking in air through the teeth indicates that there is a serious problem. Eye contact should be infrequent. While it is beneficial to make some eye contact when meeting a person for the first time, Malaysians consider frequent eye contact intrusive and rude. It is generally considered respectful to look down when speaking with senior or elder people.

Smiles do not always indicate amusement or approval. Frequently, smiling masks embarrassment, shyness, disapproval, and other feelings of distress. Accordingly, Westerners may sometimes observe Malaysians smiling or laughing at what they might consider inappropriate moments.

Initial Contacts and Meetings

Before initiating business negotiations in Malaysia, it is advantageous to identify and engage a local intermediary. This person will help bridge the cultural and communications gap, allowing you to conduct business with greater effectiveness.

Negotiations in the country can be conducted by individuals or teams of negotiators. The latter is preferable when dealing with Chinese Malaysians. It allows functional specialists on both sides to build the all-important relationships between themselves faster and more effectively, your team will bring broader functional expertise to the table, and you will be able to assign different roles to each team member, maximizing the team's impact. Each of these factors speeds up the negotiation process. It is vital that teams be well aligned, with roles clearly assigned to each member. Changing a team member may require the relationship building process to start over and should therefore be avoided. Worst case, such a change can bring negotiations to a complete halt.

If possible, schedule meetings at least three to four weeks in advance. Since Malaysians want to know whom they will be meeting, provide details on titles, positions, and responsibilities of attendees ahead of time. Schedules are usually loose and flexible, and meetings may start considerably late. However, Malaysians generally expect foreign visitors to be punctual. Avoid being more than 15 to 20 minutes late. If meeting a Chinese or anyone of higher rank, it is best to be right on time as a sign of respect. Displaying anger if you have to wait, which happens often, reflects very poorly on you.

In accordance with business protocol, people should enter the meeting room in hierarchical order. Malaysians may assume that the first foreigner to enter the room is the head of your delegation.

Because of the ethical mix of the Malaysian population, many variations in naming patterns exist. It is often best to ask people politely how to address them correctly. In that case, make sure to tell them the same for your own name. Introduce and greet older people and those of high rank first. If introducing two people, it is important to state the name of the most important person first. Introductions are accompanied by handshakes using the right hand. Some people may not want to shake hands, so it is best to wait for your counterparts to initiate handshakes, which should be light and may last as long as ten seconds. Men should wait for women to initiate handshakes. Some Malaysian women may not want to make physical contact with men, in which case it is best to just nod and smile.

After the introductions, offer your business card to everyone present. You may not always get one in return. Business cards should be printed or –preferably– embossed in English. Since many businesspeople are Chinese, it is beneficial to have the other side of your card translated into Chinese. Show advanced degrees on your card and make sure that it clearly states your professional title, especially if you have the seniority to make decisions. Present your card with both hands, with the print facing the recipient. Alternatively, use your right hand, with the left hand gently supporting your right. Accept others' cards using both hands if possible. Smile and make eye contact while doing so, then examine the card carefully. Not reading someone's card can be an insult. Next, place the card on the table in front of you or into your card case. Never stuff someone's card into your back pocket or otherwise treat it disrespectfully. Never write on a person's business card.

At the beginning of a meeting, there is normally some small talk. This allows participants to become personally acquainted. It is best to let the other side set the pace and follow along. People appreciate a sense of humor, but keep it light and friendly, and be careful not to overdo it. Business is a serious matter in Malaysia.

The primary purpose of the first meeting is to become acquainted and build relationships. It is unrealistic to expect initial meetings to lead to straight decisions.

Presentations should be short and concise. Presentation materials should be attractive, with good and clear visuals. Use diagrams and pictures wherever feasible, cut down on words, and avoid complicated expressions. Having your handout materials translated to Bahasa Melayu is not a must, but it helps in getting your messages across.

Negotiation

Attitudes and Styles - Leveraging relationships is an important element when negotiating in Malaysia. Nevertheless, Malaysians often employ distributive and contingency bargaining. While the buyer is in a superior position, both sides in a business deal own the responsibility to reach agreement. They expect long-term commitments from their business partners and will focus mostly on long-term benefits. Although the primary negotiation style is competitive, Malaysians nevertheless value long-term relationships and look for win-win solutions.

Should a dispute arise at any stage of a negotiation, you might be able to reach resolution by leveraging personal relationships and emphasizing long-term benefits to both sides. Show your commitment to the relationship and refrain from using logical reasoning or becoming argumentative since this will only make matters worse. Patience and creativity will pay strong dividends. In extreme situations, use a mediator, ideally the party who initially introduced you.

Sharing of Information - Malaysians first spend considerable time gathering information and discussing various details before the bargaining stage of a negotiation can begin. People usually do not share their information freely.

Pace of Negotiation – Expect negotiations to be slow and protracted. Relationship building, information gathering, bargaining, and decision making all take considerable time. Be prepared to make several trips if necessary to achieve your objectives. Throughout the negotiation, be patient, control your emotions, and accept that delays occur.

Malaysians generally employ a polychronic work style. They are used to pursuing multiple actions and goals in parallel. When negotiating, they often take a holistic approach and may jump back and forth between topics rather than addressing them in sequential order. Negotiators from strongly monochronic cultures, such as Germany, the United Kingdom, or the United States, may find this style confusing, irritating, and even annoying. In any case, do not show irritation or anger when encountering this behavior. Instead, keep track of the bargaining progress at all times, often emphasizing areas where agreement already exists.

Bargaining – Malaysians are used to hard bargaining but will usually haggle less extensively than other Asians. However, expect local businesspeople with international experience to use a wide array of negotiation techniques quite competently. The bargaining stage of a negotiation can be extensive. Prices may move by about 25 to 40 percent between initial offers and final agreement. Leave yourself sufficient room for concessions at different stages. Ask the other side to reciprocate if you made one. You can use the fact that aspects can be re-visited to your advantage, for instance by offering further concessions under the condition that the Malaysian side reciprocate in areas that had already been agreed upon.

Deceptive techniques might be used and it may be effective to use some of them yourself. This includes tactics such as telling lies and sending fake non-verbal messages, pretending to be disinterested in the whole deal or in single concessions, misrepresenting an item's value, or making false demands and concessions. It is advisable to verify information received from the Malaysian side through other channels if you have a chance. Similarly, they treat 'outside' information with caution. Malaysians rarely use 'good cop, bad cop;' however, it can sometimes be beneficial to use this tactic in your own negotiation approach. Carefully orchestrated, it may allow you to obtain valuable concessions without damaging the overall relationship. However, your team will need to exclude any 'bad cop' member from future negotiation rounds. Businesspeople are not likely to use the 'limited authority' technique because groups rather than individuals normally make decisions. Since you must avoid causing loss of face, be cautious when using the techniques of making false demands or false concessions. Any overt attempts to bluff your counterparts could backfire.

Negotiators may occasionally use pressure techniques that include making final offers or nibbling. Final offers may be made more than once and are almost never final. Do not use tactics such as applying time pressure or making expiring offers, since Malaysians could view these as signs that you are not willing to build a long-term relationship. They may choose to terminate the negotiation. Periods of silence in conversations are normal and may not represent an attempt to use it as a negotiation technique. Avoid pressure tactics such as opening with your best offer, opening with a written offer, or showing intransigence, since they cannot be applied effectively without running the risk of causing loss of face.

Malaysian negotiators avoid most aggressive or adversarial techniques since they affect face. The risk of using any of them yourself is rarely worth the potential gain. Using extreme openings with them may be viewed as an unfriendly act and is best avoided.

As in most strongly relationship-oriented cultures, negotiators may sometimes use emotional techniques such as attitudinal bargaining, attempting to make you feel guilty, grimacing, or appealing to personal relationships. Be cautious when doing this yourself. You might cause the other side to lose face, which could damage your negotiating position.

At times, defensive tactics such as blocking or changing the subject, asking probing questions, or making promises may be used. The exception is directness, which is rare in Malaysia. People may be shocked if you are overly direct yourself, which can be counterproductive.

Note that opening with written offers and attempting to introduce written terms and conditions as a negotiation tactic is rarely successful. In most cases, businesspeople ignore or tactfully reject them and request that each aspect be negotiated individually.

Corruption and bribery are somewhat common in Malaysia's public and private sectors. However, people may draw the line differently, viewing minor payments as rewards for getting a job done rather than as bribes. Also, keep in mind that there is a fine line between giving gifts and bribing. What you may consider a bribe, a Malaysian may view as only a nice gift.

Decision Making – Companies tend to be very hierarchical. However, decision making is normally a consensus-oriented group process in Malaysia. This can be confusing for Westerners looking to identify the 'key decision maker' in an organization, while in reality such a role may not exist at all. Decisions are often made through a process involving many stakeholders who establish consensus through a series of deliberations. This process can take a long time and requires patience. Influencing the decision making requires building strong relationships with as many of the stakeholders as you possibly can. Senior leaders orchestrate the process and secure the support of the group. Nevertheless, their input carries a lot of weight and they sometimes have the final say, so do everything you can to win their approval.

When making decisions, Malaysian businesspeople may not rely much on rules or laws. They usually consider the specific situation rather than applying universal principles. Personal feelings and experiences weigh more strongly than empirical evidence and other objective facts do. Malaysians can be quite fatalistic and are usually moderate risk takers.

Agreements and Contracts

Capturing and exchanging written understandings after meetings and at key negotiation stages is useful since oral statements are not always dependable. While these serve as tools to improve the communication and strengthen commitments, they should not be taken for final agreements. Any part of an agreement may still change significantly before both parties sign the final contract.

It is important to realize that Malaysians have a different view of written agreements and contracts than most Westerners. Businesspeople may view contracts only as general guides for conducting business, expecting that both parties are willing to change terms if there is a change of conditions. Written contracts are usually kept high-level, capturing only the primary aspects, terms, and conditions of the agreement. Writing up and signing the contract is a formality. Malaysians believe that the primary strength of an agreement lies in the partners' commitment rather than in its written documentation. Chinese Malaysians often consult astrologers and may prefer to delay signature of a contract until a 'lucky' day arrives.

It is recommended to consult a local legal expert before signing a contract. However, do not bring your attorney to the negotiation table as it may be viewed as a sign of mistrust.

Contracts are often not considered final agreements and may not be honored either. It is commonplace for negotiations to continue after a contract has already been signed. Both sides are expected to remain flexible. Your best chance to ensure that your partners follow through on their commitments is to stay in regular contact and nurture the relationship throughout your business engagement.

Women in Business

Gender equality is stronger in Malaysia than in many other Asian countries. Quite a few women can be found in leadership positions, and they generally hold positions that are more influential and enjoy more respect than elsewhere. Visiting businesswomen should have few problems in the country as long as they act professionally in business and social situations.

Other Important Things to Know

Unlike in other Asian cultures, dress codes are somewhat relaxed in Malaysia, and wearing a suit is not always required.

Malaysians are relatively punctual at most social settings. It is best to be right on time for dinners, and to arrive at parties within 15 to 30 minutes of the agreed time. Again, the length of the acceptable delay is determined by your relative status.

During small talk and other social conversations, you may be asked very personal questions. If you do not want to answer, smile or politely explain that such topics are not discussed openly in your culture.

Gift giving in business settings is rare. It is best not to bring a gift to an initial meeting in order to avoid raising suspicions about your motives.

Mexico

While some businesspeople and officials in Mexico may have only limited exposure to other cultures, many are reasonably familiar with and prepared for doing business internationally. However, that does not always mean that they will be open-minded. When negotiating business here, realize that people may expect things to be done 'their way,' in which case you should strive to understand, and occasionally emulate, their behavior in order to gain the acceptance of your Mexican counterparts.

Though the country's culture is quite homogeneous overall, business cultures differ somewhat between the North and the South. People in the North tend to be more business-focused and often have a high sense of urgency. This may be more relaxed in Southern Mexico, where the stereotypical *mañana* attitude of conducting business at a leisurely pace can still be found.

Relationships and Respect

Mexico's culture is generally group-oriented. Asserting individual preferences may be seen as less important than having a sense of belonging to a group, conforming to its norms, and maintaining harmony among its members. Building lasting and trusting personal relationships is therefore very important to most Mexicans, who often find it essential to establish strong bonds prior to closing any deals. People in this country prefer to do business with those they know, like, and trust. If they initially seem suspicious and non-committal, you may be able to overcome this with consistent friendliness and goodwill. Establishing productive business cooperation requires a long-term perspective and commitment. Proceed with serious business discussions only after your counterparts have become very comfortable with you. This can be a time-consuming process and may require several trips to strengthen the bonds. Mexicans tend to distrust people who appear unwilling to spend the time or whose motives for relationship building are unclear.

Once you have established a working relationship, the Mexicans may still prefer to keep the initial engagement small and low-risk. They view this as an opportunity for you to prove yourself. Larger-scale business engagements require time to build.

Business relationships in this country exist between people, not necessarily between companies. Even when you have won your local business partners' friendship and trust, they will not necessarily trust others from your company. That makes it very important to keep company interfaces unchanged. Changing a key contact may require the relationship building process to start over.

Families play a dominant role in Mexican society and business life. Many companies are family-owned or controlled. Mexican families can be large and may extend into powerful networks that not only include extended family but also friends, business partners, and others. Becoming integrated into such networks through personal relationships is vital to doing business in the country. Whom you know may determine whether people want to get to know you. Similarly, whether people think you are worth knowing and trusting often weighs much more strongly than how competent you are or what proposals you may have to make. Personal networks may open doors and solve problems that would otherwise be very difficult to master. Maintaining honest and cordial relations is crucial. Third party introductions can be very helpful as a starting point to building a trusting relationship with a potential partner, especially since people may initially not trust outsiders who are neither part of their family nor of their circle of friends.

While Mexicans are usually warm and friendly, most of them, especially males, are also very proud and may be easily offended by comments that leave room for misunderstandings. 'Saving face' and respecting everyone's honor and personal pride are crucial requirements for doing business in the country. Openly criticizing someone in front of others can have a devastating impact on your negotiation. Avoid open conflict, and know that politeness is crucial. In addition, showing genuine interest and compassion will win people's hearts.

In Mexico's business culture, the respect a person enjoys depends primarily on his or her status, connections, and education. Age, while respected, does not necessarily determine the seniority of a person. Admired personal traits include sincerity, integrity, charisma, and sociability.

Communication

While the country's official language is Spanish, it is notably different from the Spanish spoken in Spain. Many businesspeople speak English. Mexicans usually prefer and are more familiar with American English. Since it is different from British English to the point where misunderstandings may happen easily, familiarize yourself with the differences upfront if necessary. In any case, being able to speak Spanish is a clear advantage. With high-ranking managers, it may otherwise be useful to engage an interpreter. To avoid offending the other side, ask beforehand whether an interpreter should be present at a meeting. When communicating in English, speak in short, simple sentences and avoid using jargon and slang. It will help people with a limited command of English if you speak slowly, summarize your key points often, and pause frequently to allow for interpretation. Mexicans may not admit it if they do not understand parts of the conversation. Even when the main meeting language is English, your counterparts may frequently speak Spanish among themselves, not necessarily to shut you out from the discussion but to reduce their discomfort and ensure a common understanding among them.

While discussions may get very lively, Mexicans generally dislike loud and boisterous behavior. They may show their emotions openly. However, it is crucial that you never lose your temper or appear impatient, as there is always a risk of hurting someone's pride. People may converse in close proximity, standing only two feet or less apart. This is usually less pronounced in business situations. In any case, never back away even if your personal comfort zone calls for more space. Doing so could be read as a sign that you are uncomfortable around your local counterparts.

Communication in Mexico is somewhat indirect. People may prefer to be careful about what they say and how they say it. In addition, they may tell you what they think you want to hear rather than what they really think. They might insist that everything is in perfect order, even when this is not the case, or give seemingly ambiguous answers such as 'maybe,' 'I am not sure,' or 'we will think about it' when the message is 'no.' 'Yes' may only mean that they understood what you said, not that they agree with it. It may take extensive and unmistakable questioning to find out whether you indeed have agreement. However, some Mexicans may get straight to the point when trying to get a message across. Silence is rare and usually signals that there is a serious problem. Avoid being overly direct yourself, as your Mexican counterparts may otherwise perceive you as rude and pushy. The communication often becomes more direct and frank once a strong relationship has been established.

Gestures and body language are extensive and lively. There may be frequent physical contact with others of the same gender. The American *OK* sign, with thumb and index finger forming a circle, can be read as an obscene gesture in Mexico. Eye contact should be frequent, almost to the point of staring. This conveys sincerity and helps build trust. Anger may sometimes be masked with a smile.

Initial Contacts and Meetings

Choosing a local intermediary who can leverage existing relationships to make the initial contact is useful. This person will help bridge the gap between cultures, allowing you to conduct business with greater effectiveness and may also serve as your local interpreter.

Negotiations in the country can be conducted by individuals or teams of negotiators. It is vital that teams be well aligned, with roles clearly assigned to each member. Changing a team member may require the relationship building process to start over and should therefore be avoided. Mexican negotiation teams are usually very well aligned. If uncertain what position to support, their members will defer to the principal negotiator.

Given the strong emphasis on hierarchy in the country's business culture, a senior executive should attend the initial meeting for your company and your negotiating team should include senior leaders who know your company well. There will not be an expectation that the executive attends future meetings. Similarly, the top executive on the Mexican side, who is likely the ultimate decision maker, may attend only initially. The most senior Mexican executive to attend throughout the negotiation will likely be at a similar level in the hierarchy as your own negotiation leader.

If possible, schedule meetings at least one to two weeks in advance. Since Mexicans want to know whom they will be meeting, provide details on titles, positions, and responsibilities of attendees ahead of time. An agenda is usually set upfront, but this is only a formality. It is usually not strictly followed. Reconfirm your meeting, and be prepared for your counterparts to cancel or postpone meetings with little advance notice.

While meetings may start considerably late, Mexicans generally expect foreign visitors to be punctual. Avoid being more than 10 to 15 minutes late, and call ahead if you will be. At the same time, important people will likely make you wait. Displaying anger because of that will reflect very poorly on you. The most senior people usually arrive last. Otherwise, authority may sometimes be difficult to pick out, so watch for small hints of deference to identify the decision makers.

Names are usually given in the order of first name, family names. Most Mexicans have two family names, the first one from their father, and the second one from their mother. Use *Mr./Mrs./Miss* or *Señor/Señora/Señorita*, plus the father's family name, which is always the first one of the two family names given. If a person has an academic title, such as *Doctor* or *Professor*, or a professional title such as *Ingeniero*, *Licenciado*, or *Arquitecto*, use it instead, followed by the father's family name. You may also hear someone addressed by the titles *Don* or *Dona*. This is a show of great respect. Before calling Mexicans by their first name, it is usually better to wait until they offer it. Introduce or greet the most senior person first. Thereafter, greet everyone else individually. Introductions are accompanied by handshakes. Men should wait for women to initiate handshakes. If a woman does not seem to want to shake hands, it is best just to bow slightly.

The exchange of business cards is an essential step when meeting someone for the first time, so bring more than you need. It is recommended to use cards with one side in English and the other in Spanish. Show doctorate degrees on your card and make sure that it clearly states your professional title, especially if you have the seniority to make decisions. When presenting your card, ensure that the Spanish side is facing the recipient. Smile and keep eye contact while accepting someone else's card, then carefully examine it. Next, place the card on the table in front of you. High-ranking people may not hand out their card, which is a sign of their importance.

Business meetings usually start with some small talk intended to establish personal rapport. This may include personal questions about your background and family, allowing participants to become acquainted. It may be important to remain patient and let the other side set the pace. Initial meetings may appear very formal, but the atmosphere usually is a bit more relaxed in subsequent meetings. People appreciate a sense of humor, but keep it light and friendly, and be careful not to overdo it. Business is a serious matter in Mexico. Meetings may appear somewhat chaotic, with frequent interruptions and several parallel conversations. Do not take this personally; it also does not indicate a lack of interest.

The purpose of the first meeting, maybe also subsequent ones, is to become acquainted and build relationships. Business will be discussed, but do not try to hurry along with your agenda. Some Mexicans dislike people who try to get to the point too quickly. The goal should be to establish respect and trust between yourself and your counterparts. It is unrealistic to expect initial meetings to lead to straight decisions. In addition, it is rare to get open opinions at the conference table, so watch for subtle clues and use other opportunities such as one-on-one conversations or business dinners to learn more.

Presentations should be short and concise. Make sure your proposal is clearly structured and presented. Mexicans prefer oral communication to data exchanges, so avoid overburdening your material with many facts and details. Presentation materials should be attractive, with excellent and clear visuals. Any materials you bring, such as letters, presentation handouts, and promotional literature, should be immaculately designed and presented since initial appearances matter a lot in this country. Having your handout materials translated to Spanish is not a must, but it will be appreciated and helps in getting your messages across.

Negotiation

Attitudes and Styles - Leveraging relationships is an important element when negotiating in Mexico. Nevertheless, Mexicans often employ distributive and contingency bargaining. While the buyer is in a superior position, both sides in a business deal own the responsibility to reach agreement. They expect long-term commitments from their business partners and will focus mostly on long-term benefits. Although the primary negotiation style is competitive, Mexicans nevertheless value long-term relationships. While proposals should demonstrate the benefits to both negotiating parties, neither of them should take attempts to win competitive advantages negatively. It is critically important to remain non-confrontational and avoid direct conflict throughout the bargaining exchange. Ultimately, the culture promotes a win-win approach. You will earn your counterparts' respect by maintaining a positive, persistent attitude.

Should a dispute arise at any stage of a negotiation, you might be able to reach resolution or an acceptable compromise by leveraging personal relationships, assuming that they are strong enough.

Sharing of Information –Even when personal relationships are strong, your counterparts may be reluctant to share information openly. Many Mexicans believe that privileged information creates bargaining advantages. In addition, figures and numbers can be unreliable in this dialog-driven culture, which could make them misleading.

Pace of Negotiation – Expect negotiations to be slow and protracted. Be prepared to make several trips if necessary to achieve your objectives. Relationship building, information gathering, bargaining, and decision making may take considerable time. Attempts to rush the process are unlikely to produce better results and may be viewed as offensive. Throughout the negotiation, be patient, control your emotions, and accept the inevitable delays.

Most Mexicans prefer a polychronic work style. They are used to pursuing multiple actions and goals in parallel. When negotiating, they often take a holistic approach and may jump back and forth between topics rather than addressing them in sequential order. Negotiators from strongly monochronic cultures, such as Germany, the United Kingdom, or the United States, may find this style confusing, irritating, and even annoying. In any case, do not show irritation or anger when encountering this behavior. Instead, keep track of the bargaining progress at all times, often emphasizing areas where agreement already exists.

If your counterparts appear to be stalling the negotiation, assess carefully whether their slowing down the process indicates that they are evaluating alternatives or that they are not interested in doing business with you. Mexicans may be reluctant to deliver a final 'no,' preferring to stay in loose contact instead. However, this behavior may also either represent an attempt to create time pressure in order to obtain concessions, which happens frequently, or it simply reflects the slow decision process in the country. Again, patience and persistence are vitally important.

Bargaining – Mexicans can be very shrewd and tough negotiators. They are used to hard bargaining and often do a lot of haggling. Surprisingly strong emotions and many exaggerations may accompany the process.

The bargaining exchange can be extensive. Concessions never come easily, and although Mexicans may show interest in new ideas and concepts, they often find it difficult to change their position. Requesting a compromise may become an issue of pride if presented in the wrong way. Be respectful throughout the bargaining exchange. Rather than pushing for concessions, it may be better to re-address disagreements in follow-up meetings, which gives your counterparts the opportunity to reconsider their position without overtly losing face. Effective negotiators may be able to move prices by 40 percent or more between initial offers and final agreement. Leave yourself a lot of room for concessions at different stages. After making one, always ask the other side to reciprocate. Throughout the process, remain cool and respectful, avoid confrontation, and frequently reaffirm the relationship.

Deceptive techniques are frequent and may be effective for you to use as well. This includes tactics such as telling lies and sending fake non-verbal messages, pretending to be disinterested in the whole deal or in single concessions, misrepresenting an item's value, or making false demands and concessions. Your Mexican counterparts may play stupid or otherwise attempt to mislead you in order to obtain bargaining advantages. Even when you can see right through a lie, it would be a grave personal insult to state or even hint that your counterpart is not telling the truth. It is advisable to verify information received from the local side through other channels. Similarly, they treat 'outside' information with caution. 'Good cop, bad cop' is a tactic that Mexicans rarely use, though it could be effective on either side of the negotiation table. However, it could be devastating if the other side recognized this as a tactic, and your team will need to exclude any 'bad cop' member from future negotiation rounds. Businesspeople may claim limited authority, stating that they have to ask for their manager's approval. Mexican companies use many checks and balances in order to limit fraud, so unless you are negotiating with the head of an organization, this will often be the truth.

Negotiators in the country may use pressure techniques that include making final offers, applying time pressure, showing intransigence, or nibbling. Final offers may come more than once and are rarely final. Be careful when using tactics such as opening with your best offer or making decreasing or expiring offers. Mexicans may consider these inappropriate or even insulting. Silence can be a very effective way to signal rejection of a proposal or to obtain further concessions. Your counterparts will generally be very persistent throughout the bargaining exchange.

Mexican negotiators avoid openly aggressive or adversarial techniques. While they may make indirect threats and warnings or subtly display anger, they will be careful not to appear aggressive when doing so. Extreme openings are not frequently used since they may adversely affect the relationship, so be very cautious when using the tactic yourself. Never walk out or threaten to do so in an aggressive fashion as your counterparts will likely take this as a personal insult and may end all talks. However, threatening a 'friendly walkout' while strongly emphasizing the relationship may be very effective.

Emotional negotiation techniques, such as attitudinal bargaining or attempting to make you feel guilty, are frequent and can be effective. Be cautious not to hurt someone's personal pride when employing any of these tactics, though. Pleas to personal relationships and other emotional appeals, such as emphasizing how your proposal will add to your counterparts' personal satisfaction or heighten their honor, can be very powerful.

Mexicans may frequently employ defensive tactics such as blocking or changing the subject, asking probing or very direct questions, making promises, or keeping an inflexible position.

Corruption and bribery are somewhat common in Mexico's public and private sectors. Laws pertaining to bribery are also less stringent than in many other countries. People may draw the line differently, viewing minor payments as rewards for getting a job done or 'unofficial service charges,' rather than as bribes. Also, keep in mind that there is a fine line between giving gifts and bribing. What you may consider a bribe, a Mexican may view as only a nice gift.

Decision Making – Most companies tend to be very hierarchical, and people expect to work within clearly established lines of authority. Communication is expected to take place across similar levels in the hierarchy and it could damage the respect you enjoy if you spent much time and attention on someone you outrank. Decision makers are senior executives who are often autocratic but will consider the best interest of the group or organization. They may consult with others before making the call. Subordinates may be reluctant to accept responsibility. Decision makers also rarely delegate their authority, so it is important to deal with senior executives. Gaining access to top managers can be difficult, though. You may have to deal with subordinates who could strongly influence the final decision, which may be made behind closed doors. Maintaining good relationships with these intermediaries is crucial to your success. Decision making is often a very slow process that requires much patience. Attempts to rush or put pressure on the process are futile. However, once a decision has been reached, the remaining steps to close the agreement often happen quickly.

When making decisions, businesspeople may not rely much on rules or laws. They usually consider the specific situation rather than applying universal principles. Since Mexicans highly value intuition, personal feelings and experiences usually weigh more strongly than empirical evidence and other objective facts do, even though both may be considered. Mexicans are often uneasy with change and reluctant to take risks. If you expect them to support a risky decision, you may need to find ways for them to become comfortable with it first, for instance by explaining contingency plans, outlining areas of additional support, or by offering guarantees and warranties.

Agreements and Contracts

Capturing and exchanging written understandings after meetings and at key negotiation stages is useful. Oral commitments may sound stronger than what your Mexican counterparts may be willing to put in writing. At the same time, keep in mind that written memos or letters can already be contractually binding. Do not rely on interim agreements to be final. Any part of an agreement may still change significantly before both parties sign the final contract.

Pay particular attention to payment terms, making sure both sides know what is expected. It is common practice to use Letters of Credit, bonds, and similar instruments.

Written contracts tend to be lengthy and very legalistic. They often spell out detailed terms and conditions for the core agreements as well as for many eventualities. It is advisable to consult a local legal expert before signing a contract. Signing the contract is important from a legal perspective. However, many Mexicans believe that the primary strength of an agreement lies in the partners' commitment rather than in its written documentation.

Signed contracts may not always be honored. Payment terms are frequently violated, so expect to be paid late. Overall, the level of contract compliance depends to no small degree on the strength of the continuing relationship between the partners. It is strongly advisable to continue staying in touch and maintaining the trust of your Mexican business partner. Business partners may expect the other side to remain flexible if conditions change, which may include agreeing to modify contract terms.

Women in Business

Though this is gradually changing, *machismo* attitudes remain strong in this country. Women may be considered inferior, and they still have a hard time attaining positions of similar income and authority as men. As a visiting businesswoman, emphasize your company's importance and your role in it. A personal introduction or at least a letter of support from a senior executive within your company may help.

Female business travelers will usually have few problems in the country. However, they should graciously accept any chivalric gestures they receive, while exercising caution and acting professionally in business and social situations. Displaying confidence and some degree of assertiveness can be effective, but it is important not to appear overly bold and aggressive.

Other Important Things to Know

Formal attire is very important when doing business here. Male business visitors should wear dark suits with neckties on most occasions. First impressions can have a significant impact on how people view you.

Business dinners and all kinds of social events are frequent opportunities to get to know each other better. If business is discussed over meals at all, this will rarely be extensive. Mexicans often invite visitors to their homes. 'Mi case es su casa' (my home is your home) is still a common attitude in Mexico. Do not be surprised if someone invites you to visit 'your home' – they mean their own one.

Social events do not require strict punctuality. While it is best to arrive at dinners close to the agreed time, being late to a party by 15-30 minutes is usually acceptable. In Mexico City, where traffic delays are a common excuse for tardiness, arriving even later is rarely an issue.

Never throw documents or collateral on the business table, as this is considered highly offensive. Instead, show respect by individually handing them out to each recipient.

Gift giving in business settings is not necessary but often welcome. However, it is best not to bring a significant gift to an initial meeting in order to avoid raising suspicions about your motives. Small gifts such as pens or notebooks with your company logo are much more appropriate. For bigger occasions, such as the end of a negotiation, tasteful gifts of somewhat greater value may be exchanged.

Netherlands

Most Dutch businesspeople, especially those among younger generations, are experienced in interacting and doing business with visitors from other cultures. The country's culture is heterogeneous and strongly values tolerance towards others. Its people are usually open-minded rather than forcing their ways upon you.

The Netherlands is a nation that has been doing international business for many centuries, so expect its people to be good at it. Though in close proximity, the Dutch culture is substantially different from the German culture. Do not remark or even assume that they are similar.

Relationships and Respect

While building trust matters, business relationships are only moderately important in this country. They are usually not a necessary precondition for initial business interactions. Your counterparts' expectation may be to get to know you better as you do business together. Once the necessary trust has been established, which may take some time, there will be a sense of loyalty to you as a respected business partner, which can go a long way should a difficult situation arise.

Business relationships in this country exist between companies as well as between individuals. If your company replaces you with someone else over the course of a negotiation, it may be easy for your replacement to take things over from where you left them. Likewise, if you introduce someone else from your company into an existing business relationship, that person may quickly be accepted as a valid business partner. This does not mean that the Dutch do not care about who they are dealing with. Personal integrity and dependability are important if you want to win their trust.

The Netherlands is a very egalitarian and tolerant society. Everyone, no matter what his or her status and influence, is considered valuable and worthy of respect. It can be offensive to criticize a person in public or otherwise embarrass that person. When problems occur, however, people may be quick to blame others. At the same time, the Dutch rarely give compliments. If they do, it will be because they mean it, not so much because they want the other to feel good about it. Since treating someone preferentially is discouraged, individual rewards at work are rare. Bosses are expected to be team leaders rather than solitary decision-makers. Open competition between team members may be frowned upon.

In the country's business culture, the respect a person enjoys depends primarily on his or her achievements and education. Admired personal traits include honesty, forthrightness, discipline, attention to detail, and modesty.

Communication

The country's official language is Dutch. Frisian is also recognized in the northern part of the country; it is spoken by a small part of the population. Most businesspeople in the Netherlands speak English well. However, avoid using jargon and slang.

The Dutch usually speak neither in quiet tones nor particularly loudly. At restaurants, especially those used for business lunches and dinners, keep conversations at a quiet level. Being overly loud may be regarded as bad manners, though. Interrupting others is often considered rude. Periods of silence do not necessarily convey a negative message. Emotions are rarely shown in public, and self-control is seen as a virtue in the Netherlands. People generally converse standing about three feet apart.

Communication can be very direct in the Netherlands. The Dutch value straightforwardness and honesty much more highly than tact or diplomacy. They dislike vague statements and openly share opinions, concerns, and feelings with others. The concept of 'saving face' is not important in this country. While you want to remain respectful, pointing out mistakes is accepted and often appreciated. Being blunt is often much better than appearing evasive or deceptive. Avoid giving ambiguous answers such as 'We will consider it,' 'This will take further investigation,' or 'Perhaps' if your real answer is 'no.' If you do not want to reply with a straight 'no,' it may be best not to give any answer – the message will be clearly understood. If something is against company policy or cannot be done for other reasons, your counterparts will likely say so. They may view this as a simple statement of fact and might not understand that someone else could consider this directness insensitive. Being overly polite is a mistake - people will suspect that you are about to ask a special favor.

The Dutch use body language sparingly, although facial expressions and other clues can be quite telling, especially if they dislike an idea or proposal. They may make some physical contact, such as a backslap as a sign of friendship, but there is usually not a lot of it. Eye contact should be frequent, almost to the point of staring, as this conveys sincerity and helps build trust.

Initial Contacts and Meetings

Having a local contact can be an advantage but is usually not a necessary precondition to doing business in the Netherlands. However, introductions by reputable institutions such as a local bank or investment house may open doors faster. Having local people who could serve as a reference may also help. Negotiations in the Netherlands can be conducted by individuals or teams of negotiators.

If possible, schedule meetings at least one to two weeks in advance. Agreeing on an agenda upfront is useful. It will be strictly followed. Do not cancel a meeting on short notice since that can be viewed as very rude. At any meeting, whether business or social, it is best to be right on time. Avoid being more than 5 to 10 minutes late, and call ahead if you will be.

Names are usually given in the order of first name, family name. Use *Mr./Ms.* or *Mijnheer/Mevrouw* plus the family name. If a person has a title, such as *Doctor* or *Professor*, use it instead, followed by the family name. Only close friends call each other by their first names. You may never get to that point in a business relationship, although it is becoming more common among younger people. Introductions are accompanied by firm handshakes.

The exchange of business cards is an essential step when meeting someone for the first time, so bring more than you need. Almost all businesspeople in the Netherlands read English, so there is no need to have your card translated. Show doctorate degrees on your card and make sure that it clearly states your professional title, especially if you have the seniority to make decisions. When presenting your card, smile and keep eye contact, then take a few moments to look at the card you received.

Meetings either start with a few minutes of 'small talk' or get right down to business. A sense of humor is appreciated, but know that Dutch humor is often dry and earthy. They may not appreciate witty remarks or complicated analogies. One's private life has no place in meetings, and personal comments should be avoided. Business is a serious matter in the Netherlands, and meetings can be quite formal. While the primary purpose of the first meeting is to become acquainted, the discussion will mostly focus on business topics. It is vital to come well prepared as the Dutch hate wasting time.

Presentation materials should be attractive, with good and clear visuals. Keep your presentation succinct and methodically thought out. Since they value directness, be straightforward about both positive and negative aspects. The Dutch are generally suspicious of hype and exaggerations and may respond negatively to an aggressive sales approach that might be effective in the United States. They often look for deficiencies in your products or services and may openly draw your attention to them. Know your topic well, and use logical arguments and concrete examples to back up your proposals. Having your English-language handout materials translated to Dutch is not required, though it will be appreciated.

Negotiation

Attitudes and Styles – To the Dutch, negotiating is usually a joint problem-solving process. Buyer and seller in a business deal are equal partners who both own the responsibility to reach agreement. They may focus equally on near-term and long-term benefits. The primary negotiation style is cooperative, but people may be unwilling to agree with compromises unless it is their only option to keep the negotiation from getting stuck. Since the Dutch believe in the concept of win-win, they expect you to reciprocate their respect and trust. It is strongly advisable to be straightforward while remaining respectful and cooperative.

Should a dispute arise at any stage of a negotiation, you might be able to reach resolution by focusing on logical reasoning and facts. Depending on the situation, apologizing may also make the Dutch more conciliatory.

Sharing of Information – Dutch negotiators believe in information sharing as a way to build trust. This does not mean that they will readily reveal everything you might want to know during your negotiation. However, negotiations can become very difficult if one side appears to be hiding information from the other.

Pace of Negotiation – Expect the bargaining phase to be fairly swift, though decisions may take a long time. This assumes that enough time was available for the local side to plan and organize their approach. The Dutch are not very good at improvising. While diligent, Dutch businesspeople are less obsessive over details than Germans are and strive to conclude negotiations quickly if possible. This does not mean that they will readily accept unfavorable terms.

The Dutch generally prefer a monochronic work style. They are used to pursuing actions and goals systematically, and they dislike interruptions or digressions. When negotiating, they often work their way down a list of objectives in sequential order, bargaining for each item separately, and may be unwilling to revisit aspects that have already been agreed upon. They may show little tolerance if a more polychronic counterpart challenges this approach, which they view as systematic and effective. This rigid style may be difficult to tolerate for negotiators from highly polychronic cultures, such as most Asians, Arabs, some Southern Europeans, or most Latin Americans, who may view it as closed-minded and overly restrictive. In any case, do not show irritation or anger when encountering this behavior. Instead, be willing to bargain over some items individually. Otherwise, clearly indicate that your agreement is conditional and contingent on other items.

Bargaining – While the Dutch are not overly fond of bargaining and dislike haggling, they can be quite good at both. The bargaining stage of a negotiation may take longer than in the United States, but not excessively so. Prices rarely move by more than 20 to 30 percent between initial offers and final agreement. Leave yourself room enough for concessions and prepare alternative options since your Dutch counterparts may outright refuse some aspects of your proposal. Ask the other side to reciprocate if you make concessions. Focus your arguments on concrete facts and information. Exaggerated claims or bragging will not help your position at all.

The Dutch prefer to negotiate in a very straightforward style. They use deceptive techniques only infrequently, such as telling lies, sending fake non-verbal messages, pretending to be disinterested in the whole deal or in single concessions, misrepresenting an item's value, or making false demands and concessions. Carefully orchestrated, 'good cop, bad cop' may be an effective tactic to use in your own negotiation approach. Businesspeople rarely claim 'limited authority' since decision making is either a group process or they have the necessary empowerment. Do not use the technique yourself since the Dutch will believe they are 'talking with the wrong person.'

Negotiators in the country may use pressure techniques that include opening with their best offer, showing intransigence, making final offers, or applying time pressure. When using similar tactics yourself, clearly explain your offer and avoid being aggressive. Periods of silence in conversations are normal and may not represent an attempt to use it as a negotiation technique. Be careful when using pressure tactics such as making expiring offers or nibbling. Your counterparts may consider these inappropriate unless they are strongly interested in your offer and clearly understand the rationale behind the approach. Otherwise, while the negotiation is not necessarily over, it may become less constructive.

While Dutch negotiators may occasionally appear aggressive, this usually only reflects their direct and blunt style rather than any tactical behavior. They will not shy away from open confrontation if challenged, though. Attempts to gain advantages by being aggressive with a large Dutch company likely work against you. Threats and warnings, openly displayed anger, or walkouts may be used to some degree, but they are normally based upon calculated negotiation strategies rather than aggressive attitudes. Extreme openings are viewed as inappropriate and may upset your Dutch counterparts. It is best to open with an offer that is already in the ballpark of what you really expect.

Emotional negotiation techniques, such as attitudinal bargaining, sending dual messages, attempting to make you feel guilty, or grimacing, may occasionally be employed. It is best to remain calm. Appeals to personal relationships are very rare. Dutch businesspeople often employ defensive tactics such as changing the subject, blocking, asking probing or very direct questions, making promises, or keeping an inflexible position. When making promises, know that your counterparts will expect you to keep them. If you fail to live up to what you promised, they may lose trust and may even call off the deal.

Corruption and bribery are very rare in the Netherlands. It is strongly advisable to stay away from giving gifts of significant value or making offers that could be read as bribery.

Decision Making – Dutch companies are rarely very hierarchical. Decision making is a group process through which consensus is established and during which all team members involved get opportunities to voice their opinion. The authority to make decisions often resides with managers at lower levels of the organization without requiring further executive approval. The role of senior managers is to dispense information, provide guidance, and coordinate the decision making as needed. They do not have 'final say.' This can be confusing for negotiators from other western countries who may be looking to identify the 'key decision maker' in an organization, while in reality such a role may not exist at all. Decision making can take a long time and requires a great deal of patience. It is very important to learn about the company structure and win the support of people at all organizational levels who are involved in the negotiation, rather than focusing on upper management only. Once a decision has been made, it may be very difficult to change.

Unlike in most other cultures, there can be huge differences in the decision process depending on whether the Dutch negotiate at home or abroad. Through their tradition as traders in international markets, they have learned that success abroad may require swift decisions. Accordingly, Dutch businesspeople traveling abroad often have sufficient decision-making authority to close deals themselves. It can be advantageous to invite a Dutch counterpart to meet in your home country as a way to speed up the negotiation process.

When making decisions, businesspeople may apply universal principles rather than considering the specific situation. They often dislike 'making exceptions,' even when arguments speak in favor of doing so. Personal feelings and experiences are considered irrelevant in business negotiations, so people focus on empirical evidence, logical arguments, and objective facts. Most Dutch are moderate risk takers.

Agreements and Contracts

Capturing and exchanging meeting summaries can be an effective way to verify understanding and commitments. Oral agreements and statements of intent may already be legally binding and are usually dependable, though they do not substitute for written contracts. Actions that have been agreed upon are usually implemented immediately, even if a final contract is still pending. In general, dependability is highly valued and swift follow-up is essential.

Written contracts tend to be lengthy. They often spell out detailed terms and conditions for the core agreements as well as for many eventualities. Signing the contract is very important not only from a legal perspective, but also as a strong confirmation of your Dutch partners' commitment.

It is recommended to consult a local legal expert before signing a contract. However, do not bring your attorney to the negotiation table.

Contracts are usually dependable, and the agreed terms are viewed as binding. Your counterparts will make strong efforts to meet their commitments. Failure to meet the terms of a contract is likely to trigger legal action. However, your counterparts may occasionally ask you to reconsider aspects of the contract if conditions have changed.

Women in Business

While women enjoy similar rights as men, most Dutch women are still struggling to attain positions of similar income and authority. However, visiting businesswomen should have few problems in the country as long as they act professionally in business and social situations.

Other Important Things to Know

Formal, conservative attire is important when doing business here. Male business visitors should wear dark suits with neckties on most occasions.

While business lunches are common, dinners are not. During these events, business may or may not be discussed. Wait to see whether your counterparts bring it up.

Gift giving in business settings is rare. It is best not to bring a gift to an initial meeting in order to avoid raising suspicions about your motives.

The Dutch are often uncomfortable with secrets. Company employees expect to have access to more information than those in many other countries. Non-disclosure clauses that attempt to limit the distribution of information within a company may therefore not work well.

Nigeria

The country's very pluralistic population includes more than 250 ethnic groups, most of which have their own language. The largest groups are the Yoruba (21 percent), Hausa (20 percent), Ibo (18 percent), Ijaw (10 percent), and Fulani (9 percent). Half of Nigeria's population is Muslims and 40 percent are Christians. People usually identify themselves much more with their ethnicity and religion than their nationality. The information given in this section represents general guidelines for the country but may not always apply in full.

Businesspeople and officials in Nigeria usually have only limited exposure to other cultures. When negotiating business here, realize that people may expect things to be done 'their way.'

Relationships and Respect

Building lasting and trusting personal relationships is very important and can be crucial for your business success. People in this country usually want to do business only with those they know and like. Consequently, proceed with serious business discussions only after your counterparts have become very comfortable with you. This may include asking and answering many personal questions. Nigerians tend to distrust people who appear unwilling to spend the time or whose motives for relationship building are unclear. In addition, it may jeopardize relationships if you openly criticize someone, even in a one-on-one setting. Establishing productive business relationships is a slow process that requires a long-term perspective and commitment. As a reward, they may last forever.

Business relationships in this country exist between people, not necessarily between companies. Even when you have won your local business partners' friendship and trust, they will not necessarily trust others from your company. That makes it very important to keep company interfaces unchanged. Changing a key contact may require the relationship building process to start over.

In Nigeria's business culture, the respect a person enjoys depends primarily on his or her status, rank, and education. Admired personal traits include flexibility and humility.

Communication

More than 250 languages exist in Nigeria. While the official language is English, less than half of the population speaks it. Other languages that are spoken widely are Hausa, Yoruba, Ibo, and Fulani. When communicating in English, speak in short, simple sentences and avoid using jargon and slang.

Polite and cheerful greetings are highly valued in Nigeria and can be extensive. Conversations may get loud and passionate. However, interrupting others may be considered rude. Be careful not to read too much into it when people speak in a loud voice and look serious. It does not necessarily mean that they are angry. Nigerians usually show their emotions openly. However, never lose your temper or appear impatient. It is in your best interest to mask any negative feelings with a smile. People in the country generally converse in close proximity, standing only two feet or less apart. Never back away, even if this is much closer than your personal comfort zone allows. Doing so could be read as a sign that you are uncomfortable around them.

Communication in Nigeria can be direct and straightforward, especially among friends and close business partners. They may not find it difficult to say 'no' if they dislike a request or proposal. Early in the business relationship, people may communicate more indirectly, appearing vague and non-committal. If in doubt, watch for subtle messages that may signal issues and concerns. Silence may convey displeasure or even anger. Know that Nigerians may sometimes use English words opposite to their textbook meaning. For instance, they may call a lemon 'sweet' or a bad event 'wonderful.' This does not mean that they value sarcastic comments.

Nigerians frequently make physical contact. Men may hold hands while walking down the street, which is a sign of friendship and has no sexual connotation. However, never touch someone's head, not even that of a child. Body language and gestures may be extensive. Since Muslims consider the left hand unclean, use it only if inevitable. Eye contact should be made when initially meeting a person, but it is best to keep it infrequent thereafter, especially during meals.

Initial Contacts and Meetings

Having a local contact can be an advantage but is usually not a necessary precondition to doing business in Nigeria. Negotiations in the country can be conducted by individuals or teams of negotiators. It is vital that teams be well aligned, with roles clearly assigned to each member. Changing a team member may require the relationship building process to start over and should therefore be avoided. Worst case, such a change can bring negotiations to a complete halt.

If possible, schedule meetings at least two to three weeks in advance. Since people want to know whom they will be meeting, provide details on titles, positions, and responsibilities of attendees ahead of time. While meetings may start considerably late, Nigerians generally expect foreign visitors to be punctual. Avoid being more than 10 to 15 minutes late. Displaying anger if you have to wait, even for a considerable length of time, will reflect very poorly on you.

Names are usually given in the order of first name, family name. Nigerians may use *Mr./Mrs./Miss* together with the first name or, if they are more 'westernized,' with the family name. If a person has a professional or academic title, make sure to use it. Again, it may sometimes be used in conjunction with the first name. Do not be surprised if you see a degree with 'failed' after it on a business card. The fact that someone even got to college is an achievement. Always use the title of *Chief* if it applies to the person. Before calling Nigerians by their first name, it is best to wait until they offer it. Introductions are accompanied by handshakes.

The exchange of business cards is an essential step when meeting someone for the first time, so bring more than you need. You may not always get one in return. Show advanced degrees on your card and make sure that it clearly states your professional title, especially if you have the seniority to make decisions. Present your card with your right hand. Similarly, accept others' cards using only the right hand. Smile and make eye contact while doing so, then examine the card. Next, place the card on the table in front of you or into your card case.

Meetings start with small talk, which can be extensive. This may include inquiries about your health, family, and so on. Since family is important, asking questions about your counterpart's family yourself may be a good relationship building step. Some of the questions could be very personal. It is important to be patient and let the other side set the pace. Humor will be appreciated as long as it is not sarcastic or cynical. Generally, while Nigerians are often quite informal, it may be best to stay a bit on the formal side, at least during the initial meeting.

The primary purpose of the first meeting is to get to know each other. Business may be discussed, but do not try to hurry along with your agenda. Nigerian negotiators may try to convince you that they have the background and experience required to be successful. Businesspeople may exaggerate their capabilities or make questionable promises in order to maintain foreign contacts.

Presentation materials should be attractive, with good and clear visuals. Use diagrams and pictures wherever feasible, cut down on words, and avoid complicated expressions.

Negotiation

Attitudes and Styles - In Nigeria, the primary approach to negotiating is to employ distributive and contingency bargaining. While the buyer is in a superior position, both sides in a business deal own the responsibility to reach agreement. Nigerians expect to build long-term relationships, but rewards that lie in the far future rarely motivate them. Accordingly, they usually expect near-term benefits to result from their business engagements. The primary negotiation style is cooperative, but people may be unwilling to agree with compromises unless it is their only option to keep the negotiation from getting stuck. Win-win is not necessarily the preferred approach. Nigerians may be happy to get more out of a deal than you do. In fact, it can raise their status if they managed to trick you into accepting inferior term and conditions. Nonetheless, never show anger or other negative emotions, and do not express any frustrations. This would only work against you.

Should a dispute arise at any stage of a negotiation, you might be able to reach resolution by leveraging personal relationships and showing willingness to compromise.

Sharing of Information – Nigerians may believe in information sharing as a way to build trust. Negotiations can become very difficult if one side appears to be hiding information from the other. However, your counterparts will frequently exaggerate, so take everything you hear with a grain of salt.

In addition, beware of the many kinds of frauds found in the country. It is strongly advisable to check your counterpart's background carefully and to verify all information your may receive.

Pace of Negotiation – Expect negotiations to be slow and protracted. Relationship building, information gathering, bargaining, and decision making all take considerable time. You will likely need to make several trips to achieve your objectives. Throughout the negotiation, be patient, control your emotions, and accept that delays and changes occur.

Most Nigerians prefer a strongly polychronic work style. They are used to pursuing multiple actions and goals in parallel. When negotiating, they often take a holistic approach and may jump back and forth between topics rather than addressing them in sequential order. Negotiators from strongly monochronic cultures, such as Germany, the United Kingdom, or the United States, may find this style confusing, irritating, and even annoying. In any case, do not show irritation or anger when encountering this behavior. Instead, keep track of the bargaining progress at all times, often emphasizing areas where agreement already exists.

Bargaining – Most Nigerians love bargaining and haggling. They expect to do a lot of it during a negotiation and may be offended if you refuse to play along. The bargaining stage of a negotiation can be extensive. Prices often move more than 50 percent between initial offers and final agreement. Leave yourself sufficient room for concessions at different stages. Ask the other side to reciprocate if you made one. You can use the fact that aspects can be re-visited to your advantage, for instance by offering further concessions under the condition that the Nigerian side reciprocate in areas that had already been agreed upon.

Several deceptive techniques might be used and it may be effective to use some of them yourself. This includes tactics such as sending fake non-verbal messages, initially pretending to be disinterested in the whole deal or in single concessions, misrepresenting an item's value, or making false demands and concessions. Nigerians may occasionally use 'good cop, bad cop,' and it can be hard to see through the tactic. They may also claim limited authority, stating that they have to ask for their manager's approval. In that case, find a way to involve the manager in the negotiation since it will be important to deal with the decision maker.

Negotiators in the country may use pressure techniques that include showing intransigence, making final offers, or nibbling. Final offers may come more than once and are rarely final. Do not use tactics such as opening with your best offer, applying time pressure or making expiring offers, since Nigerians could view these as signs that you are not willing to build a long-term relationship. Silence is rarely used as a tactic, but it may be effective to employ it yourself.

Nigerian negotiators avoid most aggressive or adversarial techniques since they may overly affect the relationship. The risk of using any of them yourself is rarely worth the potential gain. As an exception, extreme openings are frequently employed as a way to start the bargaining process.

As in most relationship-oriented cultures, negotiators may sometimes use emotional techniques such as attitudinal bargaining, attempting to make you feel guilty, grimacing, or appealing to personal relationships. At times, defensive tactics such as blocking, distracting or changing the subject, asking probing or very direct questions, or making promises may also be used.

Corruption and bribery are very common in Nigeria's public and private sectors. However, people may draw the line differently, viewing minor payments as rewards for getting a job done rather than as bribes. TIPS ('To Insure Prompt Service'), or *dash*, as it is called in Nigeria, is an integral part of the culture. Tips are often collected before receiving a service. This is sometimes the case in business, too. Lastly, keep in mind that there is a fine line between giving gifts and bribing. What you may consider a bribe, a Nigerian may view as only a nice gift.

Decision Making – Companies are often very hierarchical, and people expect to work within clearly established lines of authority. Decision makers are usually senior executives who consider the best interest of the group or organization. They rarely delegate their authority to lower levels in the hierarchy, but others are often consulted in order to reach greater consensus over and support of the decision. This process can take a long time and requires much patience. Nigerians usually indicate it if they are not interested in doing business.

When making decisions, businesspeople may not rely much on rules or laws. They usually consider the specific situation rather than applying universal principles. Personal feelings and experiences may weigh much more strongly than empirical evidence and other objective facts do. Nigerians are generally risk takers and may not shy away from making bold and seemingly irrational moves.

Agreements and Contracts

Capturing and exchanging written understandings after meetings and at key negotiation stages is useful. Oral commitments may sound stronger than what your Nigerian counterparts may be willing to put in writing. However, these documents are not final agreements. Any part of an agreement may still change significantly before both parties sign the final contract. It is essential to reconfirm agreements often in order to verify understanding and commitment.

Written contracts may be created in a wide range of styles, from high-level to very detailed. Signing one is often only a formality. Nigerians believe that the primary strength of an agreement lies in the partners' commitment rather than in its written documentation.

Your legal rights are rarely enforceable. However, it is still best to consult a local legal expert before signing a contract. Do not bring an attorney to the negotiation table, though, since this may be taken as a sign that you do not trust your counterparts.

Contracts alone are not dependable and their terms may sometimes not be kept at all. Your best chance to ensure that your partners follow through on their commitments is to stay in regular contact and nurture the relationship throughout your business engagement. Business partners are expected to remain flexible if conditions change, which may include agreeing to modify some contract terms.

Women in Business

Women mostly enjoy the same rights as men and are treated almost the same at work, although many Nigerian women are still struggling to attain positions of similar income and authority. A visiting businesswoman should act professionally in business and social situations. In addition, she should be careful regarding her safety, avoiding to be alone in unknown environments.

Other Important Things to Know

Foreign visitors may be invited to special events that serve primarily to signify the importance of the host. Elaborate preparations may be made with chairs of honor being placed in the center of the room for guests to sit on. Make sure to go to great lengths to acknowledge such efforts.

Social events do not require strict punctuality. While it is best to arrive at dinners close to the agreed time, being late to a party by 15 to 30 minutes or more is perfectly acceptable.

Norway

Norwegian businesspeople, especially those among younger generations, are usually experienced in interacting and doing business with visitors from other cultures. Culturally and ethnically, the country is quite homogenous.

Norwegians tend to be proud people who may not be very open to information or assistance from outside. Their culture is close to that of Sweden, though there is a bit of a love-hate relationship between them and Norwegians may be quick to point out subtle differences. There are less similarities with Denmark, even more so with Finland, so be careful not to appear to be lumping them all into the same category.

Relationships and Respect

The Norwegian culture is not one of strong individualists, at least not in the workplace. There are rarely elements of competition across business teams, and people usually do not want to stand out in the group. Building lasting and trusting relationships is important to most people in this country. However, the existence of strong relationships is usually not a necessary precondition for doing business in this country. Although Norwegians prefer to deal with people they trust, business and personal relationships are usually kept separate. Your counterparts' expectation may be to build a relationship over the course of your business engagement. Unless past business interactions have already met their approval, Norwegians may be cautious, appearing reserved and proceeding slowly. Once the necessary trust has been established, though, there will be a sense of loyalty to you as a respected business partner, which can go a long way should a difficult situation arise.

Business relationships in this country exist between companies as well as between individuals. If your company replaces you with someone else over the course of a negotiation, it may be easy for your replacement to take things over from where you left them. Likewise, if you introduce someone else from your company into an existing business relationship, that person may quickly be accepted as a valid business partner. This does not mean that the Norwegians do not care about who they are dealing with.

Norway is a very egalitarian society. Treating someone preferentially is generally discouraged. Superiors are not necessarily considered superior and they are not empowered to be sole decision-makers. Bosses are usually easily accessible and are expected to be team members and leaders at the same time. Autocratic behavior may meet with strong disapproval. Team members usually approach management if there is a problem, not the other way round. Performance is always group performance, so reward or criticize the group, not the individual. In the country's business culture, the respect a person enjoys depends primarily on his or her achievements. Admired personal traits include honesty, sincerity and seriousness, respect, and confidence.

Communication

Norwegian, the country's official language, resembles Swedish and to a lesser degree, Danish. Most businesspeople in Norway speak English well. However, avoid using jargon and slang.

Norwegians usually speak in quiet, gentle tones. Never be loud and forceful – to the contrary, appearing reserved or even a bit shy may leave a favorable impression. Conversations may include extended periods of silence, which do not necessarily convey a negative message. Do not rush to fill in conversation pauses since your counterparts may only be taking time to formulate their thoughts. Also, interrupting others may be considered rude. Emotions are rarely shown in conversations, and the lively exuberance Americans often display can make Norwegians uncomfortable. People generally converse standing about three to four feet apart.

Norwegian communication is usually quite direct. Norwegians dislike vague statements and strive to keep business conversations focused on facts and objectives. They may ask for clarifications and do not find it difficult to say 'no' if they dislike a request or proposal.

Norwegians use body language sparingly. Avoid talking with your hands. Physical contact is rare and best avoided. The American *OK* sign, with thumb and index finger forming a circle, can be read as an obscene gesture in Norway. The thumbs-up gesture is positive as it signals approval. Eye contact should be frequent, almost to the point of staring, as this conveys sincerity and helps build trust.

Initial Contacts and Meetings

Having a local contact can be an advantage but is usually not a necessary precondition to doing business in Norway. Negotiations in Norway can be conducted by individuals or teams of negotiators. It is beneficial to make sure that your team is well aligned in order to avoid confusing and irritating your counterparts.

Scheduling meetings in advance is required. However, you can sometimes do this on short notice, especially if the parties have had previous business interactions. Since Norwegians want to know whom they will be meeting, provide details on titles, positions, and responsibilities of attendees ahead of time. Agreeing on an agenda upfront can also be useful. Avoid rescheduling meetings if you can.

Norwegians value punctuality. At any meeting, whether business or social, it is therefore best to be right on time. Arriving late, or being early, make be taken as a sign of disrespect. Expect meetings to end on or close to the scheduled time.

Names are usually given in the order of first name, family name. Some Norwegians may have two first names. Use *Mr./Mrs./Miss* or *Herr/Fru/Froken* plus the family name. If a person has an academic title, such as *Doctor* or *Professor*, use it instead, followed by the family name. Before calling Norwegians by their first name, wait until they offer it unless they introduced themselves using their first name only. Introduce and greet women first, then the oldest people in the group. Introductions are accompanied by firm handshakes.

The exchange of business cards is an essential step when meeting someone for the first time, so bring more than you need. Almost all businesspeople in Norway read English, so there is no need to have your card translated. Showing titles and advanced degrees on your card is not important. When presenting your card, smile and keep eye contact, then take a few moments to look at the card you received.

Meetings usually get right down to business with little or no small talk. Keep in mind that Norwegians are sincere people who dislike superficiality in conversation. Humor rarely has a place in business discussions, one's private life should not be discussed there at all, and personal comments should be avoided. Business is a serious matter in Norway, as are most other aspects of life. Meetings can be quite formal. While the primary purpose of the first meeting is to become acquainted, the discussion will mostly focus on business topics. It is vital to come well prepared as the Norwegians hate wasting time. Nevertheless, it is unrealistic to expect initial meetings to lead to straight decisions.

Presentations should be short and concise. Facts and figures are crucial. Allow sufficient time for questions and clarifications. The appearance of your presentation materials is not very important as long as you include good and easy-to-understand visuals. Having your English-language handout materials translated to Norwegian is not required.

Negotiation

Attitudes and Styles – To Norwegians, negotiating is usually a joint problem-solving process. Buyer and seller in a business deal are equal partners who both own the responsibility to reach agreement. They may focus equally on near-term and long-term benefits. The primary negotiation style is cooperative and people may be open to compromising if viewed helpful in order to move the negotiation forward. Since the Norwegians believe in the concept of win-win, they expect you to reciprocate their respect and trust. It is strongly advisable to avoid any open confrontation or conflict, and to remain calm, friendly, patient, and persistent.

Should a dispute arise at any stage of a negotiation, you might be able to reach resolution by focusing on logical reasoning and facts while remaining open and constructive.

Sharing of Information – Norwegian negotiators believe in information sharing as a way to build trust. This does not mean that they will readily reveal everything you might want to know during your negotiation. However, negotiations can become very difficult if one side appears to be hiding information from the other.

Pace of Negotiation – Expect negotiations to be slow. The methodical and carefully planned approach the Norwegians use in preparing for the negotiation and gathering information take considerable time, as does the effort needed to work out details of an agreement. Remain patient, control your emotions, and accept the inevitable delays.

The Norwegians generally prefer a monochronic work style. They are used to pursuing actions and goals systematically, and they dislike interruptions or digressions.

When negotiating, they often work their way down a list of objectives in sequential order, bargaining for each item separately, and may be unwilling to revisit aspects that have already been agreed upon. They may show little tolerance if a more poly-chronic counterpart challenges this approach, which they view as systematic and effective. This rigid style may be difficult to tolerate for negotiators from highly polychronic cultures, such as most Asians, Arabs, some Southern Europeans, or most Latin Americans, who may view it as closed-minded and overly restrictive. In any case, do not show irritation or anger when encountering this behavior. Instead, be willing to bargain over some items individually. Otherwise, clearly indicate that your agreement is conditional and contingent on other items.

Bargaining – Norwegians are not fond of bargaining and strongly dislike haggling. They also do not appreciate aggressive sales techniques. While the bargaining stage of a negotiation may take time and require several meetings, prices rarely move by more than 10 to 15 percent between initial offers and final agreement. The concept of fairness is very important to people, so while it is not difficult to obtain small con-cessions, your counterparts will expect reciprocity and may take it very negatively if the bargaining exchange is too one-sided.

Norwegians prefer to negotiate in a straightforward and honest style. They rarely use deceptive negotiation techniques. If they seem disinterested in a deal or in mak-ing specific concessions, they likely mean it. Realize that using any such tactics your-self, whether it is telling lies, sending fake non-verbal messages, misrepresenting an item's value, making false demands and concessions, or claiming 'limited authority,' could jeopardize the trust between the parties and damage the negotiation. 'Good cop, bad cop' is also not advisable as the tactic may lead the Norwegian side to ques-tion your trustworthiness.

Negotiators in the country use pressure techniques only as long as they can be ap-plied in a non-confrontational fashion. They may open with their best offer, show some intransigence, or make a final offer, but often remain willing to make small compromises. Norwegian negotiators may make their final offer quite early in the bargaining process, attempting to speed up the negotiation. Periods of silence in conversations are normal and may not represent an attempt to use it as a negotia-tion technique. Be very careful when using pressure tactics such as making expiring offers or nibbling. Your counterparts likely consider these inappropriate. While the negotiation will not necessarily be over because of this, the Norwegian side may become very reserved and cautious. Avoid applying time pressure, as people in this country do not like being rushed.

Avoid all aggressive tactics when negotiating with Norwegians. They will not shy away from open confrontation if challenged, but this is almost guaranteed to dete-riorate rather than strengthen your bargaining position. Opening with an extreme offer could be viewed as an unfriendly act. It is best to open with one that is already in the ballpark of what you really expect.

Other emotional negotiation techniques are also rare and should be avoided when negotiating in Norway, and appeals to personal relationships not only rarely work but also may be counterproductive. Norwegians may employ defensive tactics such as asking probing questions or making promises.

Opening with written offers and introducing written terms and conditions may be effective tactics that could help shorten the bargaining process, which your Norwegian counterparts may find desirable.

Corruption and bribery are very rare in Norway. It is strongly advisable to stay away from giving gifts of significant value or making offers that could be read as bribery.

Decision Making – Norwegian companies are much less hierarchical than most others are. Decision making is a group process through which consensus is established and during which all team members involved get opportunities to voice their opinion. The authority to make decisions often resides with managers at lower levels of the organization without requiring further executive approval. The role of senior managers is to dispense information, provide guidance, and coordinate the decision making as needed. They do not necessarily have 'final say,' and their decisions might not be followed if the group does not consent. This can be confusing for negotiators from other western countries who may be looking to identify the 'key decision maker' in an organization, while in reality such a role may not exist at all. Decision making can take a very long time and requires a great deal of patience. It is very important to learn about the company structure and win the support of people at all organizational levels who are involved in the negotiation, rather than focusing on upper management only. Once a decision has been made, it may be very difficult to change.

When making decisions, businesspeople may apply universal principles rather than considering the specific situation. They dislike 'making exceptions' even when arguments speak in favor of doing so. Personal feelings and experiences are considered irrelevant in business negotiations, so people focus on empirical evidence, logical arguments, and objective facts. Most Norwegians are moderate risk takers.

Agreements and Contracts

Capturing and exchanging meeting summaries can be an effective way to verify understanding and commitments. Handshakes and verbal agreements are often considered binding. They are normally kept, even though they are not legally binding. Nevertheless, it is best to confirm agreements in writing.

Written contracts tend to be lengthy. They often spell out detailed terms and conditions for the core agreements as well as for many eventualities. Signing the contract is very important not only from a legal perspective, but also as a strong confirmation of your Norwegian partners' commitment.

It is recommended to consult a local legal expert before signing a contract. However, do not bring your attorney to the negotiation table as it may be viewed as a sign of mistrust.

Contracts are almost always dependable, and strict adherence to the agreed terms and conditions is expected. Requests to change contract details after signature may be considered as bad faith and will meet with strong resistance.

Women in Business

Gender equality is very high in Norway. Most women are working, and many hold leadership positions that are similar in income and authority to those of men. Visiting businesswomen should have few problems in the country as long as they act professionally in business and social situations.

Other Important Things to Know

Do not expect to discuss business over meals.

Gift giving in business settings is rare. It is best not to bring a gift to an initial meeting in order to avoid raising suspicions about your motives.

Pakistan

Businesspeople and officials in Pakistan usually have only limited exposure to other cultures except for neighboring countries. Its culture is quite homogeneous. When negotiating business here, realize that people may expect things to be done 'their way,' and let them set the pace initially until you have had a chance to determine how your interactions are most effective. Always keep in mind that this is an Islamic country. Showing any disrespect for the religion could have disastrous consequences.

Relationships and Respect

Pakistan's culture is strongly group-oriented. Asserting individual preferences may be seen as less important than having a sense of belonging to a group, conforming to its norms, and maintaining harmony among its members. Building lasting and trusting personal relationships is therefore very important to most Pakistanis, who often expect to establish strong bonds prior to closing any deals. People in this country usually want to do business only with those they know and like. Establishing productive business cooperation requires a long-term perspective and commitment. Consequently, proceed with serious business discussions only after your counterparts have become comfortable with you. This is normally a slow process.

Business relationships in this country exist between people, not necessarily between companies. Even when you have won your local business partners' friendship and trust, they will not necessarily trust others from your company. That makes it very important to keep company interfaces unchanged.

Third party introductions can be very helpful as a starting point to building a trusting relationship. As a necessary ritual in the process, expect to flatter your counterparts and be flattered. Praise your business partners often and exaggerate.

In Pakistani business culture, the respect a person enjoys depends primarily on his or her age and status. It is crucial to treat elderly people with the greatest respect.

Showing status is important since people will take you more seriously. Carefully select your hotel and transportation. Use the services of others, such as a porter, to avoid being viewed as a low-ranking intermediary.

Communication

The official languages of Pakistan are English and Urdu. Most people in business speak English, often well. However, speak in short, simple sentences and avoid using jargon and slang.

Pakistanis usually speak in quiet, gentle tones. They are generally serious people who rarely smile and may seem stern. In Pakistan, humor does not have a place in business. Loud and boisterous behavior is perceived as a lack of self-control, and emotions are not shown openly. Pakistanis generally converse while standing around two to three feet apart. Never back away, even if this is much closer than your personal comfort zone allows. Doing so could be read as a sign that you are uncomfortable around them.

Communication is generally very indirect. Pakistanis often use circuitous language, which can make it difficult for Westerners to figure out the exact message. When responding to a direct question, Pakistanis may answer 'yes' only to signal that they heard what you said, not that they agree with it. Open disagreement and confrontation must be avoided, so you rarely hear a direct 'no.' Instead, they may give seemingly ambiguous answers such as 'we will try,' 'we will think about it,' or 'this will require further investigation.' Each of these could mean 'no,' as does a 'yes' that sounds hesitant or weak. Alternatively, a respondent may deliberately ignore your question. Silence is often a way to communicate a negative message. It is beneficial to use a similarly indirect approach when dealing with Pakistanis, as they may perceive you as rude and pushy if you are too direct.

Gestures are usually subtle. It is advisable to restrict your body language. Non-verbal communication is important, though, and you should carefully watch for others' small hints, just as they will be watching you. Avoid any physical contact with Pakistanis except for handshakes. Since Muslims consider the left hand unclean, use it only if inevitable. When pointing at people, use your thumb while keeping the fist closed rather than your index finger. Slapping the open hand over a fist can be read as a vulgar gesture. Eye contact should be very infrequent. While it is beneficial to make some eye contact when meeting a person for the first time, Pakistanis consider frequent eye contact intrusive and rude. It is generally considered respectful to look down when speaking with senior or elder people. Avoid any facial expressions that may suggest disagreement, such as grimacing or shaking your head.

Smiles rarely indicate amusement or approval. Instead, they may signal disapproval or other feelings of distress.

Initial Contacts and Meetings

Before initiating business negotiations in Pakistan, it is highly advantageous to identify and engage a local intermediary. This person will help bridge the cultural and communications gap, allowing you to conduct business with greater effectiveness. However, negotiations in Pakistan should preferably be conducted by individuals rather than teams. This is different from most Asian countries.

If possible, schedule meetings at least three to four weeks in advance. Since people want to know whom they will be meeting, provide details on titles, positions, and responsibilities of attendees ahead of time. Be prepared for meetings to be cancelled or postponed on short notice. Pakistanis have little sense of urgency about time and dislike being hurried. Meetings may therefore start considerably late. However, people generally expect foreign visitors to be punctual. Avoid being more than 15 to 20 minutes late. Displaying anger if you have to wait, which happens often, reflects very poorly on you.

Pakistani names are either given in the order of first name, middle name, and clan name, or clan name, first name, middle name. Other naming patterns exist as well. If you can clearly identify the names, use *Mr./Ms.* followed by the clan name, or the clan name followed by *Sahib/Begum*. Otherwise, inquire from someone upfront or politely ask the person how to address him or her correctly. In that case, make sure you do the same for your own name. Titles, such as *Doctor* or *Professor*, are highly valued. Always use them when addressing a person who carries one. Do not call Pakistanis by their first name unless they offered it, which is rare. Introduce and greet older people first. Introductions are accompanied by light handshakes using the right hand. Males should not initiate handshakes with women. However, it is usually ok for a foreign businesswoman to offer a handshake to a Pakistani man.

After the introductions, offer your business card to everyone present. It is not necessary to have it translated into Urdu. Show doctorate degrees on your card and make sure that it clearly states your professional title, especially if you have the seniority to make decisions. Present your card with your right hand, with the print facing the recipient. Similarly, accept others' cards using only the right hand. Smile and make eye contact while doing so, then examine the card carefully. Not reading someone's card can be an insult. Next, place it on the table in front of you or into your card case.

Meetings start with a lot of small talk, which may include prolonged inquiries about your health, family, and so on. This may include very personal questions. It is important to be patient and let the other side set the pace. Humor has no place at business settings, and after the initial small talk, the meeting may be rather formal and reserved. Frequent meeting interruptions are normal and do not signal a lack of interest. It is not uncommon to have additional observers sitting in on the meeting.

The primary purpose of the first meeting is to become acquainted and build relationships. Little else may happen, and you may actually not get to talk about business at all. It is unrealistic to expect initial meetings to lead to straight decisions.

Presentation materials can be simple without colorful backgrounds and fancy graphs. However, good and easy-to-understand visuals are important. Use diagrams and pictures wherever feasible, cut down on words, and avoid complicated expressions. Having your handout materials translated to Urdu is not a must.

Negotiation

Attitudes and Styles - In Pakistan, the primary approach to negotiating is to employ distributive and contingency bargaining. While the buyer is in a superior position, both sides in a business deal own the responsibility to reach agreement. They expect long-term commitments from their business partners and will focus mostly on long-term benefits. Although the primary negotiation style is competitive, Pakistanis nevertheless value long-term relationships and look for win-win solutions. They respect hard bargainers as long as they avoid creating direct conflict. Attempts to win competitive advantages should not be taken negatively. You earn your counterparts' respect by maintaining a positive, persistent attitude.

Should a dispute arise at any stage of a negotiation, you might be able to reach resolution by leveraging personal relationships and emphasizing long-term benefits. Refrain from using logical reasoning or becoming argumentative since this will only make matters worse. Patience and creativity will pay strong dividends. In extreme situations, use a mediator, ideally the party who initially introduced you.

Sharing of Information - Information is rarely shared freely, since the Pakistani believe that privileged information creates bargaining advantages.

Pace of Negotiation – Expect negotiations to be very slow and protracted. Be prepared to make several trips if necessary to achieve your objectives. Throughout the negotiation, be patient, control your emotions, and accept that delays occur. Attempts to rush the process are viewed as offensive.

Pakistanis generally employ a polychronic work style. They are used to pursuing multiple actions and goals in parallel. When negotiating, they often take a holistic approach and may jump back and forth between topics rather than addressing them in sequential order. Negotiators from strongly monochronic cultures, such as Germany, the United Kingdom, or the United States, may find this style confusing, irritating, and even annoying. In any case, do not show irritation or anger when encountering this behavior. Instead, keep track of the bargaining progress at all times, often emphasizing areas where agreement already exists.

If your counterparts appear to be stalling the negotiation, assess carefully whether their slowing down the process indicates that they are evaluating alternatives or that they are not interested in doing business with you. While such behavior could represent attempts to create time pressure in order to obtain concessions, the slow decision process in the country is far more likely causing the lack of progress. People from fast-paced cultures tend to underestimate how much time this takes and often make the mistake of trying to 'speed things up.' Again, patience and persistence are vitally important.

Bargaining – Pakistani businesspeople are often shrewd negotiators who should not be underestimated. Most of them love bargaining and haggling. They expect to do a lot of it during a negotiation and may be offended if you refuse to play along. The bargaining stage of a negotiation can be extensive. Prices often move more than 40 percent between initial offers and final agreement. Pricing usually plays a more central role in the bargaining process than services or support aspects. Leave yourself a lot of room for concessions at different stages. Ask the other side to reciprocate if you made one. It is not advisable to make significant early concessions since your counterparts expect further compromises as the bargaining continues. You can use the fact that aspects can be re-visited to your advantage, for instance by offering further concessions under the condition that the Pakistani side reciprocate in areas that had already been agreed upon.

Deceptive techniques might be used and it may be effective to use some of them yourself. This includes tactics such as telling lies and sending fake non-verbal messages, pretending to be disinterested in the whole deal or in single concessions, misrepresenting an item's value, or making false demands and concessions. Lies may be difficult to detect. It is advisable to verify information received from the local side through other channels. Similarly, Pakistanis treat 'outside' information with caution. They may claim limited authority, stating that they have to ask for their manager's approval. This could be a tactic or the truth. Since you must avoid causing loss of face, be cautious when using the techniques of making false demands or false concessions. Any overt attempts to bluff your counterparts could backfire.

Negotiators in the country may use pressure techniques that include making final offers or nibbling. Final offers may come more than once and are rarely final. Do not use tactics such as applying time pressure or making expiring offers, since Pakistanis could view these as signs that you are not willing to build a long-term relationship. They may choose to terminate the negotiation. Periods of silence are frequent and usually reflect a natural inclination rather than the intentional use of a negotiation technique.

Pakistani negotiators avoid most aggressive or adversarial techniques since they affect face. The risk of using any of them yourself is rarely worth the potential gain. As an exception, extreme openings may be used as a way to start the bargaining process. Threats and warnings may also be used. However, use these tactics with caution since they may adversely affect the relationship if employed too aggressively.

As in most strongly relationship-oriented cultures, negotiators may sometimes use emotional techniques such as attitudinal bargaining, attempting to make you feel guilty, grimacing, or appealing to personal relationships. Be cautious when using any of them yourself. You might cause the other side to lose face, which could damage your negotiating position. Also, know that Pakistanis can become very emotional during fierce bargaining. It is best to remain calm.

At times, defensive tactics such as blocking or changing the subject, asking probing questions, or making promises may be used. The exception is directness, which is rare in Pakistan. People may be offended if you are overly direct yourself, which can be very detrimental.

Corruption and bribery are common in Pakistan's public and private sectors. However, people may draw the line differently, viewing minor payments as rewards for getting a job done rather than as bribes. Also, keep in mind that there is a fine line between giving gifts and bribing. What you may consider a bribe, a Pakistani may view as only a nice gift, and so much as hinting that you view it differently could be a grave insult to the person's honor. It may help if you introduce and explain your company's policies early on, but be careful not to moralize or appear to imply that local customs are unethical.

Decision Making – Most companies tend to be very hierarchical, and people expect to work within clearly established lines of authority. Disagreeing with or criticizing superiors is unacceptable. Decision making is a very slow and deliberate process in Pakistan. Decision makers are usually senior executives who consider the best interest of the group or organization. They may consult with others before making the call. Subordinates may be reluctant to accept responsibility. Decision makers also rarely delegate their authority, so it is important to deal with senior executives.

When making decisions, Pakistani businesspeople may not rely much on rules or laws. They usually consider the specific situation rather than applying universal principles. Personal feelings and experiences weigh much more strongly than empirical evidence and other objective facts do. Pakistanis can be very fatalistic and are often reluctant to take risks. If you expect them to support a risky decision, you may need to find ways for them to become comfortable with it first. You are much more likely to succeed if the relationship with your counterparts is strong and you managed to win their trust.

Agreements and Contracts

Capturing and exchanging written understandings after meetings and at key negotiation stages is useful since oral statements are not always dependable. Never mistake interim commitments for final agreement. Any part of an agreement may still change significantly before both parties sign the final contract.

Although most businesspeople in the country understand the role of contracts well, they may view them only as general guides for conducting business, expecting that both parties are willing to change terms if there is a change of conditions. Written contracts tend to be lengthy and often spell out detailed terms and conditions for the core agreements as well as for many eventualities. Multiple signatures may be required on the Pakistani side. Nevertheless, writing up and signing the contract is a formality. Pakistanis believe that the primary strength of an agreement lies in the partners' commitment rather than in its written documentation.

Although your legal rights may not always be enforceable, it is strongly advisable to consult a local legal expert before signing a contract. However, do not bring your attorney to the negotiation table, since this may be taken as a sign that you do not trust your counterparts.

Signed contracts may not always be honored. Business partners usually expect the other side to remain somewhat flexible if conditions change, which may include agreeing to modify contract terms.

Women in Business

Pakistan remains a male-dominated society. Although some women are working, they still have a very traditional role and rarely attain positions of similar income and authority as men. The relative scarcity of women in Pakistani business may make local men uncomfortable in dealing with Western women, who should not expect to be met with the same respect as men.

As a visiting businesswoman, emphasize your company's importance and your role in it. A personal introduction or at least a letter of support from a senior executive within your company may also help. Even with these credentials, you may still not find sufficient attention, making it advisable to take a male colleague along for the trip. Female business travelers should exercise caution and act professionally in business and social situations. Displaying confidence and assertiveness can be counterproductive, and being overly bold and aggressive may create major issues. Female business travelers need to dress in accordance with local customs, which means that collarbones and knees need to be covered at all times and that clothes should not be form-fitting.

Male visitors should not bring up the subject of women with their business partners. Do not even inquire about a wife's or daughter's health.

Other Important Things to Know

Conservative attire is important when doing business here. Male business visitors should wear dark suits with neckties on most occasions. First impressions can have a significant impact on how people view you.

Social events do not require strict punctuality. While it is best to arrive at dinners close to the agreed time, being late to a party by 30 to 60 minutes or more is expected.

Topics to avoid in discussions are Pakistan's role as a nuclear power, its relationship with India, and the tensions over Kashmir, as well as issues around the U.S. war in Afghanistan.

Peru

Businesspeople and officials in Peru usually have only limited exposure to other cultures except for neighboring countries. Its culture is quite pluralistic between the most significant population groups, Amerindians, whites, and mestizos (mixed Amerindian and white). When negotiating business here, realize that people may expect things to be done 'their way.'

Relationships and Respect

Peru's culture is generally group-oriented. Asserting individual preferences may be seen as less important than having a sense of belonging to a group, conforming to its norms, and maintaining harmony among its members. Building lasting and trusting personal relationships is very important to most Peruvians, who often find it essential to establish strong bonds prior to closing any deals. People in this country usually want to do business only with those they know, like, and trust. Establishing productive business cooperation requires a long-term perspective and commitment. Proceed with serious business discussions only after your counterparts have become very comfortable with you. Even though Peruvians generally admire foreigners, this can be a time-consuming process.

Business relationships in this country exist between people, not necessarily between companies. Even when you have won your local business partners' friendship and trust, they will not necessarily trust others from your company. That makes it very important to keep company interfaces unchanged. Changing a key contact may require the relationship building process to start over.

Establishing personal relationships with others in Peru can create powerful networks and may help you a lot to achieve your business objectives. Whether people think you are worth knowing and trusting often weighs much more strongly than how competent you are or what proposals you may have to make. Personal networks may open doors and solve problems that would otherwise be difficult to master. Maintaining honest and cordial relations is crucial, as are tact and diplomacy in all your interactions with others. Third party introductions can be very helpful as a starting point to building a trusting relationship with a potential partner.

In Peru's business culture, the respect a person enjoys depends primarily on his or her status, rank, education, and age. Admired personal traits include sincerity, integrity, and sociability.

Communication

The country's official languages are Spanish and Quechua. Peruvian Spanish is notably different from the Spanish spoken in Spain. Few Peruvians speak English well, so being able to speak Spanish is a clear advantage. Otherwise, it is often useful to engage an interpreter. To avoid offending the other side, ask beforehand whether an interpreter should be present at a meeting. When communicating in English, speak in short, simple sentences and avoid using jargon and slang. It will help people with a limited command of English if you speak slowly, summarize your key points often, and pause frequently to allow for interpretation.

People in this country usually speak softly. While they may occasionally raise their voices to make a point, they dislike loud and boisterous behavior. At restaurants, keep conversations at a quiet level. People may converse in close proximity, standing only two feet or less apart. Never back away, even if this is much closer than your personal comfort zone allows. Doing so could be read as a sign that you are uncomfortable around them.

Communication in Peru is usually not overly direct. People may not get straight to the point when trying to get a message across and you may have to read between the lines to understand what is being conveyed. They may tell you what they think you want to hear rather than what they really think. Silence may express embarrassment or otherwise communicate a negative message. It is beneficial to use a similarly indirect approach when dealing with Peruvians, as they may perceive you as rude and pushy if you are too direct. The communication may become more direct and frank once a strong relationship has been established.

Gestures and body language can be lively, especially if they help underline what is being said. There may be frequent physical contact with others of the same gender. The American *OK* sign, with thumb and index finger forming a circle, can be read as an obscene gesture in Peru. Lightly tapping the head signals, 'I'm thinking.' Eye contact should be very frequent, almost to the point of staring. This conveys sincerity and helps build trust.

Initial Contacts and Meetings

Choosing a local intermediary, or *enchufado*, who can leverage existing relationships to make the initial contact is highly recommended. This person will help bridge the gap between cultures, allowing you to conduct business with greater effectiveness. Your embassy, a trade organization, a chamber of commerce, or a local legal or accounting firm may be able to provide a list of potential *enchufados*. Without such a contact, it may be very difficult to get access to the right people.

Negotiations in the country can be conducted by individuals or teams of negotiators. It is vital that teams be well aligned, with roles clearly assigned to each member. Changing a team member may require the relationship building process to start over and should therefore be avoided.

If possible, schedule meetings at least two weeks in advance. Since people want to know whom they will be meeting, provide details on titles, positions, and responsibilities of attendees ahead of time. While meetings may start considerably late, Peruvians generally expect foreign visitors to be punctual. Avoid being more than 10 to 15 minutes late, and call ahead if you will be. At the same time, showing signs of impatience if the meeting starts considerably late, which can be more than an hour after the scheduled start time, will only reflect very poorly on you. Titles and age of the Peruvian participants provide clues to their position in the company hierarchy. Otherwise, watch for small hints of deference to identify the decision makers.

Names are usually given in the order of first name, family names. Most Peruvians have two family names, the first one from their father, and the second one from their mother. Use *Mr./Mrs./Miss* or *Señor/Señora/Señorita*, plus the father's family name, which is always the first one of the two family names given. If a person has an academic title, like *Doctor* (often used for anyone with an advanced degree) or *Professor*, use it instead, followed by the father's family name. Only close friends call each other by their first names. Introductions are accompanied by handshakes.

The exchange of business cards is an essential step when meeting someone for the first time, so bring more than you need. It is recommended to use cards with one side in English and the other in Spanish. Show advanced degrees on your card and make sure that it clearly states your professional title, especially if you have the seniority to make decisions. When presenting your card, ensure that the Spanish side is facing the recipient. Smile and keep eye contact while accepting someone else's card, then carefully examine it. Next, place the card on the table in front of you.

Meetings start with small talk, which may be extensive. It is important to be patient and let the other side set the pace. People appreciate a sense of humor, but keep it light and friendly, and be careful not to overdo it. Business is a serious matter in Peru, and meetings can be very formal. At the same time, they may appear somewhat chaotic, with frequent interruptions and several parallel conversations. Do not take this personally; it also does not indicate a lack of interest.

The primary purpose of the first meeting is to become acquainted and build relationships. Business may be discussed, but do not try to hurry along with your agenda. Although the primary decision maker will usually attend, it is unrealistic to expect initial meetings to lead to straight decisions.

Presentation materials should be attractive, with good and clear visuals. Use diagrams and pictures wherever feasible, cut down on words, and avoid complicated expressions. Having your handout materials translated to Spanish is not a must, but it will be appreciated and helps in getting your messages across.

Negotiation

Attitudes and Styles - Leveraging relationships is an important element when negotiating in Peru. Nevertheless, Peruvians often employ distributive and contingency bargaining. While the buyer is in a superior position, both sides in a business deal own the responsibility to reach agreement. They expect long-term commitments from their business partners and will focus mostly on long-term benefits. The primary negotiation style is cooperative, but people may be unwilling to agree with compromises unless it is their only option to keep the negotiation from getting stuck. Nevertheless, one important function of the bargaining exchange is to build and strengthen the relationship. Since Peruvians believe in the concept of win-win, they expect you to reciprocate their respect and trust. You may be able to leverage the fact that many Peruvian businesspeople are eager to receive foreign business investments. However, it is strongly advisable to avoid aggressiveness and open confrontation, remaining calm, polite, patient, and persistent.

Should a dispute arise at any stage of a negotiation, you might be able to reach resolution by leveraging personal relationships and emphasizing long-term benefits. Patience and creativity will pay strong dividends.

Sharing of Information – Even when personal relationships are strong, your Peruvian counterparts may be reluctant to share information openly. Many believe that privileged information creates bargaining advantages. At the same time, information that may seem irrelevant may be reviewed over and over.

Pace of Negotiation – Expect negotiations to be slow and protracted. Peruvians do not hurry and dislike people who do. Be prepared to make several trips if necessary to achieve your objectives. Relationship building, information gathering, bargaining, and decision making may take considerable time. Attempts to rush the process are unlikely to produce better results and may be viewed as offensive. Throughout the negotiation, be patient, control your emotions, and accept the inevitable delays.

Most Peruvians prefer a very polychronic work style. They are used to pursuing multiple actions and goals in parallel. When negotiating, they often take a holistic approach and may jump back and forth between topics rather than addressing them in sequential order. Negotiators from strongly monochronic cultures, such as Germany, the United Kingdom, or the United States, may find this style confusing, irritating, and even annoying. In any case, do not show irritation or anger when encountering this behavior. Instead, keep track of the bargaining progress at all times, often emphasizing areas where agreement already exists.

If your counterparts appear to be stalling the negotiation, assess carefully whether their slowing down the process indicates that they are evaluating alternatives or that they are not interested in doing business with you. More likely, this behavior either represents an attempt to create time pressure in order to obtain concessions, or it simply reflects the slow decision process in the country. Again, patience and persistence are vitally important.

Bargaining – Peruvians are used to hard bargaining and haggling. The bargaining exchange can be extensive. Although people in the country may show interest in new ideas and concepts, they may find it difficult to change their position. Be respectful throughout the bargaining exchange. Rather than pushing for concessions, it may be better to re-address disagreements in follow-up meetings, which gives your counterparts the opportunity to reconsider their position without overtly losing face. Prices may move by about 25 to 35 percent between initial offer and final agreement. Leave yourself sufficient room for concessions at different stages. After making one, always ask the other side to reciprocate. Throughout the process, remain cool and respectful, avoid confrontation, and frequently reaffirm the relationship.

Deceptive techniques are frequent and can be effective. This includes tactics such as telling lies and sending fake non-verbal messages, pretending to be disinterested in the whole deal or in single concessions, misrepresenting an item's value, or making false demands and concessions. Your Peruvian counterparts may play stupid or make other attempts to mislead you in order to obtain bargaining advantages. Even when you can see right through a lie, it would be a grave personal insult to state or even hint that your counterpart is not telling the truth. It is advisable to verify information received from the local side through other channels. 'Good cop, bad cop' is a tactic that Peruvians rarely use, though it could be effective on either side of the negotiation table. However, it could be devastating if the other side recognized this as a tactic, and your team will need to exclude any 'bad cop' member from future negotiation rounds. Businesspeople may claim limited authority, stating that they have to ask for their manager's approval. This could be a tactic or the truth.

Negotiators in the country may use pressure techniques that include making final offers, showing intransigence, or nibbling. Final offers may come more than once and are rarely final. Be careful when trying to open with your best offer. Peruvians may consider this inappropriate or even insulting. Silence can be a very effective way to signal rejection of a proposal or to obtain further concessions. Do not use pressure tactics such as applying time pressure or making expiring offers as these may be taken as signs that you are not willing to build a long-term relationship. Your counterparts may even choose to terminate the negotiation.

Peruvian negotiators avoid openly aggressive or adversarial techniques. While they may make indirect threats and warnings or subtly display anger, they will be careful not to appear aggressive when doing so. Extreme openings are not frequently used since they may adversely affect the relationship, so be very cautious when using the tactic yourself. Never walk out or threaten to do so in an aggressive fashion as your counterparts will likely take this as a personal insult and may end all talks. However, threatening a 'friendly walkout' while strongly emphasizing the relationship may be very effective.

Emotional negotiation techniques, such as attitudinal bargaining or attempting to make you feel guilty, are frequent and can be effective. Be cautious not to hurt someone's personal pride when employing any of these tactics, though. Pleas to personal relationships and other emotional appeals, such as emphasizing how your proposal will add to your counterparts' personal satisfaction or heighten their honor, can be very powerful. Peruvians may frequently employ defensive tactics such as blocking or changing the subject, asking probing or very direct questions, making promises, or keeping an inflexible position.

Corruption and bribery are quite common in Peru's public and private sectors. However, people may draw the line differently, viewing minor payments as rewards for getting a job done rather than as bribes. Also, keep in mind that there is a fine line between giving gifts and bribing. What you may consider a bribe, a Peruvian may view as only a nice gift. It may help if you introduce and explain your company's policies early on, but be careful not to moralize or appear to imply that local customs are unethical.

Decision Making – Most companies are hierarchical, and people expect to work within clearly established lines of authority. Decision makers are usually senior executives who will consider the best interest of the group or organization. They may consult with others and prefer to reach consensus before making the final call. Consequently, subordinates may strongly influence the final decision and maintaining good relationships with them can be crucial to your success. Decision making can be a slow process that requires much patience. Attempts to rush or put pressure on the process are not likely to succeed.

When making decisions, businesspeople may not rely much on rules or laws. They usually consider the specific situation rather than applying universal principles. Personal feelings and experiences weigh more strongly than empirical evidence and other objective facts do. Peruvians are often uneasy with change and reluctant to take risks. If you expect them to support a risky decision, you may need to find ways for them to become comfortable with it first, for instance by explaining contingency plans, outlining areas of additional support, or by offering guarantees and warranties.

Agreements and Contracts

Capturing and exchanging written understandings after meetings and at key negotiation stages is useful. Oral commitments may sound stronger than what your Peruvian counterparts may be willing to put in writing. Do not rely on interim agreements to be final, even if they come in the form of written protocols. Any part of an agreement may still change significantly before both parties sign the final contract.

Written contracts tend to be lengthy and often spell out detailed terms and conditions for the core agreements as well as for many eventualities. Nevertheless, writing up and signing the contract is a formality. Peruvians believe that the primary strength of an agreement lies in the partners' commitment rather than in its written documentation.

It is advisable to consult a local legal expert before signing a contract. However, do not bring in your attorney until the negotiations have concluded. Peruvians may read it as a sign of mistrust if you do.

Signed contracts may not always be honored. This depends to no small degree on the strength of the continuing relationship between the contract partners. It is strongly advisable to continue staying in touch and maintaining the trust of your Peruvian business partner. Business partners usually expect the other side to remain somewhat flexible if conditions change, which may include agreeing to modify contract terms. Given the relatively unstable political and economic situation in the country, you should factor this possibility into your negotiation planning.

Women in Business

Machismo attitudes remain strong in this country. Women may be considered inferior, and they still have a hard time attaining positions of similar income and authority as men. As a visiting businesswoman, emphasize your company's importance and your role in it. A personal introduction or at least a letter of support from a senior executive within your company may help a lot.

Female business travelers should graciously accept any chivalric gestures they receive, while exercising caution and acting professionally in business and social situations. Displaying confidence and some degree of assertiveness can be effective, but it is very important not to appear overly bold and aggressive.

Other Important Things to Know

Formal, conservative attire is very important when doing business here. Male business visitors should wear dark suits with neckties on most occasions. First impressions can have a significant impact on how people view you.

Business lunches and dinners are common. Do not expect to discuss business over dinner, though.

Social events do not require strict punctuality. While it is best to arrive at dinners close to the agreed time, being late to a party by 30 minutes or more is perfectly acceptable.

Gift giving is common in social and business settings in Peru. It can be beneficial to bring a small gift, preferably something that is typical of your home country, for your initial meeting.

Do not refer to citizens of the United States as Americans. Most Latin Americans are sensitive to this point as they feel that the term includes them. They prefer to say *norteamericanos* or *North Americans*.

Philippines

Businesspeople and officials in the Philippines, especially outside of Manila, usually have only limited exposure to other cultures except for neighboring countries. The Philippines are a pluralistic society that includes many ethnic groups. When negotiating business here, realize that people may expect things to be done 'their way.' However, some, especially among younger generations, may have greater international experience and can be very open-minded.

Most Filipinos are very proud of their country. It would be a serious mistake to belittle its importance or to hint that you see yourself or your company in a superior position.

Relationships and Respect

The Filipino culture is very strongly group-oriented. Asserting individual preferences may be seen as less important than having a sense of belonging to a group, conforming to its norms, and maintaining harmony among its members. Building lasting and trusting personal relationships is therefore critically important to most Filipinos, who often expect to establish strong bonds prior to closing any deals. People in this country usually want to do business only with those they know and like. Getting to know you involves asking many questions about your family and personal background. Establishing productive business cooperation requires a long-term perspective and commitment. Proceed with serious business discussions only after your counterparts have become very comfortable with you.

Relationships are based on familiarity, respect, and personal trust, which can take a long time to establish. Business relationships in this country exist only between people, not between companies. Even when you have won your local business partners' friendship and trust, they will not necessarily trust others from your company. Accordingly, if your company replaces you with another representative, relationships need to be built anew. The only exception to this rule is if the replacement is a blood relative.

Social contacts are of primary importance in the Philippines and can create powerful networks, which are based on very strong commitments and mutual obligations. Debts must be paid back without exception. Maintaining cordial relations at all times is crucial, and showing humility is a great way to build trust. Third party introductions can be very helpful as a starting point to building a trusting relationship with a partner.

In the country's culture, 'saving face' is very essential. Every person's reputation and social standing rests on this concept. Causing embarrassment to another person may cause a *loss of face* for all parties involved and can be disastrous for the relationship. Reputation and social standing strongly depend on a person's ability to control emotions and remain friendly at all times. People believe that everyone should be treated with civility, so even snubbing a beggar may result in loss of face. Similarly, a positive attitude is mandatory since negativity of any kind can also cause loss of face. The importance of diplomatic restraint and tact cannot be overestimated.

In the Philippines' business culture, the respect a person enjoys depends primarily on his or her age and status. You will commonly find leaders in senior roles to be of advanced age. It is important to treat elderly people with great respect. Admired personal traits include humility, politeness, modesty, and graciousness.

In a way, this culture combines the Asian concept of *face* with the immense pride of the Spaniards. Filipinos are easily offended and have a reputation for violence. Do not provoke others, since people may believe they must act to regain their honor, regardless of the consequences.

Communication

The official languages of the Philippines are English and Filipino, a standardized dialect of Tagalog. However, many other languages and dialects are spoken as well. Most Filipinos speak at least some English. When communicating in English, speak in short, simple sentences and avoid using slang and jargon. It will help people with a limited command of English if you speak slowly, summarize your key points often, and pause frequently to allow for interpretation.

Filipinos can be enthusiastic conversationalists when in a happy, cheerful mood. However, people generally speak softly in the Philippines. Loud and boisterous behavior is perceived as a lack of self-control. Listen carefully when another person is talking. Interrupting others may be considered offensive. Silence is rare and may signal a problem. Filipinos generally converse while standing around two to three feet apart.

Because the concept of *face* is important in this culture, communication is generally very indirect. When responding to a direct question, Filipinos may answer 'yes' only to signal that they heard what you said, not that they agree with it. Open disagreement and confrontation must be avoided, so you rarely hear a direct 'no.' Instead, they may give seemingly ambiguous answers such as 'I am not sure,' 'we will think about it,' or 'this will require further investigation.' Each of these could mean 'no,' as does a 'yes' that sounds hesitant or weak. It is beneficial to use a similarly indirect approach when dealing with Filipinos, as they may perceive you as rude and pushy if you are too direct. No matter how a conversation goes, avoid showing negative emotions or facial expressions that could signal disagreement.

While gestures and body language are used for communication, they are usually kept subtle. Avoid any physical contact with Filipinos except for handshakes. When pointing at people, use your chin rather than a finger or your whole hand. Eye contact should be infrequent. While it is beneficial to make some eye contact when meeting a person for the first time, Filipinos consider frequent eye contact intrusive and rude.

While Filipinos do not expect foreigners to smile as often as they do, they generally respond well to happy faces and positive emotions. Smiles do not always indicate amusement or approval, though. Instead, they may mask embarrassment, disapproval, and other feelings of distress. Accordingly, Westerners may sometimes observe Filipinos smiling or laughing at what they might consider inappropriate moments.

Initial Contacts and Meetings

Before initiating business negotiations in the Philippines, it is advantageous to identify and engage a local intermediary. This person will help bridge the cultural and communications gap, allowing you to conduct business with greater effectiveness. The person may be able to leverage existing relationships. Without proper introductions, it may be very difficult to meet senior managers within any organization. The intermediary should be present at all meetings with your local counterparts.

Negotiations in the Philippines can be conducted by individuals or teams of negotiators. Teams should be well aligned, with roles clearly assigned to each member. Changing a team member may require the relationship building process to start over and should therefore be avoided. Worst case, such a change can bring negotiations to a complete halt. It is unlikely that you will meet the top executive of an organization at the first meeting, so be prepared to deal with subordinates. They may have significant influence over the final decision.

If possible, schedule meetings at least three to four weeks in advance. Since people want to know whom they will be meeting, provide details on titles, positions, and responsibilities of attendees ahead of time. Clearly communicating your objectives for the meeting and agreeing on an agenda upfront is useful, even though the latter may not be strictly followed. While punctuality is not always valued, Filipinos generally expect foreign visitors to be very punctual. Avoid being more than 5 to 10 minutes late. However, you may find that meetings start anywhere between right on time and an hour or more late.

Names are usually given in the order of first name, family names. Upper-class Filipinos often have two family names, the first one from their father and the other from their mother. Use *Mr./Mrs./Miss* plus the (father's) family name. If a person has an academic or professional title, use it instead, followed by the father's family name. Don't be surprised if you meet a person who appears to have different 'formal' and 'casual' names – the use of nicknames is widespread, and Filipinos may even show their nickname on their business cards. Introduce older people and those of higher rank first, and stand up when someone in either category enters the room. Introductions may be done by looking each other into the eye while raising eyebrows. Handshakes are also accepted, but keep them light and short. Men should wait for women to initiate handshakes. If a woman does not seem to want to shake hands, it is best just to nod your head.

After the introductions, offer your business card to everyone present. You may not always get one in return. It is not necessary to have it translated into Filipino. Make sure that it clearly states your professional title, especially if you have the seniority to make decisions. The exchange of business cards tends to be informal, which is different from most other Asian countries. Present your card with two hands, with the print facing the recipient. Accept others' cards using both hands if possible. Smile and make eye contact while doing so, then examine the card carefully. Next, remark upon the card and then place it on the table in front of you or into your card case. If a Filipino writes his or her home phone number on the card, consider this an invitation to call.

At the beginning of a meeting, there is normally some small talk. This allows participants to become personally acquainted. It is best to let the local side set the pace and follow along. Humor is often appreciated, but keep it light. The primary purpose of the first meeting is to become acquainted and build relationships. Business may or may not be discussed. Never try to hurry along with your agenda. It is unrealistic to expect initial meetings to lead to straight decisions.

Presentation materials should be attractive, with good and clear visuals. Use diagrams and pictures wherever feasible, cut down on words, and avoid complicated expressions. Having your handout materials translated to Filipino is not a must, but it will be noted favorably.

Meetings should end on a cheerful note, no matter what the outcome. Having some social conversation at the end is expected. Do not leave before the meeting has concluded.

Negotiation

Attitudes and Styles – Leveraging relationships is an important element when negotiating in the Philippines. To Filipinos, negotiating is usually a joint problem-solving process. While the buyer is in a superior position, both sides in a business deal own the responsibility to reach agreement. They expect long-term commitments from their business partners and will focus mostly on long-term benefits. The primary negotiation style is cooperative, but people may be unwilling to agree with compromises unless it is their only option to keep the negotiation from getting stuck. Maintaining harmonious relationships throughout the process is vitally important. While each party is expected to pursue their best interests, Filipinos disapprove of competitiveness and strive to find win-win solutions.

Sharing of Information - Information is rarely shared freely, since the locals believe that privileged information creates bargaining advantages.

Keep in mind that humility is a virtue in the Philippines' business culture. If you make exaggerated claims in an effort to impress the other side or to obtain concessions, they will likely investigate your claims before responding. Excessive promotions may be taken as lies and could seriously damage your counterpart's trust in you.

Pace of Negotiation – Expect negotiations to be slow and protracted. Relationship building, information gathering, bargaining, and decision making all take considerable time. In addition, Filipinos have a lower sense of urgency than a Westerner may be accustomed to. Consequently, your expectations regarding deadlines and effi-ciency may be unrealistic. Be prepared to make several trips if necessary to achieve your objectives. Throughout the negotiation, be patient, control your emotions, and accept that delays occur.

Filipinos generally employ a polychronic work style. They are used to pursuing multiple actions and goals in parallel. When negotiating, they often take a holis-tic approach and may jump back and forth between topics rather than addressing them in sequential order. Negotiators from strongly monochronic cultures, such as Germany, the United Kingdom, or the United States, may find this style confusing, irritating, and even annoying. In any case, remain positive and do not show irrita-tion or anger when encountering this behavior. Instead, keep track of the bargaining progress at all times, often emphasizing areas where agreement already exists.

If your counterparts appear to be stalling the negotiation, assess carefully whether their slowing down the process indicates that they are evaluating alternatives or that they are not interested in doing business with you. While such behavior could represent attempts to create time pressure in order to obtain concessions, the slow decision process in the country is far more likely causing the lack of progress. People from fast-paced cultures tend to underestimate how much time this takes and often make the mistake of trying to 'speed things up.' Actually, attempts to speed up the process will often prove counterproductive. Again, keep a happy face and remain patient and persistent. Your Filipino counterparts will respect this attitude, which helps in building stronger trust.

Bargaining – Most Filipinos love bargaining and haggling. They expect to do a lot of it during a negotiation and may be offended if you refuse to play along. They may use a wide array of negotiation techniques quite competently. The bargaining stage of a negotiation can be extensive. Filipinos may prefer to respond to your inputs rather than presenting ideas of their own. While they will eventually open up to new ideas, they do not easily change their opinions. Nevertheless, prices often move more than 40 percent between initial offers and final agreement. Leave yourself suf-ficient room for concessions at different stages. Ask the other side to reciprocate if you made one. You can use the fact that aspects can be re-visited to your advantage, for instance by offering further concessions under the condition that the Filipino side reciprocate in areas that had already been agreed upon.

Deceptive techniques might be used and it may be effective to use some of them yourself. This includes tactics such as telling lies and sending fake non-verbal mes-sages, initially pretending to be disinterested in the whole deal or in single conces-sions, misrepresenting an item's value, or making false demands and concessions. Lies may be difficult to detect. It is advisable to verify information received from the local side through other channels. Similarly, they treat 'outside' information with caution. Filipinos do not use 'good cop, bad cop' and it is best to avoid the tactic since the implications for relationships can be significant. They are also not likely to use the 'limited authority' technique because groups, rather than individuals, nor-mally make decisions. Since you must avoid causing loss of face, be very careful when using the techniques of making false demands or false concessions. Identifi-able attempts to bluff your counterparts will likely backfire.

Negotiators in the country may occasionally use pressure techniques that include making final offers or nibbling. Final offers may come more than once and are rarely final. Do not use tactics such as applying time pressure or making expiring offers, since Filipinos could view these as signs that you are not willing to build a long-term relationship. They may choose to terminate the negotiation. Periods of silence are frequent and usually reflect a natural inclination rather than the intentional use of a negotiation technique. Avoid pressure tactics such as opening with your best offer or showing intransigence, since they cannot be applied effectively without running the risk of causing loss of face.

Filipino negotiators avoid most aggressive or adversarial techniques since they affect face. The risk of using any of them yourself is rarely worth the potential gain. As an exception, extreme openings are frequently employed as a way to start the bargaining process. However, use the tactic with caution since it may adversely affect the relationship if employed too aggressively.

As in most strongly relationship-oriented cultures, negotiators may sometimes use emotional techniques such as attitudinal bargaining, attempting to make you feel guilty, grimacing, or appealing to personal relationships. Be cautious when doing this yourself. You might cause the other side to lose face, which could damage your negotiating position.

At times, defensive tactics such as blocking, distracting or changing the subject, asking probing questions, or making promises may be used. The exception is directness, which is very rare in this society. They may be shocked if you are overly direct yourself, which can be counterproductive.

Note that opening with written offers and attempting to introduce written terms and conditions as a negotiation tactic is rarely successful. In most cases, businesspeople ignore or tactfully reject them and request that each aspect be negotiated individually.

Corruption and bribery are quite common in the Philippines's public and private sectors. However, people may draw the line differently, viewing minor payments as rewards for getting a job done rather than as bribes. Also, keep in mind that there is a fine line between giving gifts and bribing. What you may consider a bribe, a Filipino may view as only a nice gift. It may help if you introduce and explain your company's policies early on, but be careful not to moralize or appear to imply that local customs are unethical.

Conflicts and disputes that may arise during a negotiation can be difficult to resolve because Indonesians prefer to ignore or deny them. Patience and continuous friendliness pay strong dividends. In extreme situations, use a mediator, ideally the party who initially introduced you.

Decision Making – The country's business culture is very hierarchical. However, decision making is normally a group process in the Philippines. This can be confusing for Westerners looking to identify the 'key decision maker' in an organization. While a senior manager usually makes the final decision, this is only the end of a process that involves many stakeholders who establish consensus through a series of deliberations. There is never a sense that any individual has the 'final say.' This decision process can take a long time and requires patience. Influencing the decision making requires building strong relationships with as many of the stakeholders as you possibly can.

When making decisions, Filipinos usually consider the specific situation rather than applying universal principles. Personal feelings and experiences weigh much more strongly than empirical evidence and other objective facts do. Most Filipinos are moderate risk takers.

Agreements and Contracts

Capturing and exchanging written understandings after meetings and at key negotiation stages is useful. Oral commitments may sound stronger than what your Filipino counterparts may be willing to put in writing. If possible, get a written agreement at each stage of your negotiation. Written agreements may be honored even if they are not a formal contract.

Written contracts tend to be lengthy and often spell out very detailed terms and conditions for the core agreements as well as for many eventualities. Nevertheless, writing up and signing the contract is a formality. Filipinos believe that the primary strength of an agreement lies in the partners' commitment rather than in its written documentation. Contracts need to be registered with Filipino government administration to be legal.

It is recommended to consult a local legal expert before signing a contract. However, do not bring your attorney to the negotiation table as it may be viewed as a sign of mistrust.

Contracts are usually dependable, and the agreed terms are viewed as binding. Requests to change contract details after signature may meet with strong resistance.

Signed contracts may not always be honored. This depends to no small degree on the strength of the continuing relationship between the contract partners. It is strongly advisable to continue staying in touch and maintaining the trust of your Filipino business partner. Business partners usually expect the other side to remain somewhat flexible if conditions change, which may include agreeing to modify contract terms.

Women in Business

Compared with other Asian countries, women are relatively emancipated in the Philippines. However, *machismo* attitudes remain strong. Women may be considered inferior, and they rarely attain positions of similar income and authority as men.

Female business travelers should exercise caution and act professionally in business and social situations. Displaying confidence and some degree of assertiveness can be effective, but it is very important not to appear overly bold and aggressive.

Other Important Things to Know

Proper attire is very important when doing business here. Male business visitors should wear dark suits on most occasions.

Business meals and entertainment, including breakfasts, lunches, dinners, banquets, and other evening events, are frequent. These events help advance the vital process of building strong relationships and growing your network. Business may not be discussed during these events. To prevent loss of face, always accept offers for food or drinks.

Especially with local companies that lack international expertise, business entertainment may sometimes include invitations Westerners may find inappropriate. In such cases, it will be very important to find a way to avoid the issue without openly rejecting the invitation, as this helps preserve *face* for all involved.

Social events do not require strict punctuality. While it is best to arrive at dinners close to the agreed time, being late to a party by 15 to 30 minutes or more is expected.

Gift giving is quite common in social and business settings in the Philippines. If you received one, it is best to reciprocate with an item of similar value that is typical of your home country. Fashion articles are often welcome. Do not open gifts in the presence of the giver unless your host did so first.

Topics to avoid in conversation include poverty in the country and the widespread corruption in politics and business.

Poland

Owing to the country's history within the former Eastern Bloc until the early 1990's, businesspeople and officials in Poland may have only limited exposure to other cultures except for neighboring countries. However, many Poles, especially among younger generations, have gained greater international experience since then and are open-minded.

Culturally quite homogeneous, Poland shows an interesting mix of influences from West and East. Having been seized and occupied by foreign powers many times, it always re-emerged with an even stronger sense of national pride. Poles may be less individualistic than other Eastern Europeans, leaving the entrepreneurial spirit in the country somewhat underdeveloped.

Relationships and Respect

Poland's culture expects its members to have a sense of belonging to and conforming with their group. At the same time, it leaves some room for individual preferences. Building lasting and trusting relationships is important and can be vital for the success of your business interactions. Generally, it is best to give your counterparts time to become comfortable with you. This may include asking and answering many personal questions. You may also have to prove yourself through diligent follow-up in order to gain your counterparts trust, which can be a very slow process. Patience is important in this country.

Business relationships in Poland exist both at the individual and company level. Poles usually want to do business only with those they like and trust. However, if your company replaces you with someone else over the course of a negotiation, it may be easy for your replacement to take things over from where you left them. Likewise, if you introduce someone else from your company into an existing business relationship, that person may quickly be accepted as a valid business partner.

In Poland's business culture, the respect a person enjoys depends primarily on his or her rank and achievements. Admired personal traits include persistence and resourcefulness.

Communication

The country's official language, Polish, is closely related with Czech. Many people also speak Russian. Younger businesspeople often speak English at a conversational level. With others, including older people and most high-ranking managers, it may be useful to engage an interpreter. To avoid offending the other side, ask beforehand whether an interpreter should be present at a meeting. When communicating in English, speak in short, simple sentences and avoid using slang and jargon. It will help people with a limited command of English if you speak slowly, summarize your key points often, and pause frequently to allow for interpretation.

People in this country usually speak softly. While they may occasionally raise their voices to make a point, they dislike loud and boisterous behavior. At restaurants, especially those used for business lunches and dinners, keep conversations at a quiet level. Poles generally converse while standing around three feet apart.

While the communication may initially be rather indirect, it will likely become much more direct, to the point of bluntness, once a Pole knows and trusts you. At that point, people may show emotions openly and do not find it difficult to say 'no' if they dislike a request or proposal.

Physical contact between people is infrequent. Avoid touching others. Eye contact should be frequent, as this conveys sincerity and helps build trust. However, do not stare at people.

Initial Contacts and Meetings

Choosing a local intermediary who can leverage existing relationships to make the initial contact is useful. This person will help bridge the gap between cultures, allowing you to conduct business with greater effectiveness. In addition, the person's help in getting things organized can be very important in Poland's sometimes-chaotic business environment. If you cannot find an intermediary, at least get a letter of introduction from someone who is well connected to your targeted business partners. Negotiations in Poland can be conducted by individuals or teams of negotiators.

Scheduling meetings in advance is required. However, you can sometimes do this on short notice if the parties had previous business interactions. Confirm your meeting several times, and be prepared for your counterparts to cancel or postpone meetings with little or no notice. While meetings may not always start on time, Poles expect foreign visitors to be punctual. Avoid being more than 5 to 10 minutes late.

Names are usually given in the order of first name, family name. Use *Mr./Ms.* plus the family name. If a person has an academic or professional title, it is best, though not always required, to use it instead, followed by the family name. Only close friends call each other by their first names. Introductions are accompanied by handshakes. If you did not catch the name of a person who introduced himself or herself, do not hesitate to ask for repetition. Getting the pronunciation right is important, and the effort will be appreciated.

The exchange of business cards is an essential step when meeting someone for the first time, so bring more than you need. You may not always get one in return, though. Most businesspeople in Poland read English, so there is no need to have your card translated. Show doctorate degrees on your card and make sure that it clearly states your professional title, especially if you have the seniority to make decisions. When presenting your card, smile and keep eye contact, then take a few moments to look at the card you received. Next, place the card on the table in front of you or into your card case.

Meetings usually start with some small talk intended to establish personal rapport. People appreciate a sense of humor, but keep it light and friendly, and be careful not to overdo it. Business is a serious matter in Poland. The first meeting may be very formal, but this usually gets more relaxed down the road. Its primary purpose is to become acquainted and build relationships. Business may be discussed, but do not try to hurry along with your agenda. It is unrealistic to expect initial meetings to lead to straight decisions.

Presentation materials can be simple without colorful backgrounds and fancy graphs. However, good and easy-to-understand visuals are important. Use diagrams and pictures wherever feasible, cut down on words, and avoid complicated expressions. Having your handout materials translated to Polish is not a must, but it helps in getting your messages across.

Negotiation

Attitudes and Styles – To the Poles, negotiating is usually a joint problem-solving process. While the buyer is in a superior position, both sides in a business deal own the responsibility to reach agreement. They may focus equally on near-term and long-term benefits. Although the primary negotiation style is somewhat competitive, Poles nevertheless value long-term relationships and look for win-win solutions. Polish negotiators may at times appear highly competitive and somewhat adversarial. However, even when negotiating in a fairly direct and aggressive fashion, they will ultimately be interested in finding a solution both sides can accept. It is best to remain calm, friendly, patient, and persistent, never taking anything personally.

Should a dispute arise at any stage of a negotiation, you might be able to reach resolution by focusing on logical arguments and facts. In extreme situations, use a mediator, ideally the party who initially introduced you.

Sharing of Information – Polish negotiators usually play their cards close to the chest, although some may share information as a way to build trust.

Pace of Negotiation – Although the pace of business is increasing, expect negotiations to be slow and protracted. Be patient, control your emotions, and accept that delays may occur.

If your counterparts appear to be stalling the negotiation, assess carefully whether their slowing down the process indicates that they are evaluating alternatives or that they are not interested in doing business with you. More often than not, though, this behavior indicates an attempt to create time pressure or 'wear you down' in order to obtain concessions.

Bargaining – While businesspeople in the country may have learned the ground rules of international negotiations, their experience is usually limited. Most of them are not fond of bargaining and dislike haggling. However, Poles may be patient and persistent negotiators, and it can be difficult to obtain concessions from them. The bargaining stage of a negotiation can be extensive. Concessions never come easily, and prices rarely move by more than 20 to 30 percent between initial offers and final agreement.

Deceptive techniques might be used and it may be effective to use some of them yourself. This includes tactics such as telling lies and sending fake non-verbal messages, pretending to be disinterested in the whole deal or in single concessions, misrepresenting an item's value, or making false demands and concessions. 'Good cop, bad cop' may be used on either side of the negotiation table. Poles may also claim limited authority, stating that they have to ask for their manager's approval. This could be a tactic or the truth.

Negotiators in the country may use pressure techniques that include intransigence, making final or expiring offers, or nibbling. When using similar tactics yourself, clearly explain your offer and avoid being overly aggressive. Final offers may come more than once and may or may not be final. Silence can be an effective way to signal rejection of a proposal. Be careful when using pressure tactics such as applying time pressure or making expiring offers. Your counterparts may consider these inappropriate unless they are strongly interested in your offer and clearly understand the rationale behind the approach. Otherwise, while the negotiation is not necessarily over, it may become less constructive.

Though they may appear aggressive, Polish negotiators are rarely openly adversarial. Threats and warnings may be used, but Poles rarely openly display anger or walk out of the room. Extreme openings may be viewed as unfriendly. It is best to open with an offer that is already in the ballpark of what you really expect.

Emotional negotiation techniques, such as attitudinal bargaining, sending dual messages, attempting to make you feel guilty, grimacing, or appealing to personal relationships, may occasionally be employed. It is best to remain calm. At times, Poles may also employ defensive tactics such as blocking or changing the subject, asking probing or very direct questions, making promises, or keeping an inflexible position.

Introducing written terms and conditions may be effective as this approach could lend credibility to your position.

As the country is moving from a socialist country to a free-market economy, corruption and bribery have become quite common in Poland's public and private sectors. However, people may draw the line differently, viewing minor payments as rewards for getting a job done rather than as bribes. Also, keep in mind that there is a fine line between giving gifts and bribing. What you may consider a bribe, a Pole may view as only a nice gift. It may help if you introduce and explain your company's policies early on, but be careful not to moralize or appear to imply that local customs are unethical.

Decision Making – Companies are often very hierarchical, and people expect to work within clearly established lines of authority. Openly disagreeing with or criticizing superiors is unacceptable. Decision makers are primarily senior managers who consider the best interest of the group or organization. They may sometimes delegate their authority to lower levels in the hierarchy. Others are often consulted in a committee-style process in order to reach greater consensus over and support of the decision. This process can take a long time and requires patience. Although the most senior manager involved may not be the sole decision maker, it is strongly advisable to make contact with him, seeking to get his support.

When making decisions, businesspeople usually consider not only universal principles, but also the specific situation. Empirical evidence and other objective facts weigh more strongly than personal feelings and experiences do, but they will consider all aspects. Poles are often reluctant to take risks. If you expect them to support a risky decision, you may need to find ways for them to become comfortable with it first, for instance by explaining contingency plans, outlining areas of additional support, or by offering guarantees and warranties.

Agreements and Contracts

Capturing and exchanging meeting summaries can be an effective way to verify understanding and commitments. Although Poles usually keep interim agreements, do not consider these final. Only a contract signed by both parties constitutes a binding agreement.

Written contracts tend to be lengthy. They often spell out detailed terms and conditions for the core agreements as well as for many eventualities. Signing the contract is important not only from a legal perspective, but also as a strong confirmation of your Polish partners' commitment.

It is recommended to consult a local legal expert before signing a contract. However, do not bring your attorney to the negotiation table as it may be viewed as a sign of mistrust.

Signed contracts may not always be honored. This depends to no small degree on the strength of the continuing relationship between the contract partners. It is strongly advisable to continue staying in touch and maintaining the trust of your Polish business partner. Business partners usually expect the other side to remain somewhat flexible if conditions change, which may include agreeing to modify contract terms.

Women in Business

While women enjoy the same rights as men, few Polish women have made it into senior management positions and most are still struggling to attain positions of similar income and authority as men. As a visiting businesswoman, emphasize your company's importance and your role in it. A personal introduction or at least a letter of support from a senior executive within your company may also help.

Female business travelers should exercise caution and act professionally in business and social situations. Male chivalry is a sign of good manners and should be graciously accepted. For instance, the hand-kiss is an old Polish custom which some men still follow; it should never be refused. Displaying confidence and some degree of assertiveness can be effective, but it is very important not to appear overly bold and aggressive.

Other Important Things to Know

Conservative attire is important when doing business here. Male business visitors should wear suits on most occasions. While you do not want to appear 'overdressed,' make sure shoes and suit are in good condition.

Punctuality is also valued in most social settings. It is best to be right on time for dinners, and to arrive at parties within 5 to 10 minutes of the agreed time.

Gift giving in business settings is rare. It is best not to bring a gift to an initial meeting in order to avoid raising suspicions about your motives.

Portugal

Though Portugal's culture is quite homogeneous, its businesspeople, especially those among younger generations, are usually experienced in interacting and doing business with visitors from other cultures. However, that does not always mean that they are open-minded. When negotiating business here, realize that people may expect things to be done 'their way.'

The country's business environment changed dramatically over the last 40 years. It went from being backward and mostly agrarian to becoming a market-driven economy that can be surprisingly modern. However, while more and more Portuguese companies have received foreign investment and embraced modern management techniques, other industries and enterprises still hold on the traditional style of doing business.

Most Portuguese are very proud of their country. It is advisable to familiarize yourself with some of its rich history as showing at least a little knowledge about it will be viewed very favorably.

Relationships and Respect

Portugal's culture expects its members to have a sense of belonging to and conforming with their group. At the same time, it leaves some room for individual preferences. Building lasting and trusting personal relationships is critically important to most Portuguese, who often expect to establish strong bonds prior to closing any deals. People in this country usually want to do business only with those they know, like, and trust. Establishing productive business cooperation requires a long-term perspective and commitment. Consequently, proceed with serious business discussions only after your counterparts have become very comfortable with you. This can be a time-consuming process. The Portuguese tend to distrust people who appear unwilling to spend the time or whose motives for relationship building are unclear.

Business relationships in this country exist between people, not necessarily between companies. Even when you have won your local business partners' friendship and trust, they will not necessarily trust others from your company. That makes it very important to keep company interfaces unchanged. Changing a key contact may require the relationship building process to start over.

Establishing personal relationships with others in Portugal can create powerful networks and is vital to doing business. Whether people think you are worth knowing and trusting often weighs much more strongly than what proposals you have to make. Personal networks may open doors and solve problems that would otherwise be very difficult to master. Maintaining honest and cordial relations is crucial. Third party introductions can be very helpful as a starting point to building a trusting relationship with a potential partner.

While the Portuguese are usually warm and friendly, they are also very proud. 'Saving face' and respecting everyone's honor and personal pride are crucial for doing business in the country. Openly criticizing someone in front of others, or even one-on-one, can have a devastating impact on your negotiation. The importance of diplomatic restraint and tact cannot be overestimated. Keep your cool and never show that you are upset. Avoid open conflict, and know that politeness is crucial.

In Portugal's business culture, the respect a person enjoys depends primarily on his or her status, rank, and age. It is important to treat elderly people with great respect. Admired personal traits include kindness, flexibility, and sociability.

Communication

The country's official languages are Portuguese and Mirandese. The former dominates. Many businesspeople speak at least some English. With older high-ranking managers, it may nevertheless be useful to engage an interpreter. To avoid offending the other side, ask beforehand whether an interpreter should be present at a meeting. When communicating in English, speak in short, simple sentences and avoid using jargon and slang. It will help people with a limited command of English if you speak slowly, summarize your key points often, and pause frequently to allow for interpretation.

While discussions may sometimes get lively, the Portuguese dislike loud and boisterous behavior. At restaurants, especially those used for business lunches and dinners, keep conversations at a quiet level. People may show their emotions openly. However, it is crucial that you never lose your temper or appear impatient, as there is always a risk of hurting someone's pride. People generally converse standing around two to three feet apart, which is not as close as in many Latin American cultures.

Communication in Portugal is rather indirect. The Portuguese often prefer to be careful about what they say and how they say it. People may not get straight to the point when trying to get a message across. In addition, they may tell you what they think you want to hear rather than what they really think. They might insist that everything is in perfect order, even when this is not the case. In conversations, silence is rare and usually signals that there is a problem. You may have to read between the lines or watch for non-verbal clues to understand what is being conveyed. In difficult situations, look for other contacts in your network that may be able to help you find out or interpret what is going on. It is beneficial to use a similarly indirect approach when dealing with the Portuguese, as they may perceive you as rude and pushy if you are too direct. The communication may become a little more direct and frank once a strong relationship has been established.

Gestures are usually subtle. It is advisable to restrict your body language. Non-verbal communication is important, though, and you should carefully watch for others' small hints, just as they will be watching you. Physical contact is rare and usually limited to friends. Pointing at people or objects is impolite. Instead, wave your open hand toward the object. The American *OK* sign, with thumb and index finger forming a circle, is an obscene gesture in Portugal. Eye contact should be frequent, almost to the point of staring. This conveys sincerity and helps build trust. Anger may sometimes be masked with a smile.

Initial Contacts and Meetings

Choosing a local intermediary who can leverage existing relationships to make the initial contact is useful. This person will help bridge the gap between cultures, allowing you to conduct business with greater effectiveness.

Negotiations in the country can be conducted by individuals or teams of negotiators. It is vital that teams be well aligned, with roles clearly assigned to each member. Changing a team member may require the relationship building process to start over and should therefore be avoided.

If possible, schedule meetings at least one to two weeks in advance. Since the Portuguese want to know whom they will be meeting, provide details on titles, positions, and responsibilities of attendees ahead of time. They will expect to do business with the decision-maker in your organization. The most senior executive to attend on the Portuguese side will be at a similar level in the hierarchy as your own negotiation leader. An agenda may get set upfront, but this is only a formality. It will likely not be strictly followed. While meetings often start late, people generally expect foreign visitors to be punctual. Avoid being more than 10 to 15 minutes late, and call ahead if you will be. Displaying anger if you have to wait only reflects poorly on you.

Names are usually given in the order of first name, family name. Some Portuguese may have two family names, the first one from their father and the second from their mother. Use *Mr./Ms.* or *Senhor/Senhora*, plus the person's family name. If there are two family names, use the father's. If a person has an academic title, use it instead, followed by the family name. Only close friends call each other by their first names. Introductions are accompanied by firm handshakes.

The exchange of business cards is an essential step when meeting someone for the first time, so bring more than you need. It is advantageous to use cards with one side in English and the other in Portuguese. Show doctorate degrees on your card and make sure that it clearly states your professional title, especially if you have the seniority to make decisions. Smile and keep eye contact while accepting someone else's card, then take a few moments to look at it. Next, place the card on the table in front of you.

Meetings start with small talk, which can be very extensive. It is important to be patient and let the other side set the pace. Questions should not get too personal. Initial meetings may appear somewhat formal, but the atmosphere usually is more relaxed in subsequent meetings as the relationship develops. A sense of humor will be appreciated as long as it is not sarcastic or cynical. Meetings in Portugal may appear somewhat chaotic, with frequent interruptions and several parallel conversations. Do not take this personally; it also does not indicate a lack of interest.

The primary purpose of the first meeting is to become acquainted and build relationships. Business may be discussed, but do not try to hurry along with your agenda. The goal should be to establish respect and trust between yourself and your counterparts. It is unrealistic to expect initial meetings to lead to straight decisions. In addition, it is rare to get open opinions at the conference table, so watch for subtle clues and use other opportunities such as one-on-one conversations or business dinners to learn more.

Presentation materials should be attractive, with good and clear visuals. Use diagrams and pictures wherever feasible, cut down on words, and avoid complicated expressions. Having your handout materials translated to Portuguese is not a must, but it helps in getting your messages across.

Negotiation

Attitudes and Styles – To the Portuguese, negotiating is usually a joint problem-solving process. While the buyer is in a superior position, both sides in a business deal own the responsibility to reach agreement. Although both sides must make a long-term commitment to their business engagement, the Portuguese usually expect it to result in near-term benefits. The primary negotiation style is cooperative and people may be open to compromising if viewed helpful in order to move the negotiation forward. It is vitally important to remain relaxed and non-confrontational throughout the bargaining exchange. Nevertheless, there may be attempts to win competitive advantages, which should not be taken negatively. The culture ultimately promotes a win-win approach and values reaching consensus. You will earn your counterparts' respect by maintaining a positive, persistent attitude.

Sharing of Information – Even when personal relationships are strong, your Portuguese counterparts may be reluctant to share information openly. Many believe that privileged information creates bargaining advantages or that opening up could expose weakness. If you receive information, do not take it at face value. For instance, your counterparts may signal that quality and delivery are significant decision factors even if they are only interested in price.

Pace of Negotiation – Expect negotiations to be very slow and protracted. The Portuguese do not hurry and dislike people who do. They also have little respect for deadlines. Be prepared to make several trips if necessary to achieve your objectives. Information gathering, bargaining, and decision making may take considerable time. Attempts to rush the process are unlikely to produce better results and may be viewed as offensive. Throughout the negotiation, be patient, control your emotions, and accept that delays occur.

Most Portuguese prefer a polychronic work style. They are used to pursuing multiple actions and goals in parallel. When negotiating, they often take a holistic approach and may jump back and forth between topics rather than addressing them in sequential order. Negotiators from strongly monochronic cultures, such as Germany, the United Kingdom, or the United States, may find this style confusing, irritating, and even annoying. In any case, do not show irritation or anger when encountering this behavior. Instead, keep track of the bargaining progress at all times, often emphasizing areas where agreement already exists.

Portuguese negotiators may sometimes request urgent changes. This is often a way to test your flexibility.

If your counterparts appear to be stalling the negotiation, assess carefully whether their slowing down the process indicates that they are evaluating alternatives or that they are not interested in doing business with you. While such behavior could represent attempts to create time pressure in order to obtain concessions, the slow decision process in the country is far more likely causing the lack of progress. People from fast-paced cultures tend to underestimate how much time this takes and often make the mistake of trying to 'speed things up.' Again, patience and persistence are vitally important.

Bargaining – Most of the Portuguese are used to bargaining, but many dislike haggling. Confrontation and open competition make them uncomfortable. The bargaining exchange can nevertheless be extensive, and prices may move by about 25 to 35 percent between initial offers and final agreement. Leave yourself sufficient room for concessions at different stages. The Portuguese can be very flexible when trying to find workable solutions. If needed, show willingness to compromise as a way to preserve the honor of both parties. After making concessions, always ask the other side to reciprocate. You can use the fact that aspects can be re-visited to your advantage, for instance by offering further concessions under the condition that the Portuguese side reciprocate in areas that had already been agreed upon.

Deceptive techniques are frequent and can be effective. This includes tactics such as telling lies and sending fake non-verbal messages, misrepresenting an item's value, or making false demands and concessions. Your Portuguese counterparts may make other attempts to mislead you in order to obtain bargaining advantages. Even when you can see right through a lie, it would be a grave personal insult to state or even hint that your counterpart is not telling the truth. It is advisable to verify information received from the local side through other channels. Portuguese negotiators rarely use 'good cop, bad cop' and it is best to avoid the tactic since the implications for relationships can be significant. They may claim limited authority, stating that they have to ask for their manager's approval. This could be a tactic or the truth. Since you must avoid causing loss of face, be cautious when using the techniques of making false demands or false concessions. Any overt attempts to bluff your counterparts could backfire.

Negotiators in the country may occasionally use pressure techniques that include making final offers or nibbling. Final offers should not be made too soon since your counterpart may not believe that you are serious. Do not use tactics such as applying time pressure or making expiring offers. The Portuguese could view these as signs that you are not willing to build a long-term relationship and may choose to terminate the negotiation. Avoid pressure tactics such as opening with your best offer or showing intransigence, since they cannot be applied effectively without running the risk of causing loss of face. Silence can be an effective way to signal rejection of a proposal.

Portuguese negotiators avoid most aggressive or adversarial techniques since they affect face. The risk of using any of them yourself is rarely worth the potential gain. Extreme openings may be viewed as unfriendly and will rarely work to your advantage. Never walk out or threaten to do so in an aggressive fashion as your counterparts will likely take this as a personal insult and may end all talks. However, threatening a 'friendly walkout' while strongly emphasizing the relationship may be very effective.

Emotional negotiation techniques, such as attitudinal bargaining, attempting to make you feel guilty, or appealing to personal relationships, are frequent and can be effective. Be cautious not to hurt someone's personal pride when employing any of these tactics, though. At times, defensive tactics such as blocking or changing the subject, asking probing or very direct questions, or making promises may be used.

Corruption and bribery are rare in Portugal, though not completely unheard of. Both legally and ethically, it is advisable to stay away from giving gifts of significant value or making offers that could be read as bribery.

Conflicts and disputes that may arise during a negotiation can be difficult to resolve because the Portuguese may ignore or deny them. Otherwise, you might be able to reach resolution by focusing on logical arguments and facts. Ask your counterparts to suggest alternatives if needed.

Decision Making – The country's business culture is very hierarchical and superiors enjoy strong deference. Communication is expected to take place across similar levels in the hierarchy and it could damage the respect you enjoy if you spent much time and attention on someone you outrank. Decision makers are usually senior executives who are often autocratic but will consider the best interest of the group or organization. Subordinates, and even senior managers, can be quite reluctant to accept responsibility. Decision makers rarely delegate their authority, so it is important to deal with senior executives. Decision making can take a long time and requires patience. Attempts to rush or put pressure on the process is an affront to Portuguese business protocol.

When making decisions, businesspeople usually consider the specific situation rather than applying universal principles. Personal feelings and experiences weigh much more strongly than empirical evidence and other objective facts do. The Portuguese are often uneasy with change and reluctant to take risks. If you expect them to support a risky decision, you may need to find ways for them to become comfortable with it first, for instance by explaining contingency plans, outlining areas of additional support, or by offering guarantees and warranties.

Agreements and Contracts

Capturing and exchanging meeting summaries can be an effective way to verify understanding. However, commitments may not be fulfilled even if they sounded strong. Gentle reminders between meetings are often helpful. Even when you receive written commitments during a negotiation, you may sometimes find that they are not kept. Any part of an agreement may still change significantly before both parties sign the final contract.

Written contracts tend to be lengthy and often spell out very detailed terms and conditions for the core agreements as well as for many eventualities. Nevertheless, writing up and signing the contract is a formality. The Portuguese believe that the primary strength of an agreement lies in the partners' commitment rather than in its written documentation.

It is advisable to consult a local legal expert before signing a contract. However, do not bring your attorney to the negotiation table. The Portuguese may read it as a sign of mistrust if you do.

Signed contracts may not always be honored. Since the justice system works very slowly, they are also difficult to enforce. It is important to be prepared for some frustration and to consider the possibility of being ripped off. The most important factor is the strength of the continuing relationship between the contract partners. It is strongly advisable to continue staying in touch and maintaining the trust of your Portuguese business partner. Business partners usually expect the other side to remain somewhat flexible if conditions change, which may include agreeing to modify contract terms.

Women in Business

Machismo attitudes remain strong in this country. While becoming more common in business, women still have a hard time attaining positions of similar income and authority as men. As a visiting businesswoman, emphasize your company's importance and your role in it. A personal introduction or at least a letter of support from a senior executive within your company may help a lot.

Female business travelers should graciously accept any chivalric gestures they receive, while exercising caution and acting professionally in business and social situations. Displaying confidence and some degree of assertiveness can be effective, but
it is very important not to appear overly bold and aggressive.

Other Important Things to Know

Conservative, good attire is very important when doing business here. Male business visitors should wear dark suits with neckties on most occasions.

Business meals are important opportunities for relationship building. Business is
rarely discussed over dinner.

Social events do not require strict punctuality. While it is best to arrive at dinners
close to the agreed time, being late to a party by at least 15 minutes is expected and
a longer delay is still acceptable.

Gift giving in business settings is rare, especially early in your engagement. It is
best not to bring a gift to an initial meeting in order to avoid raising suspicions
about your motives. However, partners may exchange small gifts when the contract
is signed.

Romania

Owing to the country's history within the former Eastern Bloc until 1996, many
businesspeople and officials in Romania may have only limited exposure to other
cultures except for neighboring countries. Its culture is quite homogeneous. When
negotiating business here, realize that people may expect things to be done 'their
way.' However, some among younger generations may have greater international
experience and can be open-minded.

Relationships and Respect

Though it leaves some room for individual preferences, Romania's culture expects
its members to have a sense of belonging to and conforming with their group. Building lasting and trusting personal relationships is very important and can be crucial
for your business success. People in this country usually want to do business only
with those they know and like. Consequently, proceed with serious business discussions only after your counterparts have become very comfortable with you. This
may include asking and answering many personal questions. Romanians tend to
distrust people who appear unwilling to spend the time or whose motives for relationship building are unclear. Establishing productive business relationships is a
slow process that requires a long-term perspective and commitment. As a reward,
they may last forever.

Business relationships in this country exist between people, not necessarily between
companies. Even when you have won your local business partners' friendship and
trust, they will not necessarily trust others from your company. That makes it very

important to keep company interfaces unchanged. Changing a key contact may require the relationship building process to start over.

Establishing relationships with others in Romania can create powerful networks. Maintaining cordial relations is crucial. Third party introductions can be very helpful as a starting point to building a trusting relationship with a potential partner, especially since people may initially not trust outsiders who are neither part of their family nor of their circle of friends. Always remain modest and demonstrate humility. Romanians dislike people who boast and brag.

In Romania's business culture, the respect a person enjoys depends primarily on his or her age and status. It is important to treat elderly people with great respect. Admired personal traits include modesty and humility.

Communication

The country's official language is Romanian. French is the most widely spoken foreign language. Many businesspeople speak at least some English, but often not well. Especially with older people, among them most high-ranking managers, it may be useful to engage an interpreter. To avoid offending the other side, ask beforehand whether an interpreter should be present at a meeting. When communicating in English, speak in short, simple sentences and avoid using slang and jargon. It will help people with a limited command of English if you speak slowly, summarize your key points often, and pause frequently to allow for interpretation.

People in this country usually speak softly. While they may occasionally raise their voices to make a point, they dislike loud and boisterous behavior. At restaurants, especially those used for business lunches and dinners, keep conversations at a quiet level. Emotions are not shown openly. People generally converse while standing around two to three feet apart.

As a rule, Romanians avoid being too direct as they view it as poor manners. At least initially, the communication can be quite indirect since people are cautious. Some may say what they think you want to hear. However, they may gradually open up and become more straightforward, which may then include direct 'no' responses.

Romanians keep physical contact infrequent. Body language and gestures may be extensive, though, and people may show emotions openly. The American *OK* (thumb and index finger forming a circle) sign is an obscene gestures in Romania. The thumbs-up gesture is positive as it signals approval. Eye contact should be frequent, almost to the point of staring. This conveys sincerity and helps build trust.

Initial Contacts and Meetings

Choosing a local intermediary who can leverage existing relationships to make the initial contact is useful. This person will help bridge the gap between cultures, allowing you to conduct business with greater effectiveness. In addition, the person's help in getting things organized can be very important in Romania's sometimes-chaotic business environment. Negotiations in Romania can be conducted by individuals or teams of negotiators. Although Romania's culture is generally group-oriented, meetings are often held on a one-on-one basis. You will probably not meet the top executive of an organization at the first meeting, so be prepared to deal with subordinates. They may have significant influence over the final decision.

If possible, schedule meetings at least two to three weeks in advance. Since people want to know whom they will be meeting, provide details on titles, positions, and responsibilities of attendees ahead of time. Romanians tend to be relatively punctual. Being late by more than 10 to 15 minutes without having a valid and plausible excuse can be an offense. However, displaying anger if you have to wait reflects poorly on you.

Names are usually given in the order of first name, family name. Use *Mr./Ms.* or *Domnul/Doamna*, plus the family name. If a person has an academic or professional title, always use it instead, followed by the family name. Only close friends call each other by their first names. Introductions are accompanied by handshakes.

The exchange of business cards is an essential step when meeting someone for the first time, so bring more than you need. You may not always get one in return, though. While it is beneficial to use cards with one side in English and the other in Romanian, using cards that are only in English or in French is acceptable. Show doctorate degrees on your card and make sure that it clearly states your professional title, especially if you have the seniority to make decisions. When presenting your card, smile and keep eye contact, then take a few moments to look at the card you received. Next, place the card on the table in front of you or into your card case.

Meetings usually start with some small talk intended to establish personal rapport, which could be brief. The first meeting may be very formal and reserved, but this usually gets more relaxed down the road. Its primary purpose is to become acquainted and build relationships. Business may be discussed, but do not try to hurry along with your agenda. It is unrealistic to expect initial meetings to lead to straight decisions.

Romanian negotiators may try to convince you that they have the background and experience required to be successful. Businesspeople may exaggerate their capabilities or make questionable promises in order to maintain foreign contacts.

Presentation materials can be simple without colorful backgrounds and fancy graphs. However, good and easy-to-understand visuals are important. Use diagrams and pictures wherever feasible, cut down on words, and avoid complicated expressions. Having your handout materials translated to Romanian is not a must, but it helps in getting your messages across.

Negotiation

Attitudes and Styles – To Romanians, negotiating is usually a joint problem-solving process. While the buyer is in a superior position, both sides in a business deal own the responsibility to reach agreement. Given the current turmoil in the country, negotiators may focus mostly on the near-term benefits of the business deal. Although the primary negotiation style is competitive, Romanians nevertheless value long-term relationships and look for win-win solutions. They avoid any open confrontation as it could damage relationships. It is best to remain calm, friendly, patient, and persistent, never taking anything personally.

Should a dispute arise at any stage of a negotiation, you might be able to reach resolution by focusing on logical arguments and facts. In extreme situations, use a mediator, ideally the party who initially introduced you.

Sharing of Information – Romanian negotiators usually play their cards close to the chest, although some may share information as a way to build trust.

Keep in mind that humility is a virtue in Romanian business culture. If you make exaggerated claims in an effort to impress the other side or to obtain concessions, they will likely investigate your claims before responding.

Pace of Negotiation – Expect negotiations to be slow and protracted. Relationship building, information gathering, bargaining, and decision making may all take considerable time. Be prepared to make several trips if necessary to achieve your objectives. Throughout the negotiation, be patient, show little emotion, and accept that delays occur.

Romanians generally employ a polychronic work style. They are used to pursuing multiple actions and goals in parallel. When negotiating, they often take a holistic approach and may jump back and forth between topics rather than addressing them in sequential order. Negotiators from strongly monochronic cultures, such as Germany, the United Kingdom, or the United States, may find this style confusing, irritating, and even annoying. In any case, do not show irritation or anger when encountering this behavior. Instead, keep track of the bargaining progress at all times, often emphasizing areas where agreement already exists.

If your counterparts appear to be stalling the negotiation, assess carefully whether their slowing down the process indicates that they are evaluating alternatives or that they are not interested in doing business with you. More often than not, though, this behavior indicates an attempt to create time pressure or 'wear you down' in order to obtain concessions.

Bargaining – While businesspeople in the country may have learned the ground rules of international negotiations, their experience is usually limited. They are used to bargaining but not overly fond of haggling. However, Romanians can be tough and persistent negotiators, and it may be difficult to obtain concessions from them. The bargaining stage of a negotiation can be extensive. Though concessions never come easily, prices may move by about 25 to 40 percent between initial offers and final agreement. Leave yourself sufficient room for concessions at different stages. When conceding, present this as a decision you made because you like and respect your counterpart. Ask the other side to reciprocate if you make concessions. You can use the fact that aspects can be re-visited to your advantage, for instance by offering further concessions under the condition that the Romanian side reciprocate in areas that had already been agreed upon.

Deceptive techniques might be used and it may be effective to use some of them yourself. This includes tactics such as telling lies and sending fake non-verbal messages, pretending to be disinterested in the whole deal or in single concessions, or misrepresenting an item's value. Romanians may play stupid or otherwise attempt to mislead you in order to obtain bargaining advantages. Lies may be easy to see through; otherwise, verify information received from the local side through other channels. Similarly, they treat 'outside' information with caution. When Romanians use 'good cop, bad cop,' which is rare, they may request occasional breaks so they can re-align their approach. They may claim limited authority, stating that they have to ask for their manager's approval. This could be a tactic or the truth. Be cautious when using the techniques of making false demands or false concessions. Overt attempts to bluff your counterparts could backfire.

Negotiators in Romania may use pressure techniques that include silence, making final offers, or nibbling. When using similar tactics yourself, clearly explain your offer and avoid being overly aggressive. Final offers may come more than once and are rarely final. Silence can be an effective way to signal rejection of a proposal. Be careful when using pressure tactics such as applying time pressure or making expiring offers. Your counterparts may consider these inappropriate unless they are strongly interested in your offer and clearly understand the rationale behind the approach. Otherwise, while the negotiation is not necessarily over, it may become less constructive.

Romanian negotiators avoid using overly aggressive or adversarial techniques. The risk of using any of them yourself is rarely worth the potential gain. Subtle threats and warnings may be used and often turn out to be bluffs. Since Romanians may view extreme openings as unfriendly, these are best avoided.

As in most strongly relationship-oriented cultures, negotiators may sometimes use emotional techniques such as attitudinal bargaining, attempting to make you feel guilty, grimacing, or appealing to personal relationships. Be cautious not to affect relationships when using any of them yourself.

At times, Romanians may also employ defensive tactics such as blocking or changing the subject, asking probing or direct questions, or making promises.

As the country is moving from a socialist country to a free-market economy, corruption and bribery have become quite common in Romania's public and private sectors. However, people may draw the line differently, viewing minor payments as rewards for getting a job done rather than as bribes. Also, keep in mind that there is a fine line between giving gifts and bribing. What you may consider a bribe, a Romanian may view as only a nice gift. It may help if you introduce and explain your company's policies early on, but be careful not to moralize or appear to imply that local customs are unethical.

Decision Making – Companies are often very hierarchical, and people expect to work within clearly established lines of authority. Openly disagreeing with or criticizing superiors is unacceptable. Decision makers are primarily senior managers who consider the best interest of the group or organization. They rarely delegate their authority to lower levels in the hierarchy, but others are often consulted in a committee-style process in order to reach greater consensus over and support of the decision. This process can take a long time and requires patience. Romanians usually indicate it if they are not interested in doing business.

When making decisions, businesspeople may not rely much on rules or laws. They usually consider the specific situation rather than applying universal principles. Empirical evidence and other objective facts weigh more strongly than personal feelings and experiences do, but they will consider all aspects. Romanians are often reluctant to take risks. If you expect them to support a risky decision, you may need to find ways for them to become comfortable with it first, for instance by explaining contingency plans, outlining areas of additional support, or by offering guarantees and warranties.

Agreements and Contracts

Capturing and exchanging written understandings after meetings and at key negotiation stages is useful. Oral commitments may sound stronger than what your Romanian counterparts may be willing to put in writing. However, these documents are not final agreements. Any part of an agreement may still change significantly before both parties sign the final contract.

Written contracts tend to be lengthy. They often spell out detailed terms and conditions for the core agreements as well as for many eventualities. Signing the contract is important not only from a legal perspective, but also as a strong confirmation of your Romanian partners' commitment.

Although your legal rights may not always be enforceable, you should consult a local legal expert before signing a contract. For the time being, it is wise to recognize that the country's legal system is in a transitional mode, so be prepared for laws to change on short notice. Since local financing can also be questionable, you may want to ask your counterpart for an irrevocable letter of credit from a local bank that is either a subsidiary or a correspondent of a western bank.

Signed contracts may not always be honored. This depends to no small degree on the strength of the continuing relationship between the contract partners. It is strongly advisable to continue staying in touch and maintaining the trust of your Romanian business partner. Business partners usually expect the other side to remain somewhat flexible if conditions change, which may include agreeing to modify contract terms.

Women in Business

Many Romanian women are working, and they are generally treated with extreme respect and courtesy. However, few have made it into senior management positions and most are still struggling to attain positions of similar income and authority. As a visiting businesswoman, emphasize your company's importance and your role in it. A personal introduction or at least a letter of support from a senior executive within your company may also help.

Female business travelers should exercise caution and act professionally in business and social situations. Displaying confidence and some degree of assertiveness can be effective, but it is very important not to appear overly bold and aggressive.

Other Important Things to Know

Conservative attire is important when doing business here. Male business visitors should wear suits on most occasions. While you do not want to appear 'overdressed,' make sure shoes and suit are in good condition.

Punctuality is also expected in most social settings. It is best to be right on time for dinners, and to arrive at parties within 15 minutes of the agreed time.

During small talk and other social conversations, you may be asked very personal questions. If you do not want to answer, smile or politely explain that such topics are not discussed openly in your culture.

Russia

Previously the leading state of the USSR, Russia became a separate country in 1991. Most businesspeople and officials in the country have little experience with other cultures except for its neighboring countries. There is still a widespread lack of free-market knowledge. It may be necessary to discuss and seek agreement over the definition of concepts such as fair play, good will, profit and loss, turnover, individual accountability, proprietary rights, and so forth. Even when you do, people's expectation may frequently be that things are done 'their way.'

You may find vast cultural differences within this culturally pluralistic country. Not only does the Russian Far East include a broad mix of cultural influences, but also there are notable differences between the western European region, with St. Petersburg as its most influential city, and the eastern European part around Moscow. On top of that, the dynamic political and economic changes of the past few years brought about a wide range of acceptable business behaviors. The information in this section can only provide general guidelines. When doing business in Russia, expect the unexpected.

Most Russians are very proud of their country. It would be a serious mistake to belittle its accomplishments or to refer to it as a 'loser' of the Cold War.

Relationships and Respect

Russia's culture expects its members to have a sense of belonging to and conforming with their group. At the same time, it leaves some room for individual preferences. Building lasting and trusting relationships is very important and can be crucial for your business success. If Russians engage in business without first establishing personal relationships, proceed with great caution. They may be looking to take unfair advantage of you if they get a chance. Generally, it is best to give your counterparts time to become comfortable with you. This includes letting them see your personal side, as Russians often mistrust people who are 'all business.' Relationship building is normally a slow process here, since people dislike being rushed or having to follow the fast-paced western approach. Patience is of critical importance in this country.

Business relationships in Russia usually exist both at the individual and company level. Russians may want to do business only with those they like and trust. However, if you introduce someone else from your company into an existing business relationship, that person may quickly be accepted as a valid business partner.

You may be able to establish trust by emphasizing common ground. For example, express your own distrust of authority or bureaucracy whenever there is an opportunity for it. However, refrain from praising or rewarding anyone in public. Unlike in many other cultures, it may raise suspicion about your motives.

In Russia's business culture, the respect a person enjoys depends primarily on his or her rank and status. Age and education are less important than in most other countries. Be careful never to come across as patronizing a senior Russian manager. Admired personal traits include firmness, sincerity, and dependability.

Communication

In addition to the country's official language, Russian, a number of minority languages exist. Not many businesspeople speak English fluently. In addition, Russians may insist that they understand everything you said even when this is not really the case. It may be necessary to have an interpreter. Ask beforehand whether an interpreter should be present at a meeting. However, keep in mind that even some interpreters may not speak and understand English at a fully proficient level. It may be in your best interest to bring your own interpreter, rather than depending on one provided by the Russians, to ensure an unbiased translation. When communicating in English, speak in short, simple sentences and avoid using slang and jargon. It will help people with a limited command of English if you speak slowly, summarize your key points often, and pause frequently to allow for interpretation.

While celebrations and social events can get very noisy, being loud may reflect poorly on you in most business settings. However, emotions are often shown openly. People generally converse while standing around two to three feet apart.

Communicating with Russians can be anything from very direct to rather indirect. On one hand, they may say *nyet* (no) frequently and you will have to figure out ways to get past that. In contrast, people may say things they think you want to hear as a way to lure you into a business deal.

Russians keep physical contact infrequent. While several gestures may be used, be careful to control your own. The American *OK* (thumb and index finger forming a circle) and 'V' signs are obscene gestures in Russia. Slapping the open hand over a fist can also be a vulgar gesture. Standing with your hands in your pockets may be considered rude. The thumbs-up gesture is positive as it signals approval. Eye contact should be frequent, almost to the point of staring. This conveys sincerity and helps build trust.

Initial Contacts and Meetings

Choosing a local intermediary who can leverage existing relationships to make the initial contact is useful. Assuming you identified someone who is respectable and trustworthy, this person will help bridge the gap between cultures, allowing you to conduct business with greater effectiveness. In addition, the person's help in getting things organized can be very important in Russia's sometimes-chaotic business environment. Negotiations in Russia can be conducted by individuals or teams of negotiators. Teams should be well aligned, with roles clearly assigned to each member. Russians may be very good at exploiting disagreements between members of the other team to their advantage.

If possible, schedule meetings at least two to three weeks in advance. Since Russians want to know whom they will be meeting, provide details on titles, positions, and responsibilities of attendees ahead of time. It is unlikely that you will meet the top executive of an organization at the first meeting, so be prepared to deal with subordinates. They may have significant influence over the final decision. Confirm your meeting several times, and be prepared for your counterparts to cancel or postpone meetings with little or no notice. Unless you are sure that your counterparts are sufficiently fluent in English, keeping your correspondence in Russian is strongly advisable.

While meetings may start considerably late, Russians expect foreign visitors to be punctual. Being late by more than 10 to 15 minutes without having a valid and plausible excuse can be an offense. Do not show signs of impatience if you have to wait, even if the other side is an hour or more late.

Russian names are normally given in the order of first name, middle name (derived from the father's first name, for instance *Ivanovich* = 'son of Ivan'), family name. In formal situations, the order may revert to family name, first name, middle name. People may sometimes be addressed with all three names. Otherwise, use *Mr./Ms.* plus the family name. If a person has an academic or professional title, it is very important to use it instead, followed by the family name. Before calling Russians by their first name, wait until they offer it. In that case, use a combination of first name and middle name, for example *Vladimir Ivanovich*. Introductions are accompanied by firm handshakes.

The exchange of business cards is an essential step when meeting someone for the first time, so bring more than you need. You may not always get one in return. It is beneficial to use cards with one side in English and the other in Russian. Show doctorate degrees on your card and make sure that it clearly states your professional title, especially if you have the seniority to make decisions. When presenting your card, ensure that the Russian side is facing the recipient. Smile and keep eye contact while accepting someone else's card, then take a few moments to look at it. Next, place the card on the table in front of you or into your card case.

Meetings usually start with small talk, which may range from short to extensive. Let your counterparts set the pace. The Russian side's primary objective for the initial meeting is to feel you out and assess your and your company's credibility. Remain firm and dignified without being distant, and avoid any patronizing or aggressive behavior. Business may be discussed, but do not try to hurry along with your agenda. It is unrealistic to expect initial meetings to lead to straight decisions. Meetings can often be lengthy and still not reach agreement.

Russian negotiators may try to convince you that they have the background and experience required to be successful. Businesspeople may exaggerate their capabilities or make questionable promises in order to maintain foreign contacts.

Presentations should be short and concise. Making a good first impression is at least as important as coming with a compelling proposal. It is characteristic of Russians to be pessimistic, though, so a lack of enthusiastic responses should not discourage you. Your presentation materials should be attractive, with good and clear visuals. Use diagrams and pictures wherever feasible, cut down on words, and avoid complicated expressions. Russians expect to discuss many details, so bring enough background information. Having your handout materials translated to Russian is not a must, but it helps in getting your messages across.

Negotiation

Attitudes and Styles - In Russia, the primary approach to negotiating is to employ distributive and contingency bargaining. The buyer is often in a strongly favorable position and may try to push the responsibility to reach agreement to the seller. Given the country's relatively unstable political and economic situation, negotiators may focus mostly on the near-term benefits of the business deal. The primary negotiation style in the country is very competitive and people may become outright adversarial. Most Russians view negotiating a zero-sum game in which one side's gain equals the other side's loss. Negotiations may become more personable and at least a little more cooperative if strong relationships have been established between the parties.

Should a dispute arise at any stage of a negotiation, it is advantageous first to let some time pass to allow things to blow over. Then, you might be able to reach resolution through logical arguing, presenting lots of supporting information, or making a different, though not necessarily better proposal. What you offer may be more valuable to your counterparts than is apparent from their behaviors. Russians love technology, have great respect for western expertise, and are easily impressed by size and numbers. Do not underestimate the strength of your negotiating position.

Sharing of Information - Information is rarely shared freely, since Russians believe that privileged information creates bargaining advantages.

Pace of Negotiation – Expect negotiations to be very slow and protracted. Especially during the early bargaining stages you may feel that you are making little progress; discussions often stay high-level for quite some time until your counterparts eventually decide to get down to the details of the deal. Success requires extreme patience in this country.

Russians generally employ a polychronic work style. They are used to pursuing multiple actions and goals in parallel. When negotiating, they often take a holistic approach and may jump back and forth between topics rather than addressing them in sequential order. It is not unusual for them to re-open a discussion over items that had already been agreed upon. Negotiators from strongly monochronic cultures, such as Germany, the United Kingdom, or the United States, may find this style confusing, irritating, and even annoying. It is crucial to keep track of the bargaining progress at all times.

If your counterparts appear to be stalling the negotiation, assess carefully whether their slowing down the process indicates that they are evaluating alternatives or that they are not interested in doing business with you. More often than not, though, this behavior indicates an attempt to create time pressure or 'wear you down' in order to obtain concessions.

Bargaining – While quite a few Russians are highly skilled negotiators, the majority of businesspeople in the country have only limited experience in the field. They may expect to do some bargaining and occasionally haggle a lot, but this is rare. None of this makes them easy prey, though. Russians can be extremely patient, persistent, and stubborn negotiators. It can be very difficult to obtain concessions from them. They often view compromise as a sign of weakness and may frequently refuse to change their position unless the other side offers sufficient concessions or shows exceptional firmness. Similarly, they may make minor concessions while asking for major ones in return. Negotiating with Russians inevitably includes much posturing and maneuvering. The best approach is to be polite but remain tough throughout the bargaining process.

The bargaining stage of a negotiation is usually very extensive. In spite of the Russian reluctance to compromise, prices may eventually move by 40 percent or more between initial offers and final agreement. Concessions never come easily, though. It is not advisable to make significant early concessions, since your counterparts expect further compromises as the bargaining continues.

Deceptive techniques are frequent, and Russian negotiators are prepared for you to use them, too. This includes tactics such as telling lies and sending fake non-verbal messages, pretending to be disinterested in the whole deal or in single concessions, misrepresenting an item's value, or making false demands and concessions. Russians may play stupid or otherwise attempt to mislead you in order to obtain bargaining advantages. Lies may be easy to see through; otherwise, verify information received from the local side through other channels. Similarly, they treat 'outside' information with caution. 'Good cop, bad cop' may be used on either side of the negotiation table. Russians may also claim limited authority, stating that they have to ask for their manager's approval. More often than not, this might be the truth. However, you may not always be able to force the true decision maker to participate directly in the negotiation, meaning that you may have to accept this indirect negotiation approach.

Russian negotiators often use pressure techniques that include opening with a 'best offer,' showing intransigence, making final or expiring offers, applying time pressure, or nibbling. Final offers may be made more than once and are almost never final. Time pressure can be difficult to counter. If negotiators learn that you are working against a deadline, they may exploit this knowledge to increase the pressure on you to make concessions. Even if you allowed plenty of time, they may suddenly request last-minute concessions and 'take-it-or-leave-it'-type changes near the end of a negotiation. It is important to define in advance what concessions you are willing to make. Russians may often chose to play hardball. It is ok to take a similar stance yourself; otherwise, be patient and wait it out. When using your own pressure tactics, clearly explain your offer and its benefits to your counterpart. Time pressure does not work against them since Russians can be very patient and fatalistic. However, convincing your counterparts to hold the negotiation in the West does give you a strong advantage. They will now be the ones under time pressure, which deprives them of a strong negotiation tool.

Negotiators can be aggressive or outright adversarial, and negotiations in the country often include strong confrontational elements. In extreme cases, this could include official problems and possible harassment. Extreme openings are frequent as a way to start the bargaining process. Negotiators may make direct threats and warnings, openly display anger or lose their temper, or they may walk out of the room, even several times in a row. While it is ok (and can be quite helpful) to respond in kind, you should be careful not to outdo your counterparts. While maintaining a strong and firm position is respected, it is advantageous to insist at various points that the negotiations emphasize mutual benefits and needs.

Other emotional techniques, such as attitudinal bargaining, attempting to make you feel guilty, grimacing, or appealing to personal relationships, are often used. Russians may also resort to defensive tactics. They may change subjects frequently, revisit previously agreed points, introduce all kind of distractions, or ask very direct questions, attempting to take you by surprise. Prepare well for any of these.

As the country is moving from a socialist country to a free-market economy, corruption and bribery have become quite common in Russia's public and private sectors. Personal benefits may be requested openly as part of a deal. It is important to prepare for this upfront. Keep in mind that people may draw the line differently, viewing minor payments as rewards for getting a job done rather than as bribes. Also, consider that there is a fine line between giving gifts and bribing. What you may consider a bribe, a Russian may view as only a nice gift. It may help if you introduce and explain your company's policies early on, but be careful not to moralize or appear to imply that local customs are unethical.

Decision Making – Companies can be very hierarchical, and people expect to work within clearly established lines of authority. Openly disagreeing with or criticizing superiors is unacceptable. Decision makers are usually senior executives who consider the best interest of the group or organization. They will likely consult with others before making the call. Subordinates may be reluctant to accept responsibility. Decision makers also rarely delegate their authority, so it is important to deal with senior executives. Decisions can take a long time and requires patience.

In Russia's still-shaky political and economic environment, company decisions are rarely independent of outside influences. Never underestimate the role of government officials and bureaucrats, who may have to support and approve company decisions. Similarly, crime groups have gained significant influence across many industries. It is important to come prepared to deal with these outside forces. In extreme cases, you might be well-advised to withdraw from a negotiation should you feel personally threatened. It can be advantageous to indicate to the Russian side that threats would only motivate you to look for other markets and partners.

When making decisions, businesspeople usually consider the specific situation rather than follow universal principles. Personal feelings and experiences may weigh more strongly than empirical evidence and other objective facts do. Russians are often reluctant to take risks. If you expect them to support a risky decision, you may need to find ways for them to become comfortable with it first. You are much more likely to succeed if the relationship with your counterparts is strong and you managed to win their trust.

Agreements and Contracts

Capturing and exchanging written understandings after meetings and at key negotiation stages is useful since oral statements are not always dependable. The Russian side may insist on having a *protokol* (meeting minutes) signed by both parties at the end of a meeting. It serves to record what was discussed, is not a contract, and should not be mistaken for a final agreement. Any part of an agreement may still change significantly before both parties sign the final contract.

Written contracts should be clear and concise, without too many detailed terms and conditions. Signing the contract is important not only from a legal perspective, but also as a strong confirmation of your Russian partners' commitment. Including an arbitration clause in a neutral country, for instance Sweden, is wise. Your counterparts may request that details of the contract be kept secret.

Although your legal rights may not be enforceable, you should definitely consult a local legal expert, ideally throughout the negotiation or at the very least before signing a contract. For the time being, it is wise to recognize that the country's legal system is in a transitional mode, so be prepared for laws to change on short notice. Because of that, bringing an attorney to the negotiation table may not help much, while it could make the negotiation even tougher.

After signing the contract, invite your counterparts to a lunch or dinner to celebrate the beginning of a long-lasting personal and business relationship. This will help your local partners to see you not only as a business partner, but also as a trustworthy contact.

Contracts alone are not dependable. Russians may continue to press for a better deal even after a contract has been signed, or they may ignore some of its terms. Your best chance to ensure that your partners follow through on their commitments is to stay in regular contact and nurture the relationship throughout your business engagement.

Women in Business

While in theory women enjoy the same rights as men, few Russian women have made it into senior management positions, and most are still struggling to attain positions of similar income and authority. As a visiting businesswoman, emphasize your company's importance and your role in it. This will be even more effective if you can get a male colleague to explain these aspects while emphasizing that women are treated differently in your home country. A personal introduction or at least a letter of support from a senior executive within your company may also help.

Female business travelers should exercise caution and act professionally in business and social situations. Be prepared for flattery, obsequious politeness, and apparent deference. None of this translates into clout at the negotiation table. It is also possible that you will face offensive humor or remarks with sexual connotation. While these are usually best ignored, it may sometimes help to point out that such comments are not practiced in your home country. Displaying confidence and some degree of assertiveness can be effective, but it is very important not to appear overly bold and aggressive.

Other Important Things to Know

Conservative attire is important when doing business here. Male business visitors should wear suits on most occasions. While you do not want to appear 'overdressed,' make sure shoes and suit are in good condition.

Business lunches and dinners are very common, and evening entertainment can be lavish. These events frequently include heavy alcohol consumption and may also extend to visits to the *banya* (Russian sauna). They are very important as they help advance the vital process of building relationships. Refusing to participate in these activities may be taken as a clear signal that you are not seriously interested in doing business with your counterparts. Having a drink with your Russian partners is an easy way to establish good will. However, realize that they may use the opportunity to continue negotiating. Some may even pretend to be more drunk than they really if they can use this act to their advantage.

Punctuality is expected in most social settings. It is best to be right on time for dinners, and to arrive at parties within 15 minutes of the agreed time.

Russia is a high-crime country. International visitors potentially face mugging, burglary, and even kidnapping. It is strongly advisable to dress inconspicuously and leave status symbols such as expensive watches or briefcases at home.

Saudi Arabia

Though the country's culture is quite homogeneous, Saudi businesspeople, especially those among younger generations, are usually experienced in interacting and doing business with visitors from other cultures. Until the discovery of oil, the Kingdom of Saudi Arabia produced very little, and the primary business activity was trading. This merchant culture helped them become shrewd and highly skilled bargainers. However, that does not necessarily mean that they are open-minded. When negotiating business here, realize that people may expect things to be done 'their way.'

Always keep in mind that this is an Islamic country. Showing any disrespect for the religion could have disastrous consequences.

Relationships and Respect

Saudi Arabia's culture expects its members to have a strong sense of loyalty to their group. At the same time, it leaves room for individual preferences. Building lasting and trusting personal relationships is very important to most Saudis, who often expect to establish strong bonds prior to closing any deals. People in this country prefer to do business with those they know and like. Establishing productive business cooperation requires a long-term perspective and commitment. Social interactions are just as important as business contacts, if not more. Consequently, proceed with serious business discussions only after your counterparts have become very comfortable with you. This is usually a slow process.

Business relationships in this country exist between people, not necessarily between companies. Even when you have won your local business partners' friendship and trust, they will not necessarily trust others from your company. That makes it very important to keep company interfaces unchanged. Changing a key contact may require the relationship building process to start over. Worst case, such a change may bring negotiations to a complete halt.

Establishing relationships with others in Saudi Arabia can create powerful networks, especially if they reach into the extensive royal family. Whom you know may determine whether people want to get to know you. Maintaining cordial relations is crucial. Third party introductions can be very helpful as a starting point to building a trusting relationship with a potential partner, especially since Saudis may initially not trust Westerners.

'Saving face' is very essential. Causing embarrassment to another person may cause a *loss of face* for all parties involved and can be disastrous for business negotiations. The importance of diplomatic restraint and tact cannot be overestimated. Keep your cool and never show openly that you are upset. It may be better to accept a compromise, even an unfavorable one, if the alternative means that your counterpart loses face.

In Saudi Arabia's business culture, the respect a person enjoys depends primarily on his status, rank, and age. It is vital to treat elderly people with great respect. Showing status is important since people will take you more seriously. Carefully select your hotel and transportation. Use the services of others, such as a porter, to avoid being viewed as a low-ranking intermediary. Admired personal traits include poise, sociability, and patience.

Communication

The official language of Saudi Arabia is Arabic. Many businesspeople, especially young ones and those in top positions, speak English well enough, so you rarely need an interpreter. When communicating in English, speak in short, simple sentences and avoid using jargon and slang. It will help people with a limited command of English if you speak slowly, summarize your key points often, and pause frequently to allow for interpretation.

Saudis usually speak in quiet, gentle tones. A raised voice usually indicates anger, which is a very bad signal. At restaurants, especially those used for business lunches and dinners, keep conversations at a quiet level. Being loud may be regarded as bad manners. People in the country generally converse in close proximity, standing only two feet or less apart. Never back away, even if this is much closer than your personal comfort zone allows. Doing so could be read as a sign that you are uncomfortable around them.

Communication is generally rather indirect. Saudis often use circuitous language, which can make it difficult for Westerners to figure out the exact message. They love flowery phrases, exaggerations, and other rhetoric, and generally consider eloquent people more respectable and trustworthy. Open disagreement and confrontation are rare and best avoided. You will usually not hear a direct 'no.' When a Saudi says 'yes,' he may actually mean 'possibly.' Ambiguous answers such as 'we must look into this' or 'we will think about it' usually mean 'no.' Silence is another way to communicate a negative message. It is beneficial to use a similarly indirect approach when dealing with Saudis, as they may perceive you as rude and pushy if you are too direct.

Gestures and body language are usually more restricted than in other Arab countries. Men tend to make frequent physical contact, though. They may greet each other by hugging and kissing as a sign of friendship. However, never touch someone's head, not even that of a child. Since Muslims consider the left hand unclean, use it only if inevitable. The soles of your shoes are also considered unclean and you must avoid showing them to others, even when seated on a cushion. Pointing at people or objects is impolite. Instead, wave your open hand toward the object. The thumbs-up gesture is an offensive gesture throughout the Arab world. Eye contact should be frequent, almost to the point of staring. This conveys sincerity and helps build trust. Saudis enjoy showing positive emotions as long as it is done in a controlled fashion. However, they may smile less often than some of their neighbors.

Initial Contacts and Meetings

Choosing a local intermediary who can leverage existing relationships to make the initial contact is crucially important. Having a *sponsor* is also a legal requirement for visiting the country. A person who can introduce you to the right contacts and help you build relationships is essential when doing business in this country. This person will help bridge the gap between cultures, allowing you to conduct business with greater effectiveness. Let him set the pace of your initial engagements.

Negotiations can be conducted by individuals or teams of negotiators. It is vital that teams be well aligned, with roles clearly assigned to each member. Saudis may be very good at exploiting disagreements between members of the other team to their advantage. Changing a team member may require the relationship building process to start over and should therefore be avoided. Worst case, such a change can bring negotiations to a complete halt.

If possible, schedule meetings at least three to four weeks in advance. The length of a meeting is usually unpredictable, so do not try to schedule more than one per day. Since Saudis want to know whom they will be meeting, provide details on titles, positions, and responsibilities of attendees ahead of time. Be prepared for your counterparts to cancel or postpone meetings with little or no notice. Schedules are often loose and flexible, and meetings may start considerably late. However, Saudis generally expect foreign visitors to be punctual. Avoid being more than 15 to 20 minutes late, and call ahead if you will be. Displaying anger if you have to wait, which happens often, reflects very poorly on you. The most senior meeting participants usually often arrive last.

Saudi names can have several parts and may be difficult to identify. It may be best to inquire from someone upfront or politely ask the person how to address him or her correctly. In that case, make sure you do the same for your own name. Titles, such as *Doctor* or *Professor*, are highly valued. Always use them when addressing a person who carries one. Do not call Saudis by their first name unless they offered it. Arabs may see mispronouncing their names as a sign of disrespect. Greet the most senior person first, and then greet everyone else in the room individually. Introductions and greetings are accompanied by extensive compliments as well as handshakes using the right hand. Saudi women generally do not shake hands with men. Saudi businessmen may be reluctant to shake the hand of a foreign woman.

After the introductions, offer your business card to everyone present. Cards should be in English on one side and in Arabic on the reverse, and must be in pristine condition. Show doctorate degrees on your card and make sure that it clearly states your professional title, especially if you have the seniority to make decisions. Present your card with your right hand, with the Arabic side facing the recipient. Similarly, accept others' cards using only the right hand. Smile and keep eye contact while doing so, then examine the card carefully. Next, place it on the table in front of you. Never stuff someone's card into your back pocket or otherwise treat it disrespectfully.

The first meeting may consist entirely of small talk, which may include prolonged inquiries about your health, family, and so on. This may include very personal questions. It may actually take several meetings before you even get to discuss business. Be patient and let the other side set the pace. Frequent meeting interruptions are normal and do not signal a lack of interest.

Presentations should be short and concise. Allow sufficient time for questions and clarifications. Either the decision maker is a silent observer, or that person may not attend at all. People asking many questions usually hold less important positions. Your presentation materials should be attractive, with good and clear visuals. Use diagrams and pictures wherever feasible, cut down on words, and avoid complicated expressions. Having your handout materials translated to Arabic is not a must, but it helps in getting your messages across and is thus preferable.

Negotiation

Attitudes and Styles - Leveraging relationships is an important element when negotiating in Saudi Arabia. Nevertheless, Saudis often employ distributive and contingency bargaining. While the buyer is in a superior position, both sides in a business deal own the responsibility to reach agreement. They expect long-term commitments from their business partners and will focus mostly on long-term benefits. Although the primary negotiation style is competitive, Saudis nevertheless value long-term relationships. They will ultimately look for win-win solutions and show willingness to compromise if needed. Saudi negotiators may at times appear highly competitive, fiercely bargaining for seemingly small gains. They respect hard bargainers as long as they avoid creating direct conflict. You earn your counterparts' respect by maintaining a positive, persistent attitude. It is critically important to remain calm, friendly, patient, and persistent, never taking anything personally.

Should a dispute arise at any stage of a negotiation, you might be able to reach resolution through leveraging your personal relationship with the Saudi negotiation leader in a one-on-one setting. Show your commitment to the relationship and refrain from using logical reasoning or becoming argumentative since this will only make matters worse.

Sharing of Information - Information is rarely shared freely, since the Saudis believe that privileged information creates bargaining advantages. In contrast, expect any information you share to reach your incumbent competitor. Based on their existing relationship, your Saudi counterparts will likely believe that this party must be given the right to respond to the new competitive threat.

Pace of Negotiation – Expect negotiations to be slow and protracted, and be prepared to make several trips if necessary to achieve your objectives. Throughout the negotiation, be patient, control your emotions, and accept that delays may occur. Attempts to rush the process are highly unlikely to produce better results and may be counterproductive. A Saudi proverb warns, 'Haste is of the devil,' and many Saudis may believe that whether something happens quickly, slowly, or not at all is beyond their control as it depends on Allah's will. On the other hand, do not be surprised if the pace suddenly changes from very slow to very fast – once your counterparts have made a positive decision, they may expect fast progress.

When engaging in initial business negotiations in the country, it is often crucial to take a long-term perspective over many years. It is often advisable to accept an initial deal even when its return-on-investment does not look appealing. Much bigger profits tend to come once you manage to prove yourself a worthy partner.

Most Saudis prefer a very polychronic work style. They are used to pursuing multiple actions and goals in parallel. When negotiating, they often take a holistic approach or frequently jump from one topic to another rather than addressing them in sequential order. In multi-item negotiations, people may bargain and haggle over several aspects in parallel. It is common for them to re-open a discussion over items that had already been agreed upon. In addition, they may take phone calls or interrupt meetings at critical points in a negotiation. While they may be doing all this on purpose in order to distract or confuse the other side, there are usually no bad intentions. Negotiators from strongly monochronic cultures, such as Germany, the United Kingdom, or the United States, may find this style confusing, irritating, and even annoying. Surprisingly, Saudis themselves may expect their foreign visitors to stick to the subject of conversation unless there is a logical opportunity or invitation to change topics. In any case, do not show irritation or anger when encountering this behavior. Instead, keep track of the bargaining progress at all times, often emphasizing areas where agreement already exists. Repeating your main points conveys seriousness and builds trust.

If your counterparts appear to be stalling the negotiation, assess carefully whether their slowing down the process indicates that they are evaluating alternatives or that they are not interested in doing business with you. In most cases, though, this behavior indicates an attempt to create time pressure in order to obtain concessions.

Bargaining – Saudi businesspeople are usually shrewd negotiators who should never be underestimated. Most of them thoroughly enjoy bargaining and haggling. They expect to do a lot of it during a negotiation and may be seriously offended if you refuse to play along. In addition, they may expect flexibility on your side, so avoid coming with overly narrow expectations of how a deal might be reached.

The bargaining stage of a negotiation can be very extensive. Prices often move more than 50 percent between initial offers and final agreement. Leave yourself a lot of room for concessions at many different stages. Ask the other side to reciprocate if you made one, but never make them look like the loser in the exchange. It is not advisable to make significant early concessions since your counterparts expect further compromises as the bargaining continues. You can use the fact that aspects can be re-visited to your advantage, for instance by offering further concessions under the condition that the Saudi side reciprocate in areas that had already been agreed upon.

Deceptive techniques are frequent and can be effective. This includes tactics such as telling lies and sending fake non-verbal messages, pretending to be disinterested in the whole deal or in single concessions, misrepresenting an item's value, or making false demands and concessions. Expect your Saudi counterparts to be masters at this game, playing it with many exaggerations and much enthusiasm. They may occasionally play stupid or otherwise attempt to mislead you in order to obtain bargaining advantages. Lies will be difficult to detect. It is advisable to verify information received from the local side through other channels. Similarly, they treat 'outside' information with caution. Even when you can see right through a lie, it would be a grave personal insult to state or even hint that your counterpart is not telling the truth. Saudis are usually too proud to claim or admit that they have only limited authority, even if it is true. Be cautious when using the techniques of making false demands or false concessions. Overt attempts to bluff your counterparts could backfire.

Negotiators in the country may use pressure techniques that include making final offers or nibbling. Final offers may come more than once and are rarely final. Do not use tactics such as applying time pressure, opening with your best offer, or making expiring offers, since Saudis could view these as signs that you are not willing to build a long-term relationship. They may choose to terminate the negotiation. Silence can be an effective way to signal rejection of a proposal.

Saudi negotiators avoid openly aggressive or adversarial techniques but may use more subtle versions. Making an extreme opening offer is a standard practice to start the bargaining process. Negotiators may also make indirect threats and warnings, or subtly display anger. Use these tactics with caution yourself since they may adversely affect the relationship if employed too aggressively. Do not walk out or threaten to do so as your counterpart may take this as a personal insult.

Emotional negotiation techniques, such as attitudinal bargaining, sending dual messages, attempting to make you feel guilty, grimacing, or appealing to personal relationships, are frequent and can be effective. Be cautious not to cause *loss of face* when employing any of them yourself. Also, know that Saudis can become quite emotional during fierce bargaining. It is best to remain calm. Defensive tactics such as blocking, distracting or changing the subject, asking probing or very direct questions, or making promises may also be frequent.

Corruption and bribery are quite common in Saudi Arabia's public and private sectors. However, people may draw the line differently, viewing minor payments as rewards for getting a job done rather than as bribes. Also, keep in mind that there is a fine line between giving gifts and bribing. What you may consider a bribe, a Saudi may view as only a nice gift. So much as hinting that you view this differently could be a grave insult to the person's honor. It may help if you introduce and explain your company's policies early on, but be careful not to moralize or appear to imply that local customs are unethical.

Decision Making – Company hierarchies can be very rigid, and people expect to work within clearly established lines of authority. Although the pace of business is accelerating, decision making can be a slow and deliberate process in Saudi Arabia. Decision makers are usually individuals who consider the best interest of the group or organization and may consult with others in the organization. Decisions therefore often require several layers of approval. Final decision-making authority may be delegated down, but that can change quickly if subordinates fall out of favor. Consequently, it will be important to win the support of senior executives.

When making decisions, Saudi businesspeople may not rely much on rules or laws. They usually consider the specific situation rather than applying universal principles. Personal feelings and experiences weigh more strongly than empirical evidence and other objective facts do. Saudis are often reluctant to take risks. If you expect them to support a risky decision, you may need to find ways for them to become comfortable with it first. You are much more likely to succeed if the relationship with your counterparts is strong and you managed to win their trust.

Agreements and Contracts

Capturing and exchanging meeting summaries can be an effective way to verify understanding and commitments. While these serve as tools to improve the communication and strengthen commitments, they should not be taken for final agreements. Any part of an agreement may still change significantly before both parties sign the final contract. Agreements are only final when the participants part. Until then, the Saudi side may unilaterally abrogate them, possibly even if they were already signed. Oral agreements are not binding under Saudi law.

Although businesspeople in the country understand the role of contracts well, they may view them only as general guides for conducting business, expecting that both parties are willing to change terms if there is a change of conditions. Written contracts are usually kept high-level, capturing only the primary aspects, terms, and conditions of the agreement. Writing up and signing the contract is a formality. Saudis believe that the primary strength of an agreement lies in the partners' commitment rather than in its written documentation. Accordingly, do not propose an overly detailed contract since that may cause hurt feelings.

International contracts in the country usually include 'offset' requirements, which are spelled out by law. As compensation for the gains the foreign company expects to receive from the business deal, it is required to support efforts the local economy will benefit from, such as training local staff or transferring technological know-how. Saudi law also requires having a local representative on a continuous basis. It is strongly advisable to consult a local legal expert before signing a contract. However, do not bring your attorney to the negotiation table. Saudis may read it as a sign of mistrust if you do.

Since personal honor is highly valued in Saudi Arabia, contracts are usually dependable and your partners will strive to keep their commitments. However, business partners usually expect the other side to remain somewhat flexible if conditions change, which may include agreeing to modify contract terms.

Women in Business

Saudi Arabia remains a male-dominated society. Although some women are working, they still have very traditional roles and rarely attain positions of similar income and authority as men. The relative scarcity of women in Saudi business may make local men uncomfortable in dealing with Western women, who should not expect to be met with the same respect as men. Women find themselves subjected to many restrictions in the country. Displaying confidence and assertiveness can be counterproductive. Appearing overly bold and aggressive may create major issues and must be avoided under all circumstances.

As a visiting businesswoman, emphasize your company's importance and your role in it. A personal introduction or at least a letter of support from a senior executive within your company may also help. Even with these credentials, you may still not find sufficient attention, making it advisable to take a male colleague along for the trip and act 'behind the scenes.'

Female business travelers should exercise great caution and act professionally in business and social situations. They need to dress in accordance with local customs, which means that collarbones and knees need to be covered at all times and that clothes should not be form-fitting.

Male visitors should not speak to a Saudi woman unless the situation clearly requires it. In addition, avoid bringing up the subject of women with your male business partners. Do not even inquire about a wife's or daughter's health. Furthermore, while there may be intensive contact between men, it is vitally important not to stare at any woman you may meet.

Other Important Things to Know

Impeccable appearance is very important when doing business in any of the Gulf Arab states and many other Arab countries. Male business visitors should wear conservative suits on most occasions. Always cover your whole body. Make sure shoes and suit are in excellent condition.

Saudi hospitality is world-famous. You are not expected to reciprocate at similar levels.

Tea will be served at many occasions. It would be a mistake not to accept it, even when you are not thirsty.

Social events do not require strict punctuality. While it is best to arrive at dinners close to the agreed time, being late to a party by 15 to 30 minutes or more is expected. There may be little conversation during meals, allowing everyone to relish the food. Remember that alcohol is illegal in Saudi Arabia.

Topics to avoid in discussions are Saudi Arabia's internal conflicts with Islamic extremists as well as its political role in the Gulf and Iraq wars.

Lastly, never overly praise something your host owns. He may feel obliged to give it to you, which could create a very difficult situation.

Singapore

Around three quarters of the Singaporean population is Chinese. The rest are predominantly Malays or Indians. Although they have developed many common values, their respective cultural influences remain strong and the country is culturally pluralistic. Individual cultural preferences may therefore sometimes differ from the information given in this section. In any case, Singaporean Chinese dominate the business culture of the country.

Singaporeans may appear much more 'westernized' than other Asians. However, that can be deceptive. On one hand, especially young businesspeople are usually very experienced in interacting with other cultures. Many of them are flexible and open-minded, eager to do business with foreigners. On the other hand, the country's business culture is quite ethnocentric. People of the same ethnic group may inherently trust each other much more than any 'outsider.' There also used to be a general bias against foreigners. This is gradually disappearing.

The Singaporean government is often considered to be rather 'paternal' in nature. Singaporeans may have to worry about less aspects of life and business than others, which can make it more difficult for them to think creatively and challenge the status quo. It may take some encouragement to get them to explore things outside of their own comfort zone.

Relationships and Respect

Singapore's culture is generally group-oriented. Asserting individual preferences may be seen as less important than having a sense of belonging to a group, conforming to its norms, and maintaining harmony among its members. Building lasting and trusting personal relationships is therefore very important, though to a lesser degree than in several other Asian countries. Some Singaporeans may engage in business while the relationship building process is still ongoing. However, others in the country may expect to establish strong bonds prior to closing any deals. Generally, it is beneficial to allow some time for your Singaporean counterparts to get to know and become comfortable with you prior to proceeding with serious business discussions. In any case, your local partners will expect you to be committed to the business relationship for many years.

Unlike in many western countries, business relationships in Singapore exist mostly between individuals or groups of people rather than between companies. Accordingly, if your company replaces you with another representative, relationships need to be built anew.

In Singapore's culture, 'saving face' is also critical. Causing embarrassment to another person, such as correcting him or her, disagreeing with an older person or a superior, may cause a *loss of face* for all parties involved and can be very detrimental for business negotiations. Reputation and social standing strongly depend on a person's ability to control one's emotions and remain friendly at all times. If you have to bring up an unpleasant topic with a person, never do so in public and always convey your message in ways that maintain the other's self-respect. Reserve and tact are very important. Keep your cool and never show openly that you are upset.

People in Singapore are usually very friendly and polite. This does not affect their determination to reach business goals, though, and your counterparts will patiently and persistently pursue their objectives. It is in your best interest to do the same.

In Singapore's business culture, the respect a person enjoys depends primarily on his or her status and rank, age, achievements, and education. You will commonly find leaders in senior roles to be of advanced age. It is important to treat elderly people with great respect. Long hours and hard work are expected, especially at the executive level. Admired personal traits include humility, experience, and team spirit.

Communication

Singapore has four official languages, namely Mandarin, Malay, Tamil, and English. The country has its own brand of English, known as *Singlish*, which differs from English in terms of sentence structure and grammar, as well as the frequent use of filler words such as *lah, leh, hor* and *meh*. Many businesspeople speak and understand English, often very well. Interpreters are rarely needed. However, when communicating in English, avoid using slang and jargon. It will help people with a limited command of English if you speak slowly, summarize your key points often, and pause frequently to allow for interpretation.

Businesspeople in Singapore usually speak in quiet, gentle tones. Remaining calm at all times and controlling one's emotions well is very important in this culture.

Loud and boisterous behavior is perceived as a lack of self-control. At restaurants, especially those used for business lunches and dinners, keep conversations at a quiet level. Conversations may include extended periods of silence, which do not necessarily convey a negative message. People generally converse while standing around two to three feet apart, sometimes even closer.

Because the concept of saving *face* is so important in this culture, communication is generally very indirect. When responding to a direct question, Singaporeans may answer 'yes' only to signal that they heard what you said, not that they agree with it. Open disagreement and confrontation must be avoided, so you rarely hear a direct 'no.' Instead, they may give seemingly ambiguous answers such as 'I am not sure,' 'we will think about it,' 'this will require further investigation,' or 'yes, but...' Each of these could mean 'no,' as does a 'yes' that sounds hesitant or weak. Alternatively, a respondent may deliberately ignore your question. It is beneficial to use a similarly indirect approach when dealing with Singaporeans, as they may perceive you as rude and pushy if you are too direct. Only a person with whom you have no relationship yet may occasionally give you a straight 'no.' This is a bad sign since it could mean that your counterpart is not interested in engaging in business with you.

A Singaporean who considers you a superior may tell you what he or she thinks you want to hear, especially when others are around. This is a way to save *face* and preserve honor. Candid comments and criticism may only be conveyed in private, often through a third party. Similarly, it can be effective to deliver negative responses to your negotiation counterparts through a third party, which is a more face-saving way.

Singaporeans consider it polite to offer both the positive and negative possibilities when asking a question that requires a decision. For example, they may ask 'Do you want to go back to your hotel or not?'

Gestures can be very subtle in Singapore. Non-verbal communication is important, though, and you should carefully watch for others' small hints, just as they will be watching you. Avoid any physical contact with Singaporeans except for handshakes. Most importantly, never touch someone's head, not even that of a child. When pointing at people or objects, use your open hand rather than a finger. To refer to themselves, Chinese Singaporeans put an index finger on their nose rather than pointing at their chest as Westerners do. Sucking in air through the teeth indicates that there is a serious problem. Eye contact should be infrequent. While it is beneficial to make some eye contact when meeting a person for the first time, the Singaporeans consider frequent eye contact intrusive and rude. Avoid any facial expressions that may suggest disagreement, such as grimacing or shaking your head.

Note that laughter does not always indicate amusement. Frequently, it may mask embarrassment, shyness, disapproval, and other feelings of distress. Accordingly, Westerners may sometimes observe Singaporeans smiling or laughing at what they might consider inappropriate moments.

Initial Contacts and Meetings

Having a local contact can be an advantage but is usually not a necessary precondition to doing business. While relationships matter, Singaporeans businesspeople are used to conducting international business.

It is often better to conduct negotiations in Singapore with a team of negotiators rather than to rely on a single individual. This signals importance, facilitates stronger relationship building, and may speed up the overall process. It is vital that teams be well aligned, with roles clearly assigned to each member. Singaporean negotiators may be very good at exploiting disagreements between members of the other team to their advantage. Changing a team member may require the relationship building process to start over and should therefore be avoided.

If possible, schedule meetings at least two weeks in advance. Since Singaporeans want to know whom they will be meeting, provide details on titles, positions, and responsibilities of attendees ahead of time. Punctuality is highly valued. The Chinese are especially careful not to waste others' time. Being late to a meeting or social event without having a valid and plausible excuse can be a serious affront. If a delay is inevitable, it is advisable to explain the reason and apologize profoundly, even if it is not your fault.

Chinese names are usually given in the order of family name, first name. The latter consists of two parts, the generational name and the given name. However, the two are often spoken and written as one. Many Singaporean Chinese use assumed western first names, in which case they give theirs in the order of first name followed by family name. Malay and Indian names can have several parts, and it may be hard to identify which is which. It may be best to ask people politely how to address them correctly. In that case, make sure you do the same for your own name. Singaporeans are very status-conscious. If a person has a title or doctorate degree, use it to address him or her, for example, 'Doctor Tsai' or 'Director Chan.' Otherwise, use *Mr./Ms.* plus the family name. Before calling Singaporeans by their first name, wait until they offer it.

Introduce older people and those of higher rank first, and stand up when someone in either category enters the room. Negotiating teams should line up so that the most important individuals are introduced first. If introducing two people, it is important to state the name of the most important person first. Some people may not want to shake hands, so it is best to wait for your counterparts to initiate handshakes, which should be light and may last as long as ten seconds. Men should wait for women to initiate handshakes. Some Singaporean women may not want to make physical contact with men, in which case it is best to just nod and smile.

The exchange of business cards is an essential step when meeting someone for the first time, so bring more than you need. If someone presents you with his or her card and you do not offer one in return, the person may assume that you either do not want to make their acquaintance, that your status in your company's hierarchy is very low, or, quite to the contrary, that your status is very high. There is no need to have your cards translated to a language other than English. Show doctorate degrees on your card and make sure that it clearly states your professional title, especially if you have the seniority to make decisions. Singaporeans may present their card using two hands or only the right one. If possible, use the same method your counterpart is using. Smile and make eye contact while accepting someone else's card, then examine the card carefully. Not reading someone's card can be an insult. Next, place the card on the table in front of you or into your card case. Never stuff someone's card into your back pocket or otherwise treat it disrespectfully. Never write on a person's business card.

At the beginning of a meeting, there is normally some small talk. This allows participants to become personally acquainted. It is best to let the local side set the pace and follow along. People appreciate a sense of humor, but keep it light and friendly, and be careful not to overdo it. Business is a serious matter in Singapore, and meetings, especially initial ones, may appear very formal.

The primary purpose of the first meeting is to become acquainted and build relationships. Business may be discussed, but do not try to hurry along with your agenda. It is unrealistic to expect initial meetings to lead to straight decisions.

It is good to make a presentation, but keep it simple and avoid over-designing it. Encourage questions, and verify through diplomatic questions of your own whether your audience understands you. Since saving *face* is so important to Singaporeans, people will not openly admit it in front of others if they do not understand what you are presenting.

The appearance of your presentation materials is not very important as long as you include good and easy-to-understand visuals. Having your English-language handout materials translated to any other local language is not required.

Negotiation

Attitudes and Styles - Leveraging relationships is an important element when negotiating in Singapore. Nevertheless, Singaporeans often employ distributive and contingency bargaining. While the buyer is in a superior position, both sides in a business deal own the responsibility to reach agreement. They expect long-term commitments from their business partners and will focus mostly on long-term benefits. Although the primary negotiation style is competitive, Singaporeans nevertheless value long-term relationships. They respect hard bargainers as long as they avoid creating direct conflict. Both sides remain friendly throughout the negotiation, and attempts to win competitive advantages should not be taken negatively. The culture promotes a win-win approach since this is the best way for everyone to save *face* throughout a negotiation. You earn your counterparts' respect by maintaining a positive, persistent attitude.

Should a dispute arise at any stage of a negotiation, you might be able to reach resolution through logical arguments and references to past experiences. Show your commitment to the relationship and refrain from using logical reasoning or becoming argumentative since this will only make matters worse. Patience and creativity will pay strong dividends. Although personal relationships matter a lot, referring to them alone may not be enough to resolve the conflict. In extreme situations, use a mediator, ideally the party who initially introduced you.

Sharing of Information – Singaporean negotiators are willing to spend considerable time, sometimes many weeks or even months, gathering information and discussing various details before the bargaining stage of a negotiation can begin. Some information is shared since this is viewed as a way to build trust. However, expecting your counterpart to reveal everything you might want to know during your negotiation would be naïve.

Pace of Negotiation – Expect negotiations to be slow and protracted. Relationship building, information gathering, bargaining, and decision making all take considerable time. Be prepared to make several trips if necessary to achieve your objectives. Throughout the negotiation, be patient, control your emotions, and accept that delays occur.

Singaporeans generally employ a polychronic work style. They are used to pursuing multiple actions and goals in parallel. When negotiating, they often take a holistic approach and may jump back and forth between topics rather than addressing them in sequential order. Negotiators from strongly monochronic cultures, such as Germany, the United Kingdom, or the United States, may find this style confusing, irritating, and even annoying. In any case, do not show irritation or anger when encountering this behavior. Instead, keep track of the bargaining progress at all times, often emphasizing areas where agreement already exists.

If your counterparts appear to be stalling the negotiation, assess carefully whether their slowing down the process indicates that they are evaluating alternatives or that they are not interested in doing business with you. While such behavior could represent attempts to create time pressure in order to obtain concessions, the slow decision process in the country is far more likely causing the lack of progress. People from fast-paced cultures tend to underestimate how much time this takes and often make the mistake of trying to 'speed things up.' Again, patience and persistence are important.

Bargaining – Singaporeans are often shrewd negotiators who should not be underestimated. They love bargaining and haggling, and people may use a wide array of negotiation techniques quite competently. The bargaining stage of a negotiation can be extensive. Prices often move more than 40 percent between initial offers and final agreement. Leave yourself sufficient room for concessions at different stages. Ask the other side to reciprocate if you made one. You can use the fact that aspects can be re-visited to your advantage, for instance by offering further concessions under the condition that the Singaporean side reciprocate in areas that had already been agreed upon.

Deceptive techniques might be used and it may be effective to use some of them yourself. This includes tactics such as telling lies and sending fake non-verbal messages, pretending to be disinterested in the whole deal or in single concessions, misrepresenting an item's value, or making false demands and concessions. Lies may be difficult to detect. It is advisable to verify information received from the local side through other channels. Similarly, they treat 'outside' information with caution. Singaporeans rarely use 'good cop, bad cop;' however, it can sometimes be beneficial to use this tactic in your own negotiation approach. Carefully orchestrated, it may allow you to obtain valuable concessions without damaging the overall relationship. However, your team will need to exclude any 'bad cop' member from future negotiation rounds. Businesspeople are not likely to use the 'limited authority' technique because groups rather than individuals normally make decisions. Since you must avoid causing loss of face, be cautious when using the techniques of making false demands or false concessions. Any overt attempts to bluff your counterparts could backfire.

Singaporean negotiators, especially those of Chinese heritage, may use pressure tactics such as applying time pressure or making expiring offers. If they learn that the other side is working against a deadline, they may exploit this knowledge to increase the time pressure. Most of these tactics cannot be used against them effectively since the Chinese are patient and persistent enough to overcome such challenges. Other pressure techniques such as nibbling, threats, and warnings may occasionally be used. Final offers may be made more than once and are almost never final. Periods of silence in conversations are normal and may not represent an attempt to use it as a negotiation technique. Avoid tactics such as opening with your best offer or showing intransigence, since they cannot be applied effectively without running the risk of causing loss of face.

Negotiators avoid most aggressive or adversarial techniques since they affect face. The risk of using any of them yourself is rarely worth the potential gain. Extreme openings may occasionally be used as a way to start the bargaining process. However, use the tactic only with great caution since it may adversely affect the relationship if employed too aggressively.

As in most strongly relationship-oriented cultures, negotiators may sometimes use emotional techniques such as attitudinal bargaining, sending dual messages, attempting to make you feel guilty, grimacing, or appealing to personal relationships. Singaporeans can be very compelling when acting disappointed or insulted. Be cautious when doing this yourself. You might cause the other side to lose face, which could damage your negotiating position.

At times, defensive tactics such as blocking, distracting and changing the subject, asking probing questions, or making promises may be used. The exception is directness, which is rare in Singapore. People may be shocked if you are overly direct yourself, which can be counterproductive.

Note that opening with written offers and attempting to introduce written terms and conditions as a negotiation tactic is rarely successful. In most cases, businesspeople ignore or tactfully reject them and request that each aspect be negotiated individually.

Corruption and bribery are very rare in Singapore. It is believed to have the lowest corruption rate of any Asian country. Bribery is illegal and may be punished harshly. It is strongly advisable to stay away from giving gifts of significant value or making offers that could be read as bribery.

Decision Making – Most companies tend to be very hierarchical, and people expect to work within clearly established lines of authority. Disagreeing with or criticizing superiors is unacceptable. However, decision making is normally a consensus-oriented group process in Singapore. This can be confusing for Westerners looking to identify the 'key decision maker' in an organization, while in reality such a role may not exist at all. Decisions are often made through a process involving many stakeholders who establish consensus through a series of deliberations. This process can take a long time and requires patience. Influencing the decision making requires building strong relationships with as many of the stakeholders as you possibly can. Senior leaders orchestrate the process and secure the support of the group. Nevertheless, their input carries a lot of weight and they sometimes have the final say, so do everything you can to win their approval.

When making decisions, Singaporean businesspeople usually consider the specific situation rather than applying universal principles. Personal feelings and experiences weigh more strongly than empirical evidence and other objective facts do. Most Singaporeans are moderate risk takers.

Agreements and Contracts

Capturing and exchanging written understandings after meetings and at key negotiation stages is useful since oral statements are not always dependable. While these serve as tools to improve the communication and strengthen commitments, they should not be taken for final agreements. Any part of an agreement may still change significantly before both parties sign the final contract.

Contract styles vary, but some may spell out detailed terms and conditions for the core agreements as well as for many eventualities. Nevertheless, writing up and signing the contract is a formality. Singaporeans believe that the primary strength of an agreement lies in the partners' commitment rather than in its written documentation. Ethnic Chinese often consult astrologers and may prefer to delay signature of a contract until a 'lucky' day arrives.

Your legal rights are usually enforceable. It is recommended to consult a local legal expert before signing a contract. Also, ensure that your products are patented or registered in Singapore to protect them against imitation. However, do not bring an attorney to the negotiation table, since this may be taken as a sign that you do not trust your counterparts.

Contracts are usually dependable, and the agreed terms are viewed as binding.

Women in Business

While Singapore is still a male-dominated society, there are many women in professional positions, some with significant authority and influence. At the same time, most women are still struggling to attain positions of similar income and authority as men. Nevertheless, visiting businesswomen should have few problems in the country as long as they act professionally in business and social situations. If a male local business contact asks a foreign woman out for dinner, this most likely means that he wants to talk business or intensify the business relationship rather than make personal advances.

Other Important Things to Know

Dressing very conservatively, ideally in dark suits with neckties for men, is important to convey status and poise.

Business meals and entertainment, including breakfasts, lunches, dinners, banquets, and other evening events, are important as they help advance the vital process of building strong relationships. Business may or may not be discussed during these events. Your counterparts may use them as opportunities to convey important messages or resolve disputes. Sometimes they may also try to obtain information from you that could strengthen their negotiating position. While you want to remain watchful, deflecting such inquiries if needed, never show signs of mistrust in your counterparts' intentions.

During small talk and other social conversations, you may be asked very personal questions. If you do not want to answer, smile or politely explain that such topics are not discussed openly in your culture.

Gift giving in business settings is rare, at least as long as no strong relationship exists. It is best not to bring a gift to an initial meeting in order to avoid raising suspicions about your motives.

South Africa

Businesspeople and officials in South Africa, especially outside of Johannesburg and Cape Town, usually have only limited exposure to other cultures. When negotiating business here, realize that people may expect things to be done 'their way.' However, some among younger generations may have greater international experience and can be quite open-minded.

South Africa deserves its nickname as 'The Rainbow Culture' as it is indeed one of the most multicultural nations on earth. Its culture is quite heterogeneous. The majority of the population is blacks (almost 80 percent), representing many different tribes such as the Zulu and Xhosa. In addition, 13 percent are Afrikaners (whites of Dutch origin) and 8 percent are of British decent. We will refer to the latter as *British South Africans* in the context of this section. Other important minorities include several Asian groups. There are also vast differences in business styles between urban and rural areas in South Africa. This great diversity makes preparing for specific business interactions difficult. Some business practices may deviate from the general guidelines provided in this section. Always expect the unexpected when doing business in this country.

Relationships and Respect

Building lasting and trusting relationships is important to most people in this country. However, they are usually not a necessary precondition for initial business interactions. Your counterparts' expectation may be to get to know you better as you do business together. Afrikaners and black South Africans may take relationship building even more seriously and often expect to establish strong bonds prior to closing any deals. Although people in the country may emphasize near-term results over long-range objectives, they are generally more interested in building long-term relationships than in making quick deals. Since South Africans may initially be very cautious when dealing with foreigners, gaining their trust and establishing good will is going to take time. It is very important for you to emphasize frequently the long-term benefits and your commitment to the business relationship you are seeking to build.

Business relationships in this country exist both at the individual and at the company level. Most South Africans want to do business only with those they like and trust. However, if your company replaces you with someone else over the course of a negotiation, it may be easy for your replacement to take things over from where you left them. Likewise, if you introduce someone else from your company into an existing business relationship, that person may quickly be accepted as a valid business partner.

Conventions and rules regarding race and color can be very strict. It is usually best to follow the lead of your host concerning these matters. Though Whites, particularly Afrikaners, sometimes retain a paternal or caretaker attitude toward blacks, you will rarely hear openly racist comments. When dealing with black businesspeople, try to show understanding and sensitivity toward the fact that this group long represented an oppressed majority. In addition, remember that South African blacks felt betrayed by most of the western world at some point.

In South Africa's business culture, the respect a person enjoys may depend strongly on his or her education. People of British decent highly respect status and rank, while others may be more impressed with personal knowledge and accomplishments. Admired personal traits include sincerity and dependability.

Communication

While English is widely spoken, it is only one of eleven official languages of the country. Most white South Africans are bilingual, speaking English and Afrikaans, which is closely related to Dutch. Blacks speak their own native tongue and may have a working knowledge of Afrikaans and English.

Businesspeople in this country usually speak in a controlled fashion, only occasionally raising their voices to make a point. At restaurants, especially those used for business lunches and dinners, keep conversations at a quiet level. Being loud may be regarded as bad manners. Interrupting others is often considered rude. Periods of silence do not necessarily convey a negative message. Afrikaners and British South Africans rarely show their emotions openly, but Blacks may be less restrained. People generally converse while standing around two to three feet apart, possibly closer among Blacks.

While most South Africans avoid confrontation, levels of directness may vary greatly. Afrikaners are often much more direct and may be very blunt. They do not find it difficult to say 'no' if they dislike a request or proposal. Afrikaners value straightforwardness and honesty much more highly than tact or diplomacy. They dislike vague statements and openly share opinions, concerns, and feelings with others. British South Africans are often somewhat vague and can be hard to read. While you may occasionally get a direct 'no,' evasive responses like 'I'll get back to you' could indicate a lack of interest in what you have to offer. Black South Africans, on the other hand, can be more indirect than the other groups. Instead of 'no,' they may give seemingly ambiguous answers such as 'I am not sure,' 'we will think about it,' or 'this will require further investigation.' Each of these could mean 'no,' as does a 'yes' that sounds hesitant or weak. Alternatively, a respondent may deliberately ignore your question. With Blacks, extended silence likely communicates a negative message.

Gestures are usually subtle, especially among British South Africans. Physical contact is rare among Whites but can be frequent among Blacks. However, never touch someone's head, not even that of a child. Do not use your fingers to point at others. Instead, point with your head. Eye contact should be frequent as this conveys sincerity. However, make it less frequent with a superior and do not stare at people.

Initial Contacts and Meetings

Having a local contact can be an advantage but is usually not a necessary precondition to doing business.

Negotiations in the country can be conducted by individuals or teams of negotiators. It is advisable that teams be well aligned, with roles clearly assigned to each member. With Blacks, changing a team member may require the relationship building process to start over and should therefore be avoided. It will be noted very favorably if a senior executive attends the initial meeting for your company. There will not be an expectation that the executive attends future meetings.

Scheduling meetings in advance is required. However, you can sometimes do this on short notice if the parties had previous business interactions. Since South Africans want to know whom they will be meeting, provide details on titles, positions, and responsibilities of attendees ahead of time. Agreeing on an agenda upfront can also be useful. That agenda will usually be followed. While meetings may not start on time, South Africans generally expect foreign visitors to be punctual. Avoid being more than 5 to 10 minutes late. Black South Africans may be less concerned with time. Displaying anger if you have to wait reflects poorly on you.

Names are usually given in the order of first name, family name. Use *Mr./Mrs./Miss* plus the family name. If a person has an academic title, use it instead, followed by the family name. Before calling South Africans by their first names, wait until they offer it. Introductions are accompanied by firm handshakes. Men should wait for women to initiate handshakes.

The exchange of business cards is not an essential step, but it is best to bring a sufficient supply. They may sometimes be exchanged at the end rather than the beginning of the meeting. Having your card printed in English is usually sufficient. Show doctorate degrees on your card and make sure that it clearly states your professional title, especially if you have the seniority to make decisions. Offer your card to every-one present. If someone does not give you his or her card, this may signal that the person does not want to do business with you. When presenting your card, smile and keep eye contact, then take a few moments to look at the card you received. Next, place it on the table in front of you.

Meetings usually start with some polite small talk, which may be extensive with Af-rikaners or Blacks. A sense of humor is appreciated, but know that South African hu-mor is often dry and earthy. People rarely discuss their private life around meetings and you should not inquire about their family or marital status. The overall meeting atmosphere is usually quite formal, especially early in the business relationship.

While one purpose of the initial meeting is to establish personal rapport and decide whether the other can be trusted, its primary focus will be on business topics. A first meeting will rarely lead to a straight decision.

The appearance of your presentation materials is not very important as long as you include good and easy-to-understand visuals. Keep your presentation short and to the point. South African businesspeople are not easily impressed with fancy slide presentations. Having your English-language handout materials translated into an-other local language is not required.

Negotiation

Attitudes and Styles – Negotiation approaches in South Africa may depend on your counterparts' cultural background. With Afrikaners, the primary approach to ne-gotiating is often to employ distributive and contingency bargaining. They can be quite competitive and may be unwilling to agree with compromises unless it is their only option to keep the negotiation from getting stuck. In contrast, Black and British South Africans may view negotiating as a joint problem-solving process. The lat-ter are often willing to compromise as necessary to reach agreement, while Blacks may be inclined to leverage relationships as a way to resolve disagreements. They may also focus more on the longer-term benefits of the business deal than the other groups.

With all of the groups, the buyer is in a superior position but both sides in a busi-ness deal own the responsibility to reach agreement. South Africans believe in the concept of win-win and will expect you to reciprocate their respect and trust. It is strongly advisable to avoid any open confrontation and to remain respectful and cooperative.

Should a dispute arise at any stage of a negotiation, you might be able to reach resolution through give-and-take compromising and appeals to your counterparts' fairness if you are negotiating with British South Africans. With the other groups, it can be best to leverage personal relationships and emphasize common interests and long-term benefits. Patience and creativity will pay strong dividends.

Sharing of Information – South African negotiators may spend considerable time gathering information and discussing details before the bargaining stage of a ne-gotiation can begin. Most of them believe in information sharing as a way to build trust. This does not mean that they will readily reveal everything you might want to know during your negotiation. However, negotiations can become very difficult if one side appears to be hiding information from the other.

Pace of Negotiation – How long your negotiation in South Africa may take can be hard to predict. Traditional companies may be very slow, spending considerable time gathering information, bargaining, and making decisions. Attempts to accelerate the process may be counterproductive, so be patient, and allow plenty of time. On the other hand, South Africans can be decisive and quick on their feet, so you may be able to finish the negotiation in a short time span once you have managed to win their trust.

Bargaining – Cultural influences play a big role in the bargaining stage of a negotiation in South Africa. British South Africans view bargaining as a necessary element of the process to find a compromise between the parties, but often dislike haggling. They can be tough negotiators but will strive to play a 'fair game.' Prices may only move by about 20 percent or so between initial offer and final agreement. While Afrikaners are not overly fond of bargaining and dislike haggling, they can be quite good at both. With them, prices may move by 20 to 30 percent. Of all cultural groups in the country, Blacks may be most fond of both bargaining and haggling. When negotiating with someone from this group, be prepared that prices may move by 40 percent or more.

With all groups, it is best to avoid 'hard selling' as most South Africans strongly dislike that style. At times, white South Africans may appear passive, 'taking everything in.' However, they will take control of the negotiation at an opportune moment. Leave yourself room enough for concessions and prepare alternative options. Ask the other side to reciprocate if you make concessions. Offers to provide continuing service to a South African client, in spite of long distances, can also be valuable bargaining concessions. Businesspeople in the country often find it difficult to overcome the isolation imposed on them by geography.

South Africans usually prefer to negotiate in a straightforward style. They use deceptive techniques only infrequently, such as telling lies, sending fake non-verbal messages, pretending to be disinterested in the whole deal or in single concessions, misrepresenting an item's value, or making false demands and concessions. Carefully orchestrated, 'good cop, bad cop' may be an effective tactic to use in your own negotiation approach. Businesspeople may claim limited authority, stating that they have to ask for their manager's approval. This could be a tactic or the truth.

Negotiators in the country use pressure techniques only as long as they can be applied in a non-confrontational fashion. They may open with their best offer, show some intransigence, make final offers, or attempt to nibble. Silence could simply be a part of the conversation, although it may also signal rejection of a proposal. Be very careful when attempting to apply time pressure. This may offend your counterparts, as they strongly dislike being rushed. While the negotiation will not necessarily be over, they may become very reserved and cautious. Expiring offers and ultimatums are only a last resort when negotiating with South Africans. If they fail to draw an immediate positive reaction, the deal will be over.

Avoid all aggressive tactics in South Africa. Though Afrikaners may occasionally appear aggressive, this usually only reflects their direct and blunt style rather than any tactical behavior. Responding in kind is rarely productive. People will not shy away from open confrontation if challenged, but this is likely to deteriorate rather than strengthen your bargaining position. Signs of anger, threats, or warnings usually indicate that the negotiation is not going well. They are rarely used as a tactic. Opening with an extreme offer may be viewed as ungentlemanly or even childish. It should be avoided unless you are negotiating with Blacks, who may be more receptive to this approach. With all others, it is best to open with an offer that is already in the ballpark of what you really expect.

Emotional negotiation techniques, such as attitudinal bargaining, sending dual messages, attempting to make you feel guilty, or grimacing, may be employed by Blacks but are rare with others. It is best to remain calm. Blacks, and also Afrikaners, may appeal to the personal relationship, in which case it is important to show willingness to work with them on finding an acceptable solution.

South African businesspeople may employ defensive tactics such as changing the subject, blocking, asking probing or very direct questions, making promises, or keeping an inflexible position.

Corruption and bribery are somewhat common in South Africa's public and private sectors. However, people may draw the line differently, viewing minor payments as rewards for getting a job done rather than as bribes. Also, keep in mind that there is a fine line between giving gifts and bribing. What you may consider a bribe, a South African may view as only a nice gift.

Decision Making – South African companies are often very hierarchical, and people expect to work within clearly established lines of authority. The decision maker is usually a senior executive who will consider the best interest of the group or organization. If decisions are made at lower levels, they often require top management approval, which can be time-consuming. Black managers often consult with others and carefully consider their inputs. This process can take a long time and requires patience. It is very important to learn about the company structure and win the support of people at all organizational levels who are involved in the negotiation, rather than focusing on upper management only.

With any of the cultural groups, it would be a mistake to expect decisions to be made instantly. Attempts to rush or put pressure on the process are not likely to succeed and may be counterproductive. Once a decision has been made, it may be very difficult to change.

When making decisions, white South African businesspeople may apply universal principles rather than considering the specific situation. They often dislike 'making exceptions,' even when arguments speak in favor of doing so. Personal feelings and experiences are considered mostly irrelevant in business negotiations, so people focus on empirical evidence, logical arguments, and objective facts. On the other hand, Blacks are often more interested in the specific situation at hand and may consider their feelings much more strongly than facts.

South African businesspeople are usually willing to take some risk, but often with great caution. If you expect them to support a high-risk decision, you may need to find ways for them to become comfortable with it first, for instance by explaining contingency plans, outlining areas of additional support, or by offering guarantees and warranties.

Agreements and Contracts

Capturing and exchanging meeting summaries can be an effective way to verify understanding and commitments. However, handshakes and verbal agreements may be considered binding, especially among Blacks. Verify agreement repeatedly since there is always a risk of misunderstandings, but remain flexible and do not insist that everything be put in writing. Similarly, keep your commitments, whether made orally or in writing. A foreign company that people consider a 'deal breaker' will find it very difficult to continue doing business in the country.

Written contracts may be created in a wide range of styles, from high-level to very detailed. It can be advantageous to make sure that the contract clearly spells out commitments and performance standards, drawing your counterparts' attention to these passages if necessary. Signing the contract is often only a formality. South Africans believe that the primary strength of an agreement lies in the partners' commitment rather than in its written documentation.

It is strongly recommended to consult a local legal expert before setting up a business or signing a contract. South Africans generally prefer to resolve disputes out of court, but they will not shy away from taking legal action if deemed necessary. However, do not bring your attorney to the negotiation table as it may be viewed as a sign of mistrust.

Contracts are usually dependable, though your counterparts may not meet some of the terms to the letter. Your counterparts may have a somewhat casual approach to deadlines, especially if the contract is not very strict on that point. Business partners usually expect the other side to remain somewhat flexible if conditions change, which may include agreeing to modify contract terms.

Women in Business

South Africa is still a male-dominated and chauvinistic society. Although they have equal rights in theory, women may be considered inferior and still have a hard time attaining positions of similar income and authority as men.

As a visiting businesswoman, it may help a little if you emphasize your company's importance and your role in it. However, you will still have to work hard to gain personal respect. Compliments about appearance and remarks with sexual connotation may represent little more than attempts to test your confidence. It is important to be gracious and act professionally in business and social situations. Displaying confidence and an appropriate deal of assertiveness is very important, since South Africans admire people who are tough, confident, and capable without being overly aggressive.

Other Important Things to Know

Business lunches and dinners, as well as other evening entertainment, are frequent and help in building relationships and growing your network. Business may or may not be discussed during these events. Wait to see whether your counterparts bring it up.

Social events do not require strict punctuality. While it is best to arrive at dinners close to the agreed time, being late to a party by 15 to 30 minutes is perfectly acceptable.

Gift giving in business settings is rare. It is best not to bring a gift to an initial meeting in order to avoid raising suspicions about your motives.

South Korea

Though the country's culture is quite homogeneous, South Korean businesspeople, especially those among younger generations, are often experienced in interacting with other cultures. However, that does not mean that they are open-minded. When negotiating business here, people expect that you adhere to the Korean way of doing things.

Relationships and Respect

South Korea's culture is generally group-oriented. Asserting individual preferences may be seen as less important than having a sense of belonging to a group, conforming to its norms, and maintaining harmony among its members. However, Koreans are more individualistic than their Asian neighbors. Building lasting and trusting personal relationships is very important. While members of other cultures may expect this to happen gradually over the course of a business engagement, many Koreans expect to establish strong bonds prior to closing any deals. Consequently, proceed with serious business discussions only after your counterparts have become comfortable with you. This may require significant time. Past experiences play a strong role. It is very important to emphasize frequently the long-term benefits and your commitment to the business relationship you are seeking to build. Keep in touch on a regular basis during negotiations and beyond.

Relationships are based on familiarity, respect, and personal trust. Modesty is also very important. Business relationships in this country exist between individuals or groups of people, not between companies. In spite of the group orientation of the culture and in contrast to Japan or China, it is possible to have personal discussions with your Korean business partners. However, even when you have won your local business partners' friendship and trust, they will not necessarily trust others from your company. That makes it very important to keep company interfaces unchanged. Changing a key contact may require the relationship building process to start over.

In Korean culture, 'saving face' is very essential. Harmony must be maintained at all cost, and emotional restraint is held in high esteem. Causing embarrassment to another person may cause a *loss of face* for all parties involved and can be disastrous for business negotiations. Reputation and social standing strongly depend on a person's ability to control emotions and remain friendly at all times. If you have to bring up an unpleasant topic with a person, never do so in public and always convey your message in ways that maintain the other's self-respect. The importance of diplomatic restraint and tact cannot be overestimated. Keep your cool and never show openly that you are upset. Causing embarrassment or loss of composure, even unintentionally, can seriously harm business negotiations. Moreover, refrain from criticizing your competition.

Remaining modest and doing everything you can to maintain cordial relations is crucial to your success. While Koreans view politeness and humility as essential ingredients for a successful relationship, these factors do not affect their determination to reach business goals. They are patient and persistent in pursuing their objectives. It is in your best interest to do the same.

In South Korea's business culture, the respect a person enjoys depends primarily on his or her age and status. You will commonly find leaders in senior roles to be of advanced age. It is very important to treat elderly people and superiors with the greatest respect and deference, which includes refraining from smoking and not wearing sunglasses in their presence. Admired personal traits include sincerity, persistence, and an ability to socialize.

Communication

Korean is the official language and spoken by almost everyone in the country. Not many businesspeople speak English fluently. In many cases, it is necessary to have an interpreter. Ask beforehand whether an interpreter should be present at a meeting. However, keep in mind that even professional interpreters may not always speak and understand English at a fully proficient level. When communicating in English, speak in short, simple sentences and avoid using slang and jargon. It will help people with a limited command of English if you speak slowly, summarize your key points often, and pause frequently to allow for interpretation. Do not assume that your audience readily understands you. Since saving *face* is so important in this culture, people will not admit in front of others that they are having difficulties.

Korean businesspeople usually speak in quiet, gentle tones, and conversations may include periods of silence. However, silence and distraction may also indicate that people did not understand you. In addition, people may be uncomfortable when someone is speaking for himself or herself rather than for their company or organization. Emotional restraint is held in high esteem, and loud and boisterous behavior may be perceived as a lack of self-control. At restaurants, especially those used for business lunches and dinners, keep conversations at a quiet level. Nevertheless, Koreans can get very animated and excited when entertaining visitors in more social settings. People generally converse while standing around three feet apart.

Because the concept of *face* is important in this culture, communication is generally somewhat indirect, though not nearly as much as in Japan. Koreans often acknowledge what they hear by saying 'yes' or nodding. This does not signal agreement.

Open disagreement and confrontation should be avoided. Koreans usually do not respond to a question or request with a direct 'no,' although they sometimes may. More often, they may give seemingly ambiguous answers such as 'we will think about it' or 'this will require further investigation.' Look for subtle clues that convey the true message. If you have to convey bad news to the Korean side, the more face-saving way is to use a third party instead of communicating it yourself. It is beneficial to use a similarly indirect approach when dealing with Koreans, as they may perceive you as rude and pushy if you are too direct. However, while Koreans are generally very friendly, they can also become quite direct, much more so than the Japanese or Chinese. At times, especially in the heat of a discussion or negotiation, they may be very emotional and outspoken.

Gestures are usually subtle in South Korea. It is advisable to restrict your body language. Non-verbal communication is important, though, and you should carefully watch for others' small hints, just as they will be watching you. Avoid touching other people except for handshakes. However, Korean men may hold hands, which is a sign of friendship and has no sexual connotation. When pointing at people or objects, use your open hand rather than a finger. When referring to themselves, Koreans put an index finger on their nose rather than pointing at their chest as Westerners do. Squinting the eyes or tipping the head back signals a negative response. Do not blow your nose in public since people find this repelling. Unlike in other Far East countries, eye contact should be quite frequent, although not to the point of staring. This conveys sincerity and helps build trust.

Initial Contacts and Meetings

Before initiating business negotiations in South Korea, it is advantageous to identify and engage a local intermediary. This person will help bridge the cultural and communications gap, allowing you to conduct business with greater effectiveness. The person may be able to leverage existing relationships, which could significantly shorten the time it takes until your potential partner is ready to do business with you. Koreans tend to be suspicious of people they do not know or with whom they do not have a mutual contact.

Negotiations in South Korea can be conducted by individuals or teams of negotiators. One-on-one negotiations require several rounds during which your Korean counterpart consults with the group participating in the decision-making. However, team negotiating is preferable since your team will bring broader functional expertise to the table and since you will be able to assign different roles to each team member, maximizing the team's impact. It is crucial for your team to be well aligned, with roles clearly assigned to each member and detailed strategies agreed upon upfront. Changing a team member may require the relationship building process to start over and should therefore be avoided.

Given the strong emphasis on hierarchy in the country's business culture, a senior executive should lead the negotiations for your company and your negotiating team should include senior leaders who know your company well. Find out who will participate on the Korean side, and choose people who match the rank of the Korean members. Status matters a lot, and a mismatch could be embarrassing for every-one.

If possible, schedule meetings at least three to four weeks in advance. Since Kore-ans want to know whom they will be meeting, provide details on titles, positions, and responsibilities of attendees ahead of time. Send your proposals and agree on an agenda ahead of the meeting. The agenda is usually strictly followed. Although meetings may sometimes not start on time, Koreans generally expect foreign visitors to be punctual. It is best to be right on time. If a delay is inevitable, call ahead and apologize profoundly.

In accordance with business protocol, people should enter the meeting room in hi-erarchical order. The Koreans likely assume that the first foreigner to enter the room is the head of your delegation. The same will be true on their side, allowing you to identify the most senior person within a group. That person is usually seated at the middle of the 'Korean side' of the conference table. You may get other clues by observing who receives the highest amount of deference within a group of Koreans. That way, you may actually be able to identify the hierarchical structure across the whole group.

Names are usually given in the order of family name, first name. The latter consists of two names, the generational name and the given name, separated by a hyphen. Some Koreans only give their initials, in which case they usually state their family name last, for instance 'Y.K. Kim.' Use *Mr./Ms.* plus the family name. Furthermore, Koreans are very status-conscious. If a person has a professional or academic title, use it to address him or her. Never call Koreans by their first name unless they in-sist on it. Introduce and greet older people first. Introductions are accompanied by handshakes and/or slight bows. Some people may not want to shake hands, so it is best to wait for your counterparts to initiate handshakes, which should be light.

The exchange of business cards is an essential step when meeting someone for the first time, so bring more than you need. If someone presents you with his or her card and you do not offer one in return, the person will assume that you either do not want to make their acquaintance, that your status in your company's hierarchy is very low, or, quite to the contrary, that your status is very high. Since many people are unable to read English, it is better to use cards with one side in English and the other in Korean. Show doctorate degrees on your card and make sure that it clearly states your professional title, especially if you have the seniority to make decisions. If any facts about your company are particularly noteworthy, for instance if it is the oldest or largest in your country or industry, mention this on your card since the Koreans view this very favorably.

Present your business card with two hands, and ensure that the Korean side is fac-ing the recipient. Similarly, accept others' cards using both hands if possible. Smile and keep eye contact while doing so, then examine the card carefully. Not reading someone's card can be an insult. Next, place the card on the table in front of you or into your card case. Never stuff someone's card into your back pocket or otherwise treat it disrespectfully. Also, do not write on a person's business card.

At the beginning of a meeting, there is normally some small talk. This allows participants to become personally acquainted. It is best to let the local side set the pace and follow along. There may also be an exchange of small gifts. Business meetings in South Korea are often quite formal, so be careful not to appear too relaxed and casual.

The primary purpose of the first meeting is to get to know each other, start building relationships, and gather information about the other side's areas of interest, goals, and weak points for the upcoming negotiation. In general, meetings do not serve as events for decision-making. Instead, they are opportunities to indicate interest, intensify relationships, gather and exchange more information, or to communicate decisions. It would be unrealistic to expect a meeting to lead to a straight decision.

The most senior members of your group should lead the discussion. It is good to make a presentation, but keep it simple and avoid over-designing it. Pause frequently and give the Korean side time for translation and discussion. Verify through diplomatic questions whether your audience understands you. Since saving *face* is so important, people will not openly admit it in front of others if they do not understand what you are presenting. Even if the leader of the Korean team does not speak English, make a point of addressing him occasionally.

You should bring a sufficient number of copies of anything you present, such that each attendee gets one. The appearance of your presentation materials is not very important as long as you include good and easy-to-understand visuals. Use diagrams and pictures wherever feasible, cut down on words, and avoid complicated expressions. Koreans may expect to discuss many details, so come well prepared, and bring enough background information. Having your handout materials translated to Korean is not a must, but it helps in getting your messages across.

Negotiation

Attitudes and Styles - Leveraging relationships is an important element when negotiating in South Korea. Nevertheless, South Koreans often employ distributive and contingency bargaining. While the buyer is often in a strongly favorable position, both sides are expected to 'take care of each other.' Ultimately, they are partners in a mutual dependency that is bound by their relationship. They may focus equally on near-term and long-term benefits. Although the primary negotiation style is competitive, South Koreans nevertheless value long-term relationships and look for win-win solutions.

Foreigners may perceive a dichotomy in the Korean negotiation style: on one hand, relationships matter a lot and must be maintained at all times, while on the other hand negotiations may become very emotional, aggressive, or outright adversarial. Koreans may see no conflict in this. They believe that while tough negotiating may require extreme measures, neither side should take anything personally. Adding to the challenge for foreign visitors, they are often expected to remain more controlled than the Korean side may be. Nevertheless, do not confuse the aggressive style with bad intentions. It is best to remain calm, friendly, patient, and persistent. Never allow issues during the negotiation process to create personal conflicts with your counterparts.

Should a dispute arise at any stage of a negotiation, you might be able to reach resolution through emphasizing personal relationships and re-establishing trust. It may be effective to have side discussions on a one-on-one basis with the most influential person on the Korean side. Pointing to the benefits of continuing the negotiation may also help. However, refrain from using logical reasoning or becoming argumentative since this will only make matters worse.

Sharing of Information – Korean negotiators are willing to spend considerable time gathering information and discussing various details before the bargaining stage of a negotiation can begin. In this phase, they seek to find the other side's weaknesses. Information is rarely shared freely, since the Korean believe that privileged information creates bargaining advantages. Your counterparts consider openly sharing your information foolish. However, if they have a strong and trusting relationship with you, they are usually willing to share more confidential details.

One caveat when negotiating in South Korea is that your counterparts may sometimes just be 'testing the waters.' They may only be looking to learn more about your product or service, deciding down the road that they prefer to build rather than buy. Be prepared for this turn of events and protect your intellectual property throughout your negotiation, even if the other side requests early access.

Pace of Negotiation – Expect negotiations to be slow and protracted. Relationship building, information gathering, bargaining, and decision making all take considerable time. Furthermore, negotiators often attempt to wear you down in an effort to obtain concessions. Be prepared to make several trips if necessary to achieve your objectives. Throughout the negotiation, be patient, show little emotion, and accept that delays occur.

Koreans generally employ a polychronic work style. They are used to pursuing multiple actions and goals in parallel. When negotiating, they often take a holistic approach and may jump back and forth between topics rather than addressing them in sequential order. In multi-item negotiations, people may bargain and haggle over several aspects in parallel. It is not unusual for them to re-open a discussion over items that had already been agreed upon. In addition, they may take phone calls or interrupt meetings at critical points in a negotiation. While they may be doing some of this on purpose in order to confuse the other side, there are usually no bad intentions. Negotiators from strongly monochronic cultures, such as Germany, the United Kingdom, or the United States, may nonetheless find this style highly confusing and irritating. In any case, do not show irritation or anger when encountering this behavior. Instead, keep track of the bargaining progress at all times, often emphasizing areas where agreement already exists.

If your counterparts appear to be stalling the negotiation, assess carefully whether their slowing down the process indicates that they are evaluating alternatives or that they are not interested in doing business with you. More often than not, though, this behavior indicates an attempt to create time pressure or 'wear you down' in order to obtain concessions. However, things can move fast if they see good business opportunities.

Bargaining – Korean businesspeople are often shrewd and skillful negotiators who should never be underestimated. Most of them enjoy bargaining and haggling, expect to do a lot of it during a negotiation, and may get suspicious or even offended if you refuse to play along. People in the country may use a wide array of negotiation techniques very competently. The bargaining stage of a negotiation can be very extensive. Prices often move more than 40 percent between initial offers and final agreement. Leave yourself sufficient room for concessions at many different levels and prepare several alternative options. This gives the Korean negotiators room to refuse aspects of your proposal while preserving face. Ask the other side to reciprocate if you make concessions. It is not advisable to make significant early concessions since your counterparts expect further compromises as the bargaining continues. You can use the fact that aspects can be re-visited to your advantage, for instance by offering further concessions under the condition that the Korean side reciprocate in areas that had already been agreed upon.

Deceptive techniques are frequent, and Korean negotiators may expect you to use some of them as well. This includes tactics such as telling lies and sending fake nonverbal messages, pretending to be disinterested in the whole deal or in single concessions, misrepresenting an item's value, or making false demands and concessions. Lies may be difficult to detect. It is advisable to verify information received from the local side through other channels. Similarly, they treat 'outside' information with caution. Koreans may use 'good cop, bad cop,' which is rare in other Asian cultures. It can sometimes be beneficial to use the tactic in your own negotiation approach, especially when assigning the 'bad cop' role to a legal counsel. This may allow you to separate debates over legalistic issues from the relationship. Carefully orchestrated, most deceptive techniques may allow you to obtain valuable concessions without damaging the overall relationship. Koreans will likely not use the 'limited authority' technique because groups rather than individuals normally make decisions.

Negotiators may use pressure techniques that include making final or expiring offers, applying time pressure, or nibbling. Final offers may be made more than once and are almost never final. Do not announce any of your offers as 'final'– your counterparts will likely not believe that you are serious and may turn the tactic against you. Time pressure can be difficult to counter. If Korean negotiators learn that you are working against a deadline, they may exploit this knowledge to increase the pressure on you to make concessions. Near the end of a negotiation, they may suddenly request last-minute concessions and 'compromises.' In extreme cases, they may try to renegotiate the whole deal on the final day of your visit. It is important never to take such techniques personally and to avoid open conflict. Know what concessions you are willing to make. On the other hand, time pressure techniques rarely work against them since Koreans are patient and persistent enough to overcome such challenges. However, you might be able to use these techniques should the negotiation take place on your home turf rather than in South Korea. Nibbling may prove useful in the final phases of negotiations. None of this will take your counterparts by surprise, though. Avid other common pressure tactics such as opening with your best offer or intransigence, since locals may interpret them as signs that you are disinterested in negotiating.

Korean negotiators regularly use extreme openings, hoping they can force you to reveal what you consider the real value of the items being negotiated. They do not view them as unfriendly acts as other Asians may. Counter the approach by firmly pointing out that you expect a realistic offer. Making extreme opening offers yourself may prove beneficial as it could surprise your counterparts and trigger a reaction. Be cautious not to appear overly aggressive, though. Threats and warnings may be used on both sides but should be subtle. In another tactical move, Koreans may get very emotional and show strong anger. Remaining constructive and professional usually helps refocus the negotiation. Threatened and actual walkouts should be avoided since they are too confrontational and may cause loss of face. Lastly, refrain from showing outright aggressive behavior even if you may feel that you are only reciprocating. It could prove very detrimental to your negotiation.

Other emotional techniques, such as attitudinal bargaining, attempting to make you feel guilty, grimacing, or appealing to personal relationships, are often used. If using any of them yourself, keep them subtle enough to avoid *face* issues.

Koreans often use defensive tactics. They may change subjects frequently, revisit previously agreed points, or introduce all kind of distractions. They may also ask very direct questions, attempting to take you by surprise. Prepare well for any of these.

Corruption and bribery are somewhat common in South Korea's public and private sectors. However, people may draw the line differently, viewing minor payments as rewards for getting a job done rather than as bribes. Also, keep in mind that there is a fine line between giving gifts and bribing. What you may consider a bribe, a Korean may view as only a nice gift.

Decision Making – The country's business culture is extremely hierarchical and superiors enjoy enormous deference. However, while you may encounter western-style entrepreneurs as the sole decision makers within their companies, decision making is often a consensus-oriented group process in South Korea. This can be confusing for Westerners looking to identify the 'key decision maker' in an organization, while in reality such a role may not exist at all. Decisions are often made through a process involving many stakeholders who establish consensus through a series of deliberations or exchanges of memos. This process can take a long time and requires patience. Influencing the decision making requires building strong relationships with as many of the stakeholders as you possibly can. The role of the senior leaders is to orchestrate the process, not to make decisions themselves. Nevertheless, their input carries a lot of weight and they usually have the final say, so do everything you can to win their support. At times, authority may be delegated to subordinates, making it important not to offend or ignore the lower ranks. One-on-one meetings may sometimes be set up. However, the person you meet is the contact to the group, not the one to make the decision.

When making decisions, Korean businesspeople usually consider the specific situation rather than applying universal principles. Personal feelings and experiences weigh more strongly than empirical evidence and other objective facts do, but they will consider all aspects. Some people may also be analytical and demand many data. More than most other Asians, South Koreans are able to take significant risks once they carefully assessed a proposal or situation.

Agreements and Contracts

Capturing and exchanging written understandings after meetings and at key negotiation stages is useful since oral statements are not always dependable. While these serve as tools to improve the communication and strengthen commitments, they should not be taken for final agreements. Koreans often prefer to establish general agreement, working out the necessary details later. The way they communicate agreement is by clearly stating all terms and conditions they agree with. An agreement exists only if both parties have done this, so do not simply respond with 'yes' instead of following this approach.

It is important to realize that Koreans have a very different view of written agreements and contracts from the one most Westerners have. In the traditional Korean view, agreements are just snapshots in time and contracts are similar in role to historic documents: they reflect no more than the agreement that existed at the time they were written up and signed.

Written contracts tend to be lengthy and often spell out detailed terms and conditions for the core agreements as well as for many eventualities. Nevertheless, writing up and signing the contract is a formality. Koreans believe that the primary strength of an agreement lies in the partners' commitment rather than in its written documentation. Never sign a contract in red ink.

Your legal rights are usually enforceable. Although attorneys are not common and not well regarded, it may be beneficial to consult a local legal expert before signing a contract. However, be careful when bringing your attorney to the negotiation table. Some South Koreans may read it as a sign of mistrust if you do.

Signed contracts may not always be honored. Because of their view of the role that contracts play, Koreans regularly continue to press for a better deal even after a contract has been signed. They may call 'clarification meetings' to re-discuss details. If you refuse to be flexible, allowing the relationship to deteriorate, contract terms may not be kept at all. While taking legal action is a viable option, you would be destroying any perspective of conducting future business with this partner and everyone within his or her network. Your best chance to ensure that your partners follow through on their commitments is to stay in regular contact and nurture the relationship throughout your business engagement.

Women in Business

While South Korea is still a strongly male-dominated society, gender roles have started to change some. There are many women, typically younger ones, in professional positions, although few have significant authority and influence. At the same time, most women are still struggling to attain positions of similar income and authority as men.

Most Koreans expect to deal with men in decision-making roles. Consequently, foreign women may at times find themselves in awkward or uncomfortable situations.

However, Western women are usually treated differently from Asian women. As a visiting businesswoman, emphasize your company's importance and your role in it. A personal introduction or at least a letter of support from a senior executive within your company may also help. Displaying confidence and assertiveness should be done very cautiously, and it is immensely important for women to avoid appearing overly bold and aggressive.

Other Important Things to Know

Formal attire is important when doing business here. Male business visitors should wear dark suits with neckties on most occasions.

Business meals and entertainment, in particular dinners, Karaoke singing 'contests,' and evening events that may include heavy alcohol consumption are very important as they help advance the vital process of building strong relationships. Refusing to participate in these activities may be taken as a clear signal that you are not seriously interested in doing business with your counterparts. Although business may not be discussed during these events, there could be exceptions. Your Korean counterparts may use them as opportunities to convey important messages or resolve disputes. Sometimes they may also try to obtain information from you that could strengthen their negotiating position. While you want to remain watchful, deflecting such inquiries if needed, never show signs of mistrust in your counterparts' intentions.

Punctuality is a bit more relaxed in social settings than in other East Asian countries. While it is best to be right on time for dinners, it is acceptable to arrive at parties within 20 minutes of the agreed time.

A topic to avoid in discussions is Korea's relationship with Japan. The relationship between these two countries is still overshadowed by strong animosities on both sides, especially among the older generation.

Gift giving is common in social and business settings in South Korea, including initial meetings. If you received one, it is best to reciprocate with an item of similar value that is typical of your home country. Giving a gift after signing a contract is also viewed very favorably. Give and accept gifts using both hands. Do not open gifts in the presence of the giver unless your host did so first. There are numerous potential pitfalls in what to give and how to wrap it, so prepare upfront or ask someone from the country to avoid causing embarrassment.

Cigarette smoking is very common in South Korea. Do not comment on it, and allow for cigarette breaks during meetings and negotiation sessions.

If your trip to Asia includes other countries, you should be careful not to make your counterparts feel that your visit to South Korea is one of many. The impression of making an effort only for them carry great weight. Specifically, avoid mentioning visits to Japan.

Lastly, know that the general work ethic is exceptionally strong in South Korea. Workdays may be very long, often 12 to 15 hours, and many people work on Saturdays. On average, South Koreans work about 2,400 hours per year, compared to around 2,000 in the United States.

Spain

Though the country's culture is quite homogeneous, Spanish businesspeople, especially those among younger generations, are usually experienced in interacting and doing business with visitors from other cultures. However, many may expect things to be done 'their way.' You should strive to understand, and occasionally emulate, their behavior in order to gain acceptance of your Spanish counterparts.

Ways of doing business are gradually changing in Spain. While more and more Spanish companies have received foreign investment and embraced modern management techniques, many industries and enterprises still hold on to the traditional style of doing business. The information given in this section focuses more on the latter and may thus not always apply in full.

Relationships and Respect

Building lasting and trusting personal relationships is very important to most Spaniards, who may expect to establish strong bonds prior to closing any deals. People in this country usually want to do business only with those they know, like, and trust. Establishing productive business cooperation requires a long-term perspective and commitment. Consequently, proceed with serious business discussions only after your counterparts have become very comfortable with you. This can be a time-consuming process. Spaniards tend to distrust people who appear unwilling to spend the time or whose motives for relationship building are unclear.

Business relationships in this country exist between people, not necessarily between companies. Even when you have won your local business partners' friendship and trust, they will not necessarily trust others from your company. That makes it very important to keep company interfaces unchanged. Changing a key contact may require the relationship building process to start over.

Establishing personal relationships with others in Spain can create powerful networks and is vital to doing business. Whom you know may determine whether people want to get to know you. Similarly, whether people think you are worth knowing and trusting often weighs much more strongly than what proposals you have to make. Personal networks rely mostly on strong friendships that also represent dependable mutual obligations. They may open doors and solve problems that would otherwise be very difficult to master. Maintaining honest and cordial relations is crucial. Third party introductions can be very helpful as a starting point to building a trusting relationship with a potential partner.

While Spaniards are usually warm and friendly, they are also very proud and may be easily offended by comments that leave room for misunderstandings. 'Saving face' and respecting everyone's honor and personal pride are crucial requirements for doing business in the country. Openly criticizing someone in front of others can have a devastating impact on your negotiation. The importance of diplomatic restraint and tact cannot be overestimated. Keep your cool and never show that you are upset. Avoid open conflict, and know that politeness is crucial.

In Spain's business culture, the respect a person enjoys depends primarily on his or her rank and status. Admired personal traits include confidence, poise, modesty, and sociability.

Communication

The country's official language is Castilian Spanish. There are also Catalan-, Basque-, and Galician-speaking minorities in the country. Though many businesspeople speak at least some English, it may nevertheless be useful to engage an interpreter, especially when meeting with older high-ranking managers. To avoid offending the other side, ask beforehand whether an interpreter should be present at a meeting. When communicating in English, speak in short, simple sentences and avoid using jargon and slang. It will help people with a limited command of English if you speak slowly, summarize your key points often, and pause frequently to allow for interpretation. Spaniards will rarely admit it if they do not understand parts of the conversation. Even when the main meeting language is English, your counterparts may frequently speak Spanish among themselves, not necessarily to shut you out from the discussion but to reduce their discomfort and ensure a common understanding among them.

While discussions may sometimes get lively, the Spanish dislike loud and boisterous behavior. At restaurants, especially those used for business lunches and dinners, keep conversations at a quiet level. Emotions other than passion are rarely shown in public, and self-control is seen as a virtue. Interrupting others or speaking in parallel is acceptable, though. People generally converse standing around two to three feet apart, which is not as close as in many Latin American cultures.

Communication in Spain is rather indirect. Spaniards prefer to be careful about what they say and how they say it. People may not get straight to the point when trying to get a message across. In addition, they may tell you what they think you want to hear rather than what they really think. They might insist that everything is in perfect order, even when this is not the case. Silence is rare and usually signals that there is a serious problem. You may have to read between the lines or watch for non-verbal clues to understand what is being conveyed. In difficult situations, look for other contacts in your network that may be able to help you find out or interpret what is going on. It is beneficial to use a similarly indirect approach when dealing with Spaniards, as they may perceive you as rude and pushy if you are too direct. The communication may become a little more direct and frank once a strong relationship has been established.

Gestures and body language are often lively, though not as extensive as in Italy. There may be frequent physical contact with others of the same gender. When pointing at people or objects, use your open hand rather than a finger. Eye contact should be frequent, almost to the point of staring. This conveys sincerity and helps build trust. Anger may sometimes be masked with a smile.

Initial Contacts and Meetings

Choosing a local intermediary who can leverage existing relationships to make the initial contact is useful. This person will help bridge the gap between cultures, allowing you to conduct business with greater effectiveness. However, choose your representative carefully. Once you have made your choice, it can be very difficult to switch allegiance to others.

Negotiations in the country can be conducted by individuals or teams of negotiators. It is vital that teams be well aligned, with roles clearly assigned to each member. Changing a team member may require the relationship building process to start over and should therefore be avoided.

Scheduling meetings in advance is required. However, you can sometimes do this on short notice if the parties had previous business interactions. Since Spaniards want to know whom they will be meeting, provide details on titles, positions, and responsibilities of attendees ahead of time. They will expect to do business with the decision-maker in your organization. The most senior executive to attend on the Spanish side will be at a similar level in the hierarchy as your own negotiation leader. An agenda is usually set upfront, but this is only a formality. It will not be strictly followed.

Although meetings may sometimes not start on time, Spaniards generally expect foreign visitors to be punctual. Avoid being more than 10 to 15 minutes late, and call ahead if you will be. Displaying anger if you have to wait reflects very poorly on you.

Names are usually given in the order of first name, family names. Most Spaniards have two family names, the first one from their father, and the second one from their mother. Use *Mr./Mrs./Miss* or *Señor/Señora/Señorita*, plus the father's family name, which is always the first one of the two family names given. If a person has an academic title, use it instead, followed by the family name. You may also hear someone addressed by the titles *Don* or *Dona*. This is a show of great respect. In Northern Spain, only close friends call each other by their first names. This is more relaxed in the South. Introduce or greet the most senior person first. Thereafter, greet everyone else individually. Introductions are accompanied by handshakes.

The exchange of business cards is an essential step when meeting someone for the first time, so bring more than you need. It is recommended to use cards with one side in English and the other in Spanish. Show doctorate degrees on your card and make sure that it clearly states your professional title, especially if you have the seniority to make decisions. When presenting your card, ensure that the Spanish side is facing the recipient. Smile and keep eye contact while accepting someone else's card, then take a few moments to look at it. Next, place the card on the table in front of you.

Meetings start with small talk, which can be extensive. This may include personal questions about your background and family, allowing participants to become acquainted. It is important to be patient and let the other side set the pace. Initial meetings may appear somewhat formal, but the atmosphere usually is quite casual in subsequent meetings as the relationship develops. A sense of humor will be appreciated as long as it is not sarcastic or cynical. Meetings in Spain may appear somewhat chaotic, with frequent interruptions and several parallel conversations. Do not take this personally; it also does not indicate a lack of interest.

The primary purpose of the first meeting, and maybe even the second one, is to become acquainted and build relationships. Business may be discussed, but do not try to hurry along with your agenda. The goal should be to establish respect and trust between yourself and your counterparts. It is unrealistic to expect initial meetings to lead to straight decisions. In addition, it is rare to get open opinions at the conference table, so watch for subtle clues and use other opportunities such as one-on-one conversations or business dinners to learn more.

Presentations should be short and concise. Make sure your proposal is clearly structured and presented. Spaniards prefer oral communication to data exchanges, so avoid overburdening your material with many facts and details. Presentation materials should be attractive, with good and clear visuals. Having your handout materials translated to Spanish is not a must, but it helps in getting your messages across.

Negotiation

Attitudes and Styles - Leveraging relationships is an important element when negotiating in Spain. Nevertheless, Spaniards often employ distributive and contingency bargaining. While the buyer is in a superior position, both sides in a business deal own the responsibility to reach agreement. They expect long-term commitments from their business partners and will focus mostly on long-term benefits. Although the primary negotiation style is competitive, Spaniards nevertheless value long-term relationships. While proposals should demonstrate the benefits to both negotiating parties, neither of them should take attempts to win competitive advantages negatively. It is important to remain non-confrontational throughout the bargaining exchange. Ultimately, the culture promotes a win-win approach. You will earn your counterparts' respect by maintaining a positive, persistent attitude.

Should a dispute arise at any stage of a negotiation, you might be able to reach resolution by focusing on logical arguments and facts. Ask your counterparts to suggest alternatives if needed. As a last resort, it may be effective to bring in the top managers on both sides and let them work it out.

Sharing of Information – Even when personal relationships are strong, your Spanish counterparts may be reluctant to share information openly. Many believe that privileged information creates bargaining advantages. In addition, figures and numbers can be unreliable in this dialog-driven culture, which could make them misleading.

Pace of Negotiation – Expect negotiations to be very slow and protracted. Spaniards do not hurry and dislike people who do. Be prepared to make several trips if necessary to achieve your objectives. Relationship building, information gathering, bargaining, and decision making may take considerable time. Attempts to rush the process are unlikely to produce better results and may be viewed as offensive. Throughout the negotiation, be patient, control your emotions, and accept that delays occur.

Most Spaniards prefer a polychronic work style. They are used to pursuing multiple actions and goals in parallel. When negotiating, they often take a holistic approach and may jump back and forth between topics rather than addressing them in sequential order. Negotiators from strongly monochronic cultures, such as Germany, the United Kingdom, or the United States, may find this style confusing, irritating, and even annoying. In any case, do not show irritation or anger when encountering this behavior. Instead, keep track of the bargaining progress at all times, often emphasizing areas where agreement already exists.

If your counterparts appear to be stalling the negotiation, assess carefully whether their slowing down the process indicates that they are evaluating alternatives or that they are not interested in doing business with you. While such behavior could represent attempts to create time pressure in order to obtain concessions, the slow decision process in the country is far more likely causing the lack of progress. People from fast-paced cultures tend to underestimate how much time this takes and often make the mistake of trying to 'speed things up.' Again, patience and persistence are vitally important.

Bargaining – Most Spaniards enjoy bargaining and haggling. They expect to do a lot of it during a negotiation and may get suspicious if you refuse to play along. Surprisingly strong emotions and many exaggerations may accompany the process. However, Spanish negotiators are more likely to focus on the big picture rather than negotiating point-by-point. Many will concentrate on reaching principal agreement, believing that they can always work out the details later.

The bargaining exchange can be extensive. Prices may move by 40 percent or more between initial offers and final agreement. Leave yourself a lot of room for concessions at different stages. However, concessions may not come easily, and Spaniards sometimes find it difficult to change their position. If they appear argumentative, it is important to remain cool and respectful, avoid confrontation, and frequently reaffirm the relationship. If needed, show willingness to compromise as a way to preserve the honor of both parties. However, it is best not to admit errors as doing so may hurt your credibility. After making concessions, always ask the other side to reciprocate. You can use the fact that aspects can be re-visited to your advantage, for instance by offering further concessions under the condition that the Spanish side reciprocate in areas that had already been agreed upon.

Deceptive techniques are frequent and can be effective. This includes tactics such as telling lies and sending fake non-verbal messages, pretending to be disinterested in the whole deal or in single concessions, misrepresenting an item's value, or making false demands and concessions. Your Spanish counterparts may make other attempts to mislead you in order to obtain bargaining advantages. Even when you can see right through a lie, it would be a grave personal insult to state or even hint that your counterpart is not telling the truth. It is advisable to verify information received from the local side through other channels. 'Good cop, bad cop' is a tactic that Spaniards rarely use, though it could be effective on either side of the negotiation table. However, it could be devastating if the other side recognized this as a tactic, and your team will need to exclude any 'bad cop' member from future negotiation rounds. Businesspeople are usually too proud to claim or admit that they have only limited authority, even if it is true.

Negotiators in the country may use pressure techniques that include making final offers or nibbling. Final offers may come more than once and are rarely final. Be careful when using tactics such as opening with your best offer, showing intransigence, applying time pressure, or making decreasing or expiring offers. Spaniards may consider these inappropriate or even insulting. Silence can be an effective way to signal rejection of a proposal.

Spanish negotiators avoid openly aggressive or adversarial techniques. While they may make indirect threats and warnings or subtly display anger, they will be careful not to appear aggressive when doing so. Extreme openings are not frequently used since they may adversely affect the relationship, so be very cautious when using the tactic yourself. Never walk out or threaten to do so in an aggressive fashion as your counterparts will likely take this as a personal insult and may end all talks. However, threatening a 'friendly walkout' while strongly emphasizing the relationship may be very effective.

Emotional negotiation techniques, such as attitudinal bargaining, attempting to make you feel guilty, or appealing to personal relationships, are frequent and can be effective. Be cautious not to hurt someone's personal pride when employing any of these tactics, though. At times, defensive tactics such as blocking or changing the subject, asking probing or very direct questions, or making promises may be used.

Note that opening with written offers and attempting to introduce written terms and conditions as a negotiation tactic is rarely successful. In most cases, businesspeople ignore or tactfully reject them and request that each aspect be negotiated individually.

Corruption and bribery are rare in Spain, though not completely unheard of. Both legally and ethically, it is advisable to stay away from giving gifts of significant value or making offers that could be read as bribery.

Decision Making – Most companies tend to be very hierarchical, and people expect to work within clearly established lines of authority. Communication is expected to take place across similar levels in the hierarchy and it could damage the respect you enjoy if you spent much time and attention on someone you outrank. Decision makers are usually senior executives who are often autocratic but will consider the best interest of the group or organization. They may consult with others before making the call. Subordinates may be reluctant to accept responsibility. Decision makers also rarely delegate their authority, so it is important to deal with senior executives. Gaining access to top managers can be difficult, though. You may have to deal with subordinates who could strongly influence the final decision. Maintaining good relationships with these intermediaries is crucial to your success. Decision making can take a long time and requires patience. Attempts to rush or put pressure on the process is an affront to Spanish business protocol.

When making decisions, businesspeople usually consider the specific situation rather than applying universal principles. Personal feelings and experiences weigh more strongly than empirical evidence and other objective facts do. Spaniards are often uneasy with change and reluctant to take risks. If you expect them to support a risky decision, you may need to find ways for them to become comfortable with it first, for instance by explaining contingency plans, outlining areas of additional support, or by offering guarantees and warranties.

Agreements and Contracts

Capturing and exchanging meeting summaries can be an effective way to verify understanding and commitments. Most Spaniards expect that verbal commitments be honored, although they may not be fully dependable themselves. Do not rely on interim agreements to be final, even if they come in the form of written protocols. Any part of an agreement may still change significantly before both parties sign the final contract.

Written contracts tend to be lengthy and often spell out detailed terms and conditions for the core agreements as well as for many eventualities. Nevertheless, writing up and signing the contract is a formality. Spaniards believe that the primary strength of an agreement lies in the partners' commitment rather than in its written documentation.

It is advisable to consult a local legal expert before signing a contract. However, do not bring your attorney to the negotiation table. The Spanish may read it as a sign of mistrust if you do.

Contracts are usually dependable, and the agreed terms are viewed as binding. However, it is important to stay in regular contact and nurture the relationship throughout your business engagement. In addition, business partners may expect the other side to remain somewhat flexible if conditions change, which may include agreeing to modify contract terms.

Women in Business

Machismo attitudes remain strong in this country. Women still have a hard time attaining positions of similar income and authority as men. However, businesswomen traveling to Spain will generally be treated with respect. As a visiting businesswoman, emphasize your company's importance and your role in it. A personal introduction or at least a letter of support from a senior executive within your company may help a lot.

Female business travelers should graciously accept any chivalric gestures they receive, while exercising caution and acting professionally in business and social situations. Displaying confidence and some degree of assertiveness can be effective, but it is very important not to appear overly bold and aggressive.

Other Important Things to Know

Impeccable appearance is very important when doing business here. Male business visitors should wear dark suits with neckties on most occasions. First impressions can have a significant impact on how people view you.

Working lunches are popular. Generally, business meals are important opportunities for relationship building. Business may or may not get discussed. Wait to see whether your counterparts bring it up.

Social events do not require strict punctuality. While it is best to arrive at dinners close to the agreed time, being late to a party by 15 to 30 minutes or more is perfectly acceptable.

Gift giving in business settings is rare, especially early in your engagement. It is best not to bring a gift to an initial meeting in order to avoid raising suspicions about your motives. However, partners may exchange small gifts when the contract is signed.

Sweden

Swedish businesspeople, especially those among younger generations, are usually experienced in interacting and doing business with visitors from other cultures. Culturally and ethnically, the country is quite homogenous, although immigration over the past two decades has started changing that. The Swedes tend to be proud people who may not be very open to information or assistance from outside. Their culture is close to that of Norway, though there is a bit of a love-hate relationship between them and Swedes may be quick to point out subtle differences. There are less similarities with Denmark, even more so with Finland, so be careful not to appear to be lumping them all into the same category.

Relationships and Respect

The Swedish culture is not one of strong individualists, at least not in the workplace. There are rarely elements of competition across business teams, and people usually do not want to stand out in the group. Business relationships are often only moderately important in this country and may not be a necessary precondition for initial business interactions. Your counterparts' expectation may be to get to know you better as you do business together. Unless past business interactions have already met their approval, Swedes may be cautious, appearing reserved and proceeding slowly. Once the necessary trust has been established, though, there will be a sense of loyalty to you as a respected business partner, which can go a long way should a difficult situation arise.

Business relationships in this country exist between companies as well as between individuals. If your company replaces you with someone else over the course of a negotiation, it may be easy for your replacement to take things over from where you left them. Likewise, if you introduce someone else from your company into an existing business relationship, that person may quickly be accepted as a valid business partner. This does not mean that the Swedes do not care about who they are dealing with. Personal integrity and dependability are important if you want to win their trust.

Sweden is a very egalitarian society. Treating someone preferentially is generally discouraged. Superiors are not necessarily considered superior and they are not empowered to be sole decision-makers. Bosses are often easily accessible and are expected to be team members and leaders at the same time. Autocratic behavior may meet with strong disapproval. A team member approaching management if there is a problem may be more common than the other way around. Performance is usually group performance, so it is better to reward or criticize the group, not the individual. In the country's business culture, the respect a person enjoys depends primarily on his or her achievements and education. Admired personal traits include sincerity and seriousness, knowledge, and expertise.

Communication

Swedish, the country's official language, resembles Norwegian and to a lesser degree, Danish. Most businesspeople in Sweden speak English well. However, avoid using jargon and slang.

Swedes usually speak in quiet, gentle tones. Never be loud and forceful – to the contrary, appearing reserved or even a bit shy may leave a favorable impression. Conversations may include extended periods of silence, which do not necessarily convey a negative message. Do not rush to fill in conversation pauses since your counterparts may only be taking time to formulate their thoughts. Also, interrupting others may be considered rude. Emotions are rarely shown in conversations, and the lively exuberance Americans often display can make Swedes uncomfortable. They may view it as excessive and 'over the top.' People generally converse standing about three to four feet apart.

Since confrontation is mostly avoided, Swedish communication is usually less direct than that of the Danes or Germans. However, Swedes also dislike vague statements and strive to keep business conversations focused on facts and objectives. They may ask for clarifications and do not find it difficult to say 'no' if they dislike a request or proposal.

Swedes use body language sparingly, although facial expressions may provide clues if they dislike an idea or proposal. Avoid talking with your hands. Physical contact is rare and best avoided. The thumbs-up gesture is positive as it signals approval. Eye contact should be frequent, almost to the point of staring, as this conveys sincerity and helps build trust.

Initial Contacts and Meetings

Having a local contact can be an advantage but is usually not a necessary precondition to doing business in Sweden. Negotiations can be conducted by individuals or teams of negotiators. It is beneficial to make sure that your team is well aligned in order to avoid confusing and irritating your counterparts.

Scheduling meetings in advance is required. However, you can sometimes do this on short notice, especially if the parties have had previous business interactions. Since the Swedes want to know whom they will be meeting, provide details on positions and responsibilities of attendees ahead of time. Titles are not very important, though. Agreeing on an agenda upfront can also be useful. Avoid rescheduling meetings if you can. Swedes value punctuality. At any meeting, whether business or social, it is therefore best to be right on time. Arriving late without having a valid and plausible excuse make be taken as a sign of disrespect. Expect meetings to end on or close to the scheduled time.

Names are usually given in the order of first name, family name. Some Swedes may have two first names. Addressing people with *Mr./Mrs./Miss* or *Herr/Fru/Froken* plus the family name is common only in formal situations. Normally, you address Swedish people by their first names, especially if they introduced themselves that way. Otherwise, wait until they offer it. If a person has an academic title, such as *Doctor* or *Professor*, use it instead, followed by the family name. Introductions are accompanied by firm handshakes.

The exchange of business cards is an essential step when meeting someone for the first time, so bring more than you need. Almost all businesspeople in Sweden read English, so there is no need to have your card translated. Showing titles and advanced degrees on your card is not important. Even senior executives may not always include their title on their business cards. When presenting your card, smile and keep eye contact, then take a few moments to look at the card you received.

Meetings usually get right down to business with little or no small talk. Keep in mind that Swedes are sincere people who dislike superficiality in conversation. Humor rarely has a place in business discussions, one's private life should not be discussed there at all, and personal comments should also be avoided. Business is a serious matter in Sweden, and meetings can be quite formal. While the primary purpose of the first meeting is to become acquainted, the discussion will mostly focus on business topics. It is vital to come well prepared as the Swedes hate wasting time. Nevertheless, it is unrealistic to expect initial meetings to lead to straight decisions.

Presentations should be short and concise. Facts and figures are crucial. Allow sufficient time for questions and clarifications. In some settings, for instance if most people in the audience do not know each other, you may not get any questions. The appearance of your presentation materials is not very important as long as you include good and easy-to-understand visuals. Having your English-language handout materials translated to Swedish is not required.

Negotiation

Attitudes and Styles – To the Swedes, negotiating is usually a joint problem-solving process. Buyer and seller in a business deal are equal partners who both own the responsibility to reach agreement. They may focus equally on near-term and long-term benefits. The primary negotiation style is cooperative and people may be open to compromising if viewed helpful in order to move the negotiation forward. Since the Swedes believe in the concept of win-win, they expect you to reciprocate their respect and trust. It is strongly advisable to avoid any open confrontation or conflict, and to remain calm, friendly, patient, and persistent.

Should a dispute arise at any stage of a negotiation, you might be able to reach resolution by focusing on logical reasoning and facts while remaining open and constructive.

Sharing of Information – Swedish negotiators believe in information sharing as a way to build trust. This does not mean that they will readily reveal everything you might want to know during your negotiation. However, negotiations can become very difficult if one side appears to be hiding information from the other.

Pace of Negotiation – Expect negotiations to be slow. The methodical and carefully planned approach the Swedes use in preparing for the negotiation and gathering information takes considerable time, as does the effort needed to work out details of an agreement. Remain patient, control your emotions, and accept the inevitable delays.

The Swedes generally prefer a monochronic work style. They are used to pursuing actions and goals systematically, and they dislike interruptions or digressions. When negotiating, they often work their way down a list of objectives in sequential order, bargaining for each item separately, and may be unwilling to revisit aspects that have already been agreed upon. They may show little tolerance if a more polychronic counterpart challenges this approach, which they view as systematic and effective. This rigid style may be difficult to tolerate for negotiators from highly polychronic cultures, such as most Asians, Arabs, some Southern Europeans, or most Latin Americans, who may view it as closed-minded and overly restrictive. In any case, do not show irritation or anger when encountering this behavior. Instead, be willing to bargain over some items individually. Otherwise, clearly indicate that your agreement is conditional and contingent on other items.

Bargaining – Swedes dislike bargaining and haggling. They also do not appreciate aggressive sales techniques. While the bargaining stage of a negotiation may take time and require several meetings, prices rarely move by more than 10 to 15 percent between initial offers and final agreement. The concept of fairness is very important to Swedes, so while it is not difficult to obtain small concessions, your counterparts expect reciprocity and may take it very negatively if the bargaining exchange is too one-sided.

Swedes prefer to negotiate in a straightforward and honest style. They rarely use deceptive negotiation techniques. If they seem disinterested in a deal or in making specific concessions, they likely mean it. Realize that using any such tactics yourself, whether it is telling lies, sending fake non-verbal messages, misrepresenting an item's value, making false demands and concessions, or claiming 'limited authority,' could jeopardize the trust between the parties and damage the negotiation. 'Good cop, bad cop' is also not advisable as the tactic may lead the Swedish side to question your trustworthiness.

Negotiators in the country use pressure techniques only as long as they can be applied in a non-confrontational fashion. They may open with their best offer, show some intransigence, or make a final offer, but often remain willing to make small compromises. Swedish negotiators may make their final offer quite early in the bargaining process, attempting to speed up the negotiation. Periods of silence in conversations are normal and may not represent an attempt to use it as a negotiation technique. Be very careful when using pressure tactics such as applying time pressure, making expiring offers, or nibbling. Your counterparts likely consider these inappropriate. While the negotiation will not necessarily be over because of this, the Swedish side may become very reserved and cautious.

Avoid all aggressive tactics when negotiating with Swedes. They will not shy away from open confrontation if challenged, but this is almost guaranteed to deteriorate rather than strengthen your bargaining position. Opening with an extreme offer could be viewed as an unfriendly act. It is best to open with one that is already in the ballpark of what you really expect.

Other emotional negotiation techniques are also rare and should be avoided when negotiating in Sweden, and appeals to personal relationships not only rarely work but also may be counterproductive. Swedes may employ defensive tactics such as asking probing questions or making promises.

Opening with written offers and introducing written terms and conditions may be effective tactics that could help shorten the bargaining process, which your Swedish counterparts may find desirable.

Corruption and bribery are very rare in Sweden. It is strongly advisable to stay away from giving gifts of significant value or making offers that could be read as bribery.

Decision Making – Swedish companies are much less hierarchical than most others are. Decision making is a group process through which consensus is established and during which all team members involved get opportunities to voice their opinion. The authority to make decisions often resides with managers at lower levels of the organization without requiring further executive approval. The role of senior managers is to dispense information, provide guidance, and coordinate the decision making as needed. They do not have 'final say,' and their decisions might not be followed if the group does not consent. This can be confusing for negotiators from other western countries who may be looking to identify the 'key decision maker' in an organization, while in reality such a role may not exist at all. Decision making can take a very long time and requires a great deal of patience. It is very important to learn about the company structure and win the support of people at all organizational levels who are involved in the negotiation, rather than focusing on upper management only. Once a decision has been made, it may be very difficult to change.

When making decisions, businesspeople may apply universal principles rather than considering the specific situation. They dislike 'making exceptions' even when arguments speak in favor of doing so. Personal feelings and experiences are considered irrelevant in business negotiations, so people focus on empirical evidence, logical arguments, and objective facts. Most Swedes are moderate risk takers.

Agreements and Contracts

Capturing and exchanging meeting summaries can be an effective way to verify understanding and commitments. Handshakes and verbal agreements are already considered binding and usually kept even though they are not legally binding. Nevertheless, it is best to confirm agreements in writing.

Written contracts can be lengthy, including detailed terms and conditions. Signing the contract is very important not only from a legal perspective, but also as a strong confirmation of your Swedish partners' commitment.

It is recommended to consult a local legal expert before signing a contract. However, do not bring your attorney to the negotiation table as it may be viewed as a sign of mistrust.

Contracts are almost always dependable, and the agreed terms are viewed as binding. Requests to change contract details after signature may be considered as bad faith and will meet with strong resistance.

Women in Business

Gender equality is very high in Sweden. Most women are working, and many hold leadership positions that are similar in income and authority to those of men. Quite a few Swedish women have made it into top business positions. Visiting businesswomen should have few problems in the country as long as they act professionally in business and social situations.

Other Important Things to Know

Business lunches and dinners are common. However, business is rarely discussed over dinner. Wait to see whether your counterparts bring it up. Swedes may dress up when going out for dinner, so avoid being dressed too casually yourself.

Working long hours is not necessarily interpreted as a virtue. Many Swedes may take it as an indication that a person is disorganized and incapable of finishing the job in time.

Switzerland

Swiss businesspeople are usually very experienced in interacting with other cultures. The country's population consists of a German Swiss majority, French Swiss and Italian Swiss minorities, the small group of Romansch living in the Engadin valley, and others. The German, French, and Italian parts of the population all show influences from and share traits with these respective cultures. In spite of this mix, all of the Swiss share many cultural values and are very proud of their country. Although the culture is heterogeneous, the Swiss can be somewhat ethnocentric and its members treat outside influences with caution. This is especially true outside of international business centers such as Zurich or Geneva.

Relationships and Respect

Building lasting and trusting relationships is important to most people in this country. However, they are usually not a necessary precondition for initial business interactions. Your counterparts' expectation may be to get to know you better as you do business together. Until business interactions that have met their approval have been conducted, the Swiss tend to be very cautious, appearing quite reserved and proceeding slowly. Once the necessary trust has been established, though, there will be a sense of loyalty to you as a respected business partner, which can go a long way should a difficult situation arise. Most Swiss businesspeople expect their partners to make a long-term commitment to the engagement.

Business relationships in this country exist between companies as well as between individuals. If your company replaces you with someone else over the course of a negotiation, it may be easy for your replacement to take things over from where you left them. Likewise, if you introduce someone else from your company into an existing business relationship, that person may quickly be accepted as a valid business partner. This does not mean that the Swiss do not care about who they are dealing with. Personal integrity and dependability are important if you want to win their trust.

The Swiss view it as very important to keep business and private life separate. It takes a long time to build rapport and establish personal relationships. Attempts to accelerate this process may only raise suspicion.

In Switzerland's business culture, the respect a person enjoys depends primarily on his or her rank, education, and achievements. Admired personal traits include integrity, discipline, modesty, team spirit, and experience.

Communication

The country's official languages are German, French, Italian, and Romansch. However, pronunciation and vocabulary of the German variant are significantly different and may complicate the communication for someone who learned it as a foreign language. Most Swiss businesspeople speak English well. Nevertheless, an interpreter may occasionally be useful to have. To avoid offending the other side, ask beforehand whether an interpreter should be present at a meeting. When communicating in English, speak in short, simple sentences and avoid using slang and jargon.

Businesspeople usually speak in quiet, gentle tones. Interrupting others is considered rude. Speaking slowly and clearly is a sign of authority, and loud or boisterous behavior is perceived as a lack of self-control. At restaurants, especially those used for business lunches and dinners, keep conversations at a quiet level. Conversations may include extended periods of silence, which do not necessarily convey a negative message. Emotions are not shown openly, especially in the German Swiss part of the country. People generally converse standing about three to four feet apart, closer than that in case of French and Italian Swiss.

Communication in the German part of the country is usually direct, though not as in-your-face as in Germany. German Swiss dislike vague statements and may openly share opinions and concerns with others. When communicating with them via letters or e-mail, do not waste time looking for messages 'between the lines.' There may not be any. However, most Swiss businesspeople also know how to express themselves in a more indirect and diplomatic fashion. French and Italian Swiss usually prefer this style and are considerably higher-context than the German Swiss.

The extent to which the Swiss use body language again varies. German Swiss use it sparingly and generally do not use a lot of non-verbal communication. They also make little physical contact. All of these are more extensive with French or Italian Swiss, although they may still appear more reserved than their French and Italian neighbors. The American *OK* sign, with thumb and index finger forming a circle, can be read as an obscene gesture in Switzerland. The thumbs-up gesture is positive as it signals approval. Eye contact should be frequent, almost to the point of staring, as this conveys sincerity and helps build trust.

Initial Contacts and Meetings

Having a local contact can be an advantage but is usually not a necessary precondition to doing business in Switzerland. Negotiations can be conducted by individuals or teams of negotiators. It is vital that teams be well aligned, with roles clearly assigned to each member. The Swiss are good at exploiting disagreements between members of the other team to their advantage.

If possible, schedule meetings at least one to two weeks in advance, and do not cancel one on short notice since that can be viewed as rude. The Swiss may want to know whom they will be meeting, so provide details on titles, positions, and responsibilities of attendees ahead of time. The rank of visitors does not matter as long as they are knowledgeable and have sufficient decision authority. Agreeing on an agenda upfront is common practice. That agenda is usually strictly followed. At any meeting, whether business or social, it is strongly advisable to be very punctual. This is especially true in the German Swiss part of the country. The German term for being late, 'zu spät,' translates into 'too late' in English. Being more than 10 to 15 minutes late without having a valid and plausible excuse can be a serious offense. Arriving ahead of the agreed time may be noted favorably.

Names are usually given in the order of first name, family name. Use *Mr./Ms.* or *Herr/Frau* (German), *Monsieur/Madame* (French), or *Signor/Signora* (Italian), plus the family name. If a person has an academic title, you may use it instead, followed by the family name. However, this could be considered conservative and old-fashioned. Except for people working in a multinational environment, only close friends call each other by their first names. You may never get to that point in a business relationship. Introduce high-ranking and senior people first. Introductions are accompanied by handshakes.

The exchange of business cards is an essential step when meeting someone for the first time, so bring more than you need. Most businesspeople in Switzerland read English, so there is no need to have your card translated. However, it is appreciated if you do. Show doctorate degrees on your card and make sure that it clearly states your professional title, especially if you have the seniority to make decisions. If any facts about your company are particularly noteworthy, for instance if it is very old or the largest in your country or industry, mention this on your card since the Swiss view it favorably. When presenting your card, smile and keep eye contact, then take a few moments to look at the card you received. Next, place it on the table in front of you.

Meetings with German Swiss tend to get straight down to business with little small talk, if any. It is likely more extensive when meeting with French or Italian Swiss. Humor and one's private life have no place in meetings, especially in early interactions. Business is a serious matter in Switzerland., and meetings can be quite formal. While the primary purpose of the first meeting is to become acquainted, the discussion will quickly focus on business topics. It is vital to come well prepared, as the Swiss, especially those in the German part, hate wasting time.

Presentation materials should be attractive, with good and clear visuals. Keep your presentation clear and concise. The Swiss are generally suspicious of hype and exaggerations and may respond negatively to an aggressive sales approach that might be effective in the United States. Know your topic well, and use logical arguments and concrete examples to back up your proposals.

Having your English-language handout materials translated is not required, though it will be appreciated. The Swiss are usually not impressed by high-gloss brochures and catchy slogans. Informational brochures should be serious in tone, providing a substantial amount of technical data and other hard facts. Your products are expected to conform exactly to the descriptions given.

Negotiation

Attitudes and Styles – To the Swiss, negotiating is usually a joint problem-solving process. While the buyer is in a superior position, both sides in a business deal own the responsibility to reach agreement. They may focus equally on near-term and long-term benefits. The primary negotiation style is cooperative, but people may be unwilling to agree with compromises unless it is their only option to keep the negotiation from getting stuck. Since the Swiss believe in the concept of win-win, they expect you to reciprocate their respect and trust. It is strongly advisable to avoid any open confrontation and to remain calm, friendly, patient, and persistent.

Should a dispute arise at any stage of a negotiation, you might be able to reach resolution by focusing on logical reasoning and facts while remaining open and constructive.

Sharing of Information – Swiss negotiators may share some information since this is viewed as a way to build trust. However, expecting your counterpart to reveal everything you might want to know during your negotiation would be naïve. A good part of the communication may be in writing, which the Swiss generally prefer.

Pace of Negotiation – Expect negotiations to be slow. The methodical and carefully planned approach the Swiss, in particular Swiss Germans, use in preparing for the negotiation and gathering information takes considerable time, as does the effort needed to work out details of an agreement. Remain patient, control your emotions, and accept the inevitable delays.

The Swiss generally prefer a monochronic work style. They are used to pursuing actions and goals systematically, and they dislike interruptions or digressions. When negotiating, they often work their way down a list of objectives in sequential order, bargaining for each item separately, and may be unwilling to revisit aspects that have already been agreed upon. They may show little tolerance if a more polychronic counterpart challenges this approach, which they view as systematic and effective. This rigid style may be difficult to tolerate for negotiators from highly polychronic cultures, such as most Asians, Arabs, some Southern Europeans, or most Latin Americans, who may view it as closed-minded and overly restrictive. In any case, do not show irritation or anger when encountering this behavior. Instead, be willing to bargain over some items individually. Otherwise, clearly indicate that your agreement is conditional and contingent on other items.

Bargaining – The Swiss are not fond of bargaining and strongly dislike haggling. They do not appreciate aggressive sales techniques. Although the bargaining stage of a negotiation can be extensive, prices rarely move by more than 10 to 15 percent between initial offers and final agreement. Businesspeople in this country do not make concessions easily. When selling, they focus on convincing you that their product or service is worth what they are asking. They are very good at making you believe that 'you get what you pay for.'

The Swiss prefer to negotiate in a straightforward and honest style. They rarely use deceptive negotiation techniques. If they seem disinterested in a deal or in making specific concessions, they likely mean it. Realize that using any such techniques yourself, whether it is telling lies, sending fake non-verbal messages, misrepresenting an item's value, making false demands and concessions, or claiming 'limited authority,' could jeopardize the trust between the parties and damage the negotiation. Carefully orchestrated, 'good cop, bad cop' may be an effective tactic to use, though.

Negotiators in the country may use pressure techniques that include opening with their best offer, showing intransigence, or making final offers. When using similar tactics yourself, clearly explain your offer and avoid being aggressive. Swiss negotiators may make a final offer quite early in the bargaining process. While this is not common practice, it could actually reflect a serious attempt to speed up the negotiation. Periods of silence in conversations are normal and may not represent an attempt to use it as a negotiation technique. Be very careful when using pressure tactics such as applying time pressure, making expiring offers, or nibbling. Your counterparts likely consider these inappropriate.

Avoid all aggressive tactics when negotiating with the Swiss. They will not shy away from open confrontation if challenged, but this is almost guaranteed to deteriorate rather than strengthen your bargaining position. Extreme openings are viewed as inappropriate and may upset your Swiss counterparts. It is best to open with an offer that is already in the ballpark of what you really expect.

Emotional negotiation techniques, such as attitudinal bargaining, attempting to make you feel guilty, or grimacing, may occasionally be employed. It is best to remain calm. Appeals to personal relationships rarely work. The Swiss often employ defensive tactics such as asking probing or very direct questions, making promises, or keeping an inflexible position.

Opening with written offers and introducing written terms and conditions may be effective tactics that could help shorten the bargaining process, which your Swiss counterparts often find desirable.

Corruption and bribery are very rare in Switzerland. It is strongly advisable to stay away from giving gifts of significant value or making offers that could be read as bribery.

Decision Making – Companies are often very hierarchical, even though they may initially not seem that way, and people expect to work within clearly established lines of authority. Nevertheless, the Swiss decision making process is unusual compared with most other cultures. On one hand, the deeply entrenched hierarchies demand that only senior managers make decisions. Once announced, their decisions are not discussed or questioned. On the other hand, decisions are rarely made without the consensus of the whole group they affect, and everyone involved or affected must agree. The Swiss, especially those in the German Swiss part, accomplish collaboration and teamwork within clear and respected hierarchies under the guidance of an accepted leader. This consensus-driven style and the methodical decision process that is conducted with great diligence and precision, takes much time and requires significant patience. French and Italian Swiss follow a similar but less rigid approach. Influencing the decision making requires winning the support of as many of the stakeholders as you possibly can. While this must include the top executive, that person's support alone is not sufficient. Once a decision has been made, it is extremely difficult to change.

When making decisions, businesspeople in the German and French parts of Switzerland may apply universal principles while Italian Swiss will more likely consider the specific situation. German and French Swiss tend to rely on empirical evidence and other objective facts, considering personal feelings and experiences irrelevant in business negotiations, while Italian Swiss may rely more on their subjective feelings. The Swiss are quite risk-averse and it make take extensive discussions supported by data and proven examples before they may become comfortable with a risky decision.

Agreements and Contracts

Capturing and exchanging meeting summaries is standard practice in Switzerland. It is an effective way to verify understanding and commitments. Although interim agreements are usually kept, do not consider them final. Only a final contract signed by both parties constitutes a binding agreement.

Written contracts are serious matters in Switzerland and tend to be lengthy. They often spell out detailed terms and conditions for the core agreements as well as for many eventualities. Legal aspects may be reviewed repeatedly. Signing the contract is important not only from a legal perspective, but also as a strong confirmation of your Swiss partners' commitment.

It is recommended to consult a local legal expert before signing a contract. However, do not bring your attorney to the negotiation table as it may be viewed as a sign of mistrust.

Contracts are almost always dependable, and the agreed terms are viewed as binding. Requests to change contract details after signature may be considered as bad faith and will meet with strong resistance.

Women in Business

The Swiss society is making progress towards gender equality and many women can be found in mid-level positions. Overall, few women have managed to attain positions of similar income and authority as men, though. As a visiting businesswoman, emphasize your company's importance and your role in it. A personal introduction or a letter of support from a senior executive within your company may also help.

As a female business traveler, displaying confidence and assertiveness can be effective, but it is important not to appear overly bold and aggressive.

Other Important Things to Know

Conservative attire is important when doing business here. While colored shirts are ok, male business visitors should wear dark suits with neckties on most occasions. First impressions can have a significant impact on how people view you.

Business lunches and dinners are common. Business may be discussed over meals.

Gift giving in business settings is rare. It is best not to bring a gift to an initial meeting in order to avoid raising suspicions about your motives.

Taiwan

Taiwan's mostly homogeneous culture is different from China's and Hong Kong's in several important areas. One needs to prepare separately for negotiations in Taiwan with its highly entrepreneurial and relatively fast-paced business culture. Businesspeople in the island republic are generally less long-term oriented than their brethren in the People's Republic.

Taiwanese businesspeople, especially those among younger generations, are usually very experienced in interacting with other cultures. On the other hand, assuming that Taiwan has become 'westernized' because of its many economic connections with the western world would be a mistake. People are not always open-minded. When negotiating business here, realize that some people may expect things to be done 'their way.'

Relationships and Respect

Taiwan's culture is strongly group-oriented. Asserting individual preferences may be seen as less important than having a sense of belonging to a group, conforming to its norms, and maintaining harmony among its members. Building lasting and trusting personal relationships is therefore very important. While members of other cultures may expect this to happen gradually over the course of a business engagement, many Taiwanese expect to establish strong bonds prior to closing any deals. Consequently, proceed with serious business discussions only after your counterparts have become comfortable with you. Since the Taiwanese may initially be very cautious when dealing with Westerners, gaining their trust and establishing good will is going to take time. It is very important for you to emphasize frequently the long-term benefits and your commitment to the business relationship you are seeking to build.

Relationships are based on familiarity, respect, and personal trust. Unlike in most western countries, business relationships in Taiwan exist mostly between individuals or groups of people rather than between companies. Accordingly, if your company replaces you with another representative, relationships need to be built anew.

In Taiwanese culture, 'saving face' is also critical. Harmony must be maintained at all cost, and emotional restraint is held in high esteem. Causing embarrassment to another person may cause a *loss of face* for all parties involved and can be disastrous for business negotiations. Reputation and social standing strongly depend on a person's ability to control emotions and remain friendly at all times. If you have to bring up an unpleasant topic with a person, never do so in public and always convey your message in ways that maintain the other's self-respect. The importance of diplomatic restraint and tact cannot be overestimated. Keep your cool and never show openly that you are upset.

Remaining modest and doing everything you can to maintain cordial relations is crucial to your success, especially when dealing with older people. When receiving praise, insist that you are not worthy of it or belittle your accomplishments, but thank the other for the compliment. This should not stop you from complimenting others. While the Taiwanese view politeness and humility as essential ingredients for a successful relationship, these factors do not affect their determination to reach business goals. They are patient and persistent in pursuing their objectives. It is in your best interest to do the same.

In Taiwanese business culture, the respect a person enjoys depends primarily on his or her age, title, rank, and achievements. You will commonly find leaders in senior roles to be of advanced age. It is important to treat elderly people with great respect. Admired personal traits include patience, humility, sincerity, and a willingness to work hard. However, young people's values may show greater influences of western culture.

Communication

The country's official language is Mandarin Chinese. However, people have gradually adopted native Taiwanese as the most common language. Many Taiwanese
businesspeople speak English, although not always well. It may be useful to have an
interpreter. To avoid offending the other side, ask beforehand whether an interpreter should be present at a meeting. Try to find one who speaks both Mandarin and
native Taiwanese. When communicating in English, speak in short, simple sentences
and avoid using jargon and slang. It will help people with a limited command of
English if you speak slowly, summarize your key points often, and pause frequently
to allow for interpretation.

Taiwanese businesspeople usually speak in quiet, gentle tones. At times, Taiwanese
people talking among themselves may appear emotional, but this would be misleading. To the contrary, emotional restraint is held in high esteem. Loud and boisterous
behavior is perceived as a lack of self-control. At restaurants, especially those used
for business lunches and dinners, keep conversations at a quiet level. People generally converse while standing around three feet apart.

Because the concept of 'saving face' is so important in this culture, communication
is generally very indirect. When responding to a direct question, the Taiwanese may
answer 'yes' only to signal that they heard what you said, not that they agree with
it. Open disagreement should be avoided and any kind of direct confrontation is
discouraged. People rarely respond to a question or request with a direct 'no.' Instead, they may give seemingly ambiguous answers such as 'I am not sure,' 'we may
talk again,' 'we will think about it,' or 'this will require further investigation.' Each
of these could mean 'no.' It is beneficial to use a similarly indirect approach when
dealing with the Taiwanese, as they may perceive you as rude and pushy if you are
too direct. Only a person with whom you have no relationship yet may occasionally
give you a straight 'no.' This is a bad sign since it could mean that your counterpart
is not interested in engaging in business with you. If you have to convey bad news
to the Taiwanese side, a face-saving way is to use a third party instead of communicating it yourself.

Do not take offense in the Taiwanese answering their mobile phones all the time,
even in the middle of important discussions. In this polychronic culture, interrupting one conversation to have another one and then coming back to the first one is
perfectly acceptable. It is not a sign of disrespect.

Gestures are usually subtle in Taiwan. It is advisable to restrict your body language.
Non-verbal communication is important, though, and you should carefully watch
for others' small hints, just as they will be watching you. Do not touch other people.
Avoid crossing your legs if possible since this may be viewed as a lack of self-control. Also, do not use your hands when speaking since it may distract the Taiwanese.
When pointing at people or objects, use your open hand rather than a finger. When
referring to themselves, people put an index finger on their nose rather than pointing at their chest as Westerners do. Eye contact should be infrequent. While it is
beneficial to make some eye contact when meeting a person for the first time, the
Taiwanese consider frequent eye contact intrusive and rude. Lowering one's eyes is

a sign of respect. Smiling can have several meanings, from being friendly to conceal-ing a lack of understanding, even signaling disagreement.

Initial Contacts and Meetings

Having a local contact can be an advantage but is usually not a necessary precon-dition to doing business. Many Taiwanese are experienced in doing international business.

It is often better to conduct negotiations in Taiwan with a team of negotiators than to rely on a single individual. This signals importance, facilitates stronger relation-ship building, and may speed up the overall process. In addition, Taiwanese teams usually include highly skilled negotiators who know how to outmaneuver even well prepared individual counterparts. Facing them as a team will significantly strength-en your position. It is vital that teams be well aligned, with roles clearly assigned to each member. Taiwanese negotiators may be very good at exploiting disagreements between members of the other team to their advantage. Changing a team member may require the relationship building process to start over and should therefore be avoided.

Given the strong emphasis on hierarchy in Taiwan's business culture, it is essential that a senior executive lead the negotiations for your company and that your negoti-ating team includes senior leaders who know your company well. However, while it is beneficial for your company's top management to attend the final contract signing procedure, they are not necessarily expected to participate in initial meetings.

If possible, schedule meetings at least two to three weeks in advance. Since the Tai-wanese want to know whom they will be meeting, provide details on titles, positions, and responsibilities of attendees ahead of time. Agreeing on an agenda upfront may be useful but is not required. People are careful not to waste others' time. Being late to a meeting or social event without having a valid and plausible excuse can be an affront. If a delay of more than 5 to 10 minutes happened, may sometimes be inevi-table in Taipei with its often-chaotic traffic, apologize profoundly even if it was not your fault. The most senior person on your team should enter the meeting room first.

Taiwanese names are traditionally given in the order of family name, first name, where the latter may consist of two names, the generational name and the given name. These two are usually hyphenated but may be spoken and written as one. Many people use assumed western first names, in which case they give theirs in the order of first name followed by family name ('Alan Chen'). Use *Mr./Ms.* plus the family name. If a person has an academic title, such as *Doctor* or *Professor*, use it instead, followed by the family name. Introduce and greet older people first. Before calling Taiwanese people by their first names, wait until they offer it. Greetings in-clude handshakes, which should be light.

The exchange of business cards is an essential step when meeting someone for the first time, so bring more than you need. If someone presents you with his or her card and you do not offer one in return, the person may assume that you either do not want to make their acquaintance, that your status in your company's hierarchy is very low, or, quite to the contrary, that your status is very high. Although many people are able to read English, it is preferable to use cards with one side in English and the other in Chinese. Show doctorate degrees on your card and make sure that it clearly states your professional title, especially if you have the seniority to make decisions. If any facts about your company are particularly noteworthy, for instance if it is the oldest or largest in your country or industry, mention this on your card since Taiwanese businesspeople view it very favorably. Also, consider having your company logo (but not the whole card) printed in gold ink. In Chinese culture, gold is the color of prosperity.

Present your business card with two hands, and ensure that the Chinese side is facing the recipient. Similarly, accept others' cards using both hands if possible. Smile and make eye contact while doing so, then examine the card carefully. Not reading someone's card can be an insult. Next, place the card on the table in front of you or into your card case. Never stuff someone's card into your back pocket or otherwise treat it disrespectfully.

At the beginning of a meeting, there is normally some small talk. This allows participants to become personally acquainted. It is best to let the Taiwanese side set the pace and follow along. People appreciate a sense of humor, but keep it light and friendly, and be careful not to overdo it. Business is a serious matter in Taiwan. While you will generally find the atmosphere to be pleasant at the first meeting, things may get more intense as the negotiation progresses.

The primary purpose of the first meeting is to get to know each other, start building relationships, and gather information about the other side's areas of interest, goals, and weak points for the upcoming negotiation. Your negotiating team should include senior leaders who know your company well. The most senior members of your group should lead the discussion. In Taiwanese business culture, it is inappropriate for subordinates to interrupt. It is good to make a presentation, but keep it simple and avoid over-designing it. Verify through diplomatic questions whether your audience understands you. Since saving *face* is so important in Taiwan, people will not openly admit it in front of others if they do not understand what you are presenting. If facing a question that is beyond your expertise, admit that you do not know the answer. Although this causes some loss of face, bluffing an answer can have more embarrassing consequences. Never openly criticize your competition. Doing so may turn your audience against you.

Most Taiwanese are comfortable with a high degree of initial vagueness. They may seem disinterested in clarifying many details until you have both come a long way with the business deal. Westerners may be uncomfortable with this perceived level of uncertainty. While it is acceptable and useful to try and clarify as much detail as possible even when your counterpart may not be eager to do so, do not read anything else into this style.

You should bring a sufficient number of copies such that each attendee gets one. The appearance of your presentation materials is not very important as long as you include good and easy-to-understand visuals. Use diagrams and pictures wherever feasible, cut down on words, and avoid complicated expressions. Having your handout materials translated to Chinese is not a must, but it helps in getting your messages across. However, using the traditional Chinese script that is used in the People's Republic of China is not sufficient. Bring a sufficient number of copies such that each attendee gets one.

You may have to make presentations to different levels of the organization in subsequent meetings; make sure that each is tailored to its audience. The local side may also ask you at the end of the first meeting to sign a Letter of Intent. The role of this document is to confirm the seriousness of your intentions, not to serve as a legal contract. Check it carefully, though, since the Taiwanese may abruptly terminate the negotiation if you do not strictly follow your commitments.

Negotiation

Do not refer to your negotiation with your Taiwanese counterparts by using this term. It might be viewed as too direct and offensive, so it is better to refer to the process using more neutral terms, for instance *exchange* or *discussion*.

Attitudes and Styles - In Taiwan, the primary approach to negotiating is to employ distributive and contingency bargaining. While the buyer is in a superior position, both sides in a business deal own the responsibility to reach agreement. They expect long-term commitments from their business partners and will focus mostly on long-term benefits. The primary negotiation style is competitive. Taiwanese negotiators may at times appear highly competitive or outright adversarial, fiercely bargaining for seemingly small gains. They may not believe in the value of a win-win approach, instead focusing on getting the best possible outcome for themselves. However, do not confuse the sometimes-aggressive style with bad intentions. Even when negotiating in a fairly direct and aggressive fashion, they ultimately maintain a long-term perspective and remain willing to compromise for the sake of the relationship. Nurturing relationships throughout your negotiation is therefore vital. It is best to remain calm, friendly, patient, and persistent, never taking anything personally.

The Taiwanese believe that foreign company representatives are often 'shopping around,' playing suppliers against each other in their effort to find the best possible deal. It helps your position if you avoid giving that impression. It will be very important to maintain continuity in the objectives you pursue, the messages you deliver, and the people you include in the negotiation.

Should a dispute arise at any stage of a negotiation, you might be able to reach resolution through emphasizing the benefits to both sides, remaining flexible and showing willingness to compromise. Show your commitment to the relationship and refrain from using logical reasoning or becoming argumentative since this will only make matters worse. Patience and creativity will pay strong dividends. In extreme situations, a mediator, ideally the party who initially introduced you, may help move the negotiation forward.

Sharing of Information – Taiwanese negotiators are willing to spend considerable time gathering information and discussing various details before the bargaining stage of a negotiation can begin. Information may be shared more openly than in China as many Taiwanese businesspeople have become accustomed with US negotiation styles. Nevertheless, your counterparts consider openly sharing all your information foolish. However, if you have a strong and trusting relationship with you, they are willing to share more confidential details.

Keep in mind that humility is a virtue in Chinese and Taiwanese business cultures. If you make exaggerated claims in an effort to impress the other side or to obtain concessions, they will likely investigate your claims before responding.

Pace of Negotiation – Expect negotiations to be slow and protracted, with extensive attention paid to details. Relationship building, information gathering, bargaining, and decision making may all take considerable time. Furthermore, negotiators often attempt to wear you down in an effort to obtain concessions. Be prepared to make several trips if necessary to achieve your objectives. Throughout the negotiation, be patient, show little emotion, and accept that delays occur.

The Taiwanese generally employ a polychronic work style. They are used to pursuing multiple actions and goals in parallel. When negotiating, they often take a holistic approach and may jump back and forth between topics rather than addressing them in sequential order. In multi-item negotiations, businesspeople may bargain and haggle over several aspects in parallel. It is not unusual for them to re-open a discussion over items that had already been agreed upon. In addition, they may take phone calls or interrupt meetings at critical points in a negotiation. While they may be doing some of this on purpose in order to confuse the other side, there are usually no bad intentions. Negotiators from strongly monochronic cultures, such as Germany, the United Kingdom, or the United States, may nonetheless find this style highly confusing and irritating. In any case, do not show irritation or anger when encountering this behavior. Instead, keep track of the bargaining progress at all times, often emphasizing areas where agreement already exists.

If your counterparts appear to be stalling the negotiation, assess carefully whether their slowing down the process indicates that they are evaluating alternatives or that they are not interested in doing business with you. While such behavior could represent attempts to create time pressure in order to obtain concessions, the slow decision process in the country is far more likely causing the lack of progress. People from fast-paced cultures tend to underestimate how much time this takes and often make the mistake of trying to 'speed things up.' Again, patience and persistence are vitally important.

Bargaining – Many Taiwanese businesspeople are shrewd negotiators who should not be underestimated. Bargaining and haggling are aspects of everyday life in Taiwan, and its people are often skilled in using a wide array of negotiation techniques. They generally consider all aspects of a proposed business deal rather than focusing on single details, such as the price of an item. The bargaining stage of a negotiation can be extensive. Prices often move more than 40 percent between initial offers and final agreement. Leave yourself sufficient room for concessions at many different levels and prepare several alternative options. This gives the Taiwanese negotiators room to refuse aspects of your proposal while preserving face. Ask the other side to reciprocate if you make concessions. It is not advisable to make significant early concessions since your counterparts expect further compromises as the bargaining continues. You can use the fact that aspects can be re-visited to your advantage, for instance by offering further concessions under the condition that the Taiwanese side reciprocate in areas that had already been agreed upon.

Deceptive techniques are frequent, and Taiwanese negotiators may expect you to use some of them as well. This includes tactics such as telling lies and sending fake non-verbal messages, pretending to be disinterested in the whole deal or in single concessions, misrepresenting an item's value, making false demands and concessions, or claiming limited authority. It is advisable to verify information received from the Taiwanese side through other channels if you have a chance. Similarly, they treat 'outside' information with caution. Since negotiation teams must be well aligned and always have to preserve face, the Taiwanese rarely use 'good cop, bad cop.' It can sometimes be beneficial to use this tactic in your own negotiation approach. Carefully orchestrated, it may allow you to obtain valuable concessions without damaging the overall relationship. However, it could be devastating if the other side recognized this as a tactic, and any 'bad cop' member of your team also needs to be excluded from future negotiation rounds. Be cautious when using the techniques of making false demands or false concessions. Since you must avoid causing loss of face, any overt attempts to bluff your counterparts could also backfire.

Negotiators may use pressure techniques that include keeping silent, making final or expiring offers, applying time pressure, or nibbling. Final offers may be more than once and are almost never final. Do not announce any of your offers as 'final'– your counterparts will likely not believe that you are serious and may turn the tactic against you. Time pressure can be difficult to counter. If Taiwanese negotiators learn that you are working against a deadline, they exploit this knowledge to increase the pressure on you to make concessions. Near the end of a negotiation, they may suddenly request large discounts, calling their request a 'compromise.' In extreme cases, they may try to renegotiate the whole deal on the final day of your visit. It is important never to take such techniques personally and to avoid open conflict. On the other hand, time pressure techniques rarely work against them since the Taiwanese are patient and persistent enough to overcome such challenges. However, you might be able to use these techniques should the negotiation take place on your home turf rather than in Taiwan. Silence can sometimes be effective as a way to convey displeasure, and nibbling may prove useful in the final phases of negotiations. None of this will take your counterparts by surprise, though. Avoid other common pressure tactics such as opening with your best offer or showing intransigence, since they cannot be applied effectively without running the risk of causing loss of face.

Taiwanese negotiators avoid most aggressive or adversarial techniques since they affect face. The risk of using any of them yourself is rarely worth the potential gain. Exceptions are extreme openings, which the Taiwanese use frequently, or threats and warnings. As long as an extreme opening offer is not openly aggressive, this approach can be effective. Should your counterparts appear aggressive as the bargaining gets more heated, remind yourself that they may not perceive it that way. It might be wise to deflect the pressure, for example by explaining other arrangements you have accepted for similar deals in the past.

As in most strongly relationship-oriented cultures, negotiators may sometimes use emotional techniques such as attitudinal bargaining, grimacing, or appealing to personal relationships. Be cautious when doing this yourself. You might cause the other side to lose face, which could in turn damage your negotiating position. Another emotional tactic you may encounter is if your counterpart proposes to 'split the difference.' You may often find that it is not in your best interest to accept. Politely explain why you cannot agree and make a counterproposal.

Local negotiators may use most of the standard defensive negotiation tactics. The exception is directness, which is rare in Taiwan. People may be shocked if you are overly direct yourself, which can be counterproductive.

Note that opening with written offers and attempting to introduce written terms and conditions as a negotiation tactic is rarely successful. In most cases, businesspeople ignore or tactfully reject them and request that each aspect be negotiated individually.

Corruption and bribery are quite rare in Taiwan, though not completely unheard of. Both legally and ethically, it is advisable to stay away from giving gifts of significant value or making offers that could be read as bribery.

Decision Making – While Taiwanese decision making is often a group process through which consensus is established, individuals, rather than teams, tend to make final decisions. This is especially true for entrepreneurs and younger people in progressive companies. You may therefore sometimes find it effective to meet with the key decision maker one-on-one in order to discuss and prepare a potential deal, in which case the 'official' negotiation serves primarily to finalize details and prepare the contract. In any case, it is important for the decision maker to consider the group interests and consult with others. Expect the process to take a long time and remain patient.

Most of Taiwan's companies tend to be very hierarchical, and people expect to work within clearly established lines of authority. When making decisions, businesspeople in the country usually consider the specific situation rather than applying universal principles. Personal feelings and experiences may weigh more strongly than empirical evidence, but they also consider objective facts. The Taiwanese may be reluctant to take risks. If you expect them to support a risky decision, you may need to find ways for them to become comfortable with it first. You are much more likely to succeed if the relationship with your counterparts is strong and you managed to win their trust.

Agreements and Contracts

Capturing and exchanging written understandings after meetings and at key negotiation stages is useful since oral statements are not always dependable. Do not rely on interim agreements to be final, even if they come in the form of written protocols. Any part of an agreement may still change significantly before both parties sign the final contract.

It is important to realize that the Taiwanese have a very different view of agreements and contracts than most Westerners. Legal obligations notwithstanding, many businesspeople still rely on the strength of relationships rather than any written agreements when doing business. In the traditional Chinese view, agreements are just snapshots in time. They view contracts as papers that document the intent of a working relationship at the time they were written up and signed, not as final agreements that can stand the test of litigation.

Written contracts are usually kept high-level, capturing only the primary aspects, terms, and conditions of the agreement. Writing up and signing the contract, in English and Chinese, is a formality. The Taiwanese believe that the primary strength of an agreement lies in the partners' commitment rather than in its written documentation. Before signing your contract, read it carefully. The other side may have made modifications without flagging them. While this could be perceived as bad-faith negotiation in other cultures, Taiwanese businesspeople may view the changes as clarifications.

Although it can be very slow and cumbersome to do so, your legal rights are usually enforceable. It is recommended that you consult a local legal expert before signing a contract. Also, ensure that your products are patented or registered in Taiwan to protect them against imitation. However, do not bring an attorney to the negotiation table, as this may be taken as a sign that you do not trust your counterparts.

Because of their view of the role that contracts play, the Taiwanese often continue to press for a better deal even after a contract has been signed. They may call 'clarification meetings' to re-discuss details. If pushed, the Taiwanese side will fulfill their legal obligations, but it is strongly advisable never to use legal pressure to enforce contracts with them. While you may get what the contract spells out, such a step not only destroys the business relationship, but it may also make it difficult for your company to engage with others in Taiwan because the word will get out. Your best chance to ensure that your partners follow through on their commitments is to stay in regular contact and nurture the relationship throughout your business engagement.

Do not expect your Taiwanese business partners to follow commitments to the letter. While deadlines are viewed as important, many businesspeople may claim that they have met their commitments even if they were a week or more late. Remain flexible and try to accommodate this in your own plans.

Women in Business

Gender roles in Taiwan are clearly distinct. While western-style equality is having some influence, women still rarely manage to reach positions of similar authority and salary as men.

As a visiting businesswoman, you will generally encounter few problems when visiting Taiwan, if you exercise caution and act professionally in business and social situations. Displaying confidence and some degree of assertiveness can be effective, but it is important not to appear overly bold and aggressive. If you feel that your counterparts may be questioning your competence, it can be helpful to emphasize your company's importance and your role in it. A personal introduction or at least a letter of support from a senior executive within your company may help a lot. If a negotiating team includes women, it is wise to let the Taiwanese side know about this up front so they can mentally prepare for it.

Other Important Things to Know

Business breakfasts, lunches, and dinners, as well as extensive banquets are all common and important. Taiwanese people enjoy meals and view them as great opportunities to advance the vital process of building strong relationships. Refusing to participate in these activities is a signal that you are not seriously interested in doing business with your counterparts. Although business usually does not be discussed during these events, there could be exceptions. Your Taiwanese counterparts may use them as opportunities to convey important messages or resolve disputes. Sometimes they may also try to obtain information from you that could strengthen their negotiating position. While you want to remain watchful, deflecting such inquiries if needed, never show signs of mistrust in your counterparts' intentions.

Especially with local companies that lack international expertise, business entertainment may sometimes include invitations Westerners may find highly inappropriate. In such cases, it will be very important to find a way to avoid the issue without openly rejecting the invitation, as this helps preserve *face* for all involved.

The Taiwanese value punctuality in most social settings. It is best to be right on time for dinners and banquets, and to arrive at parties within 10 to 15 minutes of the agreed time.

Common courtesy requires that you let others enter a meeting room or an elevator first.

Topics to avoid in discussions are Taiwan's relationship with China and the international diplomatic support for each country.

Gift giving is quite common in social and business settings in Taiwan. If you received one, it is best to reciprocate with an item of similar value that is typical of your home country. Giving a gift after signing a contract is viewed very favorably. Give and accept gifts using both hands. Do not open gifts in the presence of the giver unless your host did so first. There are numerous potential pitfalls in what to give and how to wrap it, so prepare upfront or ask someone from the country to avoid causing embarrassment.

Lastly, know that the general work ethic is exceptionally strong in Taiwan. Workdays may be very long, often 12 to 15 hours. Saturdays are normal workdays at many companies.

Thailand

Around 80 percent of the country's population is Ethnic Thais. The majority of the others in this pluralistic culture are Chinese. Many of the businesspeople belong to the Chinese minority. They often have strong connections back to family businesses in China, which can sometimes make it necessary to close a deal both in Thailand and China. Of all Thais, 95 percent are Buddhists and most of the others are Muslims. The country consists of two former kingdoms, Thai Lann to the North and Siam to the South. Power centers among the Thai elite still follow this division, so doing business countrywide often requires negotiating separate deals.

Businesspeople and officials in Thailand, especially outside of Bangkok, usually have only limited exposure to other cultures. When negotiating business here, realize that people may expect things to be done 'their way.' However, some among younger generations may have greater international experience and can be very open-minded.

Thailand is the only Southeast Asian country that was never under European rule. People are proud of their history. *Thai* means *free*. That notwithstanding, there is a strong allegiance to the King and his family. The country's government, though, has been the subject of many coups throughout its history. Government contracts may therefore not be secure in the long term. In addition, the country is divided into several provinces whose local governments may be very influential, especially away from Bangkok.

Relationships and Respect

Thailand's culture is strongly group-oriented. Asserting individual preferences may be seen as less important than having a sense of belonging to a group, conforming to its norms, and maintaining harmony among its members. Building lasting and trusting personal relationships is therefore very important to most Thai people, who often expect to establish strong bonds prior to closing any deals. People in this country prefer to do business with those they know and respect. Consequently, proceed with serious business discussions only after your counterparts have become somewhat comfortable with you.

Relationships are based on familiarity, respect, and personal trust, which can take a long time to establish. Business relationships in this country exist between people, not necessarily between companies. Even when you have won your local business partners' friendship and trust, they will not necessarily trust others from your company. That makes it very important to keep company interfaces unchanged. Changing a key contact may require the relationship building process to start over. Worst case, such a change may bring negotiations to a complete halt.

In Thailand's culture, 'saving face' is very essential. Harmony must be maintained at all cost, and emotional restraint is held in high esteem. Every person's reputation and social standing rests on this concept. Causing embarrassment to another person or openly criticizing others may cause a *loss of face* for all parties involved and can be disastrous for business negotiations. Reputation and social standing strongly depend on a person's ability to control emotions and remain friendly at all times. The importance of diplomatic restraint and tact cannot be overestimated. Keep your cool and never show openly that you are upset.

Thais are usually very friendly and polite. Life is there to be enjoyed and keeping a positive attitude is expected and appreciated. Never lose control of your emotions or be overly assertive.

In Thailand's business culture, the respect a person enjoys depends primarily on his or her age and rank. It is very difficult for Thais to have a conversation with a person whose status is unclear, since knowing whether someone is a superior, inferior, or equal strongly influences behaviors. Business leaders may have a high sense of self-reliance and can be very autocratic and authoritarian. Titles are very important. Admired personal traits include politeness, modesty, sincerity, honesty.

Communication

The official language of the country is Thai. Many businesspeople speak English, although not always well. It may be useful to have an interpreter. To avoid offending the other side, ask beforehand whether an interpreter should be present at a meeting. When communicating in English, speak in short, simple sentences and avoid using jargon and slang. It will help people with a limited command of English if you speak slowly, summarize your key points often, and pause frequently to allow for interpretation.

Thai people usually speak in quiet, gentle tones. Conversations may include periods of silence, which do not necessarily convey a negative message. Loud and boisterous behavior is perceived as a lack of self-control. People generally converse while standing around three feet apart.

Because being friendly and saving *face* are so important in this culture, communication is generally indirect, though slightly less so than in other Asian countries. Direct confrontation is inappropriate, and it is better to ask open questions instead of closed ones. When responding to a direct question, Thai people may answer 'yes' only to signal that they heard what you said, not that they agree with it. You rarely hear a direct 'no.' Instead, they may give seemingly ambiguous answers such as 'I am not sure,' 'we will think about it,' or 'maybe.' Each of these could mean 'no,' as does a 'yes' that sounds hesitant or weak. Alternatively, a respondent may deliberately ignore your question or pretend that he or she does not understand English. It is beneficial to use a similarly indirect approach when dealing with Thais, as they may perceive you as rude and pushy if you are too direct.

A Thai who considers you a superior will likely tell you what he or she thinks you want to hear, especially when others are around. This is a way to save *face* and preserve honor. Similarly, if asked to give constructive feedback, people may resort to highlighting only the positives, in which case you should listen carefully for what is *not* being said. Candid comments and criticism may only be conveyed in private, often through a third party. Similarly, it can be effective to deliver negative responses to your negotiation counterparts through a third party, which is a face-saving way.

Gestures are usually subtle. It is advisable to restrict your body language. Non-verbal communication is important, though, and you should carefully watch for others' small hints, just as they will be watching you. Avoid any physical contact with Thai people except for handshakes. Never touch someone's head, not even that of a child. Since Thais consider the left hand unclean, use it only if inevitable. Pointing with the index finger or the full hand is considered rude. Instead, gesticulate in the general direction of whatever you are referring to or point with your chin. Eye contact should be very infrequent. Thai people rarely look the other straight in the eye. Restrain your emotions and avoid any facial expressions that may suggest disagreement, such as grimacing or shaking your head.

Thai people do not expect foreigners to smile as often as they do. Smiles and laughter do not always indicate amusement or approval. Frequently, they may mask embarrassment, disapproval, and other feelings of distress. Accordingly, Westerners may sometimes observe Thai people smiling or laughing at what they might consider inappropriate moments.

Initial Contacts and Meetings

Before initiating business negotiations in Thailand, it is highly advantageous to identify and engage a local representative who can make the initial contact. This person will help bridge the cultural and communications gap, allowing you to conduct business with greater effectiveness. Without such an agent or business partner, even seemingly simple things such as getting items through customs can become very difficult and frustrating. Choose your representation carefully to ensure that they can accomplish what you expect them to do.

Conducting negotiations in Thailand with a team of negotiators instead of relying on a single individual may speed up the negotiation process. It is vital that teams be well aligned, with roles clearly assigned to each member. Changing a team member may require the relationship building process to start over and should therefore be avoided. Worst case, such a change can bring negotiations to a complete halt.

If possible, schedule meetings at least four weeks in advance. Since people want to know whom they will be meeting, provide details on titles, positions, and responsibilities of attendees ahead of time. While meetings may start considerably late, Thais generally expect foreign visitors to be punctual. In Bangkok with its often-chaotic traffic and resulting considerable delays, allow plenty of time to get to an appointment. Avoid being more than 10 to 15 minutes late. Displaying anger if you have to wait, which happens often, reflects very poorly on you.

Ethnic Thai names are traditionally given in the order of first name, family name. Addressing them with *Khun* plus the first name is perfectly acceptable. Using *Mr./ Ms.* plus the family name may confuse people who had little exposure to foreign cultures. Some Thais may actually call you *Mr./Ms.*, followed by your first name. Chinese people usually give their names in the order of family name, first name, where the latter consists of two names, the generational name, and the given name. These two are usually hyphenated but may be spoken (and sometimes written) as one. Some people use assumed western first names, in which case they give theirs in the order of first name followed by family name. Properly pronouncing your counterparts' names is very important. Academic and professional titles are highly valued and must be used. Introduce and greet older people first. Thais use handshakes only to greet foreigners. The local greeting is the *wai*: the hands are held together as if praying, touching your body lightly somewhere between your chest and forehead.

After the introductions, offer your business card to everyone present. Not having a card as a foreigner is viewed as unprofessional, even though you may not always get one in return. Business cards should be of high quality and printed in English, with the other side translated into Thai. Show doctorate degrees on your card and make sure that it clearly states your professional title, especially if you have the seniority to make decisions. Present your card with your right hand, with the Thai side facing the recipient. Similarly, accept others' cards using only the right hand. Smile while doing so, then examine the card carefully. Not reading someone's card can be an insult. Next, remark upon the card and then place it on the table in front of you or into your card case. Never stuff someone's card into your back pocket or otherwise treat it disrespectfully. Never write on a person's business card.

At the beginning of a meeting, there is normally some small talk. This allows participants to become personally acquainted. It is best to let the local side set the pace and follow along.

The primary purpose of the first meeting is to become acquainted and build relationships. Business may be discussed, but do not try to hurry along with your agenda. It is unrealistic to expect initial meetings to lead to straight decisions. Frequent meeting interruptions are normal and do not signal a lack of interest.

Presentation materials should be very attractive, with good and clear visuals. Use diagrams and pictures wherever feasible, cut down on words, and avoid complicated expressions. Having your handout materials translated to Thai is not a must, but it helps in getting your messages across.

Negotiation

Attitudes and Styles – Leveraging relationships is an important element when negotiating in Thailand. To Thai businesspeople, negotiating is usually a joint problem-solving process. While the buyer is in a superior position, both sides in a business deal own the responsibility to reach agreement. They expect long-term commitments from their business partners and will focus mostly on long-term benefits. The primary negotiation style is cooperative and people may be open to compromising if viewed helpful in order to move the negotiation forward. Maintaining harmonious relationships throughout the process is vitally important. While each party is expected to pursue their best interests, Thais disapprove of competitiveness and strive to find win-win solutions, avoiding confrontation and always leaving a way out for the other. In fact, Thais may prefer compromising even if there is no real need to compromise. However, keep in mind that there are often Chinese cultural influences that can affect negotiation styles.

Sharing of Information - Information is rarely shared freely, since the locals believe that privileged information creates bargaining advantages. However, it can be advantageous to share some information as a way to build trust.

Pace of Negotiation – Expect negotiations to be slow and protracted. Relationship building, information gathering, bargaining, and decision making all take considerable time. In addition, Thais have a lower sense of urgency than a Westerner may be accustomed to. Consequently, your expectations regarding deadlines and efficiency may be unrealistic. Be prepared to make several trips if necessary to achieve your objectives. Throughout the negotiation, be patient, control your emotions, and accept that delays occur.

Thai people generally employ a polychronic work style. They are used to pursuing multiple actions and goals in parallel. When negotiating, they often take a holistic approach and may jump back and forth between topics rather than addressing them in sequential order. Negotiators from strongly monochronic cultures, such as Germany, the United Kingdom, or the United States, may find this style confusing, irritating, and even annoying. In any case, do not show irritation or anger when encountering this behavior. Instead, keep track of the bargaining progress at all times, often emphasizing areas where agreement already exists.

If your counterparts appear to be stalling the negotiation, assess carefully whether their slowing down the process indicates that they are evaluating alternatives or that they are not interested in doing business with you. If small, insignificant details seem to have become major problems, realize that there may be larger problems that your counterpart is unwilling to address directly. To identify the real issue, ask open questions and try to see the bigger picture. More often than not, though, stalling behaviors are attempts to create time pressure in order to obtain concessions.

Bargaining – Thais like bargaining and haggling. They expect to do a lot of it during a negotiation and may be offended if you refuse to play along. They may use a wide array of negotiation techniques quite competently. The bargaining stage of a negotiation can be extensive. Prices often move more than 40 percent between initial offers and final agreement. Leave yourself sufficient room for concessions at different stages. Ask the other side to reciprocate if you made one. You can use the fact that aspects can be re-visited to your advantage, for instance by offering further concessions under the condition that the Thai side reciprocate in areas that had already been agreed upon. However, note that company policy is usually strictly followed, particularly in larger organizations, so be careful not to demand concessions that go against it.

Deceptive techniques might be used and it may be effective to use some of them yourself. This includes tactics such as telling lies and sending fake non-verbal messages, initially pretending to be disinterested in the whole deal or in single concessions, misrepresenting an item's value, or making false demands and concessions. Lies may be difficult to detect. It is advisable to verify information received from the local side through other channels. Similarly, they treat 'outside' information with caution. Thais rarely use 'good cop, bad cop' and it is best to avoid the tactic since the implications for relationships can be significant. They may claim limited authority, stating that they have to ask for their manager's approval. This could be a tactic or the truth. Since you must avoid causing loss of face, be cautious when using the techniques of making false demands or false concessions. While they can be very effective, any overt attempts to bluff your counterparts could backfire.

Negotiators in the country may occasionally use pressure techniques that include making final offers or nibbling. Final offers should not be made too soon since your counterpart may not believe that you are serious. Do not use tactics such as applying time pressure or making expiring offers, since Thais could view these as signs that you are not willing to build a long-term relationship. They may choose to terminate the negotiation. Avoid pressure tactics such as opening with your best offer or showing intransigence, since they cannot be applied effectively without running the risk of causing loss of face. Periods of silence in conversations are normal and may not represent an attempt to use it as a negotiation technique.

Thai negotiators avoid most aggressive or adversarial techniques since they affect face. The risk of using any of them yourself is rarely worth the potential gain. As an exception, extreme openings may be used as a way to start the bargaining process. However, use the tactic with caution since it may adversely affect the relationship if employed too aggressively.

As in most strongly relationship-oriented cultures, negotiators may sometimes use emotional techniques such as attitudinal bargaining, attempting to make you feel guilty, grimacing, or appealing to personal relationships. Be cautious when doing this yourself. You might cause the other side to lose face, which could damage your negotiating position.

At times, defensive tactics such as blocking, distracting or changing the subject, asking probing questions, or making promises may be used. The exception is directness, which is very rare in this society. They may be shocked if you are overly direct yourself, which can be counterproductive.

Note that opening with written offers and attempting to introduce written terms and conditions as a negotiation tactic is rarely successful. In most cases, businesspeople ignore or tactfully reject them and request that each aspect be negotiated individually.

Corruption and bribery are somewhat common in Thailand's public and private sectors. However, people may draw the line differently, viewing minor payments as rewards for getting a job done rather than as bribes. Also, keep in mind that there is a fine line between giving gifts and bribing. What you may consider a bribe, a Thai may view as only a nice gift. It may help if you introduce and explain your company's policies early on, but be careful not to moralize or appear to imply that local customs are unethical. Alternatively, let your local representative handle such aspects.

Conflicts and disputes that may arise during a negotiation can be difficult to resolve because Thais prefer to ignore or deny them. Patience and continuous friendliness pay strong dividends. Deepening and leveraging personal relationships may help. In extreme situations, use a mediator, ideally the party who initially introduced you.

Decision Making – The country's business culture is extremely hierarchical and superiors enjoy enormous deference. Decision making is a very slow and deliberate process in Thailand. Decision makers are usually senior executives who consider the best interest of the group or organization. They may consult with others before making the call. Subordinates may be reluctant to accept responsibility. Decision makers also rarely delegate their authority, so it is important to deal with senior executives. Gaining access to top managers can be difficult, though. You may first have to deal with layers of subordinates, many of whom could strongly influence the final decision.

In Thailand's still-shaky political and economic environment, company decisions are rarely independent of outside influences. Never underestimate the role of government officials, bureaucrats, and the military. All of them wield considerable influence across many industries. A number of criminal groups exist as well, many of which are led by high-ranking army officers. Doing business in the country can become extremely difficult and very unpleasant without the support of the 'powers-to-be.' It is important to come prepared to deal with these outside forces.

When making decisions, Thai businesspeople may not rely much on rules or laws. They usually consider the specific situation rather than applying universal principles. Personal feelings and experiences weigh much more strongly than empirical evidence and other objective facts do. Thais are often reluctant to take risks. If you expect them to support a risky decision, you may need to find ways for them to become comfortable with it first. You are much more likely to succeed if the relationship with your counterparts is strong and you managed to win their trust.

Agreements and Contracts

Capturing and exchanging written understandings after meetings and at key negotiation stages is useful. While oral commitments may be legally binding, they are rarely enforceable and may sound stronger than what your Thai counterparts may be willing to put in writing. Do not rely on interim agreements to be final. Any part of an agreement may still change significantly before both parties sign the final contract.

Written contracts are usually kept high-level, capturing only the primary aspects, terms, and conditions of the agreement. Writing up and signing the contract is a formality. Thais believe that the primary strength of an agreement lies in the partners' commitment rather than in its written documentation.

It is recommended to consult a local legal expert before signing a contract. However, do not bring your attorney to the negotiation table as it may be viewed as a sign of mistrust.

Signed contracts may not always be honored. This depends to no small degree on the strength of the continuing relationship between the contract partners. It is strongly advisable to continue staying in touch and maintaining the trust of your Thai business partner. Business partners usually expect the other side to remain somewhat flexible if conditions change, which may include agreeing to modify contract terms. Thais expect to settle all disputes out of court.

Women in Business

Thailand remains a male-dominated society. Women rarely attain positions of similar income and authority as men unless they work for the government. Otherwise, however, they mostly receive the same treatment from Thai companies.

Female business travelers should exercise caution and act professionally in business and social situations. Displaying confidence and some degree of assertiveness can be effective, but it is very important not to appear overly bold and aggressive.

Other Important Things to Know

Formal and neat attire is very important when doing business here. Male business visitors should wear dark suits with neckties on most occasions. Make sure shoes and suit are in excellent condition.

Business lunches and dinners are frequent and help advance the vital process of building strong relationships and growing your network. Business may not be discussed during these events.

Table manners are very important, especially when dealing with the Thai elite. Take your time and do not rush to eat, do not chop up your food and then eat, and above all avoid spilling food from your plate onto the table or tablecloth. Thais rarely use chopsticks, and the use of spoon and fork is commonplace. Never grimace if served something strange or unfamiliar. Leaving a little food on your plate is usually good as it signals that there was enough of it.

Especially with local companies that lack international expertise, business entertainment may sometimes include invitations Westerners may find highly inappropriate. In such cases, finding ways to avoid the issue without directly rejecting the invitation is very important as it helps preserve *face* for all involved.

Social events do not require strict punctuality. While it is best to arrive at dinners close to the agreed time, being late to a party by 30 minutes or more is perfectly acceptable.

During small talk and other social conversations, you may be asked very personal questions. If you do not want to answer, smile or politely explain that such topics are not discussed openly in your culture.

Gift giving is common in social and business settings in Thailand. If you received one, it is best to reciprocate with an item of similar value that is typical of your home country. Giving a gift after signing a contract is viewed very favorably. Give and accept gifts using both hands. Do not open gifts in the presence of the giver unless your host did so first. There are numerous potential pitfalls in what to give and how to wrap it, so prepare upfront or ask someone from the country to avoid causing embarrassment.

Turkey

Though its culture is quite homogeneous, Turkish businesspeople, especially those among younger generations, are usually experienced in interacting and doing business with visitors from other cultures. However, that does not always mean that they are open-minded. When negotiating business here, realize that people may expect things to be done 'their way.' Business practices may show European or Asian/Arabic influences. Turks are often very patriotic and can be intensely nationalistic. This is a proud nation and its people may strongly reject any critique of its ways. In addition, always keep in mind that this is an Islamic country. Showing any disrespect for the religion could have disastrous consequences.

Many businesses in Turkey are controlled by only a few powerful groups and families. It is vital to understand those influences upfront in order to determine who the real stakeholders in your negotiation are. Otherwise, you may end up wasting time without getting anywhere.

Relationships and Respect

Turkey's culture is generally group-oriented. Asserting individual preferences may be seen as less important than having a sense of belonging to a group, conforming to its norms, and maintaining harmony among its members. Building lasting and trusting personal relationships is therefore very important to most Turks, who often expect to establish strong bonds prior to closing any deals. People in this country usually want to do business only with those they know and like. Establishing productive business cooperation requires a long-term perspective and commitment. Consequently, proceed with serious business discussions only after your counterparts have become very comfortable with you. This is usually a slow process. Turks tend to distrust people who appear unwilling to spend the time or whose motives for relationship building are unclear.

Business relationships in this country exist between people, not necessarily between companies. Even when you have won your local business partners' friendship and trust, they will not necessarily trust others from your company. That makes it very important to keep company interfaces unchanged. Changing a key contact may require the relationship building process to start over.

Establishing personal relationships with others in Turkey can create powerful networks. Whom you know may determine whether people want to get to know you. Maintaining cordial relations is crucial. Third party introductions can be very helpful as a starting point to building a trusting relationship with a potential partner, especially since Turks may initially not trust outsiders who are neither part of their family nor of their circle of friends.

'Saving face' is very essential in Turkey. Causing embarrassment to another person may cause a *loss of face* for all parties involved and can be disastrous for business negotiations. The importance of diplomatic restraint and tact cannot be overestimated. Keep your cool and never show openly that you are upset. Avoid open conflict, and know that politeness is crucial. While Turks are usually very friendly, they tend to be very proud and may be easily offended.

In Turkish business culture, the respect a person enjoys depends primarily on his or her status and age. It is crucial to treat elderly people with the greatest respect. Admired personal traits include patience, flexibility, and sociability.

Communication

Turkish is the country's official language. Many businesspeople speak at least some English, French, and/or German. Especially with high-ranking managers, it may be beneficial to use an interpreter. To avoid offending the other side, ask beforehand whether an interpreter should be present at a meeting. When communicating in English, speak in short, simple sentences and avoid using jargon and slang. It will help people with a limited command of English if you speak slowly, summarize your key points often, and pause frequently to allow for interpretation.

Note that Turks dislike the use of acronyms and abbreviations. It is strongly advisable to spell out everything clearly, both in your oral and written communication.

Since they respect assertiveness, Turks usually speak forcefully, though not overly loud. They may occasionally raise their voices to make a point or demonstrate passion. Emotions are often shown openly. People in the country generally converse in close proximity, standing only two feet or less apart. Never back away, even if this is much closer than your personal comfort zone allows. Doing so could be read as a sign that you are uncomfortable around them.

Communication in Turkey may sometimes appear vague, especially early in your business interactions. Your local counterparts may become more direct and frank as the relationship strengthens. However, always watch for subtle messages that may signal issues and concerns. Silence may communicate a negative message, but it may also not mean anything, so do not read too much into it.

Gestures and body language can be extensive. It is often not a good idea to imitate them, though. There may be frequent physical contact with others of the same gender. Men may greet each other by kissing each other's cheeks as a sign of friendship. Since Muslims consider the left hand unclean, use it only if inevitable. The American OK sign, with thumb and index finger forming a circle, is an obscene gesture in Turkey. It is also rude to cross your arms while facing a person or to blow your nose in public. Eye contact should be frequent, almost to the point of staring. This conveys sincerity and helps build trust.

Shaking the head from side to side traditionally means, 'I don't understand' rather than 'no.' The Turkish way to signal 'no' is by raising the eyebrows, sometimes together with a *tsk* sound and a backward tilt of the head. A slight bow of the head traditionally signals 'yes.' However, many Turks have adopted the western way of nodding or shaking the head.

Initial Contacts and Meetings

Before initiating business negotiations in Turkey, it is advantageous to identify and engage a local intermediary. This person will help bridge the cultural and communications gap, allowing you to conduct business with greater effectiveness.

Negotiations in Turkey can be conducted by individuals or teams of negotiators. It is vital that teams be well aligned, with roles clearly assigned to each member. Turks may be very good at exploiting disagreements between members of the other team to their advantage. Changing a team member may require the relationship building process to start over and should therefore be avoided.

If possible, schedule meetings at least one to two weeks in advance. Since people want to know whom they will be meeting, provide details on titles, positions, and responsibilities of attendees ahead of time. While meetings may start considerably late, Turks generally expect foreign visitors to be punctual. Avoid being more than 15 minutes late, and call ahead if you will be. Displaying anger if you have to wait only reflects poorly on you.

Names are usually given in the order of first name, family name. However, ways to address a Turk properly differ and may depend on age, international experience, and other factors. Using *Mr./Mrs./Miss* plus the family name is usually acceptable. However, some older Turks may view this as disrespectful. It may be best to inquire from someone upfront or politely ask the person how to address him or her correctly. In that case, make sure you do the same for your own name. Titles, such as *Doctor* or *Professor*, are highly valued, and are often used without adding the person's family name. Do not call Turks by their first name unless they offered it, which is rare. Greet the most senior person first, and then greet everyone else in the room individually. Introductions are accompanied by firm handshakes using the right hand.

After the introductions, wait to see whether your Turkish counterparts want to exchange business cards. If they do, this may signal interest in building a business relationship, and you should offer your card to everyone present. You do not have to translate your cards into Turkish, but that will be appreciated. Show doctorate degrees on your card and make sure that it clearly states your professional title, especially if you have the seniority to make decisions. Present your card with your right hand, with the print facing the recipient. Similarly, accept others' cards using only the right hand. When presenting your card, smile and keep eye contact, then take a few moments to look at the card you received. Next, place it on the table in front of you.

Meetings start with small talk, which can be extensive. It is important to be patient and let the other side set the pace. Initial meetings are quite formal, and although this may get more relaxed as the relationship develops, be careful not to appear too casual. Although some humor is welcome, business is a serious matter in Turkey.

The primary purpose of the first meeting is to get to know each other. Business may or may not get discussed. Do not try to hurry along with your agenda. It is unrealistic to expect initial meetings to lead to straight decisions.

Presentations should be short and concise. Make sure your proposal is clearly structured and presented. Your presentation materials should be attractive, with good and clear visuals. Turks communicate primarily orally and visually, so avoid using too much text. Use diagrams and pictures wherever feasible, and avoid complicated expressions. Having your handout materials translated to Turkish is not a must, but it helps in getting your messages across.

Negotiation

Attitudes and Styles - In Turkey, the primary approach to negotiating is to employ distributive and contingency bargaining. It may include tough bargaining at many levels. While the buyer is in a superior position, both sides in a business deal own the responsibility to reach agreement. They expect long-term commitments from their business partners and will focus mostly on long-term benefits. Although the primary negotiation style is competitive, Turks nevertheless value long-term relationships and look for win-win solutions. While proposals should demonstrate the benefits to both negotiating parties, attempts to win competitive advantages should not be taken negatively. You earn your counterparts' respect by maintaining a positive, persistent attitude. Always consider that negotiating in Turkey may be about aspects such as power, influence, or honor as much as it is about financial benefits.

Should a dispute arise at any stage of a negotiation, you might be able to reach resolution through stating your own objections and inquiring about their concerns. Taking them seriously and showing commitment to personal relationships goes a long way even if you continue to avoid weak compromises. However, refrain from using logical reasoning or becoming argumentative since this will only make matters worse.

Sharing of Information - Information is rarely shared freely, since the Turkish believe that privileged information creates bargaining advantages. In addition, data and statistics about the country are not always reliable, even when shared with the best of intentions. Even publicly available data may be inaccurate, making it vital do conduct your own detailed research if necessary.

Pace of Negotiation – Expect negotiations to be slow and protracted, and be prepared to make several trips if necessary to achieve your objectives. Initial exchanges that precede the bargaining stage of the negotiation may be lengthy. Decisions are usually made between meetings rather than at the table. Throughout the negotiation, be patient, control your emotions, and accept that delays occur. Attempts to rush the process are unlikely to produce better results and may be viewed as offensive.

Turks generally employ a polychronic work style. They are used to pursuing multiple actions and goals in parallel. When negotiating, they often take a holistic approach and may jump back and forth between topics rather than addressing them in sequential order. Negotiators from strongly monochronic cultures, such as Germany, the United Kingdom, or the United States, may find this style confusing, irritating, and even annoying. In any case, do not show irritation or anger when encountering this behavior. Instead, keep track of the bargaining progress at all times, often emphasizing areas where agreement already exists.

If your counterparts appear to be stalling the negotiation, assess carefully whether their slowing down the process indicates that they are evaluating alternatives or that they are not interested in doing business with you. While such behavior could represent attempts to create time pressure in order to obtain concessions, the slow decision process in the country is far more likely causing the lack of progress. People from fast-paced cultures tend to underestimate how much time this takes and often make the mistake of trying to 'speed things up.' Again, patience and persistence are vitally important.

Bargaining – Most Turks enjoy bargaining and haggling. They expect to do a lot of it during a negotiation and may be seriously offended if you refuse to play along. The bargaining exchange of a negotiation can be very extensive. Opening stage and initial offers on both sides are critically important when negotiating with Turks. Many believe that the first person to quote a price will end up getting the worse part of the deal, and that initial proposals should never be accepted. Accordingly, either they may wait for you to make an initial offer and then reject it right away, or they open with an extreme offer that is far from realistic, carefully watching your response. Know your objectives, and work slowly and persistently towards them.

Prices often move 40 percent or more between initial offers and final agreement. Leave yourself a lot of room for concessions at different stages. When conceding, present this as a decision you made because you like and respect your counterpart. Always ask the other side to reciprocate. You can use the fact that aspects can be re-visited to your advantage, for instance by offering further concessions under the condition that the Turkish side reciprocate in areas that had already been agreed upon.

Deceptive techniques are frequent and can be effective. This includes tactics such as telling lies and sending fake non-verbal messages, pretending to be disinterested in the whole deal or in single concessions, misrepresenting an item's value, or making false demands and concessions. Expect your Turkish counterparts to be good at this game. They may occasionally play stupid or otherwise attempt to mislead you in order to obtain bargaining advantages. Lies will be difficult to detect. It is advisable to verify information received from the local side through other channels. Similarly, they treat 'outside' information with caution. Even when you can see right through a lie, it would be a grave personal insult to state or even hint that your counterpart is not telling the truth. Turks may claim limited authority, stating that they have to ask for their manager's approval. This could be a tactic or the truth. Be cautious when using the techniques of making false demands or false concessions. Overt attempts to bluff your counterparts could backfire.

Negotiators in the country may use pressure techniques that include making final offers or nibbling. Final offers may come more than once and are rarely final. Do not use tactics such as applying time pressure, opening with your best offer, or making decreasing or expiring offers, since your Turkish counterparts could view these as signs that you are not willing to build a long-term relationship. They may choose to terminate the negotiation. Silence can be an effective way to signal rejection of a proposal.

Turkish negotiators avoid openly aggressive or adversarial techniques but may use more subtle versions. Extreme openings are frequently employed as a way to start the bargaining process. In addition, they may make indirect threats and warnings or subtly display anger. Use these tactics with caution yourself since they may adversely affect the relationship if employed too aggressively. Do not walk out or threaten to do so as your counterparts will likely take this as a personal insult and may end all talks.

Emotional negotiation techniques, such as attitudinal bargaining, sending dual messages, attempting to make you feel guilty, grimacing, or appealing to personal relationships, are frequent and can be effective. Be cautious not to cause loss of face when employing any of them yourself. Also, know that Turks tend to exaggerate situations and can become quite emotional during fierce bargaining. It is best to remain calm. At times, defensive tactics such as blocking or changing the subject, asking probing or very direct questions, making promises, or keeping an inflexible position may be used.

Corruption and bribery are quite common in Turkey's public and private sectors. However, people may draw the line differently, viewing minor payments as rewards for getting a job done rather than as bribes. Also, keep in mind that there is a fine line between giving gifts and bribing. What you may consider a bribe, a Turk may view as only a nice gift, and so much as hinting that you view it differently could be a grave insult to the person's honor. It may help if you introduce and explain your company's policies early on, but be careful not to moralize or appear to imply that local customs are unethical.

Decision Making – Most companies tend to be very hierarchical, and people expect to work within clearly established lines of authority. Many of Turkey's businesses are still family-owned. Although the pace of business is accelerating, decision making can be a very slow process. Decision makers are usually senior executives who consider the best interest of the group or organization. They may consult with others before making the call. Subordinates may be reluctant to accept responsibility. Decision makers also rarely delegate their authority, so it is important to deal with senior executives. You may have to 'work your way up,' meeting and negotiating with less senior managers or members of a family first. Once they consider you trustworthy, you will move on to meet others who are more senior. Though this process is very time-consuming, it is vital never to lose your patience along the way.

When making decisions, businesspeople may consider the specific situation or follow universal principles. Personal feelings and experiences weigh much more strongly than empirical evidence and other objective facts do. Turks are often willing to take risks, which are seen as a way to develop self-reliance.

Agreements and Contracts

Capturing and exchanging written understandings after meetings and at key negotiation stages is useful since oral statements are not always dependable. It may be helpful to ask your counterparts to initial these write-ups as a way to document consensus. However, do not mistake them for final agreements. Any part of an agreement may still change significantly before both parties sign the contract.

Businesspeople in the country understand and respect the role of a contract. Written contracts tend to be lengthy and often spell out detailed terms and conditions for the core agreements as well as for many eventualities. Contracts may prove difficult to align between the English and the Turkish version since intentions may prove hard to translate. It is important to review all different language versions independently.

Nevertheless, writing up and signing the contract is a formality. Turks believe that the primary strength of an agreement lies in the partners' commitment rather than in its written documentation.

It is advisable to consult a local legal expert before signing a contract. However, do not bring your attorney to the negotiation table. Turks may read it as a sign of mistrust if you do.

Signed contracts may not always be honored. This depends to no small degree on the strength of the continuing relationship between the contract partners. It is strongly advisable to continue staying in touch and maintaining the trust of your Turkish business partner. Business partners usually expect the other side to remain somewhat flexible if conditions change, which may include agreeing to modify contract terms.

Women in Business

Turkey remains a male-dominated society. However, there are substantial differences across the country. In its European part, especially in Istanbul, lifestyles and gender equality may be similar to those of western countries, and many women hold professional positions, including very senior ones.

In the Asian part of the country, women are struggling to attain positions of similar income and authority as men, while many of them may not even be allowed by their families to seek employment. Men in this part of Turkey tend to be very patriarchal. As a visiting businesswoman, emphasize your company's importance and your role in it. A personal introduction or at least a letter of support from a senior executive within your company may help a lot.

No matter where in the country, female business travelers should exercise caution and act professionally in business and social situations. Avoid being alone with Turkish men. Displaying confidence and some degree of assertiveness can be effective, but it is very important not to appear overly bold and aggressive.

Other Important Things to Know

Impeccable appearance is very important when doing business here. Male business visitors should wear conservative suits with neckties on most occasions. Make sure shoes and suit are in excellent condition.

Business lunches and dinners are common and may be long. They are great opportunities to strengthen your relationships. Business may or may not get discussed. Wait to see whether your counterparts bring it up. Always keep in mind that Muslims eat no pork. It is best to avoid drinking alcohol since some Turks may take offense.

Social events do not require strict punctuality. While it is best to arrive at dinners close to the agreed time, being late to a party by 30 minutes or more is perfectly acceptable.

Turks are usually reserved about private topics. Do not inquire about family matters if your counterpart did not bring up the topic. Other topics to avoid are Turkey's relationship with Greece and the tensions over Cyprus, as well as issues around the country's minorities such as the Armenians or Kurds.

Gift giving in business settings is rare, at least as long as no strong relationship exists. It is best not to bring a gift to an initial meeting in order to avoid raising suspicions about your motives.

Ukraine

Previously a republic within the USSR, Ukraine became an independent nation in 1991. Its culture is somewhat pluralistic. The eastern part of the country and Kiev, the capital, host most of Ukraine's Russian minority of about 17 percent of the total population and show strongly influences of Russian language and culture. Numerous companies are run by Russians. In contrast, people in the western parts of the country may dislike Russian influences, strongly emphasizing Ukraine's distinct identity.

Owing to the country's historic isolation, most businesspeople and officials in Ukraine have little experience with other cultures except for neighboring countries. There is a widespread lack of free-market knowledge. It may be necessary to discuss and seek agreement over the definition of concepts such as fair play, good will, profit and loss, turnover, individual accountability, proprietary rights, and so forth. Even when you do, many people may expect that things are done 'their way.'

Relationships and Respect

Ukraine's culture expects its members to have a sense of belonging to and conforming with their group. At the same time, it leaves a lot of room for individual preferences. Building lasting and trusting relationships is very important and can be vital for the success of your business interactions. Generally, it is best to give your counterparts time to become comfortable with you. Behaving in an overly friendly fashion may be counterproductive. Ukrainians are generally serious people who rarely smile and may seem stern. They appreciate sincerity and firmness in their counterparts' trust. However, you should let them see your personal side as well, as Ukrainians often mistrust people who are 'all business.' Relationship building is normally a slow process here, since people dislike being rushed or having to follow the fast-paced western approach. Patience is of critical importance in this country.

Business relationships in Ukraine usually exist both at the individual and company level. Ukrainians may want to do business only with those they like and trust. However, if you introduce someone else from your company into an existing business relationship, that person may quickly be accepted as a valid business partner.

Refrain from praising or rewarding anyone in public. Unlike in many other cultures, it may raise suspicion about your motives.

In Ukraine's business culture, the respect a person enjoys depends primarily on his or her rank, status, and achievements. Be careful never to come across as patronizing a senior Ukrainian manager. Admired personal traits include firmness, sincerity, and dependability.

Communication

The country's official language, Ukrainian, is similar to but not identical with Russian. Communicating in Russian works well in eastern Ukraine and Kiev, but may not be appreciated in the West of the country. Not many businesspeople speak English fluently. In addition, Ukrainians may insist that they understand everything you said even when this is not really the case. It may be necessary to have an interpreter. Ask beforehand whether an interpreter should be present at a meeting. However, keep in mind that even some interpreters may not speak and understand English at a fully proficient level. It may be in your best interest to bring your own interpreter, rather than depending on one provided by the Ukrainians, to ensure an unbiased translation. When communicating in English, speak in short, simple sentences and avoid using slang and jargon. It will help people with a limited command of English if you speak slowly, summarize your key points often, and pause frequently to allow for interpretation.

People in this country usually speak softly. They may occasionally raise their voices to make a point. While celebrations and social events can get very noisy, being loud may reflect poorly on you in most business settings. People generally converse while standing around two to three feet apart.

Communicating with Ukrainians can be anything from very direct to rather indirect. On one hand, they may say 'no' frequently. In contrast, people may say things they think you want to hear as a way to lure you into a business deal.

Ukrainians keep physical contact infrequent. Avoid touching other people. While several gestures may be used, be careful to control your own. Slapping the open hand over a fist is a vulgar gesture in Ukraine, as is putting the thumb between index and middle finger in a fist. Standing with your hands in your pockets may be considered rude. The thumbs-up gesture is positive as it signals approval. Eye contact should be very frequent, almost to the point of staring, as this conveys sincerity and helps build trust.

Initial Contacts and Meetings

Choosing a local intermediary who can leverage existing relationships to make the initial contact is useful. Assuming you identified someone who is respectable and trustworthy, this person will help bridge the gap between cultures, allowing you to conduct business with greater effectiveness. In addition, the person's help in getting things organized can be very important in Ukraine's sometimes-chaotic business environment.

Negotiations in Ukraine can be conducted by individuals or teams of negotiators. Teams should be well aligned, with roles clearly assigned to each member. Ukrainians may be very good at exploiting disagreements between members of the other team to their advantage.

If possible, schedule meetings at least two to three weeks in advance. Since Ukrainians want to know whom they will be meeting, provide details on titles, positions, and responsibilities of attendees ahead of time. It is unlikely that you will meet the top executive of an organization at the first meeting, so be prepared to deal with subordinates. They may have significant influence over the final decision. Confirm your meeting several times, and be prepared for your counterparts to cancel or postpone meetings with little or no notice. Unless you are sure that your counterparts are sufficiently fluent in English, keeping your correspondence in Ukrainian is strongly advisable.

While meetings may start considerably late, Ukrainians generally expect foreign visitors to be punctual. Being late by more than 10 to 15 minutes without having a valid and plausible excuse can be an offense. Do not show signs of impatience if you have to wait, even if the other side is an hour or more late.

Ukrainian names are usually given in the order of first name, middle name (derived from the father's first name), family name. In formal situations, the order may revert to family name, first name, middle name. People may sometimes be addressed with all three names. Otherwise, use *Mr./Ms.* plus the family name. If a person has an academic or professional title, always use it instead, followed by the family name. Do not call Ukrainians by their first name unless they explicitly offered it first. In that case, use a combination of first name and middle name. Introductions are accompanied by firm handshakes.

The exchange of business cards is an essential step when meeting someone for the first time, so bring more than you need. You may not always get one in return. It is beneficial to use cards with one side in English and the other in Ukrainian. In Western Ukraine, do not use one that is in Russian – an English-only card is better in that case. Show doctorate degrees on your card and make sure that it clearly states your professional title, especially if you have the seniority to make decisions. When presenting your card, ensure that the Ukrainian side is facing the recipient. Smile and keep eye contact while accepting someone else's card, then take a few moments to look at it. Next, place the card on the table in front of you or into your card case.

Meetings usually start with some small talk intended to establish personal rapport. Let your counterparts set the pace. The primary purpose of the first meeting is to become acquainted and build relationships. In addition, your counterparts may want to feel you out and assess your and your company's credibility. Remain firm and dignified without being distant, and avoid any patronizing or aggressive behavior. Business may be discussed, but do not try to hurry along with your agenda. It is unrealistic to expect initial meetings to lead to straight decisions.

Ukrainian negotiators may try to convince you that they have the background and experience required to be successful. Businesspeople may exaggerate their capabilities or make questionable promises in order to maintain foreign contacts.

Presentations should be short and concise. Making a good first impression is at least as important as coming with a compelling proposal. It is characteristic of Ukrainians to be pessimistic, though, so a lack of enthusiastic responses should not discourage you. Your presentation materials should be attractive and colorful, with good and clear visuals. Use diagrams and pictures wherever feasible, cut down on words, and avoid complicated expressions. Having your handout materials translated to Ukrainian is not a must, but it helps in getting your messages across.

Negotiation

Attitudes and Styles - In Ukraine, the primary approach to negotiating is to employ distributive and contingency bargaining. The buyer is often in a strongly favorable position and may try to push the responsibility to reach agreement to the seller. Given the country's relatively unstable political and economic situation, negotiators may focus mostly on the near-term benefits of the business deal. The primary negotiation style in the country is very competitive and people may become outright adversarial. Most Ukrainians view negotiating a zero-sum game in which one side's gain equals the other side's loss. Negotiations may become more personable and at least a little more cooperative if strong relationships have been established between the parties.

Should a dispute arise at any stage of a negotiation, it is advantageous first to let some time pass to allow things to blow over. Then, you might be able to reach resolution through logical arguing, presenting lots of supporting information, or making a different, though not necessarily better proposal. What you offer may be more valuable to your counterparts than is apparent from their behaviors. Ukrainians have great respect for western expertise, and are easily impressed by size and numbers. Do not underestimate the strength of your negotiating position. In extreme cases, if you cannot seem to get unstuck, try using a mediator, ideally the party who initially introduced you.

Sharing of Information - Information is rarely shared freely, since Ukrainians believe that privileged information creates bargaining advantages.

Pace of Negotiation – Expect negotiations to be very slow and protracted. Especially during the early bargaining stages you may feel that you are making little progress; discussions often stay high-level for quite some time until your counterparts eventually decide to get down to the details of the deal. Success requires extreme patience in this country.

If your counterparts appear to be stalling the negotiation, assess carefully whether their slowing down the process indicates that they are evaluating alternatives or that they are not interested in doing business with you. More often than not, though, this behavior indicates an attempt to create time pressure or 'wear you down' in order to obtain concessions. Your Ukrainian intermediary may be able to find out why things have slowed down.

Bargaining – Some Ukrainians can turn out to be highly skilled negotiators, especially if they were trained by Russians. However, most businesspeople in the country have only limited experience in the field. They may expect to do some bargaining but rarely haggle a lot. None of this makes them easy prey, though. Ukrainians can be extremely patient, persistent, and stubborn negotiators. It can be very difficult to obtain concessions from them. They often view compromise as a sign of weakness and may frequently refuse to change their position unless the other side offers sufficient concessions or shows exceptional firmness. Similarly, they may make minor concessions while asking for major ones in return. Negotiating with Ukrainians inevitably includes much posturing and maneuvering. The best approach is to be polite but remain tough throughout the bargaining process. In addition, try to make your counterparts comfortable since this increases the odds of a successful outcome.

The bargaining stage of a negotiation is usually extensive. In spite of the Ukrainian reluctance to compromise, prices may eventually move by 40 percent or more between initial offers and final agreement. Concessions never come easily. It is not advisable to make significant early concessions, since your counterparts expect further compromises as the bargaining continues.

Deceptive techniques are frequent, and Ukrainian negotiators are prepared for you to use them, too. This includes tactics such as telling lies and sending fake non-verbal messages, pretending to be disinterested in the whole deal or in single concessions, misrepresenting an item's value, or making false demands and concessions. Ukrainians may play stupid or otherwise attempt to mislead you in order to obtain bargaining advantages. Lies may be easy to see through; otherwise, verify information received from the local side through other channels. Similarly, they treat 'outside' information with caution. 'Good cop, bad cop' may be used on either side of the negotiation table. Ukrainians may also claim limited authority, stating that they have to ask for their manager's approval. More often than not, this might be the truth. However, you may not always be able to force the true decision maker to participate directly in the negotiation, meaning that you may have to accept this indirect negotiation approach.

Ukrainian negotiators often use pressure techniques that include opening with a 'best offer,' showing intransigence, making final or expiring offers, applying time pressure, or nibbling. Final offers may be made more than once and are almost never final. Time pressure can be difficult to counter. If negotiators learn that you are working against a deadline, they may exploit this knowledge to increase the pressure on you to make concessions. Even if you allowed plenty of time, they may suddenly request last-minute concessions and 'take-it-or-leave-it'-type changes near the end of a negotiation. It is important to define in advance what concessions you are willing to make. Ukrainians may often chose to play hardball. It is ok to take a similar stance yourself; otherwise, be patient and wait it out. When using your own pressure tactics, clearly explain your offer and its benefits to your counterpart. Time pressure does not work against them since Ukrainians can be very patient and fatalistic. However, convincing your counterparts to hold the negotiation in the West does give you a strong advantage. They will now be the ones under time pressure, which deprives them of a strong negotiation tool.

Though not quite as confrontational as Russians, Ukrainian negotiators may be aggressive or outright adversarial. Extreme openings are frequent as a way to start the bargaining process. Negotiators may make direct threats and warnings, openly display anger or lose their temper, or they may walk out of the room, even several times in a row. While it is ok (and can be quite helpful) to respond in kind, you should be careful not to outdo your counterparts. While maintaining a strong and firm position is respected, it is advantageous to insist at various points that the negotiations emphasize mutual benefits and needs.

Other emotional techniques, such as attitudinal bargaining, attempting to make you feel guilty, grimacing, or appealing to personal relationships, are often used. Ukrainians also resort to defensive tactics. They may change subjects frequently, revisit previously agreed points, introduce all kind of distractions, or ask very direct questions, attempting to take you by surprise. Prepare well for any of these. Promises are not always kept, especially if they were made in social settings away from the negotiation table. Do not get upset over this, since your local counterparts may not consider such promises serious commitments.

As the country is moving from a socialist country to a free-market economy, corruption and bribery have become common in Ukraine's public and private sectors. However, people may draw the line differently, viewing minor payments as rewards for getting a job done rather than as bribes. Keep in mind that there is a fine line between giving gifts and bribing. What you may consider a bribe, a Ukrainian may view as only a nice gift. It may help if you introduce and explain your company's policies early on, but be careful not to moralize or appear to imply that local customs are unethical. In addition, point out that bribery is illegal in Ukraine and could get you into significant trouble.

Decision Making – Companies can be quite hierarchical, and people expect to work within clearly established lines of authority. Openly disagreeing with or criticizing superiors is unacceptable. Decision makers are usually senior executives who consider the best interest of the group or organization. While they may consult with others, bosses accept all of the responsibility. Unlike in Russia, where this is very rare, decision-making authority may sometimes be delegated to lower levels in the hierarchy. It is very important to deal with decision makers rather than with subordinates. At the same time, it can be essential to win subordinates' support since they could strongly influence the ultimate decision. Decision making can take a long time and requires patience.

In Ukraine's still-shaky political and economic environment, company decisions are rarely independent of outside influences. Never underestimate the role of government officials and bureaucrats, who may have to support and approve company decisions. Similarly, crime groups have gained significant influence across many industries. It is important to come prepared to deal with these outside forces. In extreme cases, you might be well-advised to withdraw from a negotiation should you feel personally threatened. It can be advantageous to indicate to the Ukrainian side that threats would only motivate you to look for other markets and partners.

When making decisions, businesspeople usually consider the specific situation rather than follow universal principles. Personal feelings and experiences may weigh more strongly than empirical evidence, objective facts, and even laws. Ukrainians are often reluctant to take risks. If you expect them to support a risky decision, you may need to find ways for them to become comfortable with it first. You are much more likely to succeed if the relationship with your counterparts is strong and you managed to win their trust.

Agreements and Contracts

Capturing and exchanging written understandings after meetings and at key negotiation stages is useful since oral statements are not always dependable. The Ukrainian side may insist on having a *protokol* (meeting minutes) signed by both parties at the end of a meeting. It serves to record what was discussed, is not a contract, and should not be mistaken for a final agreement. Any part of an agreement may still change significantly before both parties sign the final contract.

Written contracts should be clear and concise, without too many detailed terms and conditions. Signing the contract is important not only from a legal perspective, but also as a strong confirmation of your Ukrainian partners' commitment. Including an arbitration clause in a neutral country, for instance Sweden, is wise. Your counterparts may request that details of the contract be kept secret.

Your legal rights may not be enforceable, while local companies often have a better chance in court (or find ways to circumvent laws). You should definitely consult a local legal expert, ideally throughout the negotiation or at the very least before signing a contract. For the time being, it is wise to recognize that the country's legal system is in a transitional mode, so be prepared for laws to change on short notice. Even local businessmen may not be very familiar with applicable laws and regulations. Because of that, bringing an attorney to the negotiation table may not help much, while it could make the negotiation even tougher.

After signing the contract, invite your counterparts to a lunch or dinner to celebrate the beginning of a long-lasting personal and business relationship. This will help your local partners to see you not only as a business partner, but also as a trustworthy contact.

Contracts alone are not dependable. Ukrainians may continue to press for a better deal even after a contract has been signed, or they may ignore some of its terms. Your best chance to ensure that your partners follow through on their commitments is to stay in regular contact and nurture the relationship throughout your business engagement.

Women in Business

Ukraine is still a male-dominated society. While many women are working and a few have made it into senior positions, most are still struggling to attain positions of similar income and authority as men. As a visiting businesswoman, emphasize your company's importance and your role in it. This will be even more effective if you can get a male colleague to explain these aspects while emphasizing that women are treated differently in your home country. A personal introduction or at least a letter of support from a senior executive within your company may also help.

Female business travelers should exercise caution and act professionally in business and social situations. It is possible that you will face offensive humor or remarks with sexual connotation. While these are usually best ignored, it may sometimes help to point out that such comments are not practiced in your home country. Displaying confidence and some degree of assertiveness can be effective, but it is very important not to appear overly bold and aggressive.

Other Important Things to Know

Conservative attire is important when doing business here. Male business visitors should wear suits with neckties on most occasions. While you do not want to appear 'over-dressed,' make sure shoes and suit are in good condition.

Business lunches and dinners are very common, and evening entertainment can be lavish. These events frequently include heavy alcohol consumption and are very important as they help advance the vital process of building relationships. Refusing to participate in these activities may be taken as a clear signal that you are not seriously interested in doing business with your counterparts. Having a drink with your Ukrainian partners is an easy way to establish good will. However, realize that they may use the opportunity to continue negotiating. Some may even pretend to be more drunk than they really if they can use this act to their advantage.

Business gifts like pens, small notebooks, or similar items are usually well-received. It is ok if they carry your company logo.

Social events do not require strict punctuality. While it is best to arrive at dinners close to the agreed time, being late to a party by 30 to 60 minutes or even more is acceptable.

United Kingdom

The United Kingdom includes four constituent parts: England, Wales, Scotland, and Northern Ireland. The term *Great Britain and Northern Ireland* also refers to the U.K. People belonging to any of the four groups, the English, Welsh, Scottish, and Northern Irish, usually prefer to be called that rather than being called *British* or *Brits*. Generally, members of all four groups may emphasize that they are distinctly different from each other. People from outside of England might be highly offended if you referred to them as English. In addition, many in the U.K. do not consider themselves Europeans.

Businesspeople in the U.K., especially those among younger generations, are usually very experienced in interacting with other cultures. The reforms of the 1980s and the trend towards globalization have shaken up traditional beliefs and business attitudes. However, that does not always mean that the British are open-minded. When negotiating business here, realize that people may often expect things to be done 'their way.'

Relationships and Respect

Building lasting and trusting relationships is important to most people in this country. However, they are not a necessary precondition for initial business interactions. The British are characteristically pragmatic and may engage on a trial basis, expecting to get to know you better as you do business together. Although people in the country may emphasize near-term results over long-range objectives, they are generally more interested in building long-term relationships than in making quick deals.

Business relationships in this country exist between companies as well as between individuals. If your company replaces you with someone else over the course of a negotiation, it may be easy for your replacement to take things over from where you left them. Likewise, if you introduce someone else from your company into an existing business relationship, that person may quickly be accepted as a valid business partner. This does not mean that the British do not care about who they are dealing with. Personal integrity and dependability are important if you want to win their trust.

In Britain's business culture, the respect a person enjoys depends primarily on his or her rank, status, education, and knowledge. Age and seniority are also respected. Admired personal traits include poise and politeness.

Communication

British English is different from American English to the point where misunderstandings may happen easily. If necessary, familiarize yourself with the differences upfront.

Businesspeople in this country usually speak in a controlled fashion, only occasionally raising their voices to make a point. At restaurants, especially those used for business lunches and dinners, keep conversations at a quiet level. Being loud may be regarded as bad manners. Emotions are not shown openly as the British prefer keeping the proverbial *stiff upper lip,* so do not assume that something is not deeply felt because it is understated. People generally converse standing around three feet apart.

Levels of directness may vary greatly. This depends primarily on the strength of relationships but is also influenced by education, status, and other factors. The British tend to make vague statements that may be hard to read. Rather than responding to a direct question, they may instead tell a story, the meaning of which is left to your interpretation. While you may occasionally get a direct 'no,' evasive responses like 'I'll get back to you' could indicate a lack of interest in what you have to offer. The British are masters of understatement and often use subtle irony. It is important to listen carefully both to the tone of voice and the message that is being conveyed. In addition, pay attention to what is *not* being said. Once they have decided that they want to do business with you, the British can become much more direct, even blunt, and may openly speak their minds as long as there is no risk of direct confrontation. Silence is often a way to communicate a negative message.

Gestures are usually subtle in the U.K. It is advisable to restrict your body language. Facial expressions can be very hard to read, making it difficult figure out what your counterparts may be thinking. Physical contact is rare and best avoided. It will not be taken as a friendly gesture if you touch other people. Do not use your fingers to point at others. Instead, point with your head. Eye contact should be somewhat infrequent. While looking the other in the eye may convey sincerity, do not stare at people.

Initial Contacts and Meetings

Having a local contact who can make introductions can be a significant advantage but is not a necessary precondition to doing business. A letter of introduction from a reference in the country may also help.

It is often better to conduct negotiations in the U.K. with a team of negotiators rather than to rely on a single individual. This signals importance, facilitates stronger relationship building, and may speed up the overall process. The British side will take it as a sign that you are seriously interested in doing business with them. However, sending a team that seems too large for the task at hand will likely raise suspicions. Select older and more senior executives to represent your company. Traditional British managers may be distrustful of younger businesspeople, even if they have excellent credentials.

If possible, schedule meetings at least one to two weeks in advance. Punctuality is generally expected. Avoid being more than 5 to 10 minutes late, and call ahead if you will be.

Names are usually given in the order of first name, family name. Use *Mr./Mrs./Miss* plus the family name. If a person has an academic title, such as *Doctor* or *Professor,* use it instead, followed by the family name. Before calling people from Britain by their first name, wait until they offer it. Introductions are accompanied by handshakes. The standard greetings are 'pleased to meet you' or 'how do you do?' The latter is rhetorical and it is best to respond with the same phrase.

The exchange of business cards is not an essential step, but it is best to bring a sufficient supply. They may sometimes be exchanged at the end rather than the beginning of the meeting. Show doctorate degrees on your card and make sure that it clearly states your professional title, especially if you have the seniority to make decisions. Offer your card to everyone present. You may not always get one in return. When presenting your card, smile and keep eye contact, then take a few moments to look at the card you received. Next, place it on the table in front of you.

Meetings usually start with some polite small talk, which can be brief. People appreciate a sense of humor. British humor can be ironic or even sarcastic. They may use it to register disagreement or to ridicule an adversary. It is crucial not to take this style personally, even if some of it may feel like you are being attacked. Be careful when attempting to show your own humorous side since the British may view it as improper if you try to imitate their style. One's private life is not a subject for discussion around meetings. The overall meeting atmosphere is usually quite formal. However, meetings may appear unstructured and badly run, which often reflects the tradition of giving everyone opportunities to speak up. It is best to remain polite and cordial, listening more than speaking. While one purpose of the initial meeting is to get to know each other, its primary focus will be on business topics. A first meeting will rarely lead to a straight decision.

The highest-ranking person in a British group may be difficult to pick out. It could be the one who says the least.

Presentation materials should be attractive, with good and clear visuals. Prepare thoroughly and make sure your key messages come across clearly. Keep them straightforward, though; a presentation full of excitement and hype will make your British audience suspicious and may become an object of ridicule. Throughout your presentation, remain guarded and professional even when things appear to become more informal. Be prepared to leave copies of the material you presented as well as other collateral for further study.

Negotiation

Attitudes and Styles –To the British, negotiating is usually a joint problem-solving process. While the buyer is in a superior position, both sides in a business deal own the responsibility to reach agreement. They may focus mostly on the near-term benefits of the business deal. The primary negotiation style is cooperative and people may be open to compromising if viewed helpful in order to move the negotiation forward. Since the British believe in the concept of win-win, they expect you to reciprocate their respect and trust. It is strongly advisable to avoid any open confrontation and to remain calm, somewhat formal, patient, and persistent.

Should a dispute arise at any stage of a negotiation, you might be able to reach resolution through give-and-take compromising and appeals to your counterparts' fairness.

Sharing of Information – British negotiators may spend considerable time gathering information and discussing details before the bargaining stage of a negotiation can begin. They usually share at least some information as a way of building trust, and rarely take it negatively if you ask about sensitive details, even if they may not want to answer. It would be a mistake to give your British counterparts any misleading information or to use surprise tactics since they may view that as inappropriate or unfair. Their willingness to make concessions may otherwise deteriorate considerably.

Pace of Negotiation – How long your negotiation in the U.K. may take can be hard to predict. Traditional British companies may still be very slow, spending considerable time gathering information, bargaining, and making decisions. With them, attempts to accelerate the process may be counterproductive, so allow plenty of time. On the other hand, younger or revitalized enterprises may be interested in finishing the negotiation in a short time span, moving at sometimes-surprising speeds.

The British generally prefer a monochronic work style. They are used to pursuing actions and goals systematically, and they dislike interruptions or digressions. When negotiating, they often work their way down a list of objectives in sequential order, bargaining for each item separately, and may be unwilling to revisit aspects that have already been agreed upon. They may show little tolerance if a more polychronic counterpart challenges this approach, which they view as systematic and effective. This rigid style may be difficult to tolerate for negotiators from highly polychronic cultures, such as most Asians, Arabs, some Southern Europeans, or most Latin Americans, who may view it as closed-minded and overly restrictive. In any case, do not show irritation or anger when encountering this behavior. Instead, be willing to bargain over some items individually. Otherwise, clearly indicate that your agreement is conditional and contingent on other items. Reopening the discussion over items that had already been agreed upon will make you seem untrustworthy.

Do not make efforts to stall the negotiation to win the time needed to evaluate alternatives or to create time pressure down the road in order to obtain concessions. Worst case, your counterparts may lose interest in the deal if you do.

Bargaining – Most of the British are comfortable with bargaining but dislike haggling. While they can be tough negotiators, they are usually not out to defeat the other side and will strive to play a 'fair game.' Prices may move by about 20 to 30 percent between initial offer and final agreement. The concept of fairness is very important, so while it is not difficult to obtain small concessions, your counterparts expect reciprocity and may take it very negatively if the bargaining exchange is too one-sided. The British are quite analytical and usually receptive to 'outside' ideas, so most aspects of the deal will be open to discussion. Focus your arguments on concrete facts and information. Exaggerated claims or bragging will not help your position.

Most people in this country prefer to negotiate in a fairly straightforward and honest style. They use deceptive negotiation techniques only occasionally. This includes tactics such as telling lies and sending fake non-verbal messages, pretending to be disinterested in the whole deal or in single concessions, misrepresenting an item's value, or making false demands and concessions. Carefully orchestrated, 'good cop, bad cop' may be an effective tactic to use in your own negotiation approach. Businesspeople may claim limited authority,' stating that they have to ask for their manager's approval. This could be a tactic or the truth.

Negotiators in the country use pressure techniques only as long as they can be applied in a non-confrontational fashion. They may open with their best offer, show some intransigence, or make a final offer, but often remain willing to make small compromises. Repeatedly making final offers may trigger ridicule and harsh comments. Silence could simply be a part of the conversation, although it may also signal rejection of a proposal. Be very careful when using pressure tactics such as applying time pressure, making expiring offers, or nibbling. Your counterparts likely consider these inappropriate. While the negotiation will not necessarily be over because of this, the British side may become very reserved and cautious.

Avoid all aggressive tactics when negotiating with the British. They will not shy away from open confrontation if challenged, but this is almost guaranteed to deteriorate rather than strengthen your bargaining position. Signs of anger, threats, or warnings usually indicate that the negotiation is not going well. They are rarely used as a tactic. Opening with an extreme offer may be viewed as ungentlemanly or even childish. It should therefore be avoided.

Emotional negotiation techniques, such as attitudinal bargaining, sending dual messages, attempting to make you feel guilty, or grimacing, may occasionally be employed but are generally rare. It is best to remain calm. Appeals to personal relationships are rare. British businesspeople may employ defensive tactics such as changing the subject, blocking, asking probing or direct questions, making promises, or keeping an inflexible position.

Opening with written offers and introducing written terms and conditions may be effective tactics that could help shorten the bargaining process, which some of your British counterparts may find desirable.

Corruption and bribery are very rare in the United Kingdom. It is strongly advisable to stay away from giving gifts of significant value or making offers that could be read as bribery.

Decision Making – Levels of hierarchy in British companies may vary considerably. Older and more traditional ones are often quite hierarchical, while those working in fast-paced industries often show flat hierarchies and delegate authority to lower ranks. The decision maker is usually an individual who will consult with others and carefully consider their inputs. However, decisions made at lower levels may require top management approval, which can be time-consuming. It is often important to win the support of top managers as well as influencers in subordinate roles. Once a decision has been made, it may be very difficult to change.

When making decisions, businesspeople may apply universal principles rather than considering the specific situation. The British tend to follow established rules and practices. Empirical evidence and other objective facts weigh much more strongly than personal feelings and experiences do. Depending on their company's culture and style, British businesspeople may be low or moderate risk takers.

Agreements and Contracts

Capturing and exchanging meeting summaries can be an effective way to verify understanding and commitments. However, you should confirm that your counterparts indeed do agree with them. Handshakes and verbal agreements are often considered binding. They are normally kept, even though they are not legally binding. Nevertheless, it is best to confirm agreements in writing.

Written contracts tend to be lengthy. They often spell out detailed terms and conditions for the core agreements as well as for many eventualities. Signing the contract is important not only from a legal perspective, but also as a strong confirmation of your British partners' commitment.

It is recommended to consult a local legal expert before signing a contract. The British generally prefer to resolve disputes out of court, but they will not shy away from taking legal action if deemed necessary. However, do not bring the person to the negotiation table until you have reached the final stages of the contract discussions.

Contracts are almost always dependable, and strict adherence to the agreed terms and conditions is expected. Requests to change contract details after signature may be considered as bad faith and will meet with strong resistance.

Women in Business

While women enjoy similar rights as men and many are working, most women in the United Kingdom are still struggling to attain positions of similar income and authority. However, visiting businesswomen should have few problems in the country as long as they act professionally in business and social situations.

Other Important Things to Know

Business lunches and dinners are common. However, avoid bringing up business topics at after-work events.

Punctuality is also valued in most social settings. It is best to be right on time for dinners, and to arrive at parties within 10 to 15 minutes of the agreed time.

Gift giving in business settings is rare. It is best not to bring a gift to an initial meeting in order to avoid raising suspicions about your motives.

United States

There is probably a greater diversity of business cultures and styles in the United States than in any other country in the world. This makes preparing for specific business interactions difficult. Because of the wide spectrum of heterogeneous cultural influences, however, Americans are usually tolerant of unconventional negotiation styles and habits as long as they do not conflict with their own values. On the other hand, many share a strong belief that the country's culture and value system are superior to all others, which members of other cultures sometimes interpret as arrogant. People in the country may be convinced that the American way is the only morally acceptable one, insisting that everyone play by a common set of 'ground rules.' While we strive to explain critical beliefs throughout this section, business practices may deviate from the general guidelines provided in the following. Always expect the unexpected when doing business in this country.

Experienced American businesspeople usually have had at least some exposure to people from other countries. However, a majority of Americans have never left their country except for short vacation trips. Even senior negotiators may arrive at foreign locations with very little knowledge about other countries and cultures. On top of that, some can be surprisingly close-minded, insisting that things be done 'their way.'

The primary aspects that may influence how your American counterparts do business are worth analyzing prior to negotiating with them. The most relevant factors are as follows:

Regional Influences – Historically, there was significant variance in business practices between the country's geographic regions. Style differences across the U.S. can still be pronounced in smaller cities and rural areas. For instance, competitiveness and aggressiveness in business can be even stronger in the Northeast and at the West Coast than they are in the rest of the country. Californians are usually open to doing business with people from many different countries and cultures, while people in the northeastern states can appear regionally focused and somewhat closed-minded. Business is often conducted at a more leisurely pace in the South than elsewhere in the United States. Levels of directness also vary greatly (see **Communication**). Partly owing to the high mobility of the U.S. workforce, these differences are much less pronounced in the country's many large urban centers, where businesspeople tend to be more open-minded and tolerant of style differences.

Cultural Heritage – About 65 percent of the population is Whites (*Caucasians*), 15 percent Hispanics, 13 percent Blacks (properly referred to as *African-Americans*), and 4 percent Asians. Business styles and practices vary between these groups, which in themselves are also far from homogeneous. An estimated 10 percent of the population is foreign-born, often bringing in their own experiences of how business is conducted. However, the country's dominant culture represents a powerful integrative force and may be quickly adopted and internalized by immigrants. It is crucially important to treat everyone the same, since even unintentional behaviors that may be read as discrimination can have huge negative consequences.

Specific Industries and Company Cultures – As in all countries, matters of etiquette are influenced by the type of business a person or company engages in. For instance, people in banking, personal finance, or many consulting roles dress and act more formally than others might. Personal relationships also play a greater role in these industries. However, U.S. company cultures may show substantial differences even within the same industry. Traditional, formal, and somewhat risk-averse companies may be competing directly with others in their industry whose culture may be better described as action-oriented, youthful, and unorthodox. Stereotypes about industries or about the age or structure of companies can be misleading and may therefore not be helpful. It will be highly beneficial to familiarize yourself with the specific culture of a company you are about to engage with, for instance by talking with insiders or others who dealt with the company before.

Relationships and Respect

U.S. culture strongly encourages individualism and personal initiative. Generally, business relationships are only moderately important in this country. They are usually not a necessary precondition for initial business interactions. Your counterparts' expectation may be to get to know you better as you do business together. As long as they think the other side plays fair and does not waste their time, Americans tend to be friendly and collaborative. Otherwise, they can quickly become aggressive and somewhat hostile. In any case, most people in this country think it acceptable for partners in a productive business relationship to cooperate and compete at the same time, a view that others from strongly relationship-oriented cultures rarely share.

Even when the business relationship has become close, there will not necessarily be a strong sense of loyalty. American businesspeople tend to focus on the near-term benefits of their business engagements and may drop even a long-term partner if they believe they will get 'a better deal' elsewhere, focusing much more on the near future than on the past. Business relationships may play a greater role outside of the hectic large cities, though.

Business relationships in this country exist between companies as well as between individuals. If your company replaces you with someone else over the course of a negotiation, it is usually easy for your replacement to take things over from where you left them. Likewise, if you introduce someone else from your company into an existing business relationship, that person is likely to be accepted as a valid business partner soon. This does not mean that Americans do not care about who they are dealing with.

In the United States, money is a key priority and monetary aspects tend to dominate most arguments. Financial success may be admired more than anything else, especially if it is hard earned rather than based on inheritance. Status and personal honor play a smaller role. 'Saving face' and many of the social formalities that can be vitally important to other cultures carry little significance here.

In the country's business culture, the respect a person enjoys depends primarily on his or her achievements and to a lesser degree, education. Since age and rank play a smaller role, you may find relatively young people in American negotiation teams or in positions with decision-making authority. Admired personal traits include honesty, perseverance, and expertise, as well as good communication skills.

Communication

American English is different from British English to the point where misunderstandings may happen easily. If necessary, familiarize yourself with the differences upfront.

Businesspeople in this country may speak louder than you may be used to. A strong voice is generally associated with authority and leadership qualities. At restaurants, including those used for business lunches and dinners, conversations can get much noisier than in most other countries. Americans tend to show at least some of their emotions, though not as openly as Latin Americans. People generally converse standing around three to four feet apart.

There is a distinct difference in the level of directness between the North and the South of the country. Northerners, also many Californians, are often quite direct. They dislike vague statements and may openly share their opinions and concerns. Too much diplomacy may confuse and irritate them and can give the impression of insincerity. They may ask for clarifications and rarely find it difficult to say 'no' if they dislike a request or proposal. If something is against company policy or cannot be done for other reasons, your counterpart will likely say so. They may view this as a simple statement of fact and might not understand that someone else could consider this directness insensitive. However, Americans' intentions are almost always friendly, even when they may not appear that way.

Communication with people from the South can be a bit more indirect. They generally highlight the positives of an action or proposal before addressing issues with it in order to 'soften' the message. Rather than giving you a straight 'no,' they may word the message more indirectly to avoid appearing confrontational, for instance by saying 'I'm not sure whether I agree.' In most cases, this still expresses disagreement. 'Let me get back to you' could indicate a lack of interest in what you have to offer. Make sure you are paying attention to what is *not* being said as well. Once they have decided that they want to do business with you, Southerners can become more direct and may openly speak their minds as long as there is no risk of direct confrontation.

Owing to the culture's strong achievement orientation, Americans may perceive raising issues as negativism. As a result, people often phrase concerns very carefully and may become much more indirect when doing so. Silence is very rare in conversations and makes most Americans uncomfortable as it is perceived to convey rejection or other negative messages. When around other people, they may start or continue conversations simply to avoid silence.

Gestures are usually quite expressive, and Americans' body language can be easy to read. They may make some physical contact, such as a backslap as a sign of friendship, but there is usually not a lot of it. The thumbs-up gesture signals approval or encouragement. Thumb and index finger forming a circle means *OK*. When pointing at people, use your open hand rather than a finger. If a man puts his feet on the table, this signals that he feels he is in control of the situation. However, do not assume that the person intends to insult you. Most Americans are completely unaware that people from other countries may find this highly inappropriate. Some Americans may nod continually while making positive statements. This may be meant to confirm and strengthen the message, but it does not necessarily mean that what they say is true. Eye contact should be frequent, as this conveys sincerity and helps build trust. However, do not stare at people.

Initial Contacts and Meetings

Having a local contact can be an advantage but is usually not a necessary precondition to doing business.

Negotiations in the United States can be conducted by individuals or teams of negotiators. Both approaches have their distinct advantages. Since decisions are often made by individuals, meeting the decision-maker one-on-one may help get results quickly. On the other hand, a well-aligned team with clearly assigned roles can be quite effective when negotiating with a group of Americans. Owing to the high degree of individualism that characterizes the culture, U.S. teams are not always well aligned, which sometimes makes it easy to play one member against the other.

Scheduling meetings in advance is required. However, you can do this on short notice, even in the absence of any previous business interactions, as long as your counterparts are available. Agreeing on an agenda upfront can be useful. It will usually be followed. Punctuality is generally expected. Being more than 10 to 15 minutes late without having a valid and plausible excuse can be an offense. If you cannot avoid a delay, call ahead and apologize.

Names are usually given in the order of first name, family name. Many people also have a 'middle name,' but it is rarely used in introductions or conversations. Use *Mr./Ms.* plus the family name. Doctorate degrees are often ignored when addressing people in business, except for the first time they meet. If a person is a professor, however, use that title together with the person's family name. Before calling Americans by their first name, wait until they offer it. This may happen almost immediately since the use of first names is not a sign of intimacy. It is often helpful to let your counterpart know how you would like them to call you. Introductions may be accompanied by firm and brief handshakes. However, Americans shake hands less frequently than others do, so a handshake may often be unnecessary. When entering a room full of people, it is ok just to smile and say 'hi, everyone.' The standard greeting is 'how are you?' or, in the South, 'how're you doing?' It is rhetorical, so it is best to respond with the same phrase or to say something like 'fine, thank you,' or 'I'm doing great, and you?'

The exchange of business cards is not an essential step, but it is best to bring a sufficient supply. They may sometimes be exchanged at the end rather than the beginning of the meeting. Make sure that your card clearly states your professional title, especially if you have the seniority to make decisions. Offer your card to everyone present. You may not always get one in return. This does not necessarily signal that the person does not want to do business with you. 'Can I have one of your business cards?' is an acceptable question to ask. When presenting your card, smile and keep eye contact, then take a few moments to look at the card you received. Recipients of your card may place it on the table, into their wallet, or even into the back pocket of their pants. This means no disrespect.

Meetings usually start with some small talk intended to establish personal rapport. It is normally brief but can be more extensive in the South. Conversations often start with 'what do you do?' or 'tell me more about yourself.' In both cases, the person will expect to hear about your work background. One's private life is not a subject for discussion around meetings. Humor is considered an important way to 'break the ice,' but avoid appearing ironic, cynical, or sarcastic. The opening phase of the meeting is usually short and negotiators get straight to the point. However, the meeting atmosphere is usually casual. People may get up to stretch or leave the room for a while. This does not necessarily indicate a lack of interest.

While one purpose of the initial meeting is to get to know each other, the primary focus will be on business topics. Either the meeting leads to a straight decision or there will be a list of follow-up actions. Smaller deals may be decided and finalized at the first meeting. If the meeting concludes without next steps being defined, this may mean that there is no interest to continue the discussion.

Presentation materials should be attractive, with good and clear visuals. Focus on the 'big picture' without too much detail, and keep your presentation clear and concise. However, 'beating your chest' is not only acceptable, but often expected. It may be beneficial to praise your product or service more than you might be comfortable doing in your home country. Throughout your presentation, remain relaxed and non-confrontational. Be prepared to leave copies of the material you presented.

Negotiation

Attitudes and Styles – To Americans, negotiating is usually a joint problem-solving process. While the buyer is in a superior position, both sides in a business deal own the responsibility to reach agreement. American negotiators may focus mostly on near-term benefits. The primary negotiation style is competitive, sometimes intensely so. Although people will look for win-win solutions, they may strive to 'win more' than the other side does. Power factors such as company size and financial strength play a major role and may frequently be emphasized. When negotiating, Americans may appear fiercely competitive or even combative. However, they will ultimately be interested in finding a solution that both sides can accept. It is best to remain calm, firm, and persistent. At the same time, show a positive and constructive attitude without taking things personally.

Most people in the United States are very task-focused. They may not be willing to make concessions only for the sake of a relationship. Instead, they usually expect to get a tangible benefit in return. One of the implicit rules of this culture is that people should not take this result orientation personally.

Should a dispute arise at any stage of a negotiation, you might be able to reach resolution by analyzing and discussing the problem together with your counterparts. It will be important to emphasize common objectives, work to find mutually acceptable alternatives, and show willingness to compromise if needed. However, compromising is usually only a last resort for American negotiators.

Sharing of Information – American negotiators usually spend some time gathering information and discussing details before the bargaining stage of a negotiation can begin. However, this rarely introduces significant delays. They normally share at least some information and rarely take it negatively if you ask about sensitive details, even if they may not want to answer. Similarly, they may ask many questions themselves. They value information that is straightforward and to the point. While it can be counterproductive to appear as if you are hiding facts from your American counterparts, they will be accepting if you state openly that you do not want to share certain information. Do not provide misleading information as your counterparts will likely consider this very negatively and may try to 'get even.'

American negotiators generally keep their initial questions high-level, without too much attention paid to details. It may indicate serious interest and a willingness to close the deal if their questions get more specific and technical.

Pace of Negotiation – Negotiations in the U.S. may take less time than anywhere else in the world. 'Speed matters' and 'time is money' are beliefs most members of this culture share, and doing is usually valued much more highly than planning and analyzing. Accordingly, your counterparts will generally want to finish the negotiation in a timely manner and implement actions soon. Even complex negotiations may not require more than one trip, as follow-up negotiations are often conducted via phone and e-mail.

Americans generally prefer a monochronic work style. They are used to pursuing actions and goals systematically, and they dislike interruptions or digressions. When negotiating, they often work their way down a list of objectives in sequential order, bargaining for each item separately, and may be unwilling to revisit aspects that have already been agreed upon. They may show little tolerance if a more polychronic counterpart challenges this approach, which they view as systematic and effective. This rigid style may be difficult to tolerate for negotiators from highly polychronic cultures, such as most Asians, Arabs, some Southern Europeans, or most Latin

Americans, who may view it as closed-minded and overly restrictive. In any case, do not show irritation or anger when encountering this behavior. Instead, be willing to bargain over some items individually. Otherwise, clearly indicate that your agreement is conditional and contingent on other items. Reopening the discussion over items that had already been agreed upon will make you seem untrustworthy.

Stalling a negotiation in an attempt to create time pressure in order to obtain concessions, or to gain the time needed to evaluate alternatives, may turn out to be a big mistake. Americans hate wasting time and have little patience if they feel that the other side may be hiding or holding back something. Unlike in many other cultures, negotiators may actually become less inclined to make concessions if they feel that the overall bargaining exchange is taking too long. Worst case, your counterparts may lose interest in the deal.

On the other hand, if you have not heard back from your U.S. counterparts in a long time, this likely tells you that they are not interested in doing business with you. They may also not return your calls or respond to voicemail. This approach is more frequent in the South, where people may not be as willing to give you a direct 'no.'

Bargaining – While most Americans are comfortable with bargaining, few of them like to haggle. They can be ambitious, tough, and aggressive negotiators, though, often going for the biggest possible slice of the business. Appearing confident and assertive is essential, since facing an apparently insecure counterpart may encourage Americans to negotiate harder. State your position clearly and be willing to push for it as needed. It can be advantageous to emphasize the uniqueness of what you have to offer.

Negotiators in the U.S. often take firm positions at the beginning of the bargaining process. Once you have convinced them that you are intent on holding your own, they may become more willing to make concessions. Prices may move by about 20 to 30 percent between initial offer and final agreement. When bargaining, Americans tend to focus on areas of disagreement, so do not be surprised if there is little time spent to reaffirm consensus and emphasize commonalities.

Most people in this country expect to negotiate 'in good faith.' Nevertheless, they may use deceptive negotiation techniques such as sending fake non-verbal messages, pretending to be disinterested in the whole deal or in single concessions, misrepresenting an item's value, or making false demands and concessions. Americans may also use the tactic of telling lies. However, it would be a grave personal insult to state or even hint that your counterpart is lying. Americans may instead refer to the tactic as 'twisting things a little,' 'bending the truth,' 'leaving out a few aspects,' or by some other euphemism. Open lies are considered unacceptable. Instead, people may frequently use indirect versions of what others consider as lying, for example by making misleading statements or by omitting crucial facts.

Since 'good cop, bad cop' requires strong alignment between the players, only experienced negotiators who have spent time practicing the tactic may be using it. Carefully orchestrated, it may be effective in your own negotiation approach. Businesspeople may claim limited authority, stating that they have to ask for their manager's approval. This could be a tactic or the truth.

American negotiators may use pressure techniques that include opening with their best offer, showing intransigence, making final, decreasing, or expiring offers, or nibbling. When using similar tactics yourself, clearly explain your offer and avoid being aggressive. Silence can be a particularly effective pressure tactic to use against the U.S. side. It often makes people very uncomfortable and may stimulate them to make concessions. Be careful when attempting to create time pressure. Although it can be very effective since the Americans' sense of urgency usually works against them, their level of interest could drop and they might start considering alternatives to the deal at hand. Persistence is important, though, and you will frequently find your counterparts exploring all options to bring the negotiation to a successful close as quickly as they can.

Though negotiators in the U.S. may sometimes appear aggressive or adversarial, you should avoid being overly confrontational. They will not shy away from open confrontation if challenged, but this will rarely help your bargaining position. Using extreme openings may be viewed as unfriendly and should be done with caution. Signs of anger, threats, or warnings indicate that the negotiation is not going well. They are rarely used as a tactic. Americans will use walkouts only to make a final point, almost never as a tactic. If you walked out or threatened to do so without getting the intended reaction from your counterparts, the negotiation will likely be over.

Other emotional negotiation techniques may be more frequent. Americans may employ attitudinal bargaining, send dual messages, or grimace. It is often best simply to ignore these tactics. Attempts to make you feel guilty and appeals to personal relationships are rare since people believe that these have no place in business. However, using these tactics yourself may be surprisingly effective with some negotiators.

American businesspeople may employ defensive tactics such as changing the subject, blocking, asking probing or direct questions, making promises, or keeping an inflexible position. Attempts to change the subject repeatedly in order to confuse your counterparts may meet with resistance, though.

Introducing written terms and conditions may be effective tactics that could help shorten the bargaining process, which most of your American counterparts may find desirable. Similarly, they may frequently attempt to introduce pre-printed clauses. Unless these are based on company policies, which are usually non-negotiable, you should ignore such attempts and insist that all terms and conditions be discussed and agreed upon individually.

Corruption and bribery are rare in the United States, though not completely unheard of. Both legally and ethically, it is strongly advisable to stay away from giving gifts of significant value or making offers that could be read as bribery. If you believe you are being offered a bribe, inspect the situation carefully to make sure that you are not misreading your counterpart's intentions.

Decision Making – Levels of hierarchy in American companies vary considerably. Older and more traditional ones can be quite hierarchical, while those working in fast-paced industries often show flat hierarchies and value autonomy and self-reliance. Nevertheless, all of them likely have extensive policies and processes that may affect decision-making. They are almost always followed. Decision makers are usually individuals who may or may not consult with others in the group or organization. Establishing consensus is not necessarily required before making a decision. Managers are expected to accept responsibility for their own as well as their employees' actions. Decision-making authority is often delegated to lower levels in the hierarchy and may not require any further approval from others. Generally, the size of a deal determines how high in the organization you need to go. Once the bargaining process has concluded, decisions rarely take much time. American businesspeople are used to making up their minds quickly and decisively. It can be very difficult to get them to change their minds afterwards.

When making decisions, businesspeople may apply universal principles rather than considering the specific situation. Empirical evidence and other objective facts weigh much more strongly than personal feelings and experiences do. Americans are generally risk takers and may not shy away from making bold moves.

Agreements and Contracts

Capturing and exchanging meeting summaries can be an effective way to verify understanding and commitments. Many Americans pride themselves with being consistent, so they will likely keep their commitments, at least if they are sufficiently documented. While you should not consider interim agreements final, avoid the impression that you are not willing to hold up your commitments. Nevertheless, only a contract signed by both parties constitutes a binding agreement. Negotiators sometimes request to document the progress of a negotiation by both parties signing a Letter of Intent (LOI) or Memorandum of Understanding (MOU). While much weaker than signed contracts, these documents may have legal implications.

Written contracts tend to be lengthy and very legalistic. They often spell out detailed terms and conditions for the core agreements as well as for many eventualities. They usually represent irrevocable commitments to the terms and conditions they define and can only be changed with both partners' consent.

Always consult a legal expert who has sufficient relevant experience before signing a contract. The United States is the most litigious society in the world. There are lawyers specializing in practically every industry and segment of society. Your legal counsel may also attend negotiations to provide legal advice throughout the bargaining process. However, you should let the other side know that you intend to bring a legal expert, in which case they will likely do the same.

Contracts are almost always dependable, and strict adherence to the agreed terms and conditions is expected. Requests to change contract details after signature may be considered as bad faith and will meet with strong resistance. American companies may prefer to resolve disputes in court, which can become very costly. It is highly advisable to fulfill your contractual obligations to the letter.

Women in Business

While women enjoy the same rights in the United States as men, many are still struggling to attain positions of similar income and authority. However, they are generally treated as equals in business situations, and women can be found in senior leadership roles.

Women in the United States expect to be treated very seriously and respectfully. They can be as competitive and even as combative as men. Making improper jokes or otherwise behaving inappropriately will not only trigger sharp reprimands but may have very serious disciplinary and legal implications. It is considered highly inappropriate to ask a woman whether she is married or if she plans to have children. Generally, it is crucial to treat everyone with great respect and dignity.

A visiting businesswoman should have few problems in the country. She may often find a greater degree of freedom and flexibility than she may be used to in her home country.

Other Important Things to Know

Neat and clean attire is important when doing business here. However, dress codes can be somewhat more casual than elsewhere, especially on the West Coast.

Business lunches are more common than business dinners. Americans often discuss business during meals.

Social events do not require strict punctuality. While it is best to arrive at dinners close to the agreed time, being late to a party by 15 to 30 minutes is perfectly acceptable.

Smoking is prohibited in most offices, also in and around many public places. Since many Americans do not like being around smokers, you should always ask for permission first. You may not necessarily get it.

Gift giving in business settings is rare. It is best not to bring a gift to an initial meeting in order to avoid raising suspicions about your motives.

It is crucially important to use 'politically correct' vocabulary when working with Americans. Otherwise, you risk offending someone without realizing it. Worst case, you might have to face a tedious and costly lawsuit. Refrain from using words like *Negro* or *Oriental*. Instead, use terms such as *African-American* and *Asian-American*. The term *Latino* has also become less common and is often substituted by *Hispanic*. Older people are usually called *elderly*. If it seems that you have inadvertently offended someone, it will be best to quickly apologize to the person. If you are not sure what the offense might have been, ask one of your American counterparts later when you are in a private setting. They will be glad to help you understand what went wrong and how you might avoid similar issues in future.

Venezuela

Businesspeople and officials in Venezuela, especially outside of Caracas, usually have only limited exposure to other cultures except for neighboring countries. Its culture is quite homogeneous. When negotiating business here, realize that people may expect things to be done 'their way.' However, some among younger generations may have greater international experience and can be open-minded.

Relationships and Respect

Venezuela's culture is generally group-oriented. Asserting individual preferences may be seen as less important than having a sense of belonging to a group, conforming to its norms, and maintaining harmony among its members. Building lasting and trusting personal relationships is very important to most Venezuelans. While younger businesspeople may focus primarily on the deal at hand, most from the older generation find it essential to establish strong bonds prior to closing any deals. Generally, people may want to do business only with those they know, like, and trust. If they initially seem suspicious and non-committal, you may be able to overcome this with consistent friendliness and goodwill. Establishing productive business cooperation requires a long-term perspective and commitment. Proceed with serious business discussions only after your counterparts have become comfortable with you. This can be a time-consuming process and may require several trips to strengthen the bonds. Venezuelans tend to distrust people who appear unwilling to spend the time or whose motives for relationship building are unclear.

Business relationships in this country exist between people, not necessarily between companies. Even when you have won your local business partners' friendship and trust, they will not necessarily trust others from your company. That makes it very important to keep company interfaces unchanged. Changing a key contact may require the relationship building process to start over.

Establishing personal relationships with others in Venezuela can create powerful networks and may help you a lot to achieve your business objectives. Whom you know may determine whether people want to get to know you. Similarly, whether people think you are worth knowing and trusting often weighs much more strongly than how competent you are or what proposals you may have to make. Personal networks may open doors and solve problems that would otherwise be difficult to master. Maintaining honest and cordial relations is crucial. Third party introductions can be very helpful as a starting point to building a trusting relationship with a potential partner.

In Venezuela's business culture, the respect a person enjoys depends primarily on his or her status, rank, and education. Showing status is important since people will take you more seriously. Carefully select your hotel and transportation. Use the services of others, such as a porter, to avoid being viewed as a low-ranking intermediary. The extreme differences that exist between the rich and the poor in this society are usually accepted and people believe that those in powerful positions are entitled to the privileges they enjoy. Accordingly, showing respect to those of higher status is very important. Admired personal traits include sincerity, integrity, and charisma.

Communication

While the official language of Venezuela is Spanish, it is notably different from the Spanish spoken in Spain. Around 40 other languages are spoken in the country. Many businesspeople speak at least some English, but being able to speak Spanish is a clear advantage. With high-ranking managers, it may otherwise be useful to engage an interpreter. To avoid offending the other side, ask beforehand whether an interpreter should be present at a meeting. When communicating in English, speak in short, simple sentences and avoid using jargon and slang. It will help people with a limited command of English if you speak slowly, summarize your key points often, and pause frequently to allow for interpretation. Even when the main meeting language is English, your counterparts may frequently speak Spanish among themselves, not necessarily to shut you out from the discussion but to reduce their discomfort and ensure a common understanding among them.

People in this country usually speak softly. While they may occasionally raise their voices to make a point, they dislike loud and boisterous behavior. At restaurants, keep conversations at a quiet level. In addition, avoid dominating the conversation. Venezuelans generally converse in close proximity, standing only two feet or less apart. Never back away, even if this is much closer than your personal comfort zone allows. Doing so could be read as a sign that you are uncomfortable around them.

Communication in Venezuela can be direct and straightforward, much more so than in other Latin American countries. This is especially the case among friends and close business partners. Early in the business relationship, people may communicate more indirectly, appearing somewhat vague and non-committal. If in doubt, watch for subtle messages that may signal issues and concerns. Silence is often a way to communicate a negative message.

Gestures and body language can be lively, especially if they help underline what is being said. There may be frequent physical contact with others of the same gender. The American *OK* sign, with thumb and index finger forming a circle, can be read as an obscene gesture in Venezuela. Eye contact should be very frequent, almost to the point of staring. This conveys sincerity and helps build trust.

Initial Contacts and Meetings

Choosing a local intermediary, or *enchufado,* who can leverage existing relationships to make the initial contact is highly recommended. This person will help bridge the gap between cultures, allowing you to conduct business with greater effectiveness. Your embassy, a trade organization, a chamber of commerce, or a local legal or accounting firm may be able to provide a list of potential *enchufados*. Without such a contact, it may be difficult to gain access to the right people.

Negotiations in the country can be conducted by individuals or teams of negotiators. It is vital that teams be well aligned, with roles clearly assigned to each member. Changing a team member may require the relationship building process to start over and should therefore be avoided. Venezuelan negotiation teams are usually very well aligned. If uncertain what position to support, their members will defer to the principal negotiator.

If possible, schedule meetings at least two weeks in advance. Since people want to know whom they will be meeting, provide details on titles, positions, and responsibilities of attendees ahead of time. It may be best to send an individual to the initial meeting. Subsequent meetings may include other members of your delegation. Venezuelans generally value punctuality much more highly than other Latin Americans do. At business meetings, it is best to be right on time, since being late without having a valid and plausible excuse can be a serious affront. If a delay of more than 5 to 10 minutes happens, especially in Caracas with its sometimes-chaotic traffic, call ahead and apologize profoundly, even if it is not your fault.

Names are usually given in the order of first name, family names. Most Venezuelans have two family names, the first one from their father, and the second one from their mother. Use *Mr./Mrs./Miss* or *Señor/Señora/Señorita*, plus the father's family name, which is always the first one of the two family names given. If a person has an academic title, such as *Doctor* or *Professor*, use it instead, followed by the father's family name. Only close friends call each other by their first names. Introduce or greet the oldest person first. Introductions are accompanied by firm handshakes.

The exchange of business cards is an essential step when meeting someone for the first time, so bring more than you need. It is recommended to use cards with one side in English and the other in Spanish. Show doctorate degrees on your card and make sure that it clearly states your professional title, especially if you have the seniority to make decisions. When presenting your card, ensure that the Spanish side is facing the recipient. Smile and keep eye contact while accepting someone else's card, then carefully examine it. Next, place the card on the table in front of you. Never stuff someone's card into your back pocket or otherwise treat it disrespectfully. In addition, never write on a person's business card.

Meetings start with small talk, which may be extensive. This may include personal questions about your background and family, allowing participants to become acquainted. It is important to be patient and let the other side set the pace. People appreciate a sense of humor, but keep it light and friendly, and be careful not to overdo it. Business is a serious matter in Venezuela. Initial meetings may appear formal, but the atmosphere usually is a bit more relaxed in subsequent meetings. Meetings may also appear somewhat chaotic, with frequent interruptions and several parallel conversations. Do not take this personally; it also does not indicate a lack of interest.

The primary purpose of the first meeting is to become acquainted and build relationships. Business may be discussed, but do not try to hurry along with your agenda. It is unrealistic to expect initial meetings to lead to straight decisions.

Presentation materials should be attractive, with good and clear visuals. Use diagrams and pictures wherever feasible, cut down on words, and avoid complicated expressions. Since Venezuelans generally prefer to be 'in control,' avoid monopolizing conversations or putting pressure on your counterparts. Having your handout materials translated to Spanish is not a must, but it will be appreciated and helps in getting your messages across.

After your first business contact, it is customary for the top executive of your company to write a thank-you note to his or her Venezuelan counterpart.

Negotiation

Attitudes and Styles - Leveraging relationships is an important element when negotiating in Venezuela. Nevertheless, Venezuelans often employ distributive and contingency bargaining. While the buyer is in a superior position, both sides in a business deal own the responsibility to reach agreement. They expect long-term commitments from their business partners and will focus mostly on long-term benefits. The primary negotiation style is cooperative, but people may be unwilling to agree with compromises unless it is their only option to keep the negotiation from getting stuck. Nevertheless, one important function of the bargaining exchange is to build and strengthen the relationship. Since Venezuelans believe in the concept of win-win, they expect you to reciprocate their respect and trust. It is strongly advisable to avoid aggressiveness and open confrontation, remaining calm, friendly, patient, and persistent.

Should a dispute arise at any stage of a negotiation, you might be able to reach resolution by leveraging personal relationships and emphasizing long-term benefits. Patience and creativity will pay strong dividends.

Sharing of Information – Even when personal relationships are strong, your Venezuelan counterparts may be reluctant to share information openly. Many believe that privileged information creates bargaining advantages.

Pace of Negotiation – Expect negotiations to be slow and protracted. Venezuelans do not hurry and dislike people who do. Be prepared to make several trips if necessary to achieve your objectives. Relationship building, information gathering, bargaining, and decision making may take considerable time. Attempts to rush the process are unlikely to produce better results and may be viewed as offensive. Throughout the negotiation, be patient, control your emotions, and accept the inevitable delays.

Most Venezuelans prefer a polychronic work style. They are used to pursuing multiple actions and goals in parallel. When negotiating, they often take a holistic approach and may jump back and forth between topics rather than addressing them in sequential order. Negotiators from strongly monochronic cultures, such as Germany, the United Kingdom, or the United States, may find this style confusing, irritating, and even annoying. In any case, do not show irritation or anger when encountering this behavior. Instead, keep track of the bargaining progress at all times, often emphasizing areas where agreement already exists.

If your counterparts appear to be stalling the negotiation, assess carefully whether their slowing down the process indicates that they are evaluating alternatives or that they are not interested in doing business with you. More likely, this behavior either represents an attempt to create time pressure in order to obtain concessions, or it simply reflects the slow decision process in the country. Again, patience and persistence are vitally important.

Bargaining – Venezuelans are used to hard bargaining but generally dislike excessive haggling. The bargaining exchange can be extensive. Concessions never come easily, and although Venezuelans may show interest in new ideas and concepts, they often find it difficult to change their position. Requesting a compromise may become an issue of pride if presented in the wrong way. Be respectful throughout the bargaining exchange. Rather than pushing for concessions, it may be better to re-address disagreements in follow-up meetings, which gives your counterparts the opportunity to reconsider their position without overtly losing face. Prices may move by about 25 to 35 percent between initial offer and final agreement. Leave yourself sufficient room for concessions at different stages. After making one, always ask the other side to reciprocate. Throughout the process, remain cool and respectful, avoid confrontation, and frequently reaffirm the relationship.

Deceptive techniques are frequent and can be effective. This includes tactics such as telling lies and sending fake non-verbal messages, pretending to be disinterested in the whole deal or in single concessions, misrepresenting an item's value, or making false demands and concessions. Your Venezuelan counterparts may play stupid or make other attempts to mislead you in order to obtain bargaining advantages. Even when you can see right through a lie, it would be a grave personal insult to state or even hint that your counterpart is not telling the truth. It is advisable to verify information received from the local side through other channels. 'Good cop, bad cop' is a tactic that Venezuelans rarely use, though it could be effective on either side of the negotiation table. However, it could be devastating if the other side recognized this as a tactic, and your team will need to exclude any 'bad cop' member from future negotiation rounds. Businesspeople may claim limited authority, stating that they have to ask for their manager's approval. This is usually the truth.

Negotiators in the country may use pressure techniques that include making final offers, showing intransigence, or nibbling. Final offers may come more than once and are rarely final. Be careful when trying to open with your best offer. Venezuelans may consider this inappropriate or even insulting. Silence can be a very effective way to signal rejection of a proposal or to obtain further concessions. Do not use pressure tactics such as applying time pressure or making expiring offers as these may be taken as signs that you are not willing to build a long-term relationship. Your counterparts may even choose to terminate the negotiation.

Venezuelan negotiators avoid openly aggressive or adversarial techniques. While they may make indirect threats and warnings or subtly display anger, they will be careful not to appear aggressive when doing so. Extreme openings are not frequently used since they may adversely affect the relationship, so be very cautious when using the tactic yourself. Never walk out or threaten to do so in an aggressive fashion as your counterparts will likely take this as a personal insult and may end all talks. However, threatening a 'friendly walkout' while strongly emphasizing the relationship may be very effective.

Emotional negotiation techniques, such as attitudinal bargaining or attempting to make you feel guilty, are frequent and can be effective. Be cautious not to hurt someone's personal pride when employing any of these tactics, though. Pleas to personal relationships and other emotional appeals, such as emphasizing how your proposal will add to your counterparts' personal satisfaction or heighten their honor, can be very powerful. Venezuelans may frequently employ defensive tactics such as blocking or changing the subject, asking probing or very direct questions, making promises, or keeping an inflexible position.

Corruption and bribery are common in Venezuela's public and private sectors. However, people may draw the line differently, viewing minor payments as rewards for getting a job done rather than as bribes. Also, keep in mind that there is a fine line between giving gifts and bribing. What you may consider a bribe, a Venezuelan may view as only a nice gift. It may help if you introduce and explain your company's policies early on, but be careful not to moralize or appear to imply that local customs are unethical.

Decision Making – Most companies are hierarchical, and people expect to work within clearly established lines of authority. Many businesses in Venezuela are still family-owned. Decision makers are usually heads of family or senior executives who are often autocratic but will consider the best interest of the group or organization. They may consult with others and often prefer to reach consensus before making the final call. Subordinates may be reluctant to accept responsibility. Decision makers also rarely delegate their authority, so it is important to deal with senior executives. Gaining access to top managers can be difficult, though. You may have to deal with subordinates who could strongly influence the final decision, which may be made behind closed doors. Maintaining good relationships with these intermediaries is crucial to your success. Although the pace of business is accelerating, decision making can be a slow process that requires much patience. Attempts to rush or put pressure on the process are not likely to succeed.

When making decisions, businesspeople may not rely much on rules or laws. They usually consider the specific situation rather than applying universal principles. Personal feelings and experiences weigh more strongly than empirical evidence and other objective facts do. Venezuelans are often uneasy with change and reluctant to take risks. If you expect them to support a risky decision, you may need to find ways for them to become comfortable with it first, for instance by explaining contingency plans, outlining areas of additional support, or by offering guarantees and warranties.

Agreements and Contracts

Capturing and exchanging written understandings after meetings and at key negotiation stages is useful. Oral commitments may sound stronger than what your Venezuelan counterparts may be willing to put in writing. Do not rely on interim agreements to be final, even if they come in the form of written protocols. Any part of an agreement may still change significantly before both parties sign the final contract.

Written contracts tend to be lengthy and often spell out detailed terms and conditions for the core agreements as well as for many eventualities. Nevertheless, writing up and signing the contract is a formality. Venezuelans believe that the primary strength of an agreement lies in the partners' commitment rather than in its written documentation.

It is advisable to consult a local legal expert before signing a contract. However, do not bring in your attorney until the negotiations have concluded. Venezuelans may read it as a sign of mistrust if you do.

Signed contracts may not always be honored. This depends to no small degree on the strength of the continuing relationship between the contract partners. It is strongly advisable to continue staying in touch and maintaining the trust of your Venezuelan business partner. Business partners usually expect the other side to remain somewhat flexible if conditions change, which may include agreeing to modify contract terms. Given the relatively unstable political and economic situation in the country, you should factor this possibility into your negotiation planning.

Women in Business

Quite a few Venezuelan women hold positions of rank and authority, so men are accustomed to dealing with businesswomen. Nevertheless, *machismo* attitudes remain strong in this country. Female business travelers should graciously accept any chivalric gestures they receive, while exercising caution and acting professionally in business and social situations. Displaying confidence and some degree of assertiveness can be effective, but it is very important not to appear overly bold and aggressive.

Other Important Things to Know

Formal, conservative attire is very important when doing business here. Male business visitors should wear dark suits with neckties on most occasions. First impressions can have a significant impact on how people view you.

Business lunches and dinners are common. Business is rarely discussed over dinner, though.

Social events do not require strict punctuality. While it is best to arrive at dinners close to the agreed time, being late to a party by 15 to 30 minutes is perfectly acceptable.

Do not refer to citizens of the United States as Americans. Most Latin Americans are sensitive to this point as they feel that the term includes them. They prefer to say *norteamericanos* or *North Americans*.

References

Acuff, Frank L. 1997. *How to Negotiate Anything With Anyone Anywhere Around the World*. New York: AMACOM.

Adler, Nancy J. 2002. *International Dimensions of Organizational Behavior*. Cincinnati, OH: South-Western.

Brake, Terence, and Danielle Medina Walker, Thomas (Tim) Walker. 1995. *Doing Business Internationally – The Guide to Cross-Cultural Studies*. New York: McGraw-Hill.

Cellich, Claude, and Subhash C. Jain. 2004. *Global Business Negotiations*. Mason, OH: South-Western.

Cialdini, Robert B. 2001. *Influence. Science and Practice*. Needham Heights, MA: Allyn & Bacon.

Cleland, David I., and Roland Gareis. 1994. *Global Project Management Handbook*. New York: McGraw-Hill.

Craver, Charles. 2002. *The Intelligent Negotiator*. New York: Prima Publishing

Curry, Jeffrey Edmund. 1999. *A Short Course in International Negotiating*. San Rafael, CA: World Trade Press.

Davies, Roger J., and Osamu Ikeno. 2002. *The Japanese Mind. Understanding Contemporary Japanese Culture*. Boston: Tuttle Publishing.

Deresky, Helen. 2003. *International Management – Managing Across Borders and Cultures*. Upper Saddle River, NJ: Prentice Hall.

Deutsch, Morton. 2000. *Cooperation and Competition*, in *The Handbook of Conflict Resolution: Theory and Practice*. Edited by Morton Deutsch and Peter Coleman. San Francisco: Jossey-Bass Publishers.

Devine, Elizabeth, and Nancy L. Braganti. 1986. *The Traveler's Guide to Asian Customs & Manners*. New York: St. Martin's Press.

Fisher, Roger, and William Ury. 1991. *Getting to Yes*. New York: Penguin Books.

Foster, Dean Allen. 1992. *Bargaining Across Borders*. New York: McGraw-Hill.

Foster, Dean. 2000-2002. *The Global Etiquette Guide to xxx'* series (4 volumes), New York: Wiley.

Gundling, Ernest. 2003. *Working Globesmart*. Palo Alto, CA: Davies-Black Publishing.

Hall, Edward T. 1981. *Beyond Culture*. New York: Anchor Books.

Hampden-Turner, Charles, and Alfons Trompenaars. 1993. *The Seven Cultures of Capitalism*. New York: Doubleday.

Hendon, Donald W., and Rebecca Angeles-Hendon. 1990. *World-Class Negotiating*. New York: John Wiley & Sons.

Hofstede, Geert. 1997. *Cultures and Organizations. Software of the Mind*. New York: McGraw-Hill.

House, Robert J., and Paul J. Hanges, Mansour Javidan, Peter W. Dorfman, Vipin Gupta (editors). 2004. *Culture, Leadership, and Organizations – The GLOBE Study of 62 Societies*. Thousand Oaks, CA: Sage Publications.

Lewicki, Roy J., and David M. Saunders, John W. Minton. 2001. *Essentials of Negotiation*. New York: McGraw-Hill.

Lewicki, Roy J., and David M. Saunders, John W. Minton, Bruce Barry. 2003. *Negotiation*. New York: McGraw-Hill.

Lewis, Richard D. 1999. *When Cultures Collide*. London: Nicholas Brealey Publishing.

Nisbett, Richard E. 2003. *The Geography of Thought*. New York: The Free Press.

Morrison, Terri, and Wayne A. Conaway, George A. Borden. 1994. *Kiss, Bow, Or Shake Hands*. Holbrook, MA: Adams Media Corporation.

Morrison, Terri, and Wayne A. Conaway, Joseph J. Douress. 1997. *Dun & Bradstreet's Guide to Doing Business Around the World*. Paramus, NJ: Prentice Hall.

Putzi, Sybilla M. (managing editor). 2001. *Global Road Warrior*. Novato, CA: World Trade Press.

Rody, Raymond C. 2002. *International Business Negotiations*. Orange, CA: Oceanprises Publications.

Salacuse, Jeswald W. 2003. *The Global Negotiator*. New York: Palgrave Macmillan.

Seligman, Scott D. 1999. *Chinese Business Etiquette*. New York: Warner Books.

Schein, Edgar H. 2004. *Organizational Culture and Leadership*. San Francisco: Jossey-Bass.

Stewart, Edward C., and Milton J. Bennett. 1991. *American Cultural Patterns. A Cross-Cultural Perspective*. Yarmouth, MA: Intercultural Press.

Thomas, David C. 2002. *Essentials of International Management*. Thousand Oaks, CA: Sage Publications.

Thomas, David C., and Kerr Inkson. 2003. *Cultural Intelligence*. San Francisco: Berrett-Koehler Publishers.

Thompson, Leigh L. 2005. *The Mind and Heart of the Negotiator*. Upper Saddle River, NJ: Pearson Education, Inc.

Trompenaars, Fons, and Charles Hampden-Turner. 1998. *Riding the Waves of Culture*. New York: McGraw-Hill.

Trompenaars, Fons, and Peter Wooliams. 2003. *Business Across Cultures*. Chichester, England: Capstone.

Various authors. *Culture Shock* series (available for more than 50 different countries). Portland, OR: Graphic Arts Center Publishing Company / London: Kuperard.

Useful Websites

asia Travelinfo.com – www.asiatravelinfo.com

Austrade Industry and Country Information – www.austrade.gov.au

Centre for Intercultural Learning / E-thologies – www.e-thologies.com

Economist.com Country Briefings – www.economist.com/countries/

Economist Intelligence Unit – www.eiu.com

Executive Planet – www.executiveplanet.com

HLB International 'Doing Business in ...' booklets – www.hlbi.com/DBI_list.asp

International Business Center – www.international-business-center.com

Kwintessential Country Profiles –
www.kwintessential.co.uk/resources/country-profiles.html

Transparency International Corruptions Perception Index (CPI) – www.transparency.org/publications

U.S. Census Bureau – www.census.gov

U.S. Department of State Background Notes – www.state.gov/r/pa/ei/bgn/

The World Bank – www.worldbank.org

The World Factbook – www.odci.gov/cia/publications/factbook

These links can also be found on the web at **www.negintbiz.com**.

In addition to the information provided on these web sites, several major international accounting, banking, and legal firms offer thorough and well-researched country-specific reports and forecasts. This research is often available to clients free of charge.

Index

Made in the USA